Collins
French
Dictionary

HarperCollins Publishers
Westerhill Road
Bishopbriggs
Glasgow
G64 2QT
Great Britain

First Edition 2007

Reprint 10 9 8 7 6 5 4 3 2 1 0

© HarperCollins Publishers 2007

ISBN 978-0-00-727007-1

www.collinslanguage.com

A catalogue record for this book is available
from the British Library

Dictionary text typeset by
Wordcraft, Glasgow

Printed in Italy by Rotolito Lombarda S.p.A.

Acknowledgements
We would like to thank those authors and
publishers who kindly gave permission for
copyright material to be used in the Collins
Word Web. We would also like to thank
Times Newspapers Ltd for providing
valuable data.

CONTENTS

FIRST EDITION

Publishing Director
Lorna Sinclair Knight

Editorial Director
Michela Clari

Managing Editor
Maree Airlie

Lexicographers
Gaëlle Amiot-Cadey   Cécile Aubinière-Robb
Daphne Day   Phyllis Gautier

Illustrations
Cordelia Lilly

Computational Support
Thomas Callan   Ian Codona

We would like to give special thanks to Simon Green, Modern Languages
Advisor and Helen Morrison, teacher and author of the **Collins Primary
French Starter Pack.** We would also like to thank the many teachers
who provided us with invaluable information and advice, in particular
Janis Smith, Wendy Harris, Janette Paterson, Angela Holt, Fiona Wilson
and John de Cecco.

FOREWORD

A dictionary is not an end in itself, but a means to an end. By letting young learners have access to a dictionary, we open up for them possibilities of discovery and exploration and we enable the drive to find out and know.

I wonder if the French for dinosaur is the same as the English? How many words in French begin with the letter 'k'? Does English have a word for croissant?

This First Time French Dictionary has arrived at a most opportune time. Early language learning is firmly on the agenda, with pupils in primary schools having an entitlement to study foreign languages. This entitlement is already embedded in the National Curriculum as non-statutory guidance for Key Stage 2. Under the knowledge, skills and understanding recommended for younger learners of foreign languages there are references to "the interrelationship of sounds and writing" and "how to use dictionaries and other reference materials".

This is a dictionary for learners. The layout is appealing, the vocabulary is wide and covers both high frequency and medium frequency words with which young learners will be familiar. The text is in line with the National Literacy Strategy and it provides ready access to the spelling, meaning and usage of French that young learners need.

This is also a dictionary for teachers. It is a valuable tool in that it empowers pupils to make their own connections, seek their own meanings and find out about their own needs. It is a genuine learning resource because learners can make independent judgements about what they are looking for and they will find more than they are seeking. It is a mine of information and an instructional aid which, with guidance, can also be used to teach forms, meanings and spellings.

Let us also acknowledge that a dictionary can also be a source of fun in that odd expressions, unusual spellings, familiar friends and quirky words can enliven our learning in unexpected ways.

A dictionary is a possibility and this dictionary represents a probability that learning French can be effective, rewarding and enjoyable.

Simon Green

Modern Languages Adviser

INTRODUCTION

Collins First Time French Dictionary is a new bilingual dictionary aimed at primary school children who are learning French. With increasing numbers of primary schools introducing French, the publication of a dictionary especially designed with this age group in mind is an exciting and significant moment.

Access to an appropriate dictionary is a vital part of any language learning. As the author of the **Collins Primary French Starter Pack**, I particularly welcome the publication of the *First Time French Dictionary*, which is equally suitable for classroom or for independent use.

The dictionary reflects the key aims of the **Primary French Starter Pack**:

- to develop both language skills in French and language learning skills at Key Stage 2

- to cover the four key areas of language attainment: listening, speaking, reading and writing

- to reinforce the language knowledge and understanding pupils have acquired through the National Literacy Strategy by encouraging them to analyse how language works and to compare English and French

- to promote positive attitudes to learning a language and to prepare pupils for language learning at Key Stage 3 and beyond

- to extend cultural awareness by providing information about France

It also supports the issues identified in the National Curriculum (Guidelines for modern foreign languages at Key Stage 2), the QCA scheme of work for modern foreign languages at Key Stage 2 and the Scottish 5-14 guidelines, all of which advocate the early use of a bilingual dictionary.

The *First Time French Dictionary* supports language learning in a number of specific ways:

- it develops children's knowledge of how language works by encouraging them to understand, analyse and use simple aspects of grammar

- it supports language learning skills at Key Stage 2, developing children's individual learning skills, improving their linguistic competence and providing them with a sound foundation for future language learning either in French or in another language

- it enables children to make comparisons between French and English by encouraging them to explore the similarities and differences between the two languages and to notice the diversity of language

- it emphasizes the enjoyment of language learning

A dictionary like this one does far more than simply expand vocabulary. It is a rich source of information about language structures and patterns. It highlights the way French works in comparison with English, and offers advice on the strategies to follow when learning a language. Introducing children to a bilingual dictionary is an excellent way of building on work undertaken in literacy lessons. Amongst its many positive outcomes the National Literacy Strategy has had enormous benefits for modern foreign language learning in primary schools. Increased knowledge of the grammatical structure of their own language, and the ability to use analytical skills, provide children with a sound base for learning a new language. As an introduction to the bilingual dictionary, the *First Time French Dictionary* builds on the general dictionary skills introduced in literacy lessons, and prepares the ground for more complex bilingual dictionaries.

The *First Time French Dictionary* is presented in an easy-to-use format which is intended to appeal to children of primary school age. It provides lots of simple, relevant examples and tips on how to remember words, and how to avoid some of the pitfalls of translation. It also features key phrases, quiz-type questions, illustrations and information about life in France. Teachers, children and their parents will welcome this exciting resource, which will be an invaluable tool for anyone studying or teaching French at Key Stage 2 and beyond.

Helen Morrison
Primary Teacher
Author of **Collins Primary French Starter Pack**

USING THE DICTIONARY

▶ STEP ONE – *PICK THE RIGHT SIDE*

Remember there are 2 halves to the dictionary.

If you want to know what a French word means, look in the **French-English** half. It comes first.

If you want to translate an English word into French, look in the second half, which is **English-French**. It comes after the blue pages in the middle of the dictionary.

1 Which of these words would you look up in the **French-English** half?

   demain   brother   horse   un bonbon

2 Look at page 100 of the dictionary. Is this the French side or the English side? How can you tell?

3 Look at page 141 of the dictionary. What is shown at the top of the page next to the page number?

4 Is Internet the first or the last word on page 141?

Remember that you do not read across the whole page in a dictionary – you have to read down the <u>columns</u>.

5 Which word comes immediately after l'internat on page 141?

▶ STEP TWO – *FIND THE RIGHT WORD*

A B C D E F G H I J K L M N O P Q R S T U V W X Y Z

Words are in alphabetical order in the dictionary – like names in the phone book, and in a school register. The alphabet is shown down the edge of each page of the dictionary. You can sort words into alphabetical order by looking at the first letter of each word.

6 Can you put these names in alphabetical order?

   Chantal, Luc, Sophie, Pierre, Jean-Marie, Hélène

When two words start with the same letter, look at their second letters.

7 In alphabetical order which comes first – Hermione or Harry?

This is the order of the days of the week on a calendar:

Monday, Tuesday, Wednesday, Thursday, Friday, Saturday, Sunday

8 Which day comes first in a dictionary? Which comes last?

9 Thursday comes before Tuesday in a dictionary. Why?

10 Put the seven days of the week into alphabetical order.

If the first letters are the same, and the second letters are the same, look at the third letters.

11 June, July, August: which comes last in the dictionary?

▶ STEP THREE – PICK THE RIGHT TRANSLATION

The translations are easy to spot in this dictionary because they are underlined.

Some French words can be masculine or feminine, or even plural. In the dictionary **m**, **f**, and **pl** are the abbreviations used for these. The dictionary also shows you the French word for "the" (this can be **le**, **la**, **l'** or **les**).

doll n
la <u>poupée</u> f

When you look up doll you can see that the word for "doll" in French is <u>poupée</u>.

You can also tell that the French word for "doll" is feminine because it is given with 'la' and the dictionary says that it is f (feminine).

So "the doll" is **la poupée** and "a doll" would be **une poupée**.

Using the dictionary

> **penfriend** n
> le <u>correspondant</u> m
> la <u>correspondante</u> f

Here there are two translations, one masculine, one feminine. If your penfriend is a boy, you need the French word which is masculine (*m*) – le <u>correspondant</u>. If your penfriend is a girl, you need the French word which is feminine (*f*) – la <u>correspondante</u>.

12 If you were talking about your penfriend, which would go in the gap, **correspondant** or **correspondante**?

J'ai un _____. Il s'appelle Hugo.

> **animal** n
> l'<u>animal</u> m
> (*pl* les animaux)

Here there are two translations. The second one is plural (*pl*).

13 If you want to say that you love animals which translation would go in the gap?

J'adore les _____.

Sometimes there is more than one translation, and each one has a number. If there is more than one translation, don't just pick the first one! Check to see which is the right one.

> **ball** n
> **1** (*for tennis, golf, cricket*)
> la <u>balle</u> f
> **Hit the ball!**
> Frappe la balle!
> **2** (*for football, rugby*)
> le <u>ballon</u> m
> **Pass the ball!**
> Passe le ballon!

14 Which is the French word for a ball that you kick – **une balle**, or **un ballon**? Look for the clue.

Sometimes, to pick the right translation, you need to know the *part of speech* of a word, for example whether a word is a **noun**, an **adjective**, an **adverb** or a **verb**. In the dictionary these words are shortened to **n, adj, adv, vb**. Other abbreviations are used in the dictionary for other parts of speech – **conj** for conjunction, **excl** for exclamation, **num** for number, **prep** for preposition and **pron** for pronoun.

PARTS OF SPEECH

► NOUNS

Nouns are naming words for things or people. You often use the words "a" or "the" with a noun – eg a GIRL, a BOY, the SCHOOL, the WINDOWS.

Nouns can be singular, eg an ACCIDENT, the CANTEEN, my DAD, FOOTBALL – or plural, eg SWEETS, the CHILDREN, my FRIENDS.

15 How many nouns are there in this sentence? What are they?

The car has got a flat tyre and a big dent in the door.

► ADJECTIVES

An **adjective** is a describing word which tells you what things are like: FLAT shoes are shoes that don't have high heels. A FLAT tyre is a tyre with no air in it.

16 How many adjectives are there in this sentence? What are they?

She's got brown hair and blue eyes.

Parts of speech

Some words have a NOUN meaning and an ADJECTIVE meaning. In the dictionary there is a box to tell you about this. The different meanings have different translations in French.

---

sweet

> **sweet** can be a noun or an adjective.

Ⓐ n

1 (candy)

le <u>bonbon</u> m

a bag of sweets
un paquet de bonbons

2 (pudding)

le <u>dessert</u> m

Sweets: ice cream or chocolate mousse
Desserts: glace ou mousse au chocolat

Ⓑ adj

1 (sugary)

<u>sucré</u> m adj
<u>sucrée</u> f adj

It's too sweet.
C'est trop sucré.

---

17 You want to ask someone if they would like a sweet. Fill in the gap. How can you be sure this is the right translation?

Tu veux un _____ ?

▶ ADVERBS

An **adverb** is a word which describes a verb or an adjective: She writes NEATLY. The film was VERY good.

18 How many adverbs are in this sentence? What are they?

The children sat quietly and played happily.

Some words have an ADJECTIVE meaning and an ADVERB meaning. The different meanings have different translations in French.

hard

> **hard** can be an adjective or an adverb.

Ⓐ adj

1 *(difficult)*

difficile

This question's too hard for me.
Cette question est trop difficile pour moi.

2 *(not soft)*

dur *m adj*
dure *f adj*

This cheese is very hard.
Ce fromage est très dur.

Ⓑ adv

dur

Colette works hard.
Colette travaille dur.

19 You want to say you work hard. Fill in the gap in the sentence:

Je travaille _____.

► VERBS

Verbs are sometimes called "doing words". They often go with words like "I" and "you", and with names, eg I PLAY football, what DO you WANT?, Hugo LIKES mashed potato.

Verbs tell you about the present, eg I'M LISTENING – the past, eg I SCORED a goal – and the future, eg I'M GOING TO GET an ice cream.

20 How many verbs are there in this sentence? What are they?

School starts at nine and finishes at 3.30.

Parts of speech

Some words have an ADJECTIVE meaning and a VERB meaning. The different meanings have different translations in French.

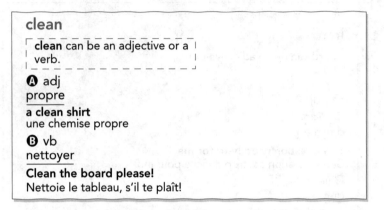

clean

clean can be an adjective or a verb.

Ⓐ adj
propre

a clean shirt
une chemise propre

Ⓑ vb
nettoyer

Clean the board please!
Nettoie le tableau, s'il te plaît!

21 If you want to ask for "a clean glass", how do you know that <u>propre</u> is the translation, not <u>nettoyer</u>?

Some words have a NOUN meaning and a VERB meaning. The different meanings have different translations in French.

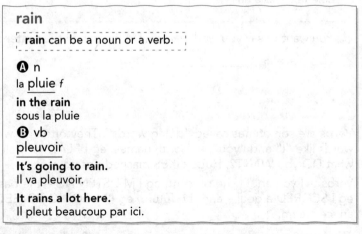

rain

rain can be a noun or a verb.

Ⓐ n
la pluie *f*

in the rain
sous la pluie

Ⓑ vb
pleuvoir

It's going to rain.
Il va pleuvoir.

It rains a lot here.
Il pleut beaucoup par ici.

22 Is "la pluie" a noun or a verb?

23 Why is "It rains a lot here." in part **Ⓑ**?

TEST YOURSELF!

A What do these abbreviations stand for in the dictionary – m, f, pl, vb, n, adj?

B Does the word "the" go with nouns or with verbs?

C Does the word "you" go with verbs or with nouns?

LEARN USEFUL PHRASES

In the dictionary you'll see phrases that are especially important in blue boxes. Try to learn these when you come across them, and you'll soon know lots of useful things to say in French.

> **What time is it?**
> Quelle heure est-il?
> **It's lunch time.**
> C'est l'heure du déjeuner.
> **How many times?**
> Combien de fois?
> **Have a good time, girls!**
> Amusez-vous bien, les filles!
> **Have a good time, Léa!**
> Amuse-toi bien, Léa!

FIND OUT ABOUT LIFE IN FRANCE

There are also boxes which tell you about French customs, and about differences between life in France and Britain.

> In France, Easter eggs are said to be brought by the Easter bells (**cloches de Pâques**) which fly from Rome and drop them in people's gardens.

EVEN MORE WORDS

At school you will learn to talk about subjects such as the time and the weather, your family, your pets, and your clothes. The most important words for talking about these subjects are shown in the dictionary itself, and <u>even more</u> words are given in **Language Plus**, the middle part of the dictionary with the blue pages. Have a look!

ANSWER KEY

1 demain and bonbon

2 It is the French side. It has French words on it and French-English written at the top.

3 French-English and Internet

4 It's the last word on page 141.

5 international

6 Chantal, Hélène, Jean-Marie, Luc, Pierre, Sophie

7 Harry. Because "a" comes before "e".

8 Friday; Wednesday

9 Because the second letter of Thursday is "h", which comes before "u", the second letter of Tuesday.

10 Friday, Monday, Saturday, Sunday, Thursday, Tuesday, Wednesday

11 June

12 correspondant

13 animaux

14 un ballon – the clue is (*for football, rugby*).

15 4 – *car, tyre, dent, door*

16 2 – *brown* and *blue*

17 bonbon; a sweet is a noun, it means "candy". The example helps too.

18 2 – *quietly* and *happily*

19 dur

20 2 – *starts* and *finishes*

21 Because "clean" is an adjective here. The example helps too.

22 It's a noun.

23 Because it's a verb.

A

a vb, *see* **avoir**

> *Don't confuse* **a** *with the preposition* **à**.

1 has

Elle a beaucoup d'amis.
She has lots of friends.

> *Sometimes* **a** *is used to show that something has happened in the past.*

Il a joué au football.
He played football.

2 is

Il a neuf ans.
He is nine years old.

il y a

> **il y a** *can either mean* **there is** *or* **there are**.

Il y a un bon film à la télé.
There's a good film on TV.

Il y a beaucoup de monde.
There are lots of people.

> **il y a** *can also mean* **ago**.

Elle est partie il y a dix minutes.
She left ten minutes ago.

> 🔑
>
> **Qu'est-ce qu'il y a?**
> What's the matter?

à prep

> *Don't confuse* **à** *with the verb form* **a**. *See also* **au** (= **à** + **le**) *and* **aux** (= **à** + **les**).

1 at

Je suis à la maison.
I am at home.

Je finis à quatre heures.
I finish at 4 o'clock.

2 in

Il est à Paris.
He is in Paris.

Elle habite au Portugal.
She lives in Portugal.

Mes grands-parents habitent à la campagne.
My grandparents live in the country.

au printemps
in the spring

au mois de juin
in June

3 to

Je vais à Paris.
I'm going to Paris.

Elle va au Portugal.
She's going to Portugal.

Cet été je vais à la campagne.
I'm going to the country this summer.

Il l'a donné à son frère.
He gave it to his brother.

Je n'ai rien à faire.
I've got nothing to do.

Ce livre est à Paul.
This book is Paul's.

4 by

Il est arrivé à bicyclette.
He arrived by bicycle.

à pied
on foot

Je vais à l'école à pied.
I walk to school.

à ... d'ici
... from here

C'est à dix kilomètres d'ici.
It's 10 kilometres from here.

... à l'heure
... an hour

cent kilomètres à l'heure
100 kilometres an hour

À samedi!
See you on Saturday!

À tout à l'heure!
See you later!

> 🔑
> **À bientôt!**
> See you soon!
> **À demain!**
> See you tomorrow!

abandonner vb
1 to abandon
2 to give up

Je veux abandonner la natation.
I want to give up swimming.

l'abeille nf
bee

abominable adj
awful

l'abord nm
d'abord
first

Je vais rentrer chez moi d'abord.
I'll go home first.

l'abricot nm
apricot

absent m adj
(f adj **absente**)
absent

absolument adv
absolutely

l'accent nm
accent

un accent aigu
an acute accent

un accent grave
a grave accent

un accent circonflexe
a circumflex

> Sometimes, French vowels have
> an accent to change their sound.
> There are three kinds of accents:
> the acute (**école**), the grave (**mère**)
> and the circumflex (**hôtel**). See
> also **aigu**, **grave**, **circonflexe**

accepter vb
to accept

l'accident nm
accident

accompagner vb
to accompany

> There is the word **accompany** in
> English, but we would often say
> something different.

Elle m'accompagne à l'école.
She takes me to school.

l'accord nm
être d'accord
to agree

Tu es d'accord avec moi?
Do you agree with me?

D'accord!
OK!

l'accordéon nm
accordion

Ray joue de l'accordéon.
Ray plays the accordion.

l'accueil nm
reception

acheter vb
to buy

l'acné nf
acne

l'acteur nm
actor

un acteur de cinéma
a film actor

actif m adj
(*f adj* active)
active

l'activité nf
activity

l'actrice nf
actress

une actrice de cinéma
a film actress

les **actualités** nfpl
news

Je regarde les actualités tous les soirs.
I watch the news every night.

l'addition nf
1 sum
2 bill

L'addition, s'il vous plaît!
Can we have the bill, please?

adhésif m adj
(*f adj* adhésive)
le ruban adhésif
sticky tape

l'adjectif nm
adjective

"grand" est un adjectif.
"grand" is an adjective.

admettre vb
1 to admit

J'admets que j'ai eu tort.
I admit I was wrong.
2 to allow

Les chiens ne sont pas admis dans le restaurant.
Dogs are not allowed in the restaurant.

l'adolescent nm
l'adolescente nf
teenager

a

adorable adj
lovely

adorer vb
to love

Elle adore le chocolat.
She loves chocolate.

J'adore jouer au tennis.
I love playing tennis.

l'**adresse** nf
address

> The French word has only one **d**, and an extra **e**.

mon adresse électronique
my email address

l'**adulte** nm/f
adult

une chambre pour deux adultes et un enfant
a room for two adults and a child

l'**adverbe** nm
adverb

"beaucoup" est un adverbe.
"beaucoup" is an adverb.

l'**adversaire** nm/f
opponent

l'**aérobic** nm
aerobics

Je fais de l'aérobic.
I do aerobics.

l'**aéroport** nm
airport

les **affaires** nfpl
1 things

Va chercher tes affaires!
Go and get your things!

Rangez vos affaires!
Put your things away!

2 business

un homme d'affaires
a business man

l'**affiche** nf
poster

affreux m adj
(f adj **affreuse**)
awful

africain m adj
(f adj **africaine**)
African

l'**Africain** nm
l'**Africaine** nf
African

l'**Afrique** nf
Africa

agacer vb
to get on somebody's nerves

Tu m'agaces!
You're getting on my nerves!

l'**âge** nm
age

Écrivez votre nom et votre âge.
Write down your name and age.

Tu as quel âge?
How old are you?
Quel âge a-t-elle?
How old is she?

âgé m adj
(f adj **âgée**)
old

l'**agence** nf
agency

une agence de voyages
a travel agency
une agence immobilière
an estate agent's

l'**agenda** nm
diary

Elle note tous ses rendez-vous dans son agenda.
She makes a note of all her appointments in her diary.

> *Be careful! The French word* **agenda** *does not mean the same as* **agenda** *in English.*

l'**agent** nm
un agent de police
a policeman

l'**agneau** nm
(*pl* les agneaux)
lamb
un gigot d'agneau
a leg of lamb

l'**agrafeuse** nf
stapler

agréable adj
nice

l'**agriculteur** nm
farmer

ai vb, *see* **avoir**
J'ai deux chats.
I have two cats.

> *Sometimes* **ai** *is used to show that something has happened in the past.*

J'ai oublié mon livre.
I've forgotten my book.

l'**aide** nf
help

aider vb
to help
Tu peux m'aider?
Can you help me?

aïe excl
ouch!

aigu m adj
un accent aigu
an acute accent

l'**aiguille** nf
needle

l'**ail** nm
garlic
Je n'aime pas l'ail.
I don't like garlic.

l'**aile** nf
wing
une aile de poulet
a chicken wing

aimable adj
nice

l'**aimant** nm
magnet

aimer vb
1 to love
Elle aime ses enfants.
She loves her children.

Je t'aime.
I love you.
2 to like

Tu aimes le chocolat?
Do you like chocolate?

J'aime bien ce garçon.
I like this boy.

J'aime bien jouer au tennis.
I like playing tennis.

aîné m adj
(*f adj* aînée)
C'est mon frère aîné.
He's my big brother.

l'**aîné** nm
l'**aînée** nf
oldest child
C'est l'aîné.
He's the oldest child.
C'est l'aînée.
She's the oldest child.

l'**air** nm
air
Tu as l'air fatiguée.
You look tired.

l'**aire de jeux** nf
playground

ajouter vb
to add

l'**alarme** nf
alarm

l'**alcool** nm
alcohol
Je ne bois pas d'alcool.
I don't drink alcohol.

l'**Algérie** nf
Algeria

algérien m adj
(*f adj* algérienne)
Algerian

l'**Algérien** nm
l'**Algérienne** nf
Algerian

l'**alimentation** nf
groceries
le rayon alimentation
the grocery department

l'**allée** nf
1 path
les allées du parc
the paths in the park
2 drive
5, allée Saint-Exupéry
5 Saint-Exupéry Drive

l'**Allemagne** nf
Germany

allemand nm, m adj
(*f adj* allemande)
German

l'**Allemand** nm
l'**Allemande** nf
German

aller

> **aller** can be a verb or a noun.

A vb
to go
Je vais à Londres.
I'm going to London.
Nous allons visiter un château.
We're going to visit a castle.
Allez! Dépêche-toi!
Come on! Hurry up!
Comment vas-tu? – Je vais bien.
How are you? – I'm fine.
Je vais mieux.
I'm feeling better.

🔑
Comment ça va? – Ça va bien.
How are you? – I'm fine.

B nm
single

Je voudrais un aller pour Angers.
I'd like a single to Angers.

un aller simple
a single

un aller retour
a return ticket

allergique adj

allergique à
allergic to

Je suis allergique aux chats.
I'm allergic to cats.

allez vb, *see* **aller**
Vous allez où?
Where are you going?

allô excl
hello!

Allô! Je voudrais parler à Monsieur Simon.
Hello! I'd like to speak to Mr Simon.

allô is only used when talking to someone on the phone.

allons vb, *see* **aller**
Nous allons coucher.
We're going to bed.

allumer vb
1 to put on

Tu peux allumer la lumière?
Can you put the light on?

2 to switch on

Allume l'ordinateur.
Switch on the computer.

3 to light

Tu peux allumer cette bougie?
Can you light this candle?

l'**allumette** nf
match

une boîte d'allumettes
a box of matches

alors adv
1 then

Alors, tu viens?
Are you coming, then?

2 so

Alors tu habites ici?
So you live here?

Et alors?
So what?

les **Alpes** nfpl
Alps

dans les Alpes
in the Alps

l'**alphabet** nm
alphabet

alphabétique adj
alphabetical

par ordre alphabétique
in alphabetical order

l'**amande** nf
almond

la pâte d'amandes
marzipan

l'**ambulance** nf
ambulance

Appelez une ambulance!
Call an ambulance!

l'**amende** nf
fine

une amende de 30 euros
a €30 fine

A B C D E F G H I J K L M N O P Q R S T U V W X Y Z

amener vb
to bring

Je peux amener un ami?
Can I bring a friend?

américain m adj
(*f adj* américaine)
American

l'**Américain** nm
l'**Américaine** nf
American

l'**Amérique** nf
America

l'**ami** nm
l'**amie** nf
friend

J'ai beaucoup d'amis.
I have lots of friends.

mon meilleur ami
my best friend

ma meilleure amie
my best friend

un petit ami
a boyfriend

une petite amie
a girlfriend

amical m adj
(*f adj* amicale)
friendly

amicalement adv
Amicalement, Pierre.
Best wishes, Pierre.

l'**amitié** nf
friendship

Amitiés, Christelle.
Best wishes, Christelle.

l'**amour** nm
love

une histoire d'amour
a love story

amoureux m adj
(*f adj* amoureuse)
in love

Il est amoureux de Naïma.
He's in love with Naïma.

l'**ampoule** nf
1 light bulb

Tu peux changer l'ampoule?
Can you change the light bulb?

2 blister

J'ai une ampoule au pied.
I've got a blister on my foot.

amusant m adj
(*f adj* amusante)
amusing

s'amuser vb
1 to play

Les enfants s'amusent dehors.
The children are playing outside.

2 to enjoy oneself

Amuse-toi bien!
Enjoy yourself!

l'**an** nm
year

Elle a douze ans.
She's twelve years old.

le premier de l'an
New Year's Day
le nouvel an
New Year

J'ai dix ans.
I'm ten years old.

l'**ananas** nm
pineapple

l'**ancêtre** nm/f
ancestor

l'**anchois** nm
anchovy

ancien m adj
(*f adj* ancienne)
1 former
C'est une ancienne élève.
She's a former pupil.
2 old
notre ancienne voiture
our old car
3 antique
un fauteuil ancien
an antique chair

l'**âne** nm
donkey

l'**ange** nm
angel

l'**angine** nf
throat infection
J'ai une angine.
I've got a throat infection.

anglais nm, m adj
(*f adj* anglaise)
English
Je suis anglais.
I'm English.

l'**Anglais** nm
l'**Anglaise** nf
English

l'**Angleterre** nf
England
J'habite en Angleterre.
I live in England.

l'**animal** nm
(*pl* les animaux)
animal
un animal domestique
a pet
Tu as un animal domestique?
Have you got a pet?

l'**animateur** nm
l'**animatrice** nf
host
Il est animateur à la télé.
He's a TV host.

animé m adj
(*f adj* animée)
lively
Cette ville est très animée.
This is a very lively town.
un dessin animé
a cartoon
J'adore les dessins animés.
I love cartoons.

l'**année** nf
year
Cette année, j'apprends le français.
I'm learning French this year.

l'**année dernière**
last year
l'**année prochaine**
next year
Bonne année!
Happy New Year!

A
B
C
D
E
F
G
H
I
J
K
L
M
N
O
P
Q
R
S
T
U
V
W
X
Y
Z

l'**anniversaire** nm

1 birthday

Aujourd'hui, c'est mon anniversaire.
It's my birthday today.

> **Quelle est la date de ton anniversaire?**
> When is your birthday?
> **Mon anniversaire, c'est le douze février.**
> My birthday is on 12 February.
> **Joyeux anniversaire!**
> Happy birthday!

2 anniversary

leur anniversaire de mariage
their wedding anniversary

l'**annonce** nf
advert

J'ai vu une annonce dans le journal.
I saw an advert in the newspaper.

les petites annonces
the small ads

annuler vb
to cancel

l'**anorak** nm
anorak

l'**antenne** nf
aerial

les **Antilles** nf
West Indies

l'**antiquité** nf
antique

un magasin d'antiquités
an antique shop

anxieux m adj
(*f adj* anxieuse)
anxious

août nm
August

en août
in August

le trois août
the third of August

apercevoir vb
to see

l'**apéritif** nm
En été, on prend l'apéritif dans le jardin.
In the summer we have drinks in the garden.

> An **apéritif** is a drink that you have before dinner. You usually have nibbles to go with it. Adults have something alcoholic and children have juice.

l'**appareil** nm
un appareil dentaire
a brace

Je dois porter un appareil dentaire.
I have to wear a brace.

un appareil photo
a camera

J'ai perdu mon appareil photo.
I've lost my camera.

l'**appartement** nm
flat

appartenir vb
Ça m'appartient.
This belongs to me.

l'**appel** nm
1 phone call

un appel d'Italie
a phone call from Italy

2 register

faire l'appel
to call the register

Silence! Je fais l'appel.
Quiet! I'm calling the register.

appeler vb
to call

Elle appelle le médecin.
She's calling the doctor.

♦ **s'appeler**
to be called

Elle s'appelle Muriel.
Her name's Muriel.

Comment ça s'appelle?
What is it called?

Comment tu t'appelles?
What's your name?
Je m'appelle Alice.
My name's Alice.

l'**appendicite** nf
appendicitis

l'**appétit** nm

Bon appétit!
Enjoy your meal!

apporter vb
to bring

Je vais apporter un gâteau.
I'm going to bring a cake.

apprendre vb
to learn

J'apprends le français.
I'm learning French.

J'apprends à faire la cuisine.
I'm learning to cook.

appris vb, see **apprendre**
Qu'est-ce que tu as appris aujourd'hui?
What have you learned today?

s'**approcher** vb
to come closer

Approchez-vous.
Come closer.

appuyer vb
to press

Il faut appuyer sur ce bouton.
You have to press this button.

après prep, adv
1 after

après le déjeuner
after lunch

2 afterwards

aussitôt après
immediately afterwards

après-demain adv
the day after tomorrow

l'**après-midi** nm/f
afternoon

A
B
C
D
E
F
G
H
I
J
K
L
M
N
O
P
Q
R
S
T
U
V
W
X
Y
Z

a
b
c
d
e
f
g
h
i
j
k
l
m
n
o
p
q
r
s
t
u
v
w
x
y
z

L'après-midi, je vais à la piscine.
In the afternoon, I go to the
swimming pool.

> 🔑
> **cet après-midi**
> this afternoon

arabe

> **arabe** can be an adjective or a
> noun.

Ⓐ adj
Arab

les pays arabes
the Arab countries

Ⓑ nm
Arabic

Il parle arabe.
He speaks Arabic.

l'araignée nf
spider

**Il y a une araignée dans la
baignoire!**
There's a spider in the bath!

l'arbitre nm
referee

l'arbre nm
tree

un arbre généalogique
a family tree

l'arc nm
bow

un arc et des flèches
a bow and arrows

l'arc-en-ciel nm
rainbow

l'argent nm
1 money

Je n'ai pas d'argent.
I haven't got any money.
l'argent de poche
pocket money
2 silver

une médaille d'argent
a silver medal

l'arme nf
weapon

l'armée nf
army

l'armoire nf
wardrobe

arranger vb
1 to arrange

**Elle arrange des fleurs dans un
vase.**
She's arranging flowers in a vase.
2 to suit

Ça m'arrange de partir plus tôt.
It suits me to leave earlier.

l'arrêt nm
stop

un arrêt de bus
a bus stop

arrêter vb

1 to stop

Tu peux arrêter la cassette?
Can you stop the tape?

Arrête!
Stop it!

Arrête de copier!
Stop copying!

2 to switch off

Il a arrêté le moteur.
He switched the engine off.

arrière

arrière can be a noun or an
adjective.

A nm
back

l'arrière de la maison
the back of the house

B m, f, pl adj
back

le siège arrière
the back seat

les roues arrière
the rear wheels

l'arrière-grand-mère nf
great-grandmother

l'arrière-grand-père nm
great-grandfather

l'arrivée nf
arrival

arriver vb

1 to arrive

J'arrive à l'école à huit heures.
I arrive at school at 8 o'clock.

2 to come

J'arrive!
I'm coming!

3 to happen

Qu'est-ce qui est arrivé à Christian?
What happened to Christian?

l'arrondissement nm
district

Paris, Lyons and Marseilles
are divided into numbered
districts called
arrondissements.

arroser vb
to water

Daphne arrose ses tomates.
Daphne is watering her
tomatoes.

l'arrosoir nm
watering can

l'artichaut nm
artichoke

l'article nm
article

un article de journal
a newspaper article

l'artiste nm/f
artist

Paul est un véritable artiste.
Paul is a real artist.

les arts plastiques nmpl
art

as

as can be part of the verb **avoir** or
a noun.

A vb, *see* **avoir**

Tu as de beaux cheveux.
You've got nice hair.

*Sometimes **as** is used to show that
something has happened in the
past.*

Tu as aimé le film?
Did you like the film?

A B C D E F G H I J K L M N O P Q R S T U V W X Y Z

B nm
ace

l'as de cœur
the ace of hearts

l'ascenseur nm
lift

Il n'y a pas d'ascenseur dans mon immeuble.
There's no lift in my building.

asiatique adj
Asiatic

la cuisine asiatique
Oriental cooking

l'Asie nf
Asia

l'asperge nf
asparagus

l'aspirateur nm
vacuum cleaner

passer l'aspirateur
to vacuum

Je déteste passer l'aspirateur!
I hate vacuuming!

l'aspirine nf
aspirin

Prenez de l'aspirine.
Take some aspirin.

l'assassin nm
murderer

assassiner vb
to murder

s'asseoir vb
to sit down

Je peux m'asseoir ici?
Can I sit here?

Asseyez-vous, tout le monde!
Sit down everybody!
Assieds-toi, Nicole!
Sit down Nicole!

assez adv
1 enough

Nous n'avons pas assez de temps.
We don't have enough time.

Est-ce qu'il y a assez de pain?
Is there enough bread?

J'en ai assez!
I've had enough!
2 quite

Il faisait assez beau.
The weather was quite nice.

l'assiette nf
plate

une assiette creuse
a soup plate

une assiette à dessert
a dessert plate

assis m adj
(f adj assise)
sitting

Il est assis par terre.
He's sitting on the floor.

l'**assistant** nm
l'**assistante** nf
assistant

Il est assistant d'anglais à Tourcoing.
He is an English assistant in Tourcoing.

Elle est assistante de français à Oxford.
She's a French assistant in Oxford.

une assistante sociale
a social worker

l'**asthme** nm
asthma

une crise d'asthme
an asthma attack

l'**atelier** nm
1 workshop

un atelier de poterie
a pottery workshop

2 studio

L'artiste est dans son atelier.
The artist is in his studio.

l'**athlète** nm/f
athlete

l'**athlétisme** nm
athletics

Je fais de l'athlétisme.
I do athletics.

l'**Atlantique** nm
Atlantic

l'**atlas** nm
atlas

attacher vb
to tie up

Elle attache ses cheveux avec un élastique.
She ties her hair up with an elastic band.

attaquer vb
to attack

attendre vb
to wait

J'attends ma copine.
I'm waiting for my friend.

Attends moi!
Wait for me!

> *Be careful! **attendre** does not mean the same as **to attend** in English.*

l'**attente** nf
wait

deux heures d'attente
two hours' wait

la salle d'attente
the waiting room

l'**attention** nf

Attention!
Watch out!

faire attention
to be careful

Il ne fait pas attention.
He's not careful.

atterrir vb
to land

l'**attraction** nf

un parc d'attractions
an amusement park

attraper vb
to catch

au prep, *see* **à**

> *au is made up of à + le.*

Je vais au cinéma.
I am going to the cinema.
au printemps
in the spring

l'aube nf
dawn

Il se lève à l'aube.
He gets up at dawn.

l'auberge de jeunesse nf
youth hostel

aucun

> **aucun** can be an adjective or a pronoun.

Ⓐ m adj
(*f adj* aucune)
no

Il n'a aucun ami.
He's got no friends.
Ⓑ m pron
(*f pron* aucune)
none

Aucune d'elles n'aime le football.
None of them like football.

au-dessous adv
downstairs

Ils habitent au-dessous.
They live au-dessous.
They live downstairs.
au-dessous de
under
au-dessous du pont
under the bridge

au-dessus adv
upstairs

J'habite au-dessus.
I live upstairs.

au-dessus de
above

au-dessus de la table
above the table

aujourd'hui adv
today

Aujourd'hui, c'est le onze juillet.
Today is 11 July.

aura, aurai, auras, aurez, aurons, auront vb, *see* **avoir**

Demain, il y aura du soleil.
It will be sunny tomorrow.

J'aurai mon nouveau vélo mardi.
I'm getting my new bike on Tuesday.

Tu auras quel âge en juillet?
How old will you be next July?

Vous n'aurez pas le temps.
You won't have time.

Nous aurons une semaine de vacances.
We'll have one week off.

Ils n'auront pas le temps de venir nous voir.
They won't have time to visit us.

aussi adv
1 too

Dors bien. – Toi aussi.
Sleep well. – You too.

Moi aussi!
Me too!

2 also

Je parle anglais et aussi français.
I speak English and also French.

aussi ... que
as ... as

Michael est aussi grand que moi.
Michael is as tall as me.

aussitôt adv

aussitôt après son retour
straight after his return

aussitôt que
as soon as

aussitôt que possible
as soon as possible

l'**Australie** nf
Australia

australien m adj
(f adj australienne)
Australian

autant adv

> **autant de** can either mean **so much** or **so many**.

Je ne veux pas autant de gâteau.
I don't want so much cake.

Je n'ai jamais vu autant de monde.
I've never seen so many people.

> **autant ... que** can either mean **as much ... as** or **as many ... as**.

J'ai autant d'argent que toi.
I've got as much money as you have.

J'ai autant d'amis que lui.
I've got as many friends as he has.

l'**auteur** nm
author

l'**auto** nf
car

l'**autobus** nm
bus

Je vais à l'école en autobus.
I go to school by bus.

l'**autocar** nm
coach

l'**autocollant** nm
sticker

l'**auto-école** nf
driving school

l'**automne** nm
autumn

en automne
in autumn

automobile

> **automobile** can be a noun or an adjective.

A nf
car

une vieille automobile
an old car

B adj

une course automobile
a motor race

l'**automobiliste** nm/f
motorist

A
B
C
D
E
F
G
H
I
J
K
L
M
N
O
P
Q
R
S
T
U
V
W
X
Y
Z

a

l'**autoradio** nm
car radio

l'**autoroute** nf
motorway

l'**auto-stop** nm
C'est dangereux de faire de
l'auto-stop.
Hitchhiking is dangerous.

autour adv
around

autour de la maison
around the house

autre adj, pron
other

Je viendrai un autre jour.
I'll come some other day.

J'ai d'autres projets.
I've got other plans.

autre chose
something else

Tu veux autre chose?
Would you like something else?

autre part
somewhere else

Je voudrais aller autre part.
I'd like to go somewhere else.

un autre
another

Tu veux un autre morceau de
gâteau?
Would you like another piece of
cake?

l'autre
the other

Non, pas celui-ci, l'autre.
No, not that one, the other one.

d'autres
others

Je t'en apporterai d'autres.
I'll bring you some others.

les autres
the others

Les autres sont arrivés plus tard.
The others arrived later.

ni l'un ni l'autre
neither of them

Je n'aime ni l'un ni l'autre.
I like neither of them.

autrefois adv
in the old days

autrement adv
1 differently
Fais-le autrement.
Do it differently.
2 otherwise
Je n'ai pas pu faire autrement.
I couldn't do otherwise.

l'**Autriche** nf
Austria

autrichien m adj
(f adj autrichienne)
Austrian

l'**Autrichien** nm
l'**Autrichienne** nf
Austrian

l'**autruche** nf
ostrich

aux prep, *see* **à**

> *aux* is made up of **à** + *les*.

Il va aux États-Unis.
He's going to the United States.

avaler vb
to swallow

l'**avance** nf

être en avance
to be early

Je suis en avance.
I am early.

à l'avance
beforehand

Il faut réserver longtemps à l'avance.
You need to book well beforehand.

d'avance
in advance

Elle a payé d'avance.
She paid in advance.

avancer vb
to go forward

Avance de trois cases.
Go forward three squares.

avant

> **avant** can be a preposition, an adjective or a noun.

Ⓐ prep
before

avant de partir
before leaving

Ⓑ m, f, pl adj
front

la roue avant
the front wheel

le siège avant
the front seat

Ⓒ nm
front

l'avant de la voiture
the front of the car

à l'avant
in front

J'aime m'asseoir à l'avant.
I like to sit in the front.

en avant
forward

Fais un pas en avant.
Take a step forward.

l'**avantage** nm
advantage

avant-dernier m adj
(*f adj* avant-dernière)
last but one

l'avant-dernière page
the last page but one

Ils sont arrivés avant-derniers.
They arrived last but one.

avant-hier adv
the day before yesterday

avec prep
with

Je joue avec mes copains.
I am playing with my friends.

Et avec ça?
Anything else?

l'**avenir** nm
future

à l'avenir
in future

l'**aventure** nf
adventure

l'**avenue** nf
avenue

J'habite au 3, avenue Pasteur.
I live at 3 Pasteur Avenue.

A B C D E F G H I J K L M N O P Q R S T U V W X Y Z

a

l'**averse** nf
shower

Il y a des averses sur toute la France.
There are showers all over France.

aveugle adj
blind

avez vb, *see* **avoir**

Vous avez des frères et sœurs?
Have you got any brothers or sisters?

*Sometimes **avez** is used to show that something has happened in the past.*

Vous avez aimé le film?
Did you like the film?

l'**avion** nm
plane

Tu préfères y aller en avion ou en train?
Would you rather go by plane or by train?

Il va en Italie en avion.
He is flying to Italy.

par avion
by airmail

l'**avis** nm
opinion

à mon avis
in my opinion

J'ai changé d'avis.
I've changed my mind.

l'**avocat** nm
1 lawyer

Il est avocat.
He's a lawyer.
2 avocado

Tu aimes les avocats?
Do you like avocados?

l'**avocate** nf
lawyer

Elle est avocate.
She's a lawyer.

l'**avoine** nf
oats

les flocons d'avoine
porridge oats

avoir vb
1 to have

Ils ont deux enfants.
They have two children.

Il a les yeux bleus.
He's got blue eyes.

avoir is used to make the past tense of most verbs.

Qu'est-ce que tu as fait hier?
What did you do yesterday?
2 to be

Il a trois ans.
He's three.

J'ai faim.
I'm hungry.
3 to get

J'ai des devoirs de maths deux fois par semaine.
I get maths homework twice a week.

a
b
c
d
e
f
g
h
i
j
k
l
m
n
o
p
q
r
s
t
u
v
w
x
y
z

Qu'est-ce que tu as eu pour Noël?
What did you get for Christmas?

il y a

> *il y a* can either mean **there is** or **there are**.

Il y a quelqu'un à la porte.
There's somebody at the door.

Il y a des chocolats sur la table.
There are some chocolates on the table.

> *il y a* can also mean **ago**.

Je l'ai rencontré il y a deux ans.
I met him two years ago.

>
> **Qu'est-ce qu'il y a?**
> What's the matter?

avons vb, *see* **avoir**

Nous avons une grande maison.
We have a big house.

> Sometimes **avons** is used to show that something has happened in the past.

Nous avons regardé la télévision.
We watched television.

avouer vb
to admit

avril nm
April

en avril
in April

le deux avril
the second of April

B

le **baby-foot** nm
table football

le **baby-sitting** nm

Ma sœur fait du baby-sitting le week-end.
My sister babysits at the weekend.

le **bac** nm = **baccalauréat**

le **baccalauréat** nm
A levels

Ma sœur passe son baccalauréat cette année.
My sister is doing her A levels this year.

> The **baccalauréat** or **bac** is an exam taken at the end of **lycée**, when French students are 17 and 18 years old.

les **bagages** nmpl
luggage

Les bagages sont dans la voiture.
The luggage is in the car.

Je déteste faire les bagages!
I hate packing!

la **bague** nf
ring

J'ai une belle bague.
I have a beautiful ring.

la **baguette** nf
stick of French bread

se **baigner** vb
to swim

J'aime me baigner.
I like swimming.

la **baignoire** nf
bath

Il y a une araignée dans la baignoire!
There's a spider in the bath!

le **bain** nm
bath

Je prends un bain.
I'm having a bath.

le **baiser** nm
kiss

donner un baiser
to give a kiss

Donne-moi un baiser!
Give me a kiss!

la **balade** nf
walk

Tu veux faire une balade?
Do you want to go for a walk?

le **baladeur** nm
Walkman®

le **balai** nm
broom

la **balançoire** nf
swing

le **balcon** nm
balcony

la **baleine** nf
whale

la **balle** nf
ball

Le chien joue avec une balle.
The dog is playing with a ball.

une balle de ping-pong
a ping-pong ball

une balle de tennis
a tennis ball

le **ballon** nm
1 ball

un ballon de football
a football
2 balloon

Je veux un ballon!
I want a balloon!

la **banane** nf
banana

le **banc** nm
bench

la **bande dessinée** nf
comic strip

J'adore les bandes dessinées!
I love comic strips!

Comic strips are very
popular in France with
people of all ages.

la **banlieue** nf
suburbs

J'habite en banlieue.
I live in the suburbs.

la **banque** nf
bank

le **banquier** nm
la **banquière** nf
banker

le **baptême** nm
christening

le **bar** nm
bar

barbant m adj
(f adj barbante)
boring

Il est vraiment barbant!
He's so boring!

la **barbe** nf
beard

Il porte la barbe.
He's got a beard.

la barbe à papa
candyfloss

le **barbecue** nm
barbecue

la **barque** nf
rowing boat

la **barrière** nf
fence

le **bar-tabac** nm

A **bar-tabac** is a café which
also sells cigarettes and
stamps. It has a red diamond-
shaped sign outside it.

le **bas** nm
bottom

le bas de la page

the bottom of the page

en bas
downstairs

La salle de bains est en bas.
The bathroom is downstairs.

le **basilic** nm
basil

le **basket** nm
basketball

Je joue au basket.
I play basketball.

les **baskets** nfpl
trainers

une paire de baskets
a pair of trainers

le **bassin** nm
pond

le **bateau** nm
(*pl* les bateaux)
boat

Je vais en France en bateau.
I'm going to France by boat.

le **bateau-mouche** nm
pleasure boat

le **bâtiment** nm
building

la **batterie** nf
drums

Je joue de la batterie.
I play the drums.

battre vb
to beat

bavard m adj
(*f adj* bavarde)
talkative

bavarder vb
to chat

le **bazar** nm
mess

Quel bazar!
What a mess!

Va ranger ton bazar!
Go and tidy up your mess!

la **BD** nf
comic strip

Rose adore les BD.
Rose loves comic strips.

beau m adj
(*m adj also* bel, *f adj* belle)

> *beau* changes to *bel* before a
> vowel sound and most words
> beginning with "h".

1 lovely

un beau cadeau
a lovely present

une belle journée
a lovely day

2 beautiful

une belle femme
a beautiful woman

3 good-looking

un beau garçon
a good-looking boy

4 handsome

un bel homme
a handsome man

> 🔑
> **Il fait beau aujourd'hui.**
> It's a nice day today.

beaucoup adv
1 a lot

Il mange beaucoup.
He eats a lot.

beaucoup de
a lot of

J'ai beaucoup de devoirs.
I have a lot of homework.

J'ai beaucoup de chance.
I am very lucky.

2 much

Je n'ai pas beaucoup d'argent.
I haven't got much money.

le **beau-fils** nm
1 son-in-law

2 stepson

le **beau-frère** nm
brother-in-law

le **beau-père** nm
1 father-in-law

2 stepfather

le **bébé** nm
baby

beige adj, nm
beige

le **beignet** nm
fritter

des beignets aux pommes
apple fritters

bel m adj, *see* **beau**

un bel été
a beautiful summer

belge adj
Belgian

le/la **Belge** nm/f
Belgian

la **Belgique** nf
Belgium

belle f adj, *see* **beau**

une belle statue
a beautiful statue

la **belle-fille** nf
1 daughter-in-law

2 stepdaughter

la **belle-mère** nf
1 mother-in-law

2 stepmother

la **belle-sœur** nf
sister-in-law

le **berceau** nm
(*pl* les berceaux)
cradle

le **berger** nm
shepherd

le **besoin** nm

Je vais avoir besoin d'aide.
I will need some help.

J'ai besoin d'un stylo.
I need a pen.

bête adj
stupid

les **bêtises** nfpl
faire des bêtises
to misbehave

Ma sœur fait toujours des bêtises.
My sister is always misbehaving.

dire des bêtises
to talk nonsense

Tu dis des bêtises!
You're talking nonsense!

la **betterave** nf
beetroot

le **beurre** nm
butter

le **biberon** nm
bottle
Ma maman donne le biberon à ma sœur.
My mum is giving my baby sister her bottle.

la **bibliothèque** nf
library

le **bic**® nm
Biro®
J'ai deux bics dans ma trousse.
I've got two Biros in my pencil case.

la **bicyclette** nf
bicycle
J'ai une nouvelle bicyclette.
I've got a new bicycle.

bien adj, adv
1 well
Daphné travaille bien.
Daphné works well.
2 good
Ce livre est vraiment bien.
This book is really good.

J'aime bien les maths.
I like maths.
Comment ça va? – Ça va bien, merci.
How are you? – Fine, thanks.

bien sûr adv
of course
Tu aimes les frites? – Oui, bien sûr!
Do you like chips? – Yes, of course!

bientôt adv
soon

À bientôt!
See you soon!

la **bienvenue** nf
welcome
Bienvenue à Paris!
Welcome to Paris!

la **bière** nf
beer

le **bijou** nm
jewel

le **billard** nm
billiards

le **bifteck** nm
steak

la **bille** nf
marble

a
b
c
d
e
f
g
h
i
j
k
l
m
n
o
p
q
r
s
t
u
v
w
x
y
z

J'aime jouer aux billes.
I like playing with marbles.

le **billet** nm
1 ticket

un billet d'avion
a plane ticket
2 banknote

un billet de 10€
a €10 note

la **biologie** nf
biology

la **biscotte** nf
toasted bread

le **biscuit** nm
biscuit

la **bise** nf
kiss

Grosses bises de Bretagne.
Love and kisses from Brittany.

Viens me faire la bise.
Come and give me a kiss.

Je fais la bise à mes copines tous les matins.
Every morning I give my friends a kiss.

> Between girls and boys, and between girls, the normal French way of saying hello and goodbye is with kisses, usually one on each cheek. Boys shake hands with each other instead.

le **bisou** nm
kiss

Viens faire un bisou à maman!
Come and give Mummy a little kiss!

bizarre adj
strange

la **blague** nf
joke

blanc

> **blanc** can be an adjective or a noun.

A m adj
(*f adj* blanche)
white

un chemisier blanc
a white blouse

une chemise blanche
a white shirt

B nm
white

Vous avez ce T-shirt en blanc?
Do you have this T-shirt in white?

blanche f adj, *see* **blanc**

de la peinture blanche
white paint

le **blé** nm
wheat

blessé m adj
(*f adj* blessée)
injured

a **b** c d e f g h i j k l m n o p q r s t u v w x y z

la **blessure** nf
injury

bleu

> **bleu** can be an adjective or a noun.

A m adj
(*f adj* bleue)
blue

une veste bleue
a blue jacket

Mon uniforme est bleu et blanc.
My uniform is blue and white.

B nm
blue

La couleur préférée de ma sœur, c'est le bleu.
Blue is my sister's favourite colour.

blond m adj
(*f adj* blonde)
blond

Andrew a les cheveux blonds.
Andrew has blond hair.

le **blouson** nm
jacket

un blouson en cuir
a leather jacket

le **bocal** nm
(*pl* les bocaux)
jar

le **bœuf** nm
beef

un rôti de bœuf
a joint of beef

bof excl
Comment ça va? – Bof! Pas terrible.
How is it going? – Oh … not too well actually.

boire vb
to drink

Je bois du jus d'orange au petit déjeuner.
I drink orange juice with my breakfast.

le **bois** nm
wood

en bois
wooden

une table en bois
a wooden table

la **boisson** nf
drink

une boisson chaude
a hot drink

la **boîte** nf
box

une boîte d'allumettes
a box of matches

une boîte aux lettres
a letter box

une boîte de conserve
a tin

une boîte de nuit
a night club

le **bol** nm
bowl

un bol de céréales
a bowl of cereal

bon m adj
(*f adj* bonne)
1 good

un bon restaurant
a good restaurant

Je suis bon en maths.
I'm good at maths.

🔑

Bonne journée!
Have a nice day!
Bonne nuit!
Good night!
Bon anniversaire!
Happy birthday!
Bon courage!
Good luck!
Bon voyage!
Have a good trip!
Bon week-end!
Have a nice weekend!
Bonne chance!
Good luck!
Bonne année!
Happy New Year!

2 right

C'est la bonne réponse.
That's the right answer.

Ah bon?
Really?

Bon, d'accord.
OK then.

le **bonbon** nm
sweet

Ma sœur aime les bonbons.
My sister likes sweets.

le **bonhomme de neige** nm
snowman

bonjour excl
1 hello!

Bonjour Madame!
Hello Miss!

2 good morning!

Bonjour, tout le monde!
Good morning everyone!

3 good afternoon!

bonjour is said in the morning and in the afternoon; in the evening bonsoir is said instead.

bonne f adj, *see* **bon**

Elle est bonne en français.
She's good at French.

le **bonnet** nm
hat

un bonnet de laine
a woolly hat

bonsoir excl
good evening!

le **bord** nm

J'habite au bord de la mer.
I live at the seaside.

Cet été, je vais au bord de la mer.
This summer, I'm going to the seaside.

bordeaux

bordeaux can be a noun or an adjective.

Ⓐ nm
Bordeaux wine

Ⓑ m, f, pl adj
maroon

une jupe bordeaux
a maroon skirt

la **bosse** nf
bump

le **bossu** nm
la **bossue** nf
hunchback

la **botte** nf
boot

une paire de bottes
a pair of boots

A
B
C
D
E
F
G
H
I
J
K
L
M
N
O
P
Q
R
S
T
U
V
W
X
Y
Z

des bottes en caoutchouc
Wellington boots

la **bouche** nf
mouth

le **boucher** nm
la **bouchère** nf
butcher

la **boucherie** nf
butcher's

Où est la boucherie?
Where is the butcher's?

le **bouchon** nm
1 top

un bouchon en plastique
a plastic top

2 cork

un bouchon de champagne
a champagne cork

3 hold-up

Il y a beaucoup de bouchons sur l'autoroute.
There are a lot of hold-ups on the motorway.

la **boucle d'oreille** nf
earring

des boucles d'oreille en or
gold earrings

bouclé m adj
(f adj bouclée)
curly

J'ai les cheveux bouclés.
I've got curly hair.

bouder vb
to sulk

le **boudin** nm
le boudin noir
black pudding

le boudin blanc
white pudding

la **boue** nf
mud

la **bouée** nf
buoy

une bouée de sauvetage
a life buoy

bouger vb
to move

la **bougie** nf
candle

la **bouillabaisse** nf
fish soup

bouillant m adj
(f adj bouillante)
boiling

de l'eau bouillante
boiling water

bouillir vb
to boil

la **bouilloire** nf
kettle

la **bouillotte** nf
hot-water bottle

le **boulanger** nm
la **boulangère** nf
baker

la **boulangerie** nf
baker's
Je vais à la boulangerie.
I'm going to the baker's.

la **boule** nf
ball
une boule de neige
a snowball

jouer aux boules
to play bowls

Mon grand-père aime jouer aux boules.
My grandad likes playing bowls.

> **boules** is played on rough ground, not smooth grass. The balls are smaller than those used in bowls, and are made of metal.

le **boulevard** nm
boulevard

la **boum** nf
party
Je vais à une boum ce week-end.
I'm going to a party this weekend.

le **bouquet** nm
bunch of flowers
un bouquet de roses
a bunch of roses

la **Bourgogne** nf
Burgundy

la **boussole** nf
compass

le **bout** nm
1 end
Elle habite au bout de la rue.
She lives at the end of the street.
2 tip
le bout du nez
the tip of the nose

la **bouteille** nf
bottle
une bouteille de limonade
a bottle of lemonade

la **boutique** nf
shop

le **bouton** nm
1 button
Appuie sur le bouton.
Press the buttton.
2 spot
Elle a des boutons.
She's got spots.

le **bowling** nm
1 tenpin bowling
J'aime aller au bowling.
I like going bowling.
2 bowling alley
Il y a un bowling près de chez moi.
There's a bowling alley near my house.

le **bracelet** nm
bracelet

A
B
C
D
E
F
G
H
I
J
K
L
M
N
O
P
Q
R
S
T
U
V
W
X
Y
Z

la **branche** nf
branch

branché m adj
(f adj branchée)
trendy

le **bras** nm
arm

J'ai mal au bras.
My arm hurts.

la **brasserie** nf
café-restaurant

bravo excl
well done!

le **Brésil** nm
Brazil

la **Bretagne** nf
Brittany

les **bretelles** nfpl
braces

Il porte des bretelles.
He's wearing braces.

breton m adj
(f adj bretonne)
Breton

le **brevet des collèges** nm
GCSE

**Mon frère passe son brevet des
collèges.**
My brother is taking his GCSEs.

The **brevet des collèges** is
an exam you take at the end
of **collège**, at the age of 15.

le **bricolage** nm
DIY

Elle aime le bricolage.
She likes doing DIY.

bricoler vb
to do DIY

Pascal aime bricoler.
Pascal loves doing DIY.

brillant m adj
(f adj brillante)
1 brilliant

une idée brillante
a brilliant idea
2 shiny

des cheveux brillants
shiny hair

briller vb
to shine

la **brioche** nf
brioche

**Je mange une brioche au petit
déjeuner.**
I have a brioche for breakfast.

brioche is a kind of sweet
bread.

la **brique** nf
brick

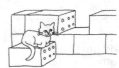

le **briquet** nm
cigarette lighter

le/la **Britannique** nm/f
Briton

britannique adj
British

Je suis britannique.
I am British.

la **brochette** nf
skewer

la **brochure** nf
brochure

la **bronchite** nf
bronchitis

le **bronze** nm
bronze

la médaille de bronze
the bronze medal

bronzer vb
to get a tan

la **brosse** nf
brush

une brosse à cheveux
a hairbrush

une brosse à dents
a toothbrush

brosser vb
to brush

se brosser les dents
to brush one's teeth

Je me brosse les dents tous les soirs.
I brush my teeth every night.

le **brouillard** nm
fog

Demain il y aura du brouillard.
It will be foggy tomorrow.

> 🔑
> **Il y a du brouillard.**
> It's foggy.

la **brouette** nf
wheelbarrow

le **bruit** nm
noise

Il y a trop de bruit!
There's too much noise!

faire du bruit
to make a noise

Cette voiture fait beaucoup de bruit.
This car makes a lot of noise.

sans bruit
without a sound

brûlant m adj
(*f adj* brûlante)
1 blazing
un soleil brûlant
a blazing sun
2 boiling
La soupe est brûlante.
The soup is boiling.

brûler vb
to burn
Ne te brûle pas!
Don't burn yourself!

la **brume** nf
mist

brun m adj
(*f adj* brune)
brown
J'ai les cheveux bruns.
I've got brown hair.

Bruxelles n
Brussels

bruyant m adj
(*f adj* bruyante)
noisy

la **bruyère** nf
heather

bu vb, *see* **boire**
J'ai bu du jus d'orange.
I drank some orange juice.

A
B
C
D
E
F
G
H
I
J
K
L
M
N
O
P
Q
R
S
T
U
V
W
X
Y
Z

a
b
c
d
e
f
g
h
i
j
k
l
m
n
o
p
q
r
s
t
u
v
w
x
y
z

la **bûche** nf

la bûche de Noël
the Yule log

Le 25 décembre, on mange de la bûche de Noël.
On December 25 we eat Yule log.

> **La bûche de Noël** is what is usually eaten in France instead of Christmas pudding.

le **buffet** nm
1 sideboard

un buffet en chêne
an oak sideboard
2 buffet

un buffet de gare
a station buffet

le **buisson** nm
bush

la **bulle** nf
bubble

le **bulletin** nm
report

un bulletin scolaire
a school report

le **bureau** nm
(*pl* les bureaux)
1 desk

Il y a un bureau dans ma chambre.
There's a desk in my room.
2 office

Ma mère travaille dans un bureau.
My mum works in an office.

un bureau de change
a bureau de change

le bureau de poste
the post office

le bureau de tabac
the tobacconist's

le **bus** nm
bus

en bus
by bus

Je vais à l'école en bus.
I go to school by bus.

le **but** nm
goal

marquer un but
to score a goal

J'ai marqué un but.
I scored a goal.

C

c' pron, see **ce**
C'est lui!
That's him!

ça pron
1 this

Je voudrais un peu de ça.
I'd like a bit of this.

2 that

Ne fais pas ça.
Don't do that.

3 it

Ça ne fait rien.
It doesn't matter.

Ça va? – Oui, ça va, merci.
How are you? – I'm fine thanks.
Ça alors!
Well, well!
C'est ça.
That's right.
Ça y est!
That's it!

la **cabane** nf
hut

la **cabine** nf
cabin

une cabine d'essayage
a fitting room

une cabine téléphonique
a phone box

le **cabinet** nm
surgery

la **cacahuète** nf
peanut

le **cacao** nm
cocoa

cache-cache nm
hide-and-seek

Tu veux jouer à cache-cache?
Do you want to play hide-and-seek?

le **cache-nez** nm
long woollen scarf

cacher means "hide" and **nez**
means "nose", so this scarf covers
your nose.

cacher vb
to hide
♦ **se cacher**
to hide

Elle s'est cachée sous la table.
She's hiding under the table.

le **cachet** nm
tablet

un cachet d'aspirine
an aspirin

la **cachette** nf
hiding place

A B C D E F G H I J K L M N O P Q R S T U V W X Y Z

le **cadavre exquis** nm
consequences

> This is a game where one player writes something on a piece of paper, folds it over and passes it on to the next player to continue the story.

le **Caddie**® nm
supermarket trolley

le **cadeau** nm
(*pl* les cadeaux)
present

un cadeau d'anniversaire
a birthday present

un cadeau de Noël
a Christmas present

Je vais faire un cadeau à ma mère.
I'm going to give my mum a present.

le **cadenas** nm
padlock

cadet m adj
(*f adj* cadette)
1 younger
2 youngest

le **cadet** nm
la **cadette** nf
youngest

Luc est le cadet de la famille.
Luc is the youngest in the family.

Muriel est la cadette de la famille.
Muriel is the youngest in the family.

le **cafard** nm
cockroach

J'ai le cafard.
I'm feeling down.

le **café** nm
1 coffee

un café au lait
a white coffee

un café crème
a strong white coffee

> If you ask for **un café**, it will not have milk in it.

2 café

Rendez-vous au café à trois heures.
Let's meet at the café at 3 o'clock.

le **café-tabac** nm

> A café-tabac is a café which also sells cigarettes and stamps; you can tell a **café-tabac** by the red diamond-shaped sign outside it.

la **cafétéria** nf
cafeteria

la **cage** nf
cage

la **cagoule** nf
balaclava

> **une cagoule** is something you wear, but on your head. It's not an anorak as it is in English.

le **cahier** nm
jotter

mon cahier de français
my French jotter

le **caillou** nm
(*pl* les cailloux)
pebble

la **caisse** nf
1 checkout

Payez à la caisse.
Pay at the checkout.
2 box

une caisse à outils
a tool box

le **caissier** nm
la **caissière** nf
cashier

la **calculatrice** nf
calculator

calculer vb
to work out
Calculez combien ça va coûter.
Work out how much it's going to cost.

la **calculette** nf
pocket calculator

le **caleçon** nm
boxer shorts

le **calendrier** nm
calendar

le **câlin** nm
cuddle

calme

> **calme** can be an adjective or a
> noun.

A adj
1 quiet
un endroit calme
a quiet place
2 calm

La mer est calme.
The sea is calm.
B nm
peace and quiet

**J'ai besoin de calme pour
travailler.**
I need peace and quiet to work.

se **calmer** vb
to calm down

Calme-toi!
Calm down!

le/la **camarade** nm/f
friend

un camarade de classe
a school friend

la **caméra** nf
camera

une caméra de télévision
a television camera

le **caméscope**® nm
camcorder

le **camion** nm
lorry

la **camionnette** nf
van

le **camp** nm
camp

la **campagne** nf
country

à la campagne
in the country

A
B
C
D
E
F
G
H
I
J
K
L
M
N
O
P
Q
R
S
T
U
V
W
X
Y
Z

camper vb
to camp

le **camping** nm
camping

Je n'aime pas le camping.
I don't like camping.

Je vais faire du camping.
I'm going camping.

un terrain de camping
a campsite

le **Canada** nm
Canada

canadien m adj
(*f adj* canadienne)
Canadian

le **Canadien** nm
la **Canadienne** nf
Canadian

le **canapé** nm
sofa

le **canard** nm
duck

le **canari** nm
canary

le **caniche** nm
poodle

le **canif** nm
penknife

la **canne** nf
walking stick

une canne à pêche
a fishing rod

la **cannelle** nf
cinnamon

le **canoë** nm
canoe

Je vais faire du canoë.
I'm going canoeing.

la **cantine** nf
canteen

Je mange à la cantine.
I eat in the canteen.

le **caoutchouc** nm
rubber

des bottes en caoutchouc
Wellington boots

le **capitaine** nm
captain

la **capitale** nf
capital

Paris est la capitale de la France.
Paris is the capital of France.

la **capuche** nf
hood

car
Ⓐ nm
coach

On va en France en car.
We're going to France by coach.

*The French **car** holds a lot more*
*people than the English **car**!*

Ⓑ conj
because

Écoutez, car c'est très important.
Listen, because it's very important.

le **caractère** nm
personality

Il a le même caractère que son père.
He's got the same personality as his father.

Il a bon caractère.
He's good-natured.

Elle a mauvais caractère.
She's bad-tempered.

la **carafe** nf
jug

les **Caraïbes** nfpl
Caribbean Islands

le **caramel** nm
toffee

la **caravane** nf
caravan

le **carême** nm
Lent

la **caresse** nf

faire des caresses
to stroke

Elle fait des caresses au chat.
She's stroking the cat.

caresser vb
to stroke

la **carie** nf

J'ai une carie.
I've got a hole in my tooth.

le **carnaval** nm
carnival

> French children usually celebrate **carnaval** on Shrove Tuesday, when they often come to school in fancy dress. There is a procession in the streets, and at the end of the day **bonhomme carnaval**, (a man made of papier mâché), is burnt on a bonfire.

le **carnet** nm
1 notebook
2 book

un carnet d'adresses
an address book

un carnet de timbres
a book of stamps

un carnet de tickets
a book of tickets

> It is cheaper to buy tickets in a book of ten for the Paris metro.

un carnet de notes
a school report

la **carotte** nf
carrot

carré

> **carré** can be an adjective or a noun.

A m adj
(*f adj* carrée)
square

un mètre carré
a square metre

B nm

un carré de chocolat
a square of chocolate

le **carreau** nm
(pl les carreaux)

1 check

une **chemise à carreaux**
a checked shirt

2 window

Maxime a cassé un carreau.
Maxime has broken a window.

3 diamonds

l'**as de carreau**
the ace of diamonds

le **carrefour** nm
junction

Tournez à gauche au carrefour.
Turn left at the junction.

le **cartable** nm
satchel

un cartable is a large, rigid
kind of satchel which school
children carry on their backs.

la **carte** nf

1 card

une **carte d'anniversaire**
a birthday card

une **carte postale**
a postcard

une **carte de vœux**
a New Year card

The French send greetings
cards (**les cartes de vœux**) in
January rather than at
Christmas, with best wishes
for the New Year.

une **carte de crédit**
a credit card

une **carte d'identité**
an identity card

une **carte téléphonique**
a phonecard

un **jeu de cartes**

*un **jeu de cartes** can either mean
a pack of cards or a card game*.

J'ai acheté un nouveau jeu de cartes.
I've bought a new pack of cards.

Tu connais ce jeu de cartes?
Do you know this card game?

2 map

une **carte de France**
a map of France

une **carte routière**
a road map

3 menu

**Je voudrais la carte, s'il vous
plaît.**
I'd like the menu, please.

le **carton** nm

1 cardboard

un **morceau de carton**
a piece of cardboard

2 cardboard box

un **carton à chaussures**
a shoe box

le **cas** nm
(pl les cas)

case

en tout cas
in any case

au cas où
just in case

Prends de l'argent au cas où.
Take some money just in case.

en cas de
in case of

En cas d'incendie, appelez ce numéro.
In case of fire, call this number.

le **casier** nm
locker

le **casque** nm
1 helmet
2 headphones
J'ai cassé mon casque.
I've broken my headphones.

la **casquette** nf
cap

le **casse-croûte** nm
snack

casse-pieds m, f, pl adj
Il est vraiment casse-pieds!
He's a real pain in the neck!

casser vb
to break

J'ai cassé un verre.
I've broken a glass.
♦ **se casser**
to break

Je me suis cassé la jambe au ski.
I broke my leg when I was skiing.

la **casserole** nf
saucepan

le **cassis** nm
blackcurrant

le **castor** nm
beaver

la **catastrophe** nf
disaster

C'est une catastrophe!
It's a disaster!

le **catéchisme** nm
catechism

la **cathédrale** nf
cathedral

catholique adj, nm/f
Catholic

le **cauchemar** nm
nightmare

J'ai fait un cauchemar.
I had a nightmare.

la **cause** nf

à cause de
because of

Il n'y a pas de courrier à cause de la grève.
There's no post because of the strike.

la **cave** nf
cellar

une cave is dark and
underground, like a cave in
English, but would contain
bottles, not stalactites!

le **CD** nm
(*pl* les CD)
CD

A
B
C
D
E
F
G
H
I
J
K
L
M
N
O
P
Q
R
S
T
U
V
W
X
Y
Z

ce

> **ce** can be an adjective or a pronoun.

A m adj
(also *m adj* cet, *f adj* cette, *pl adj* ces)

> **ce** *changes to* **cet** *before a vowel sound.*

1 this

Tu peux prendre ce livre.
You can take this book.

cet hiver
this winter

cette année
this year

cette semaine-ci
this week

2 that

Je n'aime pas du tout ce film.
I don't like that film at all.

ce livre-là
that book

cette nuit

> **cette nuit** *can either mean* **tonight** *or* **last night**.

Il va neiger cette nuit.
It's going to snow tonight.

Je n'ai pas beaucoup dormi cette nuit.
I didn't sleep much last night.

B pron

> **ce** *changes to* **c'** *before an "e".*

it

Ce n'est pas facile.
It's not easy.

c'est

> **c'est** *can either mean* **it is**, **he is** *or* **she is**.

C'est trop cher.
It's too expensive.

C'est un véritable artiste.
He's a real artist.

C'est une actrice très célèbre.
She's a very famous actress.

C'est super!
It's great!
C'est moi!
It's me!

---

ce sont
they are

Ce sont des amis à mes parents.
They're friends of my parents.

ce qui
what

C'est ce qui compte.
That's what matters.

ce que
what

Je vais lui dire ce que je pense.
I'm going to tell him what I think.

le **CE1** nm
Year 3

le **CE2** nm
Year 4

ceci pron
this

Prends ceci, tu en auras besoin.
Take this, you'll need it.

céder vb
to give in

Elle ne veut pas céder.
She won't give in.

céder à
to give in to

Je ne veux pas céder à ses caprices.
I'm not going to give in to her demands.

la **cédille** nf
cedilla

c cédille
c with a cedilla

*The cedilla looks like the number 5 with the top missing. It's attached to the bottom of the letter C as in the word **garçon**. It makes a **c** sound like an **s** rather than a **k**.*

la **ceinture** nf
belt

une ceinture en cuir
a leather belt

une ceinture de sécurité
a seatbelt

cela pron
1 it

Cela dépend.
It depends.

2 that

Je n'aime pas cela.
I don't like that.

célèbre adj
famous

célébrer vb
to celebrate

le **céleri** nm

le céleri-rave
celeriac

le céleri en branche
celery

célibataire

célibataire can be an adjective or a noun.

A adj
not married

Ma tante est célibataire.
My aunt isn't married.

B nm
bachelor

un célibataire de quarante ans
a 40 year-old bachelor

C nf
single woman

une célibataire de trente-cinq ans
a 35 year-old single woman

celle pron, *see* **celui**

celles pron, *see* **ceux**

celui m pron
(*f pron* celle)
the one

Prends celui que tu préfères.
Take the one you like best.

Ne prends pas mon appareil photo; prends celui de ma sœur!
Don't take my camera, take my sister's!

Ce n'est pas ma platine laser, c'est celle de mon frère.
This isn't my CD player, it's my brother's.

celui-ci
this one

celle-ci
this one

celui-là
that one

celle-là
that one

le **cendrier** nm
ashtray

cent num
a hundred

cent euros
a hundred euros

trois cents ans
three hundred years

cent deux kilomètres
a hundred and two kilometres

trois cent cinquante kilomètres
three hundred and fifty kilometres

la **centaine** nf
about a hundred

Il y a une centaine de personnes dans la salle.
There are about a hundred people in the hall.

des centaines de
hundreds of

J'ai des centaines de timbres dans ma collection.
I've got hundreds of stamps in my collection.

centième adj
hundredth

le **centilitre** nm
centilitre

le **centime** nm
centime

une pièce de cinquante centimes
a 50-centime coin

There are 100 **centimes** in a euro.

le **centimètre** nm
centimetre

le **centre** nm
centre

un centre commercial
a shopping centre

le **centre-ville** nm
town centre

le **cercle** nm
circle

la **céréale** nf
cereal

un bol de céréales
a bowl of cereal

la **cérémonie** nf
ceremony

le **cerf** nm
stag

le **cerf-volant** nm
kite

la **cerise** nf
cherry

le **cerisier** nm
cherry tree

certain m adj
(*f adj* certaine)
1 certain

Ce n'est pas certain.
It's not certain.
2 some

Les chiens sont interdits sur certaines plages.
Dogs are forbidden on some beaches.

certainement adv
1 definitely

C'est certainement le meilleur film de l'année.
It's definitely the best film of the year.
2 of course

Est-ce que je peux t'emprunter ton stylo? – Mais certainement!
Can I borrow your pen? – Of course!

certains pron
1 some

certains de ses amis
some of his friends
2 some people

Certains pensent que c'est difficile.
Some people think it's difficult.

le **certificat** nm
certificate

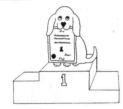

le **cerveau** nm
(*pl* les cerveaux)
brain

le **CES** nm
secondary school
Elle est au CES.
She's in secondary school.

> In France pupils go to a **CES** between the ages of 11 and 15, and then to a **lycée** until the age of 18.

ces pl adj
1 these

Tu peux prendre ces photos si tu veux.
You can have these photos if you like.

ces photos-ci
these photos
2 those

Ces montagnes sont dangereuses en hiver.
Those mountains are dangerous in winter.

ces livres-là
those books

c'est *see* **ce**

c'est-à-dire adv
that is

Est-ce que tu peux venir lundi prochain, c'est-à-dire le quinze?
Can you come next Monday, that's the 15th?

cette f adj, *see* **ce**

ceux mpl pron
(*fpl* celles)
the ones

Prends ceux que tu préfères.
Take the ones you like best.

Ne prends pas mes skis; prends ceux de ma sœur!
Don't take my skis, take my sister's!

Ce ne sont pas mes baskets, ce sont celles de mon frère.
They're not my trainers, they're my brother's.

ceux-ci
these ones

celles-ci
these ones

ceux-là
those ones

celles-là
those ones

chacun pron

1 each

Nous avons chacun donné deux euros.
We each gave 2 euros.

2 everyone

Chacun fait ce qu'il veut.
Everyone does what they like.

la chaîne nf

1 chain

une chaîne en or
a gold chain

2 channel

Le film passe sur quelle chaîne?
Which channel is the film on?

une chaîne hi-fi
a hi-fi system

une chaîne laser
a CD player

une chaîne stéréo
a music centre

la chair nf

flesh

la chair de poule
goose pimples

J'ai la chair de poule!
I've got goose pimples!

The French actually means "I've got hen's flesh"!

la chaise nf

chair

une chaise longue
a deckchair

la chaleur nf

heat

Quelle chaleur!
Phew! It's hot!

la chambre nf

room

C'est la chambre de Camille.
This is Camille's room.

une chambre à coucher
a bedroom

une chambre d'amis
a spare room

une chambre à un lit
a single room

une chambre pour une personne
a single room

une chambre pour deux personnes
a double room

"Chambres d'hôte"
"Bed and Breakfast"

le chameau nm

(*pl* les chameaux)
camel

le **champ** nm
field

le **champignon** nm
mushroom

le **champion** nm
la **championne** nf
champion

le **championnat** nm
championship
le championnat du monde
the world championship

la **chance** nf
1 luck

Tu as de la chance!
You're lucky!

Je n'ai pas de chance.
I'm unlucky.

🔑
Bonne chance!
Good luck!

2 chance
Il n'a aucune chance.
He's got no chance.

le **changement** nm
change
**Est-ce qu'il y a un changement? –
Non, c'est direct.**
Do you have to change? – No, it's a
through train.

changer vb
to change
Tu peux changer les draps?
Can you change the sheets?

Je vais me changer.
I'm going to get changed.

Tu vas te changer?
Are you going to get
changed?

la **chanson** nf
song

le **chant** nm
singing
des cours de chant
singing lessons
un chant de Noël
a Christmas carol

chanter vb
to sing

le **chanteur** nm
la **chanteuse** nf
singer

la **Chantilly** nf
whipped cream

le **chapeau** nm
(*pl* les chapeaux)
hat

le **chapitre** nm
chapter

chaque adj
every
chaque année
every year

la **charade** nf
1 riddle
2 charades
On joue aux charades?
Shall we play charades?

le **charbon** nm
coal

la **charcuterie** nf
1 delicatessen
2 cold meats

Comme entrée, je voudrais de la charcuterie.
As a starter, I would like a plate of cold meats.

le **chariot** nm
trolley

charmant m adj
(f adj charmante)
charming

la **chasse** nf
1 hunting
un chien de chasse
a hunting dog
2 shooting
la chasse au canard
duck shooting

chasser vb
to hunt

le **chasseur** nm
hunter

le **chat** nm
cat
J'ai deux chats.
I've got two cats.

la **châtaigne** nf
chestnut

le **châtaignier** nm
chestnut tree

châtain m, f, pl adj
brown
J'ai les cheveux châtain.
I've got brown hair.

le **château** nm
(pl les châteaux)
1 castle

2 palace
le château de Versailles
the palace of Versailles

le **chaton** nm
kitten

chatouiller vb
to tickle

la **chatte** nf
cat

> **te** added to the word **chat** shows you that the cat is female.

chaud m adj
(f adj chaude)
1 warm
des vêtements chauds
warm clothes
2 hot
de l'eau chaude
hot water

> **Il fait chaud.**
> It's hot.
> **J'ai chaud!**
> I'm hot!

le **chauffage** nm
heating
le chauffage central
central heating

le **chauffeur** nm

driver

un chauffeur de taxi
a taxi driver

> *An English chauffeur drives a rich person's car, but **chauffeur** in French means any kind of driver.*

la **chaussette** nf
sock

le **chausson** nm
slipper

un chausson aux pommes
an apple turnover

la **chaussure** nf
shoe

les chaussures de ski
ski boots

chauve adj
bald

la **chauve-souris** nf
bat

> *The French actually means "bald mouse"!*

le **chef** nm
■ boss

C'est toi le chef!
You're the boss!
■ chef

la spécialité du chef
the chef's speciality

un chef d'orchestre
a conductor

le **chef-d'œuvre** nm
masterpiece

le **chemin** nm
■ path
■ way

Montre-moi le chemin.
Show me the way.

en chemin
on the way

les chemins de fer
the railways

la **cheminée** nf
■ chimney
■ fireplace

la **chemise** nf
■ shirt

une chemise à carreaux
a checked shirt

une chemise de nuit
a nightdress

■ folder

le **chemisier** nm
blouse

le **chêne** nm
oak

la **chenille** nf
caterpillar

le **chèque** nm
cheque
les chèques de voyage
traveller's cheques

cher

> **cher** can be an adjective or an adverb.

A m adj
(*f adj* chère)

1 dear

Chère Mélusine …
Dear Mélusine …

2 expensive

C'est trop cher.
It's too expensive.

B adv

coûter cher
to be expensive

Cet ordinateur coûte cher.
This computer is expensive.

chercher vb

1 to look for

Je cherche mes clés.
I'm looking for my keys.

2 to look up

Cherche "apple" dans le dictionnaire.
Look up "apple" in the dictionary.

aller chercher
to go to get

Je vais chercher du pain pour le déjeuner.
I'm going to get some bread for lunch.

le **chercheur** nm
la **chercheuse** nf
scientist

chère f adj, *see* **cher**

chéri nm, m adj
(*nf, f adj* chérie)
darling

le **cheval** nm
(*pl* les chevaux)
horse

un cheval de course
a racehorse

à cheval
on horseback

Je fais du cheval le samedi.
I go riding on Saturdays.

le **chevalier** nm
knight

les **chevaux** nmpl
horses

les **cheveux** nmpl
hair

Elle a les cheveux courts.
She's got short hair.

la **cheville** nf
ankle

la **chèvre** nf
goat

le **fromage de chèvre**
goat's cheese

le **chevreuil** nm

1 roe deer

2 venison

On mange du chevreuil à Noël.
We'll eat venison at Christmas.

chez prep

> *chez means either* **at** *or* **to** *someone's house.*

On va chez moi?
Shall we go to my house?

Je vais chez Marc.
I'm going to Marc's house.

Je rentre chez moi à quatre heures.
I go home at four.

Nicole va chez elle.
Nicole is going home.

Jean-Claude reste chez lui.
Jean-Claude is staying at
home.

Tu rentres chez toi?
Are you going home?

> *chez le dentiste means either* **at the dentist's** *or* **to the dentist's**.

J'ai rendez-vous chez le dentiste.
I've got an appointment at the dentist's.

Je vais chez le dentiste.
I'm going to the dentist's.

Je suis chez moi.
I'm at home.
Je vais chez moi.
I'm going home.

chic m, f, pl adj
smart

une tenue chic
a smart outfit

le **chien** nm
dog

la **chienne** nf
bitch

C'est un chien ou une chienne?
Is it a dog or a bitch?

le **chiffon** nm
cloth

le **chiffre** nm
figure

Écris ce nombre en chiffres.
Write this number in figures.

la **chimie** nf
chemistry

la **Chine** nf
China

chinois m adj, nm
(*f adj* chinoise)
Chinese

le **Chinois** nm
Chinese man

les Chinois
the Chinese

la **Chinoise** nf
Chinese woman

le **chiot** nm
puppy

les **chips** nfpl
crisps

un paquet de chips
a packet of crisps

> *Be careful! The French word* **chips** *does not mean the same as* **chips** *in English.*

le **chirurgien** nm
surgeon

le **chocolat** nm
chocolate

un chocolat chaud
a hot chocolate

le **chœur** nm
choir

choisir vb
to choose

A
B
C
D
E
F
G
H
I
J
K
L
M
N
O
P
Q
R
S
T
U
V
W
X
Y
Z

a
b
c
d
e
f
g
h
i
j
k
l
m
n
o
p
q
r
s
t
u
v
w
x
y
z

le **choix** nm
1 choice

Je n'ai pas le choix.
I don't have a choice.

2 selection

Il n'y a pas beaucoup de choix dans ce magasin.
There's not much of a selection in this shop.

le **chômage** nm
unemployment

au chômage
unemployed

Mon père est au chômage.
My dad is unemployed.

le **chômeur** nm
la **chômeuse** nf

Il est chômeur.
He's unemployed.

Elle est chômeuse.
She's unemployed.

la **chorale** nf
choir

la **chose** nf
thing

J'ai fait beaucoup de choses pendant les vacances.
I did lots of things in the holidays.

le **chou** nm
(pl les choux)
cabbage

les choux de Bruxelles
Brussels sprouts

le **chouchou** nm
la **chouchoute** nf
teacher's pet

la **choucroute** nf
sauerkraut with sausages and ham

Sauerkraut is a kind of pickled cabbage.

chouette

chouette can be an adjective or a noun.

A adj
brilliant

Chouette alors!
Brilliant!

B nf
owl

le **chou-fleur** nm
cauliflower

chrétien m adj
(f adj chrétienne)
Christian

le **chronomètre** nm
stopwatch

le **chrysanthème** nm
chrysanthemum

People in France put chrysanthemums on graves. You wouldn't give them to someone as a present.

chuchoter vb
to whisper

chut excl
shh!

-ci adv
ce livre-ci
this book
ces bottes-ci
these boots

la **ciboulette** nf
chives

la **cicatrice** nf
scar

ci-contre adv
opposite
la page ci-contre
the opposite page

ci-dessous adv
below
la photo ci-dessous
the picture below

ci-dessus adv
above

le **cidre** nm
cider

le **ciel** nm
sky
un ciel nuageux
a cloudy sky

le **cigare** nm
cigar

la **cigarette** nf
cigarette

le **cil** nm
eyelash

le **cimetière** nm
cemetery

le **cinéma** nm
cinema

cinq num
five
Il est cinq heures du matin.
It's five in the morning.
Il a cinq ans.
He's five.

> 🔑
> **le cinq février**
> the fifth of February

la **cinquantaine** nf
about fifty
Il y a une cinquantaine de personnes dans la salle.
There are about fifty people in the hall.
Il a la cinquantaine.
He's in his fifties.

cinquante num
fifty
Il a cinquante ans.
He's fifty.
cinquante et un
fifty-one
cinquante-deux
fifty-two

cinquième

> cinquième can be an adjective or a noun.

Ⓐ adj
fifth
au cinquième étage
on the fifth floor

A B C D E F G H I J K L M N O P Q R S T U V W X Y Z

B nf
Year 8

> In French secondary schools and sixth form colleges, years are counted from the **sixième** (youngest) to **première** and **terminale** (oldest).

Mon frère est en cinquième.
My brother's in Year 8.

circonflexe adj
un accent circonflexe
a circumflex

la **circulation** nf
traffic

Il y a beaucoup de circulation.
There is a lot of traffic.

le **cirque** nm
circus

les **ciseaux** nmpl
une paire de ciseaux
a pair of scissors

la **cité** nf
estate

J'habite dans une cité.
I live on an estate.

> **une cité** is an inner-city estate.

le **citron** nm
lemon

un citron vert
a lime

un citron pressé
a fresh lemon juice

la **citrouille** nf
pumpkin

clair m adj
(*f adj* claire)
light

vert clair
light green

C'est une pièce très claire.
It's a very light room.

clairement adv
clearly

la **claque** nf
slap

claquer vb
to slam

les **claquettes** nfpl
faire des claquettes
to tap-dance

Je fais des claquettes le samedi.
I do tap on Saturdays.

la **clarinette** nf
clarinet

Élodie joue de la clarinette.
Élodie plays the clarinet.

la **classe** nf

1 class

C'est la meilleure élève de la classe.
She's the best pupil in the class.

un aller simple en première classe
a first class single

2 classroom

classer vb
to arrange

le **classeur** nm
ring binder

classique adj

1 classical

la musique classique
classical music

2 classic

le **clavier** nm
keyboard

la **clé** nf
key

la **clef** nf
key

le **client** nm
la **cliente** nf
customer

le **climat** nm
climate

le **clin d'œil** nm
wink

la **clinique** nf
private hospital

cliquer vb
to click

Clique sur une icône.
Click on an icon.

la **cloche** nf
bell

les cloches de Pâques
Easter bells

In France, Easter eggs are said to be brought by the Easter bells (**cloches de Pâques**) which fly from Rome and drop them in people's gardens.

le **clocher** nm

1 church tower

2 steeple

le **club** nm
club

le **CM1** nm
Year 5

le **CM2** nm
Year 6

le **cobaye** nm
guinea pig

le **coca** nm
Coke®

la **coccinelle** nf
ladybird

cocher vb
to tick

Cochez la bonne réponse.
Tick the right answer.

A B C D E F G H I J K L M N O P Q R S T U V W X Y Z

le **cochon** nm
pig

un cochon d'Inde
a guinea pig

le **coco** nm
une noix de coco
a coconut

cocorico excl
1 Cock-a-doodle-doo!
2 Three cheers for France!

> The symbol of France is the cockerel and so **cocorico!** is sometimes used as an expression of French national pride.

le **cœur** nm
heart

la dame de cœur
the queen of hearts

J'ai mal au cœur!
I feel sick!

Il faut l'apprendre par cœur.
You must learn it by heart.

Apprenez ce petit poème par cœur.
Learn this little poem by heart.

le **coffre** nm
car boot

un coffre à jouets
a toybox

le **coffret** nm
un coffret à bijoux
a jewellery box

coiffé m adj
(*f adj* coiffée)

Tu es bien coiffée.
Your hair looks nice.

se **coiffer** vb
Maman se coiffe.
Mum is doing her hair.

le **coiffeur** nm
la **coiffeuse** nf
hairdresser

la **coiffure** nf
hairstyle

Cette coiffure te va bien.
That hairstyle suits you.

un salon de coiffure
a hairdresser's

le **coin** nm
corner

au coin de la rue
on the corner of the street

le **col** nm
collar

la **colère** nf
anger

en colère
angry

Je suis en colère.
I'm angry.

Il va se mettre en colère.
He's going to get angry.

le **colin-maillard** nm
blind man's buff

le **colis** nm
parcel

collant

collant can be an adjective or a noun.

A m adj
(f adj collante)
sticky

B nm
tights

un collant en laine
woollen tights

la colle nf
glue

la collection nf
collection

une collection d'autocollants
a sticker collection

collectionner vb
to collect

le collège nm
secondary school

In France pupils go to a **collège** between the ages of 11 and 15, and then to a **lycée** until the age of 18.

le collégien nm
la collégienne nf
secondary school pupil

le/la collègue nm/f
colleague

coller vb
1 to stick

Colle cette feuille dans ton cahier.
Stick this piece of paper in your book.

2 to be sticky

Elle a les mains qui collent.
Her hands are sticky.

le collier nm
1 necklace

un collier de perles
a pearl necklace

2 collar

Où est le collier du chien?
Where's the dog's collar?

la colline nf
hill

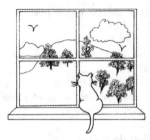

la colonie de vacances nf
summer camp

Je n'aime pas partir en colonie de vacances.
I don't like going to summer camp.

French schoolchildren often go to a **colonie de vacances** for a fortnight in the summer holidays.

la colonne nf
column

colorier vb
to colour in

combien adv
1 how much

Vous en voulez combien? Un kilo?
How much do you want? One kilo?

Combien est-ce que ça coûte?
How much does it cost?

a
b
c
d
e
f
g
h
i
j
k
l
m
n
o
p
q
r
s
t
u
v
w
x
y
z

Ça fait combien?
How much does it come to?

🔑
C'est combien?
How much is that?

2 how many

Tu en veux combien? Deux?
How many do you want? Two?

combien de

combien de can either mean how much or how many.

Tu reçois combien d'argent de poche?
How much pocket money do you get?

Tu as combien de frères et sœurs?
How many brothers and sisters have you got?

combien de temps
how long

Combien de temps est-ce que ça dure?
How long does it last?

🔑
On est le combien aujourd'hui?
What's the date today?

la **combinaison** nf
une combinaison de plongée
a wetsuit
une combinaison de ski
a ski suit

la **comédie** nf
comedy

le **comédien** nm
la **comédienne** nf
actor

Be careful! The French word comédien does not mean the same as comedian in English.

comique

comique can be an adjective or a noun.

A adj
comical
B nm
comedian

commander vb
to order

J'ai commandé un steak frites.
I ordered steak and chips.

comme conj, adv
1 like

Il est comme son père.
He's like his father.

comme ça
like this

Ça se plie comme ça.
You fold it like this.

C'était un poisson grand comme ça.
The fish was this big.

2 for

Qu'est-ce que tu veux comme dessert?
What would you like for pudding?

3 as

Elle travaille comme serveuse.
She works as a waitress.

Fais comme tu veux.
Do as you like.

4 how
Comme tu as grandi!
How you've grown!

Regarde comme c'est beau!
Look, isn't it lovely!

Comment ça va? – Comme ci comme ça.
How are you? – Okay, I suppose.

commencer vb
to start

comment adv
how

Comment dit-on "apple" en français?
How do you say "apple" in French?

Comment s'appelle-t-il?
What's his name?
Comment tu t'appelles?
What's your name?
Comment ça va?
How are you?
Comment?
What did you say?
Comment ça s'écrit?
How do you spell it?

le **commerce** nm
business

Il fait des études de commerce.
He's studying business.

commercial m adj

un centre commercial
a shopping centre

le **commissariat** nm
police station

les **commissions** nfpl
shopping

J'ai quelques commissions à faire.
I've got some shopping to do.

commode nf
chest of drawers

commun m adj
(f adj commune)

en commun
in common

Ils n'ont rien en commun.
They've got nothing in common.

les transports en commun
public transport

compact m adj
(f adj compacte)
compact

un disque compact
a compact disc

la **compagnie** nf
company

une compagnie aérienne
an airline

comparer vb
to compare

le **compartiment** nm
compartment

le **compas** nm
compasses

Je peux emprunter ton compas?
Can I borrow your compasses?

la **compétition** nf
competition

A
B
C
D
E
F
G
H
I
J
K
L
M
N
O
P
Q
R
S
T
U
V
W
X
Y
Z

une compétition de natation
a swimming competition

complet m adj
(*f adj* complète)
full

L'hôtel est complet.
The hotel is full.

"complet"
"no vacancies"

le pain complet
wholemeal bread

complètement adv
completely

compléter vb
to complete

compliqué m adj
(*f adj* compliquée)
complicated

composter vb
to punch

Tu as composté ton billet?
Have you punched your ticket?

In France you have to punch your ticket before you get on the train. If you don't you might get a fine.

la **compote** nf
stewed fruit

la compote de pommes
stewed apple

comprendre vb
to understand

Tu comprends?
Do you understand?

Je ne comprends pas!
I don't understand!

le comprimé nm
tablet

compris m adj

compris can be part of a verb or an adjective.

Ⓐ vb, *see* **comprendre**

Je n'ai pas compris.
I don't understand.
Ⓑ m adj
(*f adj* comprise)
included

Le service n'est pas compris.
Service is not included.

le/la **comptable** nm/f
accountant

le **compte** nm
account

un compte bancaire
a bank account

Ma mère travaille à son compte.
My mum is self-employed.

compter vb
to count

se **concentrer** vb
to concentrate

Il faut te concentrer!
You've got to concentrate!

le **concert** nm
concert

le/la **concierge** nm/f
caretaker

le **concombre** nm
cucumber

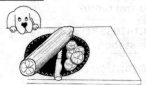

le **concours** nm
competition

un concours de chant
a singing competition

la **condition** nf
condition

Je vais le faire à une condition.
I'll do it, on one condition.

le **conducteur** nm
la **conductrice** nf
driver

conduire vb
to drive

**Ma grand-mère ne sait pas
conduire.**
My grandma can't drive.

Ma mère me conduit à l'école.
My mum drives me to school.

♦ **se conduire**
to behave

Il se conduit mal en classe.
He behaves badly in class.

les **confettis** nmpl
confetti

la **confiance** nf
trust

Tu peux avoir confiance en moi.
You can trust me.

Je n'ai pas confiance en lui.
I don't trust him.

la **confiserie** nf
sweet shop

confit m adj
(f adj confite)

des fruits confits
crystallized fruits

la **confiture** nf
jam

la confiture de fraises
strawberry jam

la confiture d'oranges
marmalade

confortable adj
comfortable

des chaussures confortables
comfortable shoes

le **congé** nm
holiday

une semaine de congé
a week's holiday

en congé
on holiday

le **congélateur** nm
freezer

connaître vb
to know

Je ne la connais pas.
I don't know her.

se **connecter** vb
to log on

**Comment est-ce qu'on se
connecte sur Internet?**
How do you log on to the internet?

connu m adj
(f adj connue)
well-known

C'est un acteur connu.
He's a well-known actor.

le **conseil** nm
advice

Je peux te demander conseil?
Can I ask you for some advice?

un conseil
a piece of advice

A B C D E F G H I J K L M N O P Q R S T U V W X Y Z

conseiller vb
1 to advise

Qu'est-ce que tu me conseilles de faire?
What do you advise me to do?
2 to recommend

Je te conseille ce livre.
I recommend this book.

le **conseiller** nm
la **conseillère** nf
adviser

le conseiller d'orientation
the careers adviser

le **conservatoire** nm
school of music

la **conserve** nf
tin

une boîte de conserve
a tin

en conserve
tinned

des petits pois en conserve
tinned peas

la **consigne** nf
left-luggage office

une consigne automatique
a left-luggage locker

la **console de jeu** nf
games console

constamment adv
constantly

construire vb
to build

contacter vb
to get in touch with

Tu peux me contacter par courrier électronique.
You can get in touch with me by email.

le **conte de fées** nm
fairy tale

content m adj
(*f adj* contente)
happy

Je suis content pour toi.
I'm happy for you.

content de
pleased with

Elle est contente de mon travail.
She is pleased with my work.

continuer vb
to carry on

Continuez sans moi!
Carry on without me!

le **contraire** nm
opposite

Il fait le contraire de ce que je demande.
He does the opposite of what I ask him to.

au contraire
on the contrary

contre prep
against

Ne mets pas ton vélo contre le mur.
Don't put your bike against the wall.

Je suis contre cette idée.
I'm against this idea.

par contre
on the other hand

la **contrebasse** nf
double bass

Je joue de la contrebasse.
I play the double bass.

le **contrôle** nm
1 control

le contrôle des passeports
passport control
2 check

un contrôle d'identité
an identity check

le contrôle des billets
ticket inspection

contrôler vb
to check

le **contrôleur** nm
la **contrôleuse** nf
ticket inspector

la **conversation** nf
conversation

cool m, f, pl adj
cool

J'adore le français. C'est vraiment cool.
I love French. It's really cool.

le **copain** nm
1 friend

C'est un bon copain.
He's a good friend.
2 boyfriend

Elle a un nouveau copain.
She's got a new boyfriend.

la **copie** nf
1 copy
2 paper

Rendez vos copies!
Hand in your papers!

copier vb
to copy

copier-coller
to copy and paste

la **copine** nf
1 friend

C'est une bonne copine.
She's a good friend.
2 girlfriend

Il a une nouvelle copine.
He's got a new girlfriend.

le **coq** nm
cockerel

The cockerel is the symbol of France.

la **coque** nf

un œuf à la coque
a soft-boiled egg

le **coquelicot** nm
poppy

le **coquillage** nm
shell

la **coquille** nf
shell

une coquille Saint-Jacques
a scallop

coquin m adj
(f adj coquine)
cheeky

le **corbeau** nm
(pl les corbeaux)
crow

la **corbeille** nf
basket

une corbeille à papier
a wastepaper basket

la **corde** nf
rope

la **cordonnerie** nf
shoe repair shop

le **cordonnier** nm
cobbler

la **cornemuse** nf
bagpipes

Je joue de la cornemuse.
I play the bagpipes.

le **cornet** nm

un cornet de frites
a bag of chips

un cornet de glace
an ice cream cone

le **cornichon** nm
gherkin

la **Cornouailles** nf
Cornwall

le **corps** nm
body

correct m adj
(f adj correcte)
correct

Est-ce que cette phrase est correcte?
Is this sentence correct?

la **correspondance** nf
connection

Il y a une correspondance pour Toulouse à dix heures.
There's a connection for Toulouse at ten o'clock.

le **correspondant** nm
la **correspondante** nf
penfriend

correspondre vb
to correspond

corriger vb
to mark

Vous pouvez corriger cet exercice?
Could you mark this exercise?

corse adj
Corsican

le/la **Corse** nm/f
Corsican

la **Corse** nf
Corsica

le **costume** nm
1 man's suit

Fabien ne porte pas souvent de costume.
Fabien doesn't often wear a suit.

2 costume

Je prépare mon costume pour carnaval.
I'm making my costume for the carnival.

la **côte** nf
1 coastline

La route longe la côte.
The road follows the coastline.

la Côte d'Azur
the French Riviera

2 hill

La maison est en haut d'une côte.
The house is at the top of a hill.

3 rib

Elle a une côte cassée.
She has a broken rib.

4 chop

une côte de porc
a pork chop

une côte de bœuf
a rib of beef

côte à côte
side by side

le **côté** nm
side

de l'autre côté
on the other side

La pharmacie est de l'autre côté de la rue.
The chemist's is on the other side of the street.

à côté de

*à côté de can either mean **next to** or **next door to**.*

La poste est à côté de la gare.
The post office is next to the station.

Il habite à côté de chez moi.
He lives next door to me.

la **côtelette** nf
chop

une côtelette d'agneau
a lamb chop

le **coton** nm
cotton

une chemise en coton
a cotton shirt

le coton hydrophile
cotton wool

le **coton-tige**® nm
cotton bud

le **cou** nm
neck

couchant m adj
le soleil couchant
the setting sun

la **couche** nf
nappy

couché m adj
(*f adj* couchée)
1 lying down

Le chien est couché sur le tapis.
The dog is lying down on the carpet.

2 in bed

Tu es déjà couché?
Are you in bed already?

le **coucher** nm
un coucher de soleil
a sunset

se **coucher** vb
1 to go to bed

Il faut se coucher tôt ce soir.
You must go to bed early tonight.

Tu te couches à quelle heure?
What time do you go to bed?

Je me couche à neuf heures.
I go to bed at nine.

2 to set

Le soleil se couche vers neuf heures.
The sun sets at around 9 o'clock.

la **couchette** nf
berth

a
b
c
d
e
f
g
h
i
j
k
l
m
n
o
p
q
r
s
t
u
v
w
x
y
z

le **coude** nm
elbow

coudre vb
to sew

Tu sais coudre?
Can you sew?

la **couette** nf
duvet

les couettes
bunches

Ma petite sœur a des couettes.
My little sister has bunches.

couler vb
1 to run

J'ai le nez qui coule.
My nose is running.

2 to flow

La rivière coule lentement.
The river flows slowly.

3 to leak

Mon stylo coule.
My pen's leaking.

4 to sink

Un bateau a coulé pendant la tempête.
A boat sank during the storm.

la **couleur** nf
colour

De quelle couleur est ton stylo?
What colour is your pen?

Elle a les yeux de quelle couleur?
What colour eyes has she got?

C'est de quelle couleur?
What colour is it?

le **couloir** nm
corridor

le **coup** nm
1 knock
2 blow

un coup sur la tête
a blow to the head

du premier coup
first time

Il a eu son permis du premier coup.
He passed his driving test first time.

coup de

There are lots of coup de combinations of words. Look through the list to find the one you need.

un coup de pied
a kick

un coup de poing
a punch

un coup de feu
a shot

un coup de fil
a ring

Donne-moi un coup de fil ce soir.
Give me a ring this evening.

Tu peux me donner un coup de main?
Can you give me a hand?

Tu vas prendre un coup de soleil!
You'll get sunburnt!

un coup de téléphone
a phone call

un coup de tonnerre
a clap of thunder

coupable

> **coupable** can be an adjective or a noun.

Ⓐ adj
guilty

Ⓑ nm/f
culprit

la **coupe** nf
cup

la coupe du monde
the World Cup

une coupe de cheveux
a haircut

une coupe de champagne
a glass of champagne

couper vb
to cut

Attention! Tu vas te couper!
Careful! You're going to cut yourself!

Je vais me faire couper les cheveux.
I'm going to get my hair cut.

le **couple** nm
couple

le **couplet** nm
verse

le premier couplet
the first verse

la **coupure** nf
cut

une coupure de courant
a power cut

la **cour** nf
yard

la cour de l'école
the school yard

courageux m adj
(f adj courageuse)
brave

couramment adv
fluently

Elle parle couramment japonais.
She speaks Japanese fluently.

courant

> **courant** can be an adjective or a noun.

Ⓐ m adj
(f adj courante)
common

'Marie' est un prénom courant.
'Marie' is a common name.

Ⓑ nm
1 current

Le courant est fort.
The current is strong.

un courant d'air
a draught

2 power

une panne de courant
a power cut

Tu es au courant?
Have you heard about it?

le **coureur** nm
la **coureuse** nf
runner

un coureur à pied
a runner

un coureur cycliste
a racing cyclist

un coureur automobile
a racing driver

A
B
C
D
E
F
G
H
I
J
K
L
M
N
O
P
Q
R
S
T
U
V
W
X
Y
Z

a
b
c
d
e
f
g
h
i
j
k
l
m
n
o
p
q
r
s
t
u
v
w
x
y
z

courir vb
to run

Ne courez pas dans le couloir.
Don't run in the corridor.

J'ai couru jusqu'à l'école.
I ran all the way to school.

la **couronne** nf
crown

courons, courez vb, *see*
courir

Courons jusqu'à la barrière!
Let's run as far as the gate!

Vous courez trop vite!
You're running too fast!

le **courrier** nm
mail

Le facteur apporte le courrier à huit heures.
The postman brings the mail at 8 o'clock.

le courrier électronique
email

le **cours** nm
1 lesson

un cours d'espagnol
a Spanish lesson

2 class

un cours du soir
an evening class

3 rate

le cours du change
the exchange rate

la **course** nf
1 running

la course de fond
long-distance running

2 race

une course hippique
a horse race

3 shopping

J'ai juste une course à faire.
I've just got a bit of shopping to do.

faire les courses
to shop
Je n'aime pas faire les courses au supermarché.
I don't like shopping in supermarkets.

court

court can be an adjective or a noun.

Ⓐ m adj
(*f adj* courte)
short
Ⓑ nm

un court de tennis
a tennis court

couru vb, *see* **courir**
J'ai couru jusqu'à la maison.
I ran all the way home.

le **couscous** nm
couscous

couscous is a spicy North African dish.

le **cousin** nm
la **cousine** nf
cousin

le **coussin** nm
cushion

le **couteau** nm
(*pl* les couteaux)
knife

coûter vb
to cost

Est-ce que ça coûte cher?
Does it cost a lot?

> 🔑
> **Combien ça coûte?**
> How much is it?

la **couture** nf
sewing

Je n'aime pas la couture.
I don't like sewing.

le **couvercle** nm
1 lid

le couvercle de la casserole
the lid of the pan
2 top

le couvercle du pot de confiture
the top of the jam jar

couvert

> **couvert** can be an adjective, a
> noun or part of the verb **couvrir**.

Ⓐ m adj
(*f adj* couverte)
overcast

Le ciel est couvert.
The sky is overcast.

couvert de
covered with

un arbre couvert de fleurs
a tree covered with blossom
Ⓑ nm
les couverts
cutlery

Les couverts sont dans le tiroir de gauche.
The cutlery is in the left-hand drawer.

Ⓒ vb, *see* **couvrir**

Il est couvert de boutons.
He's covered with spots.

la **couverture** nf
blanket

le **couvre-lit** nm
bedspread

couvrir vb
to cover

Le chien est revenu couvert de boue.
The dog came back covered with mud.

◆ **se couvrir**

> *se couvrir can either mean* **to wrap up** *or* **to cloud over**.

Couvre-toi bien: il fait froid dehors.
Wrap up well: it's cold outside.

Le ciel se couvre.
The sky's clouding over.

a

le CP nm
Year 2

b

le crabe nm
crab

c

cracher vb
to spit

d

la craie nf
chalk

e

f

craindre vb
to fear
Tu n'as rien à craindre.
You've got nothing to fear.

g

h

i

craintif m adj
(*f adj* craintive)
timid

j

k

la crampe nf
cramp
J'ai une crampe au pied.
I've got cramp in my foot.

l

m

le crapaud nm
toad

n

o

p

q

r

la cravate nf
tie

s

le crayon nm
pencil
un crayon de couleur
a coloured pencil

t

u

v

un crayon feutre
a felt-tip pen

w

la crèche nf
1 nursery
Ma petite sœur va à la crèche.
My little sister goes to a nursery.

x

y

z

2 nativity scene

créer vb
to create

la crème nf
cream
la crème anglaise
custard

la crème Chantilly
whipped cream

une crème caramel
a crème caramel

une crème au chocolat
a chocolate dessert

le crème nm
white coffee

un grand crème
a large white coffee

la crêpe nf
pancake

la crêperie nf
pancake restaurant

le cresson nm
watercress

la Crète nf
Crete

creuser vb
to dig

crevé m adj
(*f adj* crevée)
1 punctured

un pneu crevé
a puncture

2 knackered

Je suis complètement crevé!
I'm really knackered!

crever vb
1 to burst

Il a crevé mon ballon!
He's burst my balloon!
2 to have a puncture

On a crevé en route.
We had a puncture on the way.

la **crevette** nf
prawn

le **cri** nm
scream

crier vb
to shout

le **crime** nm
1 crime
2 murder

le **criquet** nm
grasshopper

la **crise** nf
attack

une crise d'asthme
an asthma attack

une crise de foie
an upset stomach

critiquer vb
to criticize

le **crocodile** nm
crocodile

croire vb
to believe

Je ne te crois pas.
I don't believe you.

Tu l'as cru?
Did you believe him?

croire que
to think that

Tu crois que c'est vrai?
Do you think that's true?

Il croit en Dieu.
He believes in God.

crois vb, see **croire**

Je crois que tu as raison.
I think you're right.

le **croisement** nm
crossroads

Tournez à gauche au croisement.
Turn left at the crossroads.

croiser vb

croiser les bras
to fold one's arms

croiser les jambes
to cross one's legs

♦ **se croiser**
to pass each other

**Nous nous croisons dans la rue
tous les matins.**
We pass each other on the street
every morning.

le **croissant** nm
croissant

croit see **croire**

Il croit encore au Père Noël!
He still believes in Santa!

la **croix** nf
cross

le **croque-madame** nm
le **croque-monsieur** nm

A **croque-monsieur** is a ham
and cheese toastie. A
croque-madame has an
added fried egg.

A B C D E F G H I J K L M N O P Q R S T U V W X Y Z

a
b
c
d
e
f
g
h
i
j
k
l
m
n
o
p
q
r
s
t
u
v
w
x
y
z

croquer vb
to munch

la **croûte** nf
1 crust

en croûte
in pastry

2 rind

Mon chat aime la croûte du fromage.
My cat likes cheese rind.

3 scab

J'ai une croûte sur le genou.
I've got a scab on my knee.

le **croûton** nm
1 end of a baguette

2 crouton

Tu veux des croûtons dans ta soupe?
Would you like some croutons in your soup?

cru
A m adj
(f adj crue)
raw

la viande crue
raw meat

le jambon cru
Parma ham

B vb, see **croire**

Je l'ai cru.
I believed him.

la **cruche** nf
jug

les **crudités** nfpl
assorted raw vegetables

cruel m adj
(f adj cruelle)
cruel

les **crustacés** nmpl
shellfish

le **cube** nm
cube

cueillir vb
to pick

J'ai cueilli des fleurs dans le jardin.
I picked some flowers in the garden.

la **cuiller** nf
la **cuillère**
spoon

une cuiller à café
a teaspoon

une cuiller à soupe
a tablespoon

la **cuillerée** nf
spoonful

le **cuir** nm
leather

un sac en cuir
a leather bag

cuire vb
to cook

faire cuire
to cook

"Faire cuire pendant une heure"
"Cook for one hour"

bien cuit
well done

trop cuit
overdone

la **cuisine** nf
1 kitchen

La cuisine est très grande.
The kitchen is very big.

2 food

Tu aimes la cuisine française?
Do you like French food?

faire la cuisine
to cook

Je ne fais jamais la cuisine.
I never cook.

cuisiner vb
to cook

J'aime beaucoup cuisiner.
I love cooking.

le **cuisinier** nm
cook

la **cuisinière** nf
1 cook

C'est une bonne cuisinière.
She's a good cook.

2 cooker

une cuisinière à gaz
a gas cooker

la **cuisse** nf
thigh

une cuisse de poulet
a chicken leg

la **cuisson** nf
cooking

"une heure de cuisson"
"cooking time: one hour"

cuit vb, see **cuire**

Est-ce que c'est cuit?
Is it cooked?

le **cuivre** nm
copper

la **culotte** nf
knickers

le **cultivateur** nm
la **cultivatrice** nf
farmer

cultiver vb
to grow

Il cultive des légumes.
He grows vegetables.

le **curé** nm
parish priest

curieux m adj
(*f adj* curieuse)
curious

le **curseur** nm
cursor

le **cybercafé** nm
internet café

cyclable adj
une piste cyclable
a cycle track

le **cyclisme** nm
cycling

le/la **cycliste** nm/f
cyclist

le **cyclone** nm
hurricane

le **cygne** nm
swan

D

d'

> **d'** can be an article or a preposition.

> *de changes to **d'** before a vowel sound.*

A article
any

Je n'ai pas d'argent.
I haven't got any money.

Je n'ai pas d'animal domestique à la maison.
I haven't got a pet.

B prep

1 of

une bouteille d'orangina
a bottle of orangina

la voiture d'Hélène
Hélène's car

un bébé d'un an
a one-year-old baby

2 from

une lettre d'Olivier
a letter from Olivier

le **daim** nm
suede

une veste en daim
a suede jacket

la **dame** nf

1 lady

une dame de service
a dinner lady

2 queen

la dame de pique
the queen of spades

les dames
draughts

un jeu de dames
a game of draughts

le **Danemark** nm
Denmark

dangereux m adj
(*f adj* dangereuse)
dangerous

danois m adj, nm
(*f adj* danoise)
Danish

le **Danois** nm
la **Danoise** nf
Dane

dans prep
in

Il est dans sa chambre.
He's in his bedroom.

dans deux mois
in two months

la **danse** nf
dance

la danse classique
ballet

Je fais de la danse.
I go to dancing classes.

danser vb
to dance

le danseur nm
la danseuse nf
dancer

la date nf
date

Quelle est ta date de naissance?
What's your date of birth?

Quelle est la date de ton anniversaire?
What date is your birthday?

> **Quelle est la date aujourd'hui?**
> What's the date today?

le dauphin nm
dolphin

de
de can be an article or a preposition.

See also du (= de + le) and des (= de + les). de changes to d' before a vowel sound.

A article

You can use de to mean either some or any.

Je voudrais de l'eau.
I'd like some water.

du pain et de la confiture
bread and jam

Il n'a pas de frères et sœurs.
He hasn't got any brothers or sisters.

Il n'y a plus de biscuits.
There aren't any more biscuits.

B prep
1 of

un paquet de biscuits
a packet of biscuits

la voiture de Paul
Paul's car

la voiture de mes parents
my parents' car

un billet de dix euros
a ten-euro note

2 from

de Londres à Paris
from London to Paris

Il vient de Londres.
He comes from London.

une lettre de Victor
a letter from Victor

3 in

à une heure de l'après-midi
at one o'clock in the afternoon

le dé nm
dice

Lance le dé.
Throw the dice.

débarrasser vb
to clear

Tu peux débarrasser la table, s'il te plaît?
Can you clear the table please?

debout adv
Debout!
Get up!

le **début** nm
beginning
au début
at the beginning
début mai
in early May

le **débutant** nm
la **débutante** nf
beginner

le **décalage horaire** nm
time difference
**Il y a une heure de décalage
horaire entre la France et la
Grande-Bretagne.**
There's an hour's time difference
between France and Britain.

décalquer vb
to trace
**Décalquez la carte de
France.**
Trace the map of France.

décapotable adj
une voiture décapotable
a convertible

décembre nm
December
en décembre
in December
le dix décembre
the tenth of December

décevoir vb
to disappoint

déchirer vb
to tear
Le poster est tout déchiré.
The poster is all torn.

décider vb
to decide
J'ai décidé d'y aller.
I've decided to go.

le **décollage** nm
takeoff

décoller vb
to take off
**L'avion a décollé avec dix minutes
de retard.**
The plane took off ten minutes late.

se **décontracter** vb
to relax
**Il fait du yoga pour se
décontracter.**
He goes to yoga to relax.

le **décorateur** nm
la **décoratrice** nf
interior decorator

les **décorations** nfpl
decorations
les décorations de Noël
the Christmas decorations

décorer vb
to decorate

découper vb
to cut out

se **décourager** vb
Ne te décourage pas!
Don't give up!

la **découverte** nf
discovery

découvrir vb
to discover
**Christophe Colomb a découvert
l'Amérique en 1492.**
Christopher Colombus discovered
America in 1492.

décrire vb
to describe
Décris quelqu'un de célèbre.
Describe somebody famous.

déçu m adj
(f adj déçue)
disappointed

dedans adv
inside
**C'est une jolie boîte: qu'est-ce
qu'il y a dedans?**
That's a nice box: what's in it?

défendre vb
1 to defend
Il ne sait pas se défendre.
He doesn't know how to defend
himself.
2 to forbid
Je te défends de lui dire.
I forbid you to tell her.

défendu m adj
(f adj défendue)
forbidden
C'est défendu.
It's not allowed.

la **défense** nf
tusk
une défense d'éléphant
an elephant's tusk

"défense de fumer"
"no smoking"

le **défilé** nm
parade
un défilé de mode
a fashion show

dégoûtant m adj
(f adj dégoûtante)
disgusting

le **degré** nm
degree
Il fait trente degrés à l'ombre.
It's thirty degrees in the shade.

le **déguisement** nm
dressing-up costume
un déguisement de sorcière
a witch's costume

se **déguiser** vb
to dress up
J'aime me déguiser.
I like dressing up.

la **dégustation** nf
tasting

dehors adv
outside
Je t'attends dehors.
I'll wait for you outside.

déjà adv
1 already
J'ai déjà fini.
I've already finished.
2 before
Tu es déjà venu en France?
Have you been to France before?

A
B
C
D
E
F
G
H
I
J
K
L
M
N
O
P
Q
R
S
T
U
V
W
X
Y
Z

déjeuner

> déjeuner can be a noun or a verb.

A nm
<u>lunch</u>

Pour le déjeuner, je mange souvent un sandwich.
I often have a sandwich for lunch.

B vb
<u>to have lunch</u>

Je déjeune à midi et demi.
I have lunch at half past twelve.

le **délégué** nm
la **déléguée** nf
<u>representative</u>

les délégués de classe
the class representatives

> In French schools, each class elects two **délégués de classe**, one boy and one girl.

délicieux m adj
(f adj délicieuse)
<u>delicious</u>

le **deltaplane** nm
<u>hang-glider</u>

J'aimerais faire du deltaplane.
I'd like to go hang-gliding.

demain adv
<u>tomorrow</u>

> **À demain!**
> See you tomorrow!

demander vb
<u>to ask for</u>

J'ai demandé la permission.
I've asked for permission.

Je vais demander à mes parents si je peux sortir.
I'll to ask my parents if I can go out.

> Be careful! **demander** does not mean **to demand**.

♦ **se demander**
to wonder

Je me demande quelle heure il est.
I wonder what time it is.

le **déménagement** nm
<u>move</u>

un camion de déménagement
a removal van

déménager vb
<u>to move house</u>

Nous déménageons dans un mois.
We're moving house in a month's time.

le **déménageur** nm
<u>removal man</u>

demi m adj
(f adj demie)
<u>half</u>

Il a trois ans et demi.
He's three and a half.

Il est trois heures et demie.
It's half past three.

> **Il est midi et demi.**
> It's half past twelve.

la **demi-baguette** nf
<u>half a baguette</u>

le **demi-cercle** nm
<u>semicircle</u>

en demi-cercle
in a semicircle

la **demi-douzaine** nf
half a dozen

une demi-douzaine d'œufs
half a dozen eggs

la **demi-finale** nf
semifinal

le **demi-frère** nm
half-brother

mon demi-frère
my half brother

la **demi-heure** nf
half an hour

dans une demi-heure
in half an hour

toutes les demi-heures
every half an hour

le **demi-litre** nm
half a litre

un demi-litre de lait
half a litre of milk

le/la **demi-pensionnaire** nm/f

In French secondary schools, pupils are either **externe** if they go home for lunch, **demi-pensionnaire** if they have a school lunch, or **interne** if they board at the school.

demi-sel m, f, pl adj
du beurre demi-sel
slightly salted butter

la **demi-sœur** nf
half-sister

ma demi-sœur
my half-sister

le **demi-tour** nm

faire demi-tour
to turn back

Il est temps de faire demi-tour.
It's time we turned back.

démodé m adj
(f adj démodée)
old-fashioned

la **demoiselle** nf
young lady

une demoiselle d'honneur
a bridesmaid

démolir vb
to demolish

la **dent** nf
tooth

une dent de lait
a milk tooth

une dent de sagesse
a wisdom tooth

la **dentelle** nf
lace

le **dentifrice** nm
toothpaste

le/la **dentiste** nm/f
dentist

la **dépanneuse** nf
breakdown lorry

le **départ** nm
departure

Le départ est à onze heures quinze.
The departure is at 11.15.

Je vais lui téléphoner la veille de son départ.
I'll phone him the day before he leaves.

le **département** nm
1 administrative region
le département du Vaucluse
the Vaucluse département

A
B
C
D
E
F
G
H
I
J
K
L
M
N
O
P
Q
R
S
T
U
V
W
X
Y
Z

a
b
c
d
e
f
g
h
i
j
k
l
m
n
o
p
q
r
s
t
u
v
w
x
y
z

France is divided into 96 **départements**, which are similar to counties in Britain.

2 department

le département d'anglais à l'université
the English department at the university

se **dépêcher** vb
to hurry

Dépêche-toi!
Hurry up!

dépendre vb
Ça dépend du temps.
It depends on the weather.

dépenser vb
to spend
J'ai dépensé tout mon argent.
I've spent all my money.

le **dépliant** nm
leaflet

déposer vb
to drop
Tu peux me déposer à la piscine?
Can you drop me at the swimming pool?

depuis prep
1 since

J'habite à Paris depuis 1998.
I've been living in Paris since 1998.

depuis que
since

Il a plu tous les jours depuis qu'elle est arrivée.
It's rained every day since she arrived.

2 for

Il habite Paris depuis cinq ans.
He's been living in Paris for five years.

3 **Tu le connais depuis combien de temps?**
How long have you known him?

Tu le connais depuis quand?
How long have you known him?

Depuis quand?
How long?
depuis 2001
since 2001
Depuis combien de temps?
How long?
depuis cinq ans
for five years

déranger vb
1 to bother

Excusez-moi de vous déranger.
I'm sorry to bother you.

2 to mess up

Ne dérange pas mes livres, s'il te plaît.
Don't mess up my books, please.

dernier m adj
(f adj dernière)
1 last

Il est arrivé dernier.
He arrived last.

la dernière fois
the last time

en dernier
last

Ajoutez le lait en dernier.
Put the milk in last.

2 latest

le dernier film de Spielberg
Spielberg's latest film

derrière

> **derrière** can be a preposition, an adverb or a noun.

A prep, adv
behind

derrière moi
behind me

derrière la porte
behind the door

Devant ou derrière?
In front or behind?

B nm

1 back

la porte de derrière
the back door

2 backside

un coup de pied dans le derrière
a kick up the backside

des article

> **des** is made up of **de + les**.

1 some

Tu veux des chips?
Would you like some crisps?

> **des** is sometimes not translated.

J'ai des cousins en France.
I have cousins in France.

pendant des mois
for months

2 any

Tu as des frères?
Have you got any brothers?

3 of the

la fin des vacances
the end of the holidays

la voiture des Durand
the Durands' car

4 from

Il arrive des États-Unis.
He's arriving from the United States.

dès prep
from

dès le mois de novembre
from November

dès le début
right from the start

dès que
as soon as

Appelle-moi dès que tu arrives.
Phone me as soon as you get there.

Je t'appelle dès mon retour.
I'll phone you as soon as I get back.

désagréable adj
unpleasant

le désastre nm
disaster

descendre vb

1 to go down

Je suis tombé en descendant l'escalier.
I fell as I was going down the stairs.

2 to come down

Attends en bas; je descends!
Wait downstairs; I'm coming down!

3 to get down

a

b

c

d

e

f

g

h

i

j

k

l

m

n

o

p

q

r

s

t

u

v

w

x

y

z

**Vous pouvez descendre ma valise,
s'il vous plaît?**
Can you get my suitcase down,
please?

■ **to get off**

**Nous descendons à la prochaine
station.**
We're getting off at the next station.

la **descente** nf
slope

une descente abrupte
a steep slope

> *descente is related to the verb
> descendre which means "to go
> down", so une descente is a
> slope that goes downhill.*

la **description** nf
description

désert

> *désert can be an adjective or a
> noun.*

A m adj
(*f adj* déserte)
deserted

**Le dimanche, le centre commercial
est désert.**
On Sundays the shopping centre is
deserted.

une île déserte
a desert island

B nm
desert

le désert du Sahara
the Sahara desert

déshabiller vb
to undress

◆ **se déshabiller**
to get undressed

**Déshabille-toi, mets ton pyjama et
vas te coucher.**
Get undressed, put on your
pyjamas and go to bed.

désirer vb
to want

**Vous désirez? – Je voudrais un
coca.**
What would you like? – I'd like a
coke.

désolé m adj
(*f adj* désolée)
sorry

Je suis vraiment désolé.
I'm very sorry.

Désolé!
Sorry!

désordonné m adj
(*f adj* désordonnée)
untidy

le **désordre** nm
untidiness

Quel désordre!
What a mess!

en désordre
in a mess

**Sa chambre est toujours en
désordre.**
His bedroom is always in a mess.

le **dessert** nm
pudding

**Qu'est-ce que vous désirez
comme dessert?**
What would you like for pudding?

le **dessin** nm
drawing

C'est un dessin de ma petite sœur.
It's a drawing my little sister did.

un dessin animé
a cartoon

un dessin humoristique
a cartoon

dessiner vb
to draw

Dessinez votre animal préféré.
Draw your favourite animal.

dessous

dessous can be an adverb or a noun.

A adv
underneath

Le prix du vase est marqué dessous.
The price of the vase is marked underneath.

ci-dessous
below

Complétez les phrases ci-dessous.
Complete the sentences below.

B nm
les voisins du dessous
the downstairs neighbours

dessus

dessus can be an adverb or a noun.

A adv
on top

un gâteau avec des bougies dessus
a cake with candles on top

au-dessus
above

au-dessus du lit
above the bed

ci-dessus
above

l'exemple ci-dessus
the example above

là-dessus
on that

Tu peux écrire là-dessus.
You can write on that.

par-dessus
over

Tu peux sauter par-dessus la barrière?
Can you jump over the gate?

B nm
les voisins du dessus
the upstairs neighbours

la **destination** nf
destination

les passagers à destination de Paris
passengers travelling to Paris

le **détail** nm
detail

en détail
in detail

le **détective** nm
detective

a

un détective privé
a private detective

b

détendre vb
to relax

c

La lecture, ça me détend.
I find reading relaxing.

d

◆ **se détendre**
to relax

e

J'écoute de la musique pour me détendre.
I listen to music to relax.

f

g

détester vb
to hate

h

Je déteste les épinards.
I hate spinach.

i

deux num
two

j

k

Il est deux heures.
It's two o'clock.

l

Elle a deux ans.
She's two.

m

deux fois
twice

n

tous les deux
both

o

Allez-y tous les deux.
Go on, both of you.

p

q

🔑

r

le deux février
the second of February

s

deuxième adj
second

t

u

au deuxième étage
on the second floor

v

devant

w

devant can be a preposition, an adverb or a noun.

x

y

Ⓐ prep
in front of

z

Il y a un grand jardin devant la maison.
There's a big garden in front of the house.

passer devant
to go past

Nous passons tous les jours devant chez lui.
We go past his house every day.

Ⓑ adv
in front

Il marche toujours devant.
He always walks in front.

Allez-y, passez devant.
Come on, you go in front.

Ⓒ nm
front

le devant de la maison
the front of the house

les pattes de devant
the front legs

développer vb
to develop

devenir vb
to become

Ça devient de plus en plus difficile.
It's becoming more and more difficult.

devez vb, see **devoir**

Vous devez attendre ici.
You've got to wait here.

deviner vb
to guess

Devine à quel animal je pense.
Guess which animal I'm thinking of.

la **devinette** nf
riddle

devoir vb
❶ to have to

Je dois partir.
I've got to go.

2 must

Tu dois être fatigué.
You must be tired.

les **devoirs** nmpl
homework

Quand je rentre de l'école, je fais mes devoirs.
When I get home from school I do my homework.

devons vb, *see* **devoir**

Nous devons partir tôt.
We have to leave early.

diabétique adj
diabetic

le **diable** nm
devil

le **diabolo** nm
fruit cordial and lemonade

un diabolo menthe
a mint cordial and lemonade

le **dialogue** nm
dialogue

le **diamant** nm
diamond

la **diapositive** nf
slide

la **diarrhée** nf
diarrhoea

J'ai la diarrhée.
I've got diarrhoea.

la **dictée** nf
dictation

La maîtresse nous fait faire une dictée tous les samedis matins.
The teacher gives us a dictation every Saturday morning.

French pupils do a lot of dictations, to help them learn to spell. French is difficult to spell because there are a lot of letters that are not pronounced – such as the "s" on the end of plurals.

dicter vb
to dictate

le **dictionnaire** nm
dictionary

Cherchez le mot "piscine" dans le dictionnaire.
Look up the word "piscine" in the dictionary.

diététique adj
un magasin diététique
a health food shop

le **dieu** nm
(*pl* les dieux)
god
Dieu
God

la **différence** nf
difference

Quelle est la différence entre les écoles françaises et anglaises?
What's the difference between French and English schools?

différent m adj
(f adj différente)
1 different

Je n'aime pas le bleu. Je voudrais une couleur différente.
I don't like blue. I'd like a different colour.

2 various

différents parfums de glace
various flavours of ice cream

difficile adj
difficult

C'est difficile à comprendre.
It's difficult to understand.

le dimanche nm
1 Sunday

Aujourd'hui, nous sommes dimanche.
It's Sunday today.

2 on Sunday

Dimanche, nous allons déjeuner chez mes grands-parents.
On Sunday we're having lunch at my grandparents'.

Le dimanche, je fais la grasse matinée.
I have a lie-in on Sundays.

> **tous les dimanches**
> every Sunday
> **le dimanche**
> on Sundays
> **dimanche dernier**
> last Sunday
> **dimanche prochain**
> next Sunday
> **À dimanche!**
> See you on Sunday!

le diminutif nm
pet name

Loulou est le diminutif de Louise.
Loulou is Louise's pet name.

la dinde nf
turkey

la dinde de Noël
the Christmas turkey

> *le dindon is a live turkey; la dinde is the bird you eat.*

le dindon nm
turkey

dîner

> *dîner can be a verb or a noun.*

A vb
to have dinner

Le soir, nous dînons à sept heures.
We have dinner at seven o'clock in the evening.

B nm
dinner

Le dîner est à quelle heure?
What time is dinner?

le diplôme nm
qualification

Il n'a aucun diplôme.
He hasn't got any qualifications.

dire vb
1 to say

Comment est-ce qu'on dit "dog" en français?
How do you say "dog" in French?

2 to tell

Je vais te dire un secret.
I'm going to tell you a secret.

Elle me dit toujours la vérité.
She always tells me the truth.

Ma mère me dit toujours de ranger ma chambre.
My mother is always telling me to tidy up my room.

Beaucoup de gens me disent que je ressemble à ma mère.
Lots of people tell me I look like my mother.

dire des bêtises
to talk nonsense

le **directeur** nm
la **directrice** nf
1 headteacher

Elle est directrice.
She's a headteacher.

2 manager

Il est directeur du personnel.
He's a personnel manager.

dis vb, *see* **dire**

Dis-moi la vérité!
Tell me the truth!

la **discothèque** nf
club

Florence aime aller danser dans les discothèques.
Florence likes going clubbing.

discuter vb
to talk

Nous discutons toujours à la récréation.
We always talk at break time.

disent vb, *see* **dire**

Qu'est-ce qu'ils disent?
What are they saying?

disons vb, *see* **dire**

Nous disons des bêtises.
We're talking nonsense.

disparaître vb
to disappear

Il peut faire disparaître le lapin.
He can make the rabbit disappear.

la **disparition** nf
disappearance

une espèce en voie de disparition
an endangered species

dispensé m adj
(*f adj* dispensée)

Elle est dispensée de gymnastique.
She's excused gym.

la **dispute** nf
argument

Depuis notre dispute, elle ne me parle plus.
She hasn't spoken to me since our argument.

se **disputer** vb
to argue

Je me dispute souvent avec ma sœur.
I often argue with my sister.

se faire disputer
to get a telling-off

Je vais me faire disputer par ma mère si je ne rentre pas maintenant.
I'll get a telling-off from my mother if I don't go home now.

le **disque** nm
record

un disque compact
a compact disc

la **disquette** nf
floppy disk

la **distance** nf
distance

Ton école est à quelle distance d'ici?
How far is your school from here?

distrait m adj
(f adj distraite)
absent-minded

distribuer vb
1 to give out

Distribue les livres, s'il te plaît.
Give out the books please.

2 to deal

Distribue les cartes, s'il te plaît.
Deal the cards please.

le **distributeur** nm

un distributeur automatique
a vending machine

un distributeur de billets
a cash dispenser

dit vb, *see* **dire**

Elle ne me dit jamais rien.
She never tells me anything.

Je te l'ai dit hier.
I told you yesterday.

dites vb, *see* **dire**

Dites-moi ce que vous pensez.
Tell me what you think.

diviser vb
to divide

Quatre divisé par deux égale deux.
4 divided by 2 equals 2.

divorcé m adj
(f adj divorcée)
divorced

Mes parents sont divorcés.
My parents are divorced.

divorcer vb
to get divorced

Ils ont décidé de divorcer.
They've decided to get divorced.

dix num
ten

Elle a dix ans.
She's ten.

Il est dix heures.
It's ten o'clock.

le dix février
the tenth of February

dix-huit num
eighteen

Elle a dix-huit ans.
She's eighteen.

Il est dix-huit heures.
It's six o'clock.

le dix-huit mars
the eighteenth of March

The 24-hour clock is used in France for travel times, appointments and other formal situations.

dixième adj
tenth

au dixième étage
on the tenth floor

dix-neuf num
nineteen

Elle a dix-neuf ans.
She's nineteen.

Il est dix-neuf heures.
It's seven o'clock.

le dix-neuf avril
the nineteenth of April

The 24-hour clock is used in France for travel times, appointments and other formal situations.

dix-sept num
seventeen

Elle a dix-sept ans.
She's seventeen.

Il est dix-sept heures.
It's five o'clock.

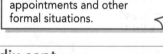

le dix-sept avril
the seventeenth of April

The 24-hour clock is used in France for travel times, appointments and other formal situations.

la dizaine nf
about ten

une dizaine de jours
about ten days

le docteur nm
doctor

Je vais chez le docteur.
I'm going to the doctor.

le documentaire nm
documentary

le/la documentaliste nm/f
librarian

le doigt nm
finger

les doigts de pied
the toes

dois, doit, doivent vb, see devoir

Je dois mettre la table.
I have to lay the table.

Il doit être tard.
It must be late.

Ils doivent rentrer à huit heures.
They have to be home at eight.

domestique

domestique can be an adjective or a noun.

Ⓐ adj
les animaux domestiques
pets

Ⓑ nm/f
servant

le domicile nm

à domicile
at home

Il travaille à domicile.
He works at home.

les dominos nmpl
dominoes

Je joue aux dominos avec ma sœur.
I play dominoes with my sister.

le **dommage** nm
C'est dommage.
It's a shame.

🔑
Quel dommage!
What a shame!

---

donc conj
so

Il fait beau, donc nous pouvons faire un pique-nique.
The weather's nice, so we can have a picnic.

donner vb
to give

Elle me donne toujours des bonbons.
She always gives me sweets.

Ça me donne faim.
That makes me feel hungry.

dont pron
1 of which

deux livres, dont l'un est en anglais
two books, one of which is in English

le prix dont il est si fier
the prize he's so proud of

2 of whom

dix blessés, dont deux grièvement
ten people injured, two of them seriously

la fille dont je t'ai parlé
the girl I told you about

doré m adj
(f adj dorée)
golden

dormir vb
1 to sleep

Tu as bien dormi?
Did you sleep well?

2 to be asleep
Ne faites pas de bruit, il dort.
Don't make a noise, he's asleep.

le **dortoir** nm
dormitory

le **dos** nm
back

dos à dos
back to back

J'ai mal au dos.
I've got backache.

dans mon dos
behind my back

Elle me critique dans mon dos.
She criticizes me behind my back.

le dos crawlé
the backstroke

le **dossier** nm
1 file

une pile de dossiers
a stack of files

2 report

un bon dossier scolaire
a good school report

3 back

le dossier de la chaise
the back of the chair

la **douane** nf
customs

un contrôle de douane
a customs inspection

le **douanier** nm
customs officer

le **double** nm

le double
twice as much

Il gagne le double.
He earns twice as much.

le double du prix normal
twice the normal price

en double
in duplicate

Garde cette photo, je l'ai en double.
Keep this photo, I've got a copy of it.

doublé m adj
(*f adj* doublée)
dubbed

un film doublé
a dubbed film

douce f adj, *see* **doux**

une peau douce
soft skin

doucement adv
1 gently

Il a frappé doucement à la porte.
He knocked gently at the door.
2 slowly

Je ne comprends pas, parle plus doucement.
I don't understand, speak more slowly.

la **douche** nf
shower

Je prends une douche tous les matins.
I have a shower every morning.

se **doucher** vb
to have a shower

Je me douche le matin.
I have a shower in the morning.

doué m adj
(*f adj* douée)
talented

Il est doué en maths.
He's good at maths.

la **douleur** nf
pain

le **doute** nm
doubt

sans doute
probably

se **douter** vb

se douter de
to suspect

Elle ne se doute de rien.
She doesn't suspect anything.

Je m'en doutais.
I thought as much.

Douvres n
Dover

doux m adj
(*f adj* douce)
1 soft

un tissu doux
soft material
2 sweet

du cidre doux
sweet cider
3 mild

Il fait doux aujourd'hui.
It's mild today.
4 gentle

C'est quelqu'un de très doux.
He's a very gentle person.

la **douzaine** nf
dozen

a
b
c
d
e
f
g
h
i
j
k
l
m
n
o
p
q
r
s
t
u
v
w
x
y
z

une douzaine d'œufs
a dozen eggs

une douzaine de personnes
about twelve people

douze num
twelve

Il a douze ans.
He's twelve.

🔑
le douze février
the twelfth of February

douzième adj
twelfth

au douzième étage
on the twelfth floor

la dragée nf
sugared almond

French people give **dragées** to family and friends at weddings and christenings.

le drap nm
sheet

le drapeau nm
(pl les drapeaux)
flag

dressé m adj
(f adj dressée)
trained

un chien bien dressé
a well-trained dog

la droguerie nf
hardware shop

droit

droit can be an adjective or a noun.

Ⓐ m adj
(f adj droite)
1 right

la jambe droite
the right leg

le côté droit
the right-hand side
2 straight

une ligne droite
a straight line

Tiens-toi droite sur ta chaise!
Sit up straight on your chair!

Allez tout droit.
Go straight on.

🔑
tout droit
straight on

Ⓑ nm
law

un étudiant en droit
a law student

Tu as le droit de sortir?
Are you allowed to go out?

Je n'ai pas le droit d'aller en ville toute seule.
I'm not allowed to go into town by myself.

la droite nf
right

sur votre droite
on your right

à droite

à droite can either mean **right** or **on the right**.

Tournez à droite.
Turn right.

Prenez la troisième rue à droite.
Take the third street on the right.

>
> **C'est à droite.**
> It's on your right.
> **la deuxième rue à droite**
> the second street on the right

droitier m adj
(*f adj* droitière)
right-handed

Elle est droitière.
She's right-handed.

drôle adj
funny

Ça n'est pas drôle.
It's not funny.

un drôle de temps
funny weather

le **dromadaire** nm
camel

du article

> *du is made up of* **de + le***.*

1 some

Tu veux du fromage?
Would you like some cheese?

2 any

Tu as du chocolat?
Have you got any chocolate?

3 of the

la porte du garage
the door of the garage

la femme du directeur
the headmaster's wife

4 from

Il rentre du Canada.
He's back from Canada.

à sept heures du soir
at seven o'clock in the evening

le **duc** nm
duke

la **duchesse** nf
duchess

dur

> **dur** can be an adjective or an adverb.

A m adj
(*f adj* dure)
hard

Il est dur avec moi.
He's hard on me.

B adv
hard

Elle travaille dur à l'école.
She works hard at school.

durant prep
1 during

durant la nuit
during the night

2 for

durant des années
for years

durer vb
to last

La leçon dure une heure.
The lesson lasts an hour.

dyslexique adj
dyslexic

A
B
C
D
E
F
G
H
I
J
K
L
M
N
O
P
Q
R
S
T
U
V
W
X
Y
Z

E

l'eau nf
water

Je voudrais de l'eau.
I'd like some water.

Qu'est-ce que tu veux boire? – De l'eau.
What would you like to drink? – Water.

l'eau minérale
mineral water

l'eau plate
still water

l'eau gazeuse
fizzy water

l'écart nm
Je sais faire le grand écart.
I can do the splits.

l'échalote nf
shallot

l'échange nm
exchange

en échange de
in exchange for

échanger vb
to swap

Je t'échange cet autocollant contre celui-là.
I'll swap you this sticker for that one.

s'**échapper** vb
to escape

l'écharpe nf
scarf

s'**échauffer** vb
to warm up

Nous allons faire quelques exercices pour nous échauffer.
We're going to do some exercises to warm up.

les **échecs** nmpl
chess

Je joue aux échecs.
I play chess.

l'échelle nf
ladder

l'éclair nm
flash of lightning

un éclair au chocolat
a chocolate éclair

l'école nf
school

aller à l'école
to go to school

Je vais à l'école avec ma sœur.
I go to school with my sister.

une école privée
a private school

une école publique
a state school

une école maternelle
a nursery school

une école primaire
a primary school

French children go to **l'école maternelle** when they are 3, and stay there until they are 6. They then go to **l'école primaire** and stay there until they are 11.

l'**écolier** nm
schoolboy

l'**écolière** nf
schoolgirl

les **économies** nfpl
savings

Je dois faire des économies.
I must save up.

économiser vb
to save up

J'économise pour m'acheter une nouvelle raquette de tennis.
I'm saving up to buy a new tennis racket.

écossais m adj
(*f adj* écossaise)
1 Scottish

Elle est écossaise.
She's Scottish.

2 tartan

une jupe écossaise
a tartan skirt

l'**Écossais** nm

l'**Écossaise** nf
Scot

les Écossais
the Scots

l'**Écosse** nf
Scotland

écouter vb
to listen to

J'aime écouter de la musique.
I like listening to music.

Écoute-moi, Bruno!
Listen Bruno!
Écoutez, tout le monde!
Listen everybody!

écraser vb
1 to crush

Écrasez une gousse d'ail.
Crush a clove of garlic.

2 to run over

Attention, tu vas te faire écraser!
Be careful or you'll get run over!

écrire vb
to write

Nous nous écrivons régulièrement.
We write to each other regularly.

Ça s'écrit comment?
How do you spell that?

l'**écriture** nf
handwriting

J'aime bien ton écriture.
I like your handwriting.

l'**écrivain** nm
writer

écru m adj
(*f adj* écrue)
off-white

l'**écureuil** nm
squirrel

A B C D **E** F G H I J K L M N O P Q R S T U V W X Y Z

Édimbourg n
Edinburgh

éducatif m adj
(f adj éducative)
educational

un jeu éducatif
an educational game

l'**éducation** nf
education

l'**éducation physique**
physical education

effacer vb
to rub out

Efface la dernière lettre.
Rub out the last letter.

l'**effort** nm
effort

Il faut faire un effort.
You've got to make an effort.

effrayant m adj
(f adj effrayante)
frightening

égal m adj
(f adj égale)
equal

une quantité égale de farine et de sucre
equal quantities of flour and sugar

ça m'est égal

> *Ça m'est égal* can either mean **I don't mind** or **I don't care**.

Tu préfères du riz ou des pâtes? – Ça m'est égal.
Would you rather have rice or pasta? – I don't mind.

Fais ce que tu veux, ça m'est égal.
Do what you like, I don't care.

égaler vb
to equal

Deux plus trois égalent cinq.
Two plus three equals five.

l'**église** nf
church

Nous allons à l'église tous les dimanches.
We go to church every Sunday.

égoïste adj
selfish

l'**Égypte** nf
Egypt

égyptien m adj
(f adj égyptienne)
Egyptian

l'**Égyptien** nm
l'**Égyptienne** nf
Egyptian

l'**élastique** nm
rubber band

l'**électricien** nm
electrician

élégant m adj
(f adj élégante)
smart

une robe élégante
a smart dress

l'**éléphant** nm
elephant

élevé m adj
(f adj élevée)

Elle est bien élevée.
She has good manners.

Il est très mal élevé.
He has very bad manners.

l'**élève** nm/f
pupil

Il y a un nouvel élève dans ma classe.
There's a new boy in my class.

éliminer vb
to eliminate

Tu es éliminé!
You're out!

elle pron
1 she

Elle est institutrice.
She is a primary school teacher.

Elle, elle est toujours en retard!
Oh, SHE's always late!

2 her

C'est ma copine; je joue toujours avec elle.
She's my friend; I always play with her.

Lui ou elle?
Him or her?

Elle l'a choisi elle-même.
She chose it herself.

elle-même
herself

3 it

Prends cette chaise: elle est plus confortable.
Take this chair: it's more comfortable.

elles pron
1 they

Où sont Anne et Rachel? – Elles sont dans le jardin.
Where are Anne and Rachel? – They're in the garden.

2 them

Julie et Aurélie ont emmené le chien avec elles.
Julie and Aurélie have taken the dog with them.

elles-mêmes
themselves

l'**Élysée** nm
Élysée Palace

The **Élysée** is the home of the French president.

l'**e-mail** nm
email

Je vais envoyer un e-mail à ma copine.
I'm going to email my friend.

embarrassant m adj
(f adj embarrassante)
embarrassing

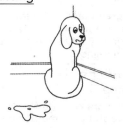

a
b
c
d
e
f
g
h
i
j
k
l
m
n
o
p
q
r
s
t
u
v
w
x
y
z

embêtant m adj
(f adj embêtante)
annoying

embêter vb
to pester
Il n'arrête pas de m'embêter.
He's always pestering me.

◆ **s'embêter**
to be bored
Qu'est-ce qu'on s'embête ici!
It's so boring here!

l'**embouteillage** nm
traffic jam

embrasser vb
to kiss
Il l'a embrassée.
He kissed her.

◆ **s'embrasser**
to kiss each other
Ils se sont embrassés.
They kissed each other.

l'**émission** nf
programme
une émission de télévision
a TV programme

emménager vb
to move in
Nous venons d'emménager dans une nouvelle maison.
We've just moved into a new house.

emmener vb
to take
Ma grand-mère m'emmène à l'école le matin.
My granny takes me to school in the morning.

empêcher vb
to stop
Tu m'empêches de travailler.
You're stopping me doing my work.

l'**emploi** nm
1 use
le mode d'emploi
instructions for use

un emploi du temps
a timetable
2 job
Il recherche un emploi.
He's looking for a job.

l'**employé** nm
l'**employée** nf
employee
un employé de bureau
an office worker

une employée de banque
a bank clerk

employer vb
to employ

empoisonner vb
to poison

emporter vb
to take
plats à emporter
take-away meals

l'**empreinte** nf
footprint

une empreinte digitale
a fingerprint

emprunter vb
to borrow
Je peux emprunter ta gomme?
Can I borrow your rubber?

en

> **en** can be a preposition or a pronoun.

Ⓐ prep

1 in

Il habite en France.
He lives in France.

2 to

Je vais en France cet été.
I'm going to France this summer.

3 by

en vélo
by bike

C'est plus rapide en voiture.
It's quicker by car.

4 made of

C'est en verre.
It's made of glass.

un bracelet en or
a gold bracelet

5 while

Il s'est coupé le doigt en ouvrant une boîte de conserve.
He cut his finger while opening a tin.

Ⓑ pron

of it

Il a un beau jardin et il en est très fier.
He's got a beautiful garden and is very proud of it.

Si tu as un problème, tu peux m'en parler.
If you've got a problem, you can talk to me about it.

Tu peux me rendre ce livre? J'en ai besoin.
Can you give me back that book? I need it.

> *When* **en** *is used with* **avoir** *and* **il y a**, *it is not translated in English.*

Tu as un dictionnaire? – Oui, j'en ai un.
Have you got a dictionary? – Yes, I've got one.

Il y a combien d'élèves dans ta classe? – Il y en a trente.
How many pupils are there in your class? – There are 30.

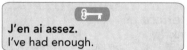

J'en ai assez.
I've had enough.

enceinte f adj

pregnant

Ma tante est enceinte de six mois.
My aunt is 6 months pregnant.

enchanté m adj

(*f adj* enchantée)

delighted

Ma mère est enchantée de sa nouvelle voiture.
My mother's delighted with her new car.

Enchanté!
Pleased to meet you!

encore adv

1 still

Il est encore au travail.
He's still at work.

Il reste encore deux morceaux de gâteau.
There are two bits of cake left.

2 even

C'est encore mieux.
That's even better.

3 again

A B C D E F G H I J K L M N O P Q R S T U V W X Y Z

a
b
c
d
e
f
g
h
i
j
k
l
m
n
o
p
q
r
s
t
u
v
w
x
y
z

Nous allons encore en Espagne cet été.
We're going to Spain again this summer.

encore une fois
once again
pas encore
not yet
Je n'ai pas encore fini.
I haven't finished yet.

l'**encre** nf
ink

l'**encyclopédie** nf
encyclopaedia

l'**endive** nf
chicory

endive is a leafy vegetable which is eaten raw in a salad, boiled, or baked with ham and cheese.

s'**endormir** vb
to go to sleep

Je m'endors vers neuf heures du soir.
I go to sleep at about nine.

l'**endroit** nm
place

C'est un endroit très tranquille.
It's a very quiet place.

à l'endroit

à l'endroit can either mean **the right way out** or **the right way up**.

Remets ton pull à l'endroit.
Turn your jumper the right way out.

Tu ne tiens pas le livre à l'endroit.
You're not holding the book the right way up.

l'**énergie** nf
energy

énerver vb
to get on someone's nerves

Il m'énerve!
He gets on my nerves!

Ne t'énerve pas!
Take it easy!

l'**enfant** nm/f
child

Ils ont trois enfants.
They've got three children.

l'**enfer** nm
hell

enfin adv
at last

Tu arrives enfin!
Here you are at last!

enflé m adj
(f adj enflée)
swollen

J'ai la cheville enflée.
I have a swollen ankle.

enlever vb
to take off

Enlève ton manteau!
Take off your coat!

enneigé m adj
(f adj enneigée)
blocked with snow

Les routes sont encore enneigées.
The roads are still blocked with snow.

---

l'**ennemi** nm
l'**ennemie** nf
enemy

---

ennuyer vb
J'espère que ça ne t'ennuie pas.
I hope this isn't a problem for you.
Ça t'ennuie?
Do you mind?
♦ **s'ennuyer**
to be bored
Je m'ennuie quand Laura n'est pas là.
I get bored when Laura isn't here.

---

ennuyeux m adj
(f adj ennuyeuse)
boring

énorme adj
huge
un énorme gâteau
a huge cake

énormément adv
Il y a énormément de neige.
There's a huge amount of snow.
Il a énormément grossi.
He's got terribly fat.

---

l'**enquête** nf
investigation

---

enquêter vb
to investigate

l'**enregistrement** nm
recording
un mauvais enregistrement
a bad recording
l'enregistrement des bagages
baggage check-in

---

enregistrer vb
1 to record
Ils viennent d'enregistrer un nouvel album.
They've just recorded a new album.
2 to check in
Combien de valises voulez-vous enregistrer?
How many bags do you want to check in?

---

enrhumé m adj
(f adj enrhumée)
Je suis enrhumé.
I've got a cold.

---

l'**enseignant** nm
l'**enseignante** nf
teacher

---

enseigner vb
to teach
Mon père enseigne les maths dans un lycée.
My father teaches maths in a secondary school.

---

ensemble

> **ensemble** can be an adverb or a noun.

A adv
together
tous ensemble
all together
B nm
outfit
Elle porte un nouvel ensemble.
She's wearing a new outfit.

ensoleillé m adj
(*f adj* ensoleillée)
<u>sunny</u>
une matinée ensoleillée
a sunny morning

ensuite adv
<u>then</u>
Nous sommes allés au cinéma et ensuite au restaurant.
We went to the cinema and then to a restaurant.

entendre vb
<u>to hear</u>
Je ne t'entends pas.
I can't hear you.
◆ **s'entendre**
to get on
Il s'entend bien avec sa sœur.
He gets on well with his sister.

entendu m adj
bien entendu
of course

l'**enterrement** nm
<u>funeral</u>

entier m adj
(*f adj* entière)
<u>whole</u>
Il a mangé une quiche entière.
He ate a whole quiche.
Je n'ai pas lu le livre en entier.
I haven't read the whole book.

dans le monde entier
in the whole wide world
le lait entier
full fat milk

entièrement adv
<u>completely</u>

l'**entorse** nf
<u>sprain</u>

entourer vb
<u>to surround</u>
Le jardin est entouré d'un mur de pierres.
The garden is surrounded by a stone wall.

l'**entraînement** nm
<u>training</u>

s'**entraîner** vb
<u>to train</u>
Il s'entraîne au foot tous les samedis matins.
He does football training every Saturday morning.

l'**entraîneur** nm
<u>trainer</u>
l'entraîneur d'une équipe de rugby
the trainer of a rugby team

entre prep
<u>between</u>
Il est assis entre son père et son oncle.
He's sitting between his father and his uncle.

l'**entrecôte** nf
rib steak

l'**entrée** nf
1 starter

Que voulez-vous comme entrée?
What would you like as a starter?
2 hall

Il y a un grand placard dans l'entrée.
There's a big cupboard in the hall.

l'**entreprise** nf
firm

entrer vb
1 to come in

Entrez!
Come in!
2 to go in

Ils sont tous entrés dans la maison.
They all went into the house.

l'**enveloppe** nf
envelope

l'**envers** nm
à l'envers
inside out

Ton pull est à l'envers.
Your jumper is inside out.

l'**envie** nf
J'ai envie de pleurer.
I feel like crying.

J'ai envie de dormir.
I want to go to sleep.

J'ai envie de faire pipi.
I need a wee.

envier vb
to envy

Je t'envie.
I envy you.

environ adv
about

C'est à soixante kilomètres environ.
It's about 60 kilometres.

l'**environnement** nm
environment

les **environs** nmpl
area

les environs de Nantes
the Nantes area

Il y a beaucoup de choses intéressantes à voir dans les environs.
There are a lot of interesting things to see in the area.

aux environs de
around

aux environs de dix-neuf heures
around 7 p.m.

s'**envoler** vb
1 to fly away

Le papillon s'est envolé.
The butterfly flew away.
2 to blow away

Attention, tes dessins vont s'envoler!
Be careful, your drawings are going to blow away!

envoyer vb
to send

Ma tante m'a envoyé une carte pour mon anniversaire.
My aunt sent me a card for my birthday.

Je vais t'envoyer un e-mail.
I'm going to email you.

épais m adj
(f adj épaisse)
thick

l'**épaule** nf
shoulder

a
b
c
d
e
f
g
h
i
j
k
l
m
n
o
p
q
r
s
t
u
v
w
x
y
z

l'**épée** nf
sword

épeler vb
to spell

Tu peux épeler ton nom s'il te plaît?
Can you spell your name please?

épicé m adj
(f adj épicée)
spicy

Ce n'est pas assez épicé.
It's not spicy enough.

l'**épicerie** nf
shop

l'**épicier** nm
l'**épicière** nf
grocer

les **épinards** nmpl
spinach

Je n'aime pas les épinards.
I don't like spinach.

éplucher vb
to peel

l'**éponge** nf
sponge

épouvantable adj
awful

l'**EPS** nm
PE

épuisé m adj
(f adj épuisée)
exhausted

l'**équilibre** nm
balance

J'ai failli perdre l'équilibre.
I nearly lost my balance.

l'**équipe** nf
team

l'**équipement** nm
equipment

l'**équitation** nf
riding

Je fais de l'équitation.
I go riding.

l'**erreur** nf
mistake

es vb, *see* **être**
Tu es très gentille.
You're very kind.

*Sometimes **es** is used to show that something has happened in the past.*

Tu es parti à quelle heure?
What time did you leave?

l'**escalade** nf
climbing

Il fait de l'escalade.
He goes climbing.

l'**escalier** nm
stairs

l'**escargot** nm
snail

l'**escrime** nf
fencing

Il fait de l'escrime.
He does fencing.

les **espadrilles** nfpl
rope-soled sandals

A lot of French people wear
espadrilles in the summer.
They are cheap and colourful
fabric sandals with soles
made of rope.

l'**Espagne** nf
Spain

espagnol m adj, nm
espagnole f adj
Spanish

l'**Espagnol** nm
l'**Espagnole** nf
Spaniard

l'**espèce** nf
sort

**Elle porte une espèce de cape en
velours.**
She's wearing a sort of velvet
cloak.

Espèce d'idiot!
You idiot!

espérer vb
to hope

**J'espère que tu passes de bonnes
vacances.**
I hope you're having a nice holiday.

J'espère bien!
I hope so!
J'espère que non.
I hope not.

l'**esquimau**® nm
(pl les esquimaux)
choc ice on a stick

l'**Esquimau** nm
l'**Esquimaude** nf
Eskimo

les Esquimaux
the Eskimos

essayer vb
1 to try

**Essaie de compter jusqu'à cent en
français.**
Try to count up to 100 in French.
2 to try on

Je peux l'essayer?
Can I try it on?

l'**essence** nf
petrol

essentiel

essentiel can be an adjective or a noun.

Ⓐ m adj
(f adj essentielle)
essential

Ⓑ nm

Tu es là: c'est l'essentiel.
You're here: that's the main thing.

essuyer vb
to wipe

Tu peux essuyer la table?
Could you wipe the table?

Il essuie la vaisselle.
He's drying the dishes.

Essuie-toi les mains avec cette serviette.
Dry your hands on this towel.

est

est can be part of the verb **être**, an adjective or a noun.

Ⓐ vb, see **être**

Elle est merveilleuse.
She's marvellous.

Sometimes est is used to show that something has happened in the past.

Hier soir, il est allé au cinéma.
He went to the cinema last night.

Ⓑ m, f, pl adj
east

la côte est des États-Unis
the east coast of the United States

Ⓒ nm
east

Je vis dans l'est de la France.
I live in the East of France.

à l'est de Paris
east of Paris

est-ce que adv

One way of asking a question in French is to use **est-ce que**.

Comment est-ce que tu t'appelles?
What's your name?

Est-ce que c'est cher?
Is it expensive?

l'**estomac** nm
stomach

et conj
and

l'**étage** nm
floor

au premier étage
on the first floor

l'**étagère** nf
shelf

étaient vb, see **être**

J'ai trouvé mes baskets: elles étaient sous mon lit.
I've found my trainers: they were under my bed.

étais, était vb, see **être**

J'étais dans le jardin.
I was in the garden.

C'était super!
It was great!

l'**étang** nm
pond

l'**état** nm
condition

en bon état
in good condition

en mauvais état
in poor condition

les **États-Unis** nmpl
United States

été

été can be a noun or part of the verb **être**.

A nm
summer

cet été
this summer

en été
in the summer

B vb, *see* **être**

Il a été puni.
He has been punished.

éteindre vb
to switch off

Éteins la lumière s'il te plaît.
Switch off the light please.

étendre vb

étendre le linge
to hang out the washing

éternuer vb
to sneeze

When you sneeze in France people say **"À tes souhaits!"**

êtes vb, *see* **être**

Vous êtes en retard.
You're late.

*Sometimes **êtes** is used to show that something has happened in the past.*

Vous êtes partis de bonne heure.
You left early.

l'**étiquette** nf
label

l'**étoile** nf
star

une étoile de mer
a starfish

une étoile filante
a shooting star

étonnant m adj
(*f adj* étonnante)
amazing

une nouvelle étonnante
amazing news

étonner vb
to surprise

Ça t'étonne?
Does that surprise you?

étourdi m adj
(*f adj* étourdie)
scatterbrained

étrange adj
strange

étranger m adj
(*f adj* étrangère)
foreign

un pays étranger
a foreign country

l'**étranger** nm
l'**étrangère** nf
1 foreigner

Il y a beaucoup d'étrangers ici.
There are lots of foreigners here.

2 stranger

Il ne faut pas parler aux étrangers.
You mustn't speak to strangers.

à l'étranger
abroad

être

> **être** can be a verb or a noun.

A vb

1 to be

Je suis heureux.
I'm happy.

Mon père est instituteur.
My father's a primary school teacher.

Il est dix heures.
It's 10 o'clock.

2 to have

> **être** is used to make the past tense of some verbs.

Il n'est pas encore arrivé.
He hasn't arrived yet.

B nm
being

un être humain
a human being

les **étrennes** nfpl

> les **étrennes** are like a Christmas box, but one that is given after Christmas, to people like the postman and the dustmen. Children sometimes get money or a gift too.

les **études** nfpl

Mon frère va faire des études de droit.
My brother is going to study law.

l'**étudiant** nm
l'**étudiante** nf
student

étudier vb
to study

l'**étui** nm
case

un étui à lunettes
a glasses case

eu vb, *see* **avoir**

J'ai eu une bonne note.
I got a good mark.

euh excl
er

Euh … je ne sais pas.
Er … I don't know.

l'**euro** nm
euro

Ça coûte 25 euros.
It costs 25 euros.

50 €
€50

l'**Europe** nf
Europe

européen m adj
(*f adj* européenne)
European

l'**Européen** nm
l'**Européenne** nf
European

eux pron
them

Je pense souvent à eux.
I often think of them.

évident m adj
(*f adj* évidente)
obvious

Elle est jalouse, c'est évident.
It's obvious she's jealous.

l'**évier** nm
sin

exactement adv
exactly

ex æquo m, f, pl adj
Huit points partout: vous êtes ex æquo.
Eight points each: it's a tie.

| **ex æquo** *is said like "ex-echo".* |

exagérer vb
to exaggerate

Il exagère toujours.
He always exaggerates.

Ça fait trois fois que tu arrives en retard: tu exagères!
That's three times you've been late: it's not good enough!

l'**examen** nm
exam

un examen de français
a French exam

excellent m adj
(*f adj* excellente)
excellent

excitant m adj
(*f adj* excitante)
exciting

l'**excuse** nf
excuse

un mot d'excuse
a note

C'est un mot d'excuse de mes parents.
This is a note from my parents.

excuser vb
excusez-moi

| **excusez-moi** *is used either to apologize, or to attract someone's attention.* |

Excusez-moi!
Sorry!

Excusez-moi, je suis en retard.
Sorry I'm late.

Excusez-moi!
Excuse me!

Excusez-moi, je cherche la poste.
Excuse me, I'm looking for the post office.

♦ **s'excuser**
to apologize

Je m'excuse.
I apologize.

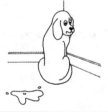

l'**exemple** nm
example

par exemple
for example

l'**exercice** nm
exercise

exister vb
to exist

Ça n'existe pas.
It doesn't exist.

exotique adj
exotic

une plante exotique
an exotic plant

un yaourt aux fruits exotiques
a tropical fruit yoghurt

l'**expéditeur** nm
sender

l'**expérience** nf

1 experience

2 experiment

une expérience de chimie
a chemistry experiment

l'**explication** nf
explanation

expliquer vb
to explain

Je vais expliquer en anglais.
I'm going to explain in English.

l'**exposition** nf
exhibition

exprès adv

1 on purpose

Je suis sûr qu'il l'a fait exprès.
I'm sure he did it on purpose.

2 specially

J'ai fait ce gâteau exprès pour toi.
I made this cake specially for you.

l'**extérieur** nm
outside

à l'extérieur
outside

Les toilettes sont à l'extérieur.
The toilet is outside.

l'**externe** nm/f

In French secondary schools, pupils are either **externe** if they go home for lunch, **demi-pensionnaire** if they have a school lunch, or **interne** if they board at the school.

extra m, f, pl adj
excellent

Ce fromage est extra!
This cheese is excellent!

l'**extrait** nm
extract

extraordinaire adj
extraordinary

extrêmement adv
extremely

l'**Extrême-Orient** nm
the Far East

F

fabriquer vb
to make

fabriqué en France
made in France

la **face** nf

en face de
opposite

Le bus s'arrête en face de chez moi.
The bus stops opposite my house.

Pile ou face? – Face.
Heads or tails? – Heads.

fâché m adj
(*f adj* fâchée)
angry

Elle est fâchée contre moi.
She's angry with me.

Elle est fâchée avec sa sœur.
She's fallen out with her sister.

se **fâcher** vb
to get angry

Je vais me fâcher.
I'm going to get angry.

Il s'est fâché avec son frère.
He's fallen out with his brother.

facile adj
easy

C'est facile à faire.
It's easy to do.

facilement adv
easily

la **façon** nf
way

Il a une drôle de façon de parler.
He has a funny way of talking.

de toute façon
anyway

le **facteur** nm
postman

faible adj
weak

Je me sens encore faible.
I still feel a bit weak.

Il est faible en maths.
He's not very good at maths.

la **faim** nf
hunger

Tu as faim?
Are you hungry?

J'ai faim.
I'm hungry.

faire vb
1 to make

a

b

c

d

e

f

g

h

i

j

k

l

m

n

o

p

q

r

s

t

u

v

w

x

y

z

Je vais faire un gâteau.
I'm going to make a cake.

Ils font trop de bruit.
They're making too much
noise.

2 to do

Qu'est-ce que tu fais?
What are you doing?

Il fait de l'italien.
He's doing Italian.

Elle fait la vaisselle.
She's doing the dishes.

3 to play

Il fait du piano.
He plays the piano.

Je fais du basket.
I play basketball.

4 to be

Il fait chaud.
It's hot.

**Ça fait combien? – Ça fait dix
euros.**
How much is that? – It's ten euros.

5 to go

Tu veux faire du vélo?
Do you want to go cycling?

Je fais du vélo.
I go cycling.

**Ça fait trois ans qu'ils habitent à
Paris.**
They've lived in Paris for three
years.

Ça ne fait rien.
It doesn't matter.

**fais, faisaient, faisais,
faisait** vb, *see* **faire**

Look at the entry **faire** *to see all
the meanings it can have.*

Ne fais pas ça!
Don't do that!

Ils faisaient beaucoup de bruit.
They were making a lot of noise.

Qu'est-ce que tu faisais?
What were you doing?

Il faisait très froid.
It was very cold.

le **faisan** nm
pheasant

**faisiez, faisions, faisons,
fait** vb, *see* **faire**

Look at the entry **faire** *to see all
the meanings it can have.*

Vous faisiez du bruit.
You were making a noise.

Qu'est-ce que nous faisions hier?
What were we doing yesterday?

Nous faisons du vélo le week-end.
We go cycling at the weekend.

Il fait des bêtises.
He does silly things.

faites vb, *see* **faire**

Look at the entry **faire** *to see all
the meanings it can have.*

Qu'est-ce que vous faites?
What are you doing?

la **falaise** nf
cliff

falloir vb, *see* **faut**

Il va falloir se dépêcher.
We'll have to hurry up.

familier m adj
(*f adj* familière)
familiar

les animaux familiers
pets

la **famille** nf
1 family

une famille nombreuse
a big family

2 relatives
Il a de la famille à Paris.
He's got relatives in Paris.

fantastique adj
fantastic

le **fantôme** nm
ghost

la **farce** nf
practical joke

farci m adj
(f adj farcie)
stuffed

des tomates farcies
stuffed tomatoes

la **farine** nf
flour

fatigant m adj
(f adj fatigante)
tiring

fatigué m adj
(f adj fatiguée)
tired
Je suis fatigué.
I'm tired.

fausse f adj
wrong
Cette réponse est fausse.
This answer's wrong.

faut vb

*faut is the present tense of **falloir**.*

Il faut faire attention.
You've got to be careful.

la **faute** nf
1 mistake
J'ai fait une faute.
I've made a mistake.
2 fault
Ce n'est pas de ma faute.
It's not my fault.

le **fauteuil** nm
armchair
un fauteuil roulant
a wheelchair

faux m adj
(f adj fausse)
1 untrue
C'est entièrement faux.
It's totally untrue.
2 wrong
Ce mot est faux.
The word is wrong.
Vrai ou faux?
True or false?

favori m adj
(f adj favorite)
favourite
Quel est ton sport favori?
What's your favourite sport?

la **fée** nf
fairy
un conte de fées
a fairy tale

les **félicitations** nfpl
congratulations

féliciter vb
to congratulate
Je te félicite pour tes bons résultats.
Congratulations on your good results!

A
B
C
D
E
F
G
H
I
J
K
L
M
N
O
P
Q
R
S
T
U
V
W
X
Y
Z

a
b
c
d
e
f
g
h
i
j
k
l
m
n
o
p
q
r
s
t
u
v
w
x
y
z

la **femelle** nf
female

féminin m adj
(*f adj* féminine)
feminine

la **femme** nf
1 woman

une jeune femme
a young woman

une femme de ménage
a cleaning woman

2 wife

C'est la femme du directeur.
She's the headmaster's wife.

une femme au foyer
a housewife

la **fenêtre** nf
window

Regardez par la fenêtre.
Look out of the window.

le **fenouil** nm
fennel

> **fenouil** is white, looks a bit like celery but has a rounded shape. It tastes of aniseed.

le **fer** nm
iron

un fer à repasser
an iron

un fer à cheval
a horseshoe

fera, ferai, feras, ferez vb,
see **faire**

> Look at the entry **faire** to see all the meanings it can have.

Marc fera la vaisselle.
Marc will do the washing up.

Je te ferai un gâteau.
I'll make you a cake.

Qu'est-ce que tu feras l'année prochaine?
What are you going to do next year?

Vous ferez du cheval pendant les vacances?
Will you go horse-riding during the holidays?

férié m adj

un jour férié
a public holiday

la **ferme** nf
farm

fermé m adj
(*f adj* fermée)
closed

La pharmacie est fermée.
The chemist's is closed.

fermer vb
1 to close

Ferme la fenêtre, s'il te plaît.
Close the window please.

2 to turn off

Ferme le robinet.
Turn the tap off.

A
B
C
D
E
F
G
H
I
J
K
L
M
N
O
P
Q
R
S
T
U
V
W
X
Y
Z

N'oublie pas de fermer la porte à clef!
Don't forget to lock the door!

la **fermeture** nf

les heures de fermeture
closing times

une fermeture éclair ®
a zip

le **fermier** nm
farmer

la **fermière** nf

1 woman farmer

2 farmer's wife

féroce adj
fierce

un animal féroce
a fierce animal

ferons, feront vb, *see* **faire**

Look at the entry **faire** *to see all the meanings it can have.*

Nous le ferons si nous avons le temps.
We'll do it if we have time.

Ils feront des quiches pour la fête.
They're going to make quiches for the party.

les **fesses** nfpl
bottom

la **fête** nf

1 party

Tu fais une fête pour ton anniversaire?
Are you having a party for your birthday?

faire la fête
to party

2 name day

C'est ma fête aujourd'hui.
It's my name day today.

Every day on a French calendar belongs to a saint. On March 15th, St Louise's day, people say "Bonne fête Louise!" to anyone with that name. Girls called Louise might get presents too.

une fête foraine
a funfair

les fêtes de fin d'année
the festive season

la Fête Nationale
Bastille Day

Bastille Day is on July 14th, when there are firework displays all over France. It marks the storming of the Bastille (a prison), at the beginning of the French Revolution in 1789.

fêter vb
to celebrate

Aujourd'hui, ma mère fête ses quarante ans.
My mum's celebrating her fortieth birthday today.

le **feu** nm
(*pl* les feux)

1 fire

Au feu!
Fire!

2 traffic light

un feu rouge
a red light

le feu vert
the green light

Tournez à gauche aux feux.
Turn left at the lights.

un feu d'artifice
a firework display

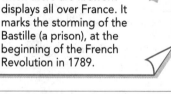

la **feuille** nf

1 leaf

des feuilles mortes
dead leaves

2 sheet

une feuille de papier
a sheet of paper

le **feuilleton** nm
soap

Tu regardes les feuilletons à la télé?
Do you watch soaps on telly?

le **feutre** nm
felt-tip pen

un stylo-feutre
a felt-tip pen

la **fève** nf
broad bean

la fève can also be a little figure which is baked in the cake that is traditionally made at Epiphany (January 6). If you find **la fève** in your slice of cake you are king (or queen) for the day.

février nm
February

en février
in February

au mois de février
in February

le six février
the sixth of February

les **fiançailles** nfpl
engagement

une bague de fiançailles
an engagement ring

fiancé m adj
(f adj fiancée)

être fiancé
to be engaged

Elle est fiancée.
She's engaged.

se **fiancer** vb
to get engaged

Luc et Claire vont se fiancer.
Luc and Claire are going to get engaged.

la **ficelle** nf
string

la **fiche** nf
form

Remplissez cette fiche, s'il vous plaît.
Fill in this form please.

le **fichier** nm
file

fier m adj
(f adj fière)
proud

Il est fier de toi.
He's proud of you.

la **fièvre** nf
fever

J'ai de la fièvre.
I've got a temperature.

la **figue** nf
fig

la **figure** nf
face

Va te laver la figure!
Go and wash your face!

le **fil** nm
<u>thread</u>

le fil de fer
wire

un coup de fil
a phone call

la **file** nf
<u>line</u>

une file de gens
a line of people

en file indienne
in single file

le **filet** nm
<u>net</u>

la **fille** nf
1 <u>girl</u>

une petite fille
a little girl

une grande fille
a big girl

une jeune fille
a young girl

2 <u>daughter</u>

C'est leur fille aînée.
She's their oldest daughter.

la **fillette** nf
<u>little girl</u>

le **filleul** nm
<u>godson</u>

la **filleule** nf
<u>goddaughter</u>

le **film** nm
<u>film</u>

un film policier
a thriller

un film d'aventures
an adventure film

un film d'horreur
a horror film

le **fils** nm
(*pl* les fils)
<u>son</u>

Ils ont deux fils et une fille.
They have two sons and one daughter.

fin

fin can be a noun or an adjective.

A nf
<u>end</u>

à la fin de la leçon
at the end of the lesson

"Fin"
"The End"

fin juin
at the end of June

B m adj
(*f adj* fine)
<u>slim</u>

Elle est fine.
She's slim.

la **finale** nf
<u>final</u>

Ils sont en finale.
They're through to the final.

les quarts de finale
the quarter finals

finalement adv
1 <u>in the end</u>

Finalement, ils ont perdu.
They lost in the end.

2 <u>after all</u>

Finalement, tu avais raison.
You were right after all.

fini m adj
(*f adj* finie)
<u>finished</u>

A
B
C
D
E
F
G
H
I
J
K
L
M
N
O
P
Q
R
S
T
U
V
W
X
Y
Z

finir vb
to finish

Le cours finit à onze heures.
The lesson finishes at 11 o'clock.

J'ai fini!
I've finished!

finlandais nm, m adj
(f adj finlandaise)
Finnish

le **Finlandais** nm
la **Finlandaise** nf
Finn

la **Finlande** nf
Finland

le **flacon** nf
bottle

les **flageolets** nmpl
small haricot beans

flamand mn, m adj
(f adj flamande)
Flemish

French is one of the
languages spoken in Belgium.
The other is Flemish; it is
similar to Dutch.

le **Flamand** nm
la **Flamande** nf
Fleming

A **Flamand** or a **Flamande** is
a Belgian person who speaks
Flemish.

la **flamme** nf
flame

en flammes
on fire

le **flan** nm
baked custard

la **flaque** nf
puddle

la **flèche** nf
arrow

les **fléchettes** nfpl
darts

J'aime jouer aux fléchettes.
I like playing darts.

la **fleur** nf
flower

un bouquet de fleurs
a bunch of flowers

Les arbres sont en fleurs.
The trees are in blossom.

le/la **fleuriste** nm/f
florist

le **fleuve** nm
river

Only big rivers are called
fleuves: the Seine, the Loire,
the Garonne and the Rhône.

le **flipper** nm
pinball machine

le **flocon** nm
flake

un flocon de neige
a snow flake

des flocons d'avoine
oat flakes

flotter vb
to float

la flûte nf
flute

Je joue de la flûte.
I play the flute.

une flûte à bec
a recorder

le **foie** nm
liver

une crise de foie
a stomach upset

le **foin** nm
hay

le rhume des foins
hay fever

la **foire** nf
fair

la **fois** nf
time

la première fois
the first time

à chaque fois
each time

deux fois deux font quatre
2 times 2 is 4

une fois
once

deux fois
twice

folklorique adj
folk

la musique folklorique
folk music

folle f adj
mad

Elle est folle!
She's mad!

foncé m adj
(*f adj* foncée)
dark

une couleur très foncée
a very dark colour

des rideaux bleu foncé
dark blue curtains

le/la **fonctionnaire** nm/f
civil servant

le **fond** nm
1 bottom

Mon porte-monnaie est au fond de mon sac.
My purse is at the bottom of my bag.
2 end

Les toilettes sont au fond du couloir.
The toilets are at the end of the corridor.

fondre vb
to melt

La neige fond.
The snow is melting.

A B C D E F G H I J K L M N O P Q R S T U V W X Y Z

a
b
c
d
e
f
g
h
i
j
k
l
m
n
o
p
q
r
s
t
u
v
w
x
y
z

fondu m adj
(f adj fondue)
melted

Ma glace est toute fondue.
My ice cream is all melted.

la **fondue** nf
fondue

> A **fondue** is a Swiss dish.
> Guests around the table dip
> bits of dry bread into a pot
> of melted cheese. If you lose
> your bread in the cheese,
> you can get a forfeit!

font vb, see **faire**

Elles font leur devoirs ensemble.
They do their homework together.

la **fontaine** nf
fountain

le **foot** nm
football

Je fais du foot avec mes copains.
I play football with my friends.

> le **foot** is a slangy way of
> saying le **football**. A more
> slangy word for "football" in
> English is "footy".

le **football** nm
football

Tu veux jouer au football?
Do you want to play football?

le **footballeur** nm
footballer

le **footing** nm
jogging

Tu veux faire du footing?
Do you want to go jogging?

forain

> **forain** can be an adjective or a
> noun.

A m adj
(f adj foraine)

une fête foraine
a funfair

B nm
fairground worker

la **force** nf
strength

**Je n'ai pas beaucoup de force
dans les bras.**
I haven't got much strength in my
arms.

la **forêt** nf
forest

la **forme** nf

être en forme
to be fit

Ça va? Tu es en forme?
How are you? Are you fit?

**Je ne suis pas en forme
aujourd'hui.**
I'm not feeling too good today.

formidable adj
great

Vous avez fini? Formidable!
Have you finished? That's great!

le **formulaire** nm
form

Tu dois remplir le formulaire.
You have to fill in the form.

fort

> **fort** can be an adjective or an
> adverb.

A m adj
(f adj forte)
1 strong

Le café est trop fort.
The coffee's too strong.
2 good

Il est très fort en maths.
He's very good at maths.
B adv
1 loud

Tu peux parler plus fort?
Can you speak louder?
2 hard

Tu dois le frapper fort.
You've got to hit it hard.

fou m adj
(f adj folle)
mad

Tu es fou?
Are you mad?

la **foudre** nf
lightning

le **foulard** nm
scarf

la **foule** nf
crowd

le **four** nm
oven

un four à micro-ondes
a microwave oven

la **fourchette** nf
fork

la **fourmi** nf
ant

J'ai des fourmis dans les jambes.
I've got pins and needles in my legs.

The French actually means "I've got ants in my legs"!

les **fournitures** nfpl

les fournitures scolaires
school stationery

la **fourrure** nf
fur

frais m adj
(f adj fraîche)
1 fresh

des œufs frais
fresh eggs
2 chilly

Il fait un peu frais ce soir.
It's a bit chilly this evening.

3 cool

des boissons fraîches
cool drinks

la **fraise** nf
strawberry

les fraises des bois
wild strawberries

la **framboise** nf
raspberry

franc

franc can be an adjective or a noun.

A m adj
(f adj franche)
frank

Pour être franc, je le trouve méchant.
To be frank, I think he's horrible.
B nm
franc

The euro replaced the franc in France, Belgium and Luxembourg in 2002.

A B C D E F G H I J K L M N O P Q R S T U V W X Y Z

français nm, m adj
(f adj **française**)
French

J'apprends le français.
I'm learning French.

le **Français** nm
Frenchman

les Français
the French

la **Française** nf
Frenchwoman

la **France** nf
France

franche f adj
frank

francophone adj
French-speaking

la **frange** nf
fringe

J'ai une frange.
I've got a fringe.

frapper vb

Frappez dans vos mains.
Clap your hands.

On frappe à la porte.
Somebody's knocking at the door.

le **frère** nm
brother

mon grand frère
my big brother

mon petit frère
my little brother

le **frigidaire**® nm
refrigerator

le **frigo** nm
fridge

frisé m adj
(f adj **frisée**)
curly

J'ai les cheveux frisés.
I've got curly hair.

frit m adj
(f adj **frite**)
fried

du poisson frit
fried fish

les **frites** nfpl
chips

J'adore le steak-frites.
I love steak and chips.

froid m adj
(f adj **froide**)
cold

La soupe est froide!
The soup is cold!

J'ai froid.
I'm cold.
Il fait froid.
It's cold.

le **fromage** nm
cheese

Tu veux du fromage ou un dessert?
Would you like some cheese or a pudding?

un sandwich au fromage
a cheese sandwich

le **front** nm
forehead

la **frontière** nf
border

le **fruit** nm
<u>fruit</u>

J'aime les fruits.
I like fruit.

un fruit
a piece of fruit

les fruits de mer
seafood

fumé m adj
(*f adj* fumée)
<u>smoked</u>

du saumon fumé
smoked salmon

la **fumée** nf
<u>smoke</u>

fumer vb
<u>to smoke</u>

Il fume la pipe.
He smokes a pipe.

le **fumeur** nm
<u>smoker</u>

un compartiment fumeurs
a smoking compartment

le **furet** nm
<u>ferret</u>

furieux m adj
(*f adj* furieuse)
<u>furious</u>

la **fusée** nf
<u>rocket</u>

le **fusil** nm
<u>gun</u>

le **futur** nm
<u>future</u>

G

le **gage** nm
forfeit

le **gagnant** nm
la **gagnante** nf
winner

gagner vb
to win

Qui a gagné?
Who won?

J'ai gagné!
I've won!

la **galerie** nf
gallery

une galerie de peinture
an art gallery

une galerie marchande
a shopping arcade

le **galet** nm
pebble

la **galette** nf

1 cake

2 biscuit

des galettes pur beurre
shortbread biscuits

la **galette des Rois**

> A **galette des Rois** is a cake
> eaten at Epiphany (January
> 6) which contains a little
> figure. The person who finds
> it is the king (or queen) and
> gets a paper crown. They
> then choose someone to be
> their queen (or king).

Galles nf
le pays de Galles
Wales

le **Gallois** nm
Welshman

les Gallois
the Welsh

gallois nm, m adj
(f adj galloise)
Welsh

la **Galloise** nf
Welshwoman

le **gant** nm
glove

des gants en laine
woollen gloves

un gant de toilette
a face cloth

le **garage** nm
garage

le **garagiste** nm
garage owner

le **garçon** nm
boy

Les garçons, levez-vous!
Stand up, boys!

garder vb
1 to keep

Tu peux garder ce crayon.
You can keep this pencil.

2 to look after

Aujourd'hui, je garde ma nièce.
I'm looking after my niece today.

la **garderie** nf
nursery

le **gardien** nm
la **gardienne** nf
caretaker

un gardien de musée
a museum attendant

un gardien de but
a goalkeeper

la **gare** nf
station

Où est la gare?
Where's the station?

la gare routière
the bus station

garer vb
to park

Où as-tu garé la voiture?
Where have you parked the car?
♦ **se garer**
to park

Gare-toi devant la maison.
Park in front of the house.

garni m adj
(f adj garnie)

un plat garni

A **plat garni** is a dish served with vegetables, salad, potatoes, chips or rice.

les **gars** nmpl
guys

Salut, les gars!
Hi guys!

gaspiller vb
to waste

le **gâteau** nm
(pl les gâteaux)
cake

un gâteau d'anniversaire
a birthday cake

un gâteau sec
a biscuit

gauche

gauche can be a noun or an adjective.

A nf
left

sur votre gauche
on your left
à gauche

à gauche can either mean **left** or **on the left**.

Tournez à gauche.
Turn left.

Prenez la troisième rue à gauche.
Take the third street on the left.

C'est à gauche.
It's on your left.
la deuxième rue à gauche
the second street on the left

B adj
<u>left</u>

Levez le bras gauche!
Put up your left arm!

gaucher m adj
(f adj gauchère)
<u>left-handed</u>

la **gaufre** nf
<u>waffle</u>

la **gaufrette** nf
<u>wafer</u>

le **Gaulois** nm
la **Gauloise** nf
<u>Gaul</u>

**J'aime les bandes dessinées
d'Astérix le Gaulois.**
I like Asterix the Gaul comic strips.

le **gaz** nm
<u>gas</u>

gazeux m adj
(f adj gazeuse)

une boisson gazeuse
a fizzy drink

de l'eau gazeuse
sparkling water

géant nm, m adj
(f adj géante)
<u>giant</u>

la **gelée** nf
<u>jelly</u>

geler vb
<u>to freeze</u>

Il gèle.
It's freezing.

le **gendarme** nm
<u>policeman</u>

la **gendarmerie** nf
<u>police station</u>

général m adj
(f adj générale)
<u>general</u>

en général
<u>usually</u>

généralement adv
<u>generally</u>

généreux m adj
(f adj généreuse)
<u>generous</u>

génial m adj
(f adj géniale)
<u>great</u>

C'est génial.
That's great.

le **génie** nm
<u>genius</u>

C'est un vrai génie.
She's a real genius.

le **genou** nm
(pl les genoux)
<u>knee</u>

Mettez-vous à genoux.
Kneel down.

le **genre** nm
1 <u>kind</u>

C'est un genre de gâteau à la crème.
It's a kind of cream cake.
2 gender

De quel genre est "chien"?
What's the gender of "chien"?

les **gens** nmpl
people

gentil m adj
(f adj gentille)
1 nice

Nos voisins sont très gentils.
Our neighbours are very nice.
2 kind

C'est gentil.
That's kind.

la **géographie** nf
geography

la **géométrie** nf
geometry

germain m adj
(f adj germaine)

Hugues est mon cousin germain.
Hugues is my first cousin.

Delphine est ma cousine germaine.
Delphine is my first cousin.

le **gigot** nm
leg of lamb

le **gilet** nm
1 cardigan
2 waistcoat

la **girafe** nf
giraffe

le **gîte** nm
holiday home

Nous avons loué un gîte pour cet été.
We've rented a holiday home for this summer.

la **glace** nf
1 ice cream

Je voudrais une glace à la fraise.
I'd like a strawberry ice cream.
2 ice

Elle a glissé sur la glace.
She slipped on the ice.
3 mirror

Il se regarde souvent dans la glace.
He often looks at himself in the mirror.

glacé m adj
(f adj glacée)
1 icy

un vent glacé
an icy wind
2 iced

un thé glacé
an iced tea

le **glaçon** nm
ice cube

glisser vb
1 to slip

Elle a glissé sur une peau de banane.
She slipped on a banana skin.
2 to be slippery

Attention, ça glisse!
Watch out, it's slippery!

le **goéland** nm
seagull

A
B
C
D
E
F
G
H
I
J
K
L
M
N
O
P
Q
R
S
T
U
V
W
X
Y
Z

a b c d e f **g** h i j k l m n o p q r s t u v w x y z

le **golf** nm

1 golf

Il joue au golf.
He plays golf.

2 golf course

C'est un golf dix-huit trous.
It's an 18-hole golf course.

la **gomme** nf
rubber

gommer vb
to rub out

la **gorge** nf
throat

J'ai mal à la gorge.
I've got a sore throat.

le **gorille** nm
gorilla

gourmand m adj
(f adj gourmande)
greedy

le **goût** nm
taste

Ça a mauvais goût.
It has a horrible taste.

Ça a un goût sucré.
It tastes sweet.

Ça a bon goût.
It tastes nice.

goûter

goûter can be a noun or a verb.

A nm
afternoon snack

C'est l'heure du goûter.
It's time for an afternoon snack.

B vb

1 to taste

Tu veux goûter?
Do you want to taste it?

2 to have an afternoon snack

Je goûte généralement vers quatre heures.
I usually have a snack around 4.

la **graine** nf
seed

la **grammaire** nf
grammar

le **gramme** nm
gramme

trois cents grammes de fromage
three hundred grammes of cheese

grand m adj
(f adj grande)

1 tall

Il est grand.
He's tall.

2 big

C'est sa grande sœur.
She's his big sister.

les grandes vacances
the summer holidays
un grand magasin
a department store

grand-chose n

pas grand-chose
not much

la **Grande-Bretagne** nf
Britain

J'habite en Grande-Bretagne.
I live in Britain.

Bretagne means "Brittany". Britain is bigger than Brittany, which is why its French name is *Grande-Bretagne*.

grandir vb
to grow

Il a beaucoup grandi.
He's grown a lot.

la **grand-mère** nf
grandmother

le **grand-père** nm
grandfather

les **grands-parents** nmpl
grandparents

gras m adj
(*f adj* grasse)
1 fatty

Évitez les aliments gras.
Avoid fatty foods.

2 greasy

J'ai les cheveux gras.
I've got greasy hair.

3 oily

J'ai une peau grasse.
I've got oily skin.

le **gratte-ciel** nm
skyscraper

gratter vb
1 to scratch

Ne gratte pas tes piqûres de moustiques!
Don't scratch your mosquito bites!

2 to be itchy

Ce pull me gratte!
This jumper's itchy.

gratuit m adj
(*f adj* gratuite)
free

entrée gratuite
admission free

grave adj
serious

C'est grave?
Is it serious?

Ce n'est pas grave.
It doesn't matter.

un accent grave
a grave accent

gravement adv
seriously

Il est gravement blessé.
He is seriously injured.

grec nm, m adj
(*f adj* grecque)
Greek

le **Grec** nm
la **Grecque** nf
Greek

la **Grèce** nf
Greece

grêler vb
to hail

Il grêle.
It's hailing.

la **grenadine** nf
grenadine

Grenadine is a popular drink with children in France. It is very pink!

A B C D E F **G** H I J K L M N O P Q R S T U V W X Y Z

le **grenier** nm
attic

la **grenouille** nf
frog

la **grève** nf
strike

en grève
on strike

Les profs sont en grève.
The teachers are on strike.

griffer vb
to scratch

Le chat m'a griffé.
The cat scratched me.

la **grillade** nf
grilled food

une grillade d'agneau
grilled lamb

le **grille-pain** nm
toaster

griller vb
1 to toast

du pain grillé
toast

2 to grill

des saucisses grillées
grilled sausages

la **grimace** nf

faire des grimaces
to make faces

Arrête de faire des grimaces.
Stop making faces.

grimper vb
to climb

grincheux m adj
(f adj grincheuse)
grumpy

la **grippe** nf
flu

Carol a la grippe.
Carol has got flu.

gris m adj
(f adj grise)
grey

grogner vb
to growl

gronder vb

se faire gronder
to get a telling off

Tu vas te faire gronder par ton père!
You're going to get a telling off
from your father!

gros m adj
(f adj grosse)
1 big

une grosse pomme
a big apple

2 fat

Il est un peu gros.
He's quite fat.

la **groseille** nf
redcurrant

la **grotte** nf
cave

le **groupe** nm
group

Mettez-vous en groupes de quatre.
Get into groups of four.

la **guêpe** nf
wasp

guérir vb
to recover

Il est complètement guéri.
He's fully recovered.

la **guerre** nf
war

la **gueule** nf
mouth

Regarde, le chat a une souris dans sa gueule!
Look, the cat has a mouse in its mouth!

le **guichet** nm
counter

le **guide** nm
guide

guider vb
to guide

la **guirlande** nf
tinsel

Nous allons décorer le sapin de Noël avec des guirlandes.
We're going to decorate the Christmas tree with tinsel.

une guirlande en papier
a paper chain

la **guitare** nf
guitar

Je joue de la guitare.
I play the guitar.

la **gym** nf
PE

le **gymnase** nm
gym

L'école a un nouveau gymnase.
The school's got a new gym.

la **gymnastique** nf
gymnastics

Je fais de la gymnastique le mercredi.
I do gymnastics on Wednesdays.

H

s'**habiller** vb
to get dressed

Je m'habille rapidement.
I get dressed quickly.

l'**habitant** nm
l'**habitante** nf
inhabitant

habiter vb
to live

Il habite à Montpellier.
He lives in Montpellier.

les **habits** nmpl
clothes

l'**habitude** nf
habit

une mauvaise habitude
a bad habit

J'ai l'habitude.
I'm used to it.

d'habitude
usually

D'habitude, je vais à la piscine le mardi.
I usually go to the pool on Tuesdays.

comme d'habitude
as usual

le **hachis** nm

le hachis Parmentier
shepherd's pie

la **haie** nf
hedge

haïr vb
to hate

Je la hais.
I hate her.

les **halles** nfpl
covered market

le **hamster** nm
hamster

la **hanche** nf
hip

le **handball** nm
handball

Le lundi, je joue au handball.
I play handball on Mondays.

handball is very popular in French schools. It is played on a similar pitch to football but players throw the ball instead of kicking it.

les **handicapés** nmpl
disabled people

handicapé m adj
(f adj handicapée)
disabled

les **haricots** nmpl
beans

les haricots verts
green beans

les haricots blancs
haricot beans

l'**harmonica** nm
mouth organ

la **harpe** nf
harp

le **hasard** nm

au hasard
at random

Choisis un numéro au hasard.
Choose a number at random.

par hasard
by chance

Je l'ai rencontrée par hasard au supermarché.
I met her at the supermarket by chance.

hausser vb

hausser les épaules
to shrug one's shoulders

haut

> **haut** can be an adjective or a noun.

Ⓐ m adj
(f adj **haute**)
high

La fenêtre est trop haute.
The window is too high.

Ⓑ nm
en haut

> **en haut** can either mean **upstairs** or **at the top**.

La salle de bain est en haut.
The bathroom is upstairs.

Le nid est tout en haut de l'arbre.
The nest is right at the top of the tree.

trois mètres de haut
three metres high

la **hauteur** nf
height

hein excl
eh?

Hein? Qu'est-ce que tu dis?
Eh? What did you say?

l'**hélicoptère** nm
helicopter

l'**herbe** nf
grass

les herbes de Provence
mixed herbs

les fines herbes
mixed herbs

le **hérisson** nm
hedgehog

l'**héroïne** nf
heroine

l'héroïne du roman
the heroine of the novel

le **héros** nm
hero

C'est le héros du film.
He's the hero of the film.

hésiter vb
to hesitate

J'hésite.
I can't decide.

J'hésite entre un hamster et un lapin.
I don't know whether to choose a hamster or a rabbit.

a
b
c
d
e
f
g
h
i
j
k
l
m
n
o
p
q
r
s
t
u
v
w
x
y
z

l'**heure** nf
1 hour

Le trajet dure six heures.
The journey lasts six hours.

2 time

Vous avez l'heure?
Have you got the time?

À quelle heure?
What time?

À quelle heure arrivons-nous?
What time do we arrive?

Elle est toujours à l'heure.
She's always on time.

3 o'clock

à deux heures du matin
at 2 o'clock in the morning

4 period

une heure de français
a period of French

> ⌐o
> **Quelle heure est-il?**
> What time is it?
> **Il est sept heures dix.**
> It's ten past seven.
> **à neuf heures**
> at nine o'clock

heureusement adv
luckily

heureux m adj
(f adj heureuse)
happy

l'**hexagone** nm
hexagon

l'**Hexagone**
France

> A hexagon has six sides.
> France is often callled
> l'**Hexagone** because of its
> six-sided shape.

le **hibou** nm
(pl les hiboux)
owl

hier adv
yesterday

avant-hier
the day before yesterday

la **hi-fi** nf

une chaîne hi-fi
a hifi

hippique adj

un club hippique
a riding centre

un concours hippique
a horse show

l'**hippopotame** nm
hippopotamus

> *L'hippopotame* is never
> shortened to "hippo" in French.

l'**hirondelle** nf
swallow

l'**histoire** nf
1 history

un cours d'histoire
a history lesson

2 story

l'**hiver** nm
winter

en hiver
in winter

le **hockey** nm
hockey

Il joue au hockey.
He plays hockey.

le hockey sur glace
ice hockey

hollandais nm, m adj
(*f adj* hollandaise)
Dutch

le **Hollandais** nm
Dutch man

les Hollandais
the Dutch

la **Hollandaise** nf
Dutch woman

la **Hollande** nf
Holland

le **homard** nm
lobster

l'**homme** nm
man

un homme d'affaires
a businessman

la **Hongrie** nf
Hungary

honnête adj
honest

la **honte** nf

avoir honte
to be ashamed

J'ai un peu honte.
I'm a bit ashamed.

l'**hôpital** nm
(*pl* les hôpitaux)
hospital

le **hoquet** nm

J'ai le hoquet.
I've got hiccups.

l'**horaire** nm
timetable

les horaires de train
the train timetable

l'**horloge** nf
clock

l'**horreur** nf

J'ai horreur du chou.
I hate cabbage.

horrible adj
horrible

le **hors-d'œuvre** nm
starter

Comme hors-d'œuvre, il y a des carottes râpées.
As a starter there's carrot salad.

l'**hôtel** nm
hotel

Nous passons une semaine à l'hôtel.
We are spending a week at a hotel.

l'hôtel de ville
the town hall

l'**hôtesse** nf

une hôtesse de l'air
an air hostess

A B C D E F G **H** I J K L M N O P Q R S T U V W X Y Z

le **houx** nm
holly

l'**huile** nf
oil

huit num
eight

Il est huit heures.
It's eight o'clock.

Il a huit ans.
He's eight.

dans huit jours
in a week's time

> **le huit février**
> the eighth of February

la **huitaine** nf

une huitaine de jours
about a week

Nous rentrons dans une huitaine de jours.
We'll be back in about a week.

huitième m adj
eighth

au huitième étage
on the eighth floor

l'**huître** nf
oyster

humain nm, m adj
(*f adj* humaine)

un être humain
a human being

l'**humeur** nf
mood

Il est de bonne humeur.
He's in a good mood.

Elle est de mauvaise humeur.
She's in a bad mood.

humide adj
damp

l'**humour** nm

avoir le sens de l'humour
to have a sense of humour

Il n'a pas le sens de l'humour.
He has no sense of humour.

hurler vb
1 to howl

Le chien des voisins hurle tous les soirs.
The neighbours' dog howls every evening.

2 to yell

Arrête de hurler comme ça!
Stop yelling like that!

hygiénique m adj
le papier hygiénique
toilet paper

l'**hypermarché** nm
hypermarket

I

ici adv
here

Viens ici.
Come here.

l'idée nf
idea

C'est une bonne idée.
It's a good idea.

idéal m adj
(f adj idéale)
ideal

Décrivez votre chambre idéale.
Describe your ideal bedroom.

identique adj
identical

l'identité nf
identity

idiot adj
(f adj idiote)
stupid

C'est vraiment une plaisanterie idiote!
It's really a stupid joke!

l'idiot nm
l'idiote nf
idiot

il pron
1 he

Il habite à Paris.
He lives in Paris.

2 it

Il pleut.
It's raining.

Attention à ce chien: il mord.
Watch that dog: it bites.

l'île nf
island

les îles Anglo-Normandes
the Channel Islands

l'île de Man
the Isle of Man

l'île de Wight
the Isle of Wight

ils pron
they

Ils sont à la piscine.
They are at the swimming pool.

l'image nf
picture

Regardez les images.
Look at the pictures.

imaginaire adj
imaginary

C'est un personnage imaginaire.
He's an imaginary character.

l'imagination nf
imagination

Elle a beaucoup d'imagination.
She's got a vivid imagination.

imaginer vb
to imagine

a
b
c
d
e
f
g
h
i
j
k
l
m
n
o
p
q
r
s
t
u
v
w
x
y
z

l'**imbécile** nm/f
idiot

C'est une imbécile.
She's an idiot.

Il fait l'imbécile en classe.
He plays the fool in the class.

imiter vb
to imitate

immédiatement adv
immediately

immense adj
huge

une maison immense
a huge house

l'**immeuble** nm
block of flats

J'habite dans un immeuble.
I live in a block of flats.

les **immigrés** nmpl
immigrants

immobilier m adj
(f adj immobilière)

une agence immobilière
an estate agent's

impair m adj

un nombre impair
an odd number

l'**impasse** nf
cul-de-sac

Ma maison est au bout d'une impasse.
My house is at the end of a cul-de-sac.

impeccable adj
1 immaculate

Elle est toujours impeccable.
She's always immaculate.
2 perfect

C'est impeccable!
That's perfect!

l'**imper** nm
raincoat

l'**imperméable** nm
raincoat

impoli m adj
(f adj impolie)
rude

l'**importance** nf

Ça n'a pas d'importance.
It doesn't matter.

important m adj
(f adj importante)
1 important

une lettre importante
an important letter
2 large

un nombre important
a large number

importer vb

Peu importe.
It doesn't matter.

impossible adj
impossible

l'**impression** nf
impression

Ce n'est qu'une impression.
It is only an impression.

avoir l'impression que
to have a feeling that

J'ai l'impression qu'il va neiger.
I have a feeling that it's going to snow.

impressionnant m adj
(*f adj* impressionnante)
impressive

impressionné m adj
(*f adj* impressionnée)
impressed
Je suis très impressionné.
I'm very impressed.

l'**imprimante** nf
printer

imprimer vb
to print

l'**incendie** nm
fire
un incendie de forêt
a forest fire

l'**incident** nm
incident

l'**inconnu** nm
l'**inconnue** nf
stranger
Ne parle pas à des inconnus.
Don't talk to strangers.

l'**inconvénient** nm
disadvantage

incorrect m adj
(*f adj* incorrecte)
incorrect
une réponse incorrecte
an incorrect answer

incroyable adj
incredible

l'**Inde** nf
India

indépendant m adj
(*f adj* indépendante)
independent

l'**index** nm
index finger

les **indications** nfpl
instructions
Suivez les indications.
Follow the instructions.

l'**indice** nm
clue
Je te donne un indice?
Shall I give you a clue?

indien m adj
(*f adj* indienne)
Indian

l'**Indien** nm
l'**Indienne** nf
Indian
les Indiens
Indians

l'**industrie** nf
industry

infirme adj
disabled

l'**infirmerie** nf
medical room
Elle est à l'infirmerie.
She's in the medical room.

l'**infirmier** nm
l'**infirmière** nf
nurse

l'**informaticien** nm
l'**informaticienne** nf
computer scientist

les **informations** nfpl

1 news

J'aime regarder les informations à la télé.
I like watching the news on the TV.

2 information

Je voudrais quelques informations, s'il vous plaît.
I'd like some information, please.

une information
a piece of information

l'**informatique** nf

1 ICT

mon prof d'informatique
my ICT teacher

2 computing

Il travaille dans l'informatique.
He works in computing.

l'**infusion** nf
herbal tea

l'**ingénieur** nm
engineer

les **initiales** nfpl
initials

Quelles sont tes initiales?
What are your initials?

l'**initiation** nf
introduction

un stage d'initiation au karaté
an introductory course in karate

injuste adj
unfair

C'est vraiment trop injuste.
It is really quite unfair.

innocent m adj
(f adj innocente)
innocent

l'**inondation** nf
flood

inquiet m adj
(f adj inquiète)
worried

s'**inquiéter** vb
to worry

Ne t'inquiète pas!
Don't worry!

l'**insecte** nm
insect

insolent m adj
(f adj insolente)
cheeky

l'**inspecteur** nm
l'**inspectrice** nf
inspector

Il y a une inspectrice à l'école.
There's an inspector in the school.

l'**instant** nm
moment

Attendez un instant.
Wait a moment.

l'**instituteur** nm
l'**institutrice** nf
primary school teacher

l'**instrument** nm
instrument

un instrument de musique
a musical instrument

insupportable adj
unbearable

intelligent m adj
(f adj intelligente)
intelligent

Mon chien est très intelligent.
My dog is very intelligent.

l'**interdiction** nf

"interdiction de fumer"
"no smoking"

"interdiction de stationner"
"no parking"

interdire vb
to forbid

Ses parents lui ont interdit de sortir.
His parents have forbidden him to go out.

interdit m adj
(*f adj* interdite)
forbidden

C'est interdit.
It's forbidden.

Il est interdit de courir dans les couloirs.
Running in the corridors is forbidden.

intéressant m adj
(*f adj* intéressante)
interesting

intéresser vb
to interest

L'histoire, ça m'intéresse.
I'm interested in history.

Je m'intéresse aux dinosaures.
I'm interested in dinosaurs.

l'**intérêt** nm

Tu as intérêt à te dépêcher.
You'd better hurry up.

C'est un film sans intérêt.
It's not a very interesting film.

l'**intérieur** nm

à l'intérieur
inside

Il fait plus frais à l'intérieur.
It's cooler inside.

l'**internat** nm
boarding school

international m adj
(*f adj* internationale)
international

l'**interne** nm/f
boarder

In French secondary schools, pupils are either **externe** if they go home for lunch, **demi-pensionnaire** if they have a school lunch, or **interne** if they board at the school.

l'**Internet** nm
Internet

sur Internet
on the Internet

l'**interprète** nm/f
interpreter

l'**interrogation** nf
test

une interrogation écrite
a written test

une interrogation orale
an oral test

interroger vb
to ask questions

interrompre vb
to interrupt

Ne m'interrompez pas.
Don't interrupt me.

intime adj

un journal intime
a diary

inutile adj
useless

inventer vb

1 to invent

J'ai inventé une machine.
I have invented a machine.

2 to make up

Elle a inventé une excuse.
She made up an excuse.

l'**inventeur** nm
inventor

inverse

| inverse can be an adjective or a noun. |

A adj

dans le sens inverse des aiguilles d'une montre
anti-clockwise

B nm

C'est l'inverse.
It's the other way round.

l'**invité** nm
l'**invitée** nf
guest

inviter vb
to invite

irai vb, see **aller**

J'irai demain au supermarché.
I'll go to the supermarket tomorrow.

l'**Irak** nm
Iraq

l'**Iran** nm
Iran

irlandais m adj
(f adj irlandaise)
Irish

l'**Irlandais** nm
Irishman

les Irlandais
the Irish

l'**Irlandaise** nf
Irishwoman

l'**Irlande** nf
Ireland

la République d'Irlande
the Irish Republic

l'Irlande du Nord
Northern Ireland

l'**ironie** nf
irony

ironique adj
ironical

irons vb, see **aller**

Nous irons à la plage cet après-midi.
We'll go to the beach this afternoon.

irrégulier m adj
(f adj irrégulière)
irregular

un verbe irrégulier
an irregular verb

irriter vb
to irritate

Elle m'irrite.
She's irritating me.

islamique adj
Islamic

l'**Islande** nf
Iceland

isolé m adj
(f adj isolée)
isolated

une ferme isolée
an isolated farm

Israël nm
Israel

israélien m adj
(f adj israélienne)
Israeli

l'**Israélien** nm
l'**Israélienne** nf
Israeli

l'**issue** nf

"issue de secours"
"emergency exit"

une voie sans issue
a dead end

l'**Italie** nf
Italy

italien nm, m adj
(f adj italienne)
Italian

l'**Italien** nm
l'**Italienne** nf
Italian

J

j' pron

j' is what je changes to before a vowel sound.

I

J'arrive!
I'm coming!

J'habite à Calais.
I live in Calais.

la **jalousie** nf
jealousy

jaloux m adj
(*f adj* jalouse)
jealous

jamais adv
never

Tu vas souvent au cinéma? – Non, jamais.
Do you go to the cinema often? – No, never.

Elle ne fait jamais la vaisselle.
She never does the washing-up.

la **jambe** nf
leg

le **jambon** nm
ham

le jambon cru
Parma ham

janvier nm
January

en janvier
in January

au mois de janvier
in January

le vingt-quatre janvier
the twenty-fourth of January

le **Japon** nm
Japan

japonais nm, m adj
(*f adj* japonaise)
Japanese

le **Japonais** nm
Japanese man

les Japonais
the Japanese

la **Japonaise** nf
Japanese woman

le **jardin** nm
garden

Nous avons un grand jardin derrière la maison.
We have a big garden at the back of the house.

un jardin d'enfants
a kindergarten

le **jardinage** nm
gardening

Le passe-temps préféré de mon père, c'est le jardinage.
My dad's favourite hobby is gardening.

le **jardinier** nm
gardener

jaune

> **jaune** can be an adjective or a noun.

Ⓐ adj
yellow

une robe jaune
a yellow dress

Ⓑ nm
yellow

Ma couleur préférée, c'est le jaune.
My favourite colour is yellow.

un jaune d'œuf
an egg yolk

le **jazz** nm
jazz

je pron

> **je** changes to **j'** before a vowel sound.

J'
Je déteste les araignées.
I hate spiders.

le **jean** nm
jeans

Elle porte un jean.
She is wearing jeans.

une veste en jean
a denim jacket

la **jeannette** nf
Brownie

> Brownies aren't as common in France as they are in Britain.

jeter vb
1 to throw

Jette ton chewing-gum à la poubelle.
Throw your chewing gum in the bin.

2 to throw away
J'ai jeté mes vieux jouets.
I've thrown away my old toys.

le **jeton** nm
counter

Je vous donne six jetons chacun.
I'm giving you six counters each.

le **jeu** nm
(pl les jeux)
game

C'est un jeu qui s'appelle "le Pendu".
It's a game called "Hangman".

un jeu de mots
a pun

un jeu de société
a board game

un jeu électronique
an electronic game

un jeu vidéo
a video game

un jeu de cartes

> **un jeu de cartes** can either mean **a pack of cards** or **a card game**.

J'ai acheté un nouveau jeu de cartes.
I've bought a new pack of cards.

Tu connais ce jeu de cartes?
Do you know this card game?

le **jeudi** nm
1 Thursday

Aujourd'hui, nous sommes jeudi.
It's Thursday today.
2 on Thursday

A B C D E F G H I **J** K L M N O P Q R S T U V W X Y Z

Il va venir jeudi.
He's coming on Thursday.

Le musée est fermé le jeudi.
The museum is closed on Thursdays.

> tous les jeudis
> every Thursday
> **le jeudi**
> on Thursdays
> **jeudi dernier**
> last Thursday
> **jeudi prochain**
> next Thursday
> **À jeudi!**
> See you on Thursday!

jeune adj
young

un jeune homme
a young man

une jeune femme
a young woman

une jeune fille
a girl

les **jeunes** nmpl
young people

la **jeunesse** nf
youth

le **jogging** nm
1 jogging

Il fait du jogging.
He goes jogging.

2 tracksuit

Clémentine porte un jogging rose.
Clémentine's wearing a pink tracksuit.

joli m adj
(f adj jolie)
pretty

la **jonquille** nf
daffodil

la **joue** nf
cheek

Elle a les joues roses.
She's got pink cheeks.

jouer vb
to play

Le soir, je joue avec ma petite sœur.
I play with my little sister in the evening.

jouer de
to play

Il joue de la guitare et du piano.
He plays the guitar and the piano.

jouer à
to play

Elle joue au tennis.
She plays tennis.

Ils jouent aux cartes.
They are playing cards.

le **jouet** nm
toy

Range tes jouets!
Tidy up your toys!

le **joueur** nm
la **joueuse** nf
player

le **jour** nm
day

On est quel jour aujourd'hui?
What day is it today?

Il fait jour.
It's daylight.

le jour de l'An
New Year's Day

un jour de congé
a day off

le jour de Noël
Christmas Day

un jour férié
a public holiday

dans huit jours
in a week
dans quinze jours
in a fortnight

le **journal** nm
(*pl* les journaux)

1 newspaper

Mon père aime lire le journal.
My dad likes to read the newspaper.

le journal télévisé
the television news

2 diary

J'écris tous les jours dans mon journal.
I write my diary every day.

le/la **journaliste** nm/f
journalist

la **journée** nf
day

Nous allons passer la journée au bord de la mer.
We are going to spend the day at the seaside.

toute la journée
all day long

joyeux m adj
(*f adj* joyeuse)
happy

des enfants joyeux
happy children

Joyeux Noël!
Merry Christmas!
Joyeux anniversaire!
Happy birthday!
Joyeuses Pâques!
Happy Easter!

le **judo** nm
judo

Le mercredi, je fais du judo.
I do judo on Wednesdays.

juif m adj
(*f adj* juive)
Jewish

juillet nm
July

en juillet
in July

le onze juillet
the eleventh of July

juin nm
June

en juin
in June

au mois de juin
in June

le vingt-trois juin
the twenty-third of June

jumeau m adj
(*f adj* jumelle)
twin

a

C'est mon frère jumeau.
He's my twin brother.

b

C'est ma sœur jumelle.
She's my twin sister.

c

Marcel et Léon sont jumeaux.
Marcel and Léon are twins.

d

les **jumeaux** nmpl
twins

e

f

Les jumeaux s'appellent Jean et Marc.
The twins are called Jean and Marc.

g

jumeler vb
to twin

h

i

Hastings est jumelée avec Béthune.
Hastings is twinned with Béthune.

j

k

les **jumelles** nfpl
1 twins

Les jumelles s'appellent Anna et Louise.
The twins are called Anna and Louise.

l

m

n

2 binoculars

o

p

q

r

s

t

u

v

w

x

y

z

la **jungle** nf
jungle

la **jupe** nf
skirt

jurer vb
to swear

Je jure que c'est vrai!
I swear it's true!

le **jus** nm
juice

un jus de fruit
a fruit juice

du jus d'orange
orange juice

jusqu'à prep
1 as far as

Allez jusqu'à la mairie et tournez à droite.
Go as far as the town hall, then turn right.
2 until

On est en vacances jusqu'à dimanche.
We're on holiday until Sunday.

juste adj
fair

Il est sévère, mais juste.
He's strict but fair.

K

kaki adj
khaki

des chaussures kaki
khaki shoes

le **kangourou** nm
kangaroo

le **karaté** nm
karate

Le lundi, je fais du karaté.
I do karate on Mondays.

la **kermesse** nf
fête

**Au mois de juin, il y a une
kermesse à mon école.**
There's a fête at our school in June.

le **kilo** nm
kilo

un kilo d'oranges
a kilo of oranges

le **kilogramme** nm
kilogramme

le **kilomètre** nm
kilometre

**Mon école est à deux kilomètres
de chez moi.**
My school is two kilometres from
my house.

le/la **kinésithérapeute** nm/f
physiotherapist

le **kiosque** nm

un kiosque à journaux
a news stand

le **koala** nm
koala

le **K-way**® nm
cagoule

A
B
C
D
E
F
G
H
I
J
K
L
M
N
O
P
Q
R
S
T
U
V
W
X
Y
Z

L

l'

l' can be an article or a pronoun.

le and la change to l' before a vowel sound.

ⓐ article
the

l'arbre
the tree

ⓑ pron

1 him

C'est un homme intelligent: je l'admire beaucoup.
He's an intelligent man: I admire him very much.

2 her

Ma maîtresse est gentille et je l'aime bien.
My teacher is nice and I like her.

3 it

J'aime bien ce T-shirt. Je l'achète.
I like this T-shirt. I'm going to buy it.

la

la can be an article or a pronoun.

ⓐ article
the

la maison
the house

ⓑ pron

1 her

C'est ma voisine: je la vois tous les jours.
This is my neighbour: I see her every day.

2 it

Prends la gomme et mets-la dans la trousse.
Take the rubber and put it in the pencil case.

là adv

1 there

Ton livre est là, sur la table.
Your book's there, on the table.

2 here

Elle n'est pas là.
She isn't here.

là-bas adv
over there

Va t'asseoir là-bas.
Go and sit over there.

le **laboratoire** nm
laboratory

le **labyrinthe** nm
maze

le **lac** nm
lake

le **lacet** nm
lace

des chaussures à lacets
lace-up shoes

là-haut adv
up there

Le ballon est là-haut sur le toit.
The ball is up there on the roof.

laid m adj
(f adj laide)
ugly

Elle est très laide.
She's very ugly.

la **laine** nf
wool

un pull en laine
a woolly jumper

laisser vb
1 to leave

Laisse ton cahier sur la table.
Leave your jotter on the table.
2 to let

Laisse-le parler.
Let him speak.

le **lait** nm
milk

Je voudrais du lait.
I'd like some milk.

un café au lait
a white coffee

la **laitue** nf
lettuce

la **lampe** nf
lamp

une lampe de poche
a torch

lancer vb
to throw

Lance-moi le ballon!
Throw me the ball!

le **landau** nm
pram

la **langouste** nf

A **langouste** is a popular kind of seafood in France and is similar to a lobster.

la **langue** nf
1 tongue

Elle m'a tiré la langue!
She stuck her tongue out at me!
2 language

une langue étrangère
a foreign language

le **lapin** nm
rabbit

le **lard** nm
streaky bacon

les **lardons** nmpl
chunks of bacon

large adj
wide

la **largeur** nf
width

le **lavabo** nm
washbasin

la **lavande** nf
lavender

laver vb
to wash

Tu peux laver la voiture?
Could you wash the car?

A B C D E F G H I J K L M N O P Q R S T U V W X Y Z

a
b
c
d
e
f
g
h
i
j
k
l
m
n
o
p
q
r
s
t
u
v
w
x
y
z

◆ **se laver**
to wash

Je me lave le matin.
I get washed in the morning.

se laver les mains
to wash one's hands

Lave-toi les mains.
Wash your hands.

le **lave-vaisselle** nm
dishwasher

le

le can be an article or a pronoun.

le changes to l' before a vowel sound.

A article
the

le livre
the book

Aujourd'hui nous sommes le douze mai.
Today is the twelfth of May.

B pron

1 him

C'est mon voisin: je le vois tous les jours.
He's my neighbour: I see him every day.

2 it

Où est mon stylo? Je ne le trouve pas.
Where's my pen? I can't find it.

lécher vb
to lick

la **leçon** nf
lesson

une leçon de piano
a piano lesson

le **lecteur** nm

un lecteur de cassettes
a cassette player

un lecteur de CD
a CD player

la **lecture** nf
reading

J'aime la lecture.
I love reading.

Be careful! The French word **lecture** does not mean the same as **lecture** in English.

léger m adj
(f adj légère)
light

un déjeuner léger
a light lunch

légèrement adv
slightly

les **légumes** nmpl
vegetables

Je n'aime pas les légumes.
I don't like vegetables.

le **lendemain** nm
next day

Il est parti le lendemain.
He left the next day.

lent m adj
(f adj lente)
slow

lentement adv
slowly

Parle plus lentement, s'il te plaît.
Please speak more slowly.

les **lentilles** nfpl

1 contact lenses

Je porte des lentilles.
I wear contact lenses.

2 lentils

un rôti de porc aux lentilles
roast pork with lentils

le **léopard** nm
leopard

les

> **les** can be an article or a pronoun.

Ⓐ article
the

les arbres
the trees

Ⓑ pron
them

J'ai deux chiens et je les promène tous les jours.
I've got two dogs and I walk them every day.

la **lessive** nf

1 washing powder

2 washing

Maman n'aime pas faire la lessive.
Mum doesn't like doing the washing.

la **lettre** nf
letter

J'écris une lettre à ma meilleure copine.
I'm writing a letter to my best friend.

leur

> **leur** can be an adjective or a pronoun.

Ⓐ adj
their

leur ami
their friend

Ⓑ pron
them

Donnez-leur le ballon.
Give them the ball.

leurs pl adj
their

leurs amis
their friends

lever vb
to raise

Levez la jambe gauche.
Raise your left leg.

Levez la main!
Put your hand up!

◆ **se lever**

> **se lever** can either mean **to get up** or **to stand up**.

Il se lève souvent à six heures.
He often gets up at 6 o'clock.

Levez-vous!
Stand up!

la **lèvre** nf
lip

le **lézard** nm
lizard

la **liberté** nf
freedom

le/la **libraire** nm/f
bookseller

la **librairie** nf
bookshop

a b c d e f g h i j k l m n o p q r s t u v w x y z

J'aime acheter des livres à la librairie.
I like to buy books in the bookshop.

> Be careful! **librairie** does not mean the same as **library**.

libre adj
free

Tu es libre de faire ce que tu veux.
You are free to do as you wish.

Avez-vous une chambre de libre?
Have you got a free room?

la **licence** nf
degree

une licence de droit
a law degree

le **lièvre** nm
hare

la **ligne** nf
line

Tracez deux lignes verticales.
Draw two vertical lines.

Mettez-vous en ligne.
Line up.

le **lilas** nm
lilac

la **limace** nf
slug

la **limonade** nf
lemonade

le **linge** nm
linen

le linge sale
dirty linen

Je vais étendre le linge
I'm going to hang out the washing.

le **lion** nm
lion

la **lionne** nf
lioness

lire vb
to read

Le soir, je lis dans mon lit.
At night I read in bed.

lis, lisent, lisez vb, see **lire**

Je lis beaucoup.
I read a lot.

Qu'est-ce que tu lis?
What are you reading?

Ils lisent des BD.
They read comics.

Lisez la première phrase.
Read the first sentence.

la **liste** nf
list

lit

> **lit** can be a noun or part of the verb **lire**.

A nm
bed

aller au lit
to go to bed

Je vais au lit à sept heures.
I go to bed at seven.

faire son lit
to make one's bed

Je fais mon lit tous les matins.
I make my bed every morning.

un grand lit
a double bed

un lit de camp
a campbed

B vb, see **lire**

Il lit des magazines.
He reads magazines.

le **litre** nm
litre

un litre de lait
a litre of milk

la **littérature** nf
literature

le **livre** nm
book

un livre de poche
a paperback

la **livre** nf
pound

Le guide coûte trois livres.
The guide book costs £3.

une livre is also a weight –
500 grams, which is nearly
the same as a British pound
(450 grams).

le **livret** nm

le livret scolaire
the school report book

logique adj
logical

loin adv
far

La gare n'est pas très loin d'ici.
The station is not very far from
here.

C'est un peu plus loin.
It's a little further on.

lointain m adj
(*f adj* lointaine)
distant

un pays lointain
a distant country

les **loisirs** nmpl
1 free time

**Qu'est-ce que tu fais d'habitude
pendant tes loisirs?**
What do you usually do in your free
time?
2 hobby

**Le ski et l'équitation sont des
loisirs coûteux.**
Skiing and riding are expensive
hobbies.

Londres n
London

J'habite à Londres.
I live in London.

Je vais à Londres.
I'm going to London.

long m adj
(*f adj* longue)
long

une longue promenade
a long walk

Elle a les cheveux longs.
She has long hair.

la **longueur** nf
length

la **loterie** nf
lottery

la loterie nationale
the National Lottery

le **lotissement** nm
housing estate

le **loto** nm
1 lottery

**Mes parents jouent au loto toutes
les semaines.**
My parents play the lottery every
week.

le loto sportif
the pools
2 bingo

On va jouer au loto.
We're going to play bingo.

la **louche** nf
ladle

louer vb

1 to let

**Ils louent des chambres à des
étudiants.**
They let rooms to students.

"à louer"
"to let"

2 to rent

**L'été, nous louons un petit
appartement au bord de la mer.**
In the summer we rent a little flat
by the sea.

3 to hire

Est-ce que vous louez des vélos?
Do you hire bikes?

le **loup** nm
wolf

la **loupe** nf
magnifying glass

lourd m adj
(*f adj* lourde)
heavy

la **loutre** nf
otter

la **luge** nf
sledge

J'aime bien faire de la luge.
I like sledging.

Quand il neige, je fais de la luge.
I go sledging when it snows.

lui pron

1 him

Voilà ton père: demande-lui!
Here's your dad – ask him!

Je pense beaucoup à lui.
I think about him a lot.

Lui, il est toujours en retard!
Oh, HE's always late!

Il a construit son bateau lui-même.
He built his boat himself.

lui-même
himself

2 to him

**Michael m'énerve, alors je ne lui
parle pas en ce moment.**
Michael's getting on my nerves so
I'm not speaking to him at the
moment.

3 her

Voilà ta mère: demande-lui!
Here's your mum – ask her!

4 to her

**C'est Julie au téléphone. Tu veux
lui parler?**
Julie's on the phone. Do you want
to speak to her?

5 it

**Cette plante ne pousse pas vite;
je vais lui donner plus d'eau.**
This plant isn't growing well; I'm
going to give it more water.

la **lumière** nf
light

**Sylvia, allume la lumière s'il te
plaît.**
Sylvia, turn on the light please.

lunatique adj
temperamental

le **lundi** nm
1 Monday

Aujourd'hui, nous sommes lundi.
It's Monday today.

le lundi de Pâques
Easter Monday
2 on Monday

Nous partons lundi.
We're leaving on Monday.

Le lundi, je vais à la piscine.
I go swimming on Mondays.

---

tous les lundis
every Monday
le lundi
on Mondays
lundi dernier
last Monday
lundi prochain
next Monday
À lundi!
See you on Monday!

---

la **lune** nf
moon

les **lunettes** nfpl
glasses

Je porte des lunettes.
I wear glasses.

des lunettes de soleil
sunglasses

des lunettes de plongée
swimming goggles

la **lutte** nf
wrestling

le **luxe** nm
luxury

de luxe
luxury

un hôtel de luxe
a luxury hotel

luxueux m adj
(f adj luxueuse)
luxurious

le **lycée** nm
secondary school

In France pupils go to a
collège between the ages of
11 and 15, and then to a
lycée until the age of 18.

un lycée technique
a technical college

le **lycéen** nm
la **lycéenne** nf
secondary school pupil

A
B
C
D
E
F
G
H
I
J
K
L
M
N
O
P
Q
R
S
T
U
V
W
X
Y
Z

M

M. abbr
Mr

M. Bernard
Mr Bernard

m' pron
me

> *m' is what the French word **me**
> changes to before a vowel sound.*

**Dominique m'invite chez elle ce
week-end.**
Dominique has invited me to her
house this weekend.

Il m'attend depuis une heure.
He's been waiting for me for an
hour.

> *m' is often not translated.*

**Je m'habille à sept heures tous les
matins.**
I get dressed at seven every morning.

ma f adj
my

ma mère
my mother

les **macaronis** nmpl
macaroni

le **machin** nm
thingy

**Passe-moi le machin pour râper
les carottes.**
Pass me the thingy for grating
carrots.

la **machine** nf
machine

une machine à sous
a fruit machine

une machine à laver
a washing machine

le **maçon** nm
bricklayer

Madame nf
(*pl* Mesdames)
1 Mrs

Madame Legall
Mrs Legall
2 Madam

Madame, ...
Dear Madam, ...

> ***Madame** is a handy way of
> attracting someone's attention.*

**Madame! Vous avez oublié votre
parapluie!**
Excuse me! You've forgotten your
umbrella!

Mademoiselle nf
(*pl* Mesdemoiselles)
Miss

Mademoiselle Martin
Miss Martin

Mademoiselle is a handy way of attracting someone's attention.

Mademoiselle! L'addition, s'il vous plaît!
Excuse me, could I have the bill?

le **magasin** nm
shop

Les magasins ouvrent à huit heures.
The shops open at 8 o'clock.

J'aime faire les magasins.
I like going shopping.

le **magazine** nm
magazine

le **magicien** nm
la **magicienne** nf
magician

la **magie** nf
magic

un tour de magie
a magic trick

magique adj
magic

une baguette magique
a magic wand

le **magnétophone** nm
tape recorder

le **magnétoscope** nm
video recorder

magnifique adj
superb

mai nm
May

en mai
in May

le trente mai
the thirtieth of May

le premier mai
the first of May

Le Premier Mai (May 1st) is a holiday in France. People give friends little bunches of lily of the valley (**muguet**) for good luck.

maigre adj
skinny

le **maillot de bain** nm
1 swimsuit

J'adore le maillot de bain de Jacqueline.
I love Jacqueline's swimsuit.

2 swimming trunks

Paul a un nouveau maillot de bain.
Paul has new swimming trunks.

la **main** nf
hand

Donne-moi la main!
Give me your hand!

se serrer la main
to shake hands

Les garçons se serrent la main en arrivant à l'école le matin.
The boys shake hands when they get to school in the morning.

maintenant adv
now

le **maire** nm
mayor

la **mairie** nf
town hall

mais conj
but

J'aime bien les maths mais c'est difficile.
I like maths, but it's difficult.

le **maïs** nm
1 sweetcorn

J'adore le maïs.
I love sweetcorn.

2 maize

la **maison** nf
house

Ils habitent dans une grande maison.
They live in a big house.

Je vais rester à la maison pendant les vacances.
I'm going to stay at home for the holidays.

rentrer à la maison
to go home

Rentrons à la maison.
Let's go home.

Viens à la maison si tu veux.
Come to the house if you want.

le **maître** nm
la **maîtresse** nf
1 teacher

Cette année, j'ai un maître au lieu d'une maîtresse.
This year I have a male teacher instead of a female one.

Maîtresse!
Miss!

2 master

Ce chien suit son maître partout.
This dog follows his master everywhere.

un maître nageur
a lifeguard

Majorque nf
Majorca

majuscule

> **majuscule** can be an adjective or a noun.

A adj
capital

un M majuscule
a capital M

B nf
capital letter

Les jours de la semaine ne prennent pas de majuscule en français.
In French the days of the week don't start with a capital letter.

mal

> **mal** can be a noun, an adjective or an adverb.

A nm
(pl les maux)
ache

J'ai mal aux dents.
I've got toothache.

J'ai mal au dos.
My back hurts.

Ça fait mal.
It hurts.

Où est-ce que tu as mal?
Where does it hurt?

> **J'ai mal à la tête.**
> I've got a headache.

B m, f, pl adj
pas mal
not bad

> **Ça va? – Oui, pas mal.**
> How are you? – Not bad.

C adv
badly
C'est mal fait.
It's badly done.

malade adj
ill

la **maladie** nf
illness

mâle adj
male

malheureusement adv
unfortunately

malin m adj
(f adj maligne)
cunning

la **maman** nf
mum

la **mamie** nf
granny

la **manche** nf
sleeve

un T-shirt à manches longues
a long-sleeved T-shirt

la Manche
the Channel

la **mandarine** nf
mandarin

le **manège** nm
merry-go-round

manger vb
to eat

Pour le petit déjeuner, je mange des céréales.
I have cereal for breakfast.

la **mangue** nf
mango

la **manifestation** nf
demonstration

le **mannequin** nm
model

manquer vb
to miss

Il manque des pages à ce livre.
There are some pages missing from this book.

Mes parents me manquent.
I miss my parents.

Ma sœur me manque.
I miss my sister.

le **manteau** nm
(*pl* les manteaux)
coat

manuel m adj
(*f adj* manuelle)
les travaux manuels
arts and crafts

le **maquereau** nm
(*pl* les maquereaux)
mackerel

la **maquette** nf
model

le **maquillage** nm
make-up

se **maquiller** vb
to put on one's make-up
J'adore me maquiller.
I love to put on make-up.

le **marchand** nm
la **marchande** nf
1 shopkeeper
un marchand de journaux
a newsagent
un marchand de fruits et légumes
a greengrocer
2 stallholder

la **marche** nf
step

Fais attention à la marche!
Mind the step!

le **marché** nm
market

marcher vb
1 to walk
Marchez deux par deux.
Walk in twos.
2 to work
L'ascenseur ne marche pas.
The lift isn't working.
Ça marche?
How are you getting on?

le **mardi** nm
1 Tuesday
Aujourd'hui, nous sommes mardi.
Today is Tuesday.
Mardi gras
Shrove Tuesday
2 on Tuesday
Ils reviennent mardi.
They're coming back on Tuesday.
Le mardi, je vais à la gym.
I go to the gym on Tuesdays.

tous les mardis
every Tuesday
le mardi
on Tuesdays
mardi dernier
last Tuesday
mardi prochain
next Tuesday
À mardi!
See you on Tuesday!

la **marelle** nf
hopscotch

la **margarine** nf
margarine

la **marge** nf
margin

Laissez une marge à droite de la page.
Leave a margin on the right-hand side of the page.

le **mari** nm
husband

son mari
her husband

le **mariage** nm
wedding

Samedi, je vais à un mariage.
I'm going to a wedding on Saturday.

marié m adj
(f adj marié)
married

Ma sœur est mariée.
My sister is married.

le **marié** nm
bridegroom

les mariés
the bride and groom

la **mariée** nf
bride

se **marier** vb
to get married

Mon frère se marie ce week-end.
My brother is getting married this weekend.

marin nm
sailor

marine m, f, pl adj
bleu marine
navy-blue

des chaussettes bleu marine
navy-blue socks

la **marionnette** nf
puppet

la **marmelade** nf
la marmelade d'oranges
marmalade

le **Maroc** nm
Morocco

marocain m adj
(f adj marocaine)
Moroccan

le **Marocain** nm
la **Marocaine** nf
Moroccan

la **marque** nf
1 mark

des marques de doigts
fingermarks

2 make

De quelle marque est ton jean?
What make are your jeans?

3 brand

une marque de lessive
a brand of washing powder

À vos marques! prêts! partez!
Ready, steady, go!

marquer vb

1 to mark

Tu peux marquer où se trouve ton village sur la carte?
Can you mark where your village is on the map?

2 to score

L'équipe irlandaise a marqué dix points.
The Irish team scored ten points.

la marraine nf
godmother

marrant m adj
(*f adj* marrante)
funny

marron

marron can be an adjective or a noun.

Ⓐ m, f, pl adj
brown

J'ai les yeux marron.
I have brown eyes.

Ⓑ nm

1 chestnut

la crème de marrons
chestnut purée

2 brown

Je n'aime pas le marron.
I don't like the colour brown.

Mars n
Mars

la planète Mars
Mars

mars nm
March

en mars
in March

le dix-huit mars
the eighteenth of March

le marteau nm
(*pl* les marteaux)
hammer

le martien nm
la martienne nf
Martian

masculin m adj
(*f adj* masculine)
masculine

le masque nm
mask

masser vb
to massage

le match nm
match

un match de football
a football match

Match nul!
It's a draw!

le matelas nm
mattress

un matelas pneumatique
an air bed

maternel m adj
(*f adj* maternelle)

ma grand-mère maternelle
my mother's mother

l'école maternelle
nursery school

la **maternelle** nf
nursery school

The **maternelle** is a state
school for 2 to 6 year-olds.

les **mathématiques** nfpl
mathematics

les **maths** nfpl
maths

J'adore les maths.
I love maths.

le **matin** nm
morning

à trois heures du matin
at 3 o'clock in the morning

ce matin
this morning

la **matinée** nf

toute la matinée
all morning

mauvais

mauvais can be an adjective or an
adverb.

A m adj
(*f adj* mauvaise)

1 bad

une mauvaise note
a bad mark

Je suis mauvais en maths.
I'm bad at maths.

Il fait mauvais.
The weather's bad.

2 wrong

Vous avez fait le mauvais numéro.
You've dialled the wrong number.

B adv

sentir mauvais
to smell

Ça sent mauvais ici!
It smells in here!

la **mayonnaise** nf
mayonnaise

me pron

1 me

Elle me téléphone tous les jours.
She phones me every day.

me changes to **m'** before a vowel
sound.

Tu peux m'aider?
Can you help me?

2 to me

Il me parle en allemand.
He talks to me in German.

me is often not translated.

**Je me lève à sept heures tous les
matins.**
I get up at 7 every morning.

le **mécanicien** nm
mechanic

méchant m adj
(*f adj* méchante)
nasty

Elle est méchante avec moi.
She's nasty to me.

la **médaille** nf
medal

la médaille de bronze
the bronze medal

le **médecin** nm
doctor

aller chez le médecin
to go to the doctor's

Ce soir, je vais chez le médecin.
I'm going to the doctor's this
evening.

le **médicament** nm
medicine

Tu as pris tes médicaments?
Have you taken your medicine?

la **Méditerranée** nf
Mediterranean

méditerranéen m adj
(f adj méditerranéenne)
Mediterranean

la **méduse** nf
jellyfish

meilleur adj
(f adj meilleure)
better

**C'est meilleur avec du fromage
râpé.**
It's better with grated cheese.

**Le livre est meilleur que le
film.**
The book is better than the
film.

le **meilleur** nm
la **meilleure** nf
the best

C'est la meilleure en sport.
She's the best at sport.

le **mélange** nm
mixture

mélanger vb
to mix

Mélangez le tout.
Mix everything together.

la **mélodie** nf
melody

le **melon** nm
melon

le **membre** nm
member

la **mémé** nf
granny

même

> **même** can be an adjective or an
> adverb.

A adj
same

J'ai la même robe.
I've got the same dress.

en même temps
at the same time

**Paul et moi, on arrive toujours en
même temps à l'école.**
Paul and I always get to school at
the same time.

B adv
even

**Je sais faire l'équilibre, et je sais
même faire la roue.**
I can do a handstand, and I can
even do a cartwheel.

le/la **même** nm/f
same one

Tiens, c'est curieux j'ai le même!
That's funny, I've got the same one!

la **mémoire** nf
memory

menacer vb
to threaten

le **ménage** nm
housework

faire le ménage
to do the housework

C'est mon père qui fait le ménage à la maison.
My father is the one who does the housework.

une femme de ménage
a cleaning lady

le **mensonge** nm
lie

Il ne faut pas dire de mensonges.
You shouldn't tell lies.

le **menteur** nm
la **menteuse** nf
liar

C'est une menteuse.
She's a liar.

la **menthe** nf
mint

des bonbons à la menthe
mints

mentir vb
to lie

Tu mens!
You're lying!

le **menton** nm
chin

le **menu** nm
menu

le menu du jour
today's menu

le **menuisier** nm
joiner

la **mer** nf
sea

la mer du Nord
the North Sea

au bord de la mer
at the seaside

merci excl
thank you

> 🔑
> **merci beaucoup**
> thank you very much

le **mercredi** nm
1 Wednesday

Aujourd'hui, nous sommes le mercredi vingt-deux février.
Today's Wednesday the twenty-second of February.
2 on Wednesday

Nous partons mercredi.
We're leaving on Wednesday.

Le musée est fermé le mercredi.
The museum is shut on Wednesdays.

> 🔑
> **tous les mercredis**
> every Wednesday
> **le mercredi**
> on Wednesdays
> **mercredi dernier**
> last Wednesday
> **mercredi prochain**
> next Wednesday
> **À mercredi!**
> See you on Wednesday!

A
B
C
D
E
F
G
H
I
J
K
L
M
N
O
P
Q
R
S
T
U
V
W
X
Y
Z

la **mère** nf
mother

Ma mère s'appelle Laura.
My mother is called Laura.

la **merguez** nf
spicy sausage

mériter vb
to deserve

le **merlan** nm
whiting

le **merle** nm
blackbird

merveilleux m adj
(*f adj* merveilleuse)
marvellous

mes pl adj
my

mes parents
my parents

Mesdames nfpl
ladies

Bonjour, Mesdames.
Good morning, ladies.

Mesdemoiselles nfpl
ladies

Bonjour, Mesdemoiselles.
Good morning, ladies.

le **message** nm
message

la **messe** nf
mass

la messe de minuit
midnight mass

Messieurs nmpl
gentlemen

Bonjour, Messieurs.
Good morning, gentlemen.

mesurer vb
to measure

Mesurez la longueur et la largeur.
Measure the length and the width.

Il mesure un mètre quatre-vingts.
He's six foot tall.

> In France people use metres and centimetres to say how tall someone is, not feet and inches.

met vb, *see* **mettre**
Il met la table.
He is laying the table.

le **métal** nm
(*pl* les métaux)
metal

la **météo** nf
weather forecast

Qu'est-ce que dit la météo pour cet après-midi?
What's the weather forecast for this afternoon?

le **métier** nm
job

Quel métier est-ce que tu aimerais faire plus tard?
What job would you like to do when you're older?

le **mètre** nm
metre

La piscine fait vingt-cinq mètres de long.
The pool is 25 metres long.

un mètre ruban
a tape measure

le **métro** nm
underground

prendre le métro
to take the underground

Je prends toujours le métro pour aller en ville.
I always take the underground into town.

mets vb, *see* **mettre**
Je ne mets jamais de jupe.
I never wear a skirt.

mettre vb
1 to put

Mets les jouets dans le placard s'il te plaît.
Put the toys in the cupboard please.

2 to put on

Je mets mon manteau et j'arrive.
I'll put on my coat and then I'll be ready.

3 to wear

Qu'est-ce que tu vas mettre pour la boum?
What are you going to wear to the party?

mettre la table
to set the table

Tu peux mettre la table?
Could you set the table?

les **meubles** nmpl
furniture

le **Mexique** nm
Mexico

miauler vb
to mew

Mon chat miaule quand il a faim.
My cat mews when he's hungry.

le **micro** nm
microphone

le **micro-ondes** nm
microwave oven

le **midi** nm
1 midday

On déjeune à midi.
We have lunch at midday.

Il est midi et demi.
It's half past twelve.

> 🔑
> **Il est midi.**
> It's midday.

2 lunchtime

Je rentre à la maison le midi.
I go home at lunchtime.

le Midi
the South of France

le **miel** nm
honey

le **mien** m pron
la **mienne** f pron
mine

Ce vélo-là, c'est le mien.
That bike's mine.

Ces baskets-là, ce sont les miennes.
Those trainers are mine.

mieux

> mieux can be an adverb, an
> adjective or a noun.

Ⓐ adv
<u>better</u>

Elle va mieux.
She's better.

Je la connais mieux que son frère.
I know her better than her brother.

Ⓑ m, f, pl adj

Il est mieux avec la moustache.
He looks better with a moustache.

Ⓒ nm
<u>best</u>

C'est la région que je connais le mieux.
It's the region I know best.

mignon m adj
(*f adj* mignonne)
<u>sweet</u>

Qu'est-ce qu'il est mignon!
Isn't he sweet!

le milieu nm
(*pl* les milieux)
<u>middle</u>

au milieu de
in the middle of

Mets le vase au milieu de la table.
Put the vase in the middle of the table.

mille num
<u>a thousand</u>

mille euros
a thousand euros

deux mille personnes
two thousand people

le millénaire nm
<u>millennium</u>

le milliard nm
<u>thousand million</u>

milliardaire nm, adj
<u>multimillionaire</u>

le millier nm
<u>thousand</u>

des milliers de personnes
thousands of people

le million nm
<u>million</u>

deux millions de personnes
two million people

millionnaire nm, adj
<u>millionaire</u>

mimer vb
<u>to mimic</u>

mince adj
<u>slim</u>

Il est grand et mince.
He's tall and slim.

Mince!
Sugar!

minéral m adj
(*f adj* minérale)
<u>mineral</u>

l'eau minérale
mineral water

mineur m adj
(*f adj* mineure)
<u>under 18</u>

Elle est mineure.
She's under 18.

les mineurs
the under-18s

le minidisque nm
Minidisc®

la **minijupe** nf
miniskirt

le **minimum** nm
minimum

au minimum
at the very least

le **ministre** nm
minister

le Premier ministre
the Prime Minister

le **Minitel**® nm

> Minitel is a mini-computer
> that is plugged into your
> phone. You can use it
> instead of a phone directory,
> as well as to book train
> tickets, etc.

la **minorité** nf
minority

Minorque nf
Minorca

minuit nm
midnight

L'avion arrive à minuit.
The plane lands at midnight.

Il est minuit et demi.
It's half past twelve.

>
> **Il est minuit.**
> It's midnight.

minuscule

> minuscule can be an adjective or
> a noun.

A adj
1 tiny

un poisson minuscule
a tiny fish

2 small

un m minuscule
a small m

B nf
small letter

**Ça s'écrit avec une minuscule, pas
une majuscule.**
You spell it with a small letter, not a
capital.

la **minute** nf
minute

le **miracle** nm
miracle

le **miroir** nm
mirror

mis vb, *see* **mettre**

Tu as mis le lait au frigo?
Have you put the milk in the fridge?

la **mi-temps** nf
half-time

La mi-temps dure quinze minutes.
Half-time lasts fifteen minutes.

à mi-temps
part-time

Elle travaille à mi-temps.
She works part-time.

Mlle abbr
(*pl* Mlles)
Miss

Mlle Renoir
Miss Renoir

Mme abbr

(*pl* Mmes)

Mrs

Mme Leroy
Mrs Leroy

la **mobylette** ® nf
moped

moche adj
horrible

Cette couleur est vraiment moche.
That colour's really horrible.

la **mode** nf
fashion

à la mode
fashionable

J'aime être à la mode.
I like to be fashionable.

Ce jean n'est pas vraiment à la mode.
These jeans aren't really fashionable.

le **modèle** nm
model

C'est le nouveau modèle.
It's the new model.

Suivez le modèle.
Follow the example.

moderne adj
modern

moi pron
me

Coucou, c'est moi!
Hello, it's me!

à moi

à moi can either mean mine or my turn.

Ce livre n'est pas à moi.
This book isn't mine.

un ami à moi
a friend of mine

C'est à moi.
It's my turn.

moi-même pron
myself

Je l'ai fait moi-même.
I did it myself.

moins

moins can be an adverb, a preposition or a noun.

Ⓐ adv

1 less

Deux cents euros? – Non, beaucoup moins.
Two hundred euros? – No, much less.

Moins de bruit, s'il vous plaît.
Less noise please.

When moins de is followed by a number it means "less than".

Ça coûte moins de deux cents euros.
It costs less than two hundred euros.

de moins is used when talking about how many years younger someone is.

Il a trois ans de moins que moi.
He's three years younger than me.

2 fewer

Il y a moins de gens aujourd'hui.
There are fewer people today.

le moins
the least

le moins changes to la moins before a feminine adjective, and les moins before a plural adjective.

C'est le modèle le moins cher.
It's the least expensive model.

C'est la plage la moins polluée.
It's the least polluted beach.

La musique, c'est la matière que j'aime le moins.
Music is my least favourite subject.

B prep

1 minus

quatre moins trois
4 minus 3

Il fait moins cinq dehors.
It's minus five outside.

2 to

Il est onze heures moins cinq.
It's five to eleven.

Il est onze heures moins le quart.
It's quarter to eleven.

C nm

au moins
at least

Il reste au moins dix bonbons dans le paquet.
There are at least ten sweets left in the packet.

le **mois** nm
month

au mois de juillet
in July

la **moitié** nf
half

une moitié de pomme
half an apple

molle f adj
soft

La margarine est plus molle que le beurre.
The margarine is softer than the butter.

le **moment** nm

1 moment

Attendez un moment.
Wait a moment.

en ce moment
at the moment

Nous avons beaucoup de travail en ce moment.
We have a lot of work to do at the moment.

2 time

C'est le moment de partir.
It's time to go.

mon m adj
(f adj ma)
my

mon frère
my brother

mon ami
my friend

ma tante
my aunt

mes parents
my parents

le **monde** nm
world

Je voudrais faire le tour du monde.
I'd like to go round the world.

Il y a du monde.
There are a lot of people.

beaucoup de monde
a lot of people

Il y a beaucoup de monde sur la plage.
There are a lot of people on the beach.

mondial m adj
(f adj mondiale)
world

un nouveau record mondial
a new world record

le **moniteur** nm

1 instructor

un moniteur de voile
a sailing instructor

2 monitor

le moniteur de mon ordinateur
my computer monitor

la **monitrice** nf
instructor

une **monitrice de ski**
a ski instructor

la **monnaie** nf
change

Voici la monnaie.
Here's the change.

une **pièce de monnaie**
a coin

le **monsieur** nm
man

Il y a un monsieur qui veut te voir.
There's a man wanting to see you.

Monsieur nm
(*pl* Messieurs)
1 Mr

Monsieur Dupont
Mr Dupont
2 Sir

Monsieur, …
Dear Sir, …

> *Monsieur is a handy way of attracting someone's attention.*

Monsieur! Vous avez laissé tomber votre billet!
Excuse me! You've dropped your ticket!

le **monstre** nm
monster

la **montagne** nf
mountain

les **montagnes russes**
the roller coaster

montagneux m adj
(*f adj* montagneuse)
mountainous

une **région montagneuse**
a mountainous area

monter vb
to go up

Montez au deuxième étage.
Go up to the second floor.

la **montre** nf
watch

montrer vb
to show

Montre la carte.
Show the card.

le **monument** nm
les **monuments de Paris**
the sights of Paris

la **moquette** nf
fitted carpet

le **morceau** nm
(*pl* les morceaux)
piece

un **morceau de pain**
a piece of bread

mordre vb
to bite

Je me suis fait mordre par un chien.
I was bitten by a dog.

mort m adj
(*f adj* morte)
dead

la **mosquée** nf
mosque

le **mot** nm
1 word

C'est un mot de six lettres.
It's a six-letter word.

des mots croisés
a crossword

le mot de passe
the password
2 note

J'écris un mot à Pierrot.
I'm writing a note to Pierrot.

la **moto** nf
motorbike

mou m adj
(f adj molle)
soft

Mon matelas est trop mou.
My mattress is too soft.

la **mouche** nf
fly

le **mouchoir** nm
handkerchief

un mouchoir en papier
a tissue

la **mouette** nf
seagull

mouillé m adj
(f adj mouillée)
wet

le **moule** nm
tin

un moule à gâteaux
a cake tin

les **moules** nfpl
mussels

le **moulin** nm
mill

un moulin à vent
a windmill

mourir vb
to die

Elle est morte.
She's dead.

la **mousse** nf

une mousse au chocolat
a chocolate mousse

la **moustache** nf
moustache

les moustaches
whiskers

le **moustique** nm
mosquito

la **moutarde** nf
mustard

le **mouton** nm
1 sheep
2 mutton

un gigot de mouton
a leg of mutton

moyen m adj
(f adj moyenne)
1 average

Je suis plutôt moyen en maths.
I'm just average at maths.
2 medium

Elle est de taille moyenne.
She's of medium height.

le moyen âge
the Middle Ages

la moyenne nf
average

la moyenne d'âge
the average age

J'espère avoir la moyenne en maths.
I hope to get a pass mark in maths.

le Moyen-Orient nm
Middle East

le muguet nm
lily of the valley

People give friends little bunches of lily of the valley on May 1st, which is a holiday in France. **Le muguet** is lucky – like white heather.

municipal m adj
(*f adj* municipale)
la bibliothèque municipale
the public library

le mur nm
wall

mûr m adj
(*f adj* mûre)
1 ripe
Ces pêches ne sont pas mûres.
These peaches aren't ripe.
2 mature
Elle est très mûre pour son âge.
She's very mature for her age.

les **mûres** nfpl
blackberries

murmurer vb
to whisper
Pense à un mot et murmure le mot à ton voisin.
You think of a word and whisper the word to the person next to you.

musclé m adj
(*f adj* musclée)
muscular

le musée nm
museum
J'adore faire les musées.
I love going round museums.

le musicien nm
la musicienne nf
musician

la musique nf
music
J'aime écouter de la musique.
I like listening to music.

musulman nm, m adj
musulmane nf, f adj
Muslim

myope adj
short-sighted

le mystère nm
mystery

mystérieux m adj
(*f adj* mystérieuse)
mysterious

N

n' adv

> **n'** is what **ne** changes to before a vowel sound.

Je n'ai pas d'argent.
I haven't got any money.

nager vb
to swim

Tu sais nager?
Can you swim?

le **nageur** nm
la **nageuse** nf
swimmer

C'est une très bonne nageuse.
She's a very good swimmer.

la **naissance** nf
birth

Quelle est ta date de naissance?
What's your date of birth?

naître vb
to be born

Il est né en 1994.
He was born in 1994.

Elle est née le 5 octobre.
She was born on 5 October.

la **natation** nf
swimming

Je fais de la natation tous les mercredis.
I go swimming every Wednesday.

national m adj
(f adj nationale)
national

Aujourd'hui, c'est le 14 juillet: c'est la fête nationale.
Today is 14 July, the national holiday.

la **nationalité** nf
nationality

Tu es de quelle nationalité?
What nationality are you?

nature

> **nature** can be a noun or an adjective.

Ⓐ nf
nature
Ⓑ adj
plain

un yaourt nature
a plain yoghurt

naturel m adj
(f adj naturelle)
natural

naturellement adv
of course

Naturellement, il est encore en retard.
He's late again, of course.

nautique adj
water

a

b

c

d

e

f

g

h

i

j

k

l

m

n

o

p

q

r

s

t

u

v

w

x

y

z

les sports nautiques
water sports

le ski nautique
water-skiing

le **navet** nm
turnip

Je n'aime pas les navets.
I don't like turnips.

la **navette** nf
shuttle

une navette spatiale
a space shuttle

ne adv

> *ne goes with **pas, personne, plus**
> and **jamais** in negatives.*

Je ne peux pas venir.
I can't come.

Ils ne vont jamais à la piscine.
They never go to the swimming pool.

Je ne connais personne ici.
I don't know anyone here.

Elle ne fait plus d'équitation.
She doesn't go riding any more.

> *ne changes to **n'** before a vowel
> sound.*

Je n'aime pas les maths.
I don't like maths.

né vb, *see* **naître**
born

Il est né en 1995.
He was born in 1995.

née vb, *see* **naître**
born

Elle est née en 1990.
She was born in 1990.

nécessaire adj
necessary

néerlandais m adj
(*f adj* néerlandaise)
Dutch

la **neige** nf
snow

une boule de neige
a snowball

un bonhomme de neige
a snowman

neiger vb
to snow

> **Il neige.**
> It's snowing.

le **Néo-Zélandais** nm
la **Néo-Zélandaise** nf
New Zealander

néo-zélandais m adj
(*f adj* néo-zélandaise)
New Zealand

Elle est néo-zélandaise.
She's from New Zealand.

nerveux m adj
(*f adj* nerveuse)
nervous

n'est-ce pas adv

> *n'est-ce pas is used to check that
> something is true.*

**Nous sommes le douze
aujourd'hui, n'est-ce pas?**
It's the 12th today, isn't it?

Elle a un chien, n'est-ce pas?
She's got a dog, hasn't she?

le Net nm
the Net

nettoyer vb
to clean

Nettoie la table, s'il te plaît.
Clean the table please.

neuf

> **neuf** can be a number or an adjective.

Ⓐ num
nine

Il est neuf heures.
It's nine o'clock.

Claire a neuf ans.
Claire's nine.

> 🔑
> **le neuf février**
> the ninth of February

Ⓑ m adj
(*f adj* neuve)
new

des chaussures neuves
new shoes

neuvième adj
ninth

au neuvième étage
on the ninth floor

le neveu nm
(*pl* les neveux)
nephew

mon neveu
my nephew

le nez nm
nose

ni conj
ni ... ni ...
neither ... nor ...

Je n'aime ni Marie ni Luc.
I like neither Marie nor Luc.

la nièce nf
niece

ma nièce
my niece

le Noël nm
Christmas

Qu'est-ce que tu as eu pour Noël?
What did you get for Christmas?

le père Noël
Father Christmas

les cadeaux de Noël
Christmas presents

> 🔑
> **Joyeux Noël!**
> Merry Christmas!

le nœud nm
knot

Fais un nœud à la corde.
Tie a knot in the rope.

un nœud papillon
a bow tie

> *The French actually means "butterfly knot"!*

noir

> **noir** can be an adjective or a noun.

Ⓐ m adj
(*f adj* noire)
1 black

une robe noire
a black dress

Elle est noire.
She's black.

2 dark

Il fait noir dehors.
It's dark outside.

B nm
1 black

J'aime le noir.
I like the colour black.

2 dark

J'ai peur du noir.
I'm afraid of the dark.

le **Noir** nm
black man

les Noirs
black people

la **Noire** nf
black woman

la **noisette** nf
hazelnut

la **noix** nf
(*pl* les noix)
walnut

une noix de coco
a coconut

les noix de cajou
cashew nuts

le **nom** nm
1 name

Écrivez votre nom en haut de la feuille.
Write your name at the top of the sheet.

mon nom de famille
my surname

2 noun

"la banane" est un nom féminin.
"la banane" is a feminine noun.

le **nombre** nm
number

un nombre pair
an even number

un nombre impair
an odd number

nombreux m adj
(*f adj* nombreuse)

Nous sommes trop nombreux.
There are too many of us.

Nous sommes peu nombreux.
There aren't many of us.

une famille nombreuse
a large family

le **nombril** nm
navel

non adv
no

Tu connais Jean-Pierre? – Non.
Do you know Jean-Pierre? – No.

Je n'aime pas les hamburgers. – Moi non plus.
I don't like burgers. – Neither do I.

nord

nord can be a noun or an adjective.

A nm
north

Ils vivent dans le nord de l'île.
They live in the north of the island.

au nord de Paris
north of Paris

l'**Afrique du Nord**
North Africa

B m, f, pl adj
le **pôle Nord**
the North Pole

le **nord-est** nm
north-east

J'habite au nord-est de Paris.
I live in north-east Paris.

le **nord-ouest** nm
north-west

J'habite au nord-ouest de Paris.
I live in north-west Paris.

normal m adj
(f adj normale)
normal

une journée normale
a normal day

> 🔑
> **C'est normal.**
> It's only natural.
> **Ce n'est pas normal!**
> That's not right!

normalement adv
normally

Normalement, il mange à midi.
He normally eats at midday.

normand m adj
(f adj normande)
from Normandy

Ma grand-mère est normande.
My grandmother is from Normandy.

la **Normandie** nf
Normandy

la **Norvège** nf
Norway

le **Norvégien** nm
la **Norvégienne** nf
Norwegian

norvégien m adj, nm
(f adj norvégienne)
Norwegian

nos pl adj
our

Où sont nos affaires?
Where are our things?

le **notaire** nm
solicitor

la **note** nf
1 mark

Vincent a de bonnes notes en maths.
Vincent gets good marks in maths.

2 bill

La note, s'il vous plaît!
The bill please!

3 note

Écoutez et prenez des notes.
Listen and take notes.

notre adj
(pl adj nos)
our

Voici notre maison.
This is our house.

le/la **nôtre** m/f pron
ours

À qui est ce chien? – C'est le nôtre.
Whose dog is it? – It's ours.

Leur voiture est rouge, la nôtre est bleue.
Their car is red, ours is blue.

Ces places-là sont les nôtres.
Those seats are ours.

les **nouilles** nfpl
noodles

le **nounours** nm
teddy

la **nourriture** nf
food

nous pron
1 we

Nous avons deux chiens.
We have two dogs.
2 us

Viens avec nous.
Come with us.

nous-mêmes
ourselves

nouveau m adj
(*f adj* nouvelle)
new

Je voudrais un nouveau vélo.
I'd like a new bike.

Nous avons une nouvelle voiture.
We've got a new car.

> *nouveau changes to **nouvel** before a vowel sound.*

Il y a un nouvel élève dans ma classe.
There's a new boy in my class.

le nouvel an
New Year

le **nouveau** nm
la **nouvelle** nf
new person

Il y a des nouveaux dans la classe.
There are new people in the class.

nouvel, nouvelle adj, *see* **nouveau**
new

la **nouvelle** nf
1 news

C'est une bonne nouvelle.
That's good news.

les nouvelles
the news

J'écoute les nouvelles à la radio.
I listen to the news on the radio.
2 short story

un livre de nouvelles
a book of short stories

la **Nouvelle-Zélande** nf
New Zealand

novembre nm
November

en novembre
in November

le vingt-deux novembre
the twenty-second of November

nu m adj
(*f adj* nue)
naked

tout nu
stark naked

le **nuage** nm
cloud

un gros nuage noir
a big black cloud

Il y a des nuages.
It's cloudy.

nuageux m adj
(*f adj* nuageuse)
cloudy

Il fait un temps nuageux.
It's cloudy.

la **nuit** nf
night

La nuit est belle.
It's a beautiful night.

la nuit
at night

Tout est calme la nuit.
Everything is quiet at night.

cette nuit
tonight

Il va rentrer cette nuit.
He'll be back tonight.

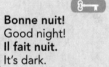

Bonne nuit!
Good night!
Il fait nuit.
It's dark.

nul m adj
(*f adj* nulle)
rubbish

Ce film est nul.
This film's rubbish.

Je suis nul en maths.
I'm rubbish at maths.

un match nul
a draw

Ils ont fait match nul.
It was a draw.

nulle part
nowhere

Je ne le vois nulle part.
I can't see it anywhere.

numérique adj
digital

le **numéro** nm
number

J'habite au numéro trois.
I live at number 3.

mon numéro de téléphone
my phone number

A
B
C
D
E
F
G
H
I
J
K
L
M
N
O
P
Q
R
S
T
U
V
W
X
Y
Z

O

l'**objet** nm
object

les objets dans la classe
classroom objects

obligé m adj
(*f adj* obligée)

Je suis obligé de rester.
I have to stay.

observer vb
to watch

J'aime bien observer les fourmis à la loupe.
I like watching ants with my magnifying glass.

l'**occasion** nf

d'occasion
second-hand

une voiture d'occasion
a second-hand car

occupé m adj
(*f adj* occupée)

1 busy

Il est très occupé.
He's very busy.

2 taken

Est-ce que cette place est occupée?
Is this seat taken?

3 engaged

Les toilettes sont occupées.
The toilet's engaged.

s'**occuper** vb

s'occuper de
to be in charge of

Elle s'occupe d'un club de sport.
She's in charge of a sports club.

l'**océan** nm
ocean

octobre nm
October

en octobre
in October

le quinze octobre
the fifteenth of October

l'**odeur** nf
smell

Il y a une drôle d'odeur ici.
There's a funny smell round here.

l'**œil** nm
(*pl* les yeux)
eye

J'ai les yeux marron.
I've got brown eyes.

Est-ce que j'ai quelque chose dans l'œil?
Have I got something in my eye?

l'**œuf** nm
egg

un œuf à la coque
a soft-boiled egg

un œuf dur
a hard-boiled egg

un œuf au plat
a fried egg

les œufs brouillés
scrambled eggs

un œuf de Pâques
an Easter egg

> In France, Easter eggs are said to be brought by the Easter bells (**cloches de Pâques**) which fly from Rome and drop them in people's gardens.

offert vb, *see* **offrir**
Elle m'a offert un CD pour mon anniversaire.
She gave me a CD for my birthday.

l'office nm
l'office du tourisme
the tourist office

offrir vb
to give
Je vais offrir des fleurs à ma mère.
I'm going to give my mum some flowers.
Elle m'a offert un appareil photo.
She gave me a camera.

l'oie nf
goose

l'oignon nm
onion

l'oiseau nm
(*pl* les oiseaux)
bird

l'olive nf
olive
l'huile d'olive
olive oil

olympique adj
les Jeux olympiques
the Olympic Games

l'omelette nf
omelette

on pron
1 we
On va à la plage demain.
We're going to the beach tomorrow.
2 someone
On m'a volé mon porte-monnaie.
Someone has stolen my purse.
3 you
On peut visiter le parc en été.
You can visit the park in the summer.

l'oncle nm
uncle
mon oncle
my uncle

l'ongle nm
nail

ont vb, *see* **avoir**
Ils ont beaucoup d'argent.
They have got lots of money.

> *Sometimes **ont** shows that something has happened in the past.*

Ils ont passé de bonnes vacances.
They had a good holiday.

onze num
eleven

A B C D E F G H I J K L M N O P Q R S T U V W X Y Z

Elle a onze ans.
She's eleven.

Il est onze heures.
It's eleven o'clock.

🔑

le onze février
the eleventh of February

onzième adj
eleventh

au onzième étage
on the eleventh floor

opérer vb

se faire opérer
to have an operation

Je dois me faire opérer.
I need to have an operation.

Elle s'est fait opérer de l'appendicite.
She's had her appendix out.

l'opticien nm
l'opticienne nf
optician

l'or nm
gold

en or
gold

un bracelet en or
a gold bracelet

l'orage nm
thunderstorm

orageux m adj
(*f adj* orageuse)
stormy

Le temps est orageux.
It's stormy.

orange

orange can be a noun or an adjective.

A nf
orange

J'adore les oranges.
I love oranges.

B nm
orange

Vous avez ce T-shirt en orange?
Do you have this tee-shirt in orange?

C m, f, pl adj
orange

des rideaux orange
orange curtains

l'orchestre nm
1 orchestra

un orchestre symphonique
a symphony orchestra
2 band

un orchestre de jazz
a jazz band

l'ordinateur nm
computer

l'ordre nm
order

par ordre alphabétique
in alphabetical order

dans l'ordre
in order

Remettez les images dans l'ordre.
Put the pictures in order.

l'**oreille** nf
ear

J'ai mal à l'oreille.
I've got earache.

l'**oreiller** nm
pillow

organiser vb
Nous organisons une tombola.
We're organizing a raffle.

l'**orgue** nm
organ

l'**orphelin** nm
l'**orpheline** nf
orphan

l'**orteil** nm
toe

l'**orthographe** nf
spelling

Je suis bon en orthographe.
I'm good at spelling.

l'**os** nm
bone

oser vb
Je n'ose pas demander.
I daren't ask.

ou conj
or

Tu veux une limonade ou un coca?
Would you like a lemonade or a coke?

où

> **où** can be an adverb or a pronoun.

A adv
where

Où est Nick?
Where's Nick?

Où vas-tu?
Where are you going?

Je sais où il est.
I know where he is.

B pron
that

Le jour où il est parti, tout le monde a pleuré.
The day that he left, everyone cried.

oublier vb
1 to forget

N'oublie pas de fermer la porte.
Don't forget to shut the door.

2 to leave

J'ai oublié mon sac chez Sabine.
I left my bag at Sabine's.

ouest

> **ouest** can be a noun or an adjective.

A nm
west

Elle vit dans l'ouest de l'Angleterre.
She lives in the West of England.

à l'ouest de Paris
west of Paris

l'Europe de l'Ouest
Western Europe

A B C D E F G H I J K L M N O P Q R S T U V W X Y Z

a
b
c
d
e
f
g
h
i
j
k
l
m
n
o
p
q
r
s
t
u
v
w
x
y
z

Ⓑ m, f, pl adj
west

la côte ouest de l'Écosse
the west coast of Scotland

ouf excl
thank heavens for that!

Ouf! J'ai retrouvé mes lunettes!
Thank heavens for that! I've found
my glasses!

oui adv
yes

Tu aimes les fraises? – Oui.
Do you like strawberries? – Yes.

l'**ours** nm
bear

un ours en peluche
a teddy bear

les **outils** nmpl
tools

une boîte à outils
a tool box

ouvert m adj
(*f adj* ouverte)
open

Le magasin est ouvert.
The shop's open.

l'**ouverture** nf

les heures d'ouverture
opening hours

l'**ouvrier** nm
l'**ouvrière** nf
worker

ouvrir vb
to open

Ouvre la porte s'il te plaît.
Open the door please.

Je peux ouvrir la fenêtre?
Can I open the window?

l'**ovni** nm
UFO

P

Pacifique adj, nm
Pacific

paf excl
wham!

la **pagaille** nf
mess

Quelle pagaille!
What a mess!

la **page** nf
page

Tournez la page.
Turn the page.

la **paille** nf
straw

le **pain** nm
bread

un morceau de pain
a piece of bread

le pain complet
wholemeal bread

le pain d'épice
gingerbread

le pain grillé
toast

pair m adj
(f adj paire)
even

un nombre pair
an even number

une jeune fille au pair
an au pair

la **paire** nf
pair

une paire de chaussures
a pair of shoes

la **paix** nf
peace

J'espère qu'ils vont faire la paix.
I hope they're going to make up.

le **palais** nm
palace

pâle adj
pale

bleu pâle
pale blue

le **palmier** nm
palm tree

le **pamplemousse** nm
grapefruit

pané m adj
(f adj panée)
fried in breadcrumbs

du poisson pané
fish fried in breadcrumbs

le **panier** nm
basket

A B C D E F G H I J K L M N O P Q R S T U V W X Y Z

a b c d e f g h i j k l m n o **p** q r s t u v w x y z

la **panique** nf
panic

Pas de panique!
Don't panic!

la **panne** nf

en panne
out of order

L'ascenseur est en panne.
The lift's not working.

tomber en panne
to break down

une panne de courant
a power cut

le **panneau** nm
(*pl* les panneaux)
sign

le **pansement** nm
1 dressing
2 sticking plaster

J'ai mis un pansement sur ma coupure.
I put a plaster on the cut.

le **pantalon** nm
trousers

Son pantalon est trop court.
His trousers are too short.

la **panthère** nf
panther

les **pantoufles** nfpl
slippers

le **paon** nm
peacock

le **papa** nm
dad

la **papeterie** nf
stationer's

On peut acheter un cahier à la papeterie.
You can buy an exercise book at the stationer's.

le **papi** nm
granddad

le **papier** nm
paper

une feuille de papier
a sheet of paper

le papier cadeau
wrapping paper

le papier hygiénique
toilet paper

le papier peint
wallpaper

le **papillon** nm
butterfly

Pâques nfpl
Easter

les vacances de Pâques
Easter holidays

un œuf de Pâques
an Easter egg

In France, Easter eggs are said to be brought by the Easter bells (**cloches de Pâques**) which fly from Rome and drop them in people's gardens.

Joyeuses Pâques!
Happy Easter!

le **paquet** nm
1 packet
2 parcel

Il y a un paquet pour toi.
There's a parcel for you.

par prep
1 by

Il s'est fait disputer par sa mère.
He was told off by his mum.

Rangez-vous deux par deux.
Get into twos.

2 with

Son nom commence par un H.
His name begins with H.

3 out of

Regardez par la fenêtre.
Look out of the window.

4 per

Le voyage coûte trois cents euros par personne.
The trip costs three hundred euros per person.

5 via

Nous passons par Paris.
We're going via Paris.

6 through

Il faut passer par la salle à manger pour aller dans la cuisine.
You have to go through the dining room to get to the kitchen.

par ici

> *par ici can either mean* **this way** *or* **near here**.

Venez par ici.
Come this way.

Il y a une boulangerie par ici?
Is there a baker's near here?

paraître vb
1 to seem

Ça paraît incroyable.
It seems incredible.

2 to look

Elle paraît plus jeune que son mari.
She looks younger than her husband.

le **parapluie** nm
umbrella

le **parc** nm
park

un parc d'attractions
an amusement park

parce que conj
because

Paul pleure parce qu'il a mal à la jambe.
Paul is crying because his leg is hurting.

pardon excl
1 sorry!

Pardon.
I'm sorry.

2 excuse me!

Pardon, madame! Je cherche la poste.
Excuse me, I'm looking for the post office.

3 pardon

Pardon? Vous pouvez répéter?
Pardon? Could you say that again?

pardonner vb
to forgive

Je te pardonne.
I forgive you.

pareil m adj
(f adj **pareille**)
the same

Ces images ne sont pas pareilles.
These pictures aren't the same.

les **parents** nmpl
parents

mes parents
my parents

paresseux m adj
(f adj paresseuse)
lazy

parfait m adj
(f adj parfaite)
perfect

parfaitement adv
perfectly

Il parle parfaitement l'arabe.
He speaks perfect Arabic.

parfois adv
sometimes

le **parfum** nm
1 perfume
2 flavour

Paris n
Paris

J'habite à Paris.
I live in Paris.

Je vais à Paris.
I'm going to Paris.

parisien m adj
(f adj parisienne)
from Paris

Elle est parisienne.
She's from Paris.

les **Parisiens** nmpl
people from Paris

le **parking** nm
car park

Be careful! The French word **parking** *does not mean the same as the English word* **parking**.

parler vb
1 to speak

Vous parlez français?
Do you speak French?

Je parle français.
I speak French.

2 to talk

Arrêtez de parler!
Stop talking!

parmi prep
among

les **paroles** nfpl
lyrics

J'aime les paroles de cette chanson.
I like the lyrics of this song.

le **parquet** nm
wooden floor

le **parrain** nm
godfather

parrainer vb
to sponsor

Tu veux me parrainer?
Will you sponsor me?

pars, part vb, *see* **partir**

Je pars demain.
I'm going tomorrow.

Le train part à quelle heure?
What time does the train leave?

la **part** nf
piece

une part de gâteau
a piece of cake

à part
except

Tout le monde va au pique-nique, à part Sandra.
Everyone except Sandra is going to the picnic.

partager vb

1 to share

Ils partagent un appartement.
They share a flat.

2 to divide

Partage le gâteau en quatre.
Divide the cake into four.

le/la partenaire nm/f
partner

la partie nf

1 game

une partie de cartes
a game of cards

2 part

une partie de la classe
part of the class

Je fais partie d'une chorale.
I belong to a choir.

partir vb

1 to go

Je dois partir.
I've got to go.

Il part travailler à sept heures.
He goes to work at seven o'clock.

partir en vacances
to go on holiday

Nous partons en vacances lundi prochain.
We're going on holiday next Monday.

2 to go away

Je pars demain et je rentre lundi.
I'm going away tomorrow and coming back on Monday.

> *partir* is related to the English word "to depart".

à partir de maintenant
from now on

partout adv
everywhere

pas

> **pas** can be an adverb or a noun.

Ⓐ adv

ne … pas
not

Il ne pleut pas.
It's not raining.

Ils n'ont pas de voiture.
They haven't got a car.

pas du tout
not at all

Je n'aime pas du tout ça.
I don't like that at all.

pas toi
not you

pas mal
not bad

> 🔑
> **Ça va? – Oui, pas mal.**
> How are you? – Not bad.

Ⓑ nm
step

Faites trois pas en avant.
Take three steps forward.

un pas en arrière
a step backwards

le passager nm
la passagère nf
passenger

le passé nm
past

le passeport nm
passport

passer vb
1 to go

Passez devant l'école et tournez à gauche.
Go past the school and turn left.

Nous passons par Paris pour aller à Tours.
We go through Paris on our way to Tours.

2 to have

Je passe de bonnes vacances.
I'm having a nice holiday.

Vous avez passé de bonnes vacances?
Did you have a nice holiday?

3 to spend

Ils passent toujours leurs vacances au Danemark.
They always spend their holidays in Denmark.

4 to pass

Passe-moi le sel, s'il te plaît.
Pass me the salt please.

5 to take

Gordon passe ses examens la semaine prochaine.
Gordon is taking his exams next week.

Be careful! **passer un examen** *does not mean* **to pass an exam.**

se passer

se passer can either mean to take place, to go or to happen.

Cette histoire se passe à New York.
This story takes place in New York.

Tout se passe bien.
Everything's going well.

Qu'est-ce qu'il s'est passé?
What happened?

Qu'est-ce qu'il se passe?
What's the matter?

le passe-temps nm
hobby

Quel est ton passe-temps préféré?
What's your favourite hobby?

passionnant m adj
(*f adj* passionnante)
gripping

la pastèque nf
watermelon

la pastille nf
cough sweet

la pâte nf
1 pastry
2 dough
3 cake mixture

la pâte à crêpes
pancake batter

la pâte à modeler
Plasticine®

la pâte d'amandes
marzipan

le pâté nm
pâté

les pâtes nfpl
pasta

J'adore les pâtes.
I love pasta.

le **patin** nm
le patin à glace
ice skating
Je fais du patin à glace tous les samedis.
I go ice skating every Saturday.
les patins à glace
ice skates
le patin à roulettes
roller skating
Je fais du patin à roulettes avec mes copains.
I go roller skating with my friends.
les patins à roulettes
roller skates

le **patinage** nm
le patinage artistique
figure skating

la **patinoire** nf
ice rink

la **pâtisserie** nf
cake shop

le **pâtissier** nm
la **pâtissière** nf
aller chez le pâtissier
to go to the cake shop

la **patte** nf
1 paw
la patte du chien
the dog's paw

2 leg
Cet oiseau a une patte cassée.
This bird has a broken leg.

pauvre adj
poor
Sa famille est pauvre.
His family is poor.

Pauvre Jean-Pierre!
Poor Jean-Pierre!

payant m adj
(f adj payante)
C'est payant.
You have to pay.

payer vb
to pay

le **pays** nm
country

le **paysage** nm
landscape

les **Pays-Bas** nmpl
Netherlands

le **pays de Galles** nm
Wales
J'habite au pays de Galles.
I live in Wales.

Cet été, je vais au pays de Galles.
I'm going to Wales this summer.

la **pêche** nf
1 peach
2 fishing
aller à la pêche
to go fishing

Il va à la pêche tous les dimanches.
He goes fishing every Sunday.

le **pêcheur** nm
fisherman

A
B
C
D
E
F
G
H
I
J
K
L
M
N
O
P
Q
R
S
T
U
V
W
X
Y
Z

a

b

c

d

e

f

g

h

i

j

k

l

m

n

o

p

q

r

s

t

u

v

w

x

y

z

le **peigne** nm
comb

peigner vb
to comb

Elle peigne sa poupée.
She's combing her doll's hair.

♦ **se peigner**
to comb one's hair

Je vais me peigner.
I'm going to comb my hair.

peindre vb
to paint

la **peine** nf

Ce n'est pas la peine.
Don't bother.

**Ce n'est pas la peine de
téléphoner.**
There's no point phoning.

le **peintre** nm
painter

la **peinture** nf
paint

la **pelle** nf
1 shovel
2 spade

la **pellicule** nf
film

une pellicule couleur
a colour film

la **pelouse** nf
lawn

la **peluche** nf
soft toy

un ours en peluche
a teddy bear

pendant prep
in

**Pendant les vacances, je fais de
l'équitation.**
I go riding in the holidays.

pendant que
while

**Ma petite sœur joue pendant que
je fais mes devoirs.**
My little sister plays while I do my
homework.

le **pendu** nm
hangman

On va jouer au pendu.
We're going to play hangman.

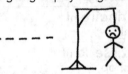

la **pendule** nf
clock

penser vb
to think

Je pense que Yann a raison.
I think Yann is right.

Je pense à mes vacances.
I'm thinking about my holidays.

la **pension** nf
boarding school

Elle est en pension.
She is at boarding school.

la **Pentecôte** nf
Whitsun

le dimanche de Pentecôte
Whit Sunday

le lundi de Pentecôte
Whit Monday

Whit Sunday is seven weeks after Easter, and the following Monday, Whit Monday, is a holiday in France.

---

le **perdant** nm
la **perdante** nf
loser

Il est mauvais perdant.
He's a bad loser.

perdre vb
to lose

Tu vas perdre!
You're going to lose!

perdu vb, *see* **perdre**

J'ai perdu ma trousse.
I've lost my pencil case.

le **père** nm
father

mon père
my father

le père Noël
Father Christmas

le **perroquet** nm
parrot

la **perruche** nf
budgie

le **persil** nm
parsley

le **personnage** nm
character

---

le personnage principal du film
the main character in the film

la **personnalité** nf
personality

personne

personne can be a noun or a pronoun.

A nf
person

la même personne
the same person

deux personnes
two people

une grande personne
an adult

une table pour quatre personnes
a table for four

B pron
1 nobody

Qui est là? – Personne.
Who's there? – Nobody.

Personne ne la connaît.
Nobody knows her.

2 anybody

Elle ne veut voir personne.
She doesn't want to see anybody.

peser vb
to weigh

Elle pèse cent kilos.
She weighs 100 kilos.

la **pétanque** nf

pétanque is a kind of bowls played on rough ground.

---

le **pétard** nm
banger

There is one kind of **pétard** that French children throw at the pavement to make a bang.

petit m adj
(*f adj* petite)

1 small

Je suis petite.
I'm small.

2 little

Phyllis a une jolie petite maison.
Phyllis has got a nice little house.

le petit déjeuner
breakfast

Je prends mon petit déjeuner à sept heures.
I have my breakfast at seven o'clock.

des petits pois
garden peas
un petit copain
a boyfriend
une petite copine
a girlfriend

la petite-fille nf
granddaughter

le petit-fils nm
grandson

les petits-enfants mpl
grandchildren

peu adv

un peu
a bit
Elle est un peu timide.
She's a bit shy.

un peu de gâteau
a bit of cake

à peu près
about

Le voyage prend à peu près deux heures.
The journey takes about two hours.

la peur nf

Tu as peur?
Are you scared?

J'ai peur!
I'm scared!

peut vb, *see* pouvoir

Il ne peut pas venir.
He can't come.

peut-être adv
perhaps

Tu viens? – Peut-être.
Are you coming? Perhaps.

Je vais peut-être aller en Corse.
I may go to Corsica.

peuvent, peux vb, *see* pouvoir

Ils ne peuvent pas venir.
They can't come.

Je ne peux pas le faire.
I can't do it.

le phare nm
lighthouse

la pharmacie nf
chemist's

Chemists in France have a big green cross outside the shop.

le **pharmacien** nm
la **pharmacienne** nf
pharmacist

aller chez le pharmacien
to go to the chemist

le **phoque** nm
seal

la **photo** nf
photograph

Tu peux m'envoyer ta photo?
Could you send me your photo?

Je veux prendre une photo.
I want to take a photo.

Je vais te prendre en photo.
I'm going to take a photo of you.

la **photocopie** nf
photocopy

photocopier vb
to photocopy

la **photocopieuse** nf
photocopier

le/la **photographe** nm/f
photographer

On va chez le photographe.
We're going to the photographer's.

la **phrase** nf
sentence

Complétez la phrase.
Complete the sentence.

physique

physique can be an adjective or a noun.

A adj
physical

l'éducation physique
physical education

B nf
physics

Il est professeur de physique.
He's a physics teacher.

le/la **pianiste** nm/f
pianist

le **piano** nm
piano

Je joue du piano.
I play the piano.

la **pièce** nf

1 room

Il y a six pièces dans ma maison.
There are six rooms in my house.

2 coin

une pièce de cinquante centimes
a fifty centime coin

une pièce de théâtre
a play
un maillot une-pièce
a one-piece swimsuit
un maillot deux-pièces
a bikini

le **pied** nm
foot

J'ai mal aux pieds.
My feet are hurting.

à pied
on foot

Je vais à l'école à pied.
I walk to school.

A B C D E F G H I J K L M N O **P** Q R S T U V W X Y Z

la pierre nf
stone

le piéton nm
la piétonne nf
pedestrian

la pieuvre nf
octopus

le pigeon nm
pigeon

pile

> pile can be a noun or an adverb.

Ⓐ nf
battery

Il faut changer les piles de mon magnétophone.
I need to change the batteries in my tape recorder.

Ⓑ adv
on the dot

à deux heures pile
at two o'clock on the dot

> 🔑
> **Pile ou face?**
> Heads or tails?

le pilote nm
pilot

un pilote de ligne
an airline pilot

un pilote de course
a racing driver

le piment nm
chilli

le pinceau nm
(pl les pinceaux)
paintbrush

le pingouin nm
penguin

le ping-pong nm
table tennis

Tu veux jouer au ping-pong?
Do you want to play table tennis?

piquant m adj
(f adj piquante)
❶ prickly

un buisson piquant
a prickly bush
❷ spicy

une sauce très piquante
a very spicy sauce

le pique nm
spades

l'as de pique
the ace of spades

le pique-nique nm
picnic

pique-niquer vb
to picnic

piquer vb
❶ to bite

J'ai été piqué par un moustique.
I have been bitten by a mosquito.
❷ to burn

Cette sauce me pique la langue.
This sauce is burning my tongue.

la piqûre nf
❶ injection

Je n'aime pas les piqûres.
I don't like injections.
❷ bite

une piqûre de moustique
a mosquito bite

3 sting

une piqûre d'abeille
a bee sting

le **pirate** nm
pirate

pire

> **pire** can be an adjective or a
> noun.

A adj
worse

C'est encore pire qu'avant.
It's even worse than before.

B nm/f
the worst

**Ce garçon est le pire de la
bande.**
That boy is the worst in the group.

la **piscine** nf
swimming pool

Tu veux aller à la piscine?
Do you want to go to the swimming
pool?

Je vais à la piscine le samedi.
I go to the swimming pool on
Saturdays.

la **pistache** nf
pistachio

une glace à la pistache
a pistachio ice cream

> Pistachio ice cream is green.

la **piste** nf

la piste de danse
the dance floor

une piste cyclable
a cycle lane

le **pistolet** nm
pistol

le **placard** nm
cupboard

la **place** nf

1 place

Vincent a eu la troisième place.
Vincent is in third place.

2 square

la place du village
the village square

3 room

Ça prend de la place.
It takes up a lot of room.

4 seat

Il reste une place.
There's one seat left.

sur place
on the spot

Courez sur place.
Run on the spot.

à la place
instead

**Je n'ai pas de bonbons; tu veux
une pomme à la place?**
I haven't got any sweets, do you
want an apple instead?

le **plafond** nm
ceiling

la **plage** nf
beach

A
B
C
D
E
F
G
H
I
J
K
L
M
N
O
P
Q
R
S
T
U
V
W
X
Y
Z

a

se **plaindre** vb

Arrête de te plaindre!
Stop complaining!

Elle se plaint tout le temps.
She's always complaining.

plaire vb

Mon cadeau me plaît beaucoup.
I like my present a lot.

Elle lui plaît.
He fancies her.

Entrez, s'il vous plaît!
Come in, please!

plaisanter vb
to joke

Je plaisante!
I'm joking!

la **plaisanterie** nf
joke

le **plaisir** nm

Ça te fait plaisir?
Are you happy?

Cette photo va faire très plaisir à ma mère.
My mum will love this photo.

plaît vb, see **plaire**

Ça te plaît?
Do you like it?

Ferme la porte, s'il te plaît.
Close the door please.

> **s'il te plaît**
> please
> **s'il vous plaît**
> please

le **plan** nm

1 map

un plan de la ville
a street map

2 plan

Voici le plan de ma maison.
This is a plan of my house.

la **planche** nf
board

une planche à repasser
an ironing board

une planche à roulettes
a skateboard

une planche à voile
a windsurfer

le **plancher** nm
floor

la **planète** nf
planet

la **plante** nf
plant

planter vb
to plant

la **plaque** nf

une plaque de chocolat
a slab of chocolate

une plaque d'immatriculation
a number plate

la **plaquette** nf

une plaquette de chocolat
a bar of chocolate

une plaquette de beurre
a pack of butter

le **plastique** nm
plastic

un sac en plastique
a carrier bag

plat

> **plat** can be a noun or an adjective.

Ⓐ nm

1 dish

un plat en verre
a glass dish

le plat du jour
the dish of the day

2 course

le plat principal
the main course

le plat de résistance
the main course

Ⓑ m adj

(*f adj* plate)

flat

La Hollande est un pays plat.
Holland is a flat country.

le **plateau** nm

(*pl* les plateaux)

tray

un plateau d'argent
a silver tray

le plateau de fromages
the cheeseboard

la **platine** nf

une platine laser
a CD player

le **plâtre** nm

plaster

J'ai le bras dans le plâtre.
I've got my arm in plaster.

plein m adj

(*f adj* pleine)

full

Ton verre est encore plein.
Your glass is still full.

à plein temps
full-time

Elle travaille à plein temps.
She works full-time.

en plein jour
in broad daylight

en pleine nuit
in the middle of the night

en plein air
in the open air

plein de
lots of

un gâteau avec plein de crème
a cake with lots of cream

pleurer vb

to cry

Pourquoi tu pleures?
Why are you crying?

pleut vb, *see* **pleuvoir**

Il ne pleut plus.
It's not raining any more.

pleuvoir vb

to rain

> **Il pleut.**
> It's raining.

plier vb

to fold

Pliez la feuille en deux.
Fold the paper in two.

le **plombier** nm

plumber

la **plongée** nf

diving

a

plonger vb
to dive

Tu sais plonger?
Can you dive?

plouf excl
splash!

plu vb, *see* **plaire, pleuvoir**

La photo lui a plu.
She loved the photo.

Il a plu toute la journée.
It rained all day.

la **pluie** nf
rain

sous la pluie
in the rain

la **plume** nf
feather

un stylo à plume
a fountain pen

plupart pron
la plupart
most of them

**Il y a quinze filles dans ma classe
et la plupart sont sympas.**
There are fifteen girls in my class
and most of them are nice.

la plupart des
most

**La plupart des gens ont peur des
serpents.**
Most people are afraid of snakes.

la plupart du temps
most of the time

le **pluriel** nm
plural

au pluriel
in the plural

plus

> **plus** can be an adverb or a
> conjunction.

A adv
more

C'est plus difficile.
It's more difficult.

Il fait plus chaud aujourd'hui.
It's warmer today.

ne ... plus
not ... any more

Je ne veux plus le voir.
I don't want to see him any more.

Je n'en ai plus.
I haven't any left.

Je n'ai plus d'argent.
I've got no money left.

plus ... que
more ... than

Elle est plus gaie que sa sœur.
She's more cheerful than her sister.

Elle est plus grande que moi.
She's bigger than me.

C'est le plus grand de la classe.
He's the tallest in the class.

plus de

> **plus de** *can either mean* **more** *or*
> **more than**.

Il nous faut plus de pain.
We need more bread.

Le voyage dure plus de six heures.
The journey takes more than six
hours.

en plus
as well

**Il est bête, et en plus il est
méchant.**
He's stupid and nasty as well.

de plus en plus
more and more

Il y a de plus en plus de touristes par ici.
There are more and more tourists round here.

Il fait de plus en plus chaud.
It's getting hotter and hotter.

B conj
plus

Quatre plus deux égalent six.
4 plus 2 is 6.

plusieurs pron
several

plusieurs personnes
several people

plutôt adv
1 quite

Elle est plutôt jolie.
She's quite pretty.

2 rather

L'eau est plutôt froide.
The water's rather cold.

3 instead

Demande-lui plutôt de rester.
Ask her to stay instead.

plutôt que
instead of

Invite Marie plutôt que Nathalie.
Invite Marie instead of Nathalie.

la poche nf
pocket

l'argent de poche
pocket money

un livre de poche
a paperback

la poêle nf
frying pan

le poème nm
poem

le poids nm
weight

le poids lourd nm
lorry

le poignet nm
wrist

le poil nm
1 hair

Il y a des poils de chat partout sur la moquette.
There are cat hairs all over the carpet.

2 fur

Ton chien a un beau poil.
Your dog's got lovely fur.

le poing nm
fist

un coup de poing
a punch

le point nm
full stop

un point d'exclamation
an exclamation mark

un point d'interrogation
a question mark

la pointe nf
sur la pointe des pieds
on tiptoe

la pointure nf
size

Quelle est ta pointure?
What size shoes do you take?

la **poire** nf
pear

le **poireau** nm
(*pl* les poireaux)
leek

les **pois** nmpl

les **petits pois**
peas

les **pois chiches**
chickpeas

à **pois**
spotted

une **robe à pois**
a spotted dress

le **poison** nm
poison

le **poisson** nm
fish

Je n'aime pas le poisson.
I don't like fish.

un poisson rouge
a goldfish

Poisson d'avril!
April fool!

> Pinning a paper fish to
> somebody's back is a
> traditional April fool joke in
> France.

la **poissonnerie** nf
fish shop

le **poissonnier** nm
fishmonger

le **poivre** nm
pepper

le **poivron** nm
pepper

un poivron rouge
a red pepper

le **pôle** nm
pole

le pôle Nord
the North Pole

le pôle Sud
the South Pole

poli m adj
(*f adj* polie)
polite

la **police** nf
police

policier

> **policier** can be a noun or an
> adjective.

A nm
policeman

B m adj
(*f adj* policière)

un roman policier
a detective novel

pollué m adj
(*f adj* polluée)
polluted

la **pollution** nf
pollution

le **polo** nm
polo shirt

la **Pologne** nf
Poland

polonais m adj, nm
(f adj polonaise)
Polish

le **Polonais** nm
la **Polonaise** nf
Pole

la **Polynésie** nf
Polynesia

la **pomme** nf
apple

les pommes de terre
potatoes

les pommes frites
chips

les pommes vapeur
boiled potatoes

le **pompier** nm
fireman

le **poney** nm
pony

le **pont** nm
bridge

populaire adj
popular

le **porc** nm
1 pig

Ils élèvent des porcs.
They breed pigs.

2 pork

du rôti de porc
roast pork

le **port** nm
harbour

le **portable** nm
mobile phone

le **portail** nm
gate

la **porte** nf
door

Ferme la porte, s'il te plaît.
Close the door, please.

le **porte-clés** nm
key ring

le **portefeuille** nm
wallet

le **portemanteau** nm
(pl les portemanteaux)
1 coat hanger
2 coat rack

le **porte-monnaie** nm
purse

porter vb
1 to carry

Tu peux me porter? – Non, tu es trop lourde!
Can you carry me? – No, you're too heavy!

A
B
C
D
E
F
G
H
I
J
K
L
M
N
O
P
Q
R
S
T
U
V
W
X
Y
Z

2 to wear

Elle porte une jolie robe bleue.
She's wearing a lovely blue dress.

portugais m adj, nm
(f adj portugaise)
Portuguese

le **Portugais** nm
la **Portugaise** nf
Portuguese

le **Portugal** nm
Portugal

poser vb
1 to put down

Posez vos crayons.
Put your pencils down.

2 to ask

Je peux te poser une question?
Can I ask you a question?

possible adj
possible

Ça n'est pas possible.
It's not possible.

le plus vite possible
as quickly as possible

la **poste** nf
post office

poster

> **poster** can be a noun or a verb.

A nm
poster

un poster de Madonna
a poster of Madonna

> When **poster** is a noun, the
> ending sounds like "air".

B vb
to post

Je vais poster ce colis.
I'm going to post this parcel.

le **pot** nm
pot

un pot de confiture
a pot of jam

un pot de yaourt
a yogurt

le **potage** nm
soup

le **potager** nm
vegetable garden

le **pot-au-feu** nm
beef stew

la **poterie** nf
pottery

la **poubelle** nf
bin

Mets ton chewing-gum à la poubelle.
Put your chewing gum in the bin.

le **pouce** nm
thumb

la **poule** nf
hen

le **poulet** nm
chicken

J'adore le poulet.
I love chicken.

la **poupée** nf
doll

pour prep
for

C'est un cadeau pour toi.
It's a present for you.

Qu'est-ce que tu veux pour ton petit déjeuner?
What would you like for breakfast?

Pour aller à la gare, s'il vous plaît?
Which way is it to the station, please?

pourquoi adv
why

Pourquoi tu pleures?
Why are you crying?

Pourquoi pas?
Why not?

pourra, pourrai, pourras, pourrez, pourrons, pourront vb, *see* **pouvoir**

Quand est-ce qu'il pourra venir?
When can he come?

Je ne pourrai pas venir.
I won't be able to come.

Tu pourras me téléphoner ce soir?
Can you ring me tonight?

Vous pourrez arrêter à cinq heures.
You can stop at 5 o'clock.

Nous pourrons faire du vélo.
We can go for bike rides.

Ils ne pourront pas faire de natation.
They won't be able to go swimming.

pousser vb
1 to push

Arrêtez de pousser.
Stop pushing.

Pousse-toi, je ne vois rien.
Move over, I can't see a thing.

2 to grow

Mes cheveux poussent vite.
My hair grows quickly.

la **poussette** nf
pushchair

le **poussin** nm
chick

pouvoir vb
can

Je peux lui téléphoner si tu veux.
I can phone her if you want.

Il ne peut pas venir.
He can't come.

pratique adj
handy

Ce sac est très pratique.
This bag's very handy.

précieux m adj
(*f adj* précieuse)
precious

préféré m adj
(*f adj* préférée)
favourite

Quel est ton sport préféré?
What's your favourite sport?

préférer vb
to prefer

Je préfère manger à la cantine.
I prefer to eat in the canteen.

Tu préfères le riz ou les pâtes?
Would you prefer rice or pasta?

préhistorique adj
prehistoric

premier

premier can be an adjective or a noun.

A m adj
(*f adj* première)
first

au premier étage
on the first floor

C'est la première fois que je viens ici.
This is the first time I've been here.

le premier avril
the first of April
le premier mai
the first of May

B nm
first

Tu veux être le premier?
Do you want to be first?

la première nf
1 first

Elle est arrivée la première.
She came first.
2 lower sixth form

Ma sœur est en première.
My sister's in the lower sixth.

In French secondary schools the years are counted from the **sixième** (youngest) to **première** and **terminale** (oldest).

prendre vb
1 to take

Prends le plus gros!
Take the biggest!

2 to get

Nous prenons le train de huit heures.
We're getting the eight o'clock train.
3 to have

Je prends mon petit déjeuner à huit heures.
I have breakfast at eight.

le prénom nm
first name

Quel est ton prénom?
What's your first name?

préparer vb
to prepare

Elle prépare le dîner.
She's preparing dinner.

près adv
près de
near

C'est près d'ici?
Is it near here?

tout près
nearby

J'habite tout près.
I live nearby.

présent

> **présent** can be an adjective or a noun.

Ⓐ m adj
(*f adj* présente)
present

Je vais faire l'appel; les garçons, répondez "présent", et les filles, répondez "présente".
I'm going to call the register. Boys, say "présent", and girls, say "présente".

Ⓑ nm
present

à présent
now

présenter vb
to present

Il va présenter le spectacle.
He's going to present the show.

Marc, je te présente Anaïs.
Marc, this is Anaïs.

presque adv
nearly

Il est presque six heures.
It's nearly 6 o'clock.

pressé m adj
(*f adj* pressée)
in a hurry

Je ne peux pas rester, je suis pressé.
I can't stay, I'm in a hurry.

une orange pressée
a glass of freshly squeezed orange juice

se presser vb
to hurry up

Allez, presse-toi, on va être en retard!
Come on, hurry up, we're going to be late!

prêt m adj
(*f adj* prête)
ready

Vous êtes prêts?
Are you ready?

prêter vb
to lend

Tu peux me prêter ta gomme?
Could you lend me your rubber?

prévenir vb

Je te préviens, il est de mauvaise humeur.
I'm warning you, he's in a bad mood.

la prière nf
prayer

primaire adj
l'école primaire
primary school

le prince nm
prince

la princesse nf
princess

principal

> **principal** can be an adjective or a noun.

Ⓐ m adj
(*f adj* principale)
main

le personnage principal
the main character

Ⓑ nm
❶ headmaster

> **le principal** is the headmaster of a **collège** – a secondary school for pupils aged 11 to 15.

2 main thing

Personne n'a été blessé; c'est le principal.
Nobody was injured; that's the main thing.

le **printemps** nm
spring

au printemps
in spring

pris vb, *see* **prendre**

Il a pris le plus gros!
He took the biggest!

la **prison** nf
prison

prisonnier m adj
(*f adj* prisonnière)
captive

le **prix** nm
1 price

Je n'arrive pas à lire le prix de ce livre.
I can't see the price of this book.

2 prize

Cécile a eu le prix de la meilleure actrice.
Cécile got the prize for best actress.

le **problème** nm
problem

prochain m adj
(*f adj* prochaine)
next

la prochaine fois
next time

À la semaine prochaine!
See you next week!

le **produit** nm
product

le/la **prof** nm/f
teacher

Elle est prof de maths.
She's a maths teacher.

> **prof** is a secondary school teacher.

le **professeur** nm
teacher

Christine est professeur d'histoire.
Christine's a history teacher.

la **profession** nf
profession

professionnel m adj
(*f adj* professionnelle)
professional

profond m adj
(*f adj* profonde)
deep

le **programmeur** nm
la **programmeuse** nf
programmer

le **progrès** nm
progress

Tu fais des progrès!
You're making progress!

progresser vb
to progress

le **projet** nm
plan

des projets de vacances
holiday plans

a b c d e f g h i j k l m n o p q r s t u v w x y z

la **promenade** nf

1 walk

Il y a de belles promenades par ici.
There are some nice walks round here.

Tu veux faire une promenade?
Do you want to go for a walk?

2 ride

Il va faire une promenade à vélo.
He's going to go for a bike ride.

Je voudrais faire une promenade en voiture.
I'd like to go for a drive.

promener vb
to take for a walk

Cordelia promène son chien tous les jours.
Cordelia takes her dog for a walk every day.

◆ **se promener**
to go for a walk

Chantal veut se promener.
Chantal wants to go for a walk.

la **promesse** nf
promise

Il m'a fait une promesse.
He made me a promise.

promettre vb
to promise

Je te promets de venir.
I promise I'll come.

Je viendrai, c'est promis.
I'll come, it's a promise.

prononcer vb
to pronounce

Le russe est difficile à prononcer.
Russian is difficult to pronounce.

la **prononciation** nf
pronunciation

propre adj
clean

Ce verre n'est pas propre.
This glass isn't clean.

le **prospectus** nm
leaflet

protéger vb
to protect

protestant m adj
(*f adj* protestante)
Protestant

le **proverbe** nm
proverb

la **province** nf
province

Ils habitent en province.
They don't live in Paris.

le **proviseur** nm
headteacher

le proviseur is the headteacher of a **lycée** – a secondary school for pupils aged 15 to 18.

prudent m adj
(*f adj* prudente)
1 careful

Sois prudent!
Be careful!

2 wise

Laisse ton passeport à la maison, c'est plus prudent.
It would be wiser to leave your passport at home.

la **prune** nf
plum

> An English "prune" is a dried plum, but a French **prune** is a fresh one.

le **pruneau** nm
(*pl* les pruneaux)
prune

le/la **psychiatre** nm/f
psychiatrist

le/la **psychologue** nm/f
psychologist

pu vb, *see* **pouvoir**

Je n'ai pas pu venir.
I couldn't come.

la **pub** nf
1 advertising

Il y a trop de pub à la télé.
There's too much advertising on TV.

2 advert

J'aime regarder les pubs à la télé.
I like watching the adverts on the telly.

> **la pub**, short for **la publicité**, is slangy.

public m adj
(*f adj* publique)
public

un jardin public
a public park

une école publique
a state school

la **publicité** nf
1 advertising

Muriel travaille dans la publicité.
Muriel works in advertising.

2 advert

Il y a trop de publicités dans ce journal.
There are too many adverts in this newspaper.

publique f adj, *see* **public**

puer vb
to stink

Ça pue le tabac ici!
It stinks of tobacco in here!

puis adv
then

Faites dorer le poulet, puis ajoutez le vin blanc.
Fry the chicken till golden, then add white wine.

puisque conj
since

Puisque c'est si cher, nous irons manger ailleurs.
Since it's so expensive, we'll eat somewhere else.

puissant m adj
(*f adj* puissante)
powerful

le **puits** nm
well

le **pull** nm
jumper

le **pull-over** nm
jumper

la **punaise** nf
drawing pin

punir vb
être puni
to be grounded
Il est puni.
He's grounded.

la **punition** nf
punishment

la **purée** nf
mashed potatoes

le **puzzle** nm
jigsaw puzzle

le **pyjama** nm
pyjamas

la **pyramide** nf
pyramid

les **Pyrénées** nfpl
Pyrenees
dans les Pyrénées
in the Pyrenees

A
B
C
D
E
F
G
H
I
J
K
L
M
N
O
P
Q
R
S
T
U
V
W
X
Y
Z

Q

quand conj
when

Quand est-ce que tu pars en vacances?
When are you going on holiday?

la **quarantaine** nf
about forty

une quarantaine de personnes
about forty people

Elle a la quarantaine.
She's in her forties.

quarante num
forty

Elle a quarante ans.
She's forty.

quarante et un
forty-one

quarante-deux
forty-two

le **quart** nm
quarter

un quart d'heure
a quarter of an hour

Il est deux heures et quart.
It's a quarter past two.
Il est dix heures moins le quart.
It's a quarter to ten.

le **quartier** nm
area

un quartier tranquille
a quiet area

quatorze num
fourteen

Il a quatorze ans.
He's fourteen.

à quatorze heures
at 2 p.m.

le quatorze février
the fourteenth of February

> The 24-hour clock is used in France for travel times, appointments and other formal situations.

quatre num
four

Il est quatre heures.
It's four o'clock.

Il a quatre ans.
He's four.

le quatre février
the fourth of February

quatre-vingts num
eighty

quatre-vingts euros
eighty euros

Elle a quatre-vingt-deux ans.
She's eighty-two.

quatre-vingt-dix
ninety

quatre-vingt-onze
ninety-one

quatre-vingt-quinze
ninety-five

quatre-vingt-dix-huit
ninety-eight

quatrième

> **quatrième** can be an adjective or a noun.

A adj
fourth

au quatrième étage
on the fourth floor

B nf
Year 9

> In French secondary schools the years are counted from the **sixième** (youngest) to **première** and **terminale** (oldest).

Mon frère est en quatrième.
My brother's in Year 9.

que

> **que** can be a conjunction or a pronoun.

A conj
that

J'espère que tu passes de bonnes vacances.
I hope that you're having a nice holiday.

plus … que
more … than

Il a plus d'argent que moi.
He's got more money than me.

Il est plus grand que moi.
He's taller than me.

aussi … que
as … as

Elle est aussi grande que moi.
She's as tall as me.

ne … que
only

Il ne boit que de l'eau.
He only drinks water.

B pron
what

Que fais-tu?
What are you doing?

Qu'est-ce que …?
What …?

Qu'est-ce que tu fais?
What are you doing?

> **Qu'est-ce que c'est?**
> What's that?

quel m adj
(*f adj* quelle)

1 who

Quel est ton chanteur préféré?
Who's your favourite singer?

2 what

Quelle est ta couleur préférée?
What's your favourite colour?

3 which

C'est quel jumeau celui-là?
Which twin is that?

> **Quelle heure est-il?**
> What time is it?

a
b
c
d
e
f
g
h
i
j
k
l
m
n
o
p
q
r
s
t
u
v
w
x
y
z

quelque adj
1 some

Il a quelques amis à Paris.
He has some friends in Paris.

2 a few

Il y a quelques tulipes dans le jardin.
There are a few tulips in the garden.

quelque chose

> *quelque chose can either mean something or anything.*

J'ai quelque chose pour toi.
I've got something for you.

Je voudrais quelque chose de moins cher.
I'd like something cheaper.

Tu veux quelque chose d'autre?
Would you like anything else?

quelquefois adv
sometimes

quelqu'un pron
1 somebody

Il y a quelqu'un à la porte.
There's somebody at the door.

2 anybody

Il y a quelqu'un?
Is there anybody there?

qu'est-ce que *see* **que**
what

qu'est-ce qui *see* **qui**
what

la **question** nf
question

le **questionnaire** nm
questionnaire

la **queue** nf
tail

Il faut faire la queue.
You have to queue.

une queue de cheval
a ponytail

> *Word for word this means 'horse's tail'.*

qui pron
1 who

Qui a téléphoné?
Who phoned?

2 that

J'aime bien les chaussures noires qui sont dans la vitrine.
I like the black shoes that are in the window.

Qu'est-ce qui …?
What …?

Qu'est-ce qui est sur la table?
What's on the table?

à qui
whose

À qui est ce sac?
Whose bag is this?

la **quille** nf
un jeu de quilles
skittles

la **quinzaine** nf
about fifteen

une quinzaine de personnes
about fifteen people

une quinzaine de jours
a fortnight

quinze num
fifteen

Elle a quinze ans.
She's fifteen.

quinze jours
a fortnight
à quinze heures
at 3 p.m.

🔑

le quinze avril
the fifteenth of April

The 24-hour clock is used in France for travel times, appointments and other formal situations.

quitter vb
to leave

Je quitte la maison à huit heures du matin.
I leave the house at 8 o'clock in the morning.

quoi pron
what?

À quoi tu penses?
What are you thinking about?

A
B
C
D
E
F
G
H
I
J
K
L
M
N
O
P
Q
R
S
T
U
V
W
X
Y
Z

R

raccompagner vb
to take home

Tu peux me raccompagner?
Can you take me home?

le **raccourci** nm
shortcut

la **race** nf
1 race

la race humaine
the human race

2 breed

De quelle race est ton chat?
What breed is your cat?

le **racisme** nm
racism

raciste adj
racist

raconter vb
to tell

**Je vais te raconter une
histoire.**
I'm going to tell you a story.

le **radiateur** nm
radiator

un radiateur électrique
an electric heater

la **radio** nf
1 radio

J'écoute la radio.
I listen to the radio.

2 X-ray

une radio des poumons
an X-ray of the lungs

le **radio-réveil** nm
clock radio

le **radis** nm
radish

French people often eat
radishes with bread and
butter as a starter.

le **ragoût** nm
stew

raide adj
1 straight

Laure a les cheveux raides.
Laure has got straight hair.

2 steep

Cette côte est raide.
This is a steep hill.

3 stiff

Son bras est encore raide.
His arm's still stiff.

le **raisin** nm
grapes

le raisin noir
black grapes

le raisin blanc
green grapes

un grain de raisin
a grape

des raisins secs
raisins

la **raison** nf
reason

Tu as raison.
You're right.

raisonnable adj
sensible

ramasser vb
1 to pick up

Ramasse le crayon, s'il te plaît.
Pick up the pencil please.

2 to collect

Paul, ramasse les cahiers s'il te plaît.
Paul, collect the books please.

ramener vb
1 to bring back

Ramène-moi un souvenir!
Bring me back a souvenir!

2 to take home

Tu me ramènes?
Will you take me home?

la **randonnée** nf

une randonnée pédestre
a ramble

une randonnée à vélo
a bike ride

le **rang** nm
row

au premier rang
in the front row

Mettez-vous en rang.
Line up.

la **rangée** nf
row

une rangée de chaises
a row of chairs

ranger vb
1 to put away

Rangez vos affaires.
Put your things away.

2 to tidy up

Va ranger ta chambre.
Go and tidy up your room.

> **Rangez-vous deux par deux.**
> Get into twos.

râper vb
to grate

le fromage râpé
grated cheese

rapide adj
fast

rapidement adv
quickly

rappeler vb
1 to call back

Je te rappelle dans cinq minutes.
I'll call you back in 5 minutes.

2 to remind

Rappelle-moi de prendre mon maillot de bain.
Remind me to take my swimming costume.

Cette chanson me rappelle mes vacances.
This song reminds me of my holiday.

Tu te rappelles?
Do you remember?

Je ne me rappelle plus.
I can't remember.

A
B
C
D
E
F
G
H
I
J
K
L
M
N
O
P
Q
R
S
T
U
V
W
X
Y
Z

rapporter vb
to bring back

N'oublie pas de rapporter la clé.
Don't forget to bring back the key.

la **raquette** nf
1 racket

une raquette de tennis
a tennis racket
2 bat

une raquette de ping-pong
a table tennis bat

se **raser** vb
to shave

Il se rase tous les matins.
He shaves every morning.

le **rasoir** nm
razor

rassembler vb
to gather

Rassemblez vos affaires!
Gather up your things!

Rassemblez-vous!
Gather round!

**Il faut se rassembler demain à huit
heures devant l'école.**
We've got to meet at 8 tomorrow
in front of the school.

rassurer vb
to reassure

Je suis rassuré.
I don't need to worry any more.

le **rat** nm
rat

raté m adj
(f adj ratée)

Mes photos sont ratées.
My photos are no good.

Le gâteau est raté.
The cake's a failure.

le **râteau** nm
(pl les râteaux)
rake

rater vb
1 to miss

Je ne veux pas rater mon train.
I don't want to miss my train.
2 to fail

**J'ai peur de rater mon examen de
maths.**
I'm afraid I'm going to fail my
maths exam.

Elle rate toujours ses gâteaux.
Her cakes are never any
good.

rayé m adj
(f adj rayée)
striped

une chemise rayée
a striped shirt

le **rayon** nm
1 ray

un rayon de soleil
a ray of sunshine
2 department

le rayon des jouets
the toy department

la **rayure** nf
stripe

**un T-shirt à rayures rouges et
blanches**
a T-shirt with red and white stripes

le/la **réceptionniste** nm/f
receptionist

la **recette** nf
recipe

recevoir vb
to get

Je suis contente quand je reçois une lettre.
I'm pleased when I get a letter.

réchauffer vb
to warm up

Un bon café va te réchauffer.
A nice cup of coffee will warm you up.

♦ **se réchauffer**
to get warm

Je vais me réchauffer près du feu.
I'll go and get warm by the fire.

la **récitation** nf
recitation

> A **récitation** is a poem which pupils have to learn off by heart and recite in front of the whole class.

réciter vb
to recite

reçois, reçoit, reçoivent vb, *see* **recevoir**

Tu reçois combien d'argent de poche?
How much pocket money do you get?

Il reçoit toujours des tas de lettres.
He always gets loads of letters.

Ils ne reçoivent jamais rien.
They never get anything.

recommencer vb
to start again

Il recommence à pleuvoir.
It's started raining again.

la **récompense** nf
reward

reconnaître vb
to recognize

Elle ne va peut-être pas me reconnaître.
She might not recognize me.

Je ne l'ai pas reconnue.
I didn't recognize her.

le **record** nm
record

J'essaie de battre le record.
I'm trying to break the record.

la **récréation** nf
break

Les élèves sont en récréation.
The pupils are having their break.

la cour de récréation
the playground

le **rectangle** nm
rectangle

reçu vb, *see* **recevoir**

J'ai reçu un colis ce matin.
I got a parcel this morning.

être reçu à un examen
to pass an exam

reculer vb
to step back

Reculez de trois cases.
Go back three spaces.

A B C D E F G H I J K L M N O P Q R S T U V W X Y Z

reculons adv
à reculons
backwards

Marchez à reculons.
Walk backwards.

la **rédaction** nf
essay

redoubler vb
to repeat a year

In French schools you
sometimes have to repeat a
year if you've not done well.

refaire vb
1 to do again

Je dois refaire mon dessin.
I'll have to do my drawing
again.
2 to start doing again

Je voudrais refaire de la gym.
I'd like to start doing gymnastics
again.

réfléchir vb
to think

Il est en train de réfléchir.
He's thinking.

la **réflexion** nf
remark

le **refrain** nm
chorus

refroidir vb
to cool

Laissez le gâteau refroidir.
Leave the cake to cool.

regarder vb
1 to look at

**Regardez l'image: qu'est-ce que
c'est?**
Look at the picture: what is it?

2 to watch
Je regarde la télévision.
I'm watching television.

le **régime** nm
diet

Il est au régime.
He's on a diet.

la **région** nf
region

la **règle** nf
ruler

regretter vb
to be sorry

Je regrette, je ne peux pas venir.
I'm sorry, I can't come.

régulier m adj
(f adj régulière)
regular

régulièrement adv
regularly

le **rein** nm
kidney

la **reine** nf
queen

le **relais** nm
relay race

se **relaxer** vb
to relax

la **religieuse** nf
1 nun

Marie est religieuse.
Marie is a nun.

2 choux cream bun

une religieuse au chocolat
a choux bun with chocolate cream
and chocolate icing

la **religion** nf
religion

relire vb
to read again

remarquable adj
remarkable

la **remarque** nf
remark

remarquer vb
to notice

**Regardez les deux dessins: que
remarquez-vous?**
Look at the two pictures: what do
you notice?

remercier vb
to thank

Je te remercie pour ton cadeau.
Thank you for your present.

remettre vb
1 to put back

**Remettez les boîtes dans le
placard, s'il vous plaît.**
Put the boxes back in the cupboard
please.

2 to put back on

Remets ton pull, il fait froid.
Put your sweater back on, it's
cold.

♦ **se remettre**
to get better

**J'espère que tu vas vite te
remettre.**
I hope you will get better soon.

les **remparts** nmpl
city walls

le **remplaçant** nm
la **remplaçante** nf
supply teacher

remplacer vb
to replace

remplacer par
to replace with

**Le premier avril, j'ai remplacé le
sel par du sucre.**
On April Fool's Day, I replaced the
salt with sugar.

Il remplace le prof de maths.
He's covering for the maths teacher.

remplir vb
to fill in

Remplissez la grille.
Fill in the grid.

remuer vb
to stir

le **renard** nm
fox

rencontrer vb
to meet

Je la rencontre souvent au marché.
I often meet her at the market.

Ils se sont rencontrés il y a deux ans.
They met two years ago.

le rendez-vous nm
appointment

J'ai rendez-vous chez le coiffeur.
I've got an appointment at the hairdresser's.

rendre vb
1 to give back

Rends-moi ma gomme.
Give me back my rubber.

2 to take back

Je vais rendre mes livres à la bibliothèque.
I'm going to take my books back to the library.

renifler vb
to sniff

le renne nm
reindeer

le renseignement nm
piece of information

Il me manque un renseignement.
There's one piece of information I still need.

des renseignements
information

Je cherche des renseignements sur l'Écosse.
I'm looking for information about Scotland.

la rentrée nf

la rentrée (des classes)
the start of the new school year

le jour de la rentrée
the day the schools go back

rentrer vb
1 to come in

Rentre, tu vas prendre froid.
Come in, you'll catch cold.

2 to get home

Il rentre à sept heures du soir.
He gets home at seven o'clock in the evening.

réparer vb
to repair

le repas nm
meal

le repas de midi
lunch

le repas du soir
dinner

le repassage nm
ironing

Ma mère déteste le repassage.
My mum hates ironing.

repasser vb
to iron

répéter vb
to repeat

Écoutez et répétez après moi.
Listen and repeat after me.

la répétition nf
rehearsal

le répondeur nm
answering machine

répondre vb
to answer

Répondez par oui ou par non.
Answer yes or no.

la **réponse** nf
answer

C'est la bonne réponse.
That's the right answer.

se **reposer** vb
to have a rest

Le week-end, je me repose.
I have a rest at the weekend.

le **représentant** nm
la **représentante** nf
rep

le **requin** nm
shark

réservé m adj
(f adj réservée)
reserved

réserver vb
to book

la **résidence** nf
block of flats

une résidence secondaire
a second home

respirer vb
to breathe

responsable adj
responsible

Elle est responsable de l'accident.
She's responsible for the accident.

ressembler vb

ressembler à
to look like

Elle ressemble à sa sœur.
She looks like her sister.

On se ressemble.
We look alike.

le **restaurant** nm
restaurant

le **reste** nm
rest

Tu peux manger le reste des pâtes.
You can eat the rest of the pasta.

les restes
the left-overs

rester vb
1 to stay

Je reste à la maison ce week-end.
I'm staying at home this weekend.
2 to be left

Il reste du pain.
There's some bread left.

le **résultat** nm
result

les résultats des examens
the exam results

le **retard** nm

Je suis en retard!
I'm late!

Tu ne dois pas être en retard.
You mustn't be late.

la **retenue** nf
detention

Gerry est en retenue.
Gerry's in detention.

A B C D E F G H I J K L M N O P Q R S T U V W X Y Z

retirer vb
to take off

Retire ton manteau.
Take your coat off.

le **retour** nm
return

Il est de retour.
He's back.

retourner vb

1 to go back

Je dois retourner chez le dentiste la semaine prochaine.
I have to go back to the dentist next week.

2 to turn over

Retourne la carte.
Turn the card over.

Retourne-toi.
Turn round.

la **retraite** nf
être à la retraite
to be retired

Mon grand-père est à la retraite.
My granddad's retired.

prendre sa retraite
to retire

Il prend sa retraite l'année prochaine.
He's retiring next year.

retraité m adj
(f adj retraitée)
retired

retrouver vb
to find

Je n'arrive pas à retrouver mes gants.
I can't find my gloves.

la **réunion** nf
meeting

réussi m adj
(f adj réussie)
successful

une soirée très réussie
a very successful party

réussir vb

réussir à un examen
to pass an exam

le **rêve** nm
dream

la maison de mes rêves
my dream house

le **réveil** nm
alarm clock

réveiller vb
to wake up

Ma mère me réveille à sept heures.
My mum wakes me up at seven o'clock.

◆ **se réveiller**
to wake up

Je me réveille à sept heures.
I wake up at seven o'clock.

le **réveillon** nm
le réveillon du jour de l'An
New Year's Eve celebrations

le réveillon de Noël
Christmas Eve celebrations

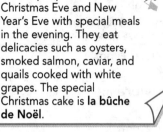

French people celebrate Christmas Eve and New Year's Eve with special meals in the evening. They eat delicacies such as oysters, smoked salmon, caviar, and quails cooked with white grapes. The special Christmas cake is **la bûche de Noël**.

réveillonner vb
1 to celebrate New Year's Eve
2 to celebrate Christmas Eve

revenez vb, *see* **revenir**
Revenez vite!
Come back soon!

revenir vb
to come back
Reviens vite!
Come back soon!

rêver vb
to dream

reviens, revient vb, *see* **revenir**
Tu reviens l'année prochaine?
Are you coming back next year?
Antoine revient souvent nous voir.
Antoine often comes back to see us.

réviser vb
to revise
Je dois réviser mon anglais.
I've got to revise my English.

revoir vb
to see again
J'aimerais bien la revoir.
I'd really like to see her again.

🔑
au revoir
goodbye

la **révolution** nf
revolution
la Révolution française
the French Revolution

le **revolver** nm
revolver

le **rez-de-chaussée** nm
ground floor
au rez-de-chaussée
on the ground floor

le **Rhin** nm
Rhine

le **rhinocéros** nm
rhinoceros

le **Rhône** nm
Rhone

la **rhubarbe** nf
rhubarb

le **rhum** nm
rum

le **rhume** nm
cold
J'ai le rhume.
I've got a cold.
le rhume des foins
hay fever

riche adj
1 well-off

Sa famille est très riche.
His family's very well-off.

2 rich

riche en vitamines
rich in vitamins

le **rideau** nm
(*pl* les rideaux)
curtain

Tire les rideaux.
Draw the curtains.

ridicule adj
ridiculous

**Je trouve ça complètement
ridicule.**
I think that's absolutely ridiculous.

rien
1 nothing

**Qu'est-ce que tu veux boire? –
Rien, merci.**
What would you like to drink? –
Nothing, thanks.

rien d'intéressant
nothing interesting

rien d'autre
nothing else

rien du tout
nothing at all

2 anything

Il ne fait rien ce soir.
He's not doing anything tonight.

Elle ne mange rien.
She's not eating anything.

De rien!
Not at all!

Merci beaucoup! – De rien!
Thank you very much! – Not at
all!

rigolo m adj
(*f adj* rigolote)
funny

rire vb
to laugh

Il me fait toujours rire.
He always makes me laugh.

le **risque** nm
risk

la **rivière** nf
river

le **riz** nm
rice

le riz au lait
rice pudding

la **robe** nf
dress

une robe de mariée
a wedding dress

une robe de chambre
a dressing gown

le **robinet** nm
tap

Ferme le robinet.
Turn off the tap.

le **robot** nm
robot

le **rocher** nm
rock

le **rock** nm
rock

un chanteur de rock
a rock singer

le **roi** nm
king

les Rois mages
the Three Wise Men

la fête des Rois
Epiphany

> January 6 is **la fête des Rois**,
> when the Three Wise Men,
> or Three Kings, came to visit
> baby Jesus. This day is also
> called Twelfth Night,
> because it is the twelfth day
> after Christmas.

les **rollers** nmpl
Rollerblades®

romain m adj
(*f adj* romaine)
Roman

des ruines romaines
Roman remains

le **roman** nm
novel

rond

> **rond** can be an adjective or a
> noun.

Ⓐ m adj
(*f adj* ronde)
round

La Terre est ronde.
The Earth is round.

Ⓑ nm
circle

Dessinez un rond.
Draw a circle.

en rond
in a circle

Asseyez-vous en rond.
Sit in a circle.

la **rondelle** nf
slice

une rondelle de citron
a slice of lemon

le **rond-point** nm
roundabout

ronfler vb
to snore

le **rosbif** nm
roast beef

rose

> **rose** can be an adjective or a
> noun.

Ⓐ adj
pink

des chaussettes roses
pink socks

Ⓑ nf
rose

une rose rouge
a red rose

Ⓒ nm
pink

Ma couleur préférée, c'est le rose.
Pink is my favourite colour.

le **rosier** nm
rose bush

rôti

> **rôti** can be a noun or an adjective.

Ⓐ nm
roast meat

un rôti de bœuf
a joint of beef

Ⓑ m adj
(*f adj* rôtie)
roast

un poulet rôti
a roast chicken

la **roue** nf
wheel

une **roue de secours**
a spare wheel

Je sais faire la roue.
I can do cartwheels.

rouge

> **rouge** can be an adjective or a noun.

A adj
red

des chaussettes rouges
red socks

B nm
red

Ma couleur préférée, c'est le rouge.
Red is my favourite colour.

un rouge à lèvres
a lipstick

> **rouge à lèvres** means "red for lips".

la **rougeole** nf
measles

rougir vb
to blush

Tu rougis!
You're blushing!

la **rouille** nf
rust

rouillé m adj
(f adj rouillée)
rusty

roulant m adj
(f adj roulante)

une table roulante
a trolley

un **fauteuil roulant**
a wheelchair

rouler vb
1 to drive

Il roule trop vite.
He drives too fast.

2 to roll up

Aide-moi à rouler le tapis.
Help me to roll up the mat.

Roulez la pâte.
Roll out the pastry.

le **Roumain** nm
la **Roumaine** nf
Romanian

roumain m adj
(f adj roumaine)
Romanian

la **Roumanie** nf
Romania

rousse

> **rousse** can be an adjective or a noun.

A f adj
red

une poule rousse
a red hen

Elle est rousse.
She's red-haired.

B nf
redhead

la **route** nf
1 road

une route nationale
an A road

au bord de la route
at the roadside

2 way

Je ne connais pas la route.
I don't know the way.

en route
on the way

On s'arrête toujours en route.
We always stop on the way.

3 journey

Bonne route!
Have a good journey!

Il y a trois heures de route.
It's a 3-hour journey.

le **routier** nm
lorry driver

roux

> **roux** can be an adjective or a noun.

A m adj
(*f adj* rousse)
red

Harry a les cheveux roux.
Harry has red hair.

Il est roux.
He's red-haired.

B nm
redhead

royal m adj
(*f adj* royale)
royal

la famille royale
the Royal Family

le **royaume** nm
kingdom

le Royaume-Uni
the United Kingdom

le **ruban** nm
ribbon

la **rubéole** nf
German measles

la **rue** nf
street

le **rugby** nm
rugby

Yann joue au rugby.
Yann plays rugby.

la **ruine** nf
ruin

les ruines de la cathédrale
the ruins of the cathedral

le **ruisseau** nm
(*pl* les ruisseaux)
stream

rusé m adj
(*f adj* rusée)
cunning

russe nm, adj
Russian

le/la **Russe** nm/f
Russian

la **Russie** nf
Russia

le **rythme** nm
rhythm

S

s' pron

> **s'** is what **se** changes to before a vowel sound.

Ils s'aiment.
They love each other.

sa f adj

1 his

Benjamin est chez sa grand-mère.
Benjamin is at his grandmother's.

2 her

Elle attend sa mère.
She's waiting for her mother.

3 its

Remets la télécommande à sa place.
Put the remote control back in its place.

le **sable** nm
sand

le **sac** nm
bag

un sac à main
a handbag

un sac à dos
a rucksack

un sac de couchage
a sleeping bag

sage adj
well-behaved

Fatima est très sage.
Fatima is very well-behaved.

Sois sage.
Be good.

saignant m adj
(f adj saignante)
rare

Saignant ou à point?
Rare or medium?

saigner vb
to bleed

Il saigne du nez.
His nose is bleeding.

saint m adj
(f adj sainte)
holy

la Saint-Sylvestre
New Year's Eve

le vendredi saint
Good Friday

le **saint** nm
la **sainte** nf
saint

Aujourd'hui, c'est la sainte Louise.
Today is Saint Louise's day.

Every day on a French calendar belongs to a saint. On March 15th, St Louise's day, people say "Bonne fête Louise!" to anyone with that name. Girls called Louise might get presents too.

sais vb, *see* **savoir**

Je ne sais pas.
I don't know.

la **saison** nf
season

sait vb, *see* **savoir**

Il sait que …
He knows that …

On ne sait jamais!
You never know!

la **salade** nf
1 lettuce

Les tortues aiment la salade.
Tortoises like lettuce.

2 salad

une salade de fruits
a fruit salad

le **saladier** nm
salad bowl

sale adj
dirty

salé m adj
(*f adj* salée)
1 salty

La soupe est trop salée.
The soup's too salty.

2 salted

du beurre salé
salted butter

3 savoury

des biscuits salés
savoury biscuits

la **salle** nf
room

la salle à manger
the dining room

la salle de séjour
the living room

la salle de bains
the bathroom

la salle d'attente
the waiting room

une salle de classe
a classroom

la salle des professeurs
the staffroom

le **salon** nm
lounge

un salon de thé
a tearoom

un salon de beauté
a beauty salon

la **salopette** nf
dungarees

salut excl
hi!

le **samedi** nm
1 Saturday

Aujourd'hui, nous sommes samedi.
It's Saturday today.

2 on Saturday

Je suis allé au cinéma samedi.
I went to the cinema on Saturday.

A
B
C
D
E
F
G
H
I
J
K
L
M
N
O
P
Q
R
S
T
U
V
W
X
Y
Z

Le magasin ferme à dix-huit heures le samedi.
The shop closes at 6 p.m. on Saturdays.

> tous les samedis
> every Saturday
> **le samedi**
> on Saturdays
> **samedi dernier**
> last Saturday
> **samedi prochain**
> next Saturday
> **À samedi!**
> See you on Saturday!

les **sandales** nfpl
sandals

le **sandwich** nm
sandwich

un sandwich au jambon
a ham sandwich

le **sang** nm
blood

le **sanglier** nm
wild boar

sans prep
without

Elle est venue sans son frère.
She came without her brother.

la **santé** nf
health

en bonne santé
in good health

> **Santé!**
> Cheers!

le **sapin** nm
fir tree

un sapin de Noël
a Christmas tree

la **sauce** nf
1 sauce

la sauce tomate
tomato sauce

2 gravy

la **saucisse** nf
sausage

le **saucisson** nm
salami

> **le saucisson sec** is a hard sausage that is eaten cold.

sauf prep
except

Tout le monde est venu sauf lui.
Everyone came except him.

sauf si
unless

Je n'irai pas sauf si tu viens.
I won't go unless you come too.

le **saumon** nm
salmon

le **saut** nm
jump

sauter vb
to jump
sauter à la corde
to skip

sauvage adj
wild
les animaux sauvages
wild animals

sauver vb
to save
Il m'a sauvé la vie.
He saved my life.

le **savant** nm
scientist

savent, savez vb, *see* **savoir**
Ils ne savent pas ce qu'ils veulent.
They don't know what they want.
Est-ce que vous savez où elle habite?
Do you know where she lives?

savoir vb
to know
Je ne sais pas où il est allé.
I don't know where he's gone.
Nous ne savons pas quoi faire.
We don't know what to do.
Tu savais que Canberra était la capitale de l'Australie?
Did you know that Canberra was the capital of Australia?

Tu sais nager?
Can you swim?

le **savon** nm
soap

la **savonnette** nf
bar of soap

savons vb, *see* **savoir**
Nous savons où tu es caché.
We know where you're hiding.

la **Scandinavie** nf
Scandinavia

la **science** nf
science
Elle est forte en sciences.
She is good at science.

scolaire adj
school
l'année scolaire
the school year
les vacances scolaires
the school holidays
mon livret scolaire
my school report

le **Scotch**® nm
adhesive tape

se pron

se changes to s' before a vowel sound.

1 himself
Il se regarde dans la glace.
He's looking at himself in the mirror.
2 herself
Elle se regarde dans la glace.
She's looking at herself in the mirror.

A B C D E F G H I J K L M N O P Q R S T U V W X Y Z

a
b
c
d
e
f
g
h
i
j
k
l
m
n
o
p
q
r
s
t
u
v
w
x
y
z

Elle s'admire dans sa nouvelle robe.
She's admiring herself in her new dress.

3 itself

Le chat se regarde dans la glace.
The cat's looking at itself in the mirror.

4 themselves

Ils se sont regardés dans la glace.
They looked at themselves in the mirror.

5 each other

Ils se détestent.
They hate each other.

Sometimes se is not translated.

Il s'appelle Paul.
His name is Paul.

Elle se brosse les dents trois fois par jour.
She brushes her teeth three times a day.

le **seau** nm
(*pl* les seaux)
bucket

sec m adj
(*f adj* sèche)
1 dry

Mon jean n'est pas encore sec.
My jeans aren't dry yet.

2 dried

des figues sèches
dried figs

le **sèche-cheveux** nm
hair dryer

le **sèche-linge** nm
tumble dryer

sécher vb
to dry

second m adj
(*f adj* seconde)
second

la **seconde** nf
1 second

Attends une seconde!
Wait a second!

2 Year 11

Ma sœur est en seconde.
My sister's in Year 11.

> In French secondary schools the years are counted from the **sixième** (youngest) to **première** and **terminale** (oldest).

le **secours** nm
help

Il est allé chercher du secours.
He went to get help.

une sortie de secours
an emergency exit

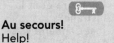

Au secours!
Help!

le **secret**

secret can be a noun or an adjective.

A nm
secret

J'ai un secret à te dire.
I have a secret to tell you.

B m adj
(*f adj* secrète)
secret

la **secrétaire** nf
secretary

le **secrétariat** nm
secretary's office

la **sécurité** nf
safety

une ceinture de sécurité
a seatbelt

seize num
sixteen

Elle a seize ans.
She's sixteen.

Il est seize heures.
It's 4 p.m.

🔑

le seize novembre
the sixteenth of November

The 24-hour clock is used in
France for travel times,
appointments and other
formal situations.

seizième adj
sixteenth

le **sel** nm
salt

le **self** nm
self-service restaurant

selon prep
according to

Ils sont répartis selon leur âge.
They're divided up according to
age.

la **semaine** nf
week

en semaine
on weekdays

le **semblant** nm
faire semblant
to pretend

Il fait semblant de dormir.
He's pretending to be asleep.

sembler vb
to seem

Le temps semble s'améliorer.
The weather seems to be
improving.

la **semoule** nf
semolina

le **sens** nm
1 sense

Il a le sens de l'humour.
He has a sense of humour.

Je n'ai pas le sens de l'orientation.
I've got no sense of direction.

Ça n'a pas de sens.
It doesn't make sense.

A
B
C
D
E
F
G
H
I
J
K
L
M
N
O
P
Q
R
S
T
U
V
W
X
Y
Z

2 direction

Elle est partie dans le mauvais sens.
She set off in the wrong direction.

dans le sens des aiguilles d'une montre
clockwise

dans le sens contraire des aiguilles d'une montre
anticlockwise

sens dessus dessous
upside down

sensible adj

sensitive

Elle est très sensible.
She's very sensitive.

> Be careful! The French word
> *sensible* does not mean the same
> as the English word **sensible**.

sentir vb

1 to smell

Ça sent bon.
That smells good.

Ça sent mauvais.
It smells horrible.

2 to smell of

Ça sent les frites ici.
It smells of chips in here.

3 to feel

Ça t'a fait mal? – Non, je n'ai rien senti.
Did it hurt? – No, I didn't feel a thing.

Je ne me sens pas bien.
I don't feel well.

séparé m adj

(*f adj* séparée)
separated

séparer vb

to separate

Séparez le blanc du jaune.
Separate the yolk from the white.

◆ **se séparer**
to separate

Mes parents se sont séparés l'année dernière.
My parents separated last year.

sept num

seven

Je me lève à sept heures.
I get up at seven o'clock.

Elle a sept ans.
She's seven.

> 🔑
> **le sept février**
> the seventh of February

septembre nm

September

en septembre
in September

le six septembre
the sixth of September

septième adj

seventh

au septième étage
on the seventh floor

sera, serai, seras, serez vb, see être

Il sera là demain.
He'll be here tomorrow.

Je serai de retour à dix heures.
I'll be back at 10 o'clock.

Tu ne seras pas toute seule.
You won't be alone.

Vous serez chez vous demain?
Will you be at home tomorrow?

la **série** nf
series

une série télévisée américaine
an American TV series

sérieux m adj
(*f adj* sérieuse)

1 serious

Il plaisante? – Non, il est sérieux.
Is he joking? – No, he's serious.

2 responsible

C'est un employé très sérieux.
He's a very responsible employee.

serons, seront vb, *see* **être**
Nous serons en vacances demain.
We'll be on holiday tomorrow.

Ils seront contents de te revoir.
They'll be happy to see you again.

le **serpent** nm
snake

se **serrer** vb
se serrer la main
to shake hands

Allez, serrez-vous la main!
Come on, shake hands!

la **serrure** nf
lock

sers, sert vb, *see* **servir**
Sers-toi.
Help yourself.
Ça ne sert à rien.
That's no use.

le **serveur** nm
waiter

la **serveuse** nf
waitress

la **serviette** nf
towel

une serviette de bain
a bath towel

servir vb
À quoi ça sert?
What's it for?

Ça ne sert à rien.
It's no use.

♦ **se servir de**
to use

Tu te sers souvent de ton vélo?
Do you use your bike a lot?

Servez-vous.
Help yourself.

ses pl adj
1 his

Il est chez ses grands-parents.
He's at his grandparents'.

2 her

Delphine joue avec ses copines.
Delphine's playing with her friends.

3 its

la chatte et ses petits
the cat and its kittens

seul

> **seul** can be an adjective or an adverb.

A m adj
(*f adj* seule)

1 only

Il reste une seule nectarine.
There's only one nectarine left.

C'est la seule chose que je n'aime pas.
It's the only thing I don't like.

2 alone

Elle vit seule.
She lives alone.

B adv
tout seul
by oneself

Elle a fait ça toute seule?
Did she do it by herself?

seulement adv
only

A
B
C
D
E
F
G
H
I
J
K
L
M
N
O
P
Q
R
S
T
U
V
W
X
Y
Z

non seulement ... mais
not only ... but

Non seulement il pleut, mais en plus il fait froid.
Not only is it raining, but it's cold as well.

sévère adj
strict

le **shampooing** nm
shampoo

le **short** nm
shorts

Il est en short.
He's wearing shorts.

si

si can be a conjunction or an adverb.

Ⓐ conj
if

si tu veux
if you like

Je me demande si elle va venir.
I wonder if she'll come.

si seulement
if only

Ⓑ adv

1 so

Elle est si gentille.
She's so kind.

2 yes actually

Tu n'es pas allé à l'école habillé comme ça? – Si.
You didn't go to school dressed like that? – Yes I did, actually.

la **Sicile** nf
Sicily

le **siècle** nm
century

le **siège** nm
seat

le **sien** m pron
la **sienne** f pron

le sien, la sienne, les siens and *les siennes* can either mean **his** or **hers**.

C'est le vélo de Paul? – Oui, c'est le sien.
Is this Paul's bike? – Yes, it's his.

C'est le vélo d'Isabelle? – Oui, c'est le sien.
Is this Isabelle's bike? – Yes, it's hers.

C'est la montre de Paul? – Oui, c'est la sienne.
Is this Paul's watch? – Yes, it's his.

Ce sont les cassettes de Christian? – Oui, ce sont les siennes.
Are these Christian's cassettes? – Yes, they're his.

la **sieste** nf
nap

faire la sieste
to have a nap

siffler vb
to whistle

le **sifflet** nm
whistle

signifier vb
to mean
Que signifie ce mot?
What does this word mean?

le **silence** nm
silence

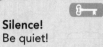
Silence!
Be quiet!

silencieux m adj
(*f adj* silencieuse)
silent

simple adj
simple

simplement adv
simply

le **singe** nm
monkey

le **singulier** nm
singular
au singulier
in the singular

sinon conj
otherwise
Dépêche-toi, sinon je pars sans toi.
Hurry up, otherwise I'll leave
without you.

la **sirène** nf
mermaid
la sirène d'alarme
the fire alarm

le **sirop** nm
cordial
du sirop de framboise
raspberry cordial

You dilute **le sirop** with
water, rather like squash.
There are all kinds of
flavours.

le sirop contre la toux
cough mixture

le **site** nm
un site Web
a website

six num
six
Il est rentré à six heures.
He got back at six o'clock.
Il a six ans.
He's six.

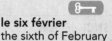
le six février
the sixth of February

sixième

sixième can be an adjective or a
noun.

Ⓐ adj
sixth
au sixième étage
on the sixth floor
Ⓑ nf
Year 7
Mon frère est en sixième.
My brother's in Year 7.

In French secondary schools
the years are counted from
the **sixième** (youngest) to
première and **terminale**
(oldest).

A
B
C
D
E
F
G
H
I
J
K
L
M
N
O
P
Q
R
S
T
U
V
W
X
Y
Z

le **ski** nm

1 ski

Mes skis sont trop petits.
My skis are too small.

2 skiing

J'adore le ski.
I love skiing.

faire du ski
to go skiing

En hiver, je fais du ski.
In winter I go skiing.

le ski nautique
water-skiing

skier vb
to ski

le **slip** nm
pants

un slip de bain
swimming trunks

la **SNCF** nf

You will see **SNCF** on trains and stations in France. It's the name of the French railways, which are state-owned.

la **société** nf

1 society
2 company

la **sœur** nf
sister

ma grande sœur
my big sister

ma petite sœur
my little sister

soi pron
oneself

rester chez soi
to stay at home

la **soie** nf
silk

la **soif** nf
thirst

Tu as soif?
Are you thirsty?

J'ai soif.
I'm thirsty.

soi-même pron
oneself

Il vaut mieux le faire soi-même.
It's better to do it oneself.

le **soin** nm
care

Prends bien soin de ce livre.
Take good care of this book.

le **soir** nm
evening

ce soir
this evening

le soir
in the evening

demain soir
tomorrow night
hier soir
last night

la **soirée** nf
evening

en tenue de soirée
in evening dress

sois vb, *see* **être**

Sois sage!
Be good!

soit conj

soit ..., soit ...
either ... or ...

soit lundi, soit mardi
either Monday or Tuesday

la **soixantaine** nf
about sixty

une soixantaine de personnes
about sixty people

Elle a la soixantaine.
She's in her sixties.

soixante num
sixty

Il a soixante ans.
He's sixty.

soixante et un
sixty-one

soixante-deux
sixty-two

soixante et onze
seventy-one

soixante-quinze
seventy-five

soixante-dix num
seventy

Il a soixante-dix ans.
He's seventy.

solaire adj
solar

le système solaire
the solar system

la crème solaire
sun cream

le **soldat** nm
soldier

le **solde** nm

en solde
reduced

Les baskets sont en solde.
The trainers are reduced.

les soldes
the sales

le **soleil** nm
sun

au soleil
in the sun

> **Il y a du soleil.**
> It's sunny.

solide adj
strong

sombre adj
dark

Il fait un peu sombre ici.
It's a little dark in here.

le **sommeil** nm
sleep

> **J'ai sommeil.**
> I'm sleepy.

sommes vb, *see* **être**

Nous sommes en vacances.
We're on holiday.

*Sometimes **sommes** shows that something has happened in the past.*

Nous sommes arrivés à une heure.
We arrived at 1 o'clock.

A B C D E F G H I J K L M N O P Q R S T U V W X Y Z

son

> **son** can be an adjective or a noun.

Ⓐ m adj
(f adj sa, *pl adj* ses)

1 his

Il est chez son grand-père.
He's at his granddad's.

2 her

Elle joue avec son frère.
She's playing with her brother.

3 its

Le chien est dans son panier.
The dog is in its basket.

Ⓑ nm
sound

Le son n'est pas très bon.
The sound's not very good.

le **sondage** nm
survey

sonner vb
to ring

Le téléphone sonne.
The phone's ringing.

la **sonnerie** nf
bell

la **sonnette** nf
bell

la sonnette d'alarme
the alarm bell

sont vb, *see* **être**

Ils sont en vacances.
They're on holiday.

> *Sometimes* **sont** *shows that
> something has happened in the
> past.*

Ils sont allés en France.
They went to France.

la **sorcière** nf
witch

le **sort** nm
spell

La sorcière lui a jeté un sort.
The witch cast a spell on him.

tirer au sort
to draw lots

la **sorte** nf
sort

C'est une sorte de gâteau.
It's a sort of cake.

la **sortie** nf
way out

Où est la sortie?
Where's the way out?

la sortie de secours
the emergency exit

Attends-moi à la sortie de l'école.
Meet me after school.

sortir vb

1 to go out

Il est sorti.
He's gone out.

2 to come out

Il sort de l'hôpital aujourd'hui.
He's coming out of hospital today.

3 to take out

Sortez vos affaires.
Take out your things.

la **soucoupe** nf
saucer

une soucoupe volante
a flying saucer

soudain

> **soudain** can be an adjective or an
> adverb.

Ⓐ m adj
(f adj soudaine)
sudden

une douleur soudaine
a sudden pain

Ⓑ adv
suddenly

Soudain, il s'est fâché.
Suddenly, he got angry.

souffler vb
1 to blow

Le vent souffle fort.
The wind's blowing hard.

2 to blow out

Souffle les bougies!
Blow out the candles!

le **souhait** nm
wish

faire un souhait
to make a wish

🔑

Atchoum! – À tes souhaits!
Atchoo! – Bless you!

souhaiter vb
to wish

Nous te souhaitons un bon Noël.
We wish you a happy Christmas.

le **soulier** nm
shoe

souligner vb
to underline

la **soupe** nf
soup

le **sourcil** nm
eyebrow

sourd m adj
(f adj sourde)
deaf

souriant m adj
(f adj souriante)
cheerful

sourire

> **sourire** can be a verb or a noun.

Ⓐ vb
to smile

Elle ne sourit jamais.
She never smiles.

Ⓑ nm
smile

Elle a un joli sourire.
She has a nice smile.

la **souris** nf
mouse

la petite souris
the tooth fairy

> French children believe that
> a little mouse (**la petite**
> **souris**) comes at night to
> take their tooth from under
> the pillow and replace it with
> money.

sous prep
under

Le chat est sous la chaise.
The cat's under the chair.

sous la pluie
in the rain

le **sous-marin** nm
submarine

le **sous-sol** nm
basement

les **sous-titres** nmpl
subtitles

sous-titré m adj
(f adj sous-titrée)
with subtitles

un film sous-titré
a film with subtitles

la **soustraction** nf
subtraction

souvenir

| **souvenir** can be a noun or a verb. |

Ⓐ nm
1 memory
2 souvenir

un souvenir de Paris
a souvenir of Paris

Ⓑ vb

◆ **se souvenir**
to remember

**Je ne me souviens pas de son
adresse.**
I can't remember his address.

**Je me souviens qu'il neigeait ce
jour-là.**
I remember it was snowing that day.

souvent adv
often

Tu vas souvent au cinéma?
Do you go to the cinema often?

soyez vb, see **être**
Soyez sages!
Be good!

la **SPA** nf
RSPCA

spécialement adv
1 specially

**Il est venu spécialement pour te
parler.**
He came specially to speak to you.

2 particularly

Ce n'est pas spécialement difficile.
It's not particularly difficult.

le **spectacle** nm
show

un spectacle de Noël
a Christmas show

splendide adj
magnificent

Il fait un temps splendide.
The weather is magnificent.

sport

| **sport** can be a noun or an adjective. |

Ⓐ nm
sport

Quel est ton sport préféré?
What's your favourite sport?

Que fais-tu comme sport?
What sport do you do?

Il fait beaucoup de sport.
He does a lot of sport.

aller aux sports d'hiver
to go on a skiing holiday

**Je vais aux sports d'hiver en
février.**
I'm going on a skiing holiday in
February.

Ⓑ adj
casual

une veste sport
a casual jacket

des vêtements sport
casual clothes

sportif m adj
(f adj sportive)
1 sporty

Elle est très sportive.
She's very sporty.

2 sports

un club sportif
a sports club

le **squelette** nm
skeleton

le **stade** nm
stadium

la **station** nf
une station de métro
an underground station

une station de ski
a ski resort

le **steak** nm
steak

un steak frites
steak and chips

un steak haché
a hamburger

stressé m adj
(f adj stressée)
stressed out

le **studio** nm
studio flat

stupide adj
stupid

le **stylo** nm
pen

un stylo bille
a ballpoint pen

un stylo-feutre
a felt-tip pen

su vb, see **savoir**
Si j'avais su …
If I'd known …

le **succès** nm
success

Ce film a beaucoup de succès en ce moment.
This film is very successful at the moment.

la **sucette** nf
lollipop

le **sucre** nm
sugar

un sucre
a sugar lump

Je prends deux sucres dans mon café.
I take two lumps of sugar in my coffee.

sucré m adj
(f adj sucrée)
sweet

Ce gâteau est un peu trop sucré.
This cake is a bit too sweet.

les **sucreries** nfpl
sweet things

sud

sud can be a noun or an adjective.

A nm
south

Ils vivent dans le sud de la France.
They live in the South of France.

au sud de Paris
south of Paris

l'Amérique du Sud
South America

B adj
south

le pôle sud
the South Pole

A B C D E F G H I J K L M N O P Q R S T U V W X Y Z

le **sud-est** nm
south-east

au sud-est
in the south-east

le **sud-ouest** nm
south-west

au sud-ouest
in the south-west

la **Suède** nf
Sweden

suédois nm, m adj
(f adj suédoise)
Swedish

le **Suédois** nm
la **Suédoise** nf
Swede

suffire vb
to be enough

Tiens, voilà cinq euros. Ça te suffit?
Here's five euros. Is that enough for you?

> **Ça suffit!**
> That's enough!

suffisamment adv
enough

suis vb, *see* **être**
Je suis écossais.
I'm Scottish.

> *Sometimes **suis** shows that something has happened in the past.*

Je suis restée chez moi.
I stayed at home.

suisse adj
Swiss

le **Suisse** nm
Swiss man

la **Suisse** nf
1 Swiss woman
2 Switzerland

la **suite** nf
rest

Je vous raconterai la suite de l'histoire demain.
I'll tell you the rest of the story tomorrow.

J'y vais tout de suite.
I'll go straightaway.

> **tout de suite**
> straightaway

suivre vb
to follow

Suivez-moi, tout le monde!
Follow me, everybody!

Suis-moi, Alice.
Follow me, Alice.

Il me suit partout.
He follows me everywhere.

super m, f, pl adj
great

C'est super!
It's great!

le **supermarché** nm
supermarket

superposé m adj

des lits superposés
bunk beds

supplémentaire adj
additional

supporter vb
to stand

Je ne supporte pas le golf.
I can't stand golf.

Je ne peux pas la supporter.
I can't stand her.

Be careful! **supporter** *does not mean the same as* **to support**.

sur prep
1 on

Pose-le sur la table.
Put it down on the table.

une émission sur les ours polaires
a programme on polar bears
2 in

une personne sur dix
1 person in 10
3 out of

J'ai eu quatorze sur vingt en maths.
I got 14 out of 20 in maths.

Tests and homework are usually marked out of 20 in French schools.

sûr m adj
(*f adj* sûre)
sure

Tu es sûr?
Are you sure?

sûrement adv
certainly

Sûrement pas!
Certainly not!

le **surnom** nm
nickname

surpris m adj
(*f adj* surprise)
surprised

Il était surpris de me voir.
He was surprised to see me.

la **surprise** nf
surprise

surtout adv
especially

Il est assez timide, surtout avec les filles.
He's rather shy, especially with girls.

surveiller vb
1 to keep an eye on

Tu peux surveiller mes bagages?
Can you keep an eye on my luggage?
2 to supervise

Nous sommes toujours surveillés pendant la récréation.
We're always supervised during break.

le **survêtement** nm
tracksuit

SVP abbr
please

le **sweat** nm
sweatshirt

sympa adj
nice

Elle est très sympa.
She's a really nice person.

sympathique adj
nice

Ce sont des gens très sympathiques.
They're very nice people.

Be careful! **sympathique** *does not mean the same as* **sympathetic**.

le **syndicat** nm
le syndicat d'initiative
the tourist information office

T

t′ pron

> t′ is what **te** changes to before a vowel sound.

Je ne t'entends pas.
I can't hear you.

Comment tu t'appelles?
What's your name?

ta f adj
your

Quel âge a ta sœur?
How old is your sister?

le **tabac** nm
tobacco

> **tabac** is also the name for a shop which sells cigarettes and stamps.

la **table** nf
table

une table de nuit
a bedside table

Mets la table, s'il te plaît.
Lay the table please.

À table!
Dinner's ready!

le **tableau** nm
(pl les tableaux)
1 painting
2 blackboard

C'est écrit au tableau.
It's on the blackboard.
3 whiteboard

la **tablette** nf
une tablette de chocolat
a bar of chocolate

le **tablier** nm
apron

le **tabouret** nm
stool

la **tache** nf
mark

Tu as une tache sur ton T-shirt.
You've got a mark on your T-shirt.

des taches de rousseur
freckles

la **taille** nf
1 waist

Elle a la taille fine.
She has a slim waist.
2 height

un homme de taille moyenne
a man of average height
3 size

Avez-vous ma taille?
Have you got my size?

le **taille-crayon** nm
pencil sharpener

se **taire** vb
to stop talking

Taisez-vous!
Stop talking!

le **tambour** nm
drum

Il joue du tambour.
He is playing the drum.

la **Tamise** nf
Thames

tant adv
so much

Je l'aime tant!
I love him so much!

tant de

> *tant de* can either mean *so much* or *so many*.

tant de nourriture
so much food

tant de livres
so many books

Tant mieux!
So much the better!
Tant pis!
Never mind!

la **tante** nf
aunt

ma tante
my aunt

taper vb
to bang

Arrêtez de taper sur la table.
Stop banging on the table.

Maman, il m'a tapé!
Mum, he hit me!

taper des pieds
to stamp one's feet

Ma petite sœur tape des pieds quand elle est en colère.
My little sister stamps her feet when she's angry.

taper des mains
to clap

Elle chante et nous tapons des mains.
She sings and we clap.

le **tapis** nm
rug

la **tapisserie** nf
wallpaper

tard adv
late

Il est tard.
It's late.

plus tard
later on

la **tarte** nf
tart

une tarte aux pommes
an apple tart

la **tartine** nf
slice of bread

une tartine de confiture
a slice of bread and jam

la **tasse** nf
cup

une tasse de thé
a cup of tea

a
b
c
d
e
f
g
h
i
j
k
l
m
n
o
p
q
r
s
t
u
v
w
x
y
z

le **taureau** nm
(*pl* les taureaux)
bull

le **taxi** nm
taxi

tchèque adj
Czech

te pron

> **te** *changes to* **t'** *before a vowel
> sound.*

1 you

Je te vois.
I can see you.

Il t'a vu?
Did he see you?

2 to you

Est-ce qu'il te parle en français?
Does he talk to you in French?

Elle t'a parlé?
Did she speak to you?

3 yourself

Tu vas te rendre malade.
You'll make yourself sick.

Ne t'en fais pas.
Don't worry yourself.

> **te** *is often not translated.*

**Je compte jusqu'à dix pendant
que tu te caches.**
I'll count to ten while you hide.

la **techno** nf
techno music

la **télé** nf
telly
à la télé
on telly

la **télécommande** nf
remote control

le **téléphérique** nm
cable car

le **téléphone** nm
telephone
Elle est au téléphone.
She's on the phone.

téléphoner vb
to phone
Je vais téléphoner à Claire.
I'll phone Claire.
Je peux téléphoner?
Can I make a phone call?

la **télévision** nf
television
à la télévision
on television

tellement adv
1 so
Andrew est tellement gentil.
Andrew's so nice.
2 so much
Il a tellement mangé que ...
He ate so much that ...
3 so many
Il y avait tellement de monde!
There were so many people!

la **température** nf
temperature

la **tempête** nf
storm

le **temps** nm
1 weather

Il fait mauvais temps.
The weather's bad.

Quel temps fait-il?
What's the weather like?

2 time

Je n'ai pas le temps.
I haven't got time.

de temps en temps
from time to time

en même temps
at the same time

Elle travaille à plein temps.
She works full time.

Elle travaille à temps partiel.
She works part-time.

tenir vb
to hold

Tu peux tenir la lampe, s'il te plaît?
Can you hold the torch, please?

Tiens, voilà un stylo.
Here's a pen.

le **tennis** nm
1 tennis

Elle joue au tennis.
She plays tennis.
2 tennis court

Il est au tennis.
He's at the tennis court.

les **tennis** nfpl
trainers

la **tente** nf
tent

tenu vb, *see* **tenir**

Il n'a pas tenu sa promesse.
He didn't keep his promise.

la **tenue** nf
clothes

en tenue de soirée
in evening dress

la **terminale** nf
upper sixth

Je suis en terminale.
I'm in the upper sixth.

In French secondary schools
the years are counted from
the **sixième** (youngest) to
première and **terminale**
(oldest).

terminer vb
to finish

♦ **se terminer**
to end

Les vacances se terminent demain.
The holidays end tomorrow.

le **terrain** nm

un terrain de camping
a campsite

un terrain de football
a football pitch

un terrain de golf
a golf course

un terrain de jeu
a playground

un terrain de sport
a sports ground

la **terrasse** nf
terrace

L'été, il y a beaucoup de gens assis aux terrasses de cafés.
In the summer there are a lot of people sitting at pavement cafés.

la **terre** nf
earth

la **Terre**
the Earth

par terre
on the floor

Asseyez-vous par terre.
Sit on the floor.

terrible adj
terrible

Quelque chose de terrible est arrivé.
Something terrible has happened.

pas terrible
nothing special

Ce film n'est pas terrible.
The film's nothing special.

tes pl adj
your

J'aime bien tes baskets.
I like your trainers.

le **têtard** nm
tadpole

la **tête** nf
head

têtu m adj
(f adj têtue)
stubborn

le **TGV** nm
high-speed train

French railways are very modern. **TGV**s go so fast that they are a good alternative to planes for long journeys.

le **thé** nm
tea

French people usually drink tea with lemon, rather than with milk.

le **théâtre** nm
theatre

J'aime aller au théâtre.
I like going to the theatre.

faire du théâtre
to act

Est-ce que tu as déjà fait du théâtre?
Have you ever acted?

la **théière** nf
teapot

le **thon** nm
tuna

un sandwich au thon mayonnaise
a tuna mayonnaise sandwich

tiède adj
warm

le **tien** m pron
la **tienne** f pron
yours

J'ai oublié mon stylo. Tu peux me prêter le tien?
I've forgotten my pen. Can you lend me yours?

Ce n'est pas ma raquette, c'est la tienne.
It's not my racket, it's yours.

Ce ne sont pas mes baskets, ce sont les tiennes.
These aren't my trainers, they're yours.

tiens vb, see **tenir**
Tiens, prends un biscuit.
Go on, have a biscuit.

le **tiers** nm
third

Un tiers de la classe a un chien.
A third of the class own a dog.

le tiers monde
the Third World

le **tigre** nm
tiger

le **timbre** nm
stamp

timide adj
shy

le **tire-bouchon** nm
corkscrew

la **tirelire** nf
money box

tirer vb
1 to pull

Il m'a tiré les cheveux.
He pulled my hair.

"Tirez"
"Pull"

2 to draw

Tire les rideaux s'il te plaît.
Draw the curtains please.

tirer au sort
to draw lots

Nous avons tiré au sort et j'ai gagné.
We drew lots and I won.

tirer les rois
to cut the galette des Rois

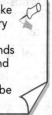

A **galette des Rois** is a cake eaten at Epiphany (January 6) which contains a little figure. The person who finds it is the king (or queen) and gets a paper crown. They then choose someone to be their queen (or king).

le **tiroir** nm
drawer

la **tisane** nf
herbal tea

le **tissu** nm
material

C'est un joli tissu.
It's nice material.

le **titre** nm
title

le **toast** nm
piece of toast

des toasts beurrés
buttered toast

le **toboggan** nm
slide

toi pron
you

Ça va? – Oui, et toi?
How are you? – Fine, and you?

J'ai faim, pas toi?
I'm hungry, aren't you?

Assieds-toi.
Sit down.

à toi

> *à toi* can mean *your turn* or *yours*.

C'est à toi de jouer.
It's your turn to play.

Est-ce que ce stylo est à toi?
Is this pen yours?

la **toile** nf
canvas

un sac de toile
a canvas bag

une toile d'araignée
a cobweb

la **toilette** nf

faire sa toilette
to have a wash

Le matin, je me lève, je fais ma toilette et je m'habille.
In the morning I get up, have a wash and get dressed.

les **toilettes** nfpl
toilet

Je peux aller aux toilettes, s'il vous plaît?
May I go to the toilet please?

toi-même pron
yourself

Tu as fait ça toi-même?
Did you do it yourself?

le **toit** nm
roof

la **tomate** nf
tomato

tomber vb
to fall

Attention, tu vas tomber!
Be careful, you'll fall!

laisser tomber

> *laisser tomber* can mean *to drop*, *to give up*, or *to let down*.

Elle a laissé tomber son stylo.
She dropped her pen.

Je vais laisser tomber le piano.
I'm going to give up the piano.

Il ne laisse jamais tomber ses amis.
He never lets his friends down.

ton m adj
(*f adj* ta, *pl adj* tes)
your

C'est ton stylo?
Is this your pen?

Ce sont tes feutres?
Are these your felt-tips?

le **tonnerre** nm
thunder

tordre vb

Je me suis tordu la cheville.
I've twisted my ankle.

la **tortue** nf
tortoise

une tortue d'eau douce
a terrapin

une tortue de mer
a turtle

tôt adv
early

Il se lève très tôt.
He gets up very early.

totalement adv
totally

toucher vb
to touch

Ne touche pas à mes livres!
Don't touch my books!

toujours adv
1 always

Il est toujours très gentil.
He's always very nice.

pour toujours
forever

2 still

Quand nous sommes revenus, il était toujours là.
When we got back he was still there.

la **tour** nf
1 tower

la Tour Eiffel
the Eiffel Tower

2 tower block

J'habite dans une tour de vingt étages.
I live in a twenty-storey tower block.

le **tour** nm
turn

C'est ton tour de jouer.
It's your turn to play.

faire un tour
to go for a walk

Allons faire un tour dans le parc.
Let's go for a walk in the park.

faire un tour en voiture
to go for a drive

faire un tour à vélo
to go for a ride

Tu veux aller faire un tour à vélo?
Do you want to go for a bike ride?

faire le tour du monde
to travel round the world

tourner vb
to turn

Tournez à droite au prochain feu.
Turn right at the lights.

le **tournesol** nm
sunflower

le **tournoi** nm
tournament

tous mpl adj, mpl pron
1 all

tous les biscuits
all the biscuits

Nous y sommes tous allés.
We all went.

2 every

tous les ans
every year

la **Toussaint** nf
All Saints' Day

La Toussaint is November 1st. On this day French people traditionally go to the cemetery to visit the graves of their relatives.

les vacances de la Toussaint
autumn half term

tousser vb
to cough

tout

> **tout** can be an adjective, an
> adverb, a pronoun or a noun.

Ⓐ m adj
(*f adj* toute)

1 all

tout le lait
all the milk

tous les livres
all the books

tout le temps
all the time

toute la journée
all day

toute la nuit
all night

tous les deux
both

**Aurélie et moi avons toutes les
deux un chien.**
Aurélie and I both have a dog.

Je les ai invités tous les trois.
I invited all three of them.

2 every

tous les jours
every day

tous les deux jours
every two days

tout le monde
everybody

tout ce qui
everything that

tout ce qui est en face de toi
everything that's in front of you

tout ce que
everything

Tu peux avoir tout ce que tu veux.
You can have everything you want.

Ⓑ adv
very

Il habite tout près.
He lives very close.

Elle est toute petite.
She's very small.

tout à l'heure

> **tout à l'heure** can either mean
> *just now* or *in a moment*.

Je l'ai vu tout à l'heure.
I saw him just now.

Je finirai ça tout à l'heure.
I'll finish it in a moment.

À tout à l'heure!
See you later!
tout de suite
straight away
tout droit
straight ahead
tout d'abord
first of all
tout à coup
suddenly
tout à fait
absolutely

Ⓒ pron
everything

Il a tout organisé.
He organized everything.

Ⓓ nm

pas du tout
not at all

toutes fpl adj, fpl pron

1 all

toutes les photos
all the photos

Je les connais toutes.
I know them all.
2 every

toutes les semaines
every week

le **tracteur** nm
tractor

traduire vb
to translate

le **train** nm
train

un train électrique
a train set

Il est en train de manger.
He's eating.

Ils sont en train de dormir.
They're sleeping.

le **traîneau** nm
(*pl* les traîneaux)
sledge

le **trait** nm
line

traiter vb

Il m'a traité d'imbécile.
He called me an idiot.

le **tramway** nm
tram

la **tranche** nf
slice

tranquille adj
quiet

Cette rue est très tranquille.
This is a very quiet street.

Tiens-toi tranquille!
Behave yourself!

Laisse-moi tranquille.
Leave me alone.

le **travail** nm
1 work

J'ai beaucoup de travail.
I've got a lot of work.
2 job

Il a un travail intéressant.
He's got an interesting job.

> *Be careful!* **travail** *does not mean the same as* **travel**.

travailler vb
to work

Elle travaille dans un bureau.
She works in an office.

> *Be careful!* **travailler** *does not mean the same as* **to travel**.

travailleur m adj
(*f adj* travailleuse)
hard-working

les **travaux** nmpl
roadworks

Il y a beaucoup de bruit à cause des travaux dans la rue.
There's a lot of noise from the roadworks.

les travaux manuels
handicrafts

le **travers** nm

à travers
through

A B C D E F G H I J K L M N O P Q R S T U V W X Y Z

Passe à travers la haie.
Go through the hedge.

la **traversée** nf
crossing

La traversée de la Manche dure une heure.
The Channel crossing takes an hour.

traverser vb
1 to cross

Traversez la rue.
Cross the street.
2 to go through

Nous avons traversé la France pour aller en Espagne.
We went through France on our way to Spain.

le **trèfle** nm
1 clover

un trèfle à quatre feuilles
a four-leaved clover
2 clubs

le roi de trèfle
the king of clubs

treize num
thirteen

Il a treize ans.
He's thirteen.

à treize heures
at 1 p.m.

le treize février
the thirteenth of February

The 24-hour clock is used in France for travel times, appointments and other formal situations.

treizième adj
thirteenth

le **tremblement de terre** nm
earthquake

trembler vb
to shake

trembler de froid
to shiver

trempé m adj
(f adj trempée)
soaking wet

la **trentaine** nf
about thirty

une trentaine de personnes
about thirty people

Il a la trentaine.
He's in his thirties.

trente num
thirty

Elle a trente ans.
She's thirty.

trente et un
thirty-one

trente-deux
thirty-two

le trente janvier
the thirtieth of January

très adv
very

le **trésor** nm
treasure

tricher vb
to cheat

Tu as triché!
You cheated!

tricolore adj
three-coloured

le drapeau tricolore
the French tricolour

le drapeau tricolore is the
French flag: its three colours
are blue, white and red.

tricoter vb
to knit

le **trimestre** nm
term

triste adj
sad

trois num
three

trois fois
three times

à trois heures du matin
at three in the morning

Elle a trois ans.
She's three.

le trois septembre
the third of September

troisième

troisième can be an adjective or a
noun.

Ⓐ adj
third

au troisième étage
on the third floor

Ⓑ nf
Year 10

Mon frère est en troisième.
My brother's in Year 10.

In French secondary schools
the years are counted from
the **sixième** (youngest) to
première and **terminale**
(oldest).

les **trois-quarts** nmpl
three-quarters

les trois-quarts de la classe
three-quarters of the class

le **trombone** nm
1 trombone

Il joue du trombone.
He plays the trombone.
2 paper clip

la **trompe** nf
trunk

A B C D E F G H I J K L M N O P Q R S T U V W X Y Z

la trompe d'un éléphant
an elephant's trunk

se **tromper** vb
to make a mistake

Je me suis trompé.
I've made a mistake.

se tromper de jour
to get the wrong day

la **trompette** nf
trumpet

Il joue de la trompette.
He plays the trumpet.

le **tronc** nm
trunk

un tronc d'arbre
a tree trunk

trop adv

1 too

Il conduit trop vite.
He drives too fast.

2 too much

J'ai trop mangé.
I've eaten too much.

trop de

> *trop de can either mean **too
> much** or **too many**.*

J'ai trop de devoirs à faire.
I've got too much homework to do.

Il y a trop de monde.
There are too many people.

le **trottoir** nm
pavement

le **trou** nm
hole

la **trousse** nf
pencil case

une trousse de toilette
a toilet bag

trouver vb

1 to find

Je ne trouve pas mes lunettes.
I can't find my glasses.

2 to think

Je trouve que c'est bête.
I think it's stupid.

♦ **se trouver**
to be

Où se trouve la poste?
Where is the post office?

le **truc** nm
thing

la **truite** nf
trout

le **T-shirt** nm
T-shirt

tu pron
you

Tu as un animal?
Have you got a pet?

le **tube** nm

1 tube

un tube de dentifrice
a tube of toothpaste

2 hit

Ça va être le tube de l'été.
It's going to be this summer's
hit.

tuer vb
to kill

la **Tunisie** nf
Tunisia

tunisien m adj
(*f adj* tunisienne)
Tunisian

le **Tunisien** nm
la **Tunisienne** nf
Tunisian

le **tunnel** nm
tunnel

le tunnel sous la Manche
the Channel Tunnel

turc nm, m adj
(*f adj* turque)
Turkish

le **Turc** nm
la **Turque** nf
Turk

la **Turquie** nf
Turkey

tutoyer vb

tutoyer quelqu'un
to call somebody "tu"

On ne doit pas tutoyer la maîtresse.
We can't call the teacher "tu".

> There are two words for "you" in French, **tu** and **vous**. Tu is the less formal one. You would call your teacher "vous" but your friend "tu".

typique adj
typical

U

l'**UE** nf
EU

un

> un can be an article or a number.

A article

> un is used in front of a masculine noun.

a

un garçon
a boy

an

un œuf
an egg

B num

> un is used for masculine nouns.

one

un citron et deux oranges
one lemon and two oranges

Combien de timbres? – Un.
How many stamps? – One.

un de mes meilleurs copains
one of my best friends

un par un
one by one

Sortez un par un.
Go out one by one.

> 🔑
>
> **Elle a un an.**
> She's one year old.

une

> une can be an article or a number.

A article

> une is used in front of a feminine noun.

a

une fille
a girl

an

une pomme
an apple

B num

> une is used for feminine nouns.

one

une pomme et deux bananes
one apple and two bananas

Combien de cartes postales? – Une.
How many postcards? – One.

une de mes meilleures copines
one of my best friends

une par une
one by one

Elles sont entrées une par une.
They went in one by one.

> 🔑
>
> **Il est une heure.**
> It's one o'clock.

l'**uniforme** nm
uniform

unique adj
unique

C'est une occasion unique.
It's a unique opportunity.

Il est fils unique.
He's an only child.
Elle est fille unique.
She's an only child.

uniquement adv
only

l'**université** nf
university

l'**usine** nf
factory

Mon père travaille dans une usine.
My dad works in a factory.

utile adj
useful

utiliser vb
to use

A
B
C
D
E
F
G
H
I
J
K
L
M
N
O
P
Q
R
S
T
U
V
W
X
Y
Z

V

va vb, see **aller**

Il va à l'école avec ses copains.
He goes to school with his friends.

Elle va partir demain.
She'll leave tomorrow.

les **vacances** nfpl
holidays

Je vais passer les vacances chez ma grand-mère.
I'm going to spend the holidays with my grandmother.

aller en vacances
to go on holiday

Où est-ce que tu vas en vacances cet été?
Where are you going on holiday this summer?

Nous partons en vacances ce soir.
We're setting off on holiday this evening.

en vacances
on holiday
les vacances de Noël
the Christmas holidays
les vacances de Pâques
the Easter holidays
les grandes vacances
the summer holidays
Bonnes vacances!
Have a good holiday!

la **vache** nf
cow

la **vague** nf
wave

le **vainqueur** nm
winner

vais vb, see **aller**

Je vais écrire à mes cousins.
I'm going to write to my cousins.

le **vaisseau** nm
(pl les vaisseaux)

un vaisseau spatial
a spaceship

la **vaisselle** nf
washing-up

Je vais faire la vaisselle.
I'll do the washing-up.

le **valet** nm
jack

le valet de carreau
the jack of diamonds

la **valise** nf
suitcase

faire sa valise
to pack

la **vallée** nf
valley

valoir vb
to be worth

Ça vaut la peine.
It's worth it.

la **vanille** nf
vanilla

vas vb, *see* **aller**

Tu vas souvent au cinéma?
Do you go to the cinema often?

vaut vb, *see* **valoir**

Ça vaut mieux.
That would be better.

le **veau** nm
(*pl* les veaux)

1 calf

la vache et son veau
the cow and her calf

2 veal

la **vedette** nf
star

une vedette de cinéma
a film star

végétarien m adj
(*f adj* végétarienne)
vegetarian

la **veille** nf
the day before

la veille de son départ
the day before he left

la **veille de Noël**
Christmas Eve

le **vélo** nm
bike

faire du vélo
to go cycling

un **vélo tout-terrain**
a mountain bike

les **vendanges** nfpl
grape harvest

le **vendeur** nm
la **vendeuse** nf
shop assistant

vendre vb
to sell

Il m'a vendu son vélo.
He sold me his bike.

"à vendre"
"for sale"

le **vendredi** nm
1 Friday

Aujourd'hui, nous sommes vendredi.
It's Friday today.

2 on Friday

Il est venu vendredi.
He came on Friday.

Je joue au foot le vendredi.
I play football on Fridays.

tous les vendredis
every Friday
le vendredi
on Fridays
vendredi dernier
last Friday
vendredi prochain
next Friday
À vendredi!
See you on Friday!
le Vendredi saint
Good Friday

vénéneux m adj
(*f adj* vénéneuse)
poisonous

venimeux m adj
(f adj venimeuse)
poisonous

un serpent venimeux
a poisonous snake

venir vb
to come

Il viendra demain.
He'll come tomorrow.

Viens t'asseoir.
Come and sit down.

venir de
to have just

Je viens de le voir.
I've just seen him.

le **vent** nm
wind

🗝
Il y a du vent.
It's windy.

le **ventre** nm
stomach

J'ai mal au ventre.
I've got tummy ache.

venu vb, see **venir**

Il est venu nous voir.
He came to see us.

le **ver** nm
worm

un ver de terre
an earthworm

le **verbe** nm
verb

le **verglas** nm
black ice

vérifier vb
to check

la **vérité** nf
truth

le **vernis** nm
varnish

le vernis à ongles
nail varnish

verra, verrai, verras vb, see
voir

on verra …
we'll see …

Je le verrai demain.
I'll see him tomorrow.

Tu verras, c'est facile.
You'll see, it's easy.

le **verre** nm
glass

une table en verre
a glass table

un verre d'eau
a glass of water

vers prep
1 towards

Il allait vers la poste.
He was going towards the post
office.

2 at about

Je me couche vers huit heures.
I go to bed at about eight o'clock.

vert

> **vert** can be an adjective or a noun.

Ⓐ m adj
(*f adj* verte)
green

J'ai les yeux verts.
I've got green eyes.
Ⓑ nm
green

J'aime le vert.
I like the colour green.

la **veste** nf
jacket

une veste en jean
a denim jacket

le **vestiaire** nm
1 changing room
2 cloakroom

les **vêtements** nmpl
clothes

le/la **vétérinaire** nm/f
vet

Il est vétérinaire.
He's a vet.

le **veuf** nm
widower

veulent, veut vb, *see*
vouloir

Ils ne veulent pas jouer.
They don't want to play.

Qui veut jouer?
Who wants to play?

la **veuve** nf
widow

veux vb, *see* **vouloir**

Tu veux aller au cinéma?
Do you want to go to the cinema?

la **viande** nf
meat

la viande hachée
mince

vide adj
empty

vidéo m, f, pl adj
video

une cassette vidéo
a video cassette

un jeu vidéo
a video game

le **vidéoclip** nm
music video

le **vidéoclub** nm
video shop

vider vb
to empty

la **vie** nf
life

vieil m adj

> **vieux** in the singular changes to
> **vieil** before a vowel sound.

old

un vieil arbre
an old tree

un vieil homme
an old man

vieille

> **vieille** can be an adjective or a noun.

Ⓐ f adj
old

une vieille dame
an old lady

Elle est plus vieille que moi.
She's older than me.

Ⓑ nf
old woman

une petite vieille
a little old lady

vieillir vb
to age

viendrai, viens vb, *see* venir

Je viendrai dès que possible.
I'll come as soon as possible.

Viens ici!
Come here!

vieux

> **vieux** can be an adjective or a noun.

Ⓐ m, mpl adj
(*f adj* vieille)
old

un vieux monsieur
an old gentleman

Il est plus vieux que moi.
He's older than me.

> **vieux** in the singular changes to **vieil** before a vowel sound.

un vieil homme
an old man

Ⓑ nm
old man

un petit vieux
a little old man

les vieux
old people

vif m adj
(*f adj* vive)
bright

rouge vif
bright red

la **vigne** nf
vine

des champs de vigne
vineyards

le **vigneron** nm
wine grower

le **vignoble** nm
vineyard

vilain m adj
(*f adj* vilaine)
1 naughty

C'est très vilain de dire des mensonges.
It's very naughty to tell lies.

2 horrible

Il a de vilaines dents.
He's got horrible teeth.

une vilaine sorcière
an evil witch

le **village** nm
village

la **ville** nf
town

Je vais en ville.
I'm going into town.

une grande ville
a city

le **vin** nm
wine

du vin blanc
white wine

du vin rouge
red wine

le **vinaigre** nm
vinegar

la **vinaigrette** nf
French dressing

vingt num
twenty

Elle a vingt ans.
She's twenty.

à vingt heures
at 8 p.m.

The 24-hour clock is used in France for travel times, appointments and other formal situations.

vingt et un
twenty-one

vingt-deux
twenty-two

le vingt février
the twentieth of February

la **vingtaine** nf
about twenty

une vingtaine de personnes
about twenty people

Il a la vingtaine.
He's about twenty.

vingtième adj
twentieth

violet

violet can be an adjective or a noun.

A m adj
(f adj violette)
purple

une robe violette
a purple dress

B nm
purple

J'aime le violet.
I like the colour purple.

le **violon** nm
violin

Je joue du violon.
I play the violin.

le **violoncelle** nm
cello

Elle joue du violoncelle.
She plays the cello.

la **vipère** nf
viper

la **virgule** nf
comma

vis vb, see **vivre**

Je vis en Écosse.
I live in Scotland.

le **visage** nm
face

Elle a le visage rond.
She's got a round face.

la **visite** nf

rendre visite à quelqu'un
to visit somebody

Je vais rendre visite à mon grand-père.
I'm going to visit my grandfather.

une visite guidée
a guided tour

visiter vb
to visit

Nous avons visité des châteaux.
We visited some castles.

vit vb, *see* **vivre**
Il vit chez ses parents.
He lives with his parents.

vite adv
1 quick

Vite, ils arrivent!
Quick, they're coming!

Prenons la voiture, ça ira plus vite.
Let's take the car, it'll be quicker.

2 fast

Il roule trop vite.
He drives too fast.

Il court plus vite que moi.
He runs faster than me.

3 soon

Il va vite oublier.
He'll soon forget.

la **vitesse** nf
1 speed

en vitesse
quickly

2 gear

J'ai un vélo à dix vitesses.
I've got a bike with ten gears.

le **viticulteur** nm
wine grower

le **vitrail** nm
(*pl* les vitraux)
stained-glass window

la **vitre** nf
window

la **vitrine** nf
shop window

vivant m adj
(*f adj* vivante)
living

vive

> **vive** can be an adjective or an exclamation.

A f adj
bright

les couleurs vives
bright colours

B excl
Vive le roi!
Long live the king!

vivement excl
Vivement les vacances!
Roll on the holidays!

vivre vb
to live

J'aimerais vivre à l'étranger.
I'd like to live abroad.

le **vocabulaire** nm
vocabulary

le **vœu** nm
(*pl* les vœux)
wish

faire un vœu
to make a wish

Meilleurs vœux de bonne année!
Best wishes for the New Year!

voici prep
this is

Voici mon frère et voilà ma sœur.
This is my brother and that's my sister.

voilà prep
1 there is

Tiens! Voilà Paul.
Look! There's Paul.

Les voilà!
There they are!

Voilà!
There you are!

2 that is

Voilà ma sœur.
That's my sister.

la **voile** nf
sailing

faire de la voile
to go sailing

un bateau à voile
a sailing boat

le **voilier** nm
sailing boat

voir vb
to see

Venez me voir quand vous serez à Paris.
Come and see me when you're in Paris.

faire voir
to show

Il m'a fait voir sa collection de timbres.
He showed me his stamp collection.

vois vb, *see* **voir**

Je n'y vois rien sans mes lunettes.
I can't see anything without my glasses.

le **voisin** nm
la **voisine** nf
neighbour

la **voiture** nf
car

une voiture de sport
a sports car

la **voix** nf
(*pl* les voix)
voice

le **vol** nm
flight

voler vb
1 to fly

2 to steal

On a volé mon appareil photo.
My camera's been stolen.

le **volet** nm
shutter

Traditional French houses have wooden shutters.

le **voleur** nm
la **voleuse** nf
thief

Au voleur!
Stop thief!

le **volley** nm
volleyball

jouer au volley
to play volleyball

le/la **volontaire** nm/f
volunteer

vomir vb
to vomit

vont vb, *see* **aller**

Ils vont à la piscine cet après-midi.
They're going to the swimming
pool this afternoon.

vos pl adj
your

Rangez vos jouets, les enfants!
Put your toys away, children.

J'ai trouvé vos clés, M. Durand.
I've found your keys, Mr Durand.

voter vb
to vote

votre adj
(*pl adj* vos)
your

**C'est votre manteau, Mme
Leblanc?**
Is this your coat, Mrs Leblanc?

Restez à votre place, les enfants!
Stay in your seats children.

le/la **vôtre** m/f pron
yours

**À qui est cette écharpe? C'est la
vôtre?**
Whose is this scarf? Is it yours?

**Ce ne sont pas mes clés, ce sont
les vôtres.**
These aren't my keys, they're yours.

voudrais vb, *see* **vouloir**

**Je voudrais deux litres de lait, s'il
vous plaît.**
I'd like two litres of milk, please.

vouloir vb
to want

Elle veut un vélo pour Noël.
She wants a bike for Christmas.

Je ne veux pas de dessert.
I don't want any pudding.

On va au cinéma? – Si tu veux.
Shall we go to the cinema? – If you
like.

voulu vb, *see* **vouloir**

Elle n'a pas voulu venir.
She didn't want to come.

vous pron

1 you

Vous voulez de l'eau, Monsieur?
Would you like some water, sir?

**Vous devez faire attention, les
enfants.**
You must be careful, children.

2 to you

Je vous écrirai bientôt.
I'll write to you soon.

3 yourself

Vous vous êtes fait mal?
Have you hurt yourself?

vous-même
yourself

Vous l'avez fait vous-même?
Did you do it yourself?

vouvoyer vb

vouvoyer quelqu'un
to call somebody "vous"

**Est-ce que je dois vouvoyer ta
sœur?**
Should I say "vous" to your sister?

*There are two words for "you" in
French, **tu** and **vous**. **Vous** is the
more formal one. You would call
your teacher "vous" but your
friend "tu".*

le **voyage** nm
journey

Avez-vous fait bon voyage?
Did you have a good journey?

Bon voyage!
Have a good trip!

---

voyager vb
to travel

---

voyez vb, *see* **voir**

Vous voyez l'arc-en-ciel là-bas?
Can you see the rainbow over there?

voyons vb, *see* **voir**

Nous ne les voyons pas souvent.
We don't see them very often.

vrai adj
true

une histoire vraie
a true story

C'est vrai?
Is that true?

---

vraiment adv
really

---

le **VTT** nm
mountain bike

---

vu vb, *see* **voir**

J'ai vu un film au cinéma.
I saw a film at the cinema.

---

la **vue** nf
1 eyesight

2 view

Il y a une belle vue d'ici.
There's a lovely view from here

A
B
C
D
E
F
G
H
I
J
K
L
M
N
O
P
Q
R
S
T
U
V
W
X
Y
Z

W

b
c
d
e
f
g
h
i
j
k
l
m
n
o
p
q
r
s
t
u
v
w
x
y
z

wallon nm, m adj
(*f adj* wallonne)
Walloon

le **Wallon** nm
la **Wallonne** nf
Walloon

les **Wallons** nmpl
Walloons

> Walloons are Belgian people
> who speak French, one of
> the two languages spoken in
> Belgium. The other language
> is Flemish, which is spoken
> by **les Flamands**.

la **Wallonie** nf
French-speaking Belgium

les **W.-C.** nmpl
toilet

Où sont les W.-C.?
Where's the toilet?

> *The French word **W.-C.** is
> pronounced "vay-say".*

le **Web** nm
Web

le **week-end** nm
weekend

Ce week-end, nous allons à Paris.
We're going to Paris this weekend.

**Qu'est-ce que tu as fait pendant
le week-end?**
What did you do at the weekend?

> **Bon week-end!**
> Have a nice weekend!

le **western** nm
western

X

le **xylophone** nm
xylophone

Elle joue du xylophone.
She plays the xylophone.

Y

y pron
1 there

Nous y sommes allés l'été dernier.
We went there last summer.

Vas-y!
Go on!

2 it

Arrête d'y penser!
Stop thinking about it!

le **yaourt** nm
yoghurt

un yaourt nature
a plain yoghurt

un yaourt aux fruits
a fruit yoghurt

les **yeux** nmpl
eyes

Elle a les yeux bleus.
She's got blue eyes.

le **yoga** nm
yoga

Elle fait du yoga.
She does yoga.

youpi excl
yippee!

le **yoyo** nm
yo-yo

Z

le **zèbre** nm
zebra

le **zéro** nm
zero

Ils ont gagné trois à zéro.
They won three-nil.

la **zone** nf
zone

une zone industrielle
an industrial estate

le **zoo** nm
zoo

zut excl
oh heck!

LANGUAGE PLUS

ANIMALS • LES ANIMAUX

● Pets

budgie *n* la perruche *f*
canary *n* le canari *m*
cat *n* le chat *m* / la chatte *f*
dog *n* le chien *m* / la chienne *f*
ferret *n* le furet *m*
gerbil *n* la gerbille *f*
goldfish *n* le poisson rouge *m*
guinea pig *n* le cochon d'Inde *m*
hamster *n* le hamster *m*
kitten *n* le chaton *m*
mouse *n* la souris *f*
parrot *n* le perroquet *m*
poodle *n* le caniche *m*
puppy *n* le chiot *m*
rabbit *n* le lapin *m*
rat *n* le rat *m*
stick insect *n* le phasme *m*
tortoise *n* la tortue *f*

● Farm animals

bull *n* le taureau *m*
calf *n* le veau *m*
chick *n* le poussin *m*
chicken *n* la poule *f*
cock *n* le coq *m*
cow *n* la vache *f*
donkey *n* l'âne *m*
duck *n* le canard *m*
goat *n* la chèvre *f*
goose *n* l'oie *f*
hen *n* la poule *f*
horse *n* le cheval *m*
lamb *n* l'agneau *m*
mare *n* la jument *f*
pig *n* le cochon *m*
pony *n* le poney *m*
ram *n* le bélier *m*
sheep *n* le mouton *m*
sheepdog *n* le chien de berger *m*
turkey *n* le dindon *m*

● Other animals

ant *n* la fourmi *f*
bat *n* la chauve-souris *f*
bear *n* l'ours *m*
bee *n* l'abeille *f*
beetle *n* le scarabée *m*
bird *n* l'oiseau *m*
butterfly *n* le papillon *m*
camel *n* le chameau *m*
crab *n* le crabe *m*
crocodile *n* le crocodile *m*
cub *n* le petit *m*
dinosaur *n* le dinosaure *m*
dolphin *n* le dauphin *m*
dragon *n* le dragon *m*
elephant *n* l'éléphant *m*
fish *n* le poisson *m*
fly *n* la mouche *f*

Animals • Les animaux

fox *n* le <u>renard</u> *m*
frog *n* la <u>grenouille</u> *f*
giraffe *n* la <u>girafe</u> *f*
gorilla *n* le <u>gorille</u> *m*
hare *n* le <u>lièvre</u> *m*
hedgehog *n* le <u>hérisson</u> *m*
hippo *n* l'<u>hippopotame</u> *m*
insect *n* l'<u>insecte</u> *m*
jellyfish *n* la <u>méduse</u> *f*
kangaroo *n* le <u>kangourou</u> *m*
ladybird *n* la <u>coccinelle</u> *f*
leopard *n* le <u>léopard</u> *m*

lion *n* le <u>lion</u> *m*
lizard *n* le <u>lézard</u> *m*
mammoth *n* le <u>mammouth</u> *m*
midge *n* le <u>moucheron</u> *m*
mole *n* la <u>taupe</u> *f*
monkey *n* le <u>singe</u> *m*
mosquito *n* le <u>moustique</u> *m*
moth *n* le <u>papillon de nuit</u> *m*
octopus *n* la <u>pieuvre</u> *f*

ostrich *n* l'<u>autruche</u> *f*
owl *n* le <u>hibou</u> *m*
panther *n* la <u>panthère</u> *f*
peacock *n* le <u>paon</u> *m*
penguin *n* le <u>pingouin</u> *m*
pheasant *n* le <u>faisan</u> *m*
pigeon *n* le <u>pigeon</u> *m*
polar bear *n* l'<u>ours blanc</u> *m*
red deer *n* le <u>cerf</u> *m*
reindeer *n* le <u>renne</u> *m*
rhinoceros *n* le <u>rhinocéros</u> *m*
seagull *n* la <u>mouette</u> *f*
seal *n* le <u>phoque</u> *m*
shark *n* le <u>requin</u> *m*
slug *n* la <u>limace</u> *f*
snail *n* l'<u>escargot</u> *m*
snake *n* le <u>serpent</u> *m*
spider *n* l'<u>araignée</u> *f*
squirrel *n* l'<u>écureuil</u> *m*
swan *n* le <u>cygne</u> *m*
tadpole *n* le <u>têtard</u> *m*
tiger *n* le <u>tigre</u> *m*
toad *n* le <u>crapaud</u> *m*
trout *n* la <u>truite</u> *f*
turtle *n* la <u>tortue</u> *f*
wasp *n* la <u>guêpe</u> *f*
whale *n* la <u>baleine</u> *f*
wolf *n* le <u>loup</u> *m*
worm *n* le <u>ver</u> *m*
zebra *n* le <u>zèbre</u> *m*

BODY • LE CORPS

ankle *n* la cheville *f*
arm *n* le bras *m*
back *n* le dos *m*
beard *n* la barbe *f*
blood *n* le sang *m*
body *n* le corps *m*
bottom *n* le derrière *m*
brain *n* le cerveau *m*
cheek *n* la joue *f*
chest *n* la poitrine *f*
chin *n* le menton *m*
ear *n* l'oreille *f*
elbow *n* le coude *m*
eye *n* l'œil *m*
eyebrow *n* le sourcil *m*
eyelash *n* le cil *m*
eyelid *n* la paupière *f*
face *n* la figure *f*
finger *n* le doigt *m*
fist *n* le poing *m*
foot *n* le pied *m*
forehead *n* le front *m*
freckles *npl* les taches de
  rousseur *fpl*
fringe *n* la frange *f*
hair *n* les cheveux *mpl*
hand *n* la main *f*
head *n* la tête *f*
heart *n* le cœur *m*
heel *n* le talon *m*
hip *n* la hanche *f*
jaw *n* la mâchoire *f*
knee *n* le genou *m*

leg *n* la jambe *f*
lip *n* la lèvre *f*
moustache *n* la moustache *f*
mouth *n* la bouche *f*
muscle *n* le muscle *m*
nail *n* l'ongle *m*
neck *n* le cou *m*
nose *n* le nez *m*
palm *n* la paume *f*
rib *n* la côte *f*
shin *n* le tibia *m*
shoulder *n* l'épaule *f*
skeleton *n* le squelette *m*
skin *n* la peau *f*
skull *n* le crâne *m*
stomach *n* l'estomac *m*
thigh *n* la cuisse *f*
throat *n* la gorge *f*
thumb *n* le pouce *m*
toe *n* le doigt de pied *m*
tongue *n* la langue *f*

tonsils *npl* les amygdales *fpl*
tooth *n* la dent *f*
tummy *n* le ventre *m*
waist *n* la taille *f*
wrist *n* le poignet *m*

CLOTHES • LES VÊTEMENTS

anorak *n* l'anorak *m*
apron *n* le tablier *m*
ballet shoes *npl* les chaussons de danse *mpl*
baseball cap *n* la casquette de base-ball *f*

belt *n* la ceinture *f*
bikini *n* le bikini *m*
blazer *n* le blazer *m*
blouse *n* le chemisier *m*
boots *npl* les bottes *fpl*
bow tie *n* le nœud papillon *m*
boxer shorts *npl* le caleçon *m*
bra *n* le soutien-gorge *m*
cagoule *n* le K-way® *m*
cap *n* la casquette *f*
cardigan *n* le cardigan *m*
clothes *npl* les vêtements *mpl*
coat *n* le manteau *m*
dinner jacket *n* le smoking *m*
dress *n* la robe *f*
dressing gown *n* la robe de chambre *f*

dungarees *npl* la salopette *f*
fleece *n* la laine polaire *f*
flippers *npl* les palmes *fpl*
football boots *npl* les chaussures de foot *fpl*
football shirt *n* le maillot de foot *m*
glasses *npl* les lunettes *fpl*
glove *n* le gant *m*
goggles *npl* les lunettes de plongée *fpl*
hat *n* le chapeau *m*
helmet *n* le casque *m*
hood *n* la capuche *f*
jacket *n* la veste *f*
jeans *npl* le jean *m*
jersey *n* le pull-over *m*
jumper *n* le pull *m*
kilt *n* le kilt *m*
knickers *npl* la culotte *f*
leather jacket *n* la veste en cuir *f*
leggings *npl* le caleçon *m*
miniskirt *n* la mini-jupe *f*
nightdress *n* la chemise de nuit *f*
nightie *n* la chemise de nuit *f*
nightshirt *n* la chemise de nuit *f*
overalls *npl* le bleu de travail *m*
panties *npl* le slip *m*
pants *npl* le slip *m*

plimsolls *npl* les chaussons de gym *mpl*

polo-neck *n* le pull à col roulé *m*

polo shirt *n* le polo *m*

pullover *n* le pull *m*

pyjamas *npl* le pyjama *m*

raincoat *n* l'imperméable *m*

sandals *npl* les sandales *fpl*

scarf *n* l'écharpe *f*

shirt *n* la chemise *f*

shoes *npl* les chaussures *fpl*

shorts *npl* le short *m*

ski boots *npl* les chaussures de ski *fpl*

skirt *n* la jupe *f*

slippers *npl* les chaussons *mpl*

sock *n* la chaussette *f*

suit *n* (for a man) le costume *m*, (for a woman) le tailleur *m*

sunglasses *npl* les lunettes de soleil *fpl*

sweater *n* le pull *m*

sweatshirt *n* le sweat *m*

swimming costume *n* le maillot de bain *m*

swimming trunks *npl* le maillot de bain *m*

swimsuit *n* le maillot de bain *m*

tee-shirt *n* le tee-shirt *m*

tie *n* la cravate *f*

tights *npl* le collant *m*

top *n* le haut *m*

tracksuit *n* le jogging *m*

trainers *npl* les baskets *fpl*

trousers *npl* le pantalon *m*

trunks *npl* le maillot de bain *m*

T-shirt *n* le tee-shirt *m*

underpants *npl* le slip *m*

underskirt *n* le jupon *m*

underwear *n* les sous-vêtements *mpl*

uniform *n* l'uniforme *m*

vest *n* le maillot de corps *m*

waistcoat *n* le gilet *m*

wellingtons *npl* les bottes en caoutchouc *fpl*

wetsuit *n* la combinaison de plongée *f*

COLOURS • LES COULEURS

beige *adj* <u>beige</u>

black *adj* <u>noir</u> *m adj* / <u>noire</u> *f adj*

blonde *adj* <u>blond</u> *m adj* / <u>blonde</u> *f adj*

blue *adj* <u>bleu</u> *m adj* / <u>bleue</u> *f adj*

brown *adj* <u>marron</u> *m, f, pl adj*

cream *adj* <u>crème</u> *m, f, pl adj*

green *adj* <u>vert</u> *m adj* / <u>verte</u> *f adj*

grey *adj* <u>gris</u> *m adj* / <u>grise</u> *f adj*

maroon *adj* <u>bordeaux</u> *m, f, pl adj*

navy *adj* <u>bleu marine</u> *m, f, pl adj*

navy blue *adj* <u>bleu marine</u> *m, f, pl adj*

orange *adj* <u>orange</u> *m, f, pl adj*

pink *adj* <u>rose</u>

purple *adj* <u>violet</u> *m adj* / <u>violette</u> *f adj*

red *adj* <u>rouge</u>

turquoise *adj* <u>turquoise</u> *m, f, pl adj*

white *adj* <u>blanc</u> *m adj* / <u>blanche</u> *f adj*

yellow *adj* <u>jaune</u>

aunt, aunty *n* la <u>tante</u> *f*
brother *n* le <u>frère</u> *m*
brother-in-law *n* le <u>beau-</u>
<u>frère</u> *m*
cousin *n* le <u>cousin</u> *m* / la
<u>cousine</u> *f*
dad *n* le <u>père</u> *m*
daddy *n* le <u>papa</u> *m*
daughter *n* la <u>fille</u> *f*
daughter-in-law *n* la <u>belle-</u>
<u>fille</u> *f*
family *n* la <u>famille</u> *f*
father *n* le <u>père</u> *m*
father-in-law *n* le <u>beau-père</u> *m*
fiancé *n* le <u>fiancé</u> *m*
fiancée *n* la <u>fiancée</u> *f*

godfather *n* le <u>parrain</u> *m*
godmother *n* la <u>marraine</u> *f*
grandchildren *npl* les <u>petits-</u>
<u>enfants</u> *mpl*
granddad *n* le <u>papi</u> *m*
granddaughter *n* la <u>petite-</u>
<u>fille</u> *f*
grandfather *n* le <u>grand-père</u> *m*

grandma *n* la <u>mamie</u> *f*
grandmother *n* la <u>grand-</u>
<u>mère</u> *f*
grandpa *n* le <u>papi</u> *m*
grandparents *npl* les
<u>grands-parents</u> *mpl*
grandson *n* le <u>petit-fils</u> *m*
granny *n* la <u>mamie</u> *f*
half-brother *n* le <u>demi-frère</u> *m*
half-sister *n* la <u>demi-sœur</u> *f*
husband *n* le <u>mari</u> *m*
mother *n* la <u>mère</u> *f*
mother-in-law *n* la <u>belle-</u>
<u>mère</u> *f*
mum *n* la <u>mère</u> *f*
mummy *n* la <u>maman</u> *f*
nephew *n* le <u>neveu</u> *m*
niece *n* la <u>nièce</u> *f*
parent *n* le <u>parent</u> *m*
sister *n* la <u>sœur</u> *f*
sister-in-law *n* la <u>belle-sœur</u> *f*
son *n* le <u>fils</u> *m*
son-in-law *n* le <u>gendre</u> *m*
stepbrother *n* le <u>demi-frère</u> *m*
stepdaughter *n* la <u>belle-fille</u> *f*
stepfather *n* le <u>beau-père</u> *m*
stepmother *n* la <u>belle-mère</u> *f*
stepsister *n* la <u>demi-sœur</u> *f*
stepson *n* le <u>beau-fils</u> *m*
uncle *n* l'<u>oncle</u> *m*
wife *n* la <u>femme</u> *f*

DAYS AND DATES •
LES JOURS ET LES DATES

● **Days of the week**
Monday lundi
Tuesday mardi
Wednesday mercredi
Thursday jeudi
Friday vendredi
Saturday samedi
Sunday dimanche

● **Months of the year**
January janvier
February février
March mars
April avril
May mai
June juin
July juillet
August août
September septembre
October octobre
November novembre
December décembre

● **Special days**
April Fool's Day n le premier avril m
Boxing Day n le lendemain de Noël m
Christmas n Noël m
Christmas Day n le jour de Noël m
Christmas Eve n la veille de Noël f
Easter n Pâques fpl
Father's Day n la fête des Pères f
Hallowe'en n la veille de la Toussaint f
Mother's Day n la fête des Mères f

New Year's Day n le premier de l'An m
New Year's Eve n la Saint-Sylvestre f
Pancake Day n le mardi gras m
Passover n la Pâque juive f
Ramadan n le ramadan m
Remembrance Day n le jour de l'Armistice m
Shrove Tuesday n le mardi gras m
Valentine's Day n la Saint-Valentin f
Whitsun n la Pentecôte f

WEATHER • LE TEMPS

It's **chilly**. Il fait froid.
It's **cloudy**. Il fait gris.
It's **cold**. Il fait froid.
It's **dull**. Il fait gris.
It's **foggy**. Il y a du brouillard.
It's **freezing**. Il gèle.
It's **frosty**. Il gèle.
It's **icy**. Il gèle.
It's **misty**. Le temps est brumeux.
It's **nice**. Il fait beau.
It's **overcast**. Le ciel est couvert.
It's **raining**. Il pleut.
It's **snowing**. Il neige.
It's **stormy**. Le temps est orageux.

It's **sunny**. Il fait du soleil.

It's **warm**. Il fait chaud.
It's **windy**. Il fait du vent.

● *Seasons*
winter *n* l'<u>hiver</u> *m*
spring *n* le <u>printemps</u> *m*
summer *n* l'<u>été</u> *m*
autumn *n* l'<u>automne</u> *m*

PLACES • LES LIEUX

● *Europe*

Alps *npl* les Alpes *fpl*

Andorra *n* Andorre *f*

Atlantic *n* l'Atlantique *m*

Austria *n* l'Autriche *f*

Belgium *n* la Belgique *f*

Britain *n* la Grande-Bretagne *f*

British Isles *npl* les îles
  Britanniques *fpl*

Brittany *n* la Bretagne *f*

Brussels *n* Bruxelles

Bulgaria *n* la Bulgarie *f*

Channel *n* la Manche *f*

Channel Islands *npl* les îles
  Anglo-Normandes *fpl*

Cornwall *n* la Cornouailles *f*

Corsica *n* la Corse *f*

Cyprus *n* Chypre *f*

Czech Republic *n* la
  République Tchèque *f*

Denmark *n* le Danemark *m*

Dover *n* Douvres

Edinburgh *n* Édimbourg

Eire *n* la République d'Irlande *f*

England *n* l'Angleterre *f*

Europe *n* l'Europe *f*

Finland *n* la Finlande *f*

France *n* la France *f*

French Riviera *n* la Côte
  d'Azur *f*

Germany *n* l'Allemagne *f*

Great Britain *n* la Grande-
  Bretagne *f*

Greece *n* la Grèce *f*

Greenland *n* le Groenland *m*

Holland *n* la Hollande *f*

Hungary *n* la Hongrie *f*

Iceland *n* l'Islande *f*

Ireland *n* l'Irlande *f*

Italy *n* l'Italie *f*

Lapland *n* la Laponie *f*

Liechtenstein *n* le
  Liechtenstein *m*

London *n* Londres

Luxembourg *n* le
  Luxembourg *m*

Majorca *n* Majorque *f*

Malta *n* Malte *f*

Mediterranean *n* la
  Méditerranée *f*

Menorca *n* Minorque *f*

Monaco *n* Monaco *m*

Netherlands *npl* les
  Pays-Bas *mpl*

Normandy *n* la Normandie *f*

Northern Ireland *n* l'Irlande
  du Nord *f*

North Sea *n* la mer du Nord *f*

Norway *n* la Norvège *f*

Orkneys *npl* les Orcades *fpl*

Poland *n* la Pologne *f*

Portugal *n* le Portugal *m*

Pyrenees *npl* les Pyrénées *fpl*

Romania *n* la Roumanie *f*

Russia *n* la Russie *f*

Scandinavia *n* la Scandinavie *f*

Scotland n l'Écosse f

Shetland Islands npl les îles Shetland fpl
Sicily n la Sicile f
Spain n l'Espagne f
Sweden n la Suède f
Switzerland n la Suisse f
Turkey n la Turquie f
UK n le Royaume-Uni m
Ulster n l'Irlande du Nord f
United Kingdom n le Royaume-Uni m
Wales n le pays de Galles m

● *Rest of the world*
Africa n l'Afrique f
Algeria n l'Algérie f
America n l'Amérique f
Australia n l'Australie f
Brazil n le Brésil m
Canada n le Canada m
Caribbean n les Caraïbes fpl
China n la Chine f
Egypt n l'Égypte f
Ethiopia n l'Éthiopie f
India n l'Inde f
Iran n l'Iran m

Iraq n l'Iraq m
Israel n Israël m
Japan n le Japon m
Jordan n la Jordanie f
Korea n la Corée f
Lebanon n le Liban m
Libya n la Libye f
Malaysia n la Malaisie f
Mexico n le Mexique m
Middle East n le Moyen-Orient m
Morocco n le Maroc m
New Zealand n la Nouvelle-Zélande f
Nigeria n le Nigéria m
North America n l'Amérique du Nord f
North Pole n le pôle Nord m
Pacific n le Pacifique m
Pakistan n le Pakistan m
Palestine n la Palestine f
Saudi Arabia n l'Arabie Saoudite f
South Africa n l'Afrique du Sud f
South America n l'Amérique du Sud f
South Pole n le pôle Sud m
Tunisia n la Tunisie f
United States n les États-Unis mpl
USA n les USA mpl
Vietnam n le Viêt-Nam m
West Indies npl les Antilles fpl

FOOD • LA NOURRITURE

● *Savoury*

bacon *n* le <u>bacon</u> *m*

baked beans *npl* les <u>haricots</u> <u>blancs en sauce</u> *mpl*

baked potato *n* la <u>pomme</u> de terre <u>cuite au four</u> *f*

beans *npl* les <u>haricots blancs</u> <u>en sauce</u> *mpl*

beef *n* le <u>bœuf</u> *m*

boiled egg *n* l'œuf à la <u>coque</u> *m*

bread *n* le <u>pain</u> *m*

breakfast *n* le <u>petit déjeuner</u> *m*

brown bread *n* le <u>pain</u> <u>complet</u> *m*

bun *n* le <u>petit pain au lait</u> *m*

burger *n* le <u>hamburger</u> *m*

butter *n* le <u>beurre</u> *m*

casserole *n* le <u>ragoût</u> *m*

cereal *n* les <u>céréales</u> *fpl*

cheese *n* le <u>fromage</u> *m*

cheeseburger *n* le <u>cheeseburger</u> *m*

chicken *n* le <u>poulet</u> *m*

chips *npl* les <u>frites</u> *fpl*

chop *n* la <u>côte</u> *f*

cod *n* le <u>cabillaud</u> *m*

coleslaw *n* la <u>salade de chou</u> cru à la mayonnaise *f*

cornflakes *npl* les <u>corn-flakes</u> *mpl*

cream cheese *n* le <u>fromage</u> à tartiner *m*

crisps *npl* les <u>chips</u> *fpl*

curry *n* le <u>curry</u> *m*

dinner *n* le <u>dîner</u> *m*

egg *n* l'<u>œuf</u> *m*

fish *n* le <u>poisson</u> *m*

fish fingers *npl* les <u>bâtonnets</u> de poisson *mpl*

flan *n* la <u>quiche</u> *f*

French fries *npl* les <u>frites</u> *fpl*

fried egg *n* l'œuf sur le plat *m*

garlic *n* l'<u>ail</u> *m*

gravy *n* la <u>sauce</u> *f*

haddock *n* l'églefin *m*

ham *n* le <u>jambon</u> *m*

hamburger *n* le <u>hamburger</u> *m*

hard-boiled egg *n* l'œuf dur *m*

herbs *npl* les <u>fines herbes</u> *fpl*

hot dog *n* le <u>hot-dog</u> *m*

jacket potato *n* la <u>pomme</u> de terre cuite au four *f*

ketchup *n* le <u>ketchup</u> *m*

lamb *n* l'<u>agneau</u> *m*

lentil *n* la <u>lentille</u> *f*

liver *n* le <u>foie</u> *m*

loaf *n* le pain *m*
lobster *n* le homard *m*
lunch *n* le déjeuner *m*
macaroni *n* les macaronis *mpl*
margarine *n* la margarine *f*
mashed potatoes *npl* la
 purée *f*
mayonnaise *n* la mayonnaise
 f
meat *n* la viande *f*
mince *n* la viande hachée *f*
muesli *n* le muesli *m*
mussel *n* la moule *f*
mustard *n* la moutarde *f*
noodles *npl* les nouilles *fpl*
olive *n* l'olive *f*
olive oil *n* l'huile d'olive *f*
omelette *n* l'omelette *f*
parsley *n* le persil *m*
pasta *n* les pâtes *fpl*
pâté *n* le pâté *m*
peanut butter *n* le beurre
 de cacahuètes *m*
pepper *n* le poivre *m*
pie *n* la tourte *f*
pizza *n* la pizza *f*
poached egg *n* l'œuf poché
 m
pork *n* le porc *m*
porridge *n* le porridge *m*
prawn cocktail *n* le cocktail
 de crevettes *m*
prawns *npl* les crevettes *fpl*
rice *n* le riz *m*

roll *n* le petit pain *m*
salad *n* la salade *f*
salad cream *n* la mayonnaise *f*
salad dressing *n* la
 vinaigrette *f*
salami *n* le salami *m*
salmon *n* le saumon *m*
salt *n* le sel *m*
sandwich *n* le sandwich *m*
sardine *n* la sardine *f*
sauce *n* la sauce *f*
sausage *n* la saucisse *f*
scampi *n* les scampi *mpl*
scrambled eggs *npl* les
 œufs brouillés *mpl*
seafood *n* les fruits de mer
 mpl

shepherd's pie *n* le hachis
 Parmentier *m*
shrimps *npl* les crevettes *fpl*
soft-boiled egg *n* l'œuf à la
 coque *m*
soup *n* la soupe *f*
soy sauce *n* la sauce de soja *f*
spaghetti *n* les spaghettis *mpl*
steak *n* le steak *m*
stew *n* le ragoût *m*

supper *n* le <u>dîner</u> *m*
toast *n* le <u>pain grillé</u> *m*
toastie *n* le <u>sandwich chaud</u> *m*
tuna *n* le <u>thon</u> *m*
turkey *n* la <u>dinde</u> *f*
vinegar *n* le <u>vinaigre</u> *m*
wholemeal bread *n* le <u>pain complet</u> *m*

● *Sweet*

afters *n* le <u>dessert</u> *m*
apple pie *n* la <u>tarte aux pommes</u> *f*
biscuit *n* le <u>gâteau sec</u> *m*
bubble gum *n* le <u>chewing-gum</u> *m*
cake *n* le <u>gâteau</u> *m*

candyfloss *n* la <u>barbe à papa</u> *f*
caramel *n* le <u>caramel</u> *m*
chewing gum *n* le <u>chewing-gum</u> *m*
chocolate *n* le <u>chocolat</u> *m*
cone *n* le <u>cornet</u> *m*
cream *n* la <u>crème</u> *f*
cream cake *n* le <u>gâteau à la crème</u> *m*
custard *n* la <u>crème anglaise</u> *f*
dessert *n* le <u>dessert</u> *m*

doughnut *n* le <u>beignet</u> *m*
flan *n* la <u>tarte</u> *f*
fruit salad *n* la <u>salade de fruits</u> *f*
honey *n* le <u>miel</u> *m*
ice cream *n* la <u>glace</u> *f*
ice lolly *n* la <u>glace à l'eau</u> *f*
jam *n* la <u>confiture</u> *f*
jelly *n* la <u>gelée</u> *f*
lollipop *n* la <u>sucette</u> *f*
marmalade *n* la <u>confiture d'oranges</u> *f*
marzipan *n* la <u>pâte d'amandes</u> *f*
meringue *n* la <u>meringue</u> *f*
mince pie *n* la <u>tartelette de Noël</u> *f*
mousse *n* la <u>mousse</u> *f*
pancake *n* la <u>crêpe</u> *f*
popcorn *n* le <u>pop-corn</u> *m*
pudding *n* le <u>dessert</u> *m*
rice pudding *n* le <u>riz au lait</u> *m*
scone *n* le <u>scone</u> *m*
sponge cake *n* le <u>biscuit de Savoie</u> *m*
sugar *n* le <u>sucre</u> *m*
tart *n* la <u>tarte</u> *f*
toffee *n* le <u>caramel</u> *m*
trifle *n* le <u>diplomate</u> *m*
vanilla *n* la <u>vanille</u> *f*
whipped cream *n* la <u>crème fouettée</u> *f*
yoghurt *n* le <u>yaourt</u> *m*

FRUIT AND VEGETABLES •
LES FRUITS ET LÉGUMES

apple *n* la pomme *f*
aubergine *n* l'aubergine *f*
avocado *n* l'avocat *m*
banana *n* la banane *f*
beetroot *n* la betterave
  rouge *f*
blackberry *n* la mûre *f*
blackcurrant *n* le cassis *m*
broccoli *n* les brocolis *mpl*
Brussels sprouts *npl* les
  choux de Bruxelles *mpl*
cabbage *n* le chou *m*
carrot *n* la carotte *f*
cauliflower *n* le chou-fleur *m*
celery *n* le céleri *m*
cherry *n* la cerise *f*
coconut *n* la noix de coco *f*
corn on the cob *n* l'épi de
  maïs *m*
courgette *n* la courgette *f*
cress *n* le cresson *m*
cucumber *n* le concombre *m*
currant *n* le raisin sec *m*
gooseberry *n* la groseille à
  maquereau *f*
grapefruit *n* le
  pamplemousse *m*
grapes *npl* le raisin *m*
green beans *npl* les haricots
  verts *mpl*
leek *n* le poireau *m*
lemon *n* le citron *m*

lettuce *n* la salade *f*
lime *n* le citron vert *m*
mango *n* la mangue *f*
melon *n* le melon *m*
mushroom *n* le champignon *m*
onion *n* l'oignon *m*
orange *n* l'orange *f*
parsnip *n* le panais *m*
pea *n* le petit pois *m*
peach *n* la pêche *f*
pear *n* la poire *f*
pepper *n* le poivron *m*
pineapple *n* l'ananas *m*
plum *n* la prune *f*
potato *n* la pomme de terre *f*
pumpkin *n* le potiron *m*
radish *n* le radis *m*
raisin *n* le raisin sec *m*
raspberry *n* la framboise *f*
redcurrant *n* la groseille *f*
rhubarb *n* la rhubarbe *f*
satsuma *n* la satsuma *f*
spinach *n* les épinards *mpl*
sprouts *npl* les choux de
  Bruxelles *mpl*
strawberry *n* la fraise *f*
sultana *n* le raisin sec *m*
sweetcorn *n* le maïs *m*
tangerine *n* la mandarine *f*
tomato *n* la tomate *f*
turnip *n* le navet *m*
watermelon *n* la pastèque *f*

DRINKS • LES BOISSONS

apple juice n le jus de pomme m

beer n la bière f

black coffee n le café m

champagne n le champagne m

cider n le cidre m

cocoa n le cacao m

coffee n le café m

Coke® n le coca m

decaffeinated coffee n le café décaféiné m

drink n la boisson f

fruit juice n le jus de fruits m

grapefruit juice n le jus de pamplemousse m

hot chocolate n le chocolat chaud m

juice n le jus m

lager n la bière blonde f

lemonade n la limonade f

milk n le lait m

milkshake n le milk-shake m

mineral water n l'eau minérale f

orange juice n le jus d'orange m

pineapple juice n le jus d'ananas m

red wine n le vin rouge m

shandy n le panaché m

soft drink n la boisson non alcoolisée f

sparkling wine n le mousseux m

tea n le thé m

tomato juice n le jus de tomate m

tonic n le Schweppes® m

water n l'eau f

whisky n le whisky m

white coffee n le café au lait m

white wine n le vin blanc m

wine n le vin m

FURNITURE • LES MEUBLES

armchair *n* le fauteuil *m*
bath *n* la baignoire *f*
bed *n* le lit *m*
bench *n* le banc *m*
bookcase *n* la bibliothèque *f*
bookshelf *n* l'étagère à livres *f*
bunk beds *npl* les lits superposés *mpl*
CD player *n* la platine laser *f*
chair *n* la chaise *f*
chest of drawers *n* la commode *f*
coffee table *n* la table basse *f*
cooker *n* la cuisinière *f*
couch *n* le canapé *m*
cupboard *n* le placard *m*

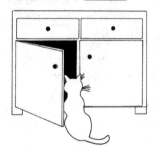

curtain *n* le rideau *m*
cushion *n* le coussin *m*

deckchair *n* la chaise longue *f*
dishwasher *n* le lave-vaisselle *m*
double bed *n* le grand lit *m*
DVD player *n* le lecteur de DVD *m*
easy chair *n* le fauteuil *m*
freezer *n* le congélateur *m*
fridge *n* le frigo *m*
microwave oven *n* le four à micro-ondes *m*
oven *n* le four *m*
refrigerator *n* le réfrigérateur *m*
rug *n* le tapis *m*
settee *n* le canapé *m*
sink *n* l'évier *m*
sofa *n* le canapé *m*
table *n* la table *f*
television *n* la télévision *f*
tumble dryer *n* le sèche-linge *m*
video recorder *n* le magnétoscope *m*
wardrobe *n* l'armoire *f*
washing machine *n* la machine à laver *f*

INSTRUMENTS • LES INSTRUMENTS

accordion *n* l'accordéon *m*

bagpipes *npl* la cornemuse *f*

bass drum *n* la grosse caisse *f*

bass guitar *n* la guitare basse *f*

bassoon *n* le basson *m*

cello *n* le violoncelle *m*

clarinet *n* la clarinette *f*

cornet *n* le cornet à pistons *m*

double bass *n* la contrebasse *f*

drum *n* le tambour *m*

drums *npl* la batterie *f*

electric guitar *n* la guitare électrique *f*

flute *n* la flûte *f*

guitar *n* la guitare *f*

horn *n* le cor *m*

keyboards *npl* le synthétiseur *m*

mouth organ *n* l'harmonica *m*

oboe *n* le hautbois *m*

organ *n* l'orgue *m*

percussion *n* la percussion *f*

piano *n* le piano *m*

pipes *npl* la cornemuse *f*

recorder *n* la flûte à bec *f*

saxophone *n* le saxophone *m*

trombone *n* le trombone *m*

trumpet *n* la trompette *f*

tuba *n* le tuba *m*

viola *n* l'alto *m*

violin *n* le violon *m*

accountant *n* le/la comptable *m/f*

actor *n* l'acteur *m*

actress *n* l'actrice *f*

air hostess *n* l'hôtesse de l'air *f*

archaeologist *n* l'archéologue *m/f*

architect *n* l'architecte *m/f*

artist *n* l'artiste *m/f*

athlete *n* l'athlète *m/f*

au pair *n* la jeune fille au pair *f*

author *n* l'auteur *m*

baker *n* le boulanger *m* / la boulangère *f*

barmaid *n* la barmaid *f*

barman *n* le barman *m*

builder *n* le maçon *m*

bus driver *n* le conducteur d'autobus *m*

butcher *n* le boucher *m*

caretaker *n* le gardien *m* / la gardienne *f*

carpenter *n* le charpentier *m*

chef *n* le chef *m*

child minder *n* la nourrice *f*

cleaner *n* la femme de ménage *f* / l'agent d'entretien *m*

computer programmer *n* le programmeur *m* / la programmeuse *f*

conductor *n* le chef d'orchestre *m*

cook *n* le cuisinier *m* / la cuisinière *f*

dancer *n* le danseur *m* / la danseuse *f*

dentist *n* le/la dentiste *m/f*

detective *n* l'inspecteur de police *m*

dinner lady *n* la dame de service *f*

disc jockey, DJ *n* le disc-jockey *m*

doctor *n* le médecin *m*

dustman *n* l'éboueur *m*

electrician *n* l'électricien *m*

engineer *n* l'ingénieur *m*

farmer *n* l'agriculteur *m* / l'agricultrice *f*

film star *n* la vedette de cinéma *f*

firefighter *n* le pompier *m*

fisherman *n* le pêcheur *m*

flight attendant *n* l'hôtesse de l'air *f* / le steward *m*

Jobs • Les professions

florist *n* le/la fleuriste *m/f*

footballer *n* le footballeur *m/* la footballeuse *f*

gardener *n* le jardinier *m*

goalkeeper *n* le gardien de but *m*

hairdresser *n* le coiffeur *m /* la coiffeuse *f*

headmaster *n* le directeur *m*

headmistress *n* la directrice *f*

housewife *n* la femme au foyer *f*

imam *n* l'imam *m*

instructor *n* le moniteur *m /* la monitrice *f*

interior designer *n* le/la designer *m/f*

interpreter *n* l'interprète *m/f*

inventor *n* l'inventeur *m /* l'inventrice *f*

janitor *n* le concierge *m*

jockey *n* le jockey *m*

joiner *n* le menuisier *m*

journalist *n* le/la journaliste *m/f*

judge *n* le juge *m*

lawyer *n* l'avocat *m /* l'avocate *f*

lecturer *n* le professeur d'université *m*

librarian *n* le/la bibliothécaire *m/f*

lorry driver *n* le routier *m*

magician *n* le prestidigitateur *m*

matron *n* l'infirmière-chef *f*

mayor *n* le maire *m*

mechanic *n* le mécanicien *m*

midwife *n* la sage-femme *f*

milkman *n* le laitier *m*

miner *n* le mineur *m*

minister *n* le pasteur *m*

model *n* le mannequin *m*

MP *n* le député *m*

musician *n* le musicien *m /* la musicienne *f*

nanny *n* la garde d'enfants *f*

nurse *n* l'infirmier *m /* l'infirmière *f*

optician *n* l'opticien *m /* l'opticienne *f*

PA *n* la secrétaire de direction *f*

painter *n* le peintre *m*

paperboy *n* le livreur de journaux *m*

papergirl *n* la livreuse de journaux *f*

pharmacist *n* le pharmacien *m /* la pharmacienne *f*

physiotherapist *n* le/la kinésithérapeute *m/f*

pilot *n* le pilote *m*
plumber *n* le plombier *m*
policeman *n* le policier *m*
policewoman *n* la femme
 policier *f*
pop star *n* la pop star *f*
postman *n* le facteur *m*
priest *n* le prêtre *m*
professor *n* le professeur
 d'université *m*
programmer *n* le
 programmeur *m* / la
 programmeuse *f*
psychiatrist *n* le/la psychiatre
 m/f
rabbi *n* le rabbin *m*
receptionist *n* le/la
 réceptionniste *m/f*
rep *n* le représentant *m* / la
 représentante *f*
reporter *n* le reporter *m*
sailor *n* le marin *m*
salesman *n* le représentant *m*
saleswoman *n* la
 représentante *f*
scientist *n* le chercheur *m* / la
 chercheuse *f*
secretary *n* le/la secrétaire *m/f*
security guard *n* l'agent de
 sécurité *m*
shop assistant *n* le vendeur
 m / la vendeuse *f*

shopkeeper *n* le commerçant
 m / la commerçante *f*
social worker *n* l'assistante
 sociale *f* / le travailleur social *m*
soldier *n* le soldat *m*
solicitor *n* l'avocat *m/f* / le
 notaire *m*
stewardess *n* l'hôtesse de
 l'air *f*
supply teacher *n* le
 suppléant *m* / la suppléante *f*
surgeon *n* le chirurgien *m*
surveyor *n* l'expert en
 bâtiment *m*
taxi driver *n* le chauffeur de
 taxi *m*
teacher *n* (*in primary school*)
 l'instituteur *m* / l'institutrice *f*,
 (*in secondary school*) le
 professeur *m*
technician *n* le technicien *m* /
 la technicienne *f*
train driver *n* le conducteur
 de train *m*
translator *n* le traducteur *m* /
 la traductrice *f*
undertaker *n* l'entrepreneur
 des pompes funèbres *m*
vet *n* le/la vétérinaire *m/f*
vicar *n* le pasteur *m*
waiter *n* le serveur *m*
waitress *n* la serveuse *f*
writer *n* l'écrivain *m*

SPORTS • LE SPORTS

aerobics *n* l'aérobic *f*

athletics *n* l'athlétisme *m*

badminton *n* le badminton *m*

baseball *n* le base-ball *m*

basketball *n* le basket *m*

bowling *n* le bowling *m*

bowls *n* les boules *fpl*

boxing *n* la boxe *f*

cricket *n* le cricket *m*

cycling *n* le cyclisme *m*

dancing *n* la danse *f*

fishing *n* la pêche *f*

football *n* le football *m*

golf *n* le golf *m*

gymnastics *n* la gymnastique *f*

handball *n* le handball *m*

hang-gliding *n* le deltaplane *m*

high jump *n* le saut en hauteur *m*

hill-walking *n* la randonnée *f*

hockey *n* le hockey *m*

ice hockey *n* le hockey sur glace *m*

ice-skating *n* le patinage sur glace *m*

judo *n* le judo *m*

karate *n* le karaté *m*

long jump *n* le saut en longueur *m*

motor racing *n* la course automobile *f*

mountaineering *n* l'alpinisme *m*

netball *n* le netball *m*

pool *n* le billard américain *m*

riding *n* l'équitation *f*

roller-blading *n* le roller *m*

roller-skating *n* le patin à roulettes *m*

rugby *n* le rugby *m*

running *n* la course *f*

sailing *n* la voile *f*

skateboarding *n* le skateboard *m*

skating *n* le patin à glace *m*

skiing *n* le ski *m*

snooker *n* le billard *m*

soccer *n* le football *m*

squash *n* le squash *m*

surfing *n* le surf *m*

swimming *n* la natation *f*

table tennis *n* le ping-pong *m*

tennis *n* le tennis *m*

tenpin bowling *n* le bowling *m*

trampolining *n* le trampoline *m*

volleyball *n* le volley-ball *m*

water-skiing *n* le ski nautique *m*

weightlifting *n* l'haltérophilie *f*

windsurfing *n* la planche à voile *f*

wrestling *n* la lutte *f*

absent *adj* <u>absent</u> *m adj*, <u>absente</u> *f adj*

assembly hall *n* la <u>salle de réunion</u> *f*

atlas *n* l'<u>atlas</u> *m*

bell *n* la <u>sonnerie</u> *f*

Biro® *n* le <u>bic</u>® *m*

blackboard *n* le <u>tableau</u> *m*

board *n* le <u>tableau</u> *m*

book *n* le <u>livre</u> *m*

break time *n* la <u>récréation</u> *f*

calculator *n* la <u>calculatrice</u> *f*

canteen *n* la <u>cantine</u> *f*

cassette player *n* le <u>lecteur de cassettes</u> *m*

CD player *n* la <u>platine laser</u> *f*

chair *n* la <u>chaise</u> *f*

chalk *n* la <u>craie</u> *f*

chart *n* le <u>tableau</u> *m*

class *n* la <u>classe</u> *f*

classroom *n* la <u>classe</u> *f*

classroom assistant *n* l'<u>aide-éducateur</u> *m* / l'<u>aide-éducatrice</u> *f*

cloakroom *n* le <u>vestiaire</u> *m*

computer *n* l'<u>ordinateur</u> *m*

computer room *n* la <u>salle d'informatique</u> *f*

corridor *n* le <u>couloir</u> *m*

curriculum *n* le <u>programme</u> *m*

deputy head *n* le <u>directeur adjoint</u> *m* / la <u>directrice adjointe</u> *f*

desk *n* le <u>pupitre</u> *m*

diagram *n* le <u>diagramme</u> *m*

dictionary *n* le <u>dictionnaire</u> *m*

dining room *n* le <u>réfectoire</u> *m*

dormitory *n* le <u>dortoir</u> *m*

drawing *n* le <u>dessin</u> *m*

drawing pin *n* la <u>punaise</u> *f*

essay *n* le <u>devoir</u> *m*

exam *n* l'<u>examen</u> *m*

exercise *n* l'<u>exercice</u> *m*

exercise book *n* le <u>cahier</u> *m*

felt-tip pen *n* le <u>stylo-feutre</u> *m*

folder *n* la <u>chemise</u> *f*

GCSE *n* le <u>brevet des collèges</u> *m*

general knowledge *n* les <u>connaissances générales</u> *fpl*

grammar *n* la <u>grammaire</u> *f*

gym hall *n* la <u>salle de gym</u> *f*

gym kit *n* les <u>affaires de gym</u> *fpl*

half term *n* les <u>petites vacances</u> *fpl*

headmaster *n* le <u>directeur</u> *m*

At school • À l'école

headmistress n la <u>directrice</u> f
homework n les <u>devoirs</u> mpl
interval n la <u>récréation</u> f
jotter n le <u>cahier</u> m
junior school n l'école
  <u>primaire</u> f
language laboratory n le
  <u>laboratoire de langues</u> m
lesson n la <u>leçon</u> f
library n la <u>bibliothèque</u> f
lower sixth n la <u>première</u> f
mouse n la <u>souris</u> f
mouse mat n le <u>tapis de
  souris</u> m
office n le <u>secrétariat</u> m
overhead projector n le
  <u>rétroprojecteur</u> m
packed lunch n le <u>casse-
  croûte</u> m
page n la <u>page</u> f
pen n le <u>stylo</u> m
pencil n le <u>crayon</u> m
pencil case n la <u>trousse</u> f
pencil sharpener n le <u>taille-
  crayon</u> m
photocopier n la
  <u>photocopieuse</u> f
photocopy n la <u>photocopie</u> f
playground n la <u>cour de
  récréation</u> f
playtime n la <u>récréation</u> f
poster n le <u>poster</u> m
primary school n l'école
  <u>primaire</u> f

printer n l'<u>imprimante</u> f
projector n le <u>projecteur</u> m
pupil n l'<u>élève</u> m/f
register n le <u>cahier d'appel</u> m
registration n l'<u>appel</u> m
rubber n la <u>gomme</u> f
ruler n la <u>règle</u> f

satchel n le <u>cartable</u> m
school n l'<u>école</u> f
school bag n le <u>cartable</u> m
schoolboy n l'<u>écolier</u> m
schoolchildren npl les
  <u>écoliers</u> mpl
schoolgirl n l'<u>écolière</u> f
school holidays npl les
  <u>vacances scolaires</u> fpl
school uniform n l'<u>uniforme
  scolaire</u> m
secondary school n (for
  11–15 year olds) le <u>collège</u> m,
  (for 15–18 year olds) le <u>lycée</u>
  m
sharpener n le <u>taille-crayon</u> m
teacher n (in primary school)
  l'<u>instituteur</u> m / l'<u>institutrice</u> f,
  (in secondary school) le
  <u>professeur</u> m

team n l'équipe f
test n le test m
textbook n le manuel m
toilets npl les toilettes fpl
upper sixth n la terminale f
whiteboard n le tableau m
worksheet n la feuille
 d'exercices f

● *School subjects*

art n les arts plastiques mpl
biology n la biologie f
chemistry n la chimie f
citizenship n la citoyenneté f
design and technology n
 la technologie f
drama n l'art dramatique m
English n l'anglais m
French n le français m
games npl le sport m
geography n la géographie f
gym n la gym f
history n l'histoire f
ICT n l'informatique f
literacy n l'éducation littéraire
 f
literature n la littérature f

maths n les maths fpl

music n la musique f
PE n l'EPS f
physics n la physique f
RE n l'éducation religieuse f
science n les sciences fpl

● *School classes*

Reception year/Primary 1
 n les moyens mpl
Year 1/Primary 2 n les
 grands mpl
Year 2/Primary 3 n le CP m
Year 3/Primary 4 n le CE1 m
Year 4/Primary 5 n le CE2 m
Year 5/Primary 6 n le CM1 m
Year 6/Primary 7 n le CM2 m
Year 7/S1 n la sixième f

NUMBERS AND TIME • LES NOMBRES ET L'HEURE

1	un/une	15	quinze	72	soixante-douze
2	deux	16	seize	80	quatre-vingts
3	trois	17	dix-sept	81	quatre-vingt-un/une
4	quatre	18	dix-huit	82	quatre-vingt-deux
5	cinq	19	dix-neuf	90	quatre-vingt-dix
6	six	20	vingt	91	quatre-vingt-onze
7	sept	21	vingt et un/une	100	cent
8	huit	22	vingt-deux	101	cent un/une
9	neuf	30	trente	200	deux cents
10	dix	40	quarante	250	deux cent cinquante
11	onze	50	cinquante		
12	douze	60	soixante	1,000	mille
13	treize	70	soixante-dix	2,000	deux mille
14	quatorze	71	soixante et onze	1,000,000	un million

Quelle heure est-il?
What time is it?

Il est …
It's …

une heure
one o'clock

une heure dix
ten past one

une heure et quart
quarter past one

une heure et demie
half past one

deux heures moins vingt
twenty to two

deux heures moins le quart
quarter to two

À quelle heure?

At what time?

à minuit
at midnight

à midi
at midday

à une heure (de l'après-midi)
at one o'clock (in the afternoon)

à huit heures (du soir)
at eight o'clock (at night)

In France times are often given in the twenty-four hour clock.

à 11.15
or
à onze heures quinze
at quarter past eleven

à 20.45
or
à vingt heures quarante-cinq
at quarter to nine

FRENCH VERBS • LES VERBES FRANÇAIS

In French the ending of the verb varies according to the person – ie the form of the verb that goes with **je** is different from the form that goes with **nous, vous** etc.

Here are the present tenses of some common verbs, with the endings highlighted. We have also shown some useful phrases which require other tenses. As the examples also make clear, a French verb may be translated in several different ways, depending on the context.

A verb form that is of particular interest to teachers is the imperative. In English *Look!, Listen! Don't do that!* can be used to a single child, or to the whole class, but in French there are always two different forms of the verb, depending on whether one, or more than one person is being spoken to. The plural form always ends in **-ez**, and this is also the polite form used to an adult. This dictionary contains many examples of imperatives that will be of use to teachers.

Some examples are given here to illustrate the past tense, and the dictionary includes translations for past tenses that children are very likely to want, such as *I got, I went, I've broken, it was* etc. Translations for these will be found at the entries for **get, go, break, be** etc.

REGARDER

je regarde	nous regardons
tu regardes	vous regardez
il regarde	ils regardent
elle regarde	elles regardent

Regarde-moi, Luc. Look at me Luc.
Regardez, les enfants! Look, children!
Regardez le tableau! Look at the board.
Je **regarde** la télé le samedi matin. I watch TV on Saturday morning.
il **a regardé** sa montre. He looked at his watch.
Elle aime **regarder** des films. She likes watching films.

FINIR

je finis	nous finissons
tu finis	vous finissez
il finit	ils finissent
elle finit	elles finissent

J'**ai fini**! I've finished!
Finis tes devoirs! Finish your homework!
Elle **a fini** sa soupe. She's finished her soup.
Il n'**a pas fini** le livre. He hasn't finished the book.
Elle va **finir** ses devoirs demain. She's going to finish her homework tomorrow.

ATTENDRE

j'attends	nous attendons
tu attends	vous attendez
il attend	ils attendent
elle attend	elles attendent

Attends-moi! Wait for me!
Attendez ici, les enfants! Wait here, children!
J'**ai attendu** deux heures. I waited for two hours.
Il m'**a attendu** à la gare. He waited for me at the station.
Je vais **attendre** ici. I'm going to wait here.

AVOIR

j'ai	nous avons
tu as	vous avez
il a	ils ont
elle a	elles ont

Je n'**ai** pas d'argent. I haven't got any money.
J'**ai** les cheveux longs. I've got long hair.
Elle **a** un vélo. She's got a bike.
Il **a eu** un accident. He's had an accident.
J'**ai eu** beaucoup de cadeaux. I got lots of presents.
Quel âge **as**-tu? How old are you?
Elle **a** cinq ans. She is five.
Il y **a** un bon film à la télé. There's a good film on TV.
Je n'**ai** pas fait mes devoirs. I haven't done my homework.
J'**ai** faim. I'm hungry.

French verbs • Les verbes français

ALLER

je vais	nous allons
tu vas	vous allez
il va	ils vont
elle va	elles vont

Je ne **vais** pas à l'école le samedi. I don't go to school on Saturday.
Je **vais** gagner. I'm going to win.
Où **vas**-tu? Where are you going?
Vas-y! Go on!
Ça **va**? Are you okay?
Il **va** pleuvoir. It's going to rain.
Je **suis allé** chez Luc. I went to Luc's house.
Où **es**-tu **allé** hier? Where did you go yesterday?
Nous **sommes allés** en France. We went to France.

FAIRE

je fais	nous faisons
tu fais	vous faites
il fait	ils font
elle fait	elles font

Je **fais** du sport. I do sport.
Ne **fais** pas ça, chéri. Don't do that, dear.
Qu'est-ce que tu **fais**? What are you doing?
Paul **fait** du judo. Paul does judo.
Deux et deux **font** quatre. Two and two make four.
Faites les gestes! Do the actions!
Je n'**ai** pas **fait** mes devoirs. I haven't done my homework.
Qui **a fait** ça? Who did that?
Quel temps **fait**-il? What's the weather like?
Il **fait** chaud. It's hot.
Il **faisait** froid. It was cold.
Je **fais** des gâteaux. I make cakes.
Ça ne **fait** rien. It doesn't matter.
Il va **faire** beau demain. It's going to be nice tomorrow.

S'APPELER

je m'appelle	nous nous appelons
tu t'appelles	vous vous appelez
il s'appelle	ils s'appellent
elle s'appelle	elles s'appellent

Je **m'appelle** Amélie. My name is Amélie.
Comment ça **s'appelle**? What is it called?
Comment tu **t'appelles**? What are you called?
Vous **vous appelez** comment? What are you called?
Tes frères **s'appellent** comment? What are your brothers called?

POUVOIR

je peux	nous pouvons
tu peux	vous pouvez
il peut	ils peuvent
elle peut	elles peuvent

Je ne **peux** pas venir. I can't come.
Vous **pouvez** commencer. You can start.
Tu **peux** te pousser un peu? Could you move a bit?
Qui **peut** répondre à la question? Who can answer the question?
Je **peux** avoir un verre d'eau? Could I have a glass of water?
Tu **pourras** venir? Will you be able to come?

ÊTRE

je suis	nous sommes
tu es	vous êtes
il est	ils sont
elle est	elles sont

Ne **sois** pas effronté! Don't be cheeky!
Je **suis** fatigué. I'm tired.
Tu **es** en retard. You're late.
C'**est** moi. It's me.
Elle **est** anglaise. She's English.
C'**était** difficile. It was difficult.
J'**étais** content. I was happy.
Nous **sommes** là. We're here.
Vous **êtes** prêts? Are you ready?
Nous **sommes** le premier mai. It's the first of May.
Mes parents **sont** au travail. My parents are at work.
Je **suis** allé à Paris. I went to Paris.
Où **es-tu** allé? Where did you go?

VOULOIR

je veux	nous voulons
tu veux	vous voulez
il veut	ils veulent
elle veut	elles veulent

Qu'est-ce que tu **veux**, Marie? What do you want, Marie?
Qu'est-ce que vous **voulez**, les garçons? What do you want, boys?
Vous **voulez** du café, Madame? Would you like some coffee, Miss?
Tu **veux** un bonbon, Louis? Would you like a sweet, Louis?
Qu'est-ce que ça **veut** dire? What does that mean?
Je **voudrais** une glace. I'd like an ice cream.

A

a article

> *Use **un** for masculine nouns, **une** for feminine nouns.*

<u>un</u> *m*

a boy
un garçon

<u>une</u> *f*

a girl
une fille

ten kilometres an hour
dix kilomètres à l'heure

able adj

Will you be able to come?
Est-ce que tu pourras venir?

I won't be able to come.
Je ne pourrai pas venir.

about

> **about** can be an adverb or a preposition.

Ⓐ adv (*approximately*)
<u>environ</u>

about sixteen girls
environ seize filles

about fourteen euros
environ quatorze euros

at about eleven o'clock
vers onze heures

Ⓑ prep (*concerning*)
<u>sur</u>

about myself
sur moi

a letter about yourself
une lettre sur toi

a song about animals
une chanson sur les animaux

How about a game of cards?
Tu veux jouer aux cartes?

above prep
1 (*higher than*)
<u>au-dessus de</u>

Hold the ball above your head.
Tiens la balle au-dessus de ta tête.

2 (*more than*)
<u>plus de</u>

above thirty degrees
plus de trente degrés

abroad adv
<u>à l'étranger</u>

We're going abroad this year.
Nous partons à l'étranger cette année.

absent adj
<u>absent</u> *m adj*
<u>absente</u> *f adj*

Who's absent today?
Qui est absent aujourd'hui?

absurd adj
<u>absurde</u>

That's absurd!
C'est absurde!

academy n
le <u>collège</u> *m*

accent n
l'<u>accent</u> *m*

He's got a good accent.
Il a un bon accent.

accident n
l'<u>accident</u> *m*

Look at Language Plus on pages 283–308 for extra vocabulary.

It was an accident.
C'était un accident.

ace n
l'as m

the ace of hearts
l'as de cœur

ache vb
My leg's aching.
J'ai mal à la jambe.

across prep
de l'autre côté de
It's across the road.
C'est de l'autre côté de la rue.

act vb
jouer
He's acting in a play.
Il joue dans une pièce.

activity n
l'activité f
outdoor activities
les activités de plein air

actor n
l'acteur m

actress n
l'actrice f

actually adv
en fait
Actually it's good fun.
En fait, c'est bien amusant.

AD abbr
ap. J.-C.
in 800 AD
en 800 ap. J.-C.

add vb
ajouter
Add some sugar.
Ajoutez du sucre.

add up vb
additionner
Add the figures up.
Additionnez les chiffres.

address n
l'adresse f
What's your address?
Quelle est votre adresse?

What's your address, Charlotte?
Quelle est ton adresse,
Charlotte?

> **address** in English has double **d**.
> The French word has only one **d**,
> and an extra **e** on the end.

adjective n
l'adjectif m

admission n
l'entrée f
"admission free"
"entrée gratuite"

adopted adj
adopté m adj
adoptée f adj

adult n
l'adulte m/f
two adults and one child
deux adultes et un enfant

advantage n
l'avantage m
**It's an advantage to be able to
speak French.**
C'est un avantage de savoir parler
français.

adventure n
l'aventure f

Harry has lots of adventures.
Harry a beaucoup d'aventures.

advice n
les conseils mpl

Could you give me some advice?
Vous pouvez me donner des conseils?

aerobics npl
l'aérobic f

I'm going to aerobics tonight.
Je vais au cours d'aérobic ce soir.

aeroplane n
l'avion m

on an aeroplane
en avion

affectionate adj
affectueux m adj
affectueuse f adj

My cat is very affectionate.
Mon chat est très affectueux.

afraid adj

to be afraid of ...
avoir peur de ...

I'm afraid of spiders.
J'ai peur des araignées.

Are you afraid of the dark?
Tu as peur du noir?

after prep
après

after me
après moi

after you
après toi

after lunch
après le déjeuner

afternoon n
l'après-midi m/f

In the morning or in the afternoon?
Le matin ou l'après-midi?

3 o'clock in the afternoon
trois heures de l'après-midi

I'm playing football on Saturday afternoon.
Je joue au foot samedi après-midi.

> **this afternoon**
> cet après-midi
> **in the afternoon**
> l'après-midi

afters n
le dessert m

What do you want for afters?
Qu'est-ce que tu veux comme dessert?

again adv
1 encore

Tamsin has won again.
Tamsin a encore gagné.
2 (one more time)
encore une fois

Try again!
Essaie encore une fois!

> *You can also add **re-** to verbs in French, to show you're doing something again. We do the same in English, eg **re**paint, **re**write.*

Let's begin again.
Recommençons.

Look at Language Plus on pages 283–308 for extra vocabulary.

Can you tell me again?
Tu peux me le redire?

Do it again!
Refais-le!

against prep
contre

Don't put your chair against the wall.
Ne mets pas ta chaise contre le mur.

age n
l'âge m

Age: twelve
Âge: douze ans

your age
ton âge

at the age of thirteen
à l'âge de treize ans

Write your name and age.
Écris ton nom et ton âge.

I am the same age as you.
J'ai le même âge que toi.

ago adv

two days ago
il y a deux jours

a week ago
il y a une semaine

a month ago
il y a un mois

a long time ago
il y a longtemps

agree vb
être d'accord

I agree!
Je suis d'accord!

I agree with Carol.
Je suis d'accord avec Carol.

ahead adv
devant

Look straight ahead!
Regardez droit devant vous!

The red team is five points ahead.
L'équipe rouge a cinq points d'avance.

air n
l'air m

Throw the ball into the air.
Lance le ballon en l'air.

I prefer to travel by air.
Je préfère voyager en avion.

air-conditioned adj
climatisé m adj
climatisée f adj

air hostess n
l'hôtesse de l'air f

airmail n

by airmail
par avion

airport n
l'aéroport m

alarm clock n
le réveil m

album n
l'album m

alcohol n
l'alcool m

I don't like alcohol.
Je n'aime pas l'alcool.

A levels npl
le <u>baccalauréat</u> *m*

My brother is taking his A levels.
Mon frère passe le baccalauréat.

The **baccalauréat** (or **bac** for short) is the equivalent in France of A levels.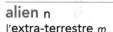

alien n
l'<u>extra-terrestre</u> *m*

alive adj
<u>vivant</u> *m adj*
<u>vivante</u> *f adj*

They're still alive.
Ils sont encore vivants.

all adj, pron, adv
<u>tout</u> *m adj*
<u>toute</u> *f adj*

all the time
tout le temps

all day
toute la journée

all my friends
tous mes amis

all the girls
toutes les filles

The score is five all.
Le score est de cinq partout.

Is that all?
C'est tout?

allergic adj
<u>allergique</u>

I'm allergic to eggs.
Je suis allergique aux œufs.

allowed adj
It's not allowed.
Ce n'est pas permis.

all right adv
1 (*not bad*)
pas mal

Great, or just all right?
Super, ou seulement pas mal?

Do you like school? – It's all right.
Tu aimes l'école? – C'est pas mal.

2 (*when agreeing*)
d'accord

I'd like a coke. – All right.
Je voudrais un coca. – D'accord.

Are you all right?
Ça va?
Is that all right?
Ça va?

almost adv
presque

Are you ready? – Almost.
Tu es prêt? – Presque.

alone adj, adv
<u>seul</u> *m adj*
<u>seule</u> *f adj*

She lives alone.
Elle habite seule.

Leave my things alone!
Ne touche pas à mes affaires!

Luc, leave Pierre alone!
Luc, laisse Pierre tranquille!

le can mean "him" and *la* can mean "her".

Leave him alone!
Laisse-le tranquille!

Leave her alone!
Laisse-la tranquille!

along prep
le long de

a walk along the beach
une promenade le long de la plage

Look at Language Plus on pages 283–308 for extra vocabulary.

aloud adv
à haute voix

Read the words aloud, children.
Lisez les mots à haute voix, les enfants.

Read the words aloud, Marcel.
Lis les mots à haute voix, Marcel.

alphabet n
l'alphabet m

alphabetical order n

in alphabetical order
par ordre alphabétique

Alps npl
les Alpes fpl

already adv
déjà

Have you finished already?
Tu as déjà fini?

also adv
aussi

alternate adj

on alternate days
tous les deux jours

alternative n
le choix m

You have no alternative.
Tu n'as pas le choix.

altogether adv
en tout

That's £20 altogether.
Ça fait vingt livres en tout.

always adv
toujours

The bus is always late.
Le bus est toujours en retard.

am vb, see **be**

a.m. abbr
du matin

at 4 a.m.
à quatre heures du matin

amazing adj
1 (surprising)
incroyable

That's amazing!
C'est incroyable!

2 (excellent)
exceptionnel m adj

exceptionnelle f adj

Vivian's an amazing cook.
Vivian est une cuisinière exceptionnelle.

amber adj

an amber light
un feu orange

ambition n
l'ambition f

It's my ambition.
C'est mon ambition.

ambulance n
l'ambulance f

America n
l'Amérique f

We're going to America.
Nous allons en Amérique.

American

> **American** can be an adjective or a noun.

Ⓐ adj
<u>américain</u> *m adj*
<u>américaine</u> *f adj*
American food
la cuisine américaine

>
>
> **He's American.**
> Il est américain.
> **She's American.**
> Elle est américaine.

Ⓑ n
l'<u>Américain</u> *m*
l'<u>Américaine</u> *f*
the Americans
les Américains

> *américain is not spelled with a capital letter except when it means an American person.*

amount n

1 *(sum of money)*
la <u>somme</u> *f*
a large amount of money
une grosse somme d'argent
2 *(quantity)*
la <u>quantité</u> *f*
a huge amount of rice
une énorme quantité de riz

amusement arcade n
la <u>salle de jeux électroniques</u>

an article

> *Use **un** for masculine nouns, **une** for feminine nouns.*

<u>un</u> *m*
an animal
un animal

<u>une</u> *f*
an apple
une pomme

and conj
<u>et</u>
you and me
toi et moi

Two and two are four.
Deux et deux font quatre.

angel n
l'<u>ange</u> *m*
You're an angel!
Tu es un ange!

angry adj
to get angry
se fâcher

Mum gets angry if I'm late.
Maman se fâche si je suis en retard.

animal n
l'<u>animal</u> *m*
(pl les animaux)

anniversary n
l'<u>anniversaire</u> *m*

my parents' wedding anniversary
l'anniversaire de mariage de mes parents

> **Happy anniversary!**
> Joyeux anniversaire de mariage!

A
B
C
D
E
F
G
H
I
J
K
L
M
N
O
P
Q
R
S
T
U
V
W
X
Y
Z

Look at Language Plus on pages 283–308 for extra vocabulary.

announcement n
l'annonce f

an important announcement
une annonce importante

anorak n
l'anorak m

my new anorak
mon nouvel anorak

another adj
un autre m
une autre f

Would you like another sandwich?
Tu veux un autre sandwich?

Do you want another card?
Tu veux une autre carte?

answer

> answer can be a verb or a noun.

Ⓐ vb
répondre

Inès, you have to answer yes or no.
Inès, tu dois répondre par oui ou par non.

Think before you answer.
Réfléchissez avant de répondre.

to answer a question
répondre à une question

Who can answer the question?
Qui peut répondre à la question?

Can you answer my question?
Peux-tu répondre à ma question?

Ⓑ n
la réponse f

the right answer
la bonne réponse

> The English words "respond" and "response" are related to **répondre** and **réponse** in French.

ant n
la fourmi f

anthem n

the national anthem
l'hymne national

any adj

> *any* can be *du*, *de la*, *de l'* or *des*, in the same way that "the" can be "le", "la", "l'" or "les".

du

Do you want any bread?
Voulez-vous du pain?

de la

Would you like any salad?
Voulez-vous de la salade?

de l'

Have you got any mineral water?
Avez-vous de l'eau minérale?

des

Have you got any brothers or sisters?
Tu as des frères et sœurs?

> In negative phrases, the French for *any* is *de* or *d'*.

de

I don't want any bread.
Je ne veux pas de pain.

d'

I haven't got any mineral water.
Je n'ai pas d'eau minérale.

I don't want any more.
Je n'en veux plus.

a b c d e f g h i j k l m n o p q r s t u v w x y z

Have you got any money?
Tu as de l'argent?
Have you got any pets?
Tu as des animaux?
I haven't got any pets.
Je n'ai pas d'animaux.
Sorry, I haven't got any.
Désolé, je n'en ai pas.

---

anybody pron
1 (in question)
quelqu'un
Does anybody want a sweet?
Quelqu'un veut un bonbon?
2 (in negative phrases)
personne
I can't see anybody.
Je ne vois personne.

anyone pron
1 (in question)
quelqu'un
Does anyone want to try?
Quelqu'un veut essayer?
2 (in negative phrases)
personne
I can't see anyone.
Je ne vois personne.

anything pron
1 (in question)
quelque chose
Do you want anything to eat?
Tu veux manger quelque chose?
2 (in negative phrases)
rien
I don't want anything.
Je ne veux rien.

apart adv
Stand with your feet apart.
Tenez-vous debout, les pieds écartés.

apartment n
l'appartement m

What are the 2 differences in spelling between the French word and the English word?

apostrophe n
l'apostrophe f
Don't forget the apostrophe!
N'oubliez pas l'apostrophe!

apple n
la pomme f
a big red apple
une grosse pomme rouge

apple juice n
le jus de pomme m

appointment n
le rendez-vous m
I've got a dental appointment.
J'ai rendez-vous chez le dentiste.

April n
avril m
April or May?
Avril ou mai?
My birthday's in April.
Mon anniversaire est en avril.

---

in April
en avril
the ninth of April
le neuf avril
The months are not spelled with a capital letter in French.

April Fool n
le poisson d'avril m

Pinning a paper fish to somebody's back is a traditional April fool joke in France.

Look at Language Plus on pages 283–308 for extra vocabulary.

a
b
c
d
e
f
g
h
i
j
k
l
m
n
o
p
q
r
s
t
u
v
w
x
y
z

April Fool's Day n
le premier avril m

apron n
le tablier m
a white apron
un tablier blanc

are vb, see **be**

area n
la région f
She lives in the Paris area.
Elle habite dans la région
parisienne.

argue vb
se disputer
Stop arguing!
Arrêtez de vous disputer!

arm n
le bras m
Swing your arms!
Balancez les bras!

armchair n
le fauteuil m

army n
l'armée f
He's in the army.
Il est dans l'armée.

around prep
(date, time)
1 vers
**I go to bed around ten
o'clock.**
Je me couche vers dix heures.

2 (nearby)
around here
près d'ici
**Is there a chemist's around
here?**
Il y a une pharmacie près d'ici?

arrive vb
arriver
**What time does the train
arrive?**
Le train arrive à quelle heure?

arrow n
la flèche f
Follow the arrows.
Suivez les flèches.

art n
(at school)
les arts plastiques mpl
Art is my favourite subject.
Ma matière préférée, c'est les arts
plastiques.

art gallery n
le musée m
The art gallery is closed.
Le musée est fermé.

artist n
l'artiste m/f

as conj, prep
(since)
puisque
**Alice, as it's your birthday you can
choose.**
Alice, tu peux choisir, puisque c'est
ton anniversaire.
**He works as a waiter in the
holidays.**
Il travaille comme serveur pendant
les vacances.

as ... as
aussi ... que
Pierre's as tall as Michel.
Pierre est aussi grand que Michel.

Write to me as soon as possible.
Écris-moi dès que possible.

ashamed adj

to be ashamed
avoir honte

You should be ashamed of yourself!
Tu devrais avoir honte!

ashtray n
le cendrier *m*

Asian

> **Asian** can be an adjective or a noun.

A adj
indo-pakistanais *m adj*
indo-pakistanaise *f adj*

He's Asian.
Il est indo-pakistanais.

She's Asian.
Elle est indo-pakistanaise.

B n
l'Indo-Pakistanais *m*
l'Indo-Pakistanaise *f*

> *indo-pakistanais is not spelled with a capital letter except when it means an Asian person.*

ask vb
1 demander

If you need help, ask!
Si tu as besoin d'aide, demande!

Ask his name.
Demande-lui son nom.

Ask her age.
Demande-lui son âge.

> *When **ask** is followed by a person, use **demander à**.*

Ask your penfriend.
Demande à ton correspondant.

Ask your friends.
Demande à tes amis.

> *to ask for is also **demander**.*

Ask for some chips and a drink.
Demandez des frites et une boisson.

Who wants to ask a question?
Qui veut poser une question?

Ask the question.
Pose la question.

2 (*invite*)
inviter

Are you going to ask Matthew to the party?
Tu vas inviter Matthew à la fête?

asleep adj

to be asleep
dormir

Are you asleep?
Tu dors?

assembly n

> There is no assembly in French schools.

assistant n
1 (*shop assistant*)
le vendeur *m*
la vendeuse *f*

Ask the assistant.
Demande à la vendeuse.

A B C D E F G H I J K L M N O P Q R S T U V W X Y Z

> Look at Language Plus on pages 283–308 for extra vocabulary.

2 (helper)
l'assistant m
l'assistante f

asthma n
l'asthme m

I've got asthma.
J'ai de l'asthme.

astronomy n
l'astronomie f

at prep
à

at Christmas
à Noël

two at a time
deux à la fois

> à + le becomes au, à + les
> becomes aux.

au

at the café
au café

aux

at the races
aux courses

at night
la nuit

What are you doing at the weekend?
Qu'est-ce que tu fais ce week-end?

> **at four o'clock**
> à quatre heures
> **at school**
> à l'école
> **at home**
> à la maison

athlete n
l'athlète m/f

He's a good athlete.
C'est un bon athlète.

Atlantic n
l'Atlantique m

atlas n
l'atlas m

attention n
l'attention f

Pay attention!
Faites attention!

Pay attention, Léon!
Fais attention, Leon!

attic n
le grenier m

attractive adj
séduisant m adj
séduisante f adj

She's very attractive.
Elle est très séduisante.

August n
août m

August or September?
Août ou septembre?

My birthday's in August.
Mon anniversaire est en août.

> **in August**
> en août
> **the fifth of August**
> le cinq août
>
> *The months are not spelled with
> a capital letter in French.*

aunt n
la tante f

my aunt
ma tante

au pair n
la jeune fille au pair f

She's an au pair.
Elle est jeune fille au pair.

You do not translate "a" when you say what someone's job is in French.

Australia n
l'Australie f

Austria n
l'Autriche f

author n
l'auteur m
J. K. Rowling is a famous author.
J. K. Rowling est un auteur connu.

autumn n
l'automne m

in autumn
en automne

avenue n
l'avenue f

average

average can be a noun or an adjective.

A n
la moyenne f
on average
en moyenne
above average
au-dessus de la moyenne
B adj
moyen m adj
moyenne f adj
the average age
l'âge moyen
I'm average height.
Je suis de taille moyenne.

away adj
(*not here*)
absent m adj
absente f adj
André's away today.
André est absent aujourd'hui.

He's away for a week.
Il est parti pour une semaine.

He's away.
Il est absent.
She's away.
Elle est absente.

awful adj
affreux m adj
affreuse f adj
That's awful!
C'est affreux!

Look at Language Plus on pages 283–308 for extra vocabulary.

B

baby n
le <u>bébé</u> m

We've got a new baby!
On a un nouveau bébé!

babysit vb
faire du <u>baby-sitting</u>

I babysit at the weekend.
Je fais du baby-sitting le weekend.

babysitter n
le/la <u>baby-sitter</u> m/f

back

> **back** can be a noun or an adjective.

Ⓐ n
1 (*of person, horse, book*)
le <u>dos</u> m

Lie on your back!
Couchez-vous sur le dos.
2 (*of room*)
le <u>fond</u> m

at the back
au fond

Luc and I sit at the back.
Luc et moi, on s'assoit au fond.

Ⓑ adj
<u>arrière</u> m, f, pl adj

the back seat
le siège arrière

the back wheels of the car
les roues arrière de la voiture

the back door
la porte de derrière

background n
l'<u>arrière-plan</u> m

a house in the background
une maison à l'arrière-plan

backstroke n
le <u>dos crawlé</u> m

I do the backstroke.
Je fais le dos crawlé.

backwards adv
<u>en arrière</u>

Take a step backwards!
Faites un pas en arrière!

bacon n
le <u>bacon</u> m

bacon and eggs
des œufs au bacon

bad adj
1 (*awful*)
<u>mauvais</u> m adj
<u>mauvaise</u> f adj

a bad film
un mauvais film

bad weather
le mauvais temps

That's not bad.
Ce n'est pas mal.

I'm bad at maths.
Je suis mauvais en maths.

> *A boy is saying this. How can you tell?*

2 (*serious*)
grave

a bad accident
un accident grave

3 (*naughty*)
vilain *m adj*
vilaine *f adj*

You bad boy!
Vilain!

not bad
pas mal
Bad luck!
Pas de chance!

---

badge n
le badge *m*

badly adv
mal

He behaved badly.
Il s'est mal comporté.

badminton n
le badminton *m*

I play badminton.
Je joue au badminton.

bag n
le sac *m*

baggy adj
ample

baggy trousers
un pantalon ample

bagpipes npl
la cornemuse *f*

Ed plays the bagpipes.
Ed joue de la cornemuse.

baked beans npl
les haricots blancs en sauce *mpl*

> *Word for word this means 'white beans in tomato sauce'.*

baked potato n
la pomme de terre cuite au four *f*

two baked potatoes
deux pommes de terre cuites au four

baker n
le boulanger *m*
la boulangère *f*

bakery n
la boulangerie *f*

balcony n
le balcon *m*

bald adj
chauve

My grandfather is bald.
Mon grand-père est chauve.

ball n
1 (*for tennis, golf, cricket*)
la balle *f*

Hit the ball!
Frappe la balle!

Look at Language Plus on pages 283–308 for extra vocabulary.

a
b
c
d
e
f
g
h
i
j
k
l
m
n
o
p
q
r
s
t
u
v
w
x
y
z

2 *(for football, rugby)*
le ballon *m*
Pass the ball!
Passe le ballon!

ballet n
la danse classique *f*
I do ballet.
Je fais de la danse classique.

> *What's the difference in spelling between the English word dance and the French word danse?*

ballet dancer n
le danseur classique *m*
la danseuse classique *f*

ballet shoes npl
les chaussons de danse *mpl*

balloon n
le ballon *m*
a red balloon
un ballon rouge

banana n
la banane *f*

band n
1 *(rock band)*
le groupe *m*
2 *(brass band)*
la fanfare *f*

bandage n
le bandage *m*

He's got a bandage round his arm.
Il a un bandage au bras.

bang

> **bang** can be a noun or a verb.

Ⓐ n
Bang! Bang!
Pan! Pan!
Ⓑ vb
Don't bang the door!
Ne claque pas la porte!

banger n
1 *(sausage)*
la saucisse *f*
bangers and mash
les saucisses à la purée
2 *(firework)*
le pétard *m*
Phyllis is scared of bangers.
Phyllis a peur des pétards.

bank n
1 *(for money)*
la banque *f*
2 *(of river, lake)*
le bord *m*

bank holiday n
le jour férié *m*

bar n
a bar of chocolate
une barre de chocolat

barbecue n
le barbecue *m*

bare adj
nu *m adj*
nue *f adj*
bare feet
les pieds nus

bargain n
l'affaire *f*

It's a bargain!
C'est une affaire!

barge n
la péniche f

bark vb
aboyer

My dog barks a lot.
Mon chien aboie beaucoup.

baseball n
le base-ball m

I play baseball.
Je joue au base-ball.

baseball cap n
la casquette de base-ball f

basement n
le sous-sol m

basin n
le lavabo m

basket n
le panier m

basketball n
le basket m

Do you play basketball?
Tu joues au basket?

bat n
1 (for cricket, rounders)
la batte f
2 (for table tennis)
la raquette f

3 (animal)
la chauve-souris f

two bats
deux chauves-souris

Make sure you pick the word for the right sort of bat!

bath n
1 (wash)
le bain m

I have a bath every night.
Je prends un bain tous les soirs.

a hot bath
un bain chaud

2 (tub)
la baignoire f

There's a spider in the bath!
Il y a une araignée dans la baignoire!

bathroom n
la salle de bains f

There are two bathrooms.
Il y a deux salles de bains.

baths npl
la piscine f

battery n
(for torch, toy)
la pile f

I need a battery.
J'ai besoin d'une pile.

battle n
la bataille f

the Battle of Hastings
la bataille de Hastings

battleships n
la bataille navale f

BC abbr
av. J.-C.

in 200 BC
en 200 av. J.-C.

be vb
1 être

It's me.
C'est moi.

Look at Language Plus on pages 283–308 for extra vocabulary.

It's easy.
C'est facile.

It's not easy.
Ce n'est pas facile.

I'm tired.
Je suis fatigué.

You're late.
Tu es en retard.

She's English.
Elle est anglaise.

We're the winners!
Nous sommes les gagnants!

Are you ready?
Vous êtes prêts?

My parents are in Paris at the moment.
Mes parents sont à Paris en ce moment.

My name is not Inès, it's Fleur.
Mon nom n'est pas Inès, c'est Fleur.

*With certain adjectives, such as "cold", "hot", "hungry" and "thirsty", you use **avoir** instead of **être**.*

I'm cold.
J'ai froid.

I'm hungry.
J'ai faim.

*When talking about ages, you use **avoir**, not **être**.*

I'm eleven.
J'ai onze ans.

My brother is thirteen.
Mon frère a treize ans.

*When talking about the weather, you use **fait**.*

It's cold.
Il fait froid.

It's too hot.
Il fait trop chaud.

It's a nice day.
Il fait beau.

It's the 28th of October today.
Aujourd'hui, nous sommes le vingt-huit octobre.

*Another way of saying this date is **Aujourd'hui, c'est le vingt-huit octobre**.*

2 (with totals)
égaler

Two times three is six.
Deux fois trois égale six.

Ten divided by two is five.
Dix divisé par deux égale cinq.

beach n
la plage f

beans n
1 (baked beans)
les haricots blancs à la sauce tomate mpl

Would you like some beans?
Tu veux des haricots blancs à la sauce tomate?

Word for word this means "white beans in tomato sauce".

2 (green beans)
les haricots verts mpl

beard n
la barbe f

beat vb
battre

We're going to beat you!
Nous allons vous battre!

A
B
C
D
E
F
G
H
I
J
K
L
M
N
O
P
Q
R
S
T
U
V
W
X
Y
Z

beautiful adj
<u>beau</u> m adj
<u>belle</u> f adj

Your garden is beautiful.
Votre jardin est beau.

Delphine is very beautiful.
Delphine est très belle.

Your hair is beautiful.
Tes cheveux sont beaux.

because conj
<u>parce que</u>

Yvette is absent because she's ill.
Yvette est absente parce qu'elle est
malade.

because of you
à cause de toi

because of the weather
à cause du temps

bed n
le <u>lit</u> m

in bed
au lit

It's time to go to bed.
Il est temps de se coucher.

I go to bed at ten o'clock.
Je me couche à dix heures.

What time do you go to bed?
À quelle heure tu te couches?

bed and breakfast n
la <u>chambre d'hôte</u> f

bedroom n
la <u>chambre</u> f

my bedroom
ma chambre

Alain's bedroom
la chambre d'Alain

bedtime n

Ten o'clock is my usual bedtime.
Je me couche généralement à dix
heures.

Bedtime!
Au lit!

bee n
l'<u>abeille</u> f

beef n
le <u>bœuf</u> m

Would you like beef or chicken?
Tu veux du bœuf ou du poulet?

roast beef
le rôti de bœuf

beefburger n
le <u>hamburger</u> m

beer n
la <u>bière</u> f

a can of beer
une canette de bière

beetle n
le <u>scarabée</u> m

beetroot n
la <u>betterave rouge</u> f

before prep, conj
<u>avant</u>

before three o'clock
avant trois heures

**Think before you answer,
Noémie!**
Réfléchis avant de répondre,
Noémie!

begin vb
<u>commencer</u>

It begins with "b".
Ça commence par un "b".

beginner n
le <u>débutant</u> m
la <u>débutante</u> f

I'm a beginner.
Je suis débutante.

> *A girl is speaking. How can you tell?*

beginning n
le <u>début</u> m

Look at Language Plus on pages 283–308 for extra vocabulary.

a

b

c

d

e

f

g

h

i

j

k

l

m

n

o

p

q

r

s

t

u

v

w

x

y

z

at the beginning
au début

behave vb
se comporter

He behaves badly.
Il se comporte mal.

Behave!
Sois sage!

behind prep
derrière

behind the television
derrière la télévision

one behind the other
l'un derrière l'autre

beige

> beige can be an adjective or a noun.

Ⓐ adj
beige

a beige skirt
une jupe beige

> Colour adjectives come after the noun in French.

Ⓑ n
le beige m

Belgian

> Belgian can be an adjective or a noun.

Ⓐ adj
belge

Belgian chocolate
le chocolat belge

Pauline is Belgian.
Pauline est belge.

> belge is not spelled with a capital letter except when it means a Belgian person.

Ⓑ n
le/la Belge m/f

the Belgians
les Belges

Belgium n
la Belgique f

believe vb
croire

I don't believe you.
Je ne te crois pas.

bell n

❶ (at school)
la sonnerie f

There's the bell!
C'est la sonnerie!

❷ (small bell)
la clochette f

My cat has a bell on his collar.
Mon chat a une clochette à son collier.

belong vb

That belongs to me.
C'est à moi.

Does this belong to you?
C'est à toi?

Who does it belong to?
C'est à qui?

The ball belongs to Mathieu.
Le ballon est à Mathieu.

below prep
au-dessous de

below ground
au-dessous du sol

ten degrees below freezing
moins dix

belt n
la <u>ceinture</u> f

bench n
le <u>banc</u> m

bend

> **bend** can be a noun or a verb.

Ⓐ n
le <u>virage</u> m

a dangerous bend
un virage dangereux

Ⓑ vb
<u>plier</u>

Bend your leg!
Pliez la jambe!

beneath prep
<u>sous</u>

beneath the table
sous la table

beret n
le <u>béret</u> m

a black beret
un béret noir

berth n
la <u>couchette</u> f

beside prep
à <u>côté de</u>

Sit beside me.
Assieds-toi à côté de moi.

> *To get the accents right in **à côté de**, remember that they form a W:*
> *`^`.*

best

> **best** can be an adjective, a noun or an adverb.

Ⓐ adj
<u>meilleur</u> m adj
<u>meilleure</u> f adj

Étienne is my best friend.
Étienne est mon meilleur ami.

Fleur and Roxanne are my best friends.
Fleur et Roxanne sont mes meilleures amies.

the best team in the world
la meilleure équipe du monde

Ⓑ n
le <u>meilleur</u> m
la <u>meilleure</u> f

He's the best in the class.
C'est le meilleur de la classe.

Ⓒ adv
le <u>mieux</u> m

Emma sings best.
C'est Emma qui chante le mieux.

> 🔑
> **Best wishes!**
> Meilleurs vœux!

best man n
le <u>garçon d'honneur</u> m

better

> **better** can be an adjective or an adverb.

Ⓐ adj
<u>meilleur</u> m adj
<u>meilleure</u> f adj

The ice cream is better than the cake.
La glace est meilleure que le gâteau.

A
B
C
D
E
F
G
H
I
J
K
L
M
N
O
P
Q
R
S
T
U
V
W
X
Y
Z

Look at Language Plus on pages 283–308 for extra vocabulary.

B adv
mieux

That's better!
C'est mieux comme ça.

Get better soon!
Remets-toi vite!

between prep
entre

a number between one and twelve
un nombre entre un et douze

Bible n
la Bible f

bicycle n
le vélo m

by bicycle
en vélo

big adj
1 (*garden, glass, plate, size*)
grand *m adj*
grande *f adj*

a big garden
un grand jardin

a big house
une grande maison

my big brother
mon grand frère

her big sister
sa grande sœur

2 (*car, animal, book, parcel*)
gros *m adj*
grosse *f adj*

a big car
une grosse voiture

bike n
le vélo m

by bike
en vélo

bikini n
le bikini m

bill n
l'addition f

Can we have the bill, please?
L'addition, s'il vous plaît.

billion n
le milliard m

bin n
la poubelle f

Put your chewing gum in the bin.
Mets ton chewing-gum à la poubelle.

bingo n
le loto m

We're going to play bingo.
On va jouer au loto.

biology n
la biologie f

bird n
l'oiseau m
(*pl* les oiseaux)

My cat catches birds.
Mon chat attrape des oiseaux.

Biro® n
le bic® m

birthday n
l'anniversaire m

My birthday is the fifth of May.
Mon anniversaire est le cinq mai.

When's your birthday?
Quelle est la date de ton anniversaire?

Happy birthday!
Bon anniversaire!

anniversaire is related to an, which is the French word for "year", and also to English words like "annual" and "anniversary".

birthday cake n
le gâteau d'anniversaire *m*

birthday card n
la carte d'anniversaire *f*

I got ten birthday cards.
J'ai eu dix cartes d'anniversaire.

birthday party n
la fête d'anniversaire *f*

Would you like to come to my birthday party?
Tu veux venir à ma fête d'anniversaire?

goûter d'anniversaire is another way of saying "birthday party".

biscuit n
le biscuit *m*

Would you like a biscuit?
Tu veux un biscuit?

bit n

a bit
un peu

I'm a bit tired.
Je suis un peu fatigué.

Wait a bit!
Attends un peu!

bite vb
mordre

My dog doesn't bite.
Mon chien ne mord pas.

black

black can be an adjective or a noun.

Ⓐ adj
noir *m adj*
noire *f adj*

She's black.
Elle est noire.

a black jacket
une veste noire

Colour adjectives come after the noun in French.

Ⓑ n
le noir *m*

He is wearing black.
Il est habillé en noir.

blackberry n
la mûre *f*

We picked blackberries.
Nous avons cueilli des mûres.

blackboard n
le tableau *m*
(*pl* les tableaux)

Look at Language Plus on pages 283–308 for extra vocabulary.

Look at the blackboard!
Regardez le tableau!

black coffee n
le café *m*

blackcurrant n
le cassis *m*

blackcurrant jam
la confiture de cassis

blank

> blank can be an adjective or a noun.

Ⓐ adj
blanc *m adj*
blanche *f adj*

a blank sheet of paper
une feuille blanche

Ⓑ n
le blanc *m*

Fill in the blanks, everyone!
Remplissez les blancs, tout le monde!

blanket n
la couverture *f*

blazer n
le blazer *m*

a navy blazer
un blazer bleu marine.

bless vb

Bless you!
À tes souhaits!

blind

> blind can be an adjective or a noun.

Ⓐ adj
aveugle

Are you blind?
Tu es aveugle?

Ⓑ n
le store *m*

Open the blinds!
Ouvrez les stores!

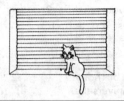

blindfold vb

I'm going to blindfold you.
Je vais te bander les yeux.

block n

a block of flats
un immeuble

blonde adj
blond *m adj*
blonde *f adj*

She's got blonde hair.
Elle a les cheveux blonds.

blood n
le sang *m*

blouse n
le chemisier *m*

a white blouse
un chemisier blanc

blow vb
souffler

The wind is blowing.
Le vent souffle.

Stop when I blow the whistle!
Arrêtez-vous quand je siffle!

Blow your nose!
Mouche-toi!

Blow out the candles!
Souffle sur les bougies!

blue

> blue can be an adjective or a noun.

Ⓐ adj
bleu *m adj*
bleue *f adj*
a blue dress
une robe bleue

> *Colour adjectives come after the noun in French.*

Ⓑ n
le bleu
Blue is my favourite colour.
Ma couleur préférée, c'est le bleu.

board n
1 (*blackboard*)
le tableau *m*
(*pl* les tableaux)

on the board
au tableau

Come to the board, Émilie.
Viens au tableau, Émilie.
2 (*for board games*)
le jeu *m*
(*pl* les jeux)

boarder n
l'interne *m/f*

board game n
le jeu de société *m*

boarding school n
I go to boarding school.
Je suis interne dans une école privée.

boat n
le bateau *m*
(*pl* les bateaux)

body n
le corps *m*

boiled adj
à l'eau *m, f, pl adj*
boiled potatoes
des pommes de terre à l'eau

boiled egg n
l'œuf à la coque *m*

two boiled eggs
deux œufs à la coque

bomb n
la bombe *f*

bonfire n
le feu *m*
(*pl* les feux)

Bonfire Night n

> The French do not celebrate **Bonfire Night**, though they have fireworks on the 14th July, Bastille Day.

book

> **book** can be a noun or a verb.

Ⓐ n
1 (*printed*)
le livre *m*
Open your books at page 10.
Ouvrez vos livres à la page 10.
2 (*exercise book*)
le cahier *m*
Write the words in your books.
Écrivez les mots dans vos cahiers.
Ⓑ vb
réserver
I want to book a seat.
Je veux réserver une place.

bookcase n
la bibliothèque *f*

booklet n
la brochure *f*

bookshelf n
l'étagère à livres *f*

Look at Language Plus on pages 283–308 for extra vocabulary.

on the bookshelves
sur les étagères à livres

bookshop n
la librairie *f*

> **librairie** is related to the English
> word "library". Both places
> contain books, but a **librairie** sells
> them, and a "library" lends them.

boot n
1 la botte *f*

I like your boots!
J'aime bien tes bottes!

football boots
des chaussures de foot

2 (of car)
le coffre *m*

It's in the boot.
C'est dans le coffre.

border n
la frontière *f*

bored adj
I'm bored.
Je m'ennuie.

Are you bored?
Tu t'ennuies?

boring adj
ennuyeux *m adj*
ennuyeuse *f adj*

a boring programme
une émission ennuyeuse

born adj
I was born in 1992.
Je suis né en 1992.

She was born in 1990.
Elle est née en 1990.

borrow vb
emprunter

Can I borrow your pen?
Je peux emprunter ton stylo?

boss n
le patron *m*
la patronne *f*

bossy adj
autoritaire

both pron
tous les deux *mpl pron*
toutes les deux *fpl pron*

**Louis and Daniel, you're both
late!**
Louis et Daniel, vous êtes tous les
deux en retard!

**Inès et Nadège have both got a
rabbit.**
Inès et Nadège ont toutes les deux
un lapin.

bother vb
déranger

I'm sorry to bother you.
Je suis désolé de vous
déranger.

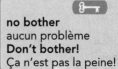

no bother
aucun problème
Don't bother!
Ça n'est pas la peine!

bottle n
la bouteille f

bottom n
1 (of page, list)
le bas m

Look at the bottom of the page.
Regardez le bas de la page.

2 (of container, bag, sea)
le fond m

My pen's in the bottom of my bag.
Mon stylo est au fond de mon sac.

bow n
1 (in ribbon)
le nœud m

Tie a bow!
Fais un nœud!

2 (for archery)
l'arc m

a bow and arrows
un arc et des flèches

bowl n
le bol m

a bowl of soup
un bol de soupe

bowling n
le bowling m

Do you want to come bowling?
Tu veux jouer au bowling?

bowls n
les boules fpl

My grandfather plays bowls.
Mon grand-père joue aux boules.

> **boules** is played on rough ground, not smooth grass. The balls are smaller than those used in bowls, and are made of metal.

box n
1 (container)
la boîte f

a box of matches
une boîte d'allumettes

a cardboard box
un carton

2 (in questionnaire)
la case f

Tick the boxes.
Cochez les cases.

boxer n
le boxeur m

boxer shorts npl
le caleçon m

> **caleçon** is a singular word.

boxing n
la boxe f

I don't like boxing.
Je n'aime pas la boxe.

Boxing Day n
le lendemain de Noël m

on Boxing Day
le lendemain de Noël

> Word for word this means "the day after Christmas".

boy n
le garçon m

Well done, boys!
Bravo les garçons!

boyfriend n
le copain m

Have you got a boyfriend?
Tu as un copain?

Look at Language Plus on pages 283–308 for extra vocabulary.

bra n
le soutien-gorge m

brace n
l'appareil m
She wears a brace.
Elle a un appareil.

bracelet n
le bracelet m

brain n
le cerveau m
(pl les cerveaux)

brainy adj
intelligent m adj
intelligente f adj
Sabine is very brainy.
Sabine est très intelligente.

branch n
la branche f

brand-new adj
tout neuf m adj
toute neuve f adj
I've got a brand-new computer.
J'ai un ordinateur tout neuf.

brass band n
la fanfare f

brave adj
courageux m adj
courageuse f adj
Be brave!
Sois courageux!

bread n
le pain m
Would you like some bread?
Tu veux du pain?

bread and butter
les tartines de pain beurrées

break

break can be a noun or a verb.

A n
la récréation f
during morning break
pendant la récréation du matin
B vb
casser
Michel has broken a window.
Michel a cassé une fenêtre.
Who broke the window?
Qui a cassé la fenêtre?
I have broken my leg.
Je me suis cassé la jambe.
Richard has broken his arm.
Richard s'est cassé le bras.

break down vb
tomber en panne
Our car broke down.
Notre voiture est tombée en panne.

breakfast n
le petit déjeuner m
Breakfast is at eight o'clock.
Le petit déjeuner est à huit heures.
I have cereal for breakfast.
Je prends des céréales au petit déjeuner.

break time n
la récréation f
at break time
à la récréation

break up vb

We break up next Wednesday.
Nos vacances commencent
mercredi.

breaststroke n

la brasse f

I can do the breaststroke.
Je sais faire la brasse.

breath n

Take a deep breath!
Respirez à fond!

brick n

la brique f

a brick wall
un mur en brique

bride n

la mariée f

bridegroom n

le marié m

bridesmaid n

la demoiselle d'honneur f

I'm going to be a bridesmaid.
Je vais être demoiselle d'honneur.

bridge n

le pont m

bright adj

vif m adj
vive f adj

a bright colour
une couleur vive

bright blue
bleu vif

a bright blue shirt
une chemise bleu vif

brilliant adj

génial m adj

géniale f adj

We're going to Paris. – Brilliant!
On va à Paris. – Génial!

bring vb

apporter

Bring the money tomorrow.
Apportez l'argent demain.

**Could you bring me a glass of
water?**
Tu peux m'apporter un verre d'eau?

bring back vb

rapporter

Bring them back!
Rapporte-les!

Britain n

la Grande-Bretagne f

in Britain
en Grande-Bretagne

When are you coming to Britain?
Quand est-ce que tu viens en
Grande-Bretagne?

British

> British can be an adjective or a
> noun.

A adj

britannique

I'm British.
Je suis britannique.

> *britannique* is not spelled with a
> capital letter except when it
> means a British person.
> *Remember that it has two **ns**.*

B n

the British
les Britanniques

Look at Language Plus on pages 283–308 for extra vocabulary.

British Isles npl
les îles Britanniques *fpl*

Brittany n
la Bretagne *f*

> *Brittany has double **t**, **Bretagne** has one **t**.*

broccoli n
les brocolis *mpl*
Would you like some broccoli?
Tu veux des brocolis?

> *What are the two differences in spelling between the French word and the English word?*

brochure n
la brochure *f*

broke vb, *see* **break**

broken adj
cassé *m adj*
cassée *f adj*
It's broken.
C'est cassé.
a broken leg
une jambe cassée
He's got a broken arm.
Il a le bras cassé.

> *If you want to say "I have broken" look at the verb to **break**.*

bronze n
le bronze *m*
the bronze medal
la médaille de bronze

brother n
le frère *m*
my big brother
mon grand frère
I've got one brother.
J'ai un frère.

I haven't got a brother.
Je n'ai pas de frère.

Have you got any brothers or sisters?
Tu as des frères et sœurs?

brown

> **brown** can be an adjective or a noun.

Ⓐ adj
1 marron *m, f, pl adj*
I've got brown eyes.
J'ai les yeux marron.
My shoes are brown.
Mes chaussures sont marron.
2 (*hair*)
brun *m adj*
brune *f adj*
I've got brown hair.
J'ai les cheveux bruns.
She's got light brown hair.
Elle a les cheveux châtain.

> *Colour adjectives come after the noun in French.*

3 (*tanned*)
bronzé *m adj*
bronzée *f adj*
Nina is very brown.
Nina est très bronzée.
Ⓑ n
le marron *m*
Do you have these shoes in brown?
Vous avez ces chaussures en marron?

brown bread n
le pain complet *m*

Brownie n
la Jeannette *f*
I'm a Brownie.
Je suis Jeannette.

I go to Brownies.
Je suis chez les Jeannettes.

Brownies aren't as common in
France as they are in Britain.

bruise n
le <u>bleu</u> m

You've got a bruise.
Tu as un bleu.

bleu is also the word for "blue".
In English "black and blue" means
"covered with bruises".

brush

brush can be a noun or a verb.

Ⓐ n
la <u>brosse</u> f

a brush and comb
une brosse et un peigne

Ⓑ vb
<u>brosser</u>

I brush my pony.
Je brosse mon poney.

I brush my hair.
Je me brosse les cheveux.

I brush my teeth every night.
Je me brosse les dents tous les soirs.

Brussels sprouts npl
les <u>choux de Bruxelles</u> mpl

Brussels has one l, *Bruxelles* has
two.

bubble gum n
le <u>chewing-gum</u> m

bucket n
le <u>seau</u> m
(*pl* les seaux)

my bucket and spade
mon seau et ma pelle

budgie n
la <u>perruche</u> f

I've got a budgie.
J'ai une perruche.

build vb
<u>construire</u>

My dad is building a garage.
Mon père construit un garage.

building n
le <u>bâtiment</u> m

a tall building
un grand bâtiment

bull n
le <u>taureau</u> m
(*pl* les taureaux)

There's a bull in the field.
Il y a un taureau dans le champ.

bully n
la <u>caïd</u> m

He's a big bully.
C'est un gros caïd.

bum n
le <u>derrière</u> m

bum bag n
la <u>banane</u> f

bun n
le <u>petit pain au lait</u> m

I'd like a bun.
Je voudrais un petit pain au lait.

bunch n

a bunch of flowers
un bouquet de fleurs

Look at Language Plus on pages 283–308 for extra vocabulary.

a
b
c
d
e
f
g
h
i
j
k
l
m
n
o
p
q
r
s
t
u
v
w
x
y
z

bunches npl
les couettes fpl
She has bunches.
Elle a des couettes.

bungalow n
le bungalow m

bunk beds npl
les lits superposés mpl

burger n
le hamburger m
a burger and chips
un hamburger avec des frites

bus n
le bus m
by bus
en bus
I go to school by bus.
Je vais à l'école en bus.
the school bus
le car scolaire

bus driver n
le conducteur de bus m

bus station n
la gare routière f

bus stop n
l'arrêt de bus m

business n
les affaires fpl
He's away on business.
Il est en voyage d'affaires.
a business trip
un voyage d'affaires

busy adj
occupé m adj
occupée f adj
My mother is always busy.
Ma mère est toujours
occupée.

but conj
mais
Thanks, but I'm not hungry.
Merci, mais je n'ai pas faim.

butcher's n
la boucherie f

butter n
le beurre m

butterfly n
le papillon m

button n
le bouton m

buy vb
acheter
What are you going to buy?
Qu'est-ce que tu vas acheter?
I'm going to buy a present for Christophe.
Je vais acheter un cadeau pour Christophe.

by prep
1 par
a meal prepared by Pierre
un repas préparé par Pierre
2 (done by)
de
a painting by Picasso
un tableau de Picasso
a book by J.K. Rowling
un livre de J.K. Rowling
3 (next to)
à côté de

Where's the library? – It's by the post office.
Où est la bibliothèque? – Elle est à côté de la poste.

> *To get the accents right in* **à côté de**, *remember that they form a W:* `` `^' ``.

4 <u>en</u>

We're going by car.
On y va en voiture.

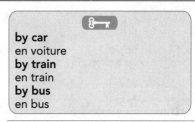

by car
en voiture
by train
en train
by bus
en bus

bye excl
<u>salut!</u>

A
B
C
D
E
F
G
H
I
J
K
L
M
N
O
P
Q
R
S
T
U
V
W
X
Y
Z

C

a
b
c
d
e
f
g
h
i
j
k
l
m
n
o
p
q
r
s
t
u
v
w
x
y
z

cab n
le <u>taxi</u> m

cabbage n
le <u>chou</u> m
(pl les choux)

cactus n
le <u>cactus</u> m

café n
le <u>café</u> m

> Cafés in France sell both
> alcoholic and non-alcoholic
> drinks.

cafeteria n
la <u>cafétéria</u> f

cage n
la <u>cage</u> f

cagoule n
le <u>K-way</u>® m

cake n
le <u>gâteau</u> m
(pl les gâteaux)

calculator n
la <u>calculatrice</u> f

calendar n
le <u>calendrier</u> m

calf n
le <u>veau</u> m
(pl les veaux)

call

> **call** can be a verb or a noun.

A vb
<u>appeler</u>
Call this number.
Appelez ce numéro.
Call the police!
Appelez la police!
I am going to call the register.
Je vais faire l'appel.

> *The l of **appeler** doubles when it
> is followed by e, es and ent.*

Everyone calls him Matt.
Tout le monde l'appelle Matt.
My cat is called Fluffy.
Mon chat s'appelle Fluffy.

What's your cat called?
Ton chat s'appelle comment?

> *The question word **comment** can
> come first or last.*

What's she called?
Comment elle s'appelle?
**What are your brothers
called?**
Tes frères s'appellent
comment?

A
B
C
D
E
F
G
H
I
J
K
L
M
N
O
P
Q
R
S
T
U
V
W
X
Y
Z

What are you called?
Comment tu t'appelles?
or
Tu t'appelles comment?
I'm called Helen.
Je m'appelle Helen.

B n
l'appel *m*
Thanks for your call.
Merci de votre appel.

Give me a call.
Appelle-moi.

call back vb
rappeler
I'll call back at six o'clock.
Je rappellerai à six heures.

call centre n
le centre d'appels *m*
My sister works in a call centre in London.
Ma sœur travaille dans un centre d'appels à Londres.

calm adj
calme

calm down vb
se calmer
Calm down, Hugo!
Calme-toi, Hugo!

Calm down, children!
Calmez-vous, les enfants!

calorie n
la calorie *f*

camcorder n
le caméscope *m*

came vb, *see* **come**

camera n
1 l'appareil photo *m*

I've got a new camera.
J'ai un nouvel appareil photo.

2 (*for filming, TV*)
la caméra *f*

camp n
le camp *m*
a cub camp
un camp de louveteaux

camping n
le camping *m*
to go camping
faire du camping
We're going camping.
Nous allons faire du camping.

campsite n
le terrain de camping *m*

can

can can be a noun or a verb.

A n
la boîte *f*
a can of coke
une boîte de coca
B vb
1 (*be able to*)
pouvoir
I can't come.
Je ne peux pas venir.
Can I help you?
Est-ce que je peux vous aider?

can is sometimes not translated.

I can't see it.
Je ne le vois pas.

Look at Language Plus on pages 283–308 for extra vocabulary.

Can you speak French? – No, I can't.
Parlez-vous français? – Non.

> 🔑
>
> **I can.**
> Je peux.
> **I can't.**
> Je ne peux pas.
> **Can you?**
> Tu peux?

2 (know how to)
savoir

I can swim.
Je sais nager.

I can make pancakes.
Je sais faire les crêpes.

Canada n
le Canada *m*

canal n
le canal *m*
(*pl* les canaux)

cancel vb
annuler

The match was cancelled.
Le match a été annulé.

cancer n
le cancer *m*

He's got cancer.
Il a le cancer.

candle n
la bougie *f*

candyfloss n
la barbe à papa *f*

canoe n
le canoë *m*

canoeing n

to go canoeing
faire du canoë

We're going canoeing.
Nous allons faire du canoë.

can-opener n
l'ouvre-boîte *m*

a can-opener
un ouvre-boîte

can't vb, *see* **can**

canteen n
la cantine *f*

I eat in the canteen.
Je mange à la cantine.

cap n
la casquette *f*

capital n
1 (city)
la capitale *f*

Cardiff is the capital of Wales.
Cardiff est la capitale du pays de Galles.

2 (letter)
la majuscule *f*

Write your address in capitals.
Écris ton adresse en majuscules.

captain n
le capitaine *m*

She's captain of the hockey team.
Elle est capitaine de l'équipe de hockey.

caption n
la légende *f*

car n
la voiture *f*

We've got a new car.
Nous avons une nouvelle voiture.

by car
en voiture

We're going there by car.
Nous y allons en voiture.

caravan n
la caravane f

caravan site n
le camping pour caravanes m

car crash n
l'accident de voiture m

card n
1 (playing card)
la carte f
2 (for birthday, Christmas etc)
la carte de vœux f

I got lots of cards.
J'ai reçu beaucoup de cartes de vœux.

French people don't send as many cards as British people.

cardboard n
le carton m

card game n
le jeu de cartes m

cardigan n
le cardigan m

a green cardigan
un cardigan vert

care

care can be a noun or a verb.

A n
le soin m

with care
avec soin

B vb

I don't care!
Ça m'est égal!

careful adj

Be careful, Gordon!
Fais attention, Gordon!

Be careful, children!
Faites attention, les enfants!

carefully adv

Think carefully, Annick!
Réfléchis bien, Annick!

Listen carefully, children!
Écoutez bien, les enfants!

careless adj

a careless mistake
une faute d'inattention

caretaker n
le gardien m
la gardienne f

My father is a caretaker.
Mon père est gardien.

You do not translate "a" when you say what someone's job is in French.

car-ferry n
le ferry m

carol n

a Christmas carol
un chant de Noël

car park n
le parking m

carpet n
la moquette f

A
B
C
D
E
F
G
H
I
J
K
L
M
N
O
P
Q
R
S
T
U
V
W
X
Y
Z

Look at Language Plus on pages 283–308 for extra vocabulary.

My bedroom carpet is blue.
La moquette de ma chambre est bleue.

carriage n
la <u>voiture</u> f

carrier bag n
le <u>sac en plastique</u> m

carrot n
la <u>carotte</u> f

> *The French word has only one r, but two t*s.

carry vb
<u>porter</u>
I'll carry your bag.
Je vais porter ton sac.

> *The French word* **porter** *is related to the English word "portable", which describes something you can carry.*

carry on vb
<u>continuer</u>
Carry on, Cécile!
Continue, Cécile!

carton n
la <u>brique</u> f

cartoon n
le <u>dessin animé</u> m
I watch cartoons on Saturdays.
Je regarde les dessins animés le samedi.

case n
la <u>valise</u> f
That's my case!
C'est ma valise!

casserole n
le <u>ragoût</u> m
I can make a casserole.
Je sais faire le ragoût.

cassette n
la <u>cassette</u> f
Listen to the cassette, children.
Écoutez la cassette, les enfants.

cassette player n
le <u>lecteur de cassettes</u> m

castle n
le <u>château</u> m
(*pl* les châteaux)
Dover Castle
le château de Douvres

> *A few other British towns have French names. Can you recognize these: Édimbourg, Cantorbéry, Londres?*

casual adj
<u>décontracté</u> m adj
<u>décontractée</u> f adj
I prefer casual clothes.
Je préfère les vêtements décontractés.

cat n
le <u>chat</u> m
la <u>chatte</u> f
Have you got a cat?
Est-ce que tu as un chat?

catch vb
1 <u>attraper</u>
Catch!
Attrape!
My cat catches birds.
Mon chat attrape des oiseaux.

2 (*bus, train*)
prendre

Which bus do you catch?
Quel bus prends-tu?

cathedral n
la cathédrale *f*

Catholic

Catholic can be an adjective or a noun.

A adj
catholique

B n
le/la catholique

I'm a Catholic.
Je suis catholique.

catholique is not spelled with a capital letter.

cauliflower n
le chou-fleur *m*

two cauliflowers
deux choux-fleurs

cave n
la grotte *f*

CD n
le CD *m*
(*pl* les CD)

CD player n
la platine laser *f*

CD-ROM n
le CD-ROM *m*

ceiling n
le plafond *m*

celebrate vb
fêter

Let's celebrate!
Il faut fêter ça!

celery n
le céleri *m*

I don't like celery.
Je n'aime pas le céleri.

cellar n
la cave *f*

a wine cellar
une cave à vins

une cave is dark and underground, like an English cave, but it would contain bottles, not stalactites!

cello n
le violoncelle *m*

I play the cello.
Je joue du violoncelle.

cemetery n
le cimetière *m*

cent n
le centime *m*

two euros and twenty cents
deux euros vingt centimes

centigrade adj
centigrade

twenty degrees centigrade
vingt degrés centigrade

centimetre n
le centimètre *m*

central heating n
le chauffage central *m*

Look at Language Plus on pages 283–308 for extra vocabulary.

centre n
le centre m

in the centre
au centre

a sports centre
un centre sportif

The office is in the centre of town.
Le bureau est en centre-ville.

century n
le siècle m

the twenty-first century
le vingt et unième siècle

cereal n
les céréales fpl

I have cereal for breakfast.
Je prends des céréales au petit déjeuner.

certain adj
certain m adj
certaine f adj

a certain person
une certaine personne

I'm not certain.
Je n'en suis pas certain.

certainly adv

Certainly not!
Certainement pas!

certificate n
le certificat m

chain n
la chaîne f

chair n
1 la chaise f

There's a table and four chairs in the kitchen.
Il y a une table et quatre chaises dans la cuisine.

2 (armchair)
le fauteuil m

There are two chairs and a sofa in the lounge.
Il y a deux fauteuils et un canapé dans le salon.

chalk n
la craie f

a stick of chalk
une craie

champagne n
le champagne m

a glass of champagne
un verre de champagne

champion n
le champion m

la championne f

Anaïs is the champion!
Anaïs est la championne!

Anaïs is a girl's name. How can you tell?

championship n
le championnat m

chance n

No chance!
Pas question!

You're taking a chance!
Tu prends un risque!

change

change *can be a verb or a noun.*

Ⓐ vb
1 changer
I'd like to change £50.
Je voudrais changer cinquante livres.
2 changer de

*Use **changer de** when you change one thing for another.*

Change places!
Changez de place!

I want to change my cards.
Je veux changer de cartes.

I've changed my mind.
J'ai changé d'avis.

B n (*money*)
la monnaie f

I haven't got any change.
Je n'ai pas de monnaie.

Keep the change!
Gardez la monnaie!

changeable adj
variable

The weather is changeable.
Le temps est variable.

changing room n
le vestiaire m

Channel n
la Manche f

> *manche* means "sleeve" in French. Do you think the Channel is sleeve-shaped?

channel n
la chaîne f

There's football on the other channel.
Il y a du football sur l'autre chaîne.

Channel Islands npl
les îles Anglo-Normandes fpl

Channel Tunnel n
le tunnel sous la Manche m

chapter n
le chapitre m

character n
le personnage m

Harry is the main character.
Harry est le personnage principal.

charge n

an extra charge
un supplément

There's no charge.
C'est gratuit.

to be in charge
être responsable

Who is in charge?
Qui est responsable?

charity n
l'association caritative f

We give the money to charity.
Nous donnons l'argent à une association caritative.

chart n
le tableau m
(*pl* les tableaux)

We're making a chart.
Nous faisons un tableau.

charter flight n
le charter m

chase vb
pourchasser

My dog chases cats.
Mon chien pourchasse les chats.

chat vb
bavarder

Pauline chats a lot.
Pauline bavarde beaucoup.

Look at Language Plus on pages 283–308 for extra vocabulary.

cheap adj
bon marché *m, f, pl adj*
cheap T-shirts
les T-shirts bon marché

cheaper adj
moins cher *m adj*
moins chère *f adj*
It's cheaper by bus.
C'est moins cher en bus.

cheat

> cheat can be a verb or a noun.

A vb
tricher
You're cheating!
Tu triches!
Don't cheat, children!
Ne trichez pas, les enfants!
B n
le tricheur *m*
la tricheuse *f*
Isabelle, you're a cheat!
Isabelle, tu es une tricheuse!

check vb
vérifier
Check the spelling.
Vérifiez l'orthographe.

check in vb
(*at airport*)
se présenter à l'enregistrement
What time do I have to check in?
À quelle heure je dois me présenter
à l'enregistrement?

checked adj
à carreaux *m, f, pl adj*
a checked shirt
une chemise à carreaux

checkout n
la caisse *f*
at the checkout
à la caisse

cheek n
la joue *f*
Yvette has got red cheeks.
Yvette a les joues rouges.

cheeky adj
effronté *m adj*
effrontée *f adj*
Don't be cheeky, Hugo!
Ne sois pas effronté, Hugo!

cheer

> cheer can be a noun or a verb.

A n
Cheers!
À la vôtre!
B vb
applaudir
Cheer your team!
Applaudissez votre équipe!

cheerful adj
gai *m adj*
gaie *f adj*

cheerio excl
salut!

cheese n
le fromage *m*
a cheese sandwich
un sandwich au fromage

chef n
le chef *m*

chemist n
la pharmacie *f*
You get it from the chemist.
Ça s'achète en pharmacie.

> Chemists in France have a
> big green cross outside the
> shop.

chemistry n
la <u>chimie</u> f

the chemistry lab
le laboratoire de chimie

cherry n
la <u>cerise</u> f

I love cherries.
J'adore les cerises.

chess n
les <u>échecs</u> mpl

I can play chess.
Je sais jouer aux échecs.

chest n
la <u>poitrine</u> f

chest of drawers n
la <u>commode</u> f

chewing gum n
le <u>chewing-gum</u> m

Put your chewing gum in the bin!
Mets ton chewing-gum à la
poubelle!

chick n
le <u>poussin</u> m

a hen and her chicks
une poule et ses poussins

chicken n
le <u>poulet</u> m

Chicken and chips, please.
Un poulet frites, s'il vous plaît.

chickenpox n
la <u>varicelle</u> f

Thibault has got chickenpox.
Thibault a la varicelle.

child n
l'<u>enfant</u> m/f

a child
un enfant

all the children
tous les enfants

child minder n
la <u>nourrice</u> f

children npl
les <u>enfants</u> mpl

Goodbye children!
Au revoir, les enfants!

chilly adj
<u>froid</u> m adj
<u>froide</u> f adj

It's chilly today.
Il fait froid aujourd'hui.

China n
la <u>Chine</u> f

Chinese

> Chinese can be an adjective or a
> noun.

Ⓐ adj
<u>chinois</u> m adj
<u>chinoise</u> f adj

a Chinese restaurant
un restaurant chinois

a Chinese man
un Chinois

a Chinese woman
une Chinoise

Chinese people
les Chinois

> *chinois is not spelled with a
> capital letter except when it
> means a Chinese person.*

Ⓑ n
the Chinese
les Chinois

A B C D E F G H I J K L M N O P Q R S T U V W X Y Z

Look at Language Plus on pages 283–308 for extra vocabulary.

a
b
c
d
e
f
g
h
i
j
k
l
m
n
o
p
q
r
s
t
u
v
w
x
y
z

chip n
la frite f
I'd like some chips.
Je voudrais des frites.

chocolate n
le chocolat m
I love chocolate.
J'adore le chocolat.

> Use **au chocolat** when something
> is chocolate-flavoured.

a chocolate cake
un gâteau au chocolat

a chocolate ice cream
une glace au chocolat

choice n
le choix m
There's lots of choice.
Il y a beaucoup de choix.

choir n
la chorale f
I sing in the school choir.
Je chante dans la chorale de
l'école.

choose vb
choisir
It's difficult to choose.
C'est difficile de choisir.

Choose the right answer.
Choisissez la bonne réponse.

chop n
la côte f
a pork chop
une côte de porc

chopsticks npl
les baguettes fpl

christening n
le baptême m

Christian name n
le prénom m

Christmas n
Noël m
at Christmas
à Noël

> **Happy Christmas!**
> Joyeux Noël!

Christmas card n
la carte de Noël f

> Christmas cards are not as
> common in France as they
> are in Britain. People
> sometimes send New Year
> cards in January.

Christmas cake n
le gâteau de Noël m

> In France people often eat
> Christmas log (**la bûche de
> Noël**) instead of Christmas
> cake.

Christmas Day m
le jour de Noël m
**Christmas Day is the twenty-fifth
of December.**
Le jour de Noël est le vingt-cinq
décembre.

Christmas dinner n
le repas de Noël m

Most French people also have a Christmas meal (**réveillon de Noël**) on Christmas Eve.

Christmas Eve n
la veille de Noël f

Christmas Eve is the twenty-fourth of December.
La veille de Noël est le vingt-quatre décembre.

Christmas tree n
le sapin de Noël m

a big Christmas tree
un grand sapin de Noël

church n
l'église f

I don't go to church every Sunday.
Je ne vais pas à l'église tous les dimanches.

cider n
le cidre m

cigarette n
la cigarette f

cinema n
le cinéma m

I'm going to the cinema this evening.
Je vais au cinéma ce soir.

circle n
le cercle m

Stand in a circle.
Mettez-vous en cercle.

circumflex n
l'accent circonflexe m

"Tête" has a circumflex.
"Tête" a un accent circonflexe.

circus n
le cirque m

citizenship n
la citoyenneté f

city n
la grande ville f

I live in a city.
J'habite dans une grande ville.

the city centre
le centre-ville

It's in the city centre.
C'est au centre-ville.

clap

clap can be a verb or a noun.

Ⓐ vb
frapper dans ses mains

Sing and clap!
Chantez et frappez dans vos mains!
Ⓑ n
Give Delphine a clap.
Applaudissez Delphine!

clarinet n
la clarinette f

Look at Language Plus on pages 283–308 for extra vocabulary.

I play the clarinet.
Je joue de la clarinette.

class n

1 (*group*)
la <u>classe</u> f

Hermione is in my class.
Hermione est dans ma classe.

2 (*lesson*)
le <u>cours</u> m

I go to dancing classes.
Je vais à des cours de danse.

classroom n
la <u>classe</u> f

classroom assistant n
l'<u>aide-éducateur</u> m
l'<u>aide-éducatrice</u> f

clean

clean can be an adjective or a
verb.

Ⓐ adj
<u>propre</u>

a clean shirt
une chemise propre

Ⓑ vb
<u>nettoyer</u>

Clean the board please!
Nettoie le tableau, s'il te plaît!

cleaner n

1 (*woman*)
la <u>femme de ménage</u> f

2 (*man*)
l'<u>agent d'entretien</u> m

clear adj
<u>clair</u> m adj
<u>claire</u> f adj

a clear explanation
une explication claire

clementine n
la <u>clémentine</u> f

clever adj
<u>intelligent</u> m adj

<u>intelligente</u> f adj

Sylvie is very clever.
Sylvie est très intelligente.

click vb
<u>cliquer</u>

Click on the icon, Luc!
Clique sur l'icône, Luc!

climate n
le <u>climat</u> m

We have a terrible climate.
Nous avons un climat terrible.

cloakroom n

1 (*for coats*)
le <u>vestiaire</u> m

2 (*toilet*)
les <u>toilettes</u> fpl

clock n

1 (*big*)
l'<u>horloge</u> f

the station clock
l'horloge de la gare

2 (*smaller*)
la <u>pendule</u> f

Look at the clock.
Regardez la pendule.

close

close can be a verb, an adjective
or an adverb.

Ⓐ vb
<u>fermer</u>

Please close the door.
Ferme la porte, s'il te plaît.

Close your books, children.
Fermez vos livres, les enfants.

What time does the pool close?
La piscine ferme à quelle heure?

B adj (near)
proche

My house is close to the school.
Ma maison est proche de l'école.

C adv

Come closer, Pierre.
Rapproche-toi, Pierre.

> *The verb, adjective and adverb*
> ***close*** *have the same spelling, but*
> *one of them is pronounced*
> *"cloze". Which one?*

closed adj
fermé *m adj*
fermée *f adj*

The door's closed.
La porte est fermée.

clothes npl
les vêtements *mpl*

I'd like some new clothes.
Je voudrais de nouveaux vêtements.

cloud n
le nuage *m*

There are some black clouds.
Il y a des nuages noirs.

cloudy adj

It's cloudy today.
Il fait gris aujourd'hui.

> ***gris*** *means "grey" – it is rather*
> *grey when it's cloudy.*

clown n
le clown *m*

club n
1 le club *m*

a football club
un club de football

2 (in cards)
clubs
le trèfle

the ace of clubs
l'as de trèfle

coach n
le car *m*

by coach
en car

We're going by coach.
Nous y allons en car.

> ***un car*** *holds a lot more people*
> *than an English car.*

coach station n
la gare routière *f*

coal n
le charbon *m*

coast n
la côte *f*

**It's on the west coast of
Scotland.**
C'est sur la côte ouest de l'Écosse.

coat n
le manteau *m*
(*pl* les manteaux)

I'm wearing a warm coat.
Je porte un manteau chaud.

cocoa n
le cacao *m*

coconut n
la noix de coco *f*

coffee n
le café *m*

I like coffee.
J'aime le café.

A cup of coffee, please.
Un café, s'il vous plaît.

coffee table n
la table basse *f*

A
B
C
D
E
F
G
H
I
J
K
L
M
N
O
P
Q
R
S
T
U
V
W
X
Y
Z

Look at Language Plus on pages 283–308 for extra vocabulary.

a b **c** d e f g h i j k l m n o p q r s t u v w x y z

coin n
la pièce de monnaie f

a two euro coin
une pièce de deux euros

Coke® n
le coca m

a can of Coke®
une boîte de coca

cold

cold can be an adjective or a noun.

Ⓐ adj
froid m adj
froide f adj

The water's cold.
L'eau est froide.

🔑

It's cold today.
Il fait froid aujourd'hui.
I'm cold.
J'ai froid.
I'm not cold.
Je n'ai pas froid.
Are you cold?
Tu as froid?

Ⓑ n (illness)
le rhume m

I've got a cold.
J'ai un rhume.

Ron's got a cold.
Ron a un rhume.

coleslaw n
la salade de chou cru à la mayonnaise f

collar n
le col m

a white collar
un col blanc

collect vb
❶ (pick up)
ramasser

Collect the books please, Natasha.
Ramasse les livres s'il te plaît, Natasha.
❷ (as hobby)
faire collection de

I collect stamps.
Je fais collection de timbres.

collection n
la collection f

college n
le lycée m

a technical college
un lycée d'enseignement technique

colour

colour can be a noun or a verb.

Ⓐ n
la couleur f
What colour eyes has he got?
Il a les yeux de quelle couleur?
Ⓑ vb
colorier

Colour it blue, children.
Coloriez en bleu, les enfants.

🔑

What colour is it?
C'est de quelle couleur?

comb n
le peigne m

come vb
1 venir

Come with me, Jean.
Viens avec moi, Jean.

Can I come too?
Est-ce que je peux venir
aussi?

I'll come with you.
Je viens avec toi.
2 (arrive)
arriver

The bus is coming.
Le bus arrive.

**The letter came this
morning.**
La lettre est arrivée ce matin.

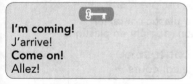

I'm coming!
J'arrive!
Come on!
Allez!

come back vb
revenir

Come back, Louise!
Reviens, Louise!

come from vb
venir de

Where do you come from?
Tu viens d'où?

come in vb
entrer

Can I come in?
Je peux entrer?

Come in!
Entrez!

comic n
l'illustré m

a comic
un illustré

comma n
la virgule f

common adj
courant m adj
courante f adj

**"Smith" is a very common
surname.**
"Smith" est un nom de famille très
courant.

communion n
la communion f

my First Communion
ma première communion

compared adj

**Oxford is small compared with
London.**
Oxford est une petite ville en
comparaison de Londres.

competition n
le concours m

competitor n
le concurrent m
la concurrente f

A
B
C
D
E
F
G
H
I
J
K
L
M
N
O
P
Q
R
S
T
U
V
W
X
Y
Z

Look at Language Plus on pages 283–308 for extra vocabulary.

a
b
c
d
e
f
g
h
i
j
k
l
m
n
o
p
q
r
s
t
u
v
w
x
y
z

complete

> **complete** can be an adjective or a verb.

A adj
complet *m adj*
complète *f adj*

B vb
finir

You must complete your homework by Friday.
Il faut finir vos devoirs pour vendredi.

completely adv
complètement

complicated adj
compliqué *m adj*
compliquée *f adj*

comprehension n
l'exercice de compréhension *f*

comprehensive school n
1 *(for pupils 11–15)*
le collège *m*

2 *(for pupils 15–18)*
le lycée *m*

> In France pupils go to a **collège** between the ages of 11 and 15, and then to a **lycée** until the age of 18.

computer n
l'ordinateur *m*

computer game n
le jeu électronique *m*

I like computer games.
J'aime les jeux électroniques.

computer room n
la salle d'informatique *f*

concert n
le concert *m*

cone n
le cornet *m*

an ice-cream cone
un cornet de glace

congratulations npl
les félicitations *fpl*

Congratulations!
Félicitations!

conjurer n
le prestidigitateur *m*

consequences n
les cadavres exquis *mpl*

conservatory n
le jardin d'hiver *m*

constant adj
constant *m adj*
constante *f adj*

contact lenses npl
les verres de contact *mpl*

container n
le récipient *m*

a plastic container
un récipient en plastique

contest n
le concours *m*

contestant n
le concurrent *m*
la concurrente *f*

continent n
le continent *m*

How many continents are there?
Il y a combien de continents?

the Continent
l'Europe

on the Continent
en Europe

A
B
C
D
E
F
G
H
I
J
K
L
M
N
O
P
Q
R
S
T
U
V
W
X
Y
Z

continental breakfast n
le petit déjeuner à la française *m*

continue vb
continuer

Continue with your work, children!
Continuez à travailler, les enfants!

convent school n
le couvent *m*

She goes to a convent school.
Elle va au couvent.

conversation n
la conversation *f*

cook

cook can be a verb or a noun.

Ⓐ vb
1 cuisiner

I can cook.
Je sais cuisiner.

I can't cook.
Je ne sais pas cuisiner.

2 (*potatoes, rice etc*)
faire cuire

Cook the pasta for ten minutes.
Faites cuire les pâtes pendant dix minutes.

Ⓑ n
le cuisinier *m*
la cuisinière *f*

Matthew's an excellent cook.
Matthew est un excellent cuisinier.

cookbook n
le livre de cuisine *m*

cooked adj
cuit *m adj*
cuite *f adj*

I don't like cooked tomatoes.
Je n'aime pas les tomates cuites.

cooker n
la cuisinière *f*

a gas cooker
une cuisinière à gaz

cooking n
I like cooking.
J'aime bien cuisiner.

cool adj
1 (*quite cold*)
frais *m adj*
fraîche *f adj*

a cool place
un endroit frais

2 (*great*)
super

copy

copy can be a noun or a verb.

Ⓐ n
la copie *f*

Make a copy.
Faites une copie.

Ⓑ vb
copier

Copy the words off the blackboard.
Copiez les mots au tableau.

cork n
le bouchon *m*

corkscrew n
le tire-bouchon *m*

corner n
le coin *m*

Look at Language Plus on pages 283–308 for extra vocabulary.

in a corner of the room
dans un coin de la pièce

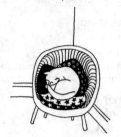

---

cornflakes npl
les corn-flakes mpl

Cornwall n
la Cornouailles f

correct

> correct can be an adjective or a verb.

A adj
exact m adj
exacte f adj
That's correct.
C'est exact.
the correct answer
la bonne réponse
B vb
corriger
Correct the spelling.
Corrigez l'orthographe.

correction n
la correction f

correctly adv
correctement

corridor n
le couloir m
in the corridor
dans le couloir

Corsica n
la Corse f

cost vb
coûter
A coke costs two euros.
Un coca coûte deux euros.

> **How much does it cost?**
> Ça coûte combien?

costume n
le costume m

cottage n
le cottage m

cotton n
le coton m
a cotton shirt
une chemise en coton

> The French word only has one **t**.

couch n
le canapé m

cough

> cough can be a noun or a verb.

A la toux f
a bad cough
une mauvaise toux
I've got a cough.
Je tousse.

B vb
tousser
I can't stop coughing.
Je n'arrête pas de tousser.

could vb
Could I have a glass of water?
Je peux avoir un verre d'eau?

A
B
C
D
E
F
G
H
I
J
K
L
M
N
O
P
Q
R
S
T
U
V
W
X
Y
Z

Could you move a bit?
Tu peux te pousser un peu?

Could you move a bit, boys?
Vous pouvez vous pousser un peu,
les garçons?

> 🔑
> **Could I ...?**
> Je peux ...?
> **Could you ...?**
> Tu peux ...?

count vb
compter

Count from one to twenty!
Comptez de un à vingt!

counter n
1 (in shop)
le comptoir m
2 (in game)
le jeton m

country n
1 (France, Britain etc)
le pays m

France is a big country.
La France est un grand pays.
2 (countryside)
la campagne f

I live in the country.
J'habite à la campagne.

country dancing n
la danse folklorique f

countryside n
la campagne f

in the countryside
à la campagne

couple n

a couple of days
deux jours

a couple of hours
deux heures

a young couple
un jeune couple

courgette n
la courgette f

course n
1 (of meal)
le plat m

the main course
le plat principal

the first course
l'entrée
2 (lessons)
le cours m

a French course
un cours de français

Do you love me? – Of course I do!
Tu m'aimes? – Bien sûr que oui!

> 🔑
> **of course**
> bien sûr

court n
le court m

There are tennis courts.
Il y a des courts de tennis.

cousin n
le cousin m
la cousine f

Jo is my favourite cousin.
Jo est ma cousine préférée.

> *Is Jo a boy or a girl? What are the
> 3 clues in the French sentence?*

cover n
la couverture f

cow n
la vache f

a big black cow
une grosse vache noire

crab n
le crabe m

Look at Language Plus on pages 283–308 for extra vocabulary.

cracker n

1 (*biscuit*)

le cracker m

2 (*Christmas cracker*)

la papillote f

> **Papillotes** are different from crackers in Britain. They consist of a sweet with a joke and a banger wrapped round it, covered in foil. You unwrap them and pull the banger.

crash n

l'accident m

a crash
un accident

crawl n

le crawl m

I can do the crawl.
Je sais nager le crawl.

crazy adj

fou m adj

folle f adj

cream

> **cream** can be a noun or an adjective.

Ⓐ n

la crème f

strawberries and cream
les fraises à la crème

Ⓑ adj (*colour*)

crème m, f, pl adj

a cream shirt
une chemise crème

> *Colour adjectives come after the noun in French.*

cream cake n

le gâteau à la crème m

two cream cakes
deux gâteaux à la crème

credit card n

la carte de crédit f

cress n

le cresson m

I'm growing cress.
Je fais pousser du cresson.

crew cut n

les cheveux en brosse mpl

He's got a crew cut.
Il a les cheveux en brosse.

cricket n

le cricket m

I play cricket.
Je joue au cricket.

> **Cricket** is not played in France.

cricket bat n

la batte de cricket f

crisps npl

les chips fpl

a bag of crisps
un paquet de chips

cross

> **cross** can be a verb, a noun or an adjective.

Ⓐ vb

traverser

Cross the road at the lights.
Traversez la rue aux feux.

B n
la <u>croix</u> f

Put a tick or a cross.
Cochez ou mettez une croix.

C adj
pas <u>content</u> m adj
pas <u>contente</u> f adj

She is cross.
Elle n'est pas contente.

crossing n
la <u>traversée</u> f

the crossing from Dover to Calais
la traversée de Douvres à Calais

crossroads n
le <u>carrefour</u> m

at the crossroads
au carrefour

crossword n
les <u>mots croisés</u> mpl

I like doing crosswords.
J'aime faire les mots croisés.

crowd n
la <u>foule</u> f

crowded adj
<u>bondé</u> m adj
<u>bondée</u> f adj

The pool is crowded on Saturdays.
La piscine est bondée le samedi.

crown n
la <u>couronne</u> f

crutch n
la <u>béquille</u> f

cry vb
<u>pleurer</u>

Why are you crying?
Pourquoi tu pleures?

CTC n
le <u>collège technique</u> m

cub n
1 (scout)
le <u>louveteau</u> m
(pl les louveteaux)

> Cubs and scouts are not as
> common in France as they
> are in Britain.

2 (young animal)
le <u>petit</u> m

cube n
le <u>cube</u> m

cucumber n
le <u>concombre</u> m

cup n
la <u>tasse</u> f

a cup of tea
une tasse de thé

a cup of coffee
un café

cupboard n
le <u>placard</u> m

What's in the cupboard?
Qu'est-ce qu'il y a dans le placard?

curious adj
<u>curieux</u> m adj
<u>curieuse</u> f adj

A B C D E F G H I J K L M N O P Q R S T U V W X Y Z

Look at Language Plus on pages 283–308 for extra vocabulary.

curly adj
1 (wavy)
bouclé m adj
bouclée f adj
2 (tightly curled)
frisé m adj
frisée f adj

currant n
le <u>raisin sec</u> m
I don't like currants.
Je n'aime pas les raisins secs.

> *raisin sec* means "dried grape" –
> which is what a currant is.

curriculum n
le <u>programme</u> m

curry n
le <u>curry</u> m

curtain n
le <u>rideau</u> m
(*pl* les rideaux)
The curtains are green and white.
Les rideaux sont verts et blancs.
Draw the curtains, please.
Tirez les rideaux, s'il vous plaît.

cushion n
le <u>coussin</u> m

custard n
la <u>crème anglaise</u> f

custom n
la <u>coutume</u> f
It's an old custom.
C'est une ancienne coutume.

customer n
le <u>client</u> m
la <u>cliente</u> f

cut vb
<u>couper</u>
I'll cut the cake.
Je vais couper le gâteau.
Mind you don't cut yourself!
Attention à ne pas te couper!

cutlery n
les <u>couverts</u> mpl

cycle vb
<u>faire du vélo</u>
I like cycling.
J'aime faire du vélo.
I cycle to school.
Je vais à l'école à vélo.

cycle lane n
la <u>piste cyclable</u> f

cycling n
le <u>cyclisme</u> m

cyclist n
le/la <u>cycliste</u> m/f

D

dad n
1 le père *m*
my dad
mon père
his dad
son père
2 (*used as a name*)
le papa *m*
Dad!
Papa!
Let's ask Dad.
On va demander à Papa.

daddy n
le papa *m*
Hello Daddy!
Bonjour Papa!

daffodil n
la jonquille *f*

daily adv
tous les jours
The pool is open daily from 9 a.m. to 6 p.m.
La piscine est ouverte tous les jours de neuf heures à dix-huit heures.

damn excl
zut!

damp adj
humide

dance

> **dance** can be a noun or a verb.

A n
1 la danse *f*
It's a new dance.
C'est une nouvelle danse.
2 le bal *m*
Are you going to the dance tonight, Marie-Thérèse?
Tu vas au bal ce soir, Marie-Thérèse?
B vb
danser
Can you dance?
Tu sais danser?
I like dancing.
J'aime danser.

dancer n
le danseur *m*
la danseuse *f*

dandelion n
le pissenlit *m*

danger n
le danger *m*
in danger
en danger
His life is in danger.
Sa vie est en danger.

dangerous adj
dangereux *m adj*
dangereuse *f adj*

Look at Language Plus on pages 283–308 for extra vocabulary.

a
b
c
d
e
f
g
h
i
j
k
l
m
n
o
p
q
r
s
t
u
v
w
x
y
z

dark

dark can be an adjective or a noun.

Ⓐ adj
1 (colour)
foncé *m adj*
foncée *f adj*

She's got dark hair.
Elle a les cheveux foncés.

a dark green sweater
un pull vert foncé
2 (at night)

It's dark at six o'clock.
Il fait nuit à six heures.

It's getting dark.
Il commence à faire nuit.

It's dark in here.
Il fait sombre ici.

Ⓑ n
le noir *m*

I'm afraid of the dark.
J'ai peur du noir.

darling n
le chéri *m*
la chérie *f*

Thank you, darling!
Merci, chéri!

dart n
la fléchette *f*

Do you want to play darts?
Tu veux jouer aux fléchettes?

date n
la date *f*

my date of birth
ma date de naissance

What date is your birthday?
Quelle est la date de ton anniversaire?

What's the date today?
Quelle est la date aujourd'hui?

daughter n
la fille *f*

day n

*There are two words for **day**: un jour is the whole 24 hours, une journée is the time you're awake.*

1 le jour *m*
I am going to Paris for three days.
Je vais à Paris pour trois jours.
2 la journée *f*

during the day
dans la journée

Marc watches TV all day.
Marc regarde la télé toute la journée.

the day before my birthday
la veille de mon anniversaire

It's Richard's birthday the day after tomorrow.
C'est l'anniversaire de Richard après-demain.

It's my day off.
C'est mon jour de congé.

the days of the week
les jours de la semaine
every day
tous les jours
all day
toute la journée
What day is it today?
Quel jour sommes-nous?
the day after tomorrow
après-demain

dead adj
mort *m adj*
morte *f adj*

deaf adj
sourd *m adj*
sourde *f adj*

deal

> **deal** can be a noun or a verb.

A n
le marché *m*

It's a deal!
Marché conclu!

a great deal
beaucoup

a great deal of money
beaucoup d'argent

B vb *(cards)*
donner

It's your turn to deal.
C'est à toi de donner.

dear adj
cher *m adj*
chère *f adj*

Dear Mrs Duval
Chère Madame Duval

death n
la mort *f*

after his death
après sa mort

> **mort** is related to the words "mortal" and "mortality" in English.

December n
décembre *m*

December or January?
Décembre ou janvier?

My birthday's in December.
Mon anniversaire est en décembre.

> 🔑
>
> **in December**
> en décembre
> **the fifth of December**
> le cinq décembre
>
> *The months are not spelled with a capital letter in French.*

decide vb
décider

I have decided to go to the party.
J'ai décidé d'aller à la fête.

I can't decide.
Je n'arrive pas à me décider.

decision n
la décision *f*

What's your decision?
Quelle est ta décision?

We need to make a decision.
On doit prendre une décision.

deck n
le pont *m*

on deck
sur le pont

deckchair n
la chaise longue *f*

decorate vb
1 décorer

We decorate the classroom for Christmas.
Nous décorons la classe pour Noël.

Look at Language Plus on pages 283–308 for extra vocabulary.

2 (a room)
peindre et tapisser
Mum's going to decorate my bedroom.
Maman va peindre et tapisser ma chambre.

*Use **peindre** alone, if you just mean "paint". Use **tapisser** alone, if you just mean "wallpaper".*

decorations npl
les décorations *fpl*
Christmas decorations
les décorations de Noël

deep adj
1 (water, hole, cut)
profond *m adj*
profonde *f adj*
Is it deep?
Est-ce que c'est profond?
2 (snow, mud)
épais *m adj*
épaisse *f adj*
The snow is deep.
La neige est épaisse.

Take a deep breath, girls!
Respirez à fond, les filles!

deer n
1 (red deer)
le cerf *m*
2 (fallow deer)
le daim *m*
3 (roe deer)
le chevreuil *m*

In French you have to say which kind of deer you mean!

defence n
la défense *f*
I play in defence.
Je joue en défense.

What are the 2 differences in spelling between the French word and the English word?

defender n
le défenseur *m*

definite adj
1 (precise)
précis *m adj*
précise *f adj*
I haven't got any definite plans.
Je n'ai pas de projets précis.
2 (certain)
sûr *m adj*
sûre *f adj*
Maybe, it's not definite.
Peut-être, ce n'est pas sûr.

definitely adv
vraiment
He's definitely the best player.
C'est vraiment lui le meilleur joueur.
Definitely!
C'est sûr!

degree n
1 (measurement)
le degré *m*
a temperature of thirty degrees
une température de trente degrés
2 (qualification)
la licence *f*
a degree in English
une licence d'anglais

delayed adj
retardé *m adj*
retardée *f adj*
All flights are delayed.
Tous les vols sont retardés.

delicatessen n
l'épicerie fine *f*

a delicatessen
une épicerie fine

delicious adj
délicieux m adj
délicieuse f adj

The mousse is delicious!
La mousse est délicieuse!

deliver vb
1 livrer

I deliver newspapers.
Je livre les journaux.
2 (letters)
distribuer

The postman delivers our mail.
Le facteur distribue notre courrier.

denim n
le jean m

a denim jacket
une veste en jean

Denmark n
le Danemark m

dentist n
le/la dentiste m/f

I'm going to the dentist.
Je vais chez le dentiste.

Catherine is a dentist.
Catherine est dentiste.

You do not translate "a" when you say what someone's job is in French.

department n
1 (in shop)
le rayon m

the shoe department
le rayon chaussures
2 (of university, school)
le département m

He works in the English department.
Il travaille dans le département d'anglais.

department store n
le grand magasin m

departure n
le départ m

departure lounge n
le hall des départs m

depend vb
It depends.
Ça dépend.

depending on the weather
selon le temps

deposit n
1 (part payment)
les arrhes fpl

You have to pay a deposit when you book.
Il faut verser des arrhes lors de la réservation.
2 (when hiring something)
la caution f

You get the deposit back when you return the bike.
On vous remboursera la caution quand vous ramènerez le vélo.

depressed adj
déprimé m adj
déprimée f adj

I feel depressed.
Je suis déprimé.

Look at Language Plus on pages 283–308 for extra vocabulary.

a
b
c
d
e
f
g
h
i
j
k
l
m
n
o
p
q
r
s
t
u
v
w
x
y
z

deputy head n
le directeur adjoint m
la directrice adjointe f

describe vb
décrire
Describe yourself.
Décris-toi.

description n
la description f

desert n
le désert m

desert island n
l'île déserte f

deserve vb
mériter
You deserve a prize, Marie.
Tu mérites un prix, Marie.

design

> **design** can be a noun or a verb.

A n (pattern)
le motif m
a simple design
un motif simple
B vb
dessiner
We're going to design a birthday card.
On va dessiner une carte d'anniversaire.

designer clothes npl
les vêtements griffés mpl

desk n
1 (in school)
le pupitre m
my desk
mon pupitre
2 (in office)
le bureau m
(pl les bureaux)

dessert n
le dessert m
for dessert
comme dessert

destination n
la destination f

detached house n
le pavillon m

detail n
le détail m
in detail
en détail

detective n
l'inspecteur de police m
He's a detective.
Il est inspecteur de police.

> You do not translate "**a**" when you say what someone's job is in French.

detective story n
le roman policier m

detention n
You'll get a detention!
Tu vas avoir une retenue!

develop vb
développer
I want to get this film developed.
Je veux faire développer ce film.

*The French word **développer** has double **p**.*

diabetic n
le/la diabétique *m/f*
I'm a diabetic.
Je suis diabétique.

diagonal adj
diagonal *m adj*
diagonale *f adj*

diagram n
le diagramme *m*

dial vb
composer
Dial the number.
Composez le numéro.

dialogue n
le dialogue *m*

diamond n
1 le diamant *m*
a diamond ring
une bague en diamant
2 (*cards*)
diamonds
le carreau
the ace of diamonds
l'as de carreau

diary n
1 l'agenda *m*
I've got her phone number in my diary.
J'ai son numéro de téléphone dans mon agenda.

2 le journal *m*
(*pl* les journaux)
I keep a diary.
Je tiens un journal.

*The French word **journal** is related to the word **jour**, which means "day". **Journal** also means "newspaper". Newspapers come out every day, and people write in their diaries every day.*

dice n
le dé *m*
Throw the dice, Leah.
Jette le dé, Leah.

dictionary n
le dictionnaire *m*
Look in the dictionary.
Cherchez dans le dictionnaire.

*The French word **dictionnaire** has double **n**.*

did vb, *see* do

die vb
mourir
He died last year.
Il est mort l'année dernière.
She died in 2002.
Elle est morte en deux mille deux.

diesel n
1 (*fuel*)
le gazole *m*
2 (*car*)
la voiture diesel *f*

diet
diet can be a noun or a verb.

Ⓐ n
1 l'alimentation *f*
a healthy diet
une alimentation saine

Look at Language Plus on pages 283–308 for extra vocabulary.

2 (for slimming)
le <u>régime</u> m

My dad's on a diet.
Mon père est au régime.

Are you on a diet?
Tu es au régime?

B vb
faire un <u>régime</u>
My mum's dieting.
Ma mère fait un régime.

difference n
la <u>différence</u> f
What's the difference?
Quelle est la différence?

different adj
<u>différent</u> m adj
<u>différente</u> f adj
We are very different.
Nous sommes très différents.

Paris is different from London.
Paris est différent de Londres.

difficult adj
<u>difficile</u>
It's difficult.
C'est difficile.

difficulty n
la <u>difficulté</u> f
without difficulty
sans difficulté

dig vb
<u>creuser</u>
My rabbit digs lots of holes.
Mon lapin creuse beaucoup de trous.

dinghy n
a rubber dinghy
un canot pneumatique

dining room n
la <u>salle à manger</u> f

> **manger** means "to eat", so word for word the French means "the room for eating".

dinner n
1 (midday meal)
le <u>déjeuner</u> m
2 (evening meal)
le <u>dîner</u> m

dinner lady n
la <u>dame de service</u> f

dinner time n
1 (midday meal)
l'<u>heure du déjeuner</u> f
2 (evening meal)
l'<u>heure du dîner</u> f

dinosaur n
le <u>dinosaure</u> m

direct adj
<u>direct</u> m adj
<u>directe</u> f adj
the most direct route
le chemin le plus direct

direction n
la <u>direction</u> f

You're going in the wrong direction.
Vous allez dans la mauvaise
direction.

dirty adj
sale

My shoes are dirty.
Mes chaussures sont sales.

disabled adj
handicapé *m adj*

handicapée *f adj*

disabled people
les handicapés

disagree vb

I disagree!
Je ne suis pas d'accord!

disappointed adj
déçu *m adj*

déçue *f adj*

disappointment n
la déception *f*

disaster n
le désastre *m*

It's a disaster!
C'est un désastre!

discipline n
la discipline *f*

disc jockey n
le disc-jockey *m*

disco n
la soirée disco *f*

**There's a disco at the school
tonight.**
Il y a une soirée disco à l'école ce
soir.

discussion n
la discussion *f*

disguise vb
déguiser

He was disguised as a policeman.
Il était déguisé en policier.

*Which consonant is missing in the
French word **déguiser**?*

disgusting adj
dégoûtant *m adj*

dégoûtante *f adj*

It looks disgusting.
Ça a l'air dégoûtant.

dish n
le plat *m*

a vegetarian dish
un plat végétarien

I always do the dishes.
Je fais toujours la vaisselle.

dishwasher n
le lave-vaisselle *m*

disk n
le disque *m*

dislike n

my likes and dislikes
ce que j'aime et ce que je n'aime pas

distance n
la distance *f*

a distance of ten kilometres
une distance de dix kilomètres

in the distance
au loin

distract vb
distraire

Don't distract him, Lulu.
Ne le distraie pas, Lulu.

Look at Language Plus on pages 283–308 for extra vocabulary.

a
b
c
d
e
f
g
h
i
j
k
l
m
n
o
p
q
r
s
t
u
v
w
x
y
z

district n

1 (of town)
le quartier m

2 (of country)
la région f

disturb vb

déranger

I'm sorry to disturb you.
Je suis désolé de vous déranger.

dive vb

plonger

I like diving.
J'aime plonger.

> *plonger* is related to the English word "plunge". When you dive, you plunge into the pool.

divide vb

diviser

Divide the pastry in half.
Divisez la pâte en deux.

Twelve divided by three is four.
Douze divisé par trois égale quatre.

Divide into two groups!
Divisez-vous en deux groupes!

diving board n

le plongeoir m

divorced adj

divorcé m adj

divorcée f adj

My parents are divorced.
Mes parents sont divorcés.

DIY n

le bricolage m

He likes doing DIY.
Il aime faire du bricolage.

dizzy adj

I feel dizzy.
J'ai la tête qui tourne.

DJ n

le disc-jockey m

do vb

> *Look carefully through the entry for **do** to find what you want to say.*

faire

I do a lot of cycling.
Je fais beaucoup de vélo.

What are you doing this evening?
Qu'est-ce que tu fais ce soir?

My brother does judo.
Mon frère fait du judo.

Do the actions.
Faites les gestes!

I haven't done my homework.
Je n'ai pas fait mes devoirs.

Who did that?
Qui a fait ça?

That'll do, thanks.
Ça ira, merci.

> *In English, **do** is often used to make questions. In French, questions are made either with* **est-ce que** ...

Do you like French food?
Est-ce que vous aimez la cuisine française?

Where does he live?
Où est-ce qu'il habite?

What do you do in your free time?
Qu'est-ce que vous faites pendant vos loisirs?

... or by reversing the order of verb and subject ...

Do you speak English?
Parlez-vous anglais?

... or by adding a question mark.

Do you speak French, Kevin?
Tu parles français, Kevin?

*Use **ne ... pas** in negative sentences.*

I don't understand.
Je ne comprends pas.

She doesn't like dogs.
Elle n'aime pas les chiens.

You go swimming on Fridays, don't you?
Tu fais de la natation le vendredi, n'est-ce pas?

What are you doing?
Qu'est-ce que tu fais?
I'm not doing anything.
Je ne fais rien.
... don't you?
... n'est-ce pas?

do up vb
1 (*tie*)
lacer
Do up your shoes!
Lace tes chaussures!
2 (*button up*)
boutonner
Do up your coat!
Boutonne ton manteau!
Do up your zip!
(*on trousers*)
Ferme ta braguette!

doctor n
le médecin m
I'm going to the doctor.
Je vais chez le médecin.

I'd like to be a doctor.
Je voudrais être médecin.
She's a doctor.
Elle est médecin.

*You do not translate "**a**" when you say what someone's job is in French.*

dodgems npl
les autos tamponneuses fpl

does vb, *see* **do**

dog n
le chien m
la chienne f
Have you got a dog?
Tu as un chien?

doll n
la poupée f

dolphin n
le dauphin m

dominoes npl
Let's have a game of dominoes.
Faisons une partie de dominos.

done vb, *see* **do**

donkey n
l'âne m
Pin the tail on the donkey!
Accroche la queue à l'âne.

door n
1 la porte f
the first door on the right
la première porte à droite

Look at Language Plus on pages 283–308 for extra vocabulary.

2 (of car, train)
la portière f

dormitory n
le dortoir m

dormitory is related to the French verb dormir, which means "to sleep". A dormitory is a place where you sleep.

dot n
le point m

double adj
double

a double helping
une double portion

double bed n
le grand lit m

double room n
la chambre pour deux personnes f

double-decker bus n
le bus à impériale m

doubt vb
I doubt it.
J'en doute.

doughnut n
le beignet m

a jam doughnut
un beignet à la confiture

Dover n
Douvres

from Dover to Boulogne
de Douvres à Boulogne

in Dover
à Douvres

down

down can be an adverb, a preposition or an adjective.

A adv
en bas

Don't look down!
Ne regarde pas en bas!

It's down in the cellar.
C'est dans la cave.

It's down there.
C'est là-bas.

B prep

I live just down the road.
J'habite tout à côté.

C adj

I'm feeling a bit down.
J'ai un peu le cafard.

The computer's down.
L'ordinateur est en panne.

download vb
télécharger

You can download the file.
Tu peux télécharger le fichier.

downstairs adv
au rez-de-chaussée

The bathroom's downstairs.
La salle de bain est au rez-de-chaussée.

I'm downstairs!
Je suis en bas!

dozen n
la douzaine f

two dozen
deux douzaines

a dozen eggs
une douzaine d'œufs

douzaine is related to the French word douze, which means "twelve". A dozen means twelve.

dragon n
le <u>dragon</u> m

drama n
l'art <u>dramatique</u> m

Drama is my favourite subject.
Ma matière préférée, c'est l'art dramatique.

drank vb, *see* drink

draughts n
les <u>dames</u> fpl

Do you want to play draughts?
Tu veux jouer aux dames?

draw

> **draw** can be a verb or a noun.

Ⓐ vb
1 (*with pencil*)
<u>dessiner</u>

I can't draw.
Je ne sais pas dessiner.

Draw a house, everyone.
Dessinez une maison, tout le monde.

Draw a picture.
Faites un dessin.
2 (*in game*)
<u>faire match nul</u>

We drew 2-2.
Nous avons fait match nul deux à deux.
Ⓑ n (*in game*)
le <u>match nul</u> m

It's a draw between the boys and the girls.
Match nul entre les garçons et les filles.

drawer n
le <u>tiroir</u> m

> *You see "Tirez" on doors in France. It means "pull".* **Un tiroir** *is something you pull out.*

drawing n
le <u>dessin</u> m

drawing pin n
la <u>punaise</u> f

dream n
le <u>rêve</u> m

Sweet dreams, darling!
Fais de beaux rêves, chérie!

a bad dream
un cauchemar

dress

> **dress** can be a noun or a verb.

Ⓐ n
la <u>robe</u> f
Élodie is wearing a white dress.
Élodie porte une robe blanche.
Ⓑ vb

to get dressed
s'habiller

I'm getting dressed.
Je m'habille.

Go and get dressed.
Va t'habiller.

dress up vb
se <u>déguiser</u>

Look at Language Plus on pages 283–308 for extra vocabulary.

a
b
c
d
e
f
g
h
i
j
k
l
m
n
o
p
q
r
s
t
u
v
w
x
y
z

I'm going to dress up as a princess.
Je vais me déguiser en princesse.

dressed adj
habillé *m adj*
habillée *f adj*

I'm not dressed yet.
Je ne suis pas encore habillé.

How was she dressed?
Comment est-ce qu'elle était habillée?

She was dressed in a green sweater and jeans.
Elle portait un pull vert et un jean.

drew vb, *see* **draw**

drink

> **drink** can be a verb or a noun.

Ⓐ vb
boire

What would you like to drink?
Qu'est-ce que vous voulez boire?

She drank three cups of tea.
Elle a bu trois tasses de thé.

Ⓑ n
1 la boisson *f*

a cold drink
une boisson fraîche

a hot drink
une boisson chaude

2 *(alcoholic)*
le verre *m*

Would you like a drink?
Vous prenez un verre?

drive

> **drive** can be a noun or a verb.

Ⓐ n
1 le tour en voiture *m*

Let's go for a drive.
Allons faire un tour en voiture.

2 *(of house)*
l'allée *f*

You can park your car in the drive.
Vous pouvez garer votre voiture dans l'allée.

Ⓑ vb
1 *(car)*
conduire

She's learning to drive.
Elle apprend à conduire.

Can you drive?
Tu sais conduire?

2 *(go by car)*
aller en voiture

Are you going by train? – No, we're driving.
Vous prenez le train? – Non, nous y allons en voiture.

3 *(take by car)*
emmener en voiture

My mother drives me to school.
Ma mère m'emmène à l'école en voiture.

driver n
1 *(of car)*
le conducteur *m*
la conductrice *f*

She's an excellent driver.
C'est une excellente conductrice.

2 *(of taxi, bus)*
le chauffeur *m*

driving licence n
le permis de conduire *m*

drop

> **drop** can be a noun or a verb.

Ⓐ n
la goutte *f*

a drop of water
une goutte d'eau

Ⓑ vb
laisser tomber

Drop the ball!
Laisse tomber la balle!

drug n
1 (*medicine*)
le médicament *m*

They need food and drugs.
Ils ont besoin de nourriture et de médicaments.

2 (*illegal*)
la drogue *f*

hard drugs
les drogues dures

Don't take drugs.
Ne vous droguez pas.

drum n
le tambour *m*

an African drum
un tambour africain

I play drums.
Je joue de la batterie.

drum kit n
la batterie *f*

drummer n
le batteur *m*
la batteuse *f*

drunk adj
ivre

dry

dry can be an adjective or a verb.

A adj
1 (*not wet*)
sec *m adj*
sèche *f adj*

The paint isn't dry yet.
La peinture n'est pas encore sèche.

2 (*weather*)
sans pluie

a long dry period
une longue période sans pluie

B vb
sécher

Let the glue dry.
Laissez sécher la colle.

I need to dry my hair.
Je dois me sécher les cheveux.

duck n
le canard *m*

due adj
The plane's due in half an hour.
L'avion doit arriver dans une demi-heure.

When's the baby due?
Le bébé est prévu pour quand?

dull adj
It's dull today.
Il fait gris aujourd'hui.

dummy n
la tétine *f*

dump n
It's a real dump!
C'est un endroit minable!

dungarees npl
la salopette *f*

salopette is a singular word.

dungeon n
le cachot *m*

Look at Language Plus on pages 283–308 for extra vocabulary.

a
b
c
d
e
f
g
h
i
j
k
l
m
n
o
p
q
r
s
t
u
v
w
x
y
z

during prep
pendant
during the day
pendant la journée

dustbin n
la poubelle f

duty-free shop n
la boutique hors taxes f

duvet n
la couette f

DVD n
le DVD m
I've got that film on DVD.
J'ai ce film en DVD.

DVD player n
le lecteur de DVD m

dwarf n
le nain m
la naine f

E

each

> **each** can be an adjective or a pronoun.

Ⓐ adj
chaque
each day
chaque jour
Ⓑ pron
chacun *m pron*
chacune *f pron*
They have 10 points each.
Ils ont dix points chacun.
The plates cost £5 each.
Les assiettes coûtent cinq livres chacune.
Take one card each.
Prenez une carte chacun.
We write to each other.
Nous nous écrivons.

ear n
l'oreille *f*

earache n
I've got earache.
J'ai mal aux oreilles.

early adv
1 (*early in the day*)
tôt
I get up early.
Je me lève tôt.
I go to bed early.
Je me couche tôt.
2 (*ahead of time*)
en avance
Come early to get a good seat.
Venez en avance pour avoir une bonne place.

earn vb
gagner
She earns £5 an hour.
Elle gagne cinq livres de l'heure.

earring n
la boucle d'oreille *f*
diamond earrings
des boucles d'oreille en diamant

earth n
la terre *f*

east

> **east** can be an adjective or a noun.

Ⓐ adj
est *m, f, pl adj*
the east coast
la côte est
Ⓑ n
l'est *m*
in the east
dans l'est

Easter n
Pâques *fpl*
at Easter
à Pâques

Look at Language Plus on pages 283–308 for extra vocabulary.

the Easter holidays
les vacances de Pâques

> 🔑
> **Happy Easter!**
> Joyeuses Pâques!

Easter egg n
l'œuf de Pâques m
a big Easter egg
un gros œuf de Pâques

> In France, Easter eggs are said to be brought by the Easter bells (**cloches de Pâques**) which fly from Rome and drop them in people's gardens.

easy adj
facile
It's easy!
C'est facile!

eat vb
manger
I eat a lot of sweets.
Je mange beaucoup de bonbons.
Would you like something to eat?
Est-ce que tu veux manger quelque chose?

edge n
le bord m

on the edge of the table
au bord de la table

Edinburgh n
Édimbourg
Andrew lives in Edinburgh.
Andrew habite à Édimbourg.

> A few British towns have French names. Can you recognize these: Douvres, Cantorbéry, Londres?

education n
l'éducation f

effect n
l'effet m
special effects
les effets spéciaux

effort n
l'effort m
You have to make an effort.
Tu dois faire un effort.

e.g. abbr
p. ex.

egg n
l'œuf m
a hard-boiled egg
un œuf dur
a soft-boiled egg
un œuf à la coque
scrambled eggs
les œufs brouillés
a fried egg
un œuf sur le plat

Eiffel Tower n
la tour Eiffel f

eight num
huit
eight euros
huit euros

She's eight.
Elle a huit ans.
*In English you can say **eight** or **eight years old**. In French you can only say **huit ans**.*

eighteen num
dix-huit

eighteen euros
dix-huit euros

He is eighteen.
Il a dix-huit ans.
*In English you can say **eighteen** or **eighteen years old**. In French you can only say **dix-huit ans**.*

eighteenth adj
dix-huitième

on the eighteenth floor
au dix-huitième étage

the eighteenth of August
le dix-huit août

eighth adj
huitième

on the eighth floor
au huitième étage

the eighth of August
le huit août

eighty num
quatre-vingts

__quatre-vingts__ is made up of two words. What does each one mean?

Eire n
la République d'Irlande f

either adv, conj, pron
non plus

I don't like milk, and I don't like eggs either.
Je n'aime pas le lait, et je n'aime pas les œufs non plus.

I haven't got any money. – I haven't either.
Je n'ai pas d'argent. – Moi non plus.

I don't like either of them.
Je n'aime ni l'un ni l'autre.

either ... or ...
soit ... soit ...

You can have either ice cream or yoghurt.
Tu peux prendre soit une glace soit un yaourt.

elastic band n
l'élastique m

an elastic band
un élastique

elder adj
aîné m adj
aînée f adj

my elder sister
ma sœur aînée

elderly adj
âgé m adj
âgée f adj

A B C D E F G H I J K L M N O P Q R S T U V W X Y Z

Look at Language Plus on pages 283–308 for extra vocabulary.

a
b
c
d
e
f
g
h
i
j
k
l
m
n
o
p
q
r
s
t
u
v
w
x
y
z

the elderly
les personnes âgées

eldest adj
aîné *m adj*
aînée *f adj*

my eldest sister
ma sœur aînée

He's the eldest.
C'est l'aîné.

election n
l'élection *f*

an election
une élection

electric adj
électrique

an electric guitar
une guitare électrique

electricity n
l'électricité *f*

electronic adj
électronique

elegant adj
élégant *m adj*
élégante *f adj*

elephant n
l'éléphant *m*

What is the difference in spelling between the French word and the English word?

eleven num
onze

eleven euros
onze euros

I'm eleven.
J'ai onze ans.
*In English you can say **eleven** or **eleven years old**. In French you can only say **onze ans**.*

eleventh adj
onzième

on the eleventh floor
au onzième étage

the eleventh of August
le onze août

else adv
d'autre

somebody else
quelqu'un d'autre

nobody else
personne d'autre

nothing else
rien d'autre

anything else
autre chose

Would you like anything else?
Désirez-vous autre chose?

I don't want anything else.
Je ne veux rien d'autre.

email

email can be a noun or a verb.

A n
l'e-mail *m*

by email
par e-mail

Send your penfriend an email.
Envoie un e-mail à ton correspondant.

B vb
envoyer un e-mail à

I'll e-mail you.
Je vais t'envoyer un e-mail.

email address n
l'adresse e-mail f

My email address is: …
Mon adresse e-mail, c'est: …

> *adresse* in French has one **d**,
> *address* in English has two **ds**.

embarrassed adj
gêné *m adj*

gênée *f adj*

I was really embarrassed.
J'étais vraiment gêné.

emergency n
l'urgence f

This is an emergency!
C'est une urgence!

in an emergency
en cas d'urgence

emergency exit n
la sortie de secours f

empty

> **empty** can be an adjective or a
> verb.

A adj
vide

The cage is empty.
La cage est vide.

B vb
vider

Empty your pockets!
Vide tes poches!

encourage vb
encourager

Encourage your team!
Encouragez votre équipe!

> *Some French words are very like
> English words!*

encyclopedia n
l'encyclopédie f

end

> **end** can be a noun or a verb.

A n
1 (final part)
la fin f

the end of the lesson
la fin du cours

2 (of place)
le bout m

at the end of the street
au bout de la rue

B vb
finir

What time does the lesson end?
À quelle heure est-ce que le cours
finit?

> *fin* and *finir* in French and *finish*
> and *final* in English are related
> words. What do they have in
> common?

ending n
la fin f

**It's a great film, especially the
ending.**
C'est un film génial, surtout la fin.

Look at Language Plus on pages 283–308 for extra vocabulary.

a
b
c
d
e
f
g
h
i
j
k
l
m
n
o
p
q
r
s
t
u
v
w
x
y
z

enemy n
l'**ennemi** m
l'**ennemie** f

> The French word has double **n**.

energetic adj
énergique

energy n
l'**énergie** f

engaged adj
1 (busy)
occupé m adj
occupée f adj

Her phone is always engaged.
Son téléphone est toujours occupé.
2 (to be married)
fiancé m adj
fiancée f adj

My brother is engaged.
Mon frère est fiancé.

My sister is engaged.
Ma sœur est fiancée.

She's engaged to Ron.
Elle est fiancée à Ron.

engagement n
les **fiançailles** fpl

engagement ring n
la **bague de fiançailles** f

engine n
le **moteur** m

> Be careful not to translate **engine** by the French word **engin**, which is a slangy word for "thing".

England n
l'**Angleterre** f

I live in England.
J'habite en Angleterre.

> 🔑
> **to England**
> en Angleterre
> **Are you coming to England?**
> Tu viens en Angleterre?

English

> **English** can be an adjective or a noun.

A adj
anglais m adj
anglaise f adj

I am English.
Je suis anglais.

English food is different.
La cuisine anglaise est différente.

English people
les Anglais
B n (language)
l'**anglais** m

Do you speak English?
Est-ce que vous parlez anglais?

the English
les Anglais

> 🔑
> **He's English.**
> Il est anglais.
> **She's English.**
> Elle est anglaise.

> **anglais** is not spelled with a capital letter except when it means an English person.

Englishman n
l'Anglais m

an Englishman
un Anglais

Englishwoman n
l'Anglaise f

an Englishwoman
une Anglaise

enjoy vb
aimer

I enjoy learning French.
J'aime apprendre le français.

Did you enjoy the film?
Est-ce que vous avez aimé le
film?

enjoyable adj
agréable

enormous adj
énorme

Benoît has got enormous feet.
Benoît a des pieds énormes.

enough

> **enough** can be an adjective or a
> pronoun.

Ⓐ adj
assez de

enough time
assez de temps

I haven't got enough money.
Je n'ai pas assez d'argent.

Ⓑ pron
assez

Have you got enough?
Tu en as assez?

I've had enough!
J'en ai assez!

That's enough.
Ça suffit.

enter vb

**I'm going to enter the
competition.**
Je vais m'inscrire à la compétition.

enthusiasm n
l'enthousiasme m

> Which extra letters does the
> French word have?

enthusiastic adj
enthousiaste

entrance n
l'entrée f

by the entrance
à l'entrée

entrance exam n
le concours d'entrée m

entry n
"no entry"
"défense d'entrer"

entry phone n
l'interphone m

envelope n
l'enveloppe f

> The English word has one **p**, and
> the French word has two **ps**.

envious adj
envieux m adj
envieuse f adj

environment n
l'environnement m

Look at Language Plus on pages 283–308 for extra vocabulary.

a
b
c
d
e
f
g
h
i
j
k
l
m
n
o
p
q
r
s
t
u
v
w
x
y
z

What are the differences in spelling between the French word and the English word?

episode n
l'épisode m

equal

equal can be an adjective or a verb.

Ⓐ adj
égal m adj
égale f adj
Divide the map into six equal squares.
Divisez la carte en six carrés égaux.
Ⓑ vb
égaler
Two times three equals six.
Deux fois trois égalent six.

equality n
l'égalité f

*Which letter does the French word have instead of **qu**?*

equalize vb
égaliser
Thierry Henry has equalized.
Thierry Henry a égalisé.

equipment n
l'équipement m
lots of equipment
beaucoup d'équipement

Which extra letter does the French word have?

error n
l'erreur f
a small error
une petite erreur

escalator n
l'escalier roulant m
Is there an escalator?
Est-ce qu'il y a un escalier roulant?

escape vb
s'échapper
A lion has escaped.
Un lion s'est échappé.

especially adv
surtout
It's very hot there, especially in summer.
Il fait très chaud là-bas, surtout en été.

essay n
le devoir m
a history essay
un devoir d'histoire

essential adj
essentiel m adj
essentielle f adj
It's essential to bring warm clothes.
Il est essentiel d'apporter des vêtements chauds.

Which vowel is different in the French word?

euro n
l'euro m
one euro
un euro

Europe n
l'Europe f

even

> **even** can be an adverb or an adjective.

A adv
même

I like all animals, even snakes.
J'aime tous les animaux, même les serpents.

B adj

an even number
un nombre pair

evening n
le soir m

at seven o'clock in the evening
à sept heures du soir

> 🔑
>
> **this evening**
> ce soir
> **in the evening**
> le soir
> **yesterday evening**
> hier soir
> **tomorrow evening**
> demain soir
> **Good evening!**
> Bonsoir!

evening class n
le cours du soir m

My mother goes to an evening class.
Ma mère va à un cours du soir.

event n
l'événement m

an important event
un événement important

ever adv

Have you ever been to France?
Est-ce que tu es déjà allé en France?

for the first time ever
pour la première fois

every adj
chaque

every pupil
chaque élève

every time
chaque fois

I talk to her every day.
Je parle avec elle tous les jours.

I do judo every week.
Je fais du judo toutes les semaines.

> 🔑
>
> **every day**
> tous les jours
> **every night**
> tous les soirs
> **every week**
> toutes les semaines

everybody pron
tout le monde

Good morning everybody!
Bonjour tout le monde!

Everybody likes sweets.
Tout le monde aime les bonbons.

everyone pron
tout le monde

Is everyone here?
Tout le monde est là?

> **everyone** is the same as **everybody**.

everything pron
tout

Everything's fine!
Tout va bien!

Is that everything?
C'est tout?

everywhere adv
partout

A B C D E F G H I J K L M N O P Q R S T U V W X Y Z

Look at Language Plus on pages 283–308 for extra vocabulary.

There are cats everywhere!
Il y a des chats partout!

exact adj
exact *m adj*
exacte *f adj*

exactly adv
exactement

Our trainers are exactly the same.
Nos baskets sont exactement les mêmes.

not exactly
pas exactement

It's exactly 10 o'clock.
Il est dix heures précises.

*In English -ly is added to **exact**. What is added to **exact** in French?*

exam n
l'examen *m*

a French exam
un examen de français

example n
l'exemple *m*

an example
un exemple

for example
par exemple

Which letter is different in French?

excellent adj
excellent *m adj*
excellente *f adj*

Excellent!
Excellent!

It was excellent fun.
C'était vraiment super.

except prep
sauf

everyone except me
tout le monde sauf moi

exchange vb
échanger

I want to exchange the book for a video.
Je veux échanger le livre contre une vidéo.

exchange rate n
le taux de change *m*

excited adj
excité *m adj*
excitée *f adj*

exciting adj
passionnant *m adj*
passionnante *f adj*

an exciting film
un film passionnant

excuse vb

Excuse me!
Pardon!

exercise n
l'exercice m

an exercise
un exercice

What is the difference in spelling between the French word and the English word?

exercise book n
le cahier m

exhausted adj
épuisé m adj
épuisée f adj

Fabrice is exhausted.
Fabrice est épuisé.

Fabrice is a boy's name. How can you tell that by looking at the sentence?

exhibition n
l'exposition f

an exhibition
une exposition

exit n
la sortie f

Where is the exit?
Où est la sortie?

expect vb
1 (wait for)
attendre

I'm expecting a phone call.
J'attends un coup de téléphone.

She's expecting a baby.
Elle attend un enfant.

2 (suppose)
supposer

I expect he wants a coke.
Je suppose qu'il veut un coca.

expedition n
l'expédition f

expensive adj
cher m adj
chère f adj

It's too expensive.
C'est trop cher.

experience n
l'expérience f

an interesting experience
une expérience intéressante

experiment n
l'expérience f

expert n
le spécialiste m
la spécialiste f

She's a computer expert.
C'est une spécialiste en informatique.

Matthew is an expert cook.
Matthew cuisine très bien.

explain vb
expliquer

I'll explain in English.
Je vais expliquer en anglais.

explanation n
l'explication f

an clear explanation
une explication claire

explode vb
exploser

It's going to explode!
Ça va exploser!

explosion n
l'explosion f

an explosion
une explosion

extension n
1 (of building)
l'annexe f
2 (phone)
le poste m

A B C D E F G H I J K L M N O P Q R S T U V W X Y Z

Look at Language Plus on pages 283–308 for extra vocabulary.

Extension 3137, please.
Poste 3137, s'il vous plaît.

> In France phone numbers are broken into pairs, so a French person would say this as "trente et un, trente-sept".

extra adj, pron, adv
supplémentaire
an extra blanket
une couverture supplémentaire
Breakfast is extra.
Il y a un supplément pour le petit déjeuner.
to pay extra
payer un supplément
It costs extra.
Il y a un supplément.

extremely adv
extrêmement

> In English -ly is added to **extreme**. What is added to **extrême** in French?

eye n
l'œil m
(pl les yeux)
I've got blue eyes.
J'ai les yeux bleus.
She's got green eyes.
Elle a les yeux verts.
What colour eyes has he got?
Il a les yeux de quelle couleur?

eyesight n
la vue f

F

fabulous adj
formidable

a fabulous show
un spectacle formidable

face n
la figure *f*

His face is red.
Il a la figure rouge.

face cloth n
le gant de toilette *m*

> *gant means "glove". A gant de toilette is a glove-shaped face cloth.*

facilities npl
l'équipement *m*

> *équipement is a singular word.*

factory n
l'usine *f*

My mum works in a factory.
Ma mère travaille dans une usine.

fail vb
rater

She's going to fail her exams.
Elle va rater ses examens.

fair

> *fair can be an adjective or a noun.*

Ⓐ adj
1 juste

That's not fair.
Ce n'est pas juste.

2 (*blonde*)
blond *m adj*
blonde *f adj*

He's got fair hair.
Il a les cheveux blonds.

Ⓑ n
la foire *f*

Are you going to the fair?
Est-ce que tu vas à la foire?

fairground n
le champ de foire *m*

fair-haired adj
Hélène is fair-haired.
Hélène a les cheveux blonds.

fairly adv
assez

That's fairly good.
C'est assez bien.

fairy n
la fée *f*

fairy tale n
le conte de fées *m*

fall vb
tomber

Look at Language Plus on pages 283–308 for extra vocabulary.

A B C D E F G H I J K L M N O P Q R S T U V W X Y Z

Mind you don't fall!
Fais attention de ne pas
tomber!

fall off vb
tomber de

He's going to fall off the wall.
Il va tomber du mur.

false adj
True or false?
Vrai ou faux?

family n
la famille f

my family
ma famille

the whole family
toute la famille

the Cooke family
la famille Cooke

> *family has one l, how many has*
> *famille got?*

famous adj
célèbre

> *There are two different accents for*
> *two different sounds.*

fan n
le/la supporter m/f

football fans
les supporters de football

fantastic adj
fantastique

far

> far can be an adjective or an adverb.

A adj (*a long way*)
loin

It's not very far.
Ce n'est pas très loin.

far from
loin de

It's not far from here.
Ce n'est pas loin d'ici.

B adv (*much*)
beaucoup

That's far better!
C'est beaucoup mieux!

> **Is it far?**
> C'est loin?
> **No, it's not far.**
> Non, ce n'est pas loin.
> **It's too far.**
> C'est trop loin.

farm n
la ferme f

farmer n
l'agriculteur m

l'agricultrice f

He's a farmer.
Il est agriculteur.

> *You do not translate "a" when you say*
> *what someone's job is in French.*

farmhouse n
la ferme f

fashion n
la mode f

fashionable adj
à la mode

Jane wears fashionable clothes.
Jane porte des vêtements à la mode.

fashion show n
le défilé m

fast

> fast can be an adverb or an adjective.

A adv
vite

You walk fast.
Tu marches vite.

B adj
rapide

a fast car
une voiture rapide

fat adj
gros m adj
grosse f adj

They're both fat.
Ils sont gros tous les deux.

father n
le père m

my father
mon père

your father
ton père

Father Christmas n
le père Noël m

Father's Day n
la fête des Pères f

favourite adj
préféré m adj
préférée f adj

David is my favourite cousin.
Mon cousin préféré, c'est David.

Blue's my favourite colour.
Ma couleur préférée, c'est le bleu.

February n
février m

next February
en février

> **in February**
> en février
> **the fifth of February**
> le cinq février
>
> *The months are not spelled with a capital letter in French.*

feed vb
donner à manger à

I'm going to feed the cat.
Je vais donner à manger au chat.

feel vb
se sentir

I don't feel well.
Je ne me sens pas bien.

I feel like …
J'ai envie de …

Do you feel like an ice cream?
Tu as envie d'une glace?

feet npl
les pieds mpl

My feet are cold.
J'ai froid aux pieds.

felt-tip pen n
le stylo-feutre m

Can I borrow your felt-tip pens?
Je peux emprunter tes stylos-feutres?

female n
la femelle f

A B C D E F G H I J K L M N O P Q R S T U V W X Y Z

a
b
c
d
e
f
g
h
i
j
k
l
m
n
o
p
q
r
s
t
u
v
w
x
y
z

Is it a male or a female?
C'est un mâle ou une femelle?

feminine adj
féminin *m ad*
féminine *f adj*

fence n
la barrière *f*

ferret n
le furet *m*

ferry n
le ferry *m*

fetch vb
aller chercher
Can you fetch my bag?
Tu peux aller chercher mon sac?

few

few can be an adjective or a pronoun.

A adj
a few
quelques
a few hours
quelques heures
quite a few people
pas mal de monde
B pron
a few
quelques-uns *mpl pron*
quelques-unes *fpl pron*

How many chips do you want? – Just a few.
Tu veux combien de frites? – Seulement quelques-unes.

fiancé n
le fiancé *m*
He's her fiancé.
C'est son fiancé.

fiancée n
la fiancée *f*
She's his fiancée.
C'est sa fiancée.

field n
1 (*in countryside*)
le champ *m*
a field of wheat
un champ de blé
2 (*for sport*)
le terrain *m*
a football field
un terrain de football

fifteen num
quinze
fifteen euros
quinze euros

I am fifteen.
J'ai quinze ans.
*In English you can say **fifteen** or **fifteen years old**. In French you can only say **quinze ans**.*

fifteenth adj
quinzième
on the fifteenth floor
au quinzième étage

the fifteenth of August
le quinze août

fifth adj
cinquième

on the fifth floor
au cinquième étage

> 🔑
> **the fifth of August**
> le cinq août

fifty num
cinquante

My aunt is fifty.
Ma tante a cinquante ans.

> In English you can say **fifty** or **fifty years old**. In French you can only say **cinquante ans**.

fight

> **fight** can be a noun or a verb.

Ⓐ n
la bagarre f
Ⓑ vb
se battre

Two boys are fighting.
Deux garçons se battent.

figure n
le chiffre m

Write down the figures.
Écrivez les chiffres.

file n
1 (folder)
la chemise f

Keep the leaflets in your files.
Gardez les brochures dans vos chemises.
2 (on computer)
le fichier m

fill vb
remplir

Can you fill the glasses?
Tu peux remplir les verres?

fill in vb
remplir

Fill in the gaps in the sentences.
Remplissez les blancs dans les phrases.

film n
1 le film m

Is it a good film?
C'est un bon film?
2 (for camera)
la pellicule f

film star n
la vedette de cinéma f

Gérard Depardieu is a film star.
Gérard Depardieu est une vedette de cinéma.

final

> **final** can be an adjective or a noun.

Ⓐ adj
dernier m adj
dernière f adj
the final minutes
les dernières minutes
Ⓑ n
la finale f

The final is tomorrow.
Demain, c'est la finale.

find vb
trouver

My brother wants to find a job.
Mon frère veut trouver du travail.
Find page fifteen.
Trouvez la page quinze.

A B C D E F G H I J K L M N O P Q R S T U V W X Y Z

Look at Language Plus on pages 283–308 for extra vocabulary.

a
b
c
d
e
f
g
h
i
j
k
l
m
n
o
p
q
r
s
t
u
v
w
x
y
z

fine adj

> 🔑
>
> **That's fine, thanks.**
> C'est très bien, merci.
> **How are you? – I'm fine.**
> Comment ça va? – Ça va bien.

finger n
le doigt *m*

my little finger
mon petit doigt

My finger is hurting.
J'ai mal au doigt.

finish

> **finish** can be a verb or a noun.

Ⓐ vb
finir

I've got to finish my homework.
Je dois finir mes devoirs.

I've finished!
J'ai fini!

Is it finished?
Ça y est?

> **finir** and **finish** are related words.
> What do they have in common?

Ⓑ n *(in board game)*
la case 'Arrivée' *f*

fire n

1 le feu *m*
(pl les feux)

There's a nice fire in the sitting room.
Il y a un bon feu dans le salon.

2 *(accidental)*
l'incendie *m*

There's a fire in the wood.
Il y a un incendie dans le bois.

fire engine n
la voiture de pompiers *f*

two fire engines
deux voitures de pompiers

fire fighter n
le pompier *m*

He's a fire fighter.
Il est pompier.

> *You do not translate "**a**" when you say what someone's job is in French.*

fire station n
la caserne de pompiers *f*

fireworks npl
le feu d'artifice *m*

There are fireworks this evening.
Il y a un feu d'artifice ce soir.

first

> **first** can be an adjective, a noun or an adverb.

Ⓐ adj
premier *m adj*

première *f adj*

the first day
le premier jour

the first time
la première fois

to come first
arriver premier

Who came first?
Qui est arrivé premier?

Who wants to be first?
Qui veut commencer?

Who's first?
Qui commence?

Me first!
C'est moi qui commence!

B n

at first
au début

It's easy at first.
Au début c'est facile.

the first of September
le premier septembre

C adv
d'abord

First write your names.
D'abord écrivez vos noms.

first of all
tout d'abord

first aid n
les premiers secours *mpl*

fir tree n
le sapin *m*

fish

fish can be a noun or a verb.

A n
le poisson *m*

I don't like fish.
Je n'aime pas le poisson.

B vb

to go fishing
aller à la pêche

Let's go fishing.
On va à la pêche?

fish fingers npl
les bâtonnets de poisson *mpl*

fishing n
la pêche *f*

I like fishing.
J'aime la pêche.

fishing boat n
le bateau de pêche *m*

fish tank n
l'aquarium *m*

fit

fit can be a verb or an adjective.

A vb
être la bonne taille

It doesn't fit.
Ce n'est pas la bonne taille.

B adj
en forme

She's fit.
Elle est en forme.

five num
cinq

five euros
cinq euros

She is five.
Elle a cinq ans.
*In English you can say **five** or **five years old**. In French you can only say **cinq ans**.*

fix vb
réparer

Can you fix my bike?
Vous pouvez réparer mon vélo?

fizzy adj
gazeux *m adj*
gazeuse *f adj*

Look at Language Plus on pages 283–308 for extra vocabulary.

a
b

I don't like fizzy drinks.
Je n'aime pas les boissons
gazeuses.

c
d

flag n
le drapeau m
(pl les drapeaux)

e

flame n
la flamme f

f

flan n
1 (sweet)
la tarte f

g
h
i

a raspberry flan
une tarte aux framboises
2 (savoury)
la quiche f

j
k
l

a cheese and onion flan
une quiche au fromage et aux
oignons

m

flannel n
le gant de toilette m

n
o

*gant means "glove". A gant de
toilette is a glove-shaped face
cloth.*

p

flash n
le flash m
(pl les flashes)

q

Has your camera got a flash?
Est-ce que ton appareil photo a un
flash?

r
s
t

a flash of lightning
un éclair

u
v
w
x
y

z

flask n
le thermos m

flat

flat can be an adjective or a noun.

A adj
1 (level)
plat m adj
plate f adj
a flat roof
un toit plat
flat shoes
des chaussures plates
2 (tyre)
crevé m adj
crevée f adj
I've got a flat tyre.
J'ai un pneu crevé.
B n
l'appartement m
She lives in a flat.
Elle habite un appartement.

*The English word apartment has
one p, how many has appartement
got?*

flavour n
le parfum m
**Which flavour of ice cream would
you like?**
Quel parfum de glace est-ce que tu
veux?

flight n
le vol m
What time is the flight to Paris?
À quelle heure est le vol pour Paris?

flippers npl
les palmes fpl

floor n
1 le sol m
a tiled floor
un sol carrelé
on the floor
par terre

Sit on the floor.
Asseyez-vous par terre.

2 (storey)
l'étage m

the first floor
le premier étage

the ground floor
le rez-de-chaussée

on the third floor
au troisième étage

floppy disk n
la disquette f

florist n
le/la fleuriste m/f

flour n
la farine f

flower n
la fleur f

flu n
la grippe f

Jean-Louis has got flu.
Jean-Louis a la grippe.

fluent adj

My sister speaks fluent French.
Ma sœur parle couramment le français.

flute n
la flûte f

I play the flute.
Je joue de la flûte.

There's an extra word in the French sentence. What is it?

fly

fly can be a verb or a noun.

A vb (go by plane)
aller en avion

I'm going to fly to Florida.
Je vais aller en Floride en avion.

B n (insect)
la mouche f

fog n
le brouillard m

foggy adj

a foggy day
un jour de brouillard

It's foggy.
Il y a du brouillard.

fold vb
plier

Fold the paper in half.
Pliez la feuille en deux.

folder n
la chemise f

follow vb
suivre

Follow me.
Suivez-moi.

food n

I like French food.
J'aime la cuisine française.

Bring some food.
Apportez à manger.

We need to buy some food.
Nous devons acheter à manger.

food processor n
le robot m

Look at Language Plus on pages 283–308 for extra vocabulary.

foot n
le pied m

My feet are hurting.
J'ai mal aux pieds.

on foot
à pied

Richard is 6 foot tall.
Richard mesure un mètre quatre-vingt.

> In France measurements are in metres and centimetres, rather than feet and inches.

football n

1 (game)
le football m

I like playing football.
J'aime jouer au football.

> You can also say **J'aime jouer au foot**, which is more slangy.

Do you want to play football, Pascal?
Tu veux jouer au foot, Pascal?

Do you want to play football, boys?
Vous voulez jouer au foot, les garçons?

2 (ball)
le ballon de foot m

Jason's got a new football.
Jason a un nouveau ballon de foot.

football boots npl
les chaussures de foot fpl

footballer n
le footballeur m
la footballeuse f

football player n
le joueur de football m
la joueuse de football f

David Beckham is a famous football player.
David Beckham est un joueur de football célèbre.

football shirt n
le maillot de foot m

footpath n
le sentier m

for prep
pour

a present for me
un cadeau pour moi

I'll do it for you.
Je vais le faire pour toi.

What's it for?
Ça sert à quoi?

What's the French for "lion"?
Comment dit-on "lion" en français?

I have been learning French for six months.
J'apprends le français depuis six mois.

forbidden adj
défendu m adj
défendue f adj

forecast n

the weather forecast
la météo

What's the forecast for today?
Il va faire quel temps aujourd'hui?

foreign adj
étranger m adj
étrangère f adj

foreigner n
l'étranger m
l'étrangère f

He's a foreigner.
C'est un étranger.

forest n
la forêt f

forget vb
oublier

Don't forget!
N'oubliez pas!

fork n
la fourchette f

form n
le formulaire m

You have to fill in the form.
Vous devez remplir le formulaire.

fortnight n

a fortnight
quinze jours

I'm going on holiday for a fortnight.
Je pars en vacances pendant quinze jours.

quinze jours actually means 15 days.

forty num
quarante

My father is forty.
Mon père a quarante ans.

*In English you can say **forty** or **forty years old**. In French you can only say **quarante ans**.*

forward adv
en avant

a step forward
un pas en avant

to move forward
avancer

Move forward two spaces.
Avancez de deux cases.

foster child n
l'enfant adoptif m
l'enfant adoptive f

fountain n
la fontaine f

four num
quatre

four euros
quatre euros

He is four.
Il a quatre ans.

*In English you can say **four** or **four years old**. In French you can only say **quatre ans**.*

fourteen num
quatorze

fourteen euros
quatorze euros

I'm fourteen.
J'ai quatorze ans.

*In English you can say **fourteen** or **fourteen years old**. In French you can only say **quatorze ans**.*

fourteenth adj
quatorzième

on the fourteenth floor
au quatorzième étage

the fourteenth of August
le quatorze août

fourth adj
quatrième

A B C D E F G H I J K L M N O P Q R S T U V W X Y Z

Look at Language Plus on pages 283–308 for extra vocabulary.

a
b
c
d
e
f
g
h
i
j
k
l
m
n
o
p
q
r
s
t
u
v
w
x
y
z

on the fourth floor
au quatrième étage

🔑

the fourth of July
le quatre juillet

fox n
le <u>renard</u> m

France n
la <u>France</u> f

I like France.
J'aime la France.

Cannes is in France.
Cannes est en France.

We're going to France.
Nous allons en France.

🔑

to France
en France
He lives in France.
Il habite en France.
They are from France.
Ils sont français.

freckles npl
les <u>taches de rousseur</u> fpl

free adj
1 (free of charge)
<u>gratuit</u> m adj
<u>gratuite</u> f adj

a free brochure
une brochure gratuite
2 (not taken)
<u>libre</u>

Excuse me, is this seat free?
Excusez-moi, la place est
libre?

freezer n
le <u>congélateur</u> m

freezing adj
I'm freezing!
Je suis gelé!

It's absolutely freezing!
Il fait un froid de canard!

French

French can be an adjective or a
noun.

Ⓐ adj
<u>français</u> m adj
<u>française</u> f adj

a French name
un nom français

a French school
une école française

our French friends
nos amis français

our French teacher
notre professeur de français

my French book
mon livre de français

French people
les Français

🔑

He's French.
Il est français.
She's French.
Elle est française.

Ⓑ n (language)
le <u>français</u> m

Do you speak French?
Est-ce que tu parles français?

the French
les Français

français is not spelled with a
capital letter except when it
means a French person.

French beans npl
les <u>haricots verts</u> mpl

French fries npl
les <u>frites</u> *fpl*

Frenchman n
le <u>Français</u> *m*

Frenchwoman n
la <u>Française</u> *f*

Friday n
le <u>vendredi</u> *m*

It's Friday today.
Aujourd'hui c'est vendredi.

> 🔑
>
> **on Friday**
> vendredi
> **on Fridays**
> le vendredi
> **every Friday**
> tous les vendredis
> **last Friday**
> vendredi dernier
> **next Friday**
> vendredi prochain
>
> *Days of the week are not spelled
> with a capital letter in French.*

fridge n
le <u>frigo</u> *m*

friend n
l'<u>ami</u> *m*
l'<u>amie</u> *f*

my friend Paul
mon ami Paul

my friend Gaëlle
mon amie Gaëlle

friendly adj
<u>gentil</u> *m adj*
<u>gentille</u> *f adj*

She's very friendly.
Elle est très gentille.

frightened adj
to be frightened
avoir peur

Anna's frightened of spiders.
Anna a peur des araignées.

> 🔑
>
> **I'm frightened!**
> J'ai peur!

fringe n
la <u>frange</u> *f*

She's got a fringe.
Elle a une frange.

Frisbee® n
le <u>Frisbee</u>® *m*

frog n
la <u>grenouille</u> *f*

frogs' legs
les cuisses de grenouille

from prep
<u>de</u>

She comes from Perth.
Elle vient de Perth.

a letter from my penfriend
une lettre de mon correspondant

from ... to ...
de ... à ...

Look at Language Plus on pages 283–308 for extra vocabulary.

from London to Paris
de Londres à Paris

the numbers from 1 to 39
les nombres de un à trente-neuf

> 🔑
> **Where do you come from?**
> Tu viens d'où?
> **I come from Birmingham.**
> Je viens de Birmingham.

front

> front can be a noun or an adjective.

Ⓐ n
le **devant** m

the front of the house
le devant de la maison

in front of
devant

in front of the house
devant la maison

Ⓑ adj
de **devant**

the front row
la rangée de devant

front door n
la **porte d'entrée** f

frost n
le **gel** m

frosty adj

a frosty morning
un matin glacial

> 🔑
> **It's frosty today.**
> Il gèle aujourd'hui.

fruit n

I like fruit.
J'aime les fruits.

a piece of fruit
un fruit

fruit juice n
le **jus de fruits** m

fruit salad n
la **salade de fruits** f

frying pan n
la **poêle** f

full adj
plein m adj
pleine f adj

The bottle's full.
La bouteille est pleine.

I'm full.
J'ai bien mangé.

full stop n
le **point** m

fun n

to have fun
s'amuser

Are you having fun?
Tu t'amuses?

> 🔑
> **It's fun!**
> C'est chouette!
> **Have fun!**
> Amuse-toi bien!

funfair n
la **fête foraine** f

funny adj
drôle

It was very funny.
C'était très drôle.

fur n
1 la **fourrure** f

a fur coat
un manteau de fourrure
2 le **poil** m

the dog's fur
le poil du chien

furious adj
<u>furieux</u> m adj
<u>furieuse</u> f adj

Dad was furious with me.
Papa était furieux contre moi.

The girls are furious.
Les filles sont furieuses.

furniture n
les <u>meubles</u> mpl

We've got new furniture.
Nous avons de nouveaux meubles.

a piece of furniture
un meuble

future n
l'<u>avenir</u> m

Be more careful in future.
Sois plus prudent à l'avenir.

Look at Language Plus on pages 283–308 for extra vocabulary.

G

game n

1 (*hangman, marbles, bingo etc*)
le jeu *m*
(*pl* les jeux)

It's a new game.
C'est un nouveau jeu.

Let's play a game.
On joue à un jeu?

2 (*match*)
le match *m*

The game is tomorrow.
Le match, c'est demain.

a game of football
un match de foot

games npl
(*at school*)
le sport *m*

I like games.
J'aime le sport.

gang n
la bande *f*

garage n
le garage *m*

garden n
le jardin *m*

We haven't got a garden.
Nous n'avons pas de
jardin.

gardening n
le jardinage *m*

garlic n
l'ail *m*

I don't like garlic.
Je n'aime pas l'ail.

gas n
le gaz *m*

gas cooker n
la cuisinière à gaz *f*

gate n

1 (*of garden, of school*)
le portail *m*

Please close the gate.
Fermez le portail, s'il vous plaît.

2 (*of field*)
la barrière *f*

There's a cow by the gate.
Il y a une vache près de la barrière.

gave vb, *see* **give**

GCSE n
le brevet des collèges *m*

Exams in France are different
from exams in Britain. **Le
brevet des collèges** is an
exam you take at the end of
the fourth year in secondary
school.

geese npl
les oies *fpl*

general knowledge n
les connaissances générales *fpl*

a general knowledge quiz
un quiz de connaissances générales

generous adj
généreux *m adj*

généreuse *f adj*

That's very generous of you.
C'est très généreux de ta part.

genius n
le génie *m*

She's a genius!
C'est un génie!

gents n
les toilettes *fpl*

Where is the 'gents', please?
Où sont les toilettes pour hommes,
s'il vous plaît?

geography n
la géographie *f*

I like geography.
J'aime la géographie.

gerbil n
la gerbille *f*

German

> **German** can be an adjective or a
> noun.

Ⓐ adj
allemand *m adj*
allemande *f adj*

a German car
une voiture allemande

German people
les Allemands

Ⓑ n (*language*)
l'allemand *m*

I can speak German.
Je parle allemand.

> *allemand* is not spelled with a
> capital letter except when it
> means a German person.

German measles n
la rubéole *f*

He's got German measles.
Il a la rubéole.

Germany n
l'Allemagne *f*

get vb
1 (*receive*)
avoir

**He always gets lots of
presents.**
Il a toujours plein de cadeaux.

**What did you get for your
birthday?**
Qu'est-ce que tu as eu pour ton
anniversaire?

I got lots of presents.
J'ai eu beaucoup de cadeaux.

**How much pocket money do you
get?**
Tu reçois combien d'argent de
poche?

I get £5 a week.
Je reçois cinq livres par semaine.

> When **I've got** means **I have**, it is
> translated by the verb **avoir**.

Look at Language Plus on pages 283–308 for extra vocabulary.

a
b
c
d
e
f
g
h
i
j
k
l
m
n
o
p
q
r
s
t
u
v
w
x
y
z

I've got a dog and two cats.
J'ai un chien et deux chats.

I haven't got a mobile phone.
Je n'ai pas de portable.

Marie hasn't got long hair.
Marie n'a pas les cheveux longs.

How many have you got?
Combien en avez-vous?

2 (buy)
acheter

Can you get me a coke?
Tu peux m'acheter un coca?

Mum's getting me a playstation.
Maman m'achète une play station.

3 (fetch)
aller chercher

Get your coats.
Allez chercher vos manteaux.

4 (go)
aller

**How do you get to the castle,
please?**
Pour aller au château, s'il vous
plaît?

5 (arrive)
arriver

What time do we get there?
À quelle heure est-ce qu'on arrive?

> When **I've got to** means **I must**, it
> is translated by the verb **devoir**.

I've got to go to the dentist.
Je dois aller chez le dentiste.

You've got to take a card, Michel.
Tu dois prendre une carte, Michel.

You've got to be careful, children.
Vous devez faire attention, les
enfants.

I've got a cat.
J'ai un chat.
I haven't got a dog.
Je n'ai pas de chien.
Have you got a sister?
Tu as une sœur?
She's got long hair.
Elle a les cheveux longs.

get away vb
s'échapper

Quick! He's getting away!
Vite! Il s'échappe!

get back vb
rentrer

What time will you get back?
Tu rentres à quelle heure?

get in vb
monter

Get in, boys!
Montez, les garçons!

Get in the car, Charlotte.
Monte dans la voiture, Charlotte.

get off vb
descendre de

Where do we get off the train?
Où est-ce que nous descendons du
train?

get on vb
1 (bus, train)
monter dans

I get on the bus at the station.
Je monte dans le bus à la gare.

2 (bike)
monter sur

I got on my bike.
Je suis monté sur mon vélo.

How are you getting on?
Comment ça marche?

get out vb
sortir

Get out!
Sortez!

Get your book out, André.
Sors ton livre, André.

Get your things out!
Sortez vos affaires!

get up vb
se lever

What time do you get up?
Tu te lèves à quelle heure?

I get up early.
Je me lève tôt.

ghost n
le fantôme m

giant n
le géant m
la géante f

gift n
le cadeau m
(pl les cadeaux)

Christmas gifts
les cadeaux de Noël

gift shop n
la boutique de cadeaux f

gigantic adj
gigantesque

ginger adj
I've got ginger hair.
J'ai les cheveux roux.

giraffe n
la girafe f

girl n
1 la fille f

Come on girls!
Allez les filles!

2 (little girl)
la petite fille f

a five-year-old girl
une petite fille de cinq ans

3 (teenager)
la jeune fille f

a sixteen-year-old girl
une jeune fille de seize ans

girlfriend n
la copine f

She's his girlfriend.
C'est sa copine.

give vb
1 donner

Give me the book, please.
Donne-moi le livre, s'il te plaît.

Give the books to Adam.
Donne les livres à Adam.

2 (gift)
offrir

What are you giving Luc?
Qu'est-ce que tu vas offrir à Luc?

My parents gave me a bike.
Mes parents m'ont offert un vélo.

give out vb
distribuer

Will you give out the books please, Christine?
Tu peux distribuer les livres, s'il te plaît, Christine?

glad adj
content m adj
contente f adj

Look at Language Plus on pages 283–308 for extra vocabulary.

a

b

c

d

e

f

g

h

i

j

k

l

m

n

o

p

q

r

s

t

u

v

w

x

y

z

I was glad to get your letter.
J'étais content de recevoir ta lettre.

glass n
le verre m
I'd like a glass of milk.
Je voudrais un verre de lait.

glasses npl
les lunettes fpl
I wear glasses.
Je porte des lunettes.

globe n
le globe m
We've got a globe in the classroom.
Nous avons un globe dans la classe.

glove n
le gant m
I've got red gloves.
J'ai des gants rouges.

glue n
la colle f

go

> **go** can be a noun or a verb.

Ⓐ n
le tour m
It's my go.
C'est mon tour.
Whose go is it?
À qui le tour?

Ⓑ vb
1 aller
I don't want to go to school.
Je ne veux pas aller à l'école.

I don't go to school on Saturday.
Je ne vais pas à l'école le samedi.

Where are you going?
Où vas-tu?

2 (talking about the future)

I'm going to win.
Je vais gagner.

We're going to visit our cousins on Friday.
On va rendre visite à nos cousins vendredi.

I'm not going to play.
Je ne vais pas jouer.

3 (talking about the past)

I went to London.
Je suis allé à Londres.

Where did you go yesterday?
Où es-tu allé hier?

I went to Luc's house.
Je suis allé chez Luc.

He's gone.
Il est parti.

She's gone.
Elle est partie.

go away vb
s'en aller

Go away, Sophie!
Vas-t'en, Sophie!

Go away!
Allez-vous-en!

go back vb
1 (in game)
reculer

Go back three spaces.
Recule de trois cases.

2 (return)
retourner

Go back to your seat, Colette!
Retourne à ta place, Colette!

Go back to your seats, boys!
Retournez à vos places, les garçons

Let's go back to the beginning.
Recommençons.

go down vb
descendre

Let's go down to the cellar.
Descendons à la cave.

go forward vb
Go forward three spaces, Alain.
Avance de trois cases, Alain.

go in vb
entrer

Let's go in.
Entrons.

go on vb
1 (continue)
continuer

Shall I go on?
Je continue?

Go on, don't stop.
Vas-y, ne t'arrête pas.
2 (happen)
se passer

What's going on?
Qu'est-ce qui se passe?

go out vb
sortir

Are you going out tonight?
Tu sors ce soir?

Melanie's going out with Matt.
Melanie sort avec Matt.

go past vb
passer devant

We're going past the cathedral.
Nous passons devant la cathédrale.

Go past the station and turn right.
Passe devant la gare et tourne à
droite.

go up vb
monter

I'm going up to my room.
Je monte dans ma chambre.

goal n
le but m

It's a goal!
C'est un but!

He's scored a goal!
Il a marqué un but!

goalkeeper n
le gardien de but m

He's the goalkeeper.
C'est le gardien de but.

goat n
la chèvre f

God n
Dieu m

godfather n
le parrain m

my godfather
mon parrain

godmother n
la marraine f

my godmother
ma marraine

goggles npl
les lunettes de plongée fpl

Look at Language Plus on pages 283–308 for extra vocabulary.

I've got new goggles.
J'ai de nouvelles lunettes de plongée.

gold adj

a gold necklace
un collier en or

goldfish n

le <u>poisson rouge</u> m

I've got five goldfish.
J'ai cinq poissons rouges.

golf n

le <u>golf</u> m

My dad plays golf.
Mon père joue au golf.

golf club n

le <u>club de golf</u> m

golf course n

le <u>terrain de golf</u> m

gone vb, see go

good adj

1 (great)

<u>bon</u> m adj
<u>bonne</u> f adj

It's a very good film.
C'est un très bon film.

We've got a good teacher.
Nous avons une bonne maîtresse.

That's a good idea.
C'est une bonne idée.

Jennifer's very good at French.
Jennifer est très bonne en français.

2 (not naughty)

<u>sage</u>

Marcel is always good.
Marcel est toujours sage.

🔑

It's good.
C'est bon.
Good morning!
Bonjour!
Good morning everyone!
Bonjour tout le monde!
Good afternoon!
Bonjour!
Good evening!
Bonsoir!
Good night!
Bonne nuit!
Good luck!
Bonne chance!
Be good, André!
Sois sage, André!

---

goodbye excl

<u>au revoir!</u>

Good Friday n

le <u>Vendredi saint</u> m

good-looking adj

<u>beau</u> m adj
<u>belle</u> f adj

Yann is very good-looking.
Yann est très beau.

---

beau changes to *bel* before a vowel sound.

---

a good-looking man
un bel homme

goose n

l'<u>oie</u> f

gorgeous adj

1 (person)

<u>beau</u> m adj
<u>belle</u> f adj

Isn't she gorgeous!
Qu'elle est belle!

2 (weather)

<u>splendide</u>

The weather's gorgeous.
Il fait un temps splendide.

got vb, *see* **get**

gradually adv
peu à peu

graffiti npl
les graffiti *mpl*

There's a lot of graffiti.
Il y a beaucoup de graffiti.

gram n
le gramme *m*

two hundred grams of cheese
deux cents grammes de fromage

grammar n
la grammaire *f*

I like grammar.
J'aime la grammaire.

grandchildren npl
les petits-enfants *mpl*

her grandchildren
ses petits-enfants

granddad n
le papi *m*

my granddad
mon papi

granddaughter n
la petite-fille *f*

He has two granddaughters.
Il a deux petites-filles.

grandfather n
le grand-père *m*

my grandfather
mon grand-père

grandma n
la mamie *f*

her grandma
sa mamie

grandmother n
la grand-mère *f*

his grandmother
sa grand-mère

grandpa n
le papi *m*

my grandpa
mon papi

grandparents npl
les grands-parents *mpl*

my grandparents
mes grands-parents

grandson n
le petit-fils *m*

her grandsons
ses petits-fils

granny n
la mamie *f*

my granny
ma mamie

grapefruit n
le pamplemousse *m*

I don't like grapefruit.
Je n'aime pas le pamplemousse.

grapefruit juice n
le jus de pamplemousse *m*

grapes npl
le raisin *m*

a kilo of grapes
un kilo de raisin.

raisin is a singular word. In English
raisins are dried grapes.

Look at Language Plus on pages 283–308 for extra vocabulary.

grass n
l'herbe f
The children are playing on the grass.
Les enfants jouent dans l'herbe.

grated adj
râpé m adj
râpée f adj
grated cheese
du fromage râpé

gravy n
I'd like some gravy.
Je voudrais de la sauce.

great adj
génial m adj
géniale f adj
We're going to France. – Great!
Nous allons en France. – Génial!

> 🔑
> **That's great!**
> C'est génial!

Great Britain n
la Grande-Bretagne f
We live in Great Britain.
Nous habitons en Grande-Bretagne.

greedy adj
gourmand m adj
gourmande f adj
Don't be so greedy Émmeline.
Ne sois pas si gourmande, Émmeline!

green

> **green** can be an adjective or a noun.

A adj
vert m adj
verte f adj
a green sweater
un pull vert
a green car
une voiture verte
I've got green eyes.
J'ai les yeux verts.

> *Colour adjectives come after the noun in French.*

B n
le vert m
Green is my favourite colour.
Ma couleur préférée, c'est le vert.

greengrocer's n
le marchand de fruits et légumes m

greenhouse n
la serre f

greetings card n
la carte de vœux f

grey

> **grey** can be an adjective or a noun.

A adj
gris m adj
grise f adj
a grey sweater
un pull gris
a grey skirt
une jupe grise
She's got grey hair.
Elle a les cheveux gris.

> *Colour adjectives come after the noun in French.*

B n
le gris m
He is dressed in grey.
Il est habillé en gris.

---

grin vb
sourire
Why are you grinning like that?
Pourquoi tu souris comme ça?

---

grocer's n
l'épicerie f
I'm going to the grocer's.
Je vais à l'épicerie.

---

groom n
le marié m

---

ground n
1 la terre f
We sat on the ground.
Nous nous sommes assis par terre.
2 (earth)
le sol m
The ground is wet.
Le sol est mouillé.
3 (sports ground)
le terrain m
Where's the football ground?
Où est le terrain de football?

on the ground
par terre

---

ground floor n
le rez-de-chaussée m
This is the ground floor.
C'est le rez-de-chaussée.
The toilets are on the ground floor.
Les toilettes sont au rez-de-chaussée.

on the ground floor
au rez-de-chaussée

---

group n
le groupe m
Get into groups of four.
Mettez-vous en groupes de quatre.

---

grow vb
1 (plant)
pousser
Grass grows fast.
L'herbe pousse vite.
2 (gardener)
faire pousser
I'm growing a sunflower.
Je fais pousser un tournesol.
3 (get bigger)
grandir
My feet have grown.
Mes pieds ont grandi.

---

grow up vb
What do you want to be when you grow up, Samir?
Samir, qu'est ce que tu veux faire quand tu seras grand?
What do want to be when you grow up, Céline?
Céline, qu'est ce que tu veux faire quand tu seras grande?

One question is to a boy, the other to a girl – how can you tell?

---

growl vb
grogner
My dog growls a lot.
Mon chien grogne beaucoup.

A B C D E F G H I J K L M N O P Q R S T U V W X Y Z

Look at Language Plus on pages 283–308 for extra vocabulary.

a

grown vb, *see* **grow**

b

grown-up n
la grande personne *f*
the grown-ups
les grandes personnes

c

d

guard dog n
le chien de garde *m*

e

f

guess vb
deviner
Guess what this is!
Devine ce que c'est!

g

h

guest n
l'invité *m*
l'invitée *f*
our French guests
nos invités français

i

j

k

guide n
1 (*tourist guide*)
le guide *m*
la guide *f*
He works as a guide at the castle.
Il travaille comme guide au château.
2 (*girl guide*)
l'éclaireuse *f*
I'm a guide.
Je suis éclaireuse.

l

m

n

o

p

q

> Guides and scouts are not as common in France as they are in Britain.

r

s

t

guidebook n
le guide *m*

u

guide dog n
le chien d'aveugle *m*

v

w

guinea pig n
le cochon d'Inde *m*

x

y

z

I've got a guinea pig.
J'ai un cochon d'Inde.

guitar n
la guitare *f*

I play the guitar.
Je joue de la guitare.

> *There is one extra letter in the French word* **guitare**. *What is it?*

gun n
le pistolet *m*

guy n
you guys
les gars
Hurry up you guys!
Dépêchez-vous les gars!

gym n
1 (*school subject*)
la gym *f*
We've got gym today.
On a gym aujourd'hui.
2 (*place*)
la salle de gym *f*
My mum goes to the gym.
Ma mère va à la salle de gym.

gymnastics n
la gymnastique *f*
I like gymnastics.
J'aime la gymnastique.
I do gymnastics.
Je fais de la gymnastique.

H

had vb, *see* **have**

hadn't = **had not**; *see* **have**

hail

> **hail** can be a noun or a verb.

A n
la grêle *f*
B vb
grêler
It's hailing.
Il grêle.

hair n
1 les cheveux *mpl*

> *cheveux* is a plural word, so you have to use a plural adjective with it.

He's got black hair.
Il a les cheveux noirs.

I've got long hair.
J'ai les cheveux longs.

I want to wash my hair.
Je veux me laver les cheveux.

You've had your hair cut!
Tu t'es fait couper les cheveux!
2 (*fur*)
le poil *m*

My cat has long hair.
Mon chat a le poil long.

hairbrush n
la brosse à cheveux *f*

hairdresser n
le coiffeur *m*
la coiffeuse *f*
He's a hairdresser.
Il est coiffeur.

> *You do not translate "a" when you say what someone's job is in French.*

hairdresser's n
le coiffeur *m*
at the hairdresser's
chez le coiffeur

hairstyle n
la coiffure *f*
You've got a new hairstyle.
Tu as une nouvelle coiffure.

hairy adj
poilu *m adj*
poilue *f adj*

half

> **half** can be a noun, an adjective or an adverb.

A n
1 (*fraction*)
la moitié *f*
half of the class
la moitié de la classe

to cut something in half
couper quelque chose en deux
2 (*ticket*)
le billet demi-tarif *m*

Look at Language Plus on pages 283–308 for extra vocabulary.

A half to York, please.
Un billet demi-tarif pour York, s'il vous plaît.

> 🔑
> **two and a half**
> deux et demi
> **half an hour**
> une demi-heure
> **half past ten**
> dix heures et demie
> **half a kilo**
> un demi kilo

B adj
a half portion
une demi-portion
C adv
à moitié
I'm half Scottish.
Je suis à moitié écossais.

half-brother n
le demi-frère m
my half-brother
mon demi-frère

half-sister n
la demi-sœur f
my half-sister
ma demi-sœur

half-term n
les vacances fpl
What are you doing at half-term?
Qu'est-ce que tu fais pendant les vacances?

> There are two half-term holidays in France: **les vacances de la Toussaint** (in October or November) and **les vacances de février** (in February).

half-time n
la mi-temps f

hall n
1 (of school)
le hall m
We have gym in the hall.
On a gym dans le hall.
2 (entrance hall)
l'entrée f

Hallowe'en n
la veille de la Toussaint f

> The French means "Eve of All Saints' Day". **Hallowe'en** is not traditionally celebrated in France, but All Saints' Day (November 1st) is a public holiday, and is the day when people often visit family graves.

ham n
le jambon m
a ham sandwich
un sandwich au jambon

hamburger n
le hamburger m

hamster n
le hamster m

hand n
1 (of person)
la main f
Put up your hands.
Levez la main.

Can you give me a hand?
Tu peux me donner un coup de main?

2 (of clock)
l'aiguille f

hand in vb
rendre
Hand in your books.
Rendez vos cahiers.

hand out vb
distribuer
Hand out the books, Ahmed.
Distribue les livres, Ahmed.

handbag n
le sac à main m

handball n
le handball m
Can we play handball?
On peut jouer au handball?

handkerchief n
le mouchoir m
Have you got a handkerchief?
Tu as un mouchoir?

handle n
la poignée f

handlebars npl
le guidon m

> *guidon* is a singular word.

handsome adj
beau m adj
belle f adj
Gaston is very handsome.
Gaston est très beau.

> *beau* changes to *bel* before a vowel sound.

a handsome man
un bel homme

handwriting n
l'écriture f
He has nice handwriting.
Il a une belle écriture.

> *écriture* is related to the French verb *écrire*, which means "to write".

hangman n
le pendu m

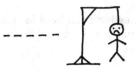

hang on vb
patienter
Hang on a minute please.
Patientez une minute, s'il vous plaît.

happen vb
se passer
What's happening?
Qu'est-ce qui se passe?

happy adj
heureux m adj
heureuse f adj
Joséphine is happy.
Joséphine est heureuse.

The children are happy.
Les enfants sont heureux.

> **Happy birthday!**
> Bon anniversaire!
> **Happy Mother's Day!**
> Bonne Fête, Maman!
> **Happy Christmas!**
> Joyeux Noël!
> **Happy New Year!**
> Bonne année!

Happy Families n
le jeu des sept familles m

harbour n
le port m

A B C D E F G **H** I J K L M N O P Q R S T U V W X Y Z

Look at Language Plus on pages 283–308 for extra vocabulary.

a
b
c
d
e
f
g
h
i
j
k
l
m
n
o
p
q
r
s
t
u
v
w
x
y
z

hard

> **hard** can be an adjective or an adverb.

A adj

1 (*difficult*)
difficile

This question's too hard for me.
Cette question est trop difficile pour moi.

2 (*not soft*)
dur *m adj*
dure *f adj*

This cheese is very hard.
Ce fromage est très dur.

B adv
dur

Colette works hard.
Colette travaille dur.

has vb, *see* **have**

hasn't = **has not**; *see* **have**

hat n
le chapeau *m*
(*pl* les chapeaux)

hate vb
détester

I hate maths.
Je déteste les maths.

> *There is an extra word in the French sentence – what is it?*

have vb

1 avoir

I've got a bike.
J'ai un vélo.

Have you got a sister?
Tu as une sœur?

No, I haven't got a sister.
Non, je n'ai pas de sœur.

He's got blue eyes.
Il a les yeux bleus.

> I have …
> J'ai …
> I have got …
> J'ai …
>
> *have* and *have got* are the same in French.

2 (*eat*)
prendre

What time do you have lunch?
À quelle heure tu prends le déjeuner?

What are you going to have?
Qu'est-ce que tu prends?

3 (*must*)
devoir

You have to be careful.
Tu dois faire attention.

Do I have to choose a card?
Est-ce que je dois choisir une carte?

Do I have to?
Est-ce que je suis vraiment obligé?

> You have to…
> Tu dois…
> You have got to…
> Tu dois…
>
> *have* and *have got* are the same in French.

haven't = **have not**; *see* **have**

he pron
il

He loves dogs.
Il aime les chiens.

head n
1 (*of person*)
la tête *f*

Mind your head!
Attention à la tête!

Heads or tails? – Heads.
Pile ou face? – Face.
2 (*headteacher*)
le directeur *m*
la directrice *f*

headache n
I've got a headache.
J'ai mal à la tête.

headmaster n
le directeur *m*

headmistress n
la directrice *f*

health n
la santé *f*

healthy adj
sain *m adj*
saine *f adj*

a healthy diet
une alimentation saine

hear vb
entendre

I can't hear.
Je n'entends pas.

I can't hear you.
Je ne vous entends pas.

Can you hear the difference?
Vous entendez la différence?

heart n
1 le cœur *m*
2 (*in cards*)

hearts
le cœur

the ace of hearts
l'as de cœur

heater n
le radiateur *m*

an electric heater
un radiateur électrique

heather n
la bruyère *f*

heavy adj
lourd *m adj*
lourde *f adj*

This bag's very heavy.
Ce sac est très lourd.

hedgehog n
le hérisson *m*

height n
la taille *f*

held vb, *see* **hold**

helicopter n
l'hélicoptère *m*

hello excl
bonjour!

helmet n
le casque *m*

Look at Language Plus on pages 283–308 for extra vocabulary.

help

> **help** can be a verb or a noun.

🅐 vb
aider

Can you help me?
Vous pouvez m'aider?

Help yourself!
Servez-vous!

> 🔑
> **Help!**
> Au secours!

🅑 n
l'**aide** f

Do you need any help?
Vous avez besoin d'aide?

hen n
la **poule** f

her

> **her** can be an adjective or a pronoun.

🅐 adj

> When you want to say something
> like "her name", "her house", or
> "her hair" in French, you need to
> know if "name", "house", and
> "hair" are masculine, feminine or
> plural, because there are three
> possible words for **her**.

son m adj
her name
son nom

sa f adj
her house
sa maison

ses pl adj
her hair
ses cheveux

> **sa** changes to **son** before a vowel
> sound.

her address
son adresse

🅑 pron
1 (object of the verb)
la

I hate her.
Je la déteste.

Do you know her?
Tu la connais?

Look at her!
Regarde-la!

> **la** becomes **l'** before a vowel
> sound.

I love her.
Je l'aime.
2 **elle**

I'm going with her.
Je vais avec elle.

It's for her.
C'est pour elle.

He's next to her.
Il est à côté d'elle.

I'm older than her.
Je suis plus âgé qu'elle.

here adv
ici

I live here.
J'habite ici.

Here's Helen.
Voici Helen.

Here are the books.
Voici les livres.

Here he is!
Le voici!

Here is …
Voici …
Here are …
Voici …

here is and *here are* are the same in French.

---

hers pron
à elle
Is this hers?
C'est à elle?

This book is hers.
Ce livre est à elle.

Whose is this? – It's hers.
C'est à qui? – À elle.

---

herself pron
se
My cat washes herself a lot.
Ma chatte se lave beaucoup.

She lives by herself.
Elle habite toute seule.

---

by herself
toute seule

---

he's = **he is**, **he has**; *see*
have

---

hi excl
salut!

---

hide vb
se cacher
Daniel is hiding under the bed.
Daniel se cache sous le lit.

Hide!
Cache-toi!

Mum hides the biscuits.
Maman cache les biscuits.

---

hide-and-seek n
cache-cache *m*

---

high adj
haut *m adj*
haute *f adj*
It's too high.
C'est trop haut.

Higher!
Plus haut!

---

high jump n
le saut en hauteur *m*

---

high-rise n
la tour *f*
I live in a high-rise.
J'habite dans une tour.

---

high school n
1 (*for pupils 11–15*)
le collège *m*
2 (*for pupils 15–18*)
le lycée *m*

In France pupils go to a
collège between the ages of
11 and 15, and then to a
lycée until the age of 18.

---

hiking n
We're going to go hiking.
Nous allons faire une
randonnée.

---

hill n
la colline *f*

Look at Language Plus on pages 283–308 for extra vocabulary.

a
b
c
d
e
f
g
h
i
j
k
l
m
n
o
p
q
r
s
t
u
v
w
x
y
z

him pron

1 (object of the verb)

<u>le</u>

I hate him.
Je le déteste.

Look at him!
Regarde-le!

> *le* changes to *l'* before a vowel sound.

I love him.
Je l'aime.

2 <u>lui</u>

I'm going with him.
Je vais avec lui.

It's for him.
C'est pour lui.

She's next to him.
Elle est à côté de lui.

I'm older than him.
Je suis plus âgé que lui.

himself pron

<u>se</u>

The cat is washing himself.
Le chat se lave.

He lives by himself.
Il habite tout seul.

> 🔑 **by himself**
> tout seul

hippo n

l'<u>hippopotame</u> m

hire vb

<u>louer</u>

You can hire bikes.
On peut louer des vélos.

his

> **his** can be an adjective or a pronoun.

Ⓐ adj

> *When you want to say something like "his name", "his house", or "his hair" in French, you need to know if "name", "house", and "hair" are masculine, feminine or plural, because there are three possible words for **his**.*

<u>son</u> *m adj*
his name
son nom

<u>sa</u> *f adj*
his house
sa maison

<u>ses</u> *pl adj*
his hair
ses cheveux

> *sa* changes to **son** before a vowel sound.

his address
son adresse

Ⓑ pron

<u>à lui</u>

Is this his?
C'est à lui?

This book is his.
Ce livre est à lui.

Whose is this? – It's his.
C'est à qui? – À lui.

history n

l'<u>histoire</u> f

hit

> **hit** can be a verb or a noun.

Ⓐ vb
frapper
Don't hit Luc, Pascal!
Ne frappe pas Luc, Pascal!
Ⓑ n *(song)*
le tube m
Westlife's latest hit
le dernier tube de Westlife

hobby n
le passe-temps m
What are your favourite hobbies?
Quels sont tes passe-temps favoris?

hockey n
le hockey m
I play hockey.
Je joue au hockey.

hold vb
tenir
Can you hold the baby?
Tu peux tenir le bébé?
Hold hands!
Donnez-vous la main!

hold on vb
Hold on a minute!
Attends un peu!

hold up vb
Hold up your hands.
Levez la main.

hole n
le trou m

holiday n
1 les vacances *fpl*
our holiday in France
nos vacances en France

When are you going on holiday?
Quand pars-tu en vacances?

We are on holiday.
Nous sommes en vacances.

in the school holidays
pendant les vacances scolaires

🔑

on holiday
en vacances
the school holidays
les vacances scolaires

---

2 *(public holiday)*
le jour férié m
Monday is a holiday.
Lundi, c'est un jour férié.

Holland n
la Hollande f

holly n
le houx m
a sprig of holly
un brin de houx

home n
la maison f
Is Charlotte at home?
Est-ce que Charlotte est à la maison?

What time do you get home?
Tu rentres à quelle heure?

I get home at five o'clock.
Je rentre à cinq heures.

to go home
rentrer à la maison
I want to go home.
Je veux rentrer à la maison.

🔑

at home
à la maison

A B C D E F G **H** I J K L M N O P Q R S T U V W X Y Z

Look at Language Plus on pages 283–308 for extra vocabulary.

homeless npl
the homeless
les sans-abri

home page n
la page d'accueil f

homework n
les devoirs mpl
We have too much homework.
Nous avons trop de devoirs.
my geography homework
mes devoirs de géographie

honey n
le miel m

honeymoon n
la lune de miel f

hood n
la capuche f

hooray excl
hourra!

hop vb
sauter à cloche-pied
Hop!
Sautez à cloche-pied!

hope vb
espérer
I hope that's okay.
J'espère que ça ira.
I'm hoping to go to France.
J'espère aller en France.

> 🔑
> **I hope so.**
> Je l'espère.
> **I hope not.**
> J'espère que non.

hopeless adj
nul m adj
nulle f adj

I'm hopeless at maths.
Je suis nul en maths.
You're hopeless, Martine!
Martine, tu es nulle!

horrible adj
horrible

horror film n
le film d'horreur m

horse n
le cheval m
(pl les chevaux)

hospital n
l'hôpital m
(pl les hôpitaux)
My grandmother is in hospital.
Ma grand-mère est à l'hôpital.

hot adj
1 (very warm)
chaud m adj
chaude f adj
a hot bath
un bain chaud
I'm too hot.
J'ai trop chaud.
It's very hot today.
Il fait très chaud aujourd'hui.

> 🔑
> **I'm hot.**
> J'ai chaud.
> **It's hot.**
> Il fait chaud.

2 *(spicy)*
épicé *m adj*

épicée *f adj*

a very hot curry
un curry très épicé

hot chocolate n
le chocolat chaud *m*

hot dog n
le hot-dog *m*

hotel n
l'hôtel *m*

hour n
l'heure *f*

an hour and ten minutes
une heure dix

> **a quarter of an hour**
> un quart d'heure
> **half an hour**
> une demi-heure
> **two and a half hours**
> deux heures et demie

house n
1 *(building)*
la maison *f*

You've got a nice house.
Vous avez une belle maison.

Do you want to play at my house?
Tu veux jouer chez moi?

> **at my house**
> chez moi

2 *(at school)*
le groupe *m*

Skye house has 180 points.
Le groupe Skye a 180 points.

housewife n
la femme au foyer *f*

She's a housewife.
Elle est femme au foyer.

> *You do not translate "a" when you say what someone's job is in French.*

how adv
comment

How do you say "apple" in French?
Comment dit-on "apple" en français?

How many …?
Combien de …?

How many pupils are there in the class?
Il y a combien d'élèves dans la classe?

How much is it?
C'est combien?

How old is your brother?
Ton frère a quel âge?

> **How are you?**
> Comment allez-vous?
> **How old are you?**
> Tu as quel âge?
> **How many?**
> Combien?
> **How much?**
> Combien?

huge adj
immense

hundred num
a hundred
cent

a hundred euros
cent euros

Look at Language Plus on pages 283–308 for extra vocabulary.

cent is spelt with an **s** when there are two or more hundreds, but not when it is followed by another number, as in "six hundred and two".

five hundred
cinq cents
five hundred and one
cinq cent un
hundreds of people
des centaines de personnes

hungry adj
Are you hungry?
Tu as faim?

I'm hungry.
J'ai faim.
I'm not hungry.
Je n'ai pas faim.

hunting n
la chasse *f*
I'm against hunting.
Je suis contre la chasse.

fox-hunting
la chasse au renard

hurry up vb
Hurry up, Gavin!
Dépêche-toi, Gavin!
Hurry up, children!
Dépêchez-vous, les enfants!

hurt vb
You're hurting me!
Tu me fais mal!
My leg hurts.
J'ai mal à la jambe.
Have you hurt yourself?
Tu t'es fait mal?
That hurts.
Ça fait mal.

husband n
le mari *m*

hymn n
le cantique *m*

hyphen n
le trait d'union *m*

I pron
1 je
I speak French.
Je parle français.

> *je changes to j' before a vowel
> sound.*

I love cats.
J'aime les chats.
2 moi
Ann and I
Ann et moi

ice n
la glace *f*
There is ice on the lake.
Il y a de la glace sur le lac.

ice cream n
la glace *f*
Would you like an ice cream?
Tu veux une glace?

vanilla ice cream
la glace à la vanille

chocolate ice cream
la glace au chocolat

> *It's "à la vanille" because **vanille** is
> feminine, and "au chocolat"
> because **chocolat** is masculine.*

ice cube n
le glaçon *m*

ice lolly n
la glace à l'eau *f*
two ice lollies
deux glaces à l'eau

ice rink n
la patinoire *f*

ice-skating n
le patin à glace *m*
I go ice-skating.
Je fais du patin à glace.

ICT n
les TIC *fpl*

icy adj
The roads are icy.
Il y a du verglas sur les routes.

idea n
l'idée *f*
Good idea!
Bonne idée!

identical adj
identique
The twins are identical.
Ces jumelles sont identiques.

if conj
si
You can have it if you like.
Tu peux le prendre si tu veux.

> *si changes to s' before il and ils.*

Do you know if he's there?
Savez-vous s'il est là?

Look at Language Plus on pages 283–308 for extra vocabulary.

a

ill adj
malade

Christelle is ill.
Christelle est malade.

b

c

imagination n
l'imagination f

d

imagine vb
imaginer

e

Imagine you have lots of money.
Imagine que tu as beaucoup
d'argent.

f

g

h

imitate vb
imiter

i

Imitate the sound.
Imitez le son.

j

k

immediately adv
immédiatement

l

I'll do it immediately.
Je vais le faire immédiatement.

m

immigrant n
l'immigré m
l'immigrée f

n

o

impatient adj
impatient m adj

p

impatiente f adj

q

Don't be so impatient, Édith.
Ne sois pas si impatiente, Édith.

r

s

t

u

v

w

important adj
important m adj

x

importante f adj

y

This is an important letter.
C'est une lettre importante.

z

Today's an important day.
Aujourd'hui est un grand jour.

impossible adj
impossible

Sorry, it's impossible.
Désolée, c'est impossible.

in

> **in** can be a preposition or an
> adverb.

Ⓐ prep

> *There are several ways of*
> *translating* **in**. *Scan the examples*
> *for one that is similar to what you*
> *want to say.*

1 dans

in the house
dans la maison

in my bag
dans mon sac

What can you see in the picture?
Que voyez-vous sur l'image?

2 à

in the country
à la campagne

in school
à l'école

in hospital
à l'hôpital

in London
à Londres

the boy in the blue shirt
le garçon à la chemise bleue

3 en

in English
en anglais

in summer
en été

in May
en mai

in 2003
en deux mille trois

A
B
C
D
E
F
G
H
I
J
K
L
M
N
O
P
Q
R
S
T
U
V
W
X
Y
Z

*When **in** refers to a country which is feminine, use **en**; when the country is masculine, use **au**; when the country is plural, use **aux**.*

in England
en Angleterre

in Portugal
au Portugal

in the United States
aux États-Unis

4 de

the tallest person in the family
le plus grand de la famille

at 6 o'clock in the morning
à six heures du matin

She's the oldest in the class.
C'est la plus vieille de la classe.

in my class
dans ma classe
in Paris
à Paris
in France
en France
in French
en français

B adv
to be in
être là

He isn't in.
Il n'est pas là.

inch n

6 inches
quinze centimètres

In France measurements are in metres and centimetres rather than feet and inches. An inch is about 2.5 centimetres.

incident n
l'incident m

an incident
un incident

included adj
compris m adj

comprise f adj
Service is not included.
Le service n'est pas compris.

incredible adj
incroyable
That's incredible!
C'est incroyable!

indeed adv
Thank you very much indeed!
Merci beaucoup!

Indian adj
indien m adj
indienne f adj

an Indian restaurant
un restaurant indien

*The adjective **Indian** is spelled with a capital letter, but **indien** is not.*

indoor adj
an indoor swimming pool
une piscine couverte

indoors adv
à l'intérieur
They're indoors.
Ils sont à l'intérieur.

Look at Language Plus on pages 283–308 for extra vocabulary.

inexpensive adj
<u>bon marché</u> *m, f, pl adj*

an inexpensive hotel
un hôtel bon marché

infant school n

He's going to start at infant school.
Il va entrer en cours préparatoire.

> **CP (cours préparatoire)** is the equivalent of first-year infants, and **CE1 (cours élémentaire de première année)** the equivalent of second-year infants.

infection n

an ear infection
une otite

a throat infection
une angine

information n
les <u>renseignements</u> *mpl*

I need some information.
J'ai besoin de renseignements.

important information
des renseignements importants

information about France
des renseignements sur la France

> *information is a singular word in English, but a plural word in French.*

ingredient n
l'<u>ingrédient</u> *m*

a list of ingredients
une liste d'ingrédients

inhabitant n
l'<u>habitant</u> *m*
l'<u>habitante</u> *f*

initials npl
les <u>initiales</u> *fpl*

My initials are GAC.
Mes initiales sont GAC.

injection n
la <u>piqûre</u> *f*

injure vb
<u>blesser</u>

Was anyone injured?
Est-ce que quelqu'un a été blessé?

injury n
la <u>blessure</u> *f*

a serious injury
une blessure grave

ink n
l'<u>encre</u> *f*

inquire vb

to inquire about something
se renseigner sur quelque chose

I'm going to inquire about train times.
Je vais me renseigner sur les horaires des trains.

inquiries npl
renseignements *mpl*

inquisitive adj
<u>curieux</u> *m adj*
<u>curieuse</u> *f adj*

insect n
l'<u>insecte</u> *m*

in-service day n
la journée de formation f

inside

> **inside** can be an adverb or a preposition.

Ⓐ adv
à l'intérieur

They're inside.
Ils sont à l'intérieur.

Do you want a table inside or outside?
Vous voulez une table à l'intérieur ou à l'extérieur?

Ⓑ prep
à l'intérieur de

inside the house
à l'intérieur de la maison

inspector n
le contrôleur m

instance n
for instance
par exemple

instantly adv
tout de suite

instead adv
à la place

There's no coke. Do you want orange juice instead?
Il n'y a pas de coca. Tu veux du jus d'orange à la place?

instead of
au lieu de

Eat fruit instead of sweets.
Mangez des fruits au lieu de bonbons.

instead of me
à ma place

instead of Manon
à la place de Manon

instructions npl
les instructions fpl

Follow the instructions.
Suivez les instructions.

instructor n
le moniteur m
la monitrice f

a skiing instructor
un moniteur de ski

instrument n
l'instrument m

Do you play an instrument?
Est-ce que tu joues d'un instrument?

intelligent adj
intelligent m adj

intelligente f adj

You're very intelligent.
Tu es très intelligente.

> *The person being spoken to is a girl. How can you tell?*

interest n
My main interest is music.
Ce qui m'intéresse le plus c'est la musique.

A
B
C
D
E
F
G
H
I
J
K
L
M
N
O
P
Q
R
S
T
U
V
W
X
Y
Z

Look at Language Plus on pages 283–308 for extra vocabulary.

a
b
c
d
e
f
g
h
i
j
k
l
m
n
o
p
q
r
s
t
u
v
w
x
y
z

interested adj
I'm not interested.
Ça ne m'intéresse pas.

I'm not interested in football.
Le football ne m'intéresse pas.

Are you interested?
Ça t'intéresse?

interesting adj
intéressant *m adj*
intéressante *f adj*

It's a very interesting story.
C'est une histoire très
intéressante.

international
international *m adj*
internationale *f adj*

an international school
une école internationale

internet n
l'Internet *m*

on the internet
sur Internet

*There's one more word in the
English sentence. What is it?*

internet café n
le cybercafé *m*

interrupt vb
interrompre
Don't interrupt Hugues!
N'interromps pas, Hugues!

interval n
1 (*cinema, theatre*)
l'entracte *m*
during the interval
pendant l'entracte
2 (*school*)
la récréation *f*

interview n
l'interview *f*

interviewer n
l'interviewer *m*

into prep
1 en
I'm going into town.
Je vais en ville.

Translate it into French.
Traduisez ça en français.

Divide into two groups.
Répartissez-vous en deux groupes.
2 (*inside*)
dans
He got into the car.
Il est monté dans la voiture.

introduce vb
présenter
Introduce yourselves.
Présentez-vous.

**I'd like to introduce Michelle
Davies.**
Je vous présente Michelle Davies.

invalid n
le/la malade *m/f*

inventor n
l'inventeur *m*
l'inventrice *f*

invisible adj
invisible

invitation n
l'invitation *f*
Thank you for the invitation.
Merci pour l'invitation.

invite vb
inviter

I'm going to invite Léon to my party.
Je vais inviter Léon à ma fête.

Ireland n
l'Irlande f

I live in Ireland.
J'habite en Irlande.

When are you coming to Ireland?
Quand est-ce que tu viens en Irlande?

I'm from Ireland.
Je suis irlandaise.

in Ireland
en Irlande
I'm going to Ireland.
Je vais en Irlande.

Irish

Irish can be an adjective or a noun.

A adj
irlandais m adj
irlandaise f adj

I am Irish.
Je suis irlandais.

Is a boy or a girl saying this? How can you tell?

I like Irish music.
J'aime la musique irlandaise.

Irish people
les Irlandais

He's Irish.
Il est irlandais.
She's Irish.
Elle est irlandaise.

B n (language)
l'irlandais m

Do you speak Irish?
Est-ce que tu parles irlandais?

the Irish
les Irlandais

irlandais is not spelled with a capital letter except when it means an Irish person.

Irishman n
l'Irlandais m

Irishwoman n
l'Irlandaise f

iron

iron can be a noun or a verb.

A n
1 (metal)
le fer m

an iron gate
un portail en fer

2 (for clothes)
le fer à repasser m

B vb
repasser

I can iron a shirt.
Je sais repasser une chemise.

irritating adj
irritant m adj
irritante f adj

is vb, see **be**

Islam n
l'Islam m

A B C D E F G H I J K L M N O P Q R S T U V W X Y Z

Look at Language Plus on pages 283–308 for extra vocabulary.

island n
l'île f

isle n
the Isle of Man
l'île de Man

the Isle of Wight
l'île de Wight

it pron

*You need to know if **it** stands for a masculine noun or a feminine noun, so that you can choose **il** or **elle**.*

il

Where's my book? – It's on the table.
Où est mon livre? – Il est sur la table.

elle

Where's my pencil case? – It's in your bag.
Où est ma trousse? – Elle est dans ton sac.

*Use **le** or **la** when **it** is the object of the sentence. **le** and **la** change to **l'** before a vowel sound.*

le

There's a croissant left. Do you want it?
Il reste un croissant. Tu le veux?

la

I don't want this apple. You can have it.
Je ne veux pas de cette pomme. Tu peux la prendre.

l'

This is my new jumper. Do you like it?
C'est mon nouveau pull. Tu l'aimes?

It's me.
C'est moi.
It's you.
C'est toi.
It's expensive.
C'est cher.
It's delicious.
C'est délicieux.

Italian

Italian can be an adjective or a noun.

A adj
italien *m adj*

italienne *f adj*

an Italian restaurant
un restaurant italien

B n (*language*)
l'italien *m*

***Italian** always has a capital letter, but **italien** doesn't.*

Italy n
l'Italie f

item n
l'article *m*

its adj

*To say something like "its name", "its place", or "its hair" in French, you need to know if "name", "place", and "hair" are masculine, feminine or plural, because there are three possible words for **its**.*

son *m adj*

What's its name?
Quel est son nom?

sa *f adj*

Every thing is in its place.
Chaque chose est à sa place.

ses *pl adj*

The dog is losing its hair.
Le chien perd ses poils.

J

jab n
la <u>piqûre</u> f

jack n
le <u>valet</u> m

the jack of hearts
le valet de cœur

jacket n
la <u>veste</u> f

a white jacket
une veste blanche

jacket potato n
la <u>pomme de terre cuite au</u>
<u>four</u> f

**There are chips and jacket
potatoes.**
Il y a des frites et des pommes de
terre cuites au four.

jam n
la <u>confiture</u> f

strawberry jam
la confiture de fraises

jam jar n
le <u>pot à confiture</u> m

janitor n
le <u>concierge</u> m

He's a janitor.
Il est concierge.

> *You do not translate "a" when you
> say what someone's job is in
> French.*

January n
<u>janvier</u> m

January or February?
Janvier ou février?

My birthday's in January.
Mon anniversaire est en janvier.

> 🔑
> **in January**
> en janvier
> **the fifth of January**
> le cinq janvier
>
> *The months are not spelled with
> a capital letter in French.*

jealous adj
<u>jaloux</u> m adj

<u>jalouse</u> f adj

Aline is jealous.
Aline est jalouse.

jeans npl
le <u>jean</u> m

I've got new jeans.
J'ai un jean neuf.

> *jeans is plural in English, but the
> French word is singular.*

Look at Language Plus on pages 283–308 for extra vocabulary.

a

b

c

d

e

f

g

h

i

j

k

l

m

n

o

p

q

r

s

t

u

v

w

x

y

z

jelly n
la <u>gelée</u> f

jersey n
le <u>pull-over</u> m

Jew n
le <u>Juif</u> m
la <u>Juive</u> f

jewellery n
les <u>bijoux</u> mpl

Jewish adj
<u>juif</u> m adj
<u>juive</u> f adj

> *Jewish* has a capital letter, but *juif* does not.

jigsaw n
le <u>puzzle</u> m
I like doing jigsaws.
J'aime faire des puzzles.

job n
l'<u>emploi</u> m
She's looking for a job.
Elle cherche un emploi.
I've got a Saturday job.
Je travaille le samedi.

jogging n
She goes jogging.
Elle fait du jogging.

joke n
la <u>plaisanterie</u> f

jotter n
le <u>cahier</u> m

journey n
le <u>voyage</u> m
I don't like long journeys.
Je n'aime pas les longs
voyages.

judge

> **judge** can be a noun or a verb.

Ⓐ n
le <u>juge</u> m
She's a judge.
Elle est juge.

> *You do not translate "a" when you say what someone's job is in French.*

Ⓑ vb
<u>juger</u>
Who's going to judge the competition?
Qui va juger le concours?

judo n
le <u>judo</u> m
I do judo.
Je fais du judo.

juggler n
le <u>jongleur</u> m
la <u>jongleuse</u> f

juice n
le <u>jus</u> m
I'd like some orange juice.
Je voudrais du jus d'orange.

July n
<u>juillet</u> m
July or August?
Juillet ou août?
My birthday is in July.
Mon anniversaire est en juillet.

> **in July**
> en juillet
> **the fourteenth of July**
> le quatorze juillet
>
> *Months are not written with a capital letter in French.*

The fourteenth of July (**la fête nationale**) is the French national holiday. There's a firework display and a military parade in Paris.

jump vb
sauter
Jump!
Saute!

jumper n
le pull *m*
a dark green jumper
un pull vert foncé

June n
juin *m*
June or July?
Juin ou juillet?

My birthday is in June.
Mon anniversaire est en juin.

> **in June**
> en juin
> **the fourth of June**
> le quatre juin
>
> *Months are not written with a capital letter in French.*

junior n
the juniors
les élèves des petites classes

junior school n
l'école primaire *f*

just adv
juste
just after Christmas
juste après Noël

just now
en ce moment

I'm busy just now.
Je suis occupé en ce moment.

I'm just coming!
J'arrive!

Just a moment, please.
Un moment, s'il vous plaît.

Look at Language Plus on pages 283–308 for extra vocabulary.

K

karaoke n
le karaoké m

karate n
le karaté m
I do karate.
Je fais du karaté.

keen adj
enthousiaste
He's not very keen.
Il n'est pas très
enthousiaste.

keep vb
1 (have)
garder
You can keep it.
Tu peux le garder.
2 (stay)
rester
Keep still!
Reste tranquille!
Keep quiet!
Tais-toi!

keep on vb
continuer
Keep on singing.
Continuez de chanter.

keep-fit n
**The keep-fit class is on
Tuesday.**
Le cours de gym, c'est mardi.

key n
la clé f
Where are my keys?
Où sont mes clés?

kick

kick can be a noun or a verb.

A n
le coup de pied m
B vb
donner un coup de pied
He kicked me!
Il m'a donné un coup de pied!

kid n
(child)
le/la gosse m/f
the kids
les gosses

kill vb
tuer
My cat kills birds.
Mon chat tue les oiseaux.

kilo n
le kilo m
two euros a kilo
deux euros le kilo

kilometre n
le kilomètre m

kilt n
le kilt *m*

kind

kind can be an adjective or a noun.

Ⓐ adj
gentil *m adj*
gentille *f adj*
That's very kind of you.
C'est très gentil.
Ⓑ n
la sorte *f*
"Saucisson" is a kind of sausage.
Le saucisson est une sorte de saucisse.

kindergarten n
l'école maternelle *f*

king n
le roi *m*
the king of hearts
le roi de cœur

kiss

kiss can be a noun or a verb.

Ⓐ n
le baiser *m*
Give me a kiss.
Donne-moi un baiser.

"bisou" and "bise" are two other words meaning kiss. At the end of a letter to a friend you could write "Bisous", or "Grosses bises".

Ⓑ vb
embrasser
Kiss me.
Embrasse-moi.

Between girls and boys, and between girls, the normal French way of saying hello and goodbye is with kisses, usually one on each cheek. Boys shake hands with each other instead.

kit n
les affaires *fpl*
Don't forget your gym kit.
N'oublie pas tes affaires de gym.

kitchen n
la cuisine *f*
She's in the kitchen.
Elle est dans la cuisine.

kite n
le cerf-volant *m*
two kites
deux cerfs-volants

kitten n
le chaton *m*

knee n
le genou *m*
(*pl* les genoux)

knickers npl
la culotte *f*
I can see your knickers!
Je vois ta culotte!

Look at Language Plus on pages 283–308 for extra vocabulary.

a pair of knickers
une culotte

> *culotte* is a singular word.

knife n
le <u>couteau</u> m
(*pl* les couteaux)

knit vb
<u>tricoter</u>
I can knit.
Je sais tricoter.

knives npl
les <u>couteaux</u> mpl
knives, forks and spoons
les couteaux, les fourchettes et les cuillères

knob n
le <u>bouton</u> m

knock vb
<u>frapper</u>
Someone's knocking at the door.
Quelqu'un frappe à la porte.

know vb
1 (*know something*)
<u>savoir</u>
It's a long way. – Yes, I know.
C'est loin. – Oui, je sais.
Who knows the answer?
Qui sait la réponse?

> **I don't know.**
> Je ne sais pas.

2 (*know someone*)
<u>connaître</u>
I know her.
Je la connais.
I don't know him.
Je ne le connais pas.
Do you know Louise?
Tu connais Louise?

Koran n
le <u>Coran</u> m

L

label n
l'étiquette f

lace n
(of shoe)
le lacet m

ladder n
l'échelle f

lady n
la dame f

a young lady
une jeune fille

Ladies and gentlemen ...
Mesdames, Messieurs ...

Where is the 'ladies'?
Où sont les toilettes pour dames?

lake n
le lac m

lamb n
l'agneau m
(pl les agneaux)

a lamb chop
une côtelette d'agneau

land

land can be a noun or a verb.

Ⓐ n
la terre f

on land
sur terre

Ⓑ vb
atterrir

The plane lands at nine o'clock.
L'avion atterrit à neuf heures.

lane n
le chemin m

a country lane
un chemin de campagne

the fast lane
la voie rapide

language n
la langue f

French isn't a difficult language.
Le français n'est pas une langue
difficile.

language laboratory n
le laboratoire de langues m

lap n
on my lap
sur mes genoux

laptop n
l'ordinateur portable m

large adj
1 (size, glass, plate, garden)
grand m adj
grande f adj

a large house
une grande maison
2 (car, animal, book, parcel)
gros m adj
grosse f adj

Look at Language Plus on pages 283–308 for extra vocabulary.

a large dog
un gros chien

last

last can be an adjective or an adverb.

A adj
<u>dernier</u> m adj
<u>dernière</u> f adj
the last time
la dernière fois

tonight and last night
ce soir et hier soir

last Friday
vendredi dernier
last week
la semaine dernière
last summer
l'été dernier
last night
hier soir
at last
enfin

B adv
<u>en dernier</u>
He always comes last.
Il arrive toujours en dernier.

late adj, adv
1 <u>en retard</u>
You're going to be late!
Tu vas être en retard!

I'm late for school.
Je suis en retard pour l'école.

Sorry I'm late!
Désolé d'être en retard!

2 (late at night)
<u>tard</u>
I go to bed late.
Je me couche tard.

later adv
<u>plus tard</u>
I'll do it later.
Je ferai ça plus tard.

See you later!
À tout à l'heure!

latest adj
<u>dernier</u> m adj
<u>dernière</u> f adj
their latest album
leur dernier album

Latin n
le <u>latin</u> m
I do Latin.
Je fais du latin.

laugh vb
<u>rire</u>
Why are you laughing?
Pourquoi tu ris?

lawn n
la <u>pelouse</u> f

lawnmower n
la <u>tondeuse à gazon</u> f

lawyer n
l'<u>avocat</u> m
l'<u>avocate</u> f
My mother's a lawyer.
Ma mère est avocate.

You do not translate "a" when you say what someone's job is in French.

lay vb
poser

Lay your cards on the table.
Posez vos cartes sur la table.

to lay the table
mettre la table

It's André's turn to lay the table.
C'est à André de mettre la table.

lazy adj
paresseux *m adj*
paresseuse *f adj*

My sister is very lazy.
Ma sœur est très paresseuse.

lead

> **lead** can be a noun or a verb.

A n
to be in the lead
être en tête

Our team is in the lead.
Notre équipe est en tête.
B vb
mener

This street leads to the station.
Cette rue mène à la gare.

leaf n
la feuille *f*

lean out vb
se pencher

Don't lean out of the window.
Ne te penche pas par la fenêtre.

lean over vb
se pencher

Don't lean over too far.
Ne te penche pas trop.

leap year n
l'année bissextile *f*

learn vb
apprendre

I'm learning to ski.
J'apprends à skier.

We're learning a lot.
Nous apprenons beaucoup.

> 🔑
> **I'm learning French.**
> J'apprends le français.

least adv, adj, pron
the least
le moins de

Who's got the least cards?
Qui a le moins de cartes?

> *When **the least** is followed by an adjective, it is translated by **le moins**, **la moins**, or **les moins**, depending on whether the noun is masculine, feminine or plural.*

the least expensive hotel
l'hôtel le moins cher

the least expensive seat
la place la moins chère

the least expensive hotels
les hôtels les moins chers

It'll cost at least £200.
Ça va coûter au moins deux cents livres.

> 🔑
> **at least**
> au moins

leather n
le cuir *m*

It's made of leather.
C'est en cuir.

Look at Language Plus on pages 283–308 for extra vocabulary.

leave vb

1 (*on purpose*)

laisser

Don't leave your bag in the car.
Ne laisse pas ton sac dans la voiture.

2 (*by mistake*)

oublier

I've left my book at home.
J'ai oublié mon livre à la maison.

3 (*depart*)

partir

The bus leaves at 8.
Le car part à huit heures.

leaves npl

les feuilles *fpl*

leek n

le poireau *m*
(*pl* les poireaux)

left vb, *see* leave

left

left can be an adjective, an adverb or a noun.

A adj

1 (*not right*)

gauche

my left hand
ma main gauche

on the left side of the road
sur le côté gauche de la route

2 (*remaining*)

How many cards have you got left?
Il te reste combien de cartes?

I haven't got any money left.
Il ne me reste plus d'argent.

B adv

à gauche

Turn left.
Tournez à gauche.

Take the next left.
Prenez la prochaine à gauche.

C n

la gauche *f*

on the left
à gauche

the house on the left
la maison à gauche

left-hand adj

the left-hand side
la gauche

It's on the left-hand side.
C'est à gauche.

left-handed adj

gaucher *m adj*

gauchère *f adj*

Annick is left-handed.
Annick est gauchère.

Annick is a girl's name – how can you tell from the translation?

left-luggage office n

la consigne *f*

leg n

la jambe *f*

She has a broken leg.
Elle a une jambe cassée.

a chicken leg
une cuisse de poulet

leisure centre n

le centre de loisirs *m*

lemon n

le citron *m*

lemonade n

la limonade *f*

A
B
C
D
E
F
G
H
I
J
K
L
M
N
O
P
Q
R
S
T
U
V
W
X
Y
Z

lend vb
prêter
Can you lend me a pencil?
Tu peux me prêter un crayon?

less

less can be an adjective or a pronoun.

Ⓐ adj
moins de
Less noise, please!
Moins de bruit, s'il vous plaît!
Ⓑ pron
moins
A bit less, please.
Un peu moins, s'il vous plaît.

I've got less than him!
J'en ai moins que lui!

*When **less than** is followed by a number the translation is **moins de**.*

It costs less than £10.
Ça coûte moins de dix livres.

lesson n
1 la leçon f
a French lesson
une leçon de français
2 (*class*)
le cours m
Each lesson lasts forty minutes.
Chaque cours dure quarante minutes.

let vb
1 (*allow*)
laisser
Let me have a look.
Laisse-moi voir.
2 (*shall we*)
Let's go to the park!
Allons au parc!

Let's go!
Allons-y!
Let's start now!
Commençons maintenant!

letter n
la lettre f

I'm writing a letter to my penfriend.
J'écris une lettre à ma correspondante.

It's a ten-letter word.
C'est un mot en dix lettres.

letterbox n
la boîte à lettres f

In France people don't usually have letter boxes in their front doors. More often they have a box outside or on the ground floor of a block of flats.

lettuce n
la salade f

liar n
le menteur m
la menteuse f

library n
la bibliothèque f

licence n
le permis m
a driving licence
un permis de conduire

Look at Language Plus on pages 283–308 for extra vocabulary.

a
b
c
d
e
f
g
h
i
j
k
l
m
n
o
p
q
r
s
t
u
v
w
x
y
z

lick vb
lécher
The dog is licking me.
Le chien me lèche.

lid n
le couvercle m

lie vb

> **lie** can be a verb or a noun.

Ⓐ vb
1 (tell lie)
mentir
She's lying.
Elle ment.
2 (lie down)
He is lying on the sofa.
Il est allongé sur le canapé.

Ⓑ n
le mensonge m
That's a lie!
C'est un mensonge!

life n
la vie f

life-saving n
le sauvetage m
I'm doing a course in life-saving.
Je prends des cours de sauvetage.

lift

> **lift** can be a verb or a noun.

Ⓐ vb
soulever
It's too heavy, I can't lift it.
C'est trop lourd, je ne peux pas le
soulever.

Ⓑ n
l'ascenseur m
The lift isn't working.
L'ascenseur est en panne.

light

> **light** can be an adjective, a noun
> or a verb.

Ⓐ adj
1 (not heavy)
léger m adj
légère f adj
as light as a feather
léger comme une plume
2 (colours)
clair m, f, pl adj
light blue socks
des chaussettes bleu clair
Ⓑ n
la lumière f
Switch on the light.
Allume la lumière.
Switch off the light
Éteins la lumière.
Ⓒ vb
allumer
Let's light the fire.
Allumons le feu.

light bulb n
l'ampoule f

lightning n
les éclairs mpl
a flash of lightning
un éclair

A
B
C
D
E
F
G
H
I
J
K
L
M
N
O
P
Q
R
S
T
U
V
W
X
Y
Z

like

like can be a verb or a preposition.

Ⓐ vb
1 (enjoy)
aimer
I like cherries.
J'aime les cerises.

There's an extra word in French, what is it?

I don't like mustard.
Je n'aime pas la moutarde.
I like riding.
J'aime faire du cheval.
2 (be fond of)
bien aimer
I like Paul.
J'aime bien Paul.
3 (want)
vouloir
Yes, if you like.
Oui, si tu veux.

To say what you'd like, use je voudrais.

I'd like an orange juice, please.
Je voudrais un jus d'orange, s'il vous plaît.
I'd like some chips.
Je voudrais des frites.

To ask what somebody would like, use vous voulez or tu veux.

What would you like, Miss?
Qu'est-ce que vous voulez, madame?
What would you like, dear?
Qu'est-ce que tu veux, mon chéri?
Would you like some tea, Miss?
Vous voulez du thé, madame?
Would you like a coke, Louis?
Tu veux un coca, Louis?

Another way to ask would you like is to put the verb first.

Would you like a coke?
Veux-tu un coca?

🔑
I'd like…
Je voudrais…

Ⓑ prep
comme
a city like Paris
une ville comme Paris
I look like my brother.
Je ressemble à mon frère.

🔑
What's the weather like?
Quel temps fait-il?

likely adj
probable
That's not very likely.
C'est peu probable.

lily of the valley n
le muguet m

On May 1st French people celebrate May Day by giving each other small bunches of lily of the valley.

line n
la ligne f
a straight line
une ligne droite
to draw a line
tirer un trait
Draw a line under each answer.
Tirez un trait après chaque réponse.

Look at Language Plus on pages 283–308 for extra vocabulary.

a
b
c
d
e
f
g
h
i
j
k
l
m
n
o
p
q
r
s
t
u
v
w
x
y
z

lion n
le <u>lion</u> m

lip n
la <u>lèvre</u> f

lipstick n
le <u>rouge à lèvres</u> m

> *Word for word, this means "red for lips".*

liquid n
le <u>liquide</u> m

list

> *list can be a noun or a verb.*

A n
la <u>liste</u> f
a shopping list
une liste de courses
B vb
<u>faire une liste de</u>
List your hobbies!
Fais une liste de tes hobbies!

listen vb
<u>écouter</u>
Are you listening, Gaëlle?
Tu écoutes, Gaëlle?

Listen to this, everybody!
Écoutez ça, tout le monde!

> 🔑
> **Listen to me, children!**
> Écoutez-moi, les enfants!

litre n
le <u>litre</u> m

litter n
les <u>détritus</u> mpl
Don't leave litter.
Ne laissez pas de détritus.

litter bin n
la <u>poubelle</u> f

little adj
petit m adj
petite f adj
a little girl
une petite fille
very little
très peu
We've got very little time.
Nous avons très peu de temps.
a little
un peu
How much would you like? – Just a little.
Combien en voulez-vous? – Juste un peu.

> *The word en means "of it".*

live vb
1 habiter
Where do you live?
Où est-ce que tu habites?

I live here.
J'habite ici.

I live in Edinburgh.
J'habite à Édimbourg.
2 vivre
I live with my grandmother.
Je vis avec ma grand-mère.

to live together
vivre ensemble

My parents don't live together any more.
Mes parents ne vivent plus ensemble.

living room n
la salle de séjour f

load n
loads of
un tas de
loads of people
un tas de gens
loads of money
un tas d'argent

loaf n
le pain m
a loaf of bread
un pain

loaves npl
les pains mpl

lock
lock can be a noun or a verb.

Ⓐ n
la serrure f
The lock is broken.
La serrure est cassée.
Ⓑ vb
fermer à clé
Lock your door.
Fermez votre porte à clé.

locker n
le casier m
Leave your books in your locker.
Laissez vos livres dans votre casier.

log n
la bûche f

log in vb
se connecter
I can't log in.
Je n'arrive pas à me connecter.

log off vb
se déconnecter
I've forgotten how to log off.
J'ai oublié comment on se déconnecte.

log on vb
se connecter
Have you logged on yet?
Ça y est, tu t'es connecté?

log out vb
se déconnecter
Please log out now.
Déconnectez-vous maintenant, s'il vous plaît.

lollipop n
la sucette f

lollipop lady n
la dame qui aide à traverser f

London n
Londres
in London
à Londres
to London
à Londres
I'm from London.
Je suis de Londres.

A few British towns have French names. Can you recognize these: Douvres, Cantorbéry, Édimbourg?

lonely adj
seul m adj
seule f adj
to feel lonely
se sentir seul
She feels lonely.
Elle se sent seule.

Look at Language Plus on pages 283–308 for extra vocabulary.

a
b
c
d
e
f
g
h
i
j
k
l
m
n
o
p
q
r
s
t
u
v
w
x
y
z

long adj
long *m adj*
longue *f adj*

There's a long queue.
Il y a une longue queue.

She's got long hair.
Elle a les cheveux longs.

*Hair is plural in French, so the
adjective has to be plural too.*

How long is the flight?
Combien de temps dure le
vol?

🔑

How long?
Combien de temps?
It takes a long time.
Ça prend du temps.

loo n
les toilettes *fpl*

Where's the loo?
Où sont les toilettes?

May I go to the loo?
Je peux aller aux toilettes?

look

look can be a noun or a verb.

A n
to have a look
regarder

Have a look at this!
Regardez ça!

B vb
1 regarder

Look, children!
Regardez, les enfants!

Look Olivier, you've broken it.
Regarde Olivier, tu l'as cassé.

to look at is also regarder.

Look at the picture.
Regardez cette image.

Look at me, Stéphane.
Regarde-moi, Stéphane.

2 (seem)
avoir l'air

That cake looks nice.
Ce gâteau a l'air bon.

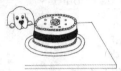

🔑

Look!
Regarde!
Look at the board.
Regardez le tableau.
Look out!
Attention!

look after vb
s'occuper de

I look after my little sister.
Je m'occupe de ma petite sœur.

look for vb
chercher

I'm looking for my rubber.
Je cherche ma gomme.

What are you looking for?
Qu'est-ce que tu cherches?

look up vb
chercher

**Look up the words in the
dictionary.**
Cherchez les mots dans le
dictionnaire.

lorry n
le camion *m*

lorry driver n
le routier *m*

He's a lorry driver.
Il est routier.

*You do not translate "**a**" when you say what someone's job is in French.*

lose vb
perdre

I've lost my purse.
J'ai perdu mon porte-monnaie.

Our team always loses.
Notre équipe perd toujours.

loser n
le perdant *m*

la perdante *f*

lost vb, *see* **lose**

lost property office n
les objets trouvés *mpl*

Word for word this means "things that have been found".

lot n
a lot
beaucoup

not a lot
pas beaucoup

That's a lot.
C'est beaucoup.

a lot of
beaucoup de

She has a lot of books.
Elle a beaucoup de livres.

lots of
un tas de

He's got lots of friends.
Il a un tas d'amis.

lottery n
le loto *m*

I hope I win the lottery.
J'espère que je vais gagner au loto.

loud adj
fort *m adj*
forte *f adj*

The television is too loud.
La télévision est trop forte.

Speak louder!
Parle plus fort!

lounge n
le salon *m*

love

love can be a noun or a verb.

A n
l'amour *m*

He's in love.
Il est amoureux.

She's in love with Paul.
Elle est amoureuse de Paul.

Give Delphine my love.
Embrasse Delphine pour moi.

Love, Rosemary.
Amitiés, Rosemary.

B vb
1 aimer

Do you love me?
Tu m'aimes?

2 *(be very fond of)*
beaucoup aimer

Everybody loves her.
Tout le monde l'aime beaucoup.

3 *(enjoy)*
adorer

I love chocolate.
J'adore le chocolat.

There is an extra word in the French sentence – what is it?

Look at Language Plus on pages 283–308 for extra vocabulary.

I love skiing.
J'adore le ski.

🔑

I love you.
Je t'aime.
Love from…
Amitiés…

---

lovely adj
It's a lovely day.
Il fait très beau aujourd'hui.
They've got a lovely house.
Ils ont une très belle maison.
Have a lovely time!
Amusez-vous bien!

---

low adj
bas *m adj*
basse *f adj*
a low price
un prix bas

---

lower sixth n
la première *f*
He's in the lower sixth.
Il est en première.

📝 *In French secondary schools the years are counted from the sixième (youngest) to première and terminale (oldest).*

---

luck n
la chance *f*
She doesn't have much luck.
Elle n'a pas beaucoup de chance.

🔑

Good luck!
Bonne chance!
Bad luck!
Pas de chance!

---

luckily adv
heureusement

---

lucky adj
You're lucky!
Tu as de la chance!
Leah is lucky, she's going to France.
Leah a de la chance, elle va en France.

---

*When you talk about things that are lucky, use **porter bonheur**.*

Black cats are lucky.
Les chats noirs portent bonheur.
a lucky horseshoe
un fer à cheval porte-bonheur

📝 *In France, a black cat crossing your path is unlucky.*

---

luggage n
les bagages *mpl*
Have you got any luggage?
Vous avez des bagages?

---

lump n
la bosse *f*
He's got a lump on his forehead.
Il a une bosse sur le front.

---

lunch n
le déjeuner *m*
I go home for lunch.
Je rentre à la maison pour le déjeuner.
It's time for lunch.
C'est l'heure du déjeuner.
to have lunch
déjeuner
We have lunch at 12.30.
Nous déjeunons à midi et demi.

Luxembourg n
le Luxembourg *m*

---

lying vb, *see* lie

M

machine n
la <u>machine</u> f

mad adj
1 (*insane*)
<u>fou</u> *m adj*
<u>folle</u> *f adj*
You're mad!
Tu es fou!

He's mad about football.
Il est dingue de foot.

She's mad about horses.
Elle adore les chevaux.

2 (*angry*)
<u>furieux</u> *m adj*
<u>furieuse</u> *f adj*
If you break it she'll be mad.
Elle sera furieuse si tu le casses pas.

madam n
<u>madame</u> *f*
Would you like to order, Madam?
Désirez-vous commander, Madame?

made vb *see* **make**

magazine n
le <u>magazine</u> *m*

magic

> **magic** can be an adjective or a noun.

A adj
1 (*magical*)
<u>magique</u>
a magic wand
une baguette magique

a magic trick
un tour de magie
2 (*brilliant*)
<u>super</u>
It was magic!
C'était super!
B n
la <u>magie</u> *f*
by magic
par magie

magician n
le <u>prestidigitateur</u> *m*

magnifying glass n
la <u>loupe</u> *f*

mail

> **mail** can be a noun or a verb.

A n
le <u>courrier</u> *m*
You've got some mail.
Tu as du courrier.
B vb
<u>envoyer un e-mail à</u>
I'll mail my friend.
Je vais envoyer un e-mail à mon copain.

Look at Language Plus on pages 283–308 for extra vocabulary.

main adj
principal _m adj_
principale _f adj_
the main problem
le principal problème

main road n
la grande route _f_
The hotel is on the main road.
L'hôtel est sur la grande route.

Majorca n
Majorque _f_

make

> **make** can be a noun or a verb.

Ⓐ n
la marque _f_
What make is that car?
De quelle marque est cette voiture?
Ⓑ vb
1 faire
I'm going to make a cake.
Je vais faire un gâteau.
Make a sentence, everyone.
Faites une phrase, tout le monde.
I make my bed every morning.
Je fais mon lit tous les matins.
2 and 2 make 4.
Deux et deux font quatre.
4 take away 2, what does that make?
Quatre moins deux, ça fait combien?
He made it himself.
Il l'a fait lui-même.
2 (_manufacture_)
fabriquer
made in France
fabriqué en France
3 (_earn_)
gagner
He makes a lot of money.
Il gagne beaucoup d'argent.

4 (_prepare_)
préparer
She's making lunch.
Elle prépare le déjeuner.

make up vb
inventer
You're making it up!
Tu inventes!

make-up n
le maquillage _m_

male adj
1 (_animal_)
mâle
a male kitten
un chaton mâle
2 (_person, on official forms_)
masculin
Sex: male.
Sexe: masculin.

man n
l'homme _m_
an old man
un vieil homme

manage vb
se débrouiller
It's okay, I can manage.
Ça va, je me débrouille.
I can't manage all that.
C'est trop pour moi.

manager n
1 (_of company_)
le directeur _m_
la directrice _f_

2 *(of shop, restaurant)*
le gérant m
la gérante f
3 *(of team)*
le manager m

manageress n
la gérante f

manners npl
les manières fpl

good manners
les bonnes manières

Her manners are appalling.
Elle a de très mauvaises manières.

It's bad manners to speak with your mouth full.
Ce n'est pas poli de parler la bouche pleine.

many adj, pron
beaucoup de

He hasn't got many friends.
Il n'a pas beaucoup d'amis.

Are many people absent?
Est-ce qu'il y a beaucoup d'absents?

How many?
Combien?

> When **how many** is followed by a noun it is translated by **combien de**.

How many sisters have you got?
Tu as combien de sœurs?

How many girls are there?
Il y a combien de filles?

How many euros do you get for £10?
Combien d'euros a-t-on pour dix livres?

How many do you want?
Combien en veux-tu?

> **en** means "of them".

That's too many.
C'est trop.

You ask too many questions!
Tu poses trop de questions!

> **How many?**
> Combien?
> **Not many.**
> Pas beaucoup.
> **Too many.**
> Trop.

map n
1 *(of country, area)*
la carte f

a map of France
une carte de France
2 *(of town)*
le plan m

a map of Paris
un plan de Paris

marathon n
le marathon m

the London marathon
le marathon de Londres

marbles n
les billes fpl

Do you want to play marbles?
Tu veux jouer aux billes?

March n
mars m

March or April?
Mars ou avril?

Look at Language Plus on pages 283–308 for extra vocabulary.

A
B
C
D
E
F
G
H
I
J
K
L
M
N
O
P
Q
R
S
T
U
V
W
X
Y
Z

My birthday's in March
Mon anniversaire est en mars.

> **in March**
> en mars
> **the fifth of March**
> le cinq mars
>
> *The months in French are not spelled with a capital letter.*

margarine n
la margarine f

margin n
la marge f

Write notes in the margin.
Écrivez vos notes dans la marge.

mark

> **mark** can be a noun or a verb.

A n (in school)
la note f

I get good marks for French.
J'ai de bonnes notes en français.
B vb
corriger

She's got books to mark.
Elle a des cahiers à corriger.

market n
le marché m

marmalade n
la confiture d'oranges f

marriage n
le mariage m

> *The English word has one more letter than the French word – what is it?*

married adj
marié m adj
mariée f adj

They are not married.
Ils ne sont pas mariés.

a married couple
un couple marié

marry vb
épouser

He wants to marry her.
Il veut l'épouser.

They want to get married.
Ils veulent se marier.

My sister's getting married in June.
Ma sœur se marie en juin.

marvellous adj
1 (excellent)
excellent m adj
excellente f adj

She's a marvellous cook.
C'est une excellente cuisinière.
2 superbe

The weather was marvellous.
Il a fait un temps superbe.

masculine adj
masculin m adj
masculine f adj

mashed potatoes npl
la purée f

sausages and mashed potatoes
des saucisses avec de la purée

> *purée is a singular word.*

mask n
le masque m

A B C D E F G H I J K L **M** N O P Q R S T U V W X Y Z

mass n

1 la <u>multitude</u> f

a mass of books and papers
une multitude de livres et de
papiers

2 (in church)
la <u>messe</u> f

We go to mass on Sunday.
Nous allons à la messe le dimanche.

massive adj
<u>énorme</u>

masterpiece n
le <u>chef-d'œuvre</u> m

mat n
le <u>paillasson</u> m

a table mat
un set de table

match

> **match** can be a noun or a verb.

Ⓐ n
1 l'<u>allumette</u> f

a box of matches
une boîte d'allumettes

2 (game)
le <u>match</u> m
(pl les matchs)

a football match
un match de foot

Ⓑ vb
1 (go with)
<u>être assorti à</u>

The jacket matches the trousers.
La veste est assortie au pantalon.

2 (put with)
<u>faire correspondre à</u>

Match the names to the pictures.
Faites correspondre les noms aux
images.

matching adj
<u>assorti</u> m adj
<u>assortie</u> f adj

**My bedroom has matching
wallpaper and curtains.**
Ma chambre a du papier peint et
des rideaux assortis.

mate n
le <u>pote</u> m

He's my mate.
C'est mon pote.

material n
le <u>tissu</u> m

It's made of red material.
C'est fait en tissu rouge.

maths n
les <u>maths</u> fpl

matter

> **matter** can be a noun or a verb.

Ⓐ n
**What's the matter? Why are you
crying?**

Qu'est-ce que tu as? Pourquoi tu
pleures?

What's the matter with him?
Qu'est-ce qu'il a?

Ⓑ vb

It doesn't matter.
Ça ne fait rien.

mattress n
le <u>matelas</u> m

Look at Language Plus on pages 283–308 for extra vocabulary.

a
b
c
d
e
f
g
h
i
j
k
l
m
n
o
p
q
r
s
t
u
v
w
x
y
z

maximum adj
maximum *m, f, pl adj*

May n
mai *m*
May or June?
Mai ou juin?
My birthday's in May.
Mon anniversaire est en mai.

> 🔑
> **in May**
> en mai
> **the fifth of May**
> le cinq mai
>
> *The months in French are not spelled with a capital letter.*

May Day n
le Premier Mai *m*

> People give friends little bunches of lily of the valley (**muguet**) on May Day.

maybe adv
peut-être
maybe not
peut-être pas
Maybe she's at home.
Elle est peut-être chez elle.

mayonnaise n
la mayonnaise *f*

mayor n
le maire *m*

maze n
le labyrinthe *m*

me pron
1 me
Could you lend me your pen, Rachid?
Tu peux me prêter ton stylo, Rachid?
Are you looking for me?
Tu me cherches?

> *me changes to m' before a vowel sound.*

Do you love me?
Tu m'aimes?
Can you help me?
Est-ce que tu peux m'aider?
2 moi

> *The French word me cannot come at the end of a sentence. Use moi instead.*

Wait for me!
Attends-moi!
Look at me, children!
Regardez-moi, les enfants!
You're after me.
Tu es après moi.
Is it for me?
C'est pour moi?

> 🔑
> **Me too!**
> Moi aussi!
> **Excuse me!**
> Excusez-moi!

meal n
le repas *m*

mean

> *mean can be a verb or an adjective.*

A vb
vouloir dire
What does "complet" mean?
Qu'est-ce que "complet" veut dire?

A
B
C
D
E
F
G
H
I
J
K
L
M
N
O
P
Q
R
S
T
U
V
W
X
Y
Z

I don't know what it means.
Je ne sais pas ce que ça veut dire.

What do you mean?
Qu'est que vous voulez dire?

That's not what I meant.
Ce n'est pas ce que je voulais dire.

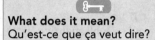

What does it mean?
Qu'est-ce que ça veut dire?

B adj
1 (with money)
radin m adj
radine f adj

He's too mean to buy presents.
Il est trop radin pour acheter des cadeaux.
2 (unkind)
méchant m adj
méchante f adj

You're being mean to me.
Tu es méchant avec moi.

meaning n
le sens m

measles n
la rougeole f

measure vb
mesurer

Measure the length.
Mesurez la longueur.

meat n
la viande f

I don't eat meat.
Je ne mange pas de viande.

Mecca n
La Mecque f

medal n
la médaille f
the gold medal
la médaille d'or

medical

medical can be an adjective or a noun.

A adj
She's a medical student.
Elle est étudiante en médecine.
B n
You have to have a medical.
Tu dois passer une visite médicale.

medicine n
le médicament m

I need some medicine.
J'ai besoin d'un médicament.

Mediterranean n
the Mediterranean
la Méditerranée

medium adj
moyen m adj
moyenne f adj

a man of medium height
un homme de taille moyenne

medium-sized adj
de taille moyenne

a medium-sized town
une ville de taille moyenne

meet vb
1 (by arrangement)
retrouver

I'm meeting my friends at the swimming pool.
Je retrouve mes amis à la piscine.

Look at Language Plus on pages 283–308 for extra vocabulary.

Let's meet in front of the tourist office.
Retrouvons-nous devant l'office de tourisme.

2 (by chance)
rencontrer

I met some French people.
J'ai rencontré des Français.

3 (pick up)
aller chercher

I'll meet you at the station.
J'irai te chercher à la gare.

meeting n
la rencontre f

their first meeting
leur première rencontre

melon n
le melon m

melt vb
fondre

The snow is melting.
La neige est en train de fondre.

member n
le membre m

a member of our club
un membre de notre club

memory n
la mémoire f

I haven't got a good memory.
Je n'ai pas une bonne mémoire.

memory game n
le jeu de mémoire m

men npl
les hommes mpl

mend vb
réparer

Can you mend it?
Vous pouvez le réparer?

mention vb
Thank you! – Don't mention it!
Merci! – Il n'y a pas de quoi!

menu n
le menu m

merry adj

🔑

Merry Christmas!
Joyeux Noël!

merry-go-round n
le manège m

mess n
le bazar m

My bedroom's a mess.
C'est le bazar dans ma chambre.

message n
le message m

met vb, see **meet**

metal n
le métal m
(pl les métaux)

method n
la méthode f

A
B
C
D
E
F
G
H
I
J
K
L
M
N
O
P
Q
R
S
T
U
V
W
X
Y
Z

metre n
le <u>mètre</u> m

I'm one metre thirty tall.
Je mesure un mètre trente.

> In France measurements are in metres and centimetres, rather than feet and inches.

metric adj
métrique

Mexican wave n
la <u>hola</u> f

mice npl
les <u>souris</u> fpl

microphone n
le <u>microphone</u> m

microwave n
le <u>four à micro-ondes</u> m

midday n
le <u>midi</u> m

It's midday.
Il est midi.

at midday
à midi

middle n
le <u>milieu</u> m

Come into the middle, Hugo.
Viens au milieu, Hugo.

in the middle of the road
au milieu de la route

in the middle of the night
au milieu de la nuit

middle-aged adj
d'un certain âge

a middle-aged man
un homme d'un certain âge

middle name n
le <u>deuxième prénom</u> m

It's my middle name.
C'est mon deuxième prénom.

midge n
le <u>moucheron</u> m

midnight n
minuit m

It's midnight.
Il est minuit.

at midnight
à minuit

might vb

I might, I might not.
Peut-être, peut-être pas.

> *peut-être* means "maybe" – you're really saying "Maybe, maybe not".

migraine n
la <u>migraine</u> f

I've got a migraine.
J'ai la migraine.

mild adj
<u>doux</u> m adj
<u>douce</u> f adj

The winters are quite mild.
Les hivers sont assez doux.

mile n

> In France distances are measured in kilometres. A mile is about 1.6 kilometres.

It's 5 miles from here.
C'est à huit kilomètres d'ici.

We walked miles!
Nous avons marché pendant des kilomètres!

Look at Language Plus on pages 283–308 for extra vocabulary.

milk n
le <u>lait</u> m

tea with milk
du thé au lait

milkman n
He's a milkman.
Il livre le lait à domicile.

> Milk is not delivered to
> people's houses in France.

milk shake n
le <u>milk-shake</u> m

millimetre n
le <u>millimètre</u> m

million n
le <u>million</u> m
two million
deux millions

millionaire n
le <u>millionnaire</u> m

mince n
la <u>viande hachée</u> f

mince pie n
la <u>tartelette de Noël</u> f

> **Mince pies** are not eaten in
> France, instead French
> people eat **papillotes**, which
> are chocolates wrapped in
> foil.

mind

> **mind** can be a verb or a noun.

Ⓐ vb

**Do you mind if I open the
window?**
Est-ce que je peux ouvrir la fenêtre?

Mind the step!
Attention à la marche!

> **I don't mind.**
> Ça ne me dérange pas.
> **Never mind!**
> Ça ne fait rien!

Ⓑ n
I've changed my mind.
J'ai changé d'avis.

mine

> **mine** can be a pronoun or a noun.

Ⓐ pron
<u>à moi</u>
This book is mine.
Ce livre est à moi.

> **It's mine.**
> C'est à moi.

Ⓑ n
la <u>mine</u> f
a coal mine
une mine de charbon

mineral water n
l'eau minérale f

minibus n
le minibus m

Minidisc® n
le minidisque m

minimum adj
minimum m, f, pl adj

miniskirt n
la mini-jupe f

minister n
1 (of church)
le pasteur m
2 (in government)
le ministre m

minor adj
mineur m adj
mineure f adj
a minor problem
un problème mineur

mint n
1 (sweet)
le bonbon à la menthe m

2 (plant)
la menthe f
mint sauce
la sauce à la menthe

minus prep
moins
16 minus 3 is 13.
Seize moins trois égale treize.

It's minus two degrees outside.
Il fait moins deux dehors.

minute n
la minute f
Wait a minute!
Attends une minute!

mirror n
le miroir m

misbehave vb
Don't misbehave, Pierre!
Sois sage, Pierre!

mischief n
les bêtises fpl
My little sister's always up to mischief.
Ma petite sœur fait constamment des bêtises.

miserable adj
1 (person)
malheureux m adj
malheureuse f adj
You look miserable.
Tu as l'air malheureux.
2 (weather)
épouvantable
The weather was miserable.
Il faisait un temps épouvantable.

Miss n
1 (teacher)
maîtresse f
Yes, Miss.
Oui, maîtresse.
2 Mademoiselle f
Miss Jones
Mademoiselle Jones

*In addresses **Miss** is **Mlle**.*

miss vb
rater
Hurry or you'll miss the bus.
Dépêche-toi ou tu vas rater le bus.

A B C D E F G H I J K L M N O P Q R S T U V W X Y Z

Look at Language Plus on pages 283–308 for extra vocabulary.

a
b
c
d
e
f
g
h
i
j
k
l
m
n
o
p
q
r
s
t
u
v
w
x
y
z

I miss you.
Tu me manques.

Miss a turn.
Passe un tour.

missing adj
manquant *m adj*
manquante *f adj*

the missing piece
la pièce manquante

My rucksack is missing.
Mon sac à dos a disparu.

Two children are missing.
Deux enfants ont disparu.

mist n
la brume *f*

mistake n
la faute *f*

Only one mistake!
Une faute seulement!

a spelling mistake
une faute d'orthographe

**Be careful not to make any
mistakes, Luc.**
Fais attention à ne pas faire de
fautes, Luc.

by mistake
par erreur

I took his bag by mistake.
J'ai pris son sac par erreur.

mistletoe n
le gui *m*

misty adj
brumeux *m adj*
brumeuse *f adj*

a misty morning
un matin brumeux

It's misty.
Le temps est brumeux.

mix vb
mélanger

Mix the flour with the sugar.
Mélangez la farine au sucre.

mix up vb
confondre

**He always mixes me up with my
sister.**
Il me confond toujours avec ma sœur.

mixed adj

a mixed salad
une salade composée

a mixed school
une école mixte

mixture n
le mélange *m*

mix-up n
la confusion *f*

mobile n
le portable *m*

I haven't got a mobile.
Je n'ai pas de portable.

mobile phone n
le portable *m*

Have you got a mobile phone?
Tu as un portable?

model

model can be a noun or an
adjective.

Ⓐ n

1 (*small version*)
la maquette f

I'm making a model of the castle.
Je fais une maquette du château.

2 (*person*)
le mannequin m

She's a famous model.
C'est un mannequin célèbre.

Ⓑ adj

a model plane
un modèle réduit d'avion

a model railway
un modèle réduit de voie ferrée

---

modern adj
moderne

What is the difference in spelling between the French word and the English word?

---

moment n
l'instant m

Wait a moment, Alain.
Attends un instant, Alain.

Could you wait a moment?
Pouvez-vous attendre un instant?

in a moment
dans un instant

Just a moment!
Un instant!
at the moment
en ce moment

Monday n
le lundi m

It's Monday today.
Aujourd'hui c'est lundi.

on Monday
lundi
on Mondays
le lundi
every Monday
tous les lundis
last Monday
lundi dernier
next Monday
lundi prochain

Days of the week are not written with a capital letter in French.

---

money n
l'argent m

I haven't got enough money.
Je n'ai pas assez d'argent.

I need to change some money.
J'ai besoin de changer de l'argent.

---

monitor n
le moniteur m

---

monk n
le moine m

---

monkey n
le singe m

---

monster n
le monstre m

---

month n
le mois m

two months
deux mois

Look at Language Plus on pages 283–308 for extra vocabulary.

a
b
c
d
e
f
g
h
i
j
k
l
m
n
o
p
q
r
s
t
u
v
w
x
y
z

at the end of the month
à la fin du mois

this month
ce mois-ci
next month
le mois prochain
last month
le mois dernier
every month
tous les mois
What month is it?
Quel mois sommes-nous?

mood n
l'humeur f

She's in a bad mood.
Elle est de mauvaise humeur.

moon n
la lune f

the moon and the stars
la lune et les étoiles

moped n
le cyclomoteur m

more adj, pron, adv
1 plus

*When comparing one thing with another, you usually use **plus**.*

more difficult
plus difficile

This model is more expensive.
Ce modèle est plus cher.

Could you speak more slowly?
Vous pourriez parler plus lentement?

more than me
plus que moi

more than that
plus que ça

He's more intelligent than me.
Il est plus intelligent que moi.

*When **plus** is followed by a noun, it becomes **plus de**.*

There are more girls in the class.
Il y a plus de filles dans la classe.

I've got more than 50 euros.
J'ai plus de cinquante euros.

There isn't any more.
Il n'y en a plus.

a bit more
un peu plus
more ... than
plus ... que

2 encore

*When you are talking about second helpings, or extra time, you use **encore**.*

Do you want some more, André?
Tu en veux encore, André?

Would you like some more, Mr Gautier?
Vous en voulez encore, M. Gautier?

Two minutes more!
Encore deux minutes!

*When **encore** is followed by a noun, it becomes **encore de**.*

Could I have some more chips?
Est-ce que je pourrais avoir encore des frites?

Do you want some more tea?
Voulez-vous encore du thé?

morning n
le <u>matin</u> m

on Saturday morning
le samedi matin

all morning
toute la matinée

Are they staying all morning?
Est-ce qu'ils vont rester toute la matinée?

> 🔑
> **this morning**
> ce matin
> **tomorrow morning**
> demain matin
> **every morning**
> tous les matins
> **in the morning**
> le matin
> **at 7 o'clock in the morning**
> à sept heures du matin

mosque n
la <u>mosquée</u> f

mosquito n
le <u>moustique</u> m

a mosquito bite
une piqûre de moustique

most adv, adj, pron

> *most of* can be translated by *la plupart de, la plupart du, la plupart de la* or *la plupart des,* depending on the following noun.

most of my friends
la plupart de mes amis

most of the time
la plupart du temps

most French people
la plupart des Français

most of the class
la majeure partie de la classe

the most
le plus

Chantal talks the most.
C'est Chantal qui parle le plus.

> *When **the most** is followed by an adjective, it is translated le plus, la plus, or les plus, depending on the following noun.*

the most expensive restaurant
le restaurant le plus cher

the most expensive seat
la place la plus chère

the most expensive restaurants
les restaurants les plus chers

the most expensive seats
les places les plus chères

at the most
au maximum

Two hours at the most.
Deux heures au maximum.

motel n
le <u>motel</u> m

moth n
le <u>papillon de nuit</u> m

> *Word for word the French means 'butterfly of the night'.*

mother n
la <u>mère</u> f

my mother
ma mère

your mother
ta mère

Look at Language Plus on pages 283–308 for extra vocabulary.

a
b
c
d
e
f
g
h
i
j
k
l
m
n
o
p
q
r
s
t
u
v
w
x
y
z

Mother's Day n
la fête des Mères f
It's Mother's Day on Sunday.
Dimanche, c'est la fête des Mères.

Happy Mother's Day!
Bonne Fête, Maman!

Mother's Day is usually on the last Sunday of May in France.

motor n
le moteur m

motorbike n
la moto f

motorboat n
le bateau à moteur m

motorcycle n
le vélomoteur m

motorcyclist n
le motard m

motorist n
l'automobiliste m/f

motorway n
l'autoroute f
on the motorway
sur l'autoroute

mountain n
la montagne f

mountain bike n
le VTT m
I've got a mountain bike.
J'ai un VTT.

mouse n
la souris f
two white mice
deux souris blanches

mouse mat n
le tapis de souris m

mousse n
la mousse f
chocolate mousse
la mousse au chocolat

moustache n
la moustache f
He's got a moustache.
Il a une moustache.

mouth n
la bouche f

move

move can be a noun or a verb.

A n
le tour m
It's your move.
C'est ton tour.

Get a move on, Marcel!
Remue-toi, Marcel!
B vb
bouger
Don't move!
Ne bouge pas!

You moved!
Tu as bougé!

Could you move your stuff please?
Tu peux pousser tes affaires, s'il te plaît?

Move forward 2 spaces!
Avance de deux cases!

move over vb
se pousser

Could you move over a bit?
Tu peux te pousser un peu?

movement n
le mouvement *m*

MP n
le député *m*

She's an MP.
Elle est député.

You do not translate "a" when you say what someone's job is in French.

mph abbr
km/h

In France, speed is measured in kilometres per hour. 50 mph is about 80 km/h.

Mr n
Monsieur *m*

In addresses Mr is M.

Mrs n
Madame *f*

In addresses Mrs is Mme.

Ms n
Madame *f*

In addresses Ms is Mme.

There isn't a specific word for Ms in French. If you are writing to somebody and don't know whether she is married, use Madame.

much adj, adv, pron
1 (*a lot*)
beaucoup

not much
pas beaucoup

I don't like sport much.
Je n'aime pas beaucoup le sport.

I don't want much.
Je n'en veux pas beaucoup.

You can also use beaucoup to say "very much".

I like France very much.
J'aime beaucoup la France.
2 (*a lot of*)
beaucoup de

I haven't got much money.
Je n'ai pas beaucoup d'argent.

You can also use beaucoup de to say "very much".

I don't want very much rice.
Je ne veux pas beaucoup de riz.

How much?
Combien?

How much does it cost?
C'est combien?

How much do you want?
Tu en veux combien?

How much is it all together?
Ça fait combien en tout?

When how much is followed by a noun it is translated by combien de.

How much money have you got?
Tu as combien d'argent?

too much
trop

Look at Language Plus on pages 283–308 for extra vocabulary.

That's too much!
C'est trop!

It costs too much.
Ça coûte trop cher.

How much?
Combien?
not much
pas beaucoup
too much
trop
Thank you very much.
Merci beaucoup.

---

mud n
la boue f

muesli n
le muesli m

mug n
la grande tasse f

Do you want a cup or a mug?
Est-ce que vous voulez une tasse
normale ou une grande tasse?

multiply vb
multiplier

Multiply 6 by 3.
Multipliez six par trois.

2 multiplied by 3 is 6.
Deux multiplié par trois égale six.

mum n
1 la mère f

my mum
ma mère

2 (used as a name)
la maman f

Mum!
Maman!

I'll ask Mum.
Je vais demander à Maman.

mummy n
la maman f

Hello Mummy!
Bonjour, Maman!

mumps n
les oreillons mpl

Thérèse has got mumps.
Thérèse a les oreillons.

murder n
le meurtre m

muscle n
le muscle m

museum n
le musée m

mushroom n
le champignon m

music n
la musique f

I like listening to music.
J'aime écouter de la musique.

musical adj
a musical instrument
un instrument de musique

musician n
le musicien m
la musicienne f

Muslim n
le musulman m
la musulmane f

He's a Muslim.
Il est musulman.

The French word is not spelled with a capital letter.

mussel n
la moule f

must vb
You must be careful, Gaëlle.
Tu dois faire attention, Gaëlle.

You must listen, children.
Vous devez écouter, les enfants.

mustard n
la moutarde f

my adj

When you want to say something like "my name", "my house", or "my hair" in French, you need to know if "name", "house", "hair" are masculine, feminine or plural, because there are three possible words for my.

mon *m adj*
my father
mon père
ma *f adj*
my aunt
ma tante
mes *pl adj*
my parents
mes parents

ma changes to mon before a vowel sound.

my friend Alice
mon amie Alice

my is not always mon, ma, or mes. Notice how my is translated in the next example.

I wash my face in the morning.
Je me lave le visage le matin.

myself pron
1 me
I've hurt myself.
Je me suis fait mal.

I like to look at myself in the mirror.
J'aime me regarder dans la glace.

me changes to m' after a vowel sound.

I'm enjoying myself.
Je m'amuse.
2 moi

After a preposition, use moi instead of me.

I'll tell you about myself.
Je vais te parler de moi.
3 moi-même
I made it myself.
Je l'ai fait moi-même.
by myself
tout seul

Use toute seule if you are a girl.

I don't like travelling by myself.
Je n'aime pas voyager toute seule.

mystery n
le mystère m

A
B
C
D
E
F
G
H
I
J
K
L
M
N
O
P
Q
R
S
T
U
V
W
X
Y
Z

Look at Language Plus on pages 283–308 for extra vocabulary.

N

nail n

1 l'ongle *m*

Don't bite your nails!
Ne te ronge pas les ongles!

2 le clou *m*

a hammer and some nails
un marteau et des clous

nailfile n

la lime à ongles *f*

nail varnish n

le vernis à ongles *m*

naked adj

nu *m adj*
nue *f adj*

name n

le nom *m*

What's your dog's name?
Comment s'appelle ton chien?

His name's Max.
Il s'appelle Max.

What's your name?
Comment tu t'appelles?

> *There are two other ways of asking this question:*
> **Tu t'appelles comment?** *and*
> **Comment t'appelles-tu?**

What's her name?
Comment elle s'appelle?

What are their names?
Ils s'appellent comment?

What's your name?
Comment tu t'appelles?
My name is Natasha.
Je m'appelle Natasha.

nanny n

la garde d'enfants *f*

She's a nanny.
C'est une garde d'enfants.

napkin n

la serviette *f*

narrow adj

étroit *m adj*
étroite *f adj*

a narrow street
une rue étroite

nasty adj

1 (*unpleasant*)
mauvais *m adj*
mauvaise *f adj*

a nasty cold
un mauvais rhume

a nasty smell
une mauvaise odeur

2 (*evil*)
méchant *m adj*
méchante *f adj*

He's a nasty man.
C'est un méchant homme.

nationality n
la nationalité *f*

natural adj
naturel *m adj*
naturelle *f adj*

nature n
la nature *f*

naughty adj
vilain *m adj*
vilaine *f adj*

Naughty girl!
Vilaine!

navy n
la marine *f*

He's in the navy.
Il est dans la marine.

navy-blue

navy-blue can be an adjective or a
noun.

A adj
bleu marine *m, f, pl adj*

a navy-blue skirt
une jupe bleu marine

*Colour adjectives come after the
noun in French.*

B n
le bleu marine *m*

near

near can be an adjective or a
preposition.

A adj
proche

It's fairly near.
C'est assez proche.

the nearest can be translated by
le plus proche, **la plus proche** or
les plus proches, depending on
the following noun.

the nearest village
le village le plus proche

**Where's the nearest service
station?**
Où est la station-service la plus
proche?

**The nearest shops are three
kilometres away.**
Les magasins les plus proches sont
à trois kilomètres.

B prep
près de

I live near Liverpool.
J'habite près de Liverpool.

near my house
près de chez moi

near here
près d'ici

Is there a bank near here?
Est-ce qu'il y a une banque près
d'ici?

nearby adv
à proximité

There's a supermarket nearby.
Il y a un supermarché à proximité.

nearly adv
presque

Dinner's nearly ready.
Le dîner est presque prêt.

I'm nearly 10.
J'ai presque dix ans.

neat adj
soigné *m adj*
soignée *f adj*

She has very neat writing.
Elle a une écriture très soignée.

necessary adj
nécessaire

A B C D E F G H I J K L M N O P Q R S T U V W X Y Z

neck n
le <u>cou</u> m

I've hurt my neck.
Je me suis fait mal au cou.

necklace n
le <u>collier</u> m

need vb
<u>avoir besoin de</u>

I need a rubber.
J'ai besoin d'une gomme.

needle n
l'<u>aiguille</u> f

neighbour n
le <u>voisin</u> m
la <u>voisine</u> f

the neighbours' garden
le jardin des voisins

neighbourhood n
le <u>quartier</u> m

neither pron, conj, adv
<u>aucun des deux</u> m
<u>aucune des deux</u> f

Carrots or peas? – Neither, thanks.
Des carottes ou des petits pois? –
Aucun des deux, merci.

neither … nor …
ni … ni …

Neither Sarah nor Tamsin is coming to the party.
Ni Sarah ni Tamsin ne viennent à la soirée.

Neither do I.
Moi non plus.
Neither have I.
Moi non plus.

---

nephew n
le <u>neveu</u> m
(pl les neveux)

her nephew
son neveu

nerve n
le <u>nerf</u> m

She gets on my nerves.
Elle me tape sur les nerfs.

Net n
le <u>Net</u> m

I like to surf the Net.
J'aime surfer sur le Net.

netball n
le <u>netball</u> m

> **Netball** is not played in France. Both boys and girls play basketball or volleyball instead.

Netherlands npl
les <u>Pays-Bas</u> mpl

never adv
1 jamais

When are you going to phone him? – Never!
Quand est-ce que tu vas l'appeler?
– Jamais!

2 ne … jamais

Add ne if the sentence contains a verb.

I never go to the cinema.
Je ne vais jamais au cinéma.

new adj

1 nouveau *m adj*
nouvelle *f adj*

a new jumper
un nouveau pull

a new dress
une nouvelle robe

2 (*brand new*)
neuf *m adj*
neuve *f adj*

We've got a new car.
Nous avons une voiture neuve.

news n

1 les nouvelles *fpl*

good news
de bonnes nouvelles

2 (*single piece of news*)
la nouvelle *f*

That's wonderful news!
Quelle bonne nouvelle!

3 (*on TV*)
les informations *fpl*

It was on the news.
C'était aux informations.

newsagent n
le marchand de journaux *m*

newspaper n
le journal *m*

(*pl* les journaux)

New Year n

New Year's Day
le premier de l'An

New Year's Eve
la Saint-Sylvestre

> 🔑
> **Happy New Year!**
> Bonne Année!

next

> **next** can be an adjective, an
> adverb or a preposition.

Ⓐ adj (*in time*)
prochain *m adj*
prochaine *f adj*

the next time
la prochaine fois

Who's next?
C'est à qui, maintenant?

I'm next.
C'est à moi, maintenant.

next door
à côté

They live next door.
Ils habitent à côté.

> 🔑
> **next Saturday**
> samedi prochain
> **next year**
> l'année prochaine
> **next summer**
> l'été prochain

Ⓑ adv (*after this*)
ensuite

What shall I do next?
Qu'est-ce que je fais ensuite?

Ⓒ prep
next to
à côté de

next to the bank
à côté de la banque

Look at Language Plus on pages 283–308 for extra vocabulary.

A
B
C
D
E
F
G
H
I
J
K
L
M
N
O
P
Q
R
S
T
U
V
W
X
Y
Z

I sit next to my friend.
Je m'asseois à côté de mon copain.

> To get the accents right in **à côté de**, remember that they form a W: `` `^` ``.

nice adj

1 (*kind*)
gentil *m adj*
gentille *f adj*

Your parents are very nice.
Tes parents sont très gentils.

2 (*pretty*)
joli *m adj*
jolie *f adj*

Aix is a nice town.
Aix est une jolie ville.

3 (*food*)
bon *m adj*
bonne *f adj*

The soup is very nice.
La soupe est très bonne.

> **Have a nice time!**
> Amuse-toi bien!
> **Have a nice time, girls!**
> Amusez-vous bien, les filles!
> **It's a nice day.**
> Il fait beau.

niece n
la nièce *f*

his niece
sa nièce

night n
1 la nuit *f*

I want a room for two nights.
Je veux une chambre pour deux nuits.

2 (*evening*)
le soir *m*

What are you doing tonight?
Qu'est-ce que tu fais ce soir?

> **last night**
> hier soir

nightie n
la chemise de nuit *f*

nightmare n
le cauchemar *m*

I have nightmares.
Je fais des cauchemars.

nightshirt n
la chemise de nuit *f*

nil n
le zéro *m*

We won one-nil.
Nous avons gagné un à zéro.

nine num
neuf

nine euros
neuf euros

> **She's nine.**
> Elle a neuf ans.
> In English you can say **nine** or **nine years old**. In French you can only say **neuf ans**.

nineteen num
dix-neuf

nineteen euros
dix-neuf euros

She's nineteen.
Elle a dix-neuf ans.
In English you can say **nineteen**
or **nineteen years old.** *In French
you can only say* **dix-neuf ans.**

nineteenth adj
dix-neuvième

on the nineteenth floor
au dix-neuvième étage

the nineteenth of August
le dix-neuf août

ninety num
quatre-vingt-dix

My gran is ninety.
Ma grand-mère a quatre-vingt-dix
ans.

*quatre-vingt-dix is made up of
three words in French – what do
they mean?*

ninth adj
neuvième

on the ninth floor
au neuvième étage

the ninth of August
le neuf août

no adv
1 non

Are you coming? – No.
Est-ce que tu viens? – Non.
2 (*not any*)
pas de

There are no trains on Sundays.
Il n'y a pas de trains le dimanche.

"no smoking"
"défense de fumer"

nobody pron
1 personne

Who's going with you? – Nobody.
Qui t'accompagne? – Personne.
2 ne … personne

*Add ne if the sentence contains a
verb.*

There's nobody in the classroom.
Il n'y a personne dans la classe.

noise n
le bruit *m*

Please make less noise.
Faites moins de bruit s'il vous plaît.

noisy adj
bruyant *m adj*
bruyante *f adj*

none pron
aucun *m pron*
aucune *f pron*

How many girls? – None.
Combien de filles? – Aucune.

There's none left.
Il n'y en a plus.

There are none left.
Il n'y en a plus.

nonsense n
les bêtises *fpl*

She talks a lot of nonsense.
Elle dit beaucoup de bêtises.

noodles npl
les nouilles *fpl*

A B C D E F G H I J K L M **N** O P Q R S T U V W X Y Z

Look at Language Plus on pages 283–308 for extra vocabulary.

a b c d e f g h i j k l m **n** o p q r s t u v w x y z

noon n
le <u>midi</u> m

It's noon.
Il est midi.

🔑

at noon
à midi

no one pron
1 personne
Who's going with you? – No one.
Qui t'accompagne? – Personne.
2 ne … personne

*Add **ne** if the sentence contains a
verb.*

There's no one in the classroom.
Il n'y a personne dans la classe.

nor conj
neither … nor
ni … ni
neither Pascal nor Yann
ni Pascal, ni Yann

🔑

Nor do I.
Moi non plus.
Nor have I.
Moi non plus.

normal adj
<u>habituel</u> m adj
<u>habituelle</u> f adj
at the normal time
à l'heure habituelle

Normandy n
la <u>Normandie</u> f
in Normandy
en Normandie
to Normandy
en Normandie

Alain is from Normandy.
Alain vient de la Normandie.

north

*north can be an adjective or a
noun.*

Ⓐ adj
<u>nord</u> m, f, pl adj
the north coast
la côte nord
Ⓑ n
le <u>nord</u> m
in the north
dans le nord

Northern Ireland n
l'<u>Irlande du Nord</u> f

in Northern Ireland
en Irlande du Nord

to Northern Ireland
en Irlande du Nord

I'm from Northern Ireland.
Je viens d'Irlande du Nord.

North Pole n
le <u>pôle Nord</u> m

North Sea n
la <u>mer du Nord</u> f

nose n
le <u>nez</u> m
(pl les nez)

nosy adj
fouineur *m adj*
fouineuse *f adj*

not adv
1 pas

Are you coming or not?
Est-ce que tu viens ou pas?

not really
pas vraiment

Do you like him? – Not at all.
Tu l'aimes bien? – Pas du tout.

Have you finished? – Not yet.
As-tu fini? – Pas encore.

2 ne … pas

*Add **ne** if **not** comes before a
verb.*

It's not raining.
Il ne pleut pas.

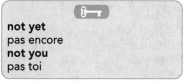

not yet
pas encore
not you
pas toi

note n
le mot *m*

I'll write her a note.
Je vais lui écrire un mot.

notebook n
le carnet *m*

notepad n
le bloc-notes *m*

notepaper n
le papier à lettres *m*

nothing n
1 rien *m*

What's wrong? – Nothing.
Qu'est-ce qui ne va pas? –
Rien.

2 ne … rien

*Add **ne** if the sentence contains a
verb.*

He does nothing.
Il ne fait rien.

notice n
l'affiche *f*

notice board n
le panneau d'affichage *m*

novel n
le roman *m*

November n
novembre *m*

October or November?
Octobre ou novembre?

My birthday's in November.
Mon anniversaire est en
novembre.

in November
en novembre
the fifth of November
le cinq novembre

*The months in French are not
spelled with a capital letter.*

now adv
maintenant

What are you doing now?
Qu'est-ce que tu fais maintenant?

I'm rather busy just now.
Je suis très occupé en ce moment.

not now
pas maintenant
just now
en ce moment

Look at Language Plus on pages 283–308 for extra vocabulary.

a

b

nowhere adv
nulle part

number n

c

1 le nombre m

d

a large number of people
un grand nombre de gens
2 (of house, telephone)

e

le numéro m

f

They live at number 5.
Ils habitent au numéro cinq.

g

What's your phone number?
Quel est votre numéro de

h

téléphone?
3 (figure)

i

le chiffre m

j

the second number
le deuxième chiffre

k

nun n

l

la religieuse f

m

I want to be a nun.
Je veux être religieuse.

n

nurse n

o

l'infirmier m
l'infirmière f

p

She's a nurse.
Elle est infirmière.

q

You do not translate "a" when you
say what someone's job is in

r

French.

s

t

u

v

w

x

y

z

nursery n
la crèche f

My sister goes to nursery.
Ma sœur va à la crèche.

nursery school n
l'école maternelle f

**My little sister goes to nursery
school.**

Ma petite sœur va à l'école
maternelle.

The **école maternelle** is a
state school for children
between the ages of 3 and 6.

nut n

1 (peanut)
la cacahuète f
2 (hazelnut)
la noisette f
3 (walnut)
la noix f
(pl les noix)

You have to say which kind of nut
you mean, because there is no
*general word for **nut** in French.*

O

oats n
l'avoine f

> *avoine* is a singular word.

obedient adj
obéissant *m adj*
obéissante *f adj*

obey vb
You must obey the rules of the game.
Vous devez respecter les règles du jeu.

object n
l'objet *m*
classroom objects
les objets de la classe

obvious adj
évident *m adj*
évidente *f adj*
That's obvious!
C'est évident!

occasion n
l'occasion f
a special occasion
une occasion spéciale

on several occasions
à plusieurs reprises

occasionally adv
de temps en temps

occupation n
la profession f

ocean n
l'océan *m*

o'clock adv
at four o'clock
à quatre heures

> **It's five o'clock.**
> Il est cinq heures.

October n
octobre *m*

October or November?
Octobre ou novembre?

My birthday's in October.
Mon anniversaire est en octobre.

> **in October**
> en octobre
> **the fifth of October**
> le cinq octobre
>
> *The months in French are not spelled with a capital letter.*

odd adj
bizarre
That's odd!
C'est bizarre!

Look at Language Plus on pages 283–308 for extra vocabulary.

a
b
c
d
e
f
g
h
i
j
k
l
m
n
o
p
q
r
s
t
u
v
w
x
y
z

of prep
de

some photos of my family
des photos de ma famille

a boy of ten
un garçon de dix ans

a picture of the school
une photo de l'école

a friend of mine
un de mes amis

That's very kind of you.
C'est très gentil de votre part.

> *de* changes to *d'* before a vowel sound.

a kilo of oranges
un kilo d'oranges

> *de + le* changes to *du*, and *de + les* changes to *des*.

the end of the film
la fin du film

the end of the holidays
la fin des vacances

> *of it*, *of that* and *of them* is translated by *en*.

Do you want half of it?
Tu en veux la moitié?

Can I have half of that?
Je peux en avoir la moitié?

Do you want some of them?
Tu en veux?

off

> *off* can be an adjective, a preposition or an adverb.

A adj
1 (switched off)
éteint *m adj*
éteinte *f adj*

The light is off.
La lumière est éteinte.

2 (turned off)
fermé *m adj*
fermée *f adj*

Is the tap off?
Est-ce que le robinet est fermé?

3 (cancelled)
annulé *m adj*
annulée *f adj*

The match is off.
Le match est annulé.

4 (absent)
absent *m adj*
absente *f adj*

He's off today.
Il est absent aujourd'hui.

B prep

She's off school today.
Elle n'est pas à l'école aujourd'hui.

C adv

Off you go, Jack!
Vas-y, Jack!

offer vb
offrir

Offer Melanie something to drink.
Offre quelque chose à boire à Melanie.

office n
le bureau *m*
(*pl* les bureaux)

She works in an office.
Elle travaille dans un bureau.

often adv
souvent

We often go to London.
Nous allons souvent à Londres.

It often rains.
Il pleut souvent.

oil n
l'huile f

okay excl, adj
1 (in agreement)
d'accord

I'll come tomorrow. – Okay!
Je viens demain. – D'accord!

Is that okay?
C'est d'accord?
2 (not bad)
pas mal

Do you like school? – It's okay.
Tu aimes l'école? – C'est pas mal.

I'm okay thanks.
Ça va, merci.

Is everything okay?
Tout va bien?

> 🔑
> **Okay!**
> D'accord!
> **Are you okay?**
> Ça va?

old adj
vieux m adj
vieille f adj

an old dog
un vieux chien

an old house
une vieille maison

old clothes
des vieux vêtements

old shoes
des vieilles chaussures

> In the singular **vieux** changes to
> **vieil** before a vowel sound.

an old man
un vieil homme

> **âgé** and **âgée** are more polite
> than **vieux** and **vieille**.

old people
les personnes âgées

I'm older than you.
Je suis plus âgée que toi.

Léa is older than Richard.
Léa est plus âgée que Richard.

She's two years older than me.
Elle a deux ans de plus que moi.

How old are you, Max?
Tu as quel âge, Max?

> Another way of asking this
> question is **Quel âge as-tu, Max?**

> 🔑
> **How old are you?**
> Tu as quel âge?
> **How old are you, Miss?**
> Quel âge avez-vous, Maîtresse?
> **He's ten years old.**
> Il a dix ans.

old age pensioner n
le retraité m
la retraitée f

She's an old age pensioner.
Elle est retraitée.

oldest adj
aîné m adj
aînée f adj

my oldest brother
mon frère aîné

Look at Language Plus on pages 283–308 for extra vocabulary.

a
b
c
d
e
f
g
h
i
j
k
l
m
n
o
p
q
r
s
t
u
v
w
x
y
z

*To say that someone is the oldest use **le plus âgé** for a boy and **la plus âgée** for a girl.*

Hugo's the oldest in the class.
Hugo est le plus âgé de la classe.

She's the oldest.
C'est la plus âgée.

Olympic adj
olympique

the Olympics
les Jeux olympiques

omelette n
l'omelette f

on

on can be adjective or a preposition. There are a lot of translations – skim down the page to find the right one.

Ⓐ adj
1 (switched on)
allumé m adj
allumée f adj

The light is on.
La lumière est allumée.

2 (turned on)
ouvert m adj
ouverte f adj

The tap is on.
Le robinet est ouvert.

Ⓑ prep
1 à

on the left
à gauche

I go to school on my bike.
Je vais à l'école à vélo.

on TV
à la télé

*à + **le** changes to **au**.*

on the phone
au téléphone

on the 2nd floor
au deuxième étage

2 (on top of)
sur

on the table
sur la table

3 en

They're on holiday.
Ils sont en vacances.

*Notice how **on** is translated in days and dates.*

on Christmas Day
le jour de Noël

on my birthday
le jour de mon anniversaire

on Friday
vendredi
on Fridays
le vendredi
on June 20th
le vingt juin
on holiday
en vacances

once adv
une fois

once a week
une fois par semaine

only once
juste une fois

at once
tout de suite

once more
encore une fois

one num

*Use **un** for masculine nouns and **une** for feminine nouns.*

un *m*

one day
un jour

une *f*

one minute
une minute

I've got one brother and one sister.
J'ai un frère et une sœur.

onion n
l'oignon *m*

only

only can be an adjective or an adverb.

A adj
seul *m adj*
seule *f adj*

my only clean T-shirt
mon seul tee-shirt propre

my only dress
ma seule robe

I'm an only child.
Je suis fils unique.

Danielle is an only child.
Danielle est fille unique.

B adv
1 seulement

only 10 euros
seulement dix euros
2 *(with a verb)*
ne … que

I've only got two cards.
Je n'ai que deux cartes.

He's only three.
Il n'a que trois ans.

open

open can be an adjective or a verb.

A adj
ouvert *m adj*
ouverte *f adj*

The baker's is open on Sunday morning.
La boulangerie est ouverte le dimanche matin.

B vb
ouvrir

Can I open the window?
Est-ce que je peux ouvrir la fenêtre?

Open your books.
Ouvrez vos livres.

opening hours npl
les heures d'ouverture *fpl*

opinion n
l'avis *m*

in my opinion
à mon avis

What's your opinion?
Qu'est-ce que vous en pensez?

opinion poll n
le sondage *m*

opponent n
l'adversaire *m/f*

opportunity n
l'occasion *f*

It's a good opportunity.
C'est une bonne occasion.

Look at Language Plus on pages 283–308 for extra vocabulary.

opposite

> **opposite** can be an adjective, an adverb or a preposition.

A adj
opposé *m adj*

opposée *f adj*

It's in the opposite direction.
C'est dans la direction opposée.

B adv
en face

They live opposite.
Ils habitent en face.

C prep
en face de

the girl sitting opposite me
la fille assise en face de moi

optimistic adj
optimiste

or conj

1 ou

Would you like tea or coffee?
Tu veux du thé ou du café?

2 ni … ni

> Use **ni … ni** in negative sentences.

I don't eat meat or fish.
Je ne mange ni viande, ni poisson.

3 (otherwise)
sinon

Hurry up or you'll miss the bus.
Dépêche-toi, sinon tu vas rater le bus.

oral n
l'oral *m*
(*pl* les oraux)

I've got my French oral soon.
Je vais bientôt passer mon oral de français.

orange

> **orange** can be a noun or an adjective.

A n
1 l'orange *f*

a big orange
une grosse orange

2 l'orange *m*

Orange is my favourite colour.
Ma couleur préférée, c'est l'orange.

B adj
orange *m, f, pl adj*

orange curtains
des rideaux orange

> *Colour adjectives come after the noun in French.*

orange juice n
le jus d'orange *m*

orchard n
le verger *m*

orchestra n
l'orchestre *m*

I play in the school orchestra.
Je joue dans l'orchestre de l'école.

order

> **order** can be a noun or a verb.

A n
1 (sequence)
l'ordre *m*

Put the words in alphabetical order, children.
Rangez ces mots par ordre alphabétique, les enfants.

The words are not in the right order.
Les mots ne sont pas dans le bon ordre.

2 (in restaurant)
la commande f

The waiter took our order.
Le serveur a pris notre commande.

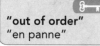
"out of order"
"en panne"

B vb
commander

Are you ready to order?
Vous êtes prêt à commander?

ordinary adj
ordinaire

an ordinary day
une journée ordinaire

organ n
l'orgue m

I play the organ.
Je joue de l'orgue.

organize vb
organiser

Could you help to organize the party?
Vous pouvez aider à organiser la fête?

original adj
original m adj

originale f adj

It's a very original idea.
C'est une idée très originale.

Orkneys npl
les Orcades fpl

orphan n
l'orphelin m

l'orpheline f

other

other can be an adjective or a pronoun.

A adj
autre

on the other side of the street
de l'autre côté de la rue

the other day
l'autre jour

the other one
l'autre

This one? – No, the other one.
Celui-ci? – Non, l'autre.

B pron
l'autre m/f pron

Get into twos, one behind the other.
Mettez-vous par deux, l'un derrière l'autre.

Where are the others?
Où sont les autres?

our adj
notre m/f adj

nos pl adj

Our house is quite big.
Notre maison est plutôt grande.

They are our friends.
Ce sont nos amis.

ours pron
à nous

Is this ours?
C'est à nous?

Whose is this? – It's ours.
C'est à qui? – À nous.

Look at Language Plus on pages 283–308 for extra vocabulary.

out

> **out** can be an adverb or an adjective.

Ⓐ adv
1 *(not at home)*
sorti *m*
sortie *f*

Gaston's out.
Gaston est sorti.

I'm going out.
Je sors.

2 *(in game)*
éliminé *m*
éliminée *f*

You're out Lucie!
Tu es éliminée, Lucie!

🔑
"way out"
"sortie"

Ⓑ adj *(turned off)*
éteint *m adj*
éteinte *f adj*

All the lights are out.
Toutes les lumières sont éteintes.

outdoor adj
en plein air

an outdoor swimming pool
une piscine en plein air

outdoor activities
les activités de plein air

outdoors adv
au grand air

outer space n
l'espace *m*

a monster from outer space
un monstre de l'espace

outside

> **outside** can be an adverb or a preposition.

Ⓐ adv
dehors

It's very cold outside.
Il fait très froid dehors.

Ⓑ prep
en dehors de

outside the school
en dehors de l'école

oven n
le four *m*

over

> **over** can be a preposition or an adjective.

Ⓐ prep
1 *(more than)*
plus de

Are you over ten?
Tu as plus de dix ans?

The temperature is over thirty degrees.
Il fait une température de plus de trente degrés.

2 *(during)*
pendant

over Christmas
pendant les fêtes de Noël

3 *(across)*
de l'autre côté de

The baker's is over the road.
La boulangerie est de l'autre côté de la rue.

over here
ici
over there
là-bas
all over Scotland
dans toute l'Écosse

B adj *(finished)*
terminé *m adj*
terminée *f adj*

The match is over.
Le match est terminé.

overcast adj
couvert *m adj*
couverte *f adj*

The sky was overcast.
Le ciel était couvert.

overhead projector n
le rétroprojecteur *m*

owl n
le hibou *m*
(*pl* les hiboux)

own adj
propre

I've got my own bathroom.
J'ai ma propre salle de bain.

I'd like a room of my own.
J'aimerais avoir une chambre à moi.

on his own
tout seul
on her own
toute seule

owner n
le/la propriétaire *m/f*

Look at Language Plus on pages 283–308 for extra vocabulary.

P

pack

pack can be a verb or a noun.

A vb
faire ses bagages

I need to pack.
Je dois faire mes bagages.

B n
a pack of cards
un jeu de cartes

packed lunch n
le casse-croûte m

I take a packed lunch to school.
J'apporte un casse-croûte à l'école
pour le déjeuner.

> French schoolchildren do not
> take packed lunches to
> school. They either eat at
> the canteen or go home for
> lunch.

packet n
le paquet m

a packet of crisps
un paquet de chips

page n
la page f

on page ten
page dix

Look at page six, everyone.
Regardez page six, tout le monde.

paid vb, see pay

pain n
1 la douleur f

a terrible pain
une douleur insupportable

I've got a pain in my stomach.
J'ai mal à l'estomac.

2 (a nuisance)
le/la casse-pieds m/f

My little sister is a pain.
Ma petite sœur est casse-pieds.

paint

paint can be a noun or a verb.

A n
la peinture f

"wet paint"
"attention, peinture fraîche"

B vb
peindre

I'm going to paint it green.
Je vais le peindre en vert.

painting n
le tableau m
(pl les tableaux)

a painting by Picasso
un tableau de Picasso

I like painting.
J'aime faire de la peinture.

pair n
la paire f

a pair of shoes
une paire de chaussures

a pair of trousers
un pantalon

a pair of jeans
un jean

in pairs
deux par deux

We work in pairs.
Nous travaillons deux par
deux.

Pakistan n
le Pakistan m

Pakistani

Pakistani can be a noun or an
adjective.

Ⓐ n
le Pakistanais m
la Pakistanaise f

Ⓑ adj
pakistanais m adj

pakistanaise f adj

*pakistanais is not spelled with a
capital letter when it is an
adjective.*

pal n
le copain m

la copine f

my pal Ronan
mon copain Ronan

my pal Elsa
ma copine Elsa

You're my best pal.
Tu es mon meilleur copain.

*This "best pal" is a boy. How can
you tell?*

palace n
le palais m

pale adj
pâle

a pale blue shirt
une chemise bleu pâle

pan n
1 (saucepan)
la casserole f

2 (frying pan)
la poêle f

pancake n
la crêpe f

Pancake Day n
le mardi gras m

Pancake Day is celebrated
in France as well. Children
dress up and eat pancakes
(**crêpes**).

panic vb
Don't panic!
Pas de panique!

pantomime n
le spectacle de Noël pour
enfants m

Pantomimes don't exist in
France.

pants npl
le slip m

a pair of pants
un slip

paper n
1 le papier m

**Have you got a pencil and some
paper?**
Tu as un crayon et du papier?

a piece of paper
du papier

Look at Language Plus on pages 283–308 for extra vocabulary.

a
b
c
d
e
f
g
h
i
j
k
l
m
n
o
p
q
r
s
t
u
v
w
x
y
z

a paper towel
une serviette en papier

2 (*newspaper*)
le journal *m*
(*pl* les journaux)

paper boy n
le livreur de journaux *m*

paper girl n
la livreuse de journaux *f*

paper round n
la tournée de distribution de journaux *f*

parade n
le défilé *m*

paragraph n
le paragraphe *m*

parcel n
le colis *m*

pardon n
Pardon?
Pardon?

parent n
le parent *m*

my parents
mes parents

Paris n
Paris

in Paris
à Paris

to Paris
à Paris

Gilles is from Paris.
Gilles est parisien.

Inès is from Paris.
Inès est parisienne.

Parisian n
le Parisien *m*
la Parisienne *f*

park

park can be a noun or a verb.

Ⓐ n
le parc *m*

There's a nice park.
Il y a un beau parc.

Ⓑ vb
se garer

It's difficult to park.
C'est difficile de se garer.

parking n
"no parking"
"stationnement interdit"

parrot n
le perroquet *m*

part n
la partie *f*

The first part is easy.
La première partie est facile.

partly adv
en partie

partner n
1 (*in game, role play*)
le/la partenaire *m/f*
2 (*in dance*)
le cavalier *m*
la cavalière *f*

part-time adj, adv
à temps partiel

a part-time job
un travail à temps partiel

She works part-time.
Elle travaille à temps partiel.

party n
1 la fête *f*
a birthday party
une fête d'anniversaire

> In France, a children's party held
> in the afternoon is called **un**
> **goûter d'anniversaire**.

a Christmas party
une fête de Noël

a New Year party
une fête du Nouvel An
2 (*more formal*)
la soirée *f*

I'm going to a party on Saturday.
Je vais à une soirée samedi.

pass vb
1 (*hand*)
passer

Pass the ball, Nina!
Passe le ballon, Nina!

Could you pass me the salt?
Vous pouvez me passer le sel?
2 (*go*)
passer devant

You pass the post office.
Vous passez devant la poste.

passenger n
le passager *m*
la passagère *f*

Passover n
la Pâque juive *f*

at Passover
à la Pâque juive

passport n
le passeport *m*

password n
le mot de passe *m*

past

> **past** can be a preposition or a
> noun.

A prep
1 (*after*)
après

**It's on the right, just past the
station.**
C'est sur la droite, juste après la
gare.

2 (*with times*)

It's half past ten exactly.
Il est exactement dix heures et
demie.

It's quarter past nine.
Il est neuf heures et quart.

It's ten past eight.
Il est huit heures dix.

> **half past eight**
> huit heures et demie
> **quarter past ten**
> dix heures et quart

B n
le passé *m*

in the past
dans le passé

pasta n
les pâtes *fpl*

Pasta is easy to cook.
Les pâtes sont faciles à préparer.

A B C D E F G H I J K L M N O P Q R S T U V W X Y Z

Look at Language Plus on pages 283–308 for extra vocabulary.

pâté n
le pâté m

path n
1 (footpath)
le chemin m
Follow the path.
Suivez le chemin.
2 (in garden, park)
l'allée f

patience n
1 la patience f
He hasn't got much patience.
Il n'a pas beaucoup de patience.
2 (card game)
la réussite f
I sometimes play patience.
Quelquefois je fais une réussite.

patient

> **patient** can be a noun or an adjective.

Ⓐ n
le patient m
la patiente f
Ⓑ adj
patient m adj
patiente f adj
The teacher is very patient.
La maîtresse est très patiente.

patio n
le patio m

pattern n
le motif m
a simple pattern
un motif simple

pause n
la pause f

pavement n
le trottoir m

on the pavement
sur le trottoir

paw n
la patte f

pay

> **pay** can be a noun or a verb.

Ⓐ n
le salaire m
What is the pay?
Le salaire est de combien?
Ⓑ vb
payer
Who's going to pay?
Qui va payer?
Where do I pay?
Où est-ce que je dois payer?

> **pay for** is also translated by **payer**.

I've paid for my ticket.
J'ai payé mon billet.
I paid 10 euros for it.
Je l'ai payé dix euros.

Pay attention, Christophe!
Fais attention, Christophe!
Pay attention, everybody!
Faites attention, tout le monde!

PC n
le PC m

I have a PC at home.
J'ai un PC chez moi.

PE n
l'EPS f

We have PE twice a week.
Nous avons EPS deux fois par semaine.

pea n
le petit pois m

Peas or beans?
Des petits pois ou des haricots?

peach n
la pêche f

a kilo of peaches
un kilo de pêches

peanut n
la cacahuète f

a packet of peanuts
un paquet de cacahuètes

peanut butter n
le beurre de cacahuètes m

a peanut butter sandwich
un sandwich au beurre de cacahuètes

pear n
la poire f

Which would you like, a pear or an apple?
Qu'est-ce que tu veux: une poire ou une pomme?

pebble n
le galet m

a pebble beach
une plage de galets

pedal n
la pédale f

pedigree adj
de race

a pedigree dog
un chien de race

peg n
1 (for coats)
le portemanteau m
(pl les portemanteaux)
2 (clothes peg)
l'épingle à linge f

pen n
le stylo m

Can I borrow your pen?
Je peux emprunter ton stylo?

pencil n
le crayon m

in pencil
au crayon

coloured pencils
les crayons de couleur

pencil case n
la trousse f

pencil sharpener n
le taille-crayon m

penfriend n
le correspondant m

la correspondante f

I'm Emma, your English penfriend.
Je suis Emma, ta correspondante anglaise.

*What is the difference between the English word **correspondent** and the French word **correspondant**?*

A
B
C
D
E
F
G
H
I
J
K
L
M
N
O
P
Q
R
S
T
U
V
W
X
Y
Z

Look at Language Plus on pages 283–308 for extra vocabulary.

penknife n
le canif *m*

pensioner n
le retraité *m*
la retraitée *f*

people npl
1 les gens *mpl*

The people are nice.
Les gens sont sympathiques.

a lot of people
beaucoup de gens

2 (*individuals*)
les personnes *fpl*

Four people can play.
Quatre personnes peuvent jouer.

How many people are there in your family?
Vous êtes combien dans votre famille?

> In English you usually say "tall people", "rich people", etc. In French you say "the tall", "the rich", etc.

tall people
les grands

French people
les Français

pepper n
1 (*spice*)
le poivre *m*

Pass the pepper, please.
Passez-moi le poivre, s'il vous plaît.

2 (*vegetable*)
le poivron *m*

a green pepper
un poivron vert

per prep
par

per day
par jour

per cent adv
pour cent

fifty per cent
cinquante pour cent

perfect adj
parfait *m adj*
parfaite *f adj*

Chantal speaks perfect English.
Chantal parle un anglais parfait.

performance n
le spectacle *m*

The performance starts at two o'clock.
Le spectacle commence à deux heures.

perfume n
le parfum *m*

perhaps adv
peut-être

Perhaps he's ill.
Il est peut-être malade.

period n
la période *f*

the holiday period
la période des vacances

permission n
la permission f

Have you got permission?
Tu as la permission?

person n
la personne f

She's a very nice person.
C'est une personne très
sympathique.

*There are two more letters in the
French word – what are they?*

personality n
la personnalité f

personal stereo n
le walkman® m

pessimistic adj
pessimiste

pet n
l'animal m
(pl les animaux)

Have you got a pet?
Tu as un animal?

petrol n
l'essence f

unleaded petrol
l'essence sans plomb

phone

phone can be a noun or a verb.

Ⓐ n
le téléphone m

Where's the phone?
Où est le téléphone?

by phone
par téléphone

on the phone
au téléphone

Can I use the phone, please?
Je peux téléphoner, s'il vous plaît?

Ⓑ vb
téléphoner à

I have to phone my Mum.
Je dois téléphoner à ma mère.

phone box n
la cabine téléphonique f

phone call n
l'appel m

She gets lots of phone calls.
Elle reçoit beaucoup d'appels.

Can I make a phone call?
Est-ce que je peux téléphoner?

phonecard n
la carte de téléphone f

phone number n
le numéro de téléphone m

What's your phone number?
Quel est ton numéro de téléphone?

photo n
la photo f

This is a photo of my family.
Voici une photo de ma famille.

I want to take some photos.
Je veux prendre des photos.

I want to take a photo of you.
Je veux te prendre en photo.

photocopier n
la photocopieuse f

photocopy

photocopy can be a noun or a
verb.

Ⓐ n
la photocopie f

It's only a photocopy.
Ce n'est qu'une photocopie.

Ⓑ vb
photocopier

You can photocopy it.
Vous pouvez le photocopier.

A B C D E F G H I J K L M N O P Q R S T U V W X Y Z

Look at Language Plus on pages 283–308 for extra vocabulary.

a
b
c
d
e
f
g
h
i
j
k
l
m
n
o
p
q
r
s
t
u
v
w
x
y
z

photograph n
la photo f

phrase book n
le guide de conversation m

physics n
la physique f

She teaches physics.
Elle enseigne la physique.

pianist n
le/la pianiste m/f

piano n
le piano m

I play the piano.
Je joue du piano.

I have piano lessons.
Je prends des leçons de piano.

pick

> **pick** can be a noun or a verb.

Ⓐ n
Take your pick!
Faites votre choix!

Ⓑ vb
1 (choose)
choisir

Pick a card, Jean!
Choisis une carte, Jean!

Pick three girls and three boys.
Choisis trois filles et trois garçons.

2 (fruit, flowers)
cueillir

I like picking strawberries.
J'aime bien cueillir des fraises.

pick up vb
1 (collect)
venir chercher

We can come to the airport to pick you up.
Nous pouvons venir vous chercher à l'aéroport.

2 tirer

Pick up another card, Susie!
Tire une autre carte, Susie!

3 (learn)
apprendre

I hope I'll pick up some French.
J'espère apprendre quelques mots de français.

picnic n
le pique-nique m

I like picnics.
J'aime les pique-niques.

to have a picnic
pique-niquer

We had a picnic on the beach.
Nous avons pique-niqué sur la plage.

picture n
1 l'image f

Look at the picture.
Regarde l'image.

There are pictures in this dictionary.
Il a des images dans ce dictionnaire.

2 la photo f

This is a picture of my family.
Voici une photo de ma famille.

3 (painting)
le tableau m
(pl les tableaux)

a famous picture
un tableau célèbre

4 (drawing)
le dessin m

I'll draw a picture.
Je vais faire un dessin.

Draw a picture of your pet, Lisa.
Dessine ton animal, Lisa.

pie n
la <u>tourte</u> f

an apple pie
une tourte aux pommes

piece n
le <u>morceau</u> m
(pl les morceaux)

A small piece, please.
Un petit morceau, s'il vous plaît.

pierced adj
<u>percé</u> m adj

<u>percée</u> f adj

I've got pierced ears.
J'ai les oreilles percées.

pig n
le <u>cochon</u> m

pigeon n
le <u>pigeon</u> m

piggy bank n
la <u>tirelire</u> f

pigtail n
la <u>natte</u> f

She's got pigtails.
Elle a des nattes.

pile n
la <u>pile</u> f

pill n
la <u>pilule</u> f

pillow n
l'<u>oreiller</u> m

a pillow
un oreiller

pilot n
le <u>pilote</u> m

pinball n
le <u>flipper</u> m

Do you want to play pinball?
Tu veux jouer au flipper?

pineapple n
l'<u>ananas</u> m

pink

> **pink** can be an adjective or a noun.

A adj
<u>rose</u>

a pink blouse
un chemisier rose

> *Colour adjectives come after the noun in French.*

B n
le <u>rose</u> m

Pink is my favourite colour.
Ma couleur préférée, c'est le rose.

pint n

a pint of milk
un demi-litre de lait

> In France measurements are in litres and centilitres. A pint is about 0.6 litres.

pipe n
la <u>pipe</u> f

He smokes a pipe.
Il fume la pipe.

pitch n
le <u>terrain</u> m

a football pitch
un terrain de football

A
B
C
D
E
F
G
H
I
J
K
L
M
N
O
P
Q
R
S
T
U
V
W
X
Y
Z

Look at Language Plus on pages 283–308 for extra vocabulary.

pity n

What a pity she can't come.
Quel dommage! Elle ne peut pas venir.

> 🔑
>
> **What a pity!**
> Quel dommage!

pizza n
la pizza f

place n
1 (location)
l'endroit m

It's a quiet place.
C'est un endroit tranquille.

There are a lot of interesting places to visit.
Il y a beaucoup d'endroits intéressants à visiter.
2 (position)
la place f

Can I change places?
Je peux changer de place?

Léon, change places with Nina!
Léon, change de place avec Nina!

plain adj
simple

a plain white blouse
un chemisier blanc simple

plain chocolate n
le chocolat à croquer m

plait n
la natte f

She wears her hair in a plait.
Elle a une natte.

plan

> **plan** can be a noun or a verb.

Ⓐ n
1 le projet m

Have you got plans for the holidays?
Tu as des projets pour les vacances?
2 (map)
le plan m

a plan of the school
un plan de l'école
Ⓑ vb
préparer

We're planning a trip to France.
Nous préparons un voyage en France.

plane n
l'avion m

by plane
en avion

plant n
la plante f

plastic adj
en plastique

a plastic bag
un sac en plastique

plate n
l'assiette f

platform n
le quai m

on platform 7
sur le quai numéro sept

play

> **play** can be a noun or a verb.

A n
la pièce f

a play by Shakespeare
une pièce de Shakespeare

B vb

1 jouer

He's playing with his friends.
Il joue avec ses amis.

What sort of music do they play?
Quel genre de musique jouent-ils?

2 (sport, game)
jouer à

I play hockey.
Je joue au hockey.

Can you play chess?
Tu sais jouer aux échecs?

3 (instrument)
jouer de

I play the guitar.
Je joue de la guitare.

player n
le joueur m
la joueuse f

a football player
un joueur de football

playground n

1 (at school)
la cour de récréation f

2 (in park)
l'aire de jeux f

playgroup n
la garderie f

playing card n
la carte à jouer f

playing field n
le terrain de sport m

playtime n
la récréation f

at playtime
à la récréation

please excl

1 (polite form)
s'il vous plaît

Two coffees, please.
Deux cafés, s'il vous plaît.

2 (familiar form)
s'il te plaît

Please write back soon.
Réponds vite, s'il te plaît.

> **Yes please!**
> Oui, merci.

pleased adj
content m adj
contente f adj

My mother's not pleased.
Ma mère n'est pas contente.

pleasure n
le plaisir m

with pleasure
avec plaisir

plenty n
largement assez

I've got plenty.
J'en ai largement assez.

You've got plenty of time.
Vous avez largement le temps.

> **That's plenty, thanks.**
> Ça suffit largement, merci.

Look at Language Plus on pages 283–308 for extra vocabulary.

a

plug in vb
brancher

Is it plugged in?
Est-ce que c'est branché?

It's not plugged in.
Ce n'est pas branché.

b

c

d

plum n
la prune f

plum jam
la confiture de prunes

e

f

plump adj
dodu m adj
dodue f adj

g

h

plural n
le pluriel m

i

j

plus prep
plus

4 plus 3 equals 7.
Quatre plus trois égalent sept.

k

l

m

p.m. abbr

at 8 p.m.
à huit heures du soir

at 2 p.m.
à quatorze heures

n

o

In France times are often
given using the 24-hour
clock.

p

q

r

s

poached egg n
l'œuf poché m

a poached egg
un œuf poché

t

u

pocket n
la poche f

v

w

pocket calculator n
la calculette f

x

pocket money n
l'argent de poche m

y

z

I get £2 a week pocket money.
Je reçois deux livres d'argent de
poche par semaine.

poem n
le poème m

point

point can be a noun or a verb.

Ⓐ n

1 (in game)
le point m

You've got 5 points.
Vous avez cinq points.

What's the point?
À quoi bon?

**What's the point of leaving so
early?**
À quoi bon partir si tôt?

2 (in decimal numbers)
la virgule f

two point five (2.5)
deux virgule cinq (2,5)

In decimal numbers, the
French use a comma instead
of a point.

Ⓑ vb

**Which cake? You can point to
it.**
Quel gâteau? Vous pouvez le
montrer du doigt.

**The guide pointed out Notre-
Dame to us.**
Le guide nous a montré Notre-
Dame.

poison n
le poison m

poisonous adj

1 (snake)
venimeux m adj
venimeuse f adj

a poisonous snake
un serpent venimeux

2 (mushroom, berry)
vénéneux *m adj*
vénéneuse *f adj*

Don't eat it, it's poisonous!
Ne mange pas ça, c'est
vénéneux!

polica npl

police npl
la police *f*

police is a singular word in French.

police car n
la voiture de police *f*

policeman n
le policier *m*

policewoman n
la femme policier *f*

polite adj
poli *m adj*

polie *f adj*

He's a very polite boy.
C'est un garçon très poli.

politely adv
poliment

polluted adj
pollué *m adj*

polluée *f adj*

pollution n
la pollution *f*

polo shirt n
le polo *m*

pond n
le bassin *m*

There's a pond in the garden.
Il y a un bassin dans le jardin.

pony n
le poney *m*

What extra letter does the French word have?

ponytail n
la queue de cheval *f*

I've got a ponytail.
J'ai une queue de cheval.

pony trekking n

I go pony trekking.
Je fais des randonnées à dos de
poney.

poodle n
le caniche *m*

pool n
1 (swimming pool)
la piscine *f*

There's a pool.
Il y a une piscine.
2 (game)
le billard américain *m*

Can you play pool?
Tu sais jouer au billard américain?

poor adj
pauvre

Poor David, he's very unlucky!
Le pauvre David, il n'a vraiment pas
de chance!

A
B
C
D
E
F
G
H
I
J
K
L
M
N
O
P
Q
R
S
T
U
V
W
X
Y
Z

Look at Language Plus on pages 283–308 for extra vocabulary.

popcorn n
le pop-corn *m*

pope n
le pape *m*

pop group n
le groupe pop *m*
What's your favourite pop group?
Quel est ton groupe pop préféré?

pop music n
la musique pop *f*

poppy n
le coquelicot *m*

pop song n
la chanson pop *f*

pop star n
la pop star *f*
Who's your favourite pop star?
Qui est ta pop star préférée?

popular adj
populaire
She's a very popular girl.
C'est une fille très populaire.

porch n
le porche *m*

pork n
le porc *m*
a pork chop
une côtelette de porc
I don't eat pork.
Je ne mange pas de porc.

port n
le port *m*

portable adj
portable
a portable TV
un téléviseur portable

> If something is **portable** you can carry it. The French for "to carry" is **porter**.

portion n
la portion *f*
a large portion of chips
une grosse portion de frites

Portugal n
le Portugal *m*

posh adj
chic *m, f, pl adj*
a posh hotel
un hôtel chic

positive adj
certain *m adj*
certaine *f adj*
Are you positive, Joëlle?
Tu en es certaine, Joëlle?

possibility n
It's a possibility.
C'est possible.

possible adj
possible
as soon as possible
aussitôt que possible

post

> **post** can be a noun or a verb.

A n (*letters*)
le courrier *m*
Is there any post for me?
Est-ce qu'il y a du courrier pour moi?

B vb
poster

I've got some cards to post.
J'ai quelques cartes à poster.

postbox n
la boîte aux lettres f

French postboxes are yellow.

postcard n
la carte postale f

Thank you for the postcard, Charlotte.
Merci pour la carte postale, Charlotte.

postcode n
le code postal m

What is your postcode?
Quel est ton code postal?

poster n
le poster m

I've got posters on my bedroom walls.
J'ai des posters sur les murs de ma chambre.

In French you pronounce **poster** as "post-air".

postman n
le facteur m

He's a postman.
Il est facteur.

You do not translate "**a**" when you say what someone's job is in French.

post office n
la poste f

Where's the post office, please?
Où est la poste, s'il vous plaît?

potato n
la pomme de terre f

Rice or potatoes?
Du riz ou des pommes de terre?

mashed potatoes
la purée

boiled potatoes
les pommes vapeur

a baked potato
une pomme de terre cuite au four

potato salad n
la salade de pommes de terre f

pottery n
la poterie f

pound n
la livre f

How many euros do you get for a pound?
Combien d'euros a-t-on pour une livre?

a pound of potatoes
une livre de pommes de terre

pour vb
pleuvoir à verse

It's pouring.
Il pleut à verse.

Look at Language Plus on pages 283–308 for extra vocabulary.

powerful adj
puissant *m adj*

puissante *f adj*

practically adv
pratiquement

It's practically impossible.
C'est pratiquement impossible.

practice n
(for sport)
l'entraînement *m*

football practice
l'entraînement de foot

I've got to do my piano practice.
Je dois travailler mon piano.

practise vb
1 *(instrument)*
travailler

I practise my flute every evening.
Je travaille ma flûte tous les soirs.

2 *(language)*
pratiquer

I like practising my French.
J'aime pratiquer mon français.

3 *(sport)*
s'entraîner

The team practises on Thursdays.
L'équipe s'entraîne le jeudi.

prawn n
la crevette *f*

pray vb
prier

Let us pray.
Prions.

prayer n
la prière *f*

precisely adv
at 10 a.m. precisely
à dix heures précises

prefer vb
préférer

Which would you prefer?
Lequel préfères-tu?

Which do you prefer, tennis or football?
Tu préfères le tennis ou le football?

I prefer French to geography.
Je préfère le français à la géographie.

pregnant adj
enceinte

She's six months pregnant.
Elle est enceinte de six mois.

prep n
les devoirs *mpl*

history prep
les devoirs d'histoire

prepare vb
préparer

She has to prepare lessons in the evening.
Elle doit préparer ses cours le soir.

prep school n
l'école primaire privée *f*

present

> **present** can be an adjective or a noun.

A adj
présent *m adj*

présente *f adj*

Ten present, two absent.
Dix présents, deux absents.

the present tense
le présent

B n
1 *(gift)*
le cadeau *m*
(*pl* les cadeaux)

I'm going to give Julie a present.
Je vais offrir un cadeau à Julie.

I got lots of presents.
J'ai eu beaucoup de cadeaux.

priest n
le prêtre *m*

He's a priest.
Il est prêtre.

You do not translate "a" when you say what someone's job is in French.

2 (time)
le présent *m*

the present and the future
le présent et le futur

president n
le président *m*

la présidente *f*

pretend vb

Pretend you are in a café.
Imagine que tu es dans un café.

pretty

pretty can be an adjective or an adverb.

Ⓐ adj
joli *m adj*
jolie *f adj*

She's very pretty.
Elle est très jolie.

Ⓑ adv
plutôt

It's pretty old.
C'est plutôt vieux.

The weather was pretty awful.
Il faisait un temps minable.

previous adj
précédent *m adj*

précédente *f adj*

the previous day
le jour précédent

price n
le prix *m*

primary adj
primaire

I'm in primary 7.
Je suis au CM2.

primary school n
l'école primaire *f*

I am at primary school.
Je suis à l'école primaire.

*In France children start primary school at the age of 6. The first year is **CP**, followed by **CE1** and **CE2**. The last two years are **CM1** and **CM2**.*

prince n
le prince *m*

the Prince of Wales
le prince de Galles

There are no princes in France, because France is a republic, not a monarchy like Britain.

princess n
la princesse *f*

Princess Anne
la princesse Anne

print vb
écrire en majuscules

Print your name.
Écris ton nom en majuscules.

Look at Language Plus on pages 283–308 for extra vocabulary.

prison n
la prison f

in prison
en prison

private adj
privé m adj

privée f adj

a private school
une école privée

I have private lessons.
Je prends des cours particuliers.

private school n
l'école privée f

prize n
le prix m

The prize is one hundred euros.
C'est un prix de cent euros.

You can win a prize.
Tu peux gagner un prix.

prize-giving n
la distribution des prix f

prizewinner n
le gagnant m
la gagnante f

probably adv
probablement

probably not
probablement pas

problem n
le problème m

Is there a problem?
Il y a un problème?

What's the problem?
Qu'est-ce qui ne va pas?

No problem!
Pas de problème!

procession n
la procession f

profession n
la profession f

professor n
le professeur d'université m

profit n
le bénéfice m

program n
le programme m

a computer program
un programme informatique

programme n
1 (on TV, radio)
l'émission f

my favourite programme
mon émission préférée
2 (booklet)
le programme m

Would you like a programme?
Tu veux un programme?

progress n
le progrès m

You're making progress, Éric!
Tu fais des progrès, Éric!

projector n
le projecteur m

promise

promise can be a noun or a verb.

Ⓐ n
la promesse f

I'll make you a promise.
Je te fais une promesse.

That's a promise!
C'est promis!

Ⓑ vb
promettre

I promise!
Je te le promets!

I'll write, I promise!
J'écrirai, c'est promis!

prompt

prompt can be an adjective or an
adverb.

Ⓐ adj
rapide

a prompt reply
une réponse rapide

Ⓑ adv
at eight o'clock prompt
à huit heures précises

pronoun n
le pronom m

pronounce vb
prononcer

How do you pronounce that word?
Comment on prononce ce mot?

pronunciation n
la prononciation f

Your pronunciation is good!
Tu as une bonne prononciation!

Which vowel is different in the
French word?

proper adj
vrai m adj
vraie f adj

proper French bread
du vrai pain français

properly adv
comme il faut

I can't pronounce it properly.
Je n'arrive pas à le prononcer
comme il faut.

Protestant

Protestant can be an adjective or
a noun.

Ⓐ adj
protestant m adj
protestante f adj

Ⓑ n
le protestant m
la protestante f

I'm a Protestant.
Je suis protestant.

In French **protestant** is not
spelled with a capital letter.

proud adj
fier m adj
fière f adj

Her parents are proud of her.
Ses parents sont fiers d'elle.

prune n
le pruneau m
(pl les pruneaux)

Be careful! There is a word **prune**
in French, but it means "plum". A
prune in English is a dried plum.

A B C D E F G H I J K L M N O **P** Q R S T U V W X Y Z

Look at Language Plus on pages 283–308 for extra vocabulary.

a
b
c
d
e
f
g
h
i
j
k
l
m
n
o
p
q
r
s
t
u
v
w
x
y
z

PTO abbr
T.S.V.P.

T.S.V.P. stands for "Tournez s'il vous plaît". What does PTO stand for?

pub n
le pub m

public
Ⓐ n
le public m

The castle is open to the public.
Le château est ouvert au public.
Ⓑ adj
public m adj

publique f adj

a public swimming pool
une piscine publique

publicity n
la publicité f

public school n
l'école privée f

public transport n
les transports en commun mpl

by public transport
en transports en commun

pudding n
le dessert m

Would you like a pudding?
Tu veux un dessert?

What's for pudding?
Qu'est-ce qu'il y a comme dessert?

pull vb
tirer

Pull!
Tirez!

pullover n
le pull m

What colour is your pullover?
De quelle couleur est ton pull?

pump n
1 (for bike)
la pompe f

a bicycle pump
une pompe à vélo
2 (shoe)
le chausson de gym m

Have you got your pumps?
Tu as tes chaussons de gym?

pump up vb
gonfler

Pump up your tyres!
Gonfle tes pneus!

punch vb
1 (hit)
donner un coup de poing à

He punched me!
Il m'a donné un coup de poing!
2 (in ticket machine)
composter

Punch your ticket before you get on the train.
Compostez votre billet avant de monter dans le train.

In France, you have to punch your ticket before you get on the train. If you don't, you can be fined.

punctual adj
Be punctual!
Soyez à l'heure!

punctuation n
la ponctuation f

There is a different vowel in the French word – what is it?

punishment n
la punition f

pupil n
l'élève m/f

There are 22 pupils in my class.
Il y a vingt-deux élèves dans ma classe.

puppet n
la marionnette f

puppy n
le chiot m

pure adj
pur m adj
pure f adj

It's pure orange juice.
C'est du jus d'orange pur.

purple

purple can be an adjective or a noun.

A adj
violet m adj
violette f adj

a purple skirt
une jupe violette

Colour adjectives come after the noun in French.

B n
le violet m

Purple is my favourite colour.
Ma couleur préférée, c'est le violet.

purpose n

on purpose
exprès

You're doing it on purpose.
Tu le fais exprès.

purr vb
ronronner

The cat is purring.
Le chat ronronne.

purse n
le porte-monnaie m

I've lost my purse.
J'ai perdu mon porte-monnaie.

pursuit n
l'activité f

outdoor pursuits
les activités de plein air

push vb
pousser

Don't push, boys!
Arrêtez de pousser, les garçons!

Push!
Poussez!

pushchair n
la poussette f

put vb
1 (place)
mettre

Put your chewing gum in the bin.
Mets ton chewing-gum à la poubelle.

Where shall I put my things?
Où est-ce que je peux mettre mes affaires?

She's putting the baby to bed.
Elle met le bébé au lit.

2 (write)
écrire

Don't forget to put your name on the paper.
N'oubliez pas d'écrire votre nom sur la feuille.

put away vb
ranger

Put your things away, children.
Rangez vos affaires, les enfants.

A B C D E F G H I J K L M N O **P** Q R S T U V W X Y Z

Look at Language Plus on pages 283–308 for extra vocabulary.

a

put back vb
remettre en place

Don't forget to put it back.
N'oublie pas de le remettre en
place.

b

c

put down vb
poser

Put down a card.
Pose une carte.

Put down your hands.
Baissez la main.

d

e

f

g

put off vb
1 (switch off)
éteindre

Shall I put the light off?
Est-ce que j'éteins la lumière?
2 (distract)
déranger

Stop putting me off!
Arrête de me déranger!

h

i

j

k

l

put on vb
1 (clothes)
mettre

I'll put my coat on.
Je vais mettre mon manteau.
2 (switch on)
allumer

Shall I put the light on?
J'allume la lumière?

m

n

o

p

put up vb
1 (pin up)
mettre

I'll put the poster up on my wall.
Je vais mettre le poster au mur.
2 (raise)
lever

Put up your hands.
Levez la main.
3 (increase)
augmenter

q

r

s

t

u

v

w

x

y

z

They've put up the price.
Ils ont augmenté le prix.

puzzle n
le puzzle m

puzzled adj
perplexe

You look puzzled!
Tu as l'air perplexe!

pyjamas npl
le pyjama m

my pyjamas
mon pyjama

I've got new pyjamas.
J'ai un nouveau pyjama.

a pair of pyjamas
un pyjama

In French, **pyjama** is a singular
word.

Pyrenees npl
les Pyrénées f

in the Pyrenees
dans les Pyrénées

We went to the Pyrenees.
Nous sommes allés dans les
Pyrénées.

Q

quality n
la qualité f

quantity n
la quantité f

quarrel vb
se disputer

Don't quarrel!
Ne vous disputez pas!

quarter n
le quart m

a quarter of the class
un quart de la classe

It's quarter past six.
Il est six heures et quart.

at quarter to eight
à huit heures moins le quart

three quarters
trois quarts
a quarter of an hour
un quart d'heure
three quarters of an hour
trois quarts d'heure
a quarter past ten
dix heures et quart
a quarter to eleven
onze heures moins le quart

quarter final n
le quart de finale m

queen n
1 la reine f

Queen Elizabeth
la reine Élisabeth

2 (card)
la dame f

the queen of hearts
la dame de cœur

question n
la question f

Can I ask a question?
Est-ce que je peux poser une question?

Are there any questions?
Vous avez des questions?

That's a difficult question.
C'est une question difficile.

questionnaire n
le questionnaire m

queue

queue can be a noun or a verb.

A n
la queue f

There's a long queue.
Il y a une longue queue.

B vb
faire la queue

You have to queue.
Il faut faire la queue.

Look at Language Plus on pages 283–308 for extra vocabulary.

quick adj
rapide

a quick lunch
un déjeuner rapide

It's quicker by train.
C'est plus rapide en train.

> 🔑
>
> **Be quick, Laurent!**
> Dépêche-toi, Laurent!
> **Be quick, girls!**
> Dépêchez-vous, les filles!

quickly adv
vite

Am I speaking too quickly?
Je parle trop vite?

quiet adj
1 (not chatty)
silencieux m adj
silencieuse f adj

You're very quiet, Daphne.
Tu es bien silencieuse, Daphne.

2 (peaceful)
tranquille

a quiet little town
une petite ville tranquille

a quiet weekend
un week-end tranquille

Be quiet, I'm thinking!
Tais-toi, je réfléchis!

> 🔑
>
> **Quiet!**
> Silence!

quietly adv
doucement

Talk quietly.
Parlez doucement.

Shut the door quietly.
Fermez doucement la porte.

quilt n
la couette f

quite adv
1 (rather)
assez

It's quite warm today.
Il fait assez chaud aujourd'hui.

It's quite a long way.
C'est assez loin.

It's quite expensive.
C'est assez cher.

quite a lot of money
pas mal d'argent

2 (completely)
tout à fait

I'm quite sure he's coming.
Je suis tout à fait sûr qu'il va venir.

Are you ready, Lola? – Not quite.
Tu es prête, Lola? – Pas tout à fait.

> 🔑
>
> **quite good**
> pas mal

quiz n
le jeu-concours m

R

rabbi n
le <u>rabbin</u> m

rabbit n
le <u>lapin</u> m

race n
la <u>course</u> f

a cycle race
une course cycliste

Let's have a race!
On fait la course?

racer n
le <u>vélo de course</u> m

I've got a new racer.
J'ai un nouveau vélo de course.

racing car n
la <u>voiture de course</u> f

two racing cars
deux voitures de course

racket n
la <u>raquette</u> f

my tennis racket
ma raquette de tennis

radiator n
le <u>radiateur</u> m

My coat's on the radiator.
Mon manteau est sur le
radiateur.

radio n
la <u>radio</u> f

on the radio
à la radio

radio cassette n
le <u>radiocassette</u> m

radio-controlled adj
<u>téléguidé</u> m adj
<u>téléguidée</u> f adj

raffle n
la <u>tombola</u> f

raffle ticket n
le <u>billet de tombola</u> m

**Do you want to buy a raffle
ticket?**
Tu veux acheter un billet de
tombola?

rage n

to be in a rage
être furieux

She's in a rage.
Elle est furieuse.

rail n

by rail
en train

railway n
le <u>chemin de fer</u> m

railway line n
le <u>chemin de fer</u> m

railway station n
la <u>gare</u> f

Look at Language Plus on pages 283–308 for extra vocabulary.

a

rain

> **rain** can be a noun or a verb.

Ⓐ n
la pluie *f*

in the rain
sous la pluie

Ⓑ vb
pleuvoir

It's going to rain.
Il va pleuvoir.

It rains a lot here.
Il pleut beaucoup par ici.

It's raining.
Il pleut.

rainbow n
l'arc-en-ciel *m*

raincoat n
l'imperméable *m*

rainy adj
pluvieux *m adj*

pluvieuse *f adj*

a rainy day
une journée pluvieuse

raise vb
lever

Raise your right arm, everyone.
Levez le bras droit, tout le monde.

to raise money
collecter des fonds

We're raising money for a new gym.
Nous collectons des fonds pour un nouveau gymnase.

raisin n
le raisin sec *m*

> **raisin** in French means "grape".
> An English **raisin** is a dried grape,
> which is what **raisin sec** means.

Ramadan n
le ramadan *m*

ramp n
la rampe d'accès *f*

ran vb, *see* **run**

random adj

at random
au hasard

Pick a card at random.
Choisis une carte au hasard.

rang vb, *see* **ring**

range n
le choix *m*

There's a wide range of colours.
Il y a un grand choix de coloris.

rap n
le rap *m*

rare adj
rare

rasher n
la tranche *f*

an egg and two rashers of bacon
un œuf et deux tranches de bacon

raspberry n
la framboise *f*

raspberry jam
la confiture de framboises

rat n
le rat *m*

rather adv
<u>plutôt</u>

£20! That's rather expensive!
Vingt livres! C'est plutôt cher!

I'd rather …
J'aimerais mieux …

I'd rather stay in tonight.
J'aimerais mieux rester à la maison ce soir.

Would you like a sweet? – I'd rather have an apple.
Tu veux un bonbon? – J'aimerais mieux une pomme.

Which would you rather have?
Qu'est-ce que tu préfères?

Would you rather have water or coke?
Tu préfères boire de l'eau ou du coca?

ravenous adj
I'm ravenous!
J'ai une faim de loup!

> *un loup* is a wolf, so word for word this means "I'm as hungry as a wolf".

raw adj
<u>cru</u> *m adj*
<u>crue</u> *f adj*

razor n
le <u>rasoir</u> *m*

RE n
l'<u>éducation religieuse</u> *f*

reach

> **reach** can be a noun or a verb.

Ⓐ n
Mum keeps the biscuits out of reach.
Maman garde les biscuits hors de portée.

The hotel is within easy reach of the town centre.
L'hôtel se trouve à proximité du centre-ville.

Ⓑ vb
(get to)
<u>arriver à</u>

I can't reach the top shelf.
Je n'arrive pas à atteindre l'étagère du haut.

We hope to reach Paris tomorrow evening.
Nous espérons arriver à Paris demain soir.

read vb
<u>lire</u>

I don't read much.
Je ne lis pas beaucoup.

Have you read "The Prisoner of Azkaban"?
Est-ce que tu as lu "le Prisonnier d'Azkaban"?

read out vb
<u>lire</u>

I'll read out the names.
Je vais lire les noms.

reading n
la <u>lecture</u> *f*

Reading is one of my hobbies.
La lecture est l'un de mes passe-temps.

ready adj
<u>prêt</u> *m adj*
<u>prête</u> *f adj*

Look at Language Plus on pages 283–308 for extra vocabulary.

A B C D E F G H I J K L M N O P Q **R** S T U V W X Y Z

a

Lunch is ready.
Le déjeuner est prêt.

b

She's nearly ready.
Elle est presque prête.

c

Are you ready, children?
Vous êtes prêts, les enfants?

d

e

🔑

Ready, steady, go!
À vos marques, prêts, partez!

f

g

real adj

h

1 (true)
vrai m adj
vraie f adj

i

Her real name is Cordelia.
Son vrai nom, c'est Cordelia.

j

2 véritable

k

It's real leather.
C'est du cuir véritable.

l

really adv

m

vraiment

n

She's really nice.
Elle est vraiment sympa.

o

Do you want to go? – Not really.
Tu veux y aller? – Pas vraiment.

p

reason n

q

la raison f

r

reasonable adj
raisonnable

s

Be reasonable, Marie!
Sois raisonnable, Marie!

t

receipt n

u

le ticket de caisse m

v

Take your receipt.
Prenez votre ticket de caisse.

w

receive vb

x

recevoir

y

I received your letter yesterday.
J'ai reçu ta lettre hier.

z

recent adj
récent m adj
récente f adj

recently adv
ces derniers temps

He's been ill a lot recently.
Il est souvent malade ces derniers temps.

reception n
la réception f

Please leave your key at reception.
Merci de laisser votre clé à la réception.

The reception will be at a big hotel.
La réception aura lieu dans un grand hôtel.

receptionist n
le/la réceptionniste m/f

In French **réceptionniste** has double **n**.

recipe n
la recette f

reckon vb
penser

What do you reckon?
Qu'est-ce que tu en penses?

recognize vb
reconnaître

Do you recognize this boy?
Tu reconnais ce garçon?

recommend vb
conseiller

What do you recommend?
Qu'est-ce que vous me conseillez?

I recommend the soup.
Je vous conseille la soupe.

record

> **record** can be a noun or a verb.

Ⓐ n *(sport)*
le record *m*

the world record
le record du monde

Ⓑ vb
enregistrer

We'll record the song.
On va enregistrer la chanson.

recorder n
la flûte à bec *f*

I play the recorder.
Je joue de la flûte à bec.

rectangle n
le rectangle *m*

red

> **red** can be an adjective or a noun.

Ⓐ adj
1 rouge

a red rose
une rose rouge

The lights are red.
Le feu est au rouge.

2 *(hair)*
roux *m adj*
rousse *f adj*

Tamsin's got red hair.
Tamsin a les cheveux roux.

Colour adjectives come after the noun in French.

Ⓑ n
le rouge *m*

Red is my favourite colour.
Ma couleur préférée, c'est le rouge.

redecorate vb
1 *(with wallpaper)*
retapisser

Mum is helping me redecorate my room.
Maman m'aide à retapisser ma chambre.

2 *(with paint)*
refaire les peintures

Mum is helping me redecorate my room.
Maman m'aide à refaire les peintures de ma chambre.

red-haired adj
roux *m adj*
rousse *f adj*

redhead n
le roux *m*
la rousse *f*

redo vb
refaire

I need to redo my homework.
Je dois refaire mes devoirs.

reduced adj
at a reduced price
à prix réduit

reduction n
la réduction *f*

Look at Language Plus on pages 283–308 for extra vocabulary.

a 5% reduction
une réduction de cinq pour cent

referee n
l'arbitre m

reflexive adj
a reflexive verb
un verbe réfléchi

refreshments npl
les rafraîchissements mpl

refrigerator n
le réfrigérateur m

refugee n
le réfugié m
la réfugiée f

refuse vb
refuser
He refuses to help.
Il refuse d'aider.

regards npl
Give my regards to Luc.
Transmets mon bon souvenir à Luc.
Jean-Louis sends his regards.
Vous avez le bonjour de Jean-Louis.

region n
la région f
in this region
dans cette région

register n
I'm going to call the register.
Je vais faire l'appel.

registration n
l'appel m
after registration
après l'appel

regular adj
1 régulier m adj
régulière f adj
at regular intervals
à intervalles réguliers

a regular verb
un verbe régulier

You should take regular exercise.
Il faut faire régulièrement de
l'exercice.
2 (medium)
normal m adj
normale f adj

a regular portion of fries
une portion de frites normale

rehearsal n
la répétition f

reindeer n
le renne m

relation n
my relations
ma famille
I've got relations in London.
J'ai de la famille à Londres.

relative n
all her relatives
toute sa famille
I've got relatives in Manchester.
J'ai de la famille à Manchester.

relax vb
Relax! Everything's fine.
Ne t'en fais pas! Tout va bien.

relaxed adj
détendu m adj
détendue f adj

relaxing adj
reposant m adj
reposante f adj

I find cooking relaxing.
Cela me détend de faire la cuisine.

relay race n
la course de relais f

We won the relay race.
Nous avons gagné la course de relais.

reliable adj
fiable

a reliable car
une voiture fiable

He's not very reliable.
Il n'est pas très fiable.

religion n
la religion f

What religion are you?
Quelle est votre religion?

religious adj
religieux m adj

religieuse f adj

a religious school
une école religieuse

My parents are very religious.
Mes parents sont très religieux.

remark n
la remarque f

remember vb
se souvenir de

Who remembers this word?
Qui se souvient de ce mot?

Do you remember the rules of the game?
Tu te souviens des règles du jeu?

I can't remember his name.
Je ne me souviens pas de son nom.

*In French you often say "don't forget" instead of **remember**.*

Remember your passport!
N'oublie pas ton passeport!

Remember this word is feminine.
N'oublie pas que ce mot est féminin.

Remember to write your name on the form, children.
N'oubliez pas d'écrire votre nom sur le formulaire, les enfants.

Sorry, I can't remember.
Désolé, je ne m'en souviens pas.

Remembrance Day n
le jour de l'Armistice m

on Remembrance Day
le jour de l'Armistice

remind vb
rappeler

Remind me to speak to Daniel.
Rappelle-moi de parler à Daniel.

remote adj
isolé m adj

isolée f adj

a remote village
un village isolé

remote control n
la télécommande f

remove vb
enlever

Please remove your bag from my seat.
Est-ce que vous pouvez enlever votre sac de mon siège?

rent

rent can be a noun or a verb.

A n
le loyer m

She has to pay the rent.
Elle doit payer le loyer.

Look at Language Plus on pages 283–308 for extra vocabulary.

B vb
louer

We are going to rent a car.
Nous allons louer une voiture.

repair vb
réparer

Can you repair them?
Vous pouvez les réparer?

repeat vb
répéter

Repeat after me, everyone.
Répétez après moi, tout le monde.

reply

reply can be a noun or a verb.

A n
la réponse f

I got no reply to my letter.
Je n'ai pas eu de réponse à ma lettre.

B vb
répondre

I hope you will reply soon.
J'espère que tu vas vite répondre.

report n
le bulletin scolaire m

I usually get a good report.
D'habitude, j'ai un bon bulletin scolaire.

republic n
la république f

France is a republic.
La France est une république.

request n
la demande f

another request
une autre demande

reservation n
la réservation f

I've got a reservation.
J'ai une réservation.

I'd like to make a reservation for this evening.
J'aimerais faire une réservation pour ce soir.

reserve

reserve can be a noun or a verb.

A n
le remplaçant m
la remplaçante f

I was reserve in the game last Saturday.
J'étais remplaçant dans le match de samedi dernier.

B vb
réserver

I'd like to reserve a table for tomorrow evening.
J'aimerais réserver une table pour demain soir.

reserved adj
réservé m adj
réservée f adj

a reserved seat
une place réservée

resolution n
la <u>résolution</u> f

Have you made any New Year's resolutions?
Tu as pris de bonnes résolutions pour l'année nouvelle?

resort n
la <u>station balnéaire</u> f

It's a resort on the Costa del Sol.
C'est une station balnéaire sur la Costa del Sol.

a ski resort
une station de ski

responsibility n
la <u>responsabilité</u> f

It's your responsibility.
C'est ta responsabilité.

> *What are the differences in spelling between the French and the English word?*

responsible adj
<u>responsable</u>

He's responsible for booking the tickets.
Il est responsable de la réservation des billets.

It's a responsible job.
C'est un poste à responsabilités.

> *The i in **responsible** becomes an a in the French word **responsable**.*

rest

> **rest** can be a noun or a verb.

Ⓐ n

1 le <u>repos</u> m

five minutes' rest
cinq minutes de repos

Can we have a rest?
On peut se reposer?

I need a rest.
J'ai besoin de me reposer.

2 *(remainder)*

the rest
le reste

I'll do the rest.
Je ferai le reste.

the rest of the money
le reste de l'argent

Ⓑ vb
se <u>reposer</u>

She's resting in her room.
Elle se repose dans sa chambre.

restaurant n
le <u>restaurant</u> m

We don't often go to restaurants.
Nous n'allons pas souvent au restaurant.

restaurant car n
le <u>wagon-restaurant</u> m

result n
le <u>résultat</u> m

my exam results
mes résultats d'examen

What was the result? – One-nil.
Quel a été le résultat? – Un à zéro.

retire vb
<u>prendre sa retraite</u>

He's going to retire.
Il va prendre sa retraite.

retired adj
<u>retraité</u> m adj
<u>retraitée</u> f adj

She's retired.
Elle est retraitée.

retirement n
la <u>retraite</u> f

return

> **return** can be a noun or a verb.

Ⓐ n

1 le <u>retour</u> m

A B C D E F G H I J K L M N O P Q **R** S T U V W X Y Z

Look at Language Plus on pages 283–308 for extra vocabulary.

after our return
à notre retour

the return journey
le voyage de retour

2 (*ticket*)
l'aller retour *m*

A return to Avignon, please.
Un aller retour pour Avignon, s'il vous plaît.

> 🔑
> **Many happy returns!**
> Bon anniversaire!

Ⓑ vb

1 (*come back*)
revenir

I've just returned from holiday.
Je viens de revenir de vacances.

2 (*give back*)
rendre

I've got to return this book to the library.
Je dois rendre ce livre à la bibliothèque.

reverse adj
inverse

in reverse order
dans l'ordre inverse

10 9 8 7 6

revise vb
réviser

I haven't started revising yet.
Je n'ai pas encore commencé à réviser.

revision n
les révisions *fpl*

Have you done a lot of revision?
Est-ce que tu as fait beaucoup de révisions?

revolution n
la révolution *f*

the French Revolution
la Révolution française

reward n
la récompense *f*

There's a €1000 reward.
Il y a une récompense de 1000€.

MISSING

€1000

rewind vb
rembobiner

Can you rewind the tape?
Tu peux rembobiner la cassette?

rhubarb n
la rhubarbe *f*

a rhubarb tart
une tarte à la rhubarbe

rhythm n
le rythme *m*

Which consonant is missing in the French word?

rib n
la côte *f*

ribbon n
le ruban *m*

rice n
le riz *m*

Would you like some rice?
Vous voulez du riz?

rich adj
riche

rid vb
to get rid of
se débarrasser de
I need to get rid of my chewing gum.
Je dois me débarrasser de mon
chewing gum.

ride n

> **ride** can be a noun or a verb.

Ⓐ n (*on horse*)
la promenade à cheval f
Would you like to go for a ride?
Tu veux faire une promenade à
cheval?

a bike ride
un tour en vélo
I'm going to go for a bike ride.
Je vais faire un tour en vélo.
Ⓑ vb (*on horse*)
monter à cheval
I'm learning to ride.
J'apprends à monter à cheval.

to ride a bike
faire du vélo
Can you ride a bike?
Tu sais faire du vélo?

rider n
le cavalier m
la cavalière f
She's a good rider.
C'est une bonne cavalière.

ridiculous adj
ridicule
Don't be ridiculous, Fiona!
Ne sois pas ridicule, Fiona!

riding n
l'équitation f

I like riding.
J'aime l'équitation.

to go riding
faire de l'équitation
I'd like to go riding.
Je voudrais faire de l'équitation.

riding school n
l'école d'équitation f

right

> **right** can be an adjective, an
> adverb or a noun.

Ⓐ adj
1 (*correct*)
bon m adj
bonne f adj
That's the right answer!
C'est la bonne réponse!
It isn't the right size.
Ce n'est pas la bonne taille.
We're on the right train.
Nous sommes dans le bon train.
2 (*true*)
vrai m adj
vraie f adj
That's right!
C'est vrai!
3 (*not left*)
droit m adj
droite f adj
my right hand
ma main droite

Look at Language Plus on pages 283–308 for extra vocabulary.

a
b
c
d
e
f
g
h
i
j
k
l
m
n
o
p
q
r
s
t
u
v
w
x
y
z

ⓑ adv

1 *(correctly)*

correctement

Am I pronouncing it right?
Est-ce que je prononce ça
correctement?

2 *(to the right)*

à droite

Turn right at the traffic lights.
Tournez à droite aux prochains feux.

ⓒ n *(not left)*

on the right
à droite

a step to the right
un pas à droite

> **You're right, Léa.**
> Tu as raison, Léa.
> **You're right, sir.**
> Vous avez raison, monsieur.
> **Right! Let's get started.**
> Bon! On commence.
> **Go right.**
> Allez à droite.

right-hand adj
the right-hand side
la droite

It's on the right-hand side.
C'est à droite.

right-handed adj
droitier *m adj*
droitière *f adj*

ring

> **ring** can be a noun or a verb.

ⓐ n

1 *(jewellery)*

la bague *f*

a gold ring
une bague en or

a diamond ring
une bague de diamants

a wedding ring
une alliance

2 *(circle)*

le cercle *m*

Stand in a ring.
Mettez-vous en cercle.

ⓑ vb

1 *(phone)*

appeler

You can ring me at home.
Tu peux m'appeler à la maison.

2 *(make sound)*

sonner

The phone's ringing.
Le téléphone sonne.

rink n

1 *(for ice-skating)*

la patinoire *f*

2 *(for roller-skating)*

la piste *f*

ripe adj
mûr *m adj*
mûre *f adj*

a ripe peach
une pêche mûre

risk n
le risque *m*

It's a big risk.
C'est un gros risque.

rival

> **rival** can be a noun or an
> adjective.

A n
le <u>rival</u> m
la <u>rivale</u> f

our rivals
nos rivaux

B adj
<u>rival</u> m adj
<u>rivale</u> f adj

a rival gang
une bande rivale

river n
la <u>rivière</u> f

across the river
de l'autre côté de la rivière

> **fleuve** is the French word for
> major rivers that flow into
> the sea. The five **fleuves** in
> France are the Seine, the
> Rhine, the Rhône, the Loire
> and the Garonne.

the river Amazon
le fleuve Amazone

Riviera n

the French Riviera
la Côte d'Azur

road n

1 la <u>route</u> f

There's traffic on the roads.
Il y a de la circulation sur les routes.

the main road
la grande route

2 (street)
la <u>rue</u> f

They live across the road.
Ils habitent de l'autre côté de la rue.

road sign n
le <u>panneau</u> m
(pl les panneaux)

Ducks crossing

roadworks npl
les <u>travaux</u> mpl

roast adj
<u>rôti</u> m adj
<u>rôtie</u> f adj

roast chicken
le poulet rôti

roast potatoes
les pommes de terre rôties

roast pork
le rôti de porc

roast beef
le rôti de bœuf

robber n
le <u>voleur</u> m

a bank robber
un cambrioleur de banques

robbery n
le <u>vol</u> m

a bank robbery
un hold-up

robot n
le <u>robot</u> m

rock n

1 (boulder)
le <u>rocher</u> m

Shall we sit on this rock?
On s'asseoit sur ce rocher?

2 (music)
le <u>rock</u> m

a rock concert
un concert de rock

He's a rock star.
C'est une rock star.

Look at Language Plus on pages 283–308 for extra vocabulary.

A
B
C
D
E
F
G
H
I
J
K
L
M
N
O
P
Q
R
S
T
U
V
W
X
Y
Z

3 (*sweet*)
le sucre d'orge *m*

a stick of rock
un bâton de sucre d'orge

rocket n
la fusée *f*

rod n
la canne à pêche *f*

role play n
le jeu de rôle *m*

We're going to do a role play.
Nous allons faire un jeu de rôle.

roll

> **roll** can be a noun or a verb.

A n (*bread*)
le petit pain *m*

B vb
rouler

Roll the truffles in cocoa powder.
Roulez les truffes dans la poudre de cacao.

> 🔑
> **Roll the dice.**
> Lance le dé.

roll call n
l'appel *m*

Rollerblade® n
le roller *m*

a pair of Rollerblades
une paire de rollers

rollercoaster n
les montagnes russes *fpl*

roller skates npl
les patins à roulettes *mpl*

roller-skating n
le patin à roulettes *m*

Do you want to go roller-skating?
Tu veux faire du patin à roulettes?

Roman n
the Romans
les Romains

Roman Catholic n
le/la catholique *m/f*

He's a Roman Catholic.
Il est catholique.

> *catholique* is not spelled with a capital letter.

romantic adj
romantique

roof n
le toit *m*

room n
1 la pièce *f*

the biggest room in the house
la plus grande pièce de la maison

2 (*bedroom*)
la chambre *f*

My room is the smallest.
Ma chambre est la plus petite.

a single room
une chambre pour une personne

a double room
une chambre pour deux personnes

3 (*in school*)
la salle *f*

the music room
la salle de musique

4 (*space*)
la place *f*

A
B
C
D
E
F
G
H
I
J
K
L
M
N
O
P
Q
R
S
T
U
V
W
X
Y
Z

Is there room for me?
Est-ce qu'il y a de la place pour moi?

rope n
la <u>corde</u> f

rose n
la <u>rose</u> f

a bunch of roses
un bouquet de roses

rotten adj

rotten weather
un temps pourri

rough adj
<u>violent</u> m adj

<u>violente</u> f adj

roughly adv
<u>à peu près</u>

It weighs roughly 20 kilos.
Ça pèse à peu près vingt kilos.

round

> **round** can be an adjective, a preposition or a noun.

A adj
<u>rond</u> m adj
<u>ronde</u> f adj

a round table
une table ronde

B prep
<u>autour de</u>

Sit round the table.
Asseyez-vous autour de la table.

It's just round the corner.
C'est tout près.

round here
près d'ici

Is there a chemist's round here?
Il y a une pharmacie près d'ici?

C n (of tournament)
la <u>manche</u> f

the next round
la prochaine manche

a round of golf
une partie de golf

roundabout n
le <u>manège</u> m

rounders n

Rounders is a bit like baseball.
Le "rounders" ressemble un peu au base-ball.

> **Rounders** is not played in France.

row

> **row** can be a noun or a verb.

A n
1 la <u>rangée</u> f

a row of houses
une rangée de maisons
2 (of seats)
le <u>rang</u> m

Our seats are in the front row.
Nos places se trouvent au premier rang.
3 (noise)
le <u>vacarme</u> m

What a row!
Quel vacarme!

B vb
<u>ramer</u>

Look at Language Plus on pages 283–308 for extra vocabulary.

I can row.
Je sais ramer.

> *row* can be pronounced in two ways – be careful to pick the right translation!

rowing boat n
le bateau à rames *m*

royal adj
royal *m adj*
royale *f adj*
the royal family
la famille royale

rubber n
la gomme *f*
Can I borrow your rubber?
Je peux emprunter ta gomme?

rubber band n
l'élastique *m*

rubbish

> *rubbish* can be a noun or an adjective.

A n
1 (*garbage*)
les ordures *fpl*
Where shall I put the rubbish?
Où est-ce que je mets les ordures?
2 (*nonsense*)
les bêtises *fpl*
Don't talk rubbish!
Ne dis pas de bêtises!
B adj (*useless*)
nul *m adj*
nulle *f adj*
They're a rubbish team!
Cette équipe est nulle!
The film was rubbish.
Le film était nul.

rubbish bin n
la poubelle *f*

rucksack n
le sac à dos *m*

rude adj
impoli *m adj*
impolie *f adj*
Don't be rude!
Ne sois pas impoli!
a rude word
un gros mot

rug n
1 (*carpet*)
le tapis *m*
a Persian rug
un tapis persan
2 (*blanket*)
la couverture *f*
a tartan rug
une couverture écossaise

> *The word for **tartan** is **écossaise**, which means "Scottish".*

rugby n
le rugby *m*
I play rugby.
Je joue au rugby.

ruin

> *ruin* can be a noun or a verb.

A n
la ruine *f*
the ruins of the castle
les ruines du château
B vb
abîmer
You'll ruin your shoes.
Tu vas abîmer tes chaussures.

rule n
1 (*of game*)
la règle *f*
the rules of the game
les règles du jeu

2 (*regulation*)
the rules
le règlement

It's against the rules.
C'est contre le réglement.

ruler n
la règle *f*

Can I borrow your ruler?
Je peux emprunter ta règle?

run

| run can be a noun or a verb. |

A n

Do you want to go for a run?
Tu veux courir?

I go for a run every morning.
Je cours tous les matins.

I did a ten-kilometre run.
J'ai couru dix kilomètres.

B vb

1 courir

Run!
Cours!

I ran two kilometres.
J'ai couru deux kilomètres.

2 (*organize*)
organiser

They run French courses.
Ils organisent des cours de français.

runner n
le coureur *m*
la coureuse *f*

runner-up n
le second *m*
la seconde *f*

running n
la course *f*

Running is my favourite sport.
Mon sport préféré, c'est la course.

rush

| rush can be a noun or a verb. |

A n
la hâte *f*

in a rush
à la hâte

B vb
se dépêcher

There's no need to rush.
Ce n'est pas la peine de se dépêcher.

rush hour n
les heures de pointe *fpl*

in the rush hour
aux heures de pointe

A B C D E F G H I J K L M N O P Q R S T U V W X Y Z

Look at Language Plus on pages 283–308 for extra vocabulary.

S

Sabbath n
1 (*Christian*)
le dimanche m
2 (*Jewish*)
le sabbat m

sack n
le sac m

sad adj
triste

saddle n
la selle f

sadly adv
tristement

safe adj
1 (*not dangerous*)
sans danger m, f, pl adj
Don't worry, it's perfectly safe.
Ne vous inquiétez pas, c'est absolument sans danger.
2 (*secure*)
sûr m adj
sûre f adj
Put it in a safe place.
Mets-le en lieu sûr.

safely adv
The parcel arrived safely.
Le paquet est bien arrivé.

safety n
la sécurité f

said vb, *see* **say**

sailing n
la voile f

His hobby is sailing.
Son passe-temps, c'est la voile.

to go sailing
faire de la voile

I'd like to go sailing.
J'aimerais faire de la voile.

sailing boat n
le voilier m

saint n
le saint m
la sainte f

salad n
la salade f

Would you like some salad?
Tu veux de la salade?

salad cream n
la mayonnaise f

salad dressing n
la vinaigrette f

salary n
le salaire m

sale n
"for sale"
"à vendre"

salmon n
le saumon m

salt n
le <u>sel</u> m

same

> **same** can be an adjective or a pronoun.

Ⓐ adj
<u>même</u>

the same class
la même classe

at the same time
en même temps

We've got the same colour T-shirts.
Nous avons des T-shirts de la même couleur.

Ⓑ pron

the same
pareil

They're exactly the same.
Ils sont exactement pareils.

It's not the same.
Ça n'est pas pareil.

> *Use **pareille** for something feminine.*

Our trainers are the same.
Nos baskets sont pareilles.

sand n
le <u>sable</u> m

sandal n
la <u>sandale</u> f

a pair of sandals
une paire de sandales

sand castle n
le <u>château de sable</u> m

sandwich n
le <u>sandwich</u> m

a cheese sandwich
un sandwich au fromage

sang vb, *see* **sing**

Santa Claus n
le <u>père Noël</u> m

> French children don't leave anything for Santa to eat!

satchel n
le <u>cartable</u> m

My satchel is black.
Mon cartable est noir.

satisfied adj
<u>satisfait</u> m adj
<u>satisfaite</u> f adj

Saturday n
le <u>samedi</u> m

It's Saturday today.
Aujourd'hui c'est samedi.

I've got a Saturday job.
Je travaille le samedi.

> **on Saturday**
> samedi
> **on Saturdays**
> le samedi
> **every Saturday**
> tous les samedis
> **last Saturday**
> samedi dernier
> **next Saturday**
> samedi prochain
>
> *Days of the week are not written with a capital letter in French.*

Look at Language Plus on pages 283–308 for extra vocabulary.

sauce n
la <u>sauce</u> f

saucepan n
la <u>casserole</u> f

saucer n
la <u>soucoupe</u> f

sausage n
la <u>saucisse</u> f

sausage and chips
une saucisse-frites

a sausage roll
un friand à la saucisse

save vb

1 (save up)

<u>mettre de l'argent de côté</u>

I'm saving for a new bike.
Je mets de l'argent de côté pour un nouveau vélo.

2 (rescue)

<u>sauver</u>

He saved my life.
Il m'a sauvé la vie.

3 (on computer)

<u>sauvegarder</u>

I saved the file.
J'ai sauvegardé le fichier.

to save time
gagner du temps

It'll save time.
Ça nous fera gagner du temps.

save up vb
<u>mettre de l'argent de côté</u>

I'm saving up for a new bike.
Je mets de l'argent de côté pour un nouveau vélo.

savoury adj
<u>salé</u> m adj
<u>salée</u> f adj

Is it sweet or savoury?
C'est sucré ou salé?

saw vb, see **see**

say vb
<u>dire</u>

I don't know how to say it in French.
Je ne sais pas comment ça se dit en français.

Say hello, Donald.
Dis bonjour, Donald.

Say hello, children.
Dites bonjour, les enfants.

What did you say?
Qu'est-ce que tu as dit?

I said no.
J'ai dit non.

How do you say "Sorry" in French?
Comment dit-on "Sorry" en français?

Say the words again, children.
Répétez ces mots, les enfants.

Say it after me, Aurélie.
Répète après moi, Aurélie.

Could you say that again, please?
Pourriez-vous répéter, s'il vous plaît?

scampi n
les <u>scampi</u> mpl

scared adj

to be scared
avoir peur

I'm scared of dogs.
J'ai peur des chiens.

I'm scared!
J'ai peur !

scarf n
l'écharpe f

a hat and scarf
un bonnet et une écharpe

scary adj
effrayant m adj
effrayante f adj

It was really scary.
C'était vraiment effrayant.

scenery n
le paysage m

school n
l'école f

I love school.
J'adore l'école.

the school library
la bibliothèque de l'école

I go to school with Marc.
Je vais à l'école avec Marc.

at school
à l'école

school bag n
le cartable m

schoolboy n
l'écolier m

schoolchildren npl
les écoliers mpl

schoolgirl n
l'écolière f

school holidays npl
les vacances scolaires fpl

school uniform n
l'uniforme scolaire m

 French children don't wear school uniform.

science n
la science f

scientist n
le chercheur m
la chercheuse f

scissors npl
les ciseaux mpl

a pair of scissors
une paire de ciseaux

scooter n
1 (for children)
la trottinette f
2 (motorbike)
le scooter m

score

score can be a noun or a verb.

Ⓐ n
le score m

What's the score?
Quel est le score ?

The score is three-nil.
Le score est de trois à zéro.

Ⓑ vb
1 (goal, point)
marquer

A B C D E F G H I J K L M N O P Q R S T U V W X Y Z

Look at Language Plus on pages 283–308 for extra vocabulary.

a

I scored a goal.
J'ai marqué un but.

b

2 (keep score)
compter les points

c

Who's going to score?
Qui va compter les points?

d

e

Scot n
l'Écossais m

f

l'Écossaise f

Scottish always has a capital
letter, but **écossais** doesn't.

g

Scotland n

h

l'Écosse f

Stirling is in Scotland.
Stirling est en Écosse.

i

j

When are you coming to
Scotland?

k

Quand est-ce que tu viens en
Écosse?

l

m

Tommy is from Scotland.
Tommy est écossais.

n

Elspeth is from Scotland.
Elspeth est écossaise.

o

p

in Scotland
en Écosse

q

to Scotland
en Écosse

r

I'm from Scotland.
Je suis écossais.

s

t

Scotsman n

u

l'Écossais m

Scotswoman n

v

l'Écossaise f

w

Scottish adj

x

écossais m adj
écossaise f adj

y

a Scottish accent
un accent écossais

z

Scout n
le scout m

I'm in the Scouts.
Je suis scout.

Guides and scouts are not as
common in France as they
are in Britain.

scrambled eggs npl
les œufs brouillés mpl

scrapbook n
l'album m

scream vb
hurler

Simon says "Scream!"
Jacques a dit "Hurlez!"

screen n
l'écran m

sea n
la mer f

I live by the sea.
J'habite au bord de la mer.

seafood n
les fruits de mer mpl

seagull n
la mouette f

seashore n
le bord de la mer m

on the seashore
au bord de la mer

seasick adj
I get seasick.
J'ai le mal de mer.

seaside n
le bord de la mer m
at the seaside
au bord de la mer

season n
la saison f
What's your favourite season?
Quelle est ta saison préférée?

season ticket n
la carte d'abonnement f

seat n
le siège m
I'd like a seat by the window.
Je voudrais un siège côté fenêtre.
Go back to your seat, Michel!
Retourne à ta place, Michel!

second

second can be an adjective or a
noun.

A adj
deuxième
on the second page
à la deuxième page
I came second.
Je suis arrivé deuxième.
B n
la seconde f
It'll only take a second.
Ça va prendre juste une
seconde.

the second of March
le deux mars

secondary school n
1 (for pupils 11–15)
le collège m
2 (for pupils 15–18)
le lycée m

In France pupils go to a
collège between the ages of
11 and 15, and then to a
lycée until the age of 18.

secret

secret can be a noun or an
adjective.

A n
le secret m
It's a secret.
C'est un secret.

Can you keep a secret?
Tu sais garder un secret?
in secret
en secret
B adj
secret m adj
secrète f adj
a secret passage
un passage secret

secretary n
le/la secrétaire m/f
She's a secretary.
Elle est secrétaire.

A
B
C
D
E
F
G
H
I
J
K
L
M
N
O
P
Q
R
S
T
U
V
W
X
Y
Z

Look at Language Plus on pages 283–308 for extra vocabulary.

a

You do not translate "a" when you say what someone's job is in French.

b

c

d

secretly n
secrètement

e

see vb
voir

f

I can see her car.
Je vois sa voiture.

g

Can you see the difference?
Est-ce que tu vois la différence?

h

We're going to see Granny and Grandpa.
On va voir Papi et Mamie.

i

j

I saw Denis yesterday.
J'ai vu Denis hier.

k

Have you seen Pascal?
Est-ce que tu as vu Pascal?

l

m

See you!
Salut!
See you tomorrow!
À demain!
See you soon!
À bientôt!

n

o

p

q

seed n
la graine f

r

sunflower seeds
des graines de tournesol

seem vb
There seems to be a problem.
Il semble y avoir un problème.

s

seen vb *see* **see**

t

seesaw n
le tapecul m

u

*tapecul is made up of the words **tape** (meaning "bang") and **cul** (meaning "bottom"). This is what a seesaw sometimes does to you.*

v

w

x

y

z

selfish adj
égoïste

Don't be so selfish, Charles.
Ne sois pas si égoïste, Charles.

self-service adj

The café is self-service.
Le café est un self-service.

a self-service restaurant
un self

sell vb
vendre

He's selling his car.
Il vend sa voiture.

The tickets are all sold out.
Il ne reste plus de billets.

*The English word "vendor" is related to the French word **vendre**. A vendor is someone who is selling something.*

Sellotape® n
le scotch® m

semicircle n
le demi-cercle m

Get into a semicircle.
Mettez-vous en demi-cercle.

semi-final n
la demi-finale f

send vb
envoyer

I'm going to send Magali a postcard.
Je vais envoyer une carte postale à Magali.

Send me an e-mail.
Envoie-moi un e-mail.

My penfriend has sent me some photos.
Ma correspondante m'a envoyé des photos.

senior adj
senior school
le lycée

sense n
sense of humour
le sens de l'humour

Our teacher has a sense of humour.
Notre maîtresse a le sens de l'humour.

He's got no sense of humour.
Il n'a aucun sens de l'humour.

sensible adj
raisonnable

Be sensible, Brigitte!
Sois raisonnable, Brigitte!

Be sensible, children!
Soyez raisonnables, les enfants!

raisonnable is similar to the English word "reasonable", but it has two **ns**. Can you see another difference?

sent vb, *see* send

sentence n
la phrase *f*

What does this sentence mean?
Que veut dire cette phrase?

separate adj
a separate piece of paper
une feuille différente

Put the green cards in a separate pile.
Fais une pile à part avec les cartes vertes.

September n
septembre *m*

September or October?
Septembre ou octobre?

My birthday's in September.
Mon anniversaire est en septembre.

> **in September**
> en septembre
> **the fifth of September**
> le cinq septembre
>
> *The months in French are not spelled with a capital letter.*

sequence n
l'ordre *m*
Put the pictures in sequence, Paul.
Mets les images dans l'ordre, Paul.

series n
la série *f*

a TV series
une série télévisée

serious adj
sérieux *m adj*
sérieuse *f adj*
You look very serious.
Tu as l'air sérieux.

A B C D E F G H I J K L M N O P Q R S T U V W X Y Z

Look at Language Plus on pages 283–308 for extra vocabulary.

a

b **Are you serious?**
Sérieusement?

c **serve** vb
<u>servir</u>

d **They're serving lunch now.**
On sert le déjeuner en ce moment.

e **It serves you right.**
C'est bien fait pour toi.

f **service** n
1 (*in restaurant*)
g le <u>service</u> m

h **Service is included.**
Le service est compris.
i **2** (*in church*)
l'<u>office</u> m

j **service charge** n
k le <u>service</u> m

l **There's no service charge.**
Le service est compris.

m **service station** n
la <u>station-service</u> f

n **serviette** n
o la <u>serviette</u> f

p **set** vb
<u>se coucher</u>

q **The sun is setting.**
Le soleil se couche.
r **to set the table**
mettre le couvert
s **Could you set the table?**
Tu peux mettre la table?
t

u **set off** vb
<u>partir</u>

v **What time are you setting off?**
À quelle heure tu pars?

w **settee** n
x le <u>canapé</u> m

y **settle down** vb
Settle down, children!
z Du calme, les enfants!

seven num
sept

seven euros
sept euros

She's seven.
Elle a sept ans.

*In English you can say **seven** or
seven years old. In French you
can only say **sept ans**.*

seventeen num
dix-sept

seventeen euros
dix-sept euros

He's seventeen.
Il a dix-sept ans.

*In English you can say **seventeen**
or **seventeen years old**. In French
you can only say **dix-sept ans**.*

seventeenth adj
dix-septième

on the seventeenth floor
au dix-septième étage

the seventeenth of August
le dix-sept août

seventh adj
septième

on the seventh floor
au septième étage

the seventh of August
le sept août

seventy num
soixante-dix

The French word consists of two numbers, what are they?

French boys shake hands with their friends when they arrive at school in the morning.

several pron
plusieurs

Several children are absent.
Plusieurs enfants sont absents.

sewing n
la couture f

I like sewing.
J'aime faire de la couture.

shade n
l'ombre f

It was 35 degrees in the shade.
Il faisait trente-cinq à l'ombre.

shadow n
l'ombre f

shake vb

to shake hands with somebody
serrer la main à quelqu'un

Simon says "Shake hands with your best friend!"
Jacques a dit "Serrez la main à votre meilleur ami!"

French people shake hands a lot.
Les Français se serrent beaucoup la main.

shall vb

Shall I shut the window?
Je ferme la fenêtre?

Shall I go first?
Je commence?

Shall I put the light on?
J'allume?

To ask if you should do something, you can make a question by changing your tone of voice. Try it!

shame n

What a shame! She can't come.
Quel dommage! Elle ne peut pas venir!

What a shame!
Quel dommage!

shampoo n
le shampooing m

a bottle of shampoo
une bouteille de shampooing

shape n
la forme f

Look at Language Plus on pages 283–308 for extra vocabulary.

a b c d e f g h i j k l m n o p q r s t u v w x y z

share vb
partager
I share a room with Léa.
Je partage ma chambre avec Léa.

sharp adj
coupant m adj
coupante f adj
Be careful, it's sharp.
Attention, c'est coupant.

she pron
elle
She's very nice.
Elle est très gentille.

sheep n
le mouton m

sheet n
le drap m
clean sheets
des draps propres
a sheet of paper
une feuille de papier

shelf n
l'étagère f

shell n
le coquillage m

shelves npl
les étagères fpl

she's = she is, she has

Shetland Islands npl
les îles Shetland fpl

shine vb
briller
The sun is shining.
Le soleil brille.

*The French word **briller** is related to the English word "brilliant", which can describe something that shines brightly.*

ship n
le bateau m
(pl les bateaux)

shirt n
1 (man's)
la chemise f
a white shirt
une chemise blanche
2 (footballer's)
le maillot m

shocking adj
choquant m adj
choquante f adj
It's shocking!
C'est choquant!

shoe n
la chaussure f
I've got new shoes.
J'ai de nouvelles chaussures.

shoe shop n
le magasin de chaussures m

shooting n
la chasse f
He goes shooting.
Il va à la chasse.

shop n
le magasin m
The shop is shut.
Le magasin est fermé.
a sports shop
un magasin de sports

shop assistant n
le vendeur m
la vendeuse f
She's a shop assistant.
Elle est vendeuse.

You do not translate "a" when you say what someone's job is in French.

shopkeeper n
le commerçant m
la commerçante f

shopping n
les courses fpl

Can you get the shopping from the car?
Tu peux aller chercher les courses dans la voiture?

If you're shopping for food you say Je fais les courses. If you're looking round the shops you say Je fais les magasins.

I do the shopping for my granny.
Je fais les courses pour ma grandmère.

I go shopping with my friends.
Je fais les magasins avec mes amies.

shopping bag n
le sac à provisions m

shopping centre n
le centre commercial m

short adj
1 (in length)
court m adj
courte f adj

a short skirt
une jupe courte

short hair
les cheveux courts

2 (in time)
petit m adj
petite f adj

a short walk
une petite promenade

shorts npl
le short m

My shorts are green.
Mon short est vert.

a pair of shorts
un short

short is a singular word in French.

short-sighted adj
myope

shoulder n
l'épaule f

should vb

You should try it.
Tu devrais essayer.

You shouldn't do that.
Tu ne devrais pas faire ça.

shout vb
crier

Don't shout, children!
Ne criez pas, les enfants!

show vb
montrer

Show me!
Montrez-moi!

Shall I show you the photos?
Je te montre les photos?

shower n
la douche f

I'm going to have a shower.
Je vais prendre une douche.

Shrove Tuesday n
le mardi gras m

Shrove Tuesday is the same as **Pancake Day** and is celebrated in France as well. French children dress up and eat pancakes (**crêpes**).

Look at Language Plus on pages 283–308 for extra vocabulary.

a
b
c
d
e
f
g
h
i
j
k
l
m
n
o
p
q
r
s
t
u
v
w
x
y
z

shrug vb

Simon says "Shrug your shoulders!"
Jacques a dit "Haussez les épaules!"

shuffle vb

You have to shuffle the cards.
Il faut battre les cartes.

shut

shut can be a verb or an adjective.

Ⓐ vb
fermer

Shut your books, children.
Fermez vos livres, les enfants.

Open your mouth and shut your eyes.
Ouvre la bouche et ferme les yeux.

What time do the shops shut?
Les magasins ferment à quelle heure?

🔑

Shut up!
Tais-toi!

Ⓑ adj
fermé m adj
fermée f adj

The door is shut.
La porte est fermée.

The shop is shut.
Le magasin est fermé.

shutters npl
les volets mpl

shy adj
timide

sick adj
malade

He is sick.
Il est malade.

to be sick
vomir

I'm going to be sick.
Je vais vomir.

I feel sick.
J'ai envie de vomir.

side n

1 (of object, building, car)
le côté m

on this side
de ce côté

It's on this side of the street.
C'est de ce côté de la rue.

It's on the other side.
C'est de l'autre côté.

2 (team)
l'équipe f

He's on my side.
Il est dans mon équipe.

sightseeing n
le tourisme m

We're going to go sightseeing.
Nous allons faire du tourisme.

sign

sign can be a noun or a verb.

Ⓐ n
a road sign
un panneau

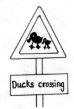

Ducks crossing

Ⓑ vb
signer

Sign here, please.
Signez ici, s'il vous plaît.

signal n
le signal m
(pl les signaux)

signature n
la signature f

sign language n
le langage des signes m

silence n
le silence m

silent adj
silencieux m adj
silencieuse f adj

silk adj
en soie

a silk scarf
un foulard en soie

silly adj
bête

Don't be silly, Nadège!
Ne sois pas bête, Nadège!

silver

silver can be a noun or an adjective.

A n
l'argent m

gold and silver
l'or et l'argent

B adj
en argent

a silver chain
une chaîne en argent

a silver medal
une médaille d'argent

Simon says n
Jacques a dit

simple adj
simple

It's very simple.
C'est très simple.

since prep
depuis

since Christmas
depuis Noël

since then
depuis ce moment-là

sincerely adv
Yours sincerely ...
Cordialement ...

sing vb
chanter

I sing in the choir.
Je chante dans la chorale.

Sing everyone!
Allez, chantez!

singer n
le chanteur m
la chanteuse f

single

single can be an adjective or a noun.

A adj
a single room
une chambre pour une personne
B n (ticket)
l'aller simple m

A single to Toulouse, please.
Un aller simple pour Toulouse, s'il vous plaît.

singular n
le singulier m

in the singular
au singulier

Look at Language Plus on pages 283–308 for extra vocabulary.

a
b
c
d
e
f
g
h
i
j
k
l
m
n
o
p
q
r
s
t
u
v
w
x
y
z

sink n
l'évier m

sir n
monsieur m

Yes sir.
Oui, Monsieur.

sister n
la sœur f

my little sister
ma petite sœur

I've got one sister.
J'ai une sœur.

I haven't got a sister.
Je n'ai pas de sœur.

> 🔑
> **Have you got any brothers or sisters?**
> Tu as des frères et sœurs?

sit vb
s'asseoir

I want to sit beside my friend.
Je veux m'asseoir à côté de mon amie.

Can I sit here?
Je peux m'asseoir ici?

Jean-Pierre sits next to Christelle.
Jean-Pierre s'assoit à côté de Christelle.

sit down vb
s'asseoir

Sit down, Mathilde.
Assieds-toi, Mathilde.

You can sit down now, Mathieu.
Tu peux t'asseoir maintenant, Mathieu.

> 🔑
> **Sit down, children.**
> Asseyez-vous, les enfants.

site n
1 (campsite)
le camping m

2 (website)
le site web m

sitting room n
le salon m

situation n
la situation f

six num
six

six euros
six euros

> 🔑
> **She's six.**
> Elle a six ans.
>
> *In English you can say six or six years old. In French you can only say six ans.*

sixteen num
seize

sixteen euros
seize euros

> 🔑
> **He's sixteen.**
> Il a seize ans.
>
> *In English you can say sixteen or sixteen years old. In French you can only say seize ans.*

sixteenth adj
seizième

on the sixteenth floor
au seizième étage

> 🔑
> **the sixteenth of August**
> le seize août

sixth adj
sixième

on the sixth floor
au sixième étage

the sixth of August
le six août

sixth form n
le lycée n

sixty num
soixante

My aunt is sixty.
Ma tante a soixante ans.

*In English you can say **sixty** or **sixty years old**. In French you can only say **soixante ans**.*

size n
la taille f

It's the right size.
C'est la bonne taille.

skate vb
faire du patin à glace

I like to skate.
J'aime faire du patin à glace.

skateboard n
le skateboard m

skateboarding n
le skateboard m

I like skateboarding.
J'aime le skateboard.

I go skateboarding with Kieran.
Je fais du skateboard avec Kieran.

skating n
le patin à glace m

I like skating.
J'aime le patin à glace.

I go skating.
Je fais du patin à glace.

skeleton n
le squelette m

ski

ski can be a verb or a noun.

A vb
skier

Can you ski?
Tu sais skier?

B n
le ski m

ski boots npl
les chaussures de ski fpl

ski lift n
le remonte-pente m

ski slope n
la piste de ski f

skiing n
le ski m

Do you like skiing?
Tu aimes le ski?

I'd like to go skiing.
J'aimerais faire du ski.

I'm going on a skiing holiday.
Je vais aux sports d'hiver.

skin n
la peau f

skinny adj
maigre

A B C D E F G H I J K L M N O P Q R S T U V W X Y Z

Look at Language Plus on pages 283–308 for extra vocabulary.

skipping rope n
la corde à sauter f

skirt n
la jupe f

a black skirt
une jupe noire

sky n
le ciel m

The sky is blue.
Le ciel est bleu.

slam vb
claquer

Don't slam the door.
Ne claque pas la porte.

sledge n
la luge f

sledging n

Let's go sledging!
Allons faire de la luge!

sleep vb
dormir

My cat sleeps in a box.
Mon chat dort dans une boîte.

Did you sleep well, Cyril?
Tu as bien dormi, Cyril?

sleeping bag n
le sac de couchage m

sleepover n

My friend is coming for a sleepover tonight.
Mon amie vient dormir chez moi ce soir.

We're going to Jasmine's for a sleepover.
On va dormir chez Jasmine.

sleepy adj

I'm sleepy.
J'ai sommeil.

sleeve n
la manche f

a shirt with long sleeves
une chemise à manches longues

a shirt with short sleeves
une chemise à manches courtes

slice n
la tranche f

slide n
1 (in playground)
le toboggan m
2 (hair slide)
la barrette f
3 (photo)
la diapositive f

slight adj
léger m adj
légère f adj

a slight problem
un léger problème

slightly adv
légèrement

slim

slim can be an adjective or a verb.

A adj
mince

You're slim!
Tu es mince!
B vb (be on a diet)
faire un régime

I'm slimming.
Je fais un régime.

slipper n
le chausson m

a pair of slippers
des chaussons

slow adj
lent m adj
lente f adj

The music is too slow.
La musique est trop lente.

slowly adv
lentement

Could you speak more slowly?
Vous pouvez parler plus
lentement?

smack n
la tape f

small adj
petit m adj
petite f adj

smart adj
1 chic m, f, pl adj

smart clothes
des vêtements chic

2 (clever)
intelligent m adj
intelligente f adj

She's very smart.
Elle est très intelligente.

smell

> **smell** can be a noun or a verb.

A n
l'odeur f

a nice smell
une bonne odeur

B vb
sentir

Mmm, that smells nice!
Mmm, ça sent bon!

smile

> **smile** can be a noun or a verb.

A n
le sourire m

a beautiful smile
un beau sourire

B vb
sourire

Why are you smiling?
Pourquoi tu souris?

smoke vb
fumer

I don't smoke.
Je ne fume pas.

smoking n

Smoking is bad for you.
Le tabac est mauvais pour la santé.

"no smoking"
"défense de fumer"

snack n
le casse-croûte m

You can get a snack in the canteen.
On peut s'acheter un casse-croûte à
la cantine.

snack bar n
le snack-bar m

snail n
l'escargot m

snake n
le serpent m

snooker n
le billard m

I play snooker.
Je joue au billard.

Look at Language Plus on pages 283–308 for extra vocabulary.

A
B
C
D
E
F
G
H
I
J
K
L
M
N
O
P
Q
R
S
T
U
V
W
X
Y
Z

snow

snow can be a noun or a verb.

Ⓐ n
la neige f

Ⓑ vb
neiger

It's going to snow.
Il va neiger.

It snows a lot in the mountains.
Il neige beaucoup à la montagne.

> 🔑
> **It's snowing.**
> Il neige.

snowball n
la boule de neige f

lots of snowballs
beaucoup de boules de neige

snowflake n
le flocon de neige m

snowman n
le bonhomme de neige m

I'm going to make a snowman.
Je vais faire un bonhomme de neige.

so

so can be an adverb or a conjunction.

Ⓐ adv

1 si

Don't eat so fast!
Ne mange pas si vite!

2 (too)
tellement

You talk so fast.
Tu parles tellement vite.

It's so difficult.
C'est tellement difficile.

I love you so much.
Je t'aime tellement.

Ⓑ conj
alors

It's Luc's birthday, so I've got him a present.
C'est l'anniversaire de Luc, alors je lui ai acheté un cadeau.

> 🔑
> **So do I.**
> Moi aussi.
> **So have I.**
> Moi aussi.
> **So am I.**
> Moi aussi.
> **I think so.**
> Je crois.
> **I hope so.**
> J'espère bien.

soap n
le savon m

soccer n
le football m

sock n
la chaussette f

I'm wearing white socks.
Je porte des chaussettes blanches.

sofa n
le canapé m

soft adj
1 (voice, texture)
doux m adj
douce f adj
2 (pillow, bed, ball)
mou m adj
molle f adj

soft drink n
la boisson non alcoolisée f

soil n
la terre f

sold adj
vendu m adj
vendue f adj

soldier n
le soldat m

He's a soldier.
Il est soldat.

You do not translate "a" when you say what someone's job is in French.

some

some can be an adjective or a pronoun.

Ⓐ adj
1 (a certain amount of)

*Some can be **du**, **de la**, **de l'** and **des** in the same way that **the** can be **le**, **la**, **l'** or **les**.*

du
Would you like some bread?
Voulez-vous du pain?

de la
Would you like some soup?
Voulez-vous de la soupe?

de l'
Have you got some mineral water?
Avez-vous de l'eau minérale?

des
I've got some sweets.
J'ai des bonbons.
2 (certain)
des
Some children are absent.
Il y a des enfants absents.

Ⓑ pron
1 (certain ones)
certains mpl pron
certaines fpl pron
some of my friends
certains de mes amis
Have you got all her books? – I've got some.
Tu as tous ses livres? – J'en ai certains.
2 (some, not all)
quelques-uns mpl pron
quelques-unes fpl pron
I've got some, but not many.
J'en ai quelques-uns, mais pas beaucoup.
3 en

*The word **en** can mean "some of them", or "some of it". Notice its position in the sentences.*

Chips? – No thanks, I've got some.
Des frites? – Non merci, j'en ai déjà.

A
B
C
D
E
F
G
H
I
J
K
L
M
N
O
P
Q
R
S
T
U
V
W
X
Y
Z

Look at Language Plus on pages 283–308 for extra vocabulary.

a
b
c
d
e
f
g
h
i
j
k
l
m
n
o
p
q
r
s
t
u
v
w
x
y
z

I've got a bar of chocolate. Do you want some?
J'ai une barre de chocolat. Tu en veux?

I've got some.
J'en ai.
Would you like some?
Tu en veux?

somebody pron
quelqu'un

Somebody is going to win £100!
Quelqu'un va gagner cent livres!

someone pron
quelqu'un

Someone is going to win £100!
Quelqu'un va gagner cent livres!

something pron
quelque chose

Are you looking for something?
Tu cherches quelque chose?

something special
quelque chose de spécial

something hot
quelque chose de chaud

I can see something green.
Je vois quelque chose de vert.

sometimes adv
quelquefois

sometimes, but not very often
quelquefois, mais pas très souvent

somewhere adv
quelque part

It's somewhere in the classroom.
C'est quelque part dans la classe.

son n
le fils m

her son
son fils

song n
la chanson f

We're going to sing a song.
Nous allons chanter une chanson.

I know some French songs.
Je connais des chansons françaises.

soon adv
bientôt

It'll soon be lunchtime.
C'est bientôt l'heure du déjeuner.

very soon
très bientôt

as soon as possible
aussitôt que possible
Write soon!
Écris-moi vite!

sorcerer n
le sorcier m

sore adj

It's sore.
Ça fait mal.

My head is sore.
J'ai mal à la tête.

sorry adj
désolé *m adj*
désolée *f adj*

I'm really sorry.
Je suis vraiment désolé.

I'm sorry I'm late.
Je suis désolé d'être en retard.

I'm sorry, I can't.
Je suis désolé, je ne peux pas.

Sorry!
Pardon!

sort n
la sorte *f*

What sort of bike have you got?
Quelle sorte de vélo as-tu?

sound

sound can be a noun or a verb.

A n
1 (*noise*)
le bruit *m*

Don't make a sound!
Pas un bruit!

2 (*volume*)
le son *m*

Can I turn the sound down?
Je peux baisser le son?

B vb

That sounds interesting.
Ça a l'air intéressant.

That sounds like a good idea.
C'est une bonne idée.

soup n
la soupe *f*

vegetable soup
la soupe aux légumes

sour adj
aigre

south

south can be an adjective or a noun.

A adj
sud *m, f, pl adj*

the south coast
la côte sud

B n
le sud *m*

in the south
dans le sud

the South of France
le sud de la France

Arles is in the South of France.
Arles est dans le sud de la France.

southern adj
Southern England
le sud de l'Angleterre

South Pole n
le pôle Sud *m*

South Wales n
le sud du Pays de Galles *m*

souvenir n
le souvenir *m*

a souvenir shop
une boutique de souvenirs

space n
1 (*room*)
la place *f*

There's lots of space.
Il y a beaucoup de place.

2 (*gap*)
l'espace *m*

Leave a space for a picture.
Laissez un espace pour le dessin.

3 (*in game*)
la case *f*

Go back three spaces.
Recule de trois cases.

4 (*outer space*)
l'espace *m*

Look at Language Plus on pages 283–308 for extra vocabulary.

A B C D E F G H I J K L M N O P Q R S T U V W X Y Z

spaceship n
le vaisseau spatial *m*

spade n
1 (*shovel*)
la pelle *f*
a bucket and spade
un seau et une pelle
2 (*in cards*)
spades
le pique
the ace of spades
l'as de pique

Spain n
l'Espagne *f*

Spanish

> Spanish can be an adjective or a noun.

Ⓐ adj
espagnol *m adj*
espagnole *f adj*
He's Spanish.
Il est espagnol.
She's Spanish.
Elle est espagnole.
Ⓑ n (*language*)
l'espagnol *m*

> **Spanish** always has a capital letter, but **espagnol** doesn't.

spare room n
la chambre d'amis *f*

spare time n
le temps libre *m*

What do you do in your spare time?
Qu'est-ce que tu fais pendant ton temps libre?

sparkling adj
pétillant *m adj*
pétillante *f adj*
a bottle of sparkling water
une bouteille d'eau pétillante

sparkling wine
le mousseux

speak vb
parler
Please could you speak more slowly.
Vous pouvez parler plus lentement, s'il vous plaît?

> 🗝
> **I speak French.**
> Je parle français.
> **Do you speak English?**
> Vous parlez anglais?

special adj
spécial *m adj*
spéciale *f adj*

speciality n
la spécialité *f*

specially adv
surtout

It rains a lot, specially in winter.
Il pleut beaucoup, surtout en hiver.

spectator n
le spectateur m
la spectatrice f

speech n
le discours m

speed n
la vitesse f

a ten-speed bike
un vélo à dix vitesses

speedboat n
la vedette f

spell vb
1 (in writing)
écrire
How do you spell that?
Comment ça s'écrit?

> You can also say **Ça s'écrit
> comment?** or **Comment est-ce
> que ça s'écrit?**

2 (out loud)
épeler
Can you spell that please?
Est-ce que vous pouvez l'épeler, s'il
vous plaît?

spelling n
l'orthographe f
a spelling mistake
une faute d'orthographe

spend vb
1 (money)
dépenser
I spent £10 on presents.
J'ai dépensé dix livres en cadeaux.

2 (time)
passer
**We are going to spend two weeks
in France.**
Nous allons passer deux semaines
en France.

spicy adj
épicé m adj
épicée f adj

spider n
l'araignée f

spinach n
les épinards mpl

spite n
in spite of
malgré
in spite of the weather
malgré le temps

split vb
1 (divide)
se séparer
Split into two groups.
Séparez-vous en deux groupes.
2 (share)
partager
Let's split the money between us.
Partageons l'argent entre nous.

spoiled adj
gâté m adj
gâtée f adj
a spoiled child
un enfant gâté

spoilsport n
le/la trouble-fête m, f, pl
Don't be a spoilsport!
Ne joue pas les trouble-fête!

spoilt adj
gâté m adj
gâtée f adj

A B C D E F G H I J K L M N O P Q R **S** T U V W X Y Z

a spoilt child
un enfant gâté

sponge n
l'éponge f

sponge bag n
la trousse de toilette f

sponge cake n
le biscuit de Savoie m

sponsor vb
parrainer

Twenty people are sponsoring me.
Vingt personnes me parrainent.

> Getting sponsored for
> charity is not very common
> in France.

spoon n
la cuillère f

I haven't got a spoon.
Je n'ai pas de cuillère.

sport n
le sport m

What's your favourite sport?
Quel est ton sport préféré?

It's my favourite sport.
C'est mon sport préféré.

What sports do you play?
Qu'est-ce que tu fais comme sport?

sports bag n
le sac de sport m

sports car n
la voiture de sport f

spot

> **spot** can be a noun or a verb.

Ⓐ n
1 (dot)
le pois m

a red dress with white spots
une robe rouge à pois blancs
2 (pimple)
le bouton m

He's covered in spots.
Il est couvert de boutons.
Ⓑ vb
trouver

Can you spot the odd one out?
Trouvez-vous l'intrus?

spring n
le printemps m

It's the first day of spring.
C'est le premier jour du printemps.

in spring
au printemps

springtime n
le printemps m

in springtime
au printemps

sprouts npl
les choux de Bruxelles mpl

square n
1 (shape)
le carré m

a square and a triangle
un carré et un triangle

2 (*in town*)
la place *f*

There's a statue in the middle of the square.
Il y a une statue au centre de la place.

squash n
1 (*drink*)
orange squash
l'orangeade
2 (*sport*)
le squash *m*

I play squash.
Je joue au squash.

squirrel n
l'écureuil *m*

stable n
l'écurie *f*

stack n
la pile *f*

a stack of books
une pile de livres

stadium n
le stade *m*

staff n
1 (*in primary school*)
les instituteurs *mpl*
2 (*in secondary school*)
les professeurs *mpl*

staffroom n
la salle des profs *f*

staircase n
l'escalier *m*

stairs npl
l'escalier *m*

Go down the stairs.
Descends l'escalier.

> *escalier is a singular word.*

stamp

> **stamp** can be a noun or a verb.

A n
le timbre *m*

a French stamp
un timbre français

My hobby is stamp collecting.
Je collectionne les timbres.
B vb
taper du pied

Stamp your feet, everyone!
Tapez des pieds, tout le monde!

stamp album n
l'album de timbres *m*

stamp collection n
la collection de timbres *f*

stand vb

Stand in a line.
Mettez-vous en rang.

Stand over there, Alain.
Mets-toi là, Alain.

stand for vb
être l'abréviation de

"SVP" stands for "s'il vous plaît".
"SVP" est l'abréviation de "s'il vous plaît".

> *What are the two differences in the spelling of the French word abréviation and the English word abbreviation?*

stand up vb
se lever

A
B
C
D
E
F
G
H
I
J
K
L
M
N
O
P
Q
R
S
T
U
V
W
X
Y
Z

Look at Language Plus on pages 283–308 for extra vocabulary.

a

Stand up, Élodie!
Lève-toi, Élodie!

b

Stand up, children!
Levez-vous, les enfants!

c

star n

d

1 (*in sky*)
l'**étoile** f

e

the moon and the stars
la lune et les étoiles

f

g

h

i

j

2 (*person*)
la **vedette** f

k

He's a TV star.
C'est une vedette de la télé.

l

start

m

> **start** can be a verb or a noun.

n

A vb

o

1 (*begin*)
commencer

p

What time does it start?
Ça commence à quelle heure?

q

It starts with a P.
Ça commence par un P.

r

I'll start again.
Je recommence.

s

> When **start** is followed by another
> verb it is translated by
> **commencer à**.

t

u

Let's start playing.
On commence à jouer.

v

You can start writing now.
Vous pouvez commencer à écrire
maintenant.

w

x

Don't start being silly, Anne.
Ne commence pas à faire l'imbécile,

y

Anne.

z

🔑

Let's start.
On commence.
Start now, children.
Commencez maintenant, les
enfants.
Fleur, you start.
Commence, Fleur.

2 (*set up*)
créer

We want to start a French club.
On veut créer un club de français.

B n

1 le **début** m

at the start of December
début décembre

Shall we make a start?
On commence?

2 (*of race*)
le **départ** m

starter n
l'**entrée** f

starve vb

I'm starving!
Je meurs de faim!

station n
la **gare** f

Where is the station?
Où est la gare?

statue n
la **statue** f

stay

> **stay** can be a verb or a noun.

A vb
1 (remain)
rester

Stay here, Michelle!
Reste ici, Michelle!

Stay in the garden, children.
Restez dans le jardin, les enfants.
2 (spend the night)
loger

We're going to stay with friends.
Nous allons loger chez des amis.

Where are you staying?
Où est-ce que vous logez?

We stayed in Paris for three days.
Nous avons passé trois jours à Paris.
B n
le séjour m

my stay in France
mon séjour en France

stay in vb
rester à la maison

I'm staying in tonight.
Ce soir je reste à la maison.

steak n
le steak m

I'd like steak and chips.
Je voudrais un steak-frites.

steal vb
voler

Who's stolen my pencil case?
Qui a volé ma trousse?

step n
1 (pace)
le pas m

a step backwards
un pas en arrière

Take a step forward, boys.
Faites un pas en avant, les garçons.

2 (stair)
la marche f

Mind the step.
Attention à la marche.

stepbrother n
le demi-frère m

his stepbrother
son demi-frère

stepfather n
le beau-père m

my stepfather
mon beau-père

stepmother n
la belle-mère f

my stepmother
ma belle-mère

stepsister n
la demi-sœur f

her stepsister
sa demi-sœur

stew n
le ragoût m

stewardess n
l'hôtesse de l'air f

stick vb
coller

Stick the stamps on the envelope.
Collez les timbres sur l'enveloppe.

stick out vb

Don't stick out your tongue!
Ne tire pas la langue!

sticker n
l'autocollant m

still

> **still** can be an adverb or an adjective.

A adv
encore

A
B
C
D
E
F
G
H
I
J
K
L
M
N
O
P
Q
R
S
T
U
V
W
X
Y
Z

Look at Language Plus on pages 283–308 for extra vocabulary.

You've still got two cards.
Tu as encore deux cartes.

I'm still hungry.
J'ai encore faim.

B adj

Keep still, Charlotte!
Ne bouge pas, Charlotte!

Sit still, David!
Reste tranquille, David!

stitch n
le point de suture m

I've got five stitches.
J'ai cinq points de suture.

stomach n
l'estomac m

stomachache n

I've got stomachache.
J'ai mal au ventre.

stone n

1 (rock)
la pierre f

a stone wall
un mur en pierre

2 (in weight)

I weigh five stone.
Je pèse trente kilos.

> In France, weight is given in
> kilos. A **stone** is about
> 6.3 kg.

stool n
le tabouret m

stop

stop can be a verb or a noun.

A vb
arrêter

Stop, that's enough!
Arrête, ça suffit!

Stop talking, children.
Arrêtez de parler, les enfants.

Stop it!
Arrête!

B n
l'arrêt m

a bus stop
un arrêt de bus

storey n
l'étage m

a three-storey building
un immeuble à trois étages

storm n

1 (with strong winds)
la tempête f

2 (thunderstorm)
l'orage m

stormy adj

stormy weather
un temps orageux

story n
l'histoire f

I'm going to tell you a story.
Je vais vous raconter une histoire.

stove n
la <u>cuisinière</u> f

straight

> **straight** can be an adjective or an adverb.

Ⓐ adj
1 <u>droit</u> m adj
<u>droite</u> f adj

a straight line
une ligne droite
2 (hair)
<u>raide</u>

I've got straight hair.
J'ai les cheveux raides.
Ⓑ adv

straight away
tout de suite

straight on
tout droit

> 🔑
> **Go straight on.**
> Allez tout droit.

strange adj
<u>bizarre</u>
That's strange!
C'est bizarre!

stranger n
l'<u>inconnu</u> m
l'<u>inconnue</u> f

Don't talk to strangers.
Ne parle pas aux inconnus.

I'm a stranger here.
Je ne suis pas d'ici.

strap n
le <u>bracelet</u> m

I need a new strap for my watch.
J'ai besoin d'un nouveau bracelet pour ma montre.

straw n
la <u>paille</u> f

strawberry n
la <u>fraise</u> f

strawberry jam
la confiture de fraises

a strawberry ice cream
une glace à la fraise

stream n
le <u>ruisseau</u> m
(pl les ruisseaux)

street n
la <u>rue</u> f

in the street
dans la rue

stretch vb
Stretch up high!
Étirez-vous!

Stretch out your arms!
Tendez les bras!

strict adj
<u>strict</u> m adj
<u>stricte</u> f adj

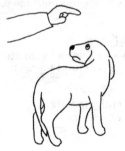

strike n
la <u>grève</u> f
They are on strike.
Ils sont en grève.

striker n
le <u>buteur</u> m

A
B
C
D
E
F
G
H
I
J
K
L
M
N
O
P
Q
R
S
T
U
V
W
X
Y
Z

Look at Language Plus on pages 283–308 for extra vocabulary.

string n

1 la ficelle f

a piece of string
un bout de ficelle

2 (of violin, guitar)
la corde f

stripe n
la rayure f

stripy adj
rayé m adj
rayée f adj

a stripy shirt
une chemise rayée

strong adj
fort m adj
forte f adj

She's very strong.
Elle est très forte.

student n
l'étudiant m
l'étudiante f

study vb

My sister's studying for her exams.
Ma sœur révise pour ses examens.

stuff n
les affaires fpl

Have you got all your stuff?
Est-ce que tu as toutes tes affaires?

stuffy adj

It's stuffy in here.
On étouffe ici.

stupid adj
stupide

a stupid joke
une plaisanterie stupide

subject n
la matière f

What's your favourite subject?
Quelle est ta matière préférée?

subtitles npl
les sous-titres mpl

a French film with English subtitles
un film français avec des sous-titres en anglais

subtract vb
retrancher

Subtract 3 from 5.
Retranchez trois à cinq.

suburb n
la banlieue f

a suburb of Paris
une banlieue de Paris

They live in the suburbs.
Ils habitent en banlieue.

success n
le succès m

another wonderful success
encore un formidable succès

The party was a great success.
La soirée était très réussie.

such adv
si

such nice people
des gens si gentils

such a long journey
un voyage si long

such as
comme

towns such as Avignon and Arles
des villes comme Avignon et Arles

sudden adj
soudain m adj
soudaine f adj

a sudden change
un changement soudain

suede n
le daim m

a suede jacket
une veste en daim

sugar n
le sucre m

Do you take sugar?
Est-ce que vous prenez du sucre?

More sugar?
Encore un peu de sucre?

suggestion n
la suggestion f

Have you got any suggestions?
Vous avez des suggestions?

suit

> *suit* can be a noun or a verb.

Ⓐ n
1 (man's)
le costume m
2 (woman's)
le tailleur m
Ⓑ vb
That dress suits you.
Cette robe te va bien.

suitcase n
la valise f

sums npl
le calcul m

She's good at sums.
Elle est bonne en calcul.

> *calcul* is a singular word.

summer n
l'été m

We're going to France this summer.
Nous allons en France cet été.

in summer
en été
this summer
cet été
last summer
l'été dernier

summer holidays npl
les vacances d'été fpl

in the summer holidays
pendant les vacances d'été

summertime n
l'été m

in summertime
en été

summit n
le sommet m

sun n
le soleil m

in the sun
au soleil

sunbathe vb
se faire bronzer
I like sunbathing.
J'aime me faire bronzer.

Look at Language Plus on pages 283–308 for extra vocabulary.

sunburnt adj

I got sunburnt.
J'ai attrapé un coup de soleil.

sun cream n

la crème solaire f

Sunday n

le dimanche m

It's Sunday today.
Aujourd'hui, c'est dimanche.

on Sunday
dimanche
on Sundays
le dimanche
every Sunday
tous les dimanches
last Sunday
dimanche dernier
next Sunday
dimanche prochain

Days of the week are not written with a capital letter in French.

Sunday school n

le catéchisme m

In France **le catéchisme** is on Wednesday mornings, when most children don't have ordinary school.

sunflower n

le tournesol m

sunglasses npl

les lunettes de soleil fpl

a pair of sunglasses
une pair de lunettes de soleil

sunny adj
It's a sunny day.
C'est une belle journée.

It's sunny.
Il fait du soleil.

sunset n

le coucher du soleil m

at sunset
au coucher du soleil

sunshine n

le soleil m

lots of sunshine
beaucoup de soleil

super adj
formidable

supermarket n
le supermarché m

supper n
le dîner m

supply teacher n

le suppléant m

la suppléante f

She's a supply teacher.
Elle est suppléante.

You do not translate "a" when you say what someone's job is in French.

support vb
être supporter de

I support Manchester United.
Je suis supporter de Manchester United.

What team do you support?
Tu es supporter de quelle équipe?

supporter n
le supporter *m*

a Liverpool supporter
un supporter de Liverpool

suppose vb
imaginer

I suppose he's late.
J'imagine qu'il est en retard.

You're not supposed to do that, Thérèse.
Tu n'es pas censée faire ça, Thérèse.

sure adj
sûr *m adj*
sûre *f adj*

Are you sure, Inès?
Tu es sûre, Inès?

I'm not sure.
Je ne suis pas sûr.

surface n
la surface *f*

surfboard n
la planche de surf *f*

surfing n
le surf *m*

I go surfing.
Je fais du surf.

surname n
le nom de famille *m*

What's your surname?
Quel est votre nom de famille?

surprise n
la surprise *f*

What a surprise!
Quelle surprise!

survey n
le sondage *m*

We're doing a survey on pets.
On fait un sondage sur les animaux domestiques.

suspend vb
He's been suspended.
Il s'est fait exclure.

swam vb, *see* **swim**

swan n
le cygne *m*

swap vb
échanger

Do you want to swap?
Tu veux échanger?

Let's swap places.
Changeons de place.

sweater n
le pull *m*

a white sweater
un pull blanc

sweatshirt n
le sweat *m*

a dark green sweatshirt
un sweat vert foncé

A B C D E F G H I J K L M N O P Q R S T U V W X Y Z

Look at Language Plus on pages 283–308 for extra vocabulary.

sweet

> **sweet** can be a noun or an adjective.

Ⓐ n

1 (candy)

le <u>bonbon</u> m

a bag of sweets
un paquet de bonbons

2 (pudding)

le <u>dessert</u> m

Sweets: ice cream or chocolate mousse
Desserts: glace ou mousse au chocolat

Ⓑ adj

1 (sugary)

sucré m adj

sucrée f adj

It's too sweet.
C'est trop sucré.

2 (kind)

gentil m adj

gentille f adj

She's a sweet person.
Elle est gentille.

3 (cute)

mignon m adj

mignonne f adj

Isn't she sweet!
Comme elle est mignonne!

sweetcorn n

le <u>maïs doux</u> m

sweetie n

le <u>bonbon</u> m

swim

> **swim** can be a verb or a noun.

Ⓐ vb

<u>nager</u>

Can you swim?
Tu sais nager?

I can swim·
Je sais nager.

I can't swim.
Je ne sais pas nager.

Ⓑ n

I want to go for a swim.
Je veux aller me baigner.

swimmer n

le <u>nageur</u> m

la <u>nageuse</u> f

She's a good swimmer.
C'est une bonne nageuse.

swimming n

la <u>natation</u> f

Do you like swimming?
Tu aimes la natation?

I go swimming on Wednesdays.
Je vais à la piscine le mercredi.

swimming costume n

le <u>maillot de bain</u> m

swimming pool n

la <u>piscine</u> f

swimming trunks npl

le <u>maillot de bain</u> m

I've got new swimming trunks.
J'ai un nouveau maillot de bain.

> **maillot de bain** is a singular word.

swimsuit n

le <u>maillot de bain</u> m

swing n

la <u>balançoire</u> f

Swiss adj
suisse

Sabine is Swiss.
Sabine est suisse.

> *Swiss is always written with a capital letter, suisse is not.*

switch

> *switch can be a noun or a verb.*

Ⓐ n
le bouton *m*

Where's the switch?
Où est le bouton?

Ⓑ vb
changer de

Switch partners!
Changez de partenaire!

switch off vb
éteindre

Switch off the computer, Nina.
Éteins l'ordinateur, Nina.

switch on vb
allumer

Switch on the light, Pierre.
Allume la lumière, Pierre.

Switzerland n
la Suisse *f*

swop vb
échanger

Do you want to swop?
Tu veux échanger?

Let's swop places.
Changeons de place.

symbol n
le symbole *m*

sympathetic adj
compréhensif *m adj*
compréhensive *f adj*

A
B
C
D
E
F
G
H
I
J
K
L
M
N
O
P
Q
R
S
T
U
V
W
X
Y
Z

Look at Language Plus on pages 283–308 for extra vocabulary.

T

table n
la <u>table</u> f

It's on the table.
C'est sur la table.

the three times table
la table de trois

tablecloth n
la <u>nappe</u> f

tablespoon n
la <u>grande cuillère</u> f

table tennis n
le <u>ping-pong</u> m

tail n
la <u>queue</u> f

Pin the tail on the donkey.
Accroche la queue à l'âne.

> *la queue* also has the same
> meaning as "queue" in English.
> Queues are often long and thin –
> like a tail.

🔑
Heads or tails?
Pile ou face?

take
1 (*thing*)
prendre

Take a card, Luc.
Prends une carte, Luc.

Take one card each.
Prenez une carte chacun.

I don't take sugar.
Je ne prends pas de sucre.

It takes about an hour.
Ça prend environ une heure.

Who's taken my ruler?
Qui a pris ma règle?

2 (*person*)
emmener

Mum's going to take me to the funfair.
Maman va m'emmener à la fête foraine.

take away vb
30 take away 9 is 21.
Trente moins neuf égale vingt et un.

take back vb
rapporter

I'm going to take this book back to the library.
Je vais rapporter ce livre à la bibliothèque.

take down vb
enlever

Take the posters down.
Enlève les posters.

taken vb, *see* **take**

take off vb
enlever

Take your coats off.
Enlevez vos manteaux.

takeoff n
le décollage *m*

take out vb
sortir

I take the dog out at about six o'clock.
Je sors le chien vers six heures.

talk

talk can be a verb or a noun.

Ⓐ vb
parler

You talk too much.
Tu parles trop.

Today we're going to talk about Paris.
Aujourd'hui nous allons parler de Paris.

Ⓑ n

Let's have a talk about it.
Parlons-en.

talkative adj
bavard *m adj*
bavarde *f adj*

tall adj
1 (person, tree)
grand *m adj*
grande *f adj*

Clément is tall.
Clément est grand.

Yvette is tall.
Yvette est grande.

2 (building)
haut *m adj*
haute *f adj*

a very tall building
un très haut immeuble

> 🔑
>
> **How tall are you?**
> Tu mesures combien?
> **I'm one metre thirty tall.**
> Je mesure un mètre trente.

tan n
le bronzage *m*

She's got an amazing tan.
Elle a un bronzage superbe.

tangerine n
la mandarine *f*

tap n
le robinet *m*

Turn on the tap.
Ouvre le robinet.

tap-dancing n
les claquettes *fpl*

I do tap-dancing.
Je fais des claquettes.

tape

tape can be a verb or a noun.

Ⓐ vb
enregistrer

I'm going to tape the song.
Je vais enregistrer la chanson.

Ⓑ n
la cassette *f*

a tape of Kylie Minogue
une cassette de Kylie Minogue

Look at Language Plus on pages 283–308 for extra vocabulary.

A
B
C
D
E
F
G
H
I
J
K
L
M
N
O
P
Q
R
S
T
U
V
W
X
Y
Z

tape recorder n
le magnétophone m

target n
la cible f

tart n
la tarte f

an apple tart
une tarte aux pommes

tartan adj
écossais m adj
écossaise f adj

a tartan scarf
une écharpe écossaise

écossais can also mean *Scottish*.

taste

taste can be a noun or a verb.

Ⓐ n
le goût m

It's got a strange taste.
Ça a un goût bizarre.

Would you like a taste?
Tu veux goûter?

Ⓑ vb
goûter

Would you like to taste it?
Vous voulez y goûter?

tasty adj
savoureux m adj
savoureuse f adj

tattoo n
le tatouage m

taxi n
le taxi m

by taxi
en taxi

taxi driver n
le chauffeur de taxi m

tea n
1 (*drink*)
le thé m

a cup of tea
une tasse de thé

tea with milk
thé au lait

> In France it is more common to have lemon with your tea.

2 (*evening meal*)
le dîner m

We were having tea.
Nous étions en train de dîner.

tea bag n
le sachet de thé m

teach vb
1 (*in school*)
enseigner

Mrs Morrison teaches us French.
Madame Morrison nous enseigne le français.

2 apprendre

My cousin is teaching me the guitar.
Ma cousine m'apprend la guitare.

teacher n
1 (*in primary school*)
l'instituteur m
l'institutrice f

Mr Price is our teacher.
Mr Price est notre instituteur.

2 (*in secondary school*)
le professeur *m*

a maths teacher
un professeur de maths

She's a teacher.
Elle est professeur.

> *You do not translate "a" when you say what someone's job is in French.*

team n
l'équipe *f*

a football team
une équipe de football

She's in my team.
Elle est dans mon équipe.

We're going to divide the class into two teams.
On va diviser la classe en deux équipes.

teaspoon n
la petite cuillère *f*

teatime n
l'heure du dîner *f*

at teatime
à l'heure du dîner

tea towel n
le torchon *m*

technology n
la technologie *f*

teddy bear n
le nounours *m*

teenager n
l'adolescent *m*
l'adolescente *f*

teens npl

She's in her teens.
C'est une adolescente.

He's in his teens.
C'est un adolescent.

tee-shirt n
le tee-shirt *m*

teeth npl
les dents *fpl*

I clean my teeth three times a day.
Je me brosse les dents trois fois par jour.

telephone n
le téléphone *m*

on the telephone
au téléphone

telephone call n
le coup de téléphone *m*

telephone number n
le numéro de téléphone *m*

television n
la télévision *f*

on television
à la télévision

television programme n
l'émission de télévision *f*

tell vb
1 dire

A B C D E F G H I J K L M N O P Q R S T U V W X Y Z

a

Tell me why, Marc.
Dis-moi pourquoi, Marc.

b

Tell me your names.
Dites-moi vos noms.

c

I'm going to tell my mum.
Je vais le dire à ma maman.

d

I told you to wait.
Je t'ai dit d'attendre.

e

2 (talk about)
parler

f

I'll tell you about myself.
Je vais te parler de moi.

g

Tell your penfriends about yourselves.
Parlez de vous à vos correspondants.

h

3 (story)
raconter

i

I'm going to tell you a story.
Je vais vous raconter une histoire.

j

k

tell off vb
gronder

l

She tells me off if I'm late.
Elle me gronde si je suis en retard.

m

telly n
la télé f

n

I watch telly a lot.
Je regarde beaucoup la télé.

o

on telly
à la télé

p

temperature n
I've got a temperature.
J'ai de la fièvre.

q

ten num
dix

r

ten euros
dix euros

s

It's ten to three.
Il est trois heures moins dix.

t

It's ten past two.
Il est deux heures dix.

u

v

w

x

y

z

I'm ten.
J'ai dix ans.

*In English you can say **ten** or **ten years old**. In French you can only say **dix ans**.*

---

tennis n
le tennis m

I play tennis.
Je joue au tennis.

tennis ball n
la balle de tennis f

tennis court n
le court de tennis m

tennis racket n
la raquette de tennis f

tennis player n
le joueur de tennis m
la joueuse de tennis f

tenpin bowling n
le bowling m

Do you want to go tenpin bowling?
Tu veux jouer au bowling?

tent n
la tente f

What extra vowel does the French word have?

tenth adj
dixième

on the tenth floor
au dixième étage

---

the tenth of August
le dix août

term n
le <u>trimestre</u> m

It'll soon be the end of term.
C'est bientôt la fin du trimestre.

terrible adj
<u>épouvantable</u>

My French is terrible.
Mon français est épouvantable.

terrified adj
<u>terrifié</u> m adj
<u>terrifiée</u> f adj

I was terrified!
J'étais terrifié!

test n
l'<u>interrogation</u> f

I've got a test tomorrow.
J'ai une interrogation demain.

textbook n
le <u>manuel</u> m

a French textbook
un manuel de français

than conj
<u>que</u>

She's taller than me.
Elle est plus grande que moi.

Are you older than him?
Tu es plus vieux que lui?

thank you excl
<u>merci!</u>

Thank you very much.
Merci beaucoup.

thanks excl
<u>merci!</u>

No thanks.
Non merci.

that

> **that** can be a pronoun, an
> adjective or a conjunction.

Ⓐ pron
<u>ça</u>

Do you see that?
Tu vois ça?

That's my brother.
C'est mon frère.

That's my friend Bernadette.
C'est mon amie Bernadette.

That's right! Well done.
C'est ça! Bravo!

> **What's that?**
> Qu'est-ce que c'est?
> **How much is that?**
> C'est combien?
> **Who's that?**
> C'est qui?
> **I know that.**
> Je le sais.
> **Is that him?**
> C'est lui?
> **Is that her?**
> C'est elle?

Ⓑ adj
<u>ce</u> m adj
<u>cette</u> f adj

that dog
ce chien

that woman
cette femme

> *Ce* changes to *cet* with masculine
> nouns starting with a vowel sound.

that man
cet homme

Look at Language Plus on pages 283–308 for extra vocabulary.

that bird
cet oiseau

that one

> When you say **that one** when you are pointing, use **celui-là** if the French noun is masculine, and **celle-là** if it is feminine.

This man? – No, that one.
Cet homme-ci? – Non, celui-là.

This colour? – No, that one.
Cette couleur? – Non, celle-là.

Ⓒ conj
que

I think that you're right.
Je pense que tu as raison.

I think that it's raining.
Je crois qu'il pleut.

I think that Henri is ill.
Je crois qu'Henri est malade.

the article

> Use **le** with a masculine noun, and **la** with a feminine noun. Use **l'** before a vowel sound. For plural nouns always use **les**.

le
the boy
le garçon

l'
the man
l'homme

the orange
l'orange

la
the girl
la fille

les
the children
les enfants

theatre n
le théâtre m

their adj
leur m, f adj
leurs pl adj

their house
leur maison

their parents
leurs parents

theirs pron
à eux mpl pron
à elles fpl pron

This car is theirs.
Cette voiture est à eux.

Whose is this? – It's theirs.
C'est à qui? – À eux.

them pron
1 les

I can't see them.
Je ne les vois pas.

Do you want them?
Tu les veux?

2 (for them, to them)
leur

I'm going to buy them a present.
Je vais leur acheter un cadeau.

Can you give them a message?
Tu peux leur donner un message?

3 (after a preposition)
eux mpl pron
elles fpl pron

It's not for you, it's for them.
Ce n'est pas pour toi, c'est pour eux.

Ann and Sophie are here, and Graham's with them.
Ann et Sophie sont là, et Graham est avec elles.

theme park n
le parc d'attractions m

themselves pron

1 se
They're enjoying themselves.
Ils s'amusent.

2 (by themselves)
eux-mêmes mpl pron
elles-mêmes fpl pron
They did it themselves.
Ils l'ont fait eux-mêmes.

then conj
ensuite

I get dressed. Then I have breakfast.
Je m'habille. Ensuite je prends mon petit déjeuner.

there adv

1 là
Put it there, on the table.
Mets-le là, sur la table.

up there
là-haut

down there
là-bas

2 (to there)
y
I'm going there on Friday.
J'y vais vendredi.

*To say either **there is** or **there are** use **il y a**.*

There's a new boy in the class.
Il y a un nouveau dans la classe.

There are five people in my family.
Il y a cinq personnes dans ma famille.

How many biscuits are there?
Il y a combien de biscuits?

There are lots.
Il y en a beaucoup.

There aren't many.
Il n'y en a pas beaucoup.

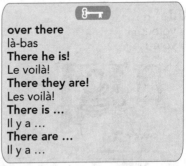

over there
là-bas
There he is!
Le voilà!
There they are!
Les voilà!
There is …
Il y a …
There are …
Il y a …

these

these can be an adjective or a pronoun.

A adj
ces

these shoes
ces chaussures

B pron
ceux-ci mpl pron
celles-ci fpl pron

Which sweets do you want? – These.
Quels bonbons veux-tu? – Ceux-ci.

Which seats are free? – These.
Quelles places sont libres? – Celles-ci.

they pron

*Check if **they** stands for a masculine or feminine noun; **ils** is used for masculine nouns and **elles** for feminine nouns.*

ils mpl pron

Look at Language Plus on pages 283–308 for extra vocabulary.

A
B
C
D
E
F
G
H
I
J
K
L
M
N
O
P
Q
R
S
T
U
V
W
X
Y
Z

a

b

c

d

e

f

g

h

i

j

k

l

m

n

o

p

q

r

s

t

u

v

w

x

y

z

Where are your friends? – They're over there.
Où sont tes amis? – Ils sont là-bas.

elles *fpl pron*

Are your socks white? – No, they're grey.
Tes chaussettes sont blanches? – Non, elles sont grises.

thief n
le voleur *m*
la voleuse *f*

thin adj
1 (*person, slice*)
mince

I'm quite thin.
Je suis assez mince.

2 (*skinny*)
maigre

She's got very thin legs.
Elle a les jambes très maigres.

thing n
1 la chose *f*

I've got lots of things to do.
J'ai beaucoup de choses à faire.

There are beautiful things in the museum.
Il y a de belles choses au musée.

2 (*belongings*)
my things
mes affaires

think
1 (*believe*)
penser

I think he's here.
Je pense qu'il est là.

> 🔑
> **I think so.**
> Oui, je crois.
> **I don't think so.**
> Je ne crois pas.

2 (*spend time thinking*)
réfléchir

Think carefully, Jason.
Réfléchis bien, Jason.

Think carefully, children.
Réfléchissez bien, les enfants.

I'll think about it.
Je vais y réfléchir.

third adj
troisième

It's the third time.
C'est la troisième fois.

I came third.
Je suis arrivé troisième.

> 🔑
> **the third of March**
> le trois mars

thirsty adj
Are you thirsty?
Tu as soif?

I'm not thirsty.
Je n'ai pas soif.

> 🔑
> **I'm thirsty.**
> J'ai soif.

thirteen num
<u>treize</u>

thirteen euros
treize euros

I'm thirteen.
J'ai treize ans.

*In English you can say **thirteen** or
thirteen years old. In French you
can only say **treize ans**.*

thirteenth adj
<u>treizième</u>

on the thirteenth floor
au treizième étage

the thirteenth of August
le treize août

thirty num
<u>trente</u>

My aunt is thirty.
Ma tante a trente ans.

*In English you can say **thirty** or
thirty years old. In French you
can only say **trente ans**.*

this

*this can be an adjective or a
pronoun.*

A adj
<u>ce</u> *m adj*
<u>cette</u> *f adj*

this book
ce livre

this time
cette fois

*Use **cet** with masculine nouns
starting with a vowel sound.*

this man
cet homme

this one

*For **this one** use **celui-ci** if the
French noun it refers to is
masculine, and **celle-ci** if it is
feminine.*

**Which T-shirt do you want? – This
one.**
Quel tee-shirt veux-tu? – Celui-ci.

That card? – No, this one.
Cette carte-là? – Non, celle-ci.

B pron
<u>ça</u>

Look at this.
Regarde ça.

this morning
ce matin
this year
cette année
this afternoon
cet après-midi
What's this?
Qu'est-ce que c'est?

those

*those can be an adjective or a
pronoun.*

A adj
<u>ces</u>

those shoes
ces chaussures

B pron
<u>ceux-là</u> *mpl pron*
<u>celles-là</u> *fpl pron*

**Which sweets do you want? –
Those.**
Quels bonbons veux-tu? –
Ceux-là.

Which seats are free? – Those.
Quelles places sont libres? –
Celles-là.

Look at Language Plus on pages 283–308 for extra vocabulary.

a
b
c
d
e
f
g
h
i
j
k
l
m
n
o
p
q
r
s
t
u
v
w
x
y
z

thousand num

a thousand
mille

a thousand euros
mille euros

thousands of people
des milliers de personnes

three num
trois

three euros
trois euros

> She's three.
> Elle a trois ans.
>
> *In English you can say **three** or **three years old**. In French you can only say **trois ans**.*

throat n
la gorge f

I've got a sore throat.
J'ai mal à la gorge.

through prep
par

through the window
par la fenêtre

throw vb
lancer

Throw me the ball.
Lance-moi la balle.

throw away vb
jeter

Don't throw it away!
Ne le jette pas!

thumb n
le pouce m

thunder n
le tonnerre m

There was thunder and lightning.
Il y avait du tonnerre et des éclairs.

thunderstorm n
l'orage m

Thursday n
le jeudi m

It's Thursday today.
Aujourd'hui c'est jeudi.

> **on Thursday**
> jeudi
> **on Thursdays**
> le jeudi
> **every Thursday**
> tous les jeudis
> **last Thursday**
> jeudi dernier
> **next Thursday**
> jeudi prochain
>
> *Days of the week are not written with a capital letter in French.*

tick

> **tick** can be a noun or a verb.

A n
Put a tick or a cross.
Cochez ou mettez une croix.

B vb
cocher

Tick the right box.
Cochez la bonne case.

ticket n

1 *(for bus, tube, cinema, museum)*
le ticket m

a bus ticket
un ticket de bus

2 (for plane, train, concert)
le **billet** m

ticket office n
le **guichet** m

tidy

> **tidy** can be an adjective or a verb.

A adj (place)
bien **rangé** m adj

bien **rangée** f adj

My room is tidy.
Ma chambre est bien rangée.

B vb
ranger

Go and tidy your room.
Va ranger ta chambre.

tidy up vb
ranger

Don't forget to tidy up afterwards, children.
N'oubliez pas de ranger après, les enfants.

tie

> **tie** can be a noun or a verb.

A n
la **cravate** f

B vb
nouer

Tie your laces.
Noue tes lacets.

tiger n
le **tigre** m

tight adj
1 (tight-fitting)
moulant m adj

moulante f adj

a tight skirt
une jupe moulante

2 (too tight)
juste

This dress is a bit tight.
Cette robe est un peu juste.

tights npl
le **collant** m

I'm wearing black tights.
Je porte un collant noir.

> **collant** is a singular word.

till

> **till** can be a noun or a preposition.

A n
la **caisse** f

at the till
à la caisse

B prep
1 **jusqu'à**

He's staying till Monday.
Il reste jusqu'à lundi.

2 (with "not")
avant

not till tomorrow
pas avant demain

3 **à**

from nine till five
de neuf heures à cinq heures

> 🔑
> **from Monday till Friday**
> du lundi au vendredi

time n
1 (on clock)
l'**heure** f

Look at Language Plus on pages 283–308 for extra vocabulary.

A B C D E F G H I J K L M N O P Q R S **T** U V W X Y Z

What time is it?
Quelle heure est-il?

> *You can also say: **Il est quelle heure?***

What time?
à quelle heure?

What time do you get up?
À quelle heure tu te lèves?

What time does the train arrive?
Le train arrive à quelle heure?

2 (amount of time)
le temps *m*

I'm sorry, I haven't got time.
Je suis désolé, je n'ai pas le temps.

It's time to go.
Il est temps de partir.

3 (occasion)
la fois *f*

this time
cette fois

next time
la prochaine fois

the first time
la première fois

two at a time
deux à la fois

2 times 2 is 4.
deux fois deux égalent quatre.

> **🔑**
>
> **What time is it?**
> Quelle heure est-il?
> **It's lunch time.**
> C'est l'heure du déjeuner.
> **How many times?**
> Combien de fois?
> **Have a good time, girls!**
> Amusez-vous bien, les filles!
> **Have a good time, Léa!**
> Amuse-toi bien, Léa!

timetable n
1 (at school)
l'emploi du temps *m*
2 (for train, bus)

l'horaire *m*

tin n
la boîte *f*

a tin of soup
une boîte de soupe

tin opener n
l'ouvre-boîte *m*

tinsel n
les guirlandes de Noël *fpl*

tip n
le pourboire *m*

It's a tip for the waiter.
C'est un pourboire pour le serveur.

tiptoe n
on tiptoe
sur la pointe des pieds

tired adj
fatigué *m adj*

fatiguée *f adj*

I'm tired.
Je suis fatigué.

tiring adj
fatigant *m adj*

fatigante *f adj*

tissue n
le kleenex® *m*

Have you got a tissue?
Tu as un kleenex?

title n
le titre *m*

to prep

> *à + le changes to au. à + les changes to aux.*

1 à

We're going to London.
Nous allons à Londres.

I go to school with my friend.
Je vais à l'école avec mon amie.

We're ready to start.
Nous sommes prêts à commencer.

from nine o'clock to half past three
de neuf heures à trois heures et demie

au

We're going to a restaurant.
Nous allons au restaurant.

aux

Can I go to the toilet?
Je peux aller aux toilettes?

> *To talk about going to a country, use au if the country is masculine, en if the country is feminine, and aux if the country is plural.*

We're going to Wales.
Nous allons au pays de Galles.

I'm going to Scotland.
Je vais en Écosse.

We're going to the United States.
Nous allons aux États-Unis.

2 de

the train to London
le train de Londres

the plane to Paris
l'avion pour Paris

3 *(to someone's house)*
chez

I'm going to Anne's house.
Je vais chez Anne.

Let's go to mine.
Allons chez moi.

I'm going to the doctor.
Je vais chez le docteur.

4 *(up to)*
jusqu'à

Count to ten, everyone.
Comptez jusqu'à dix, tout le monde.

to Paris
à Paris
to France
en France
to Portugal
au Portugal
to the swimming pool
à la piscine
to the supermarket
au supermarché
to my house
chez moi

toad n
le crapaud *m*

toast n
le pain grillé *m*

a piece of toast
une tranche de pain grillé

toastie n
le sandwich chaud *m*

today adv
aujourd'hui

What's the date today?
Quelle est la date aujourd'hui?

It's Monday today.
Aujourd'hui c'est lundi.

Look at Language Plus on pages 283–308 for extra vocabulary.

a
b
c
d
e
f
g
h
i
j
k
l
m
n
o
p
q
r
s
t
u
v
w
x
y
z

toe n
le <u>doigt de pied</u> m

> **doigt** also means "finger". The French **doigt de pied** actually means "foot finger"!

toffee n
le <u>caramel</u> m

together adv
<u>ensemble</u>

toilet n
les <u>toilettes</u> fpl

Can I go to the toilet?
Je peux aller aux toilettes?

token n
a gift token
un bon-cadeau

told vb, see **tell**

tomato n
la <u>tomate</u> f

tomato soup
la soupe à la tomate

tomato sauce n
la <u>sauce tomate</u> f

tomorrow adv
<u>demain</u>

Let's go swimming tomorrow.
Allons nager demain.

tomorrow night
demain soir

> 🔑
>
> **tomorrow morning**
> demain matin
> **the day after tomorrow**
> après-demain
> **tomorrow night**
> demain soir
> **See you tomorrow.**
> À demain.

tongue n
la <u>langue</u> f

> **la langue** is related to the word "language". You use your tongue to speak a language.

tonight adv
ce soir

Are you going out tonight?
Tu sors ce soir?

tonsillitis n
l'angine f

too adv
1 (as well)
<u>aussi</u>

My sister is coming too.
Ma sœur vient aussi.
2 (very)
<u>trop</u>

The water's too hot.
L'eau est trop chaude.

You're too late.
Tu arrives trop tard.

> You can use **trop** with a verb, to mean **too much**.

Danielle, you talk too much.
Danielle, tu parles trop.

It costs too much.
Ça coûte trop cher.

> You can use **trop de** with a noun, to mean **too much** or **too many**.

too much noise
trop de bruit

A B C D E F G H I J K L M N O P Q R S T U V W X Y Z

too many mistakes
trop d'erreurs

Me too.
Moi aussi.

tooth n
la dent f

la dent is related to the word "dentist". A dentist looks after your teeth.

toothache n

I've got toothache.
J'ai mal aux dents.

toothbrush n
la brosse à dents f

toothpaste n
le dentifrice m

top

top can be a noun or an adjective.

A n
1 le haut m

a black skirt and a white top
une jupe noire et un haut blanc

at the top of the page
en haut de la page

2 (of mountain)
le sommet m

the top of Snowdon
le sommet de Snowdon

on top of
sur

on top of the fridge
sur le frigo

B adj

He always gets top marks in French.
Il a toujours d'excellentes notes en français.

the top floor
le dernier étage

on the top floor
au dernier étage

torch n
la lampe de poche f

tortoise n
la tortue f

total n
le total m
(*pl* les totaux)

touch vb
toucher

Don't touch that!
N'y touche pas!

tour n
la visite f

a tour of the museum
une visite du musée

tourism n
le tourisme m

tourist n
le touriste m
la touriste f

There are lots of tourists.
Il y a beaucoup de touristes.

tourist information office n
l'office du tourisme m

towards prep
vers

Come towards me.
Viens vers moi.

Look at Language Plus on pages 283–308 for extra vocabulary.

towel n
la <u>serviette</u> f

tower n
la <u>tour</u> f

a tower block
une tour

town n
la <u>ville</u> f

I'm going into town.
Je vais en ville.

the town centre
le centre-ville

toy n
le <u>jouet</u> m

> The noun **le jouet** is related to the
> verb **jouer**, which means "to
> play".

toy shop n
le <u>magasin de jouets</u> m

tracksuit n
le <u>jogging</u> m

tractor n
le <u>tracteur</u> m

tradition n
la <u>tradition</u> f

traffic n
la <u>circulation</u> f

There's a lot of traffic.
Il y a beaucoup de circulation.

traffic lights npl
les <u>feux</u> mpl

train n
le <u>train</u> m

by train
en train

We're going by train.
Nous y allons en train.

trainers npl
les <u>baskets</u> fpl

a pair of trainers
une paire de baskets

tram n
le <u>tramway</u> m

trampoline n
le <u>trampoline</u> m

translate vb
<u>traduire</u>

I can translate the menu into English.
Je sais traduire le menu en anglais.

translation n
la <u>traduction</u> f

travel agent's n
l'<u>agence de voyages</u> f

travelling n
I love travelling.
J'adore les voyages.

treasure n
le <u>trésor</u> m

tree n
l'<u>arbre</u> m

triangle n
le <u>triangle</u> m

trick n
le <u>tour</u> m

I can do magic tricks.
Je sais faire des tours de magie.

trip n
le voyage m

We're going on a trip to London.
Nous faisons un voyage à Londres.

Have a good trip!
Bon voyage!

trolley n
le chariot m

trouble n
le problème m

The trouble is, it's too expensive.
Le problème, c'est que c'est trop cher.

Éric is always getting into trouble.
Éric fait tout le temps des bêtises.

trousers npl
le pantalon m

I'm wearing black trousers.
Je porte un pantalon noir.

pantalon is a singular word.

trout n
la truite f

truck n
le camion m

true adj
vrai m adj
vraie f adj

That's true.
C'est vrai.

That's not true.
Ce n'est pas vrai.

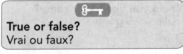
True or false?
Vrai ou faux?

trumpet n
la trompette f

She plays the trumpet.
Elle joue de la trompette.

trunks npl
le maillot de bain m

I've got new trunks.
J'ai un nouveau maillot de bain.

maillot de bain is a singular word.

truth n
la vérité f

Tell me the truth.
Dis-moi la vérité.

try

try can be a verb or a noun.

Ⓐ vb
1 *(attempt)*
essayer

I'm going to try.
Je vais essayer.

Try to remember.
Essaie de te souvenir.

Try again, everyone.
Encore une fois, toute la classe.

You're not trying, Éric.
Tu ne fais pas d'efforts, Éric.

Look at Language Plus on pages 283–308 for extra vocabulary.

2 (taste)
goûter

Would you like to try some?
Voulez-vous goûter?

B n
l'essai m

his third try
son troisième essai

🔑

Good try!
Pas mal!
Can I have a try?
Je peux essayer?

---

try on vb
essayer

Can I try it on?
Je peux l'essayer?

T-shirt n
le tee-shirt m

tube n
the Tube
le métro

Tuesday n
le mardi m

It's Tuesday today.
Aujourd'hui, c'est mardi.

🔑

on Tuesday
mardi
on Tuesdays
le mardi
every Tuesday
tous les mardis
last Tuesday
mardi dernier
next Tuesday
mardi prochain

*Days of the week are not written
with a capital letter in French.*

---

tummy n
le ventre m

tummy ache n
I've got tummy ache.
J'ai mal au ventre.

tuna n
le thon m

a tuna salad
une salade de thon

tune n
l'air m

I know the tune.
Je connais l'air.

tunnel n
le tunnel m

the Channel Tunnel
le tunnel sous la Manche

turkey n
1 (meat)
la dinde f
2 (bird)
le dindon m

turn

turn can be a noun or a verb.

A n (go)
le tour m

You miss a turn.
Passe ton tour.

🔑

Whose turn is it?
C'est à qui le tour?
It's my turn!
C'est mon tour!

B vb
tourner

Turn right at the lights.
Tournez à droite aux feux.

turn off vb
éteindre

Could you turn off the light?
Tu peux éteindre?

turn on vb
allumer

Could you turn on the light?
Tu peux allumer?

turn over vb
retourner

Turn over the cards, everyone.
Retournez les cartes, tout le monde.

turn round vb
se retourner

Turn round, children!
Retournez-vous, les enfants!

turquoise

turquoise can be an adjective or a noun.

Ⓐ adj
turquoise m, f, pl adj

a turquoise top
un haut turquoise

Colour adjectives come after the noun in French.

Ⓑ n
le turquoise m

Turquoise is my favourite colour.
Ma couleur préférée, c'est le turquoise.

TV n
la télé f

on TV
à la télé

twelfth adj
douzième

on the twelfth floor
au douzième étage

> 🔑
> **the twelfth of August**
> le douze août

twelve num
douze

twelve euros
douze euros

I have lunch at twelve o'clock.
Je déjeune à midi.

It is twelve thirty.
Il est midi et demi.

> 🔑
> **twelve o'clock**
> midi
> **twelve o'clock at night**
> minuit
> **I'm twelve.**
> J'ai douze ans.

*In English you can say **twelve** or **twelve years old**. In French you can only say **douze ans**.*

twentieth adj
vingtième

the twentieth time
la vingtième fois

> 🔑
> **the twentieth of May**
> le vingt mai

twenty num
vingt

twenty euros
vingt euros

It's twenty to three.
Il est trois heures moins vingt.

Look at Language Plus on pages 283–308 for extra vocabulary.

It's twenty past eleven.
Il est onze heures vingt.

> 🔑
>
> **He's twenty.**
> Il a vingt ans.
>
> *In English you can say **twenty** or **twenty years old**. In French you can only say **vingt ans**.*

twice adv
deux fois

twin n
le jumeau *m*
(*pl* les jumeaux)
la jumelle *f*
(*pl* les jumelles)

my twin brother
mon frère jumeau

her twin sister
sa sœur jumelle

identical twins
les vrais jumeaux

twin room n
la chambre à deux lits *f*

twinned adj
jumelé *m adj*
jumelée *f adj*

Stroud is twinned with Châteaubriant.
Stroud est jumelée avec Châteaubriant.

two num
deux

two euros
deux euros

Get into twos.
Mettez-vous deux par deux.

> 🔑
>
> **She's two.**
> Elle a deux ans.
>
> *In English you can say **two** or **two years old**. In French you can only say **deux ans**.*

type n
le type *m*
What type of camera have you got?
Quel type d'appareil photo as-tu?

tyre n
le pneu *m*

U

UFO n
l'OVNI m

ugly adj
laid m adj
laide f adj

UK n
le Royaume-Uni m

in the UK
au Royaume-Uni

to the UK
au Royaume-Uni

I live in the UK.
J'habite au Royaume-Uni.

Ulster n
l'Irlande du Nord f

in Ulster
en Irlande du Nord

umbrella n
1 le parapluie m

*The French for rain is "pluie". **un parapluie** is something that keeps the rain off you.*

2 (sunshade)
le parasol m

umpire n
1 (in tennis)
le juge de chaise m
2 (in cricket)
l'arbitre m

unbeatable adj
imbattable

unbelievable adj
incroyable

That's unbelievable!
C'est incroyable!

uncle n
l'oncle m

my uncle
mon oncle

uncomfortable adj
pas confortable

The seats are rather uncomfortable.
Les sièges ne sont pas très confortables.

under prep
1 (beneath)
sous

The cat's under the table.
Le chat est sous la table.

Look at Language Plus on pages 283–308 for extra vocabulary.

a

b The tunnel goes under the
Channel.
c Le tunnel passe sous la Manche.

d **under there**
là-dessous

e **What's under there?**
Qu'est-ce qu'il y a là-dessous?
f **2** (less than)
moins de
g
It costs under £10.
h Ça coûte moins de dix livres.

i **children under 10**
les enfants de moins de dix ans

j ## underground

k | underground can be a noun, an
adjective or an adverb. |
l

m **Ⓐ** n
le métro m

n **by underground**
en métro
o **Ⓑ** adj
souterrain m adj
p souterraine f adj

q **an underground car park**
un parking souterrain
r **Ⓒ** adv
sous terre
s
Moles live underground.
t Les taupes vivent sous
terre.
u
underneath
v
| underneath can be a preposition
w or an adverb. |

x **Ⓐ** prep
sous
y
underneath the carpet
z sous la moquette
Ⓑ adv
dessous

Look underneath, Pierre!
Regarde dessous, Pierre!

understand vb
comprendre

| *The English words "comprehend"
and "comprehension" are related
to* **comprendre**. *Comprehension
exercises test your understanding
of something.* |

Do you all understand?
Vous comprenez tous?

**Do you understand,
Richard?**
Tu comprends, Richard?

**I don't understand this
word.**
Je ne comprends pas ce
mot.

**I understood almost
everything.**
J'ai presque tout compris.

It's easy to understand.
C'est facile à comprendre.

🔑

I don't understand.
Je ne comprends pas.
Did you understand, Claire?
Tu as compris, Claire?
Did you understand, children?
Vous avez compris, les enfants?

---

understood vb, see
understand

underwear n
les sous-vêtements mpl

undone adj
défait m adj

défaite f adj

Your laces are undone.
Tes lacets sont défaits.

undressed adj
to get undressed
se déshabiller

A
B
C
D
E
F
G
H
I
J
K
L
M
N
O
P
Q
R
S
T
U
V
W
X
Y
Z

I'm getting undressed.
Je me déshabille.

> *Je m'habille* means "I'm getting dressed". By adding **dés** to the start of the French verb you make the opposite. In English you add **un** to make the opposite.

unemployed adj
au chômage

He's unemployed.
Il est au chômage.

unfair adj
injuste

That's unfair!
C'est injuste!

unfashionable adj
démodé *m adj*
démodée *f adj*

unfold vb
déplier

Unfold the map.
Déplie la carte.

> *plier* means "to fold". By adding **dé** to the start of the French verb you make the opposite. In English you add **un** to make the opposite.

unforgettable adj
inoubliable

unfortunately adv
malheureusement

Unfortunately it's too late.
Malheureusement, c'est trop tard.

Unfortunately not.
Malheureusement, non.

unhappy adj
malheureux *m adj*
malheureuse *f adj*

He's unhappy at school.
Il est malheureux à l'école.

You look unhappy.
Tu as l'air triste.

uni n
la fac *f*

She's at uni.
Elle est à la fac.

uniform n
l'uniforme *m*

We wear school uniform.
Nous portons un uniforme scolaire.

> French children don't wear school uniform.

Union Jack n
le drapeau du Royaume-Uni *m*

> **le drapeau tricolore** is the French flag: its three colours are blue, white and red.

United Kingdom n
le Royaume-Uni *m*

to the United Kingdom
au Royaume-Uni

in the United Kingdom
au Royaume-Uni

United States n
les États-Unis *mpl*

in the United States
aux États-Unis

Look at Language Plus on pages 283–308 for extra vocabulary.

a b c d e f g h i j k l m n o p q r s t u v w x y z

to the United States
aux États-Unis

universe n
l'univers *m*

university n
l'université *f*

She's at university.
Elle va à l'université.

Do you want to go to university?
Tu veux aller à l'université?

Lancaster University
l'université de Lancaster

unless conj

Don't do it unless I say "Simon says".
Ne le faites pas si je ne dis pas "Jacques a dit".

I'll have that biscuit, unless you want it.
Je veux bien ce biscuit si tu n'en veux pas.

unlikely adj
peu probable

It's possible, but unlikely.
C'est possible, mais peu probable.

unlucky adj
1 (*person*)

If you are unlucky, try again.
Si tu n'as pas de chance, recommence.

I'm always unlucky.
Je n'ai jamais de chance.

2 (*number, animal*)

Thirteen is an unlucky number.
Le nombre treize porte malheur.

It's unlucky to walk under a ladder.
Ça porte malheur de passer sous une échelle.

French people think black cats are unlucky.

unnecessary adj
inutile

unpack vb
défaire

I'm going to unpack my suitcase.
Je vais défaire ma valise.

> *Je fais ma valise* means "I'm packing my case". By adding *dé* to the start of the French verb you make the opposite. In English you add *un* to make the opposite.

unpleasant adj
désagréable

unpopular adj
impopulaire

unpredictable adj
imprévisible

The weather is unpredictable.
Le temps est imprévisible.

unreliable adj
pas fiable

Our car is unreliable.
Notre voiture n'est pas fiable.

unsuitable adj
inapproprié *m adj*
inappropriée *f adj*

untidy adj
en désordre

My bedroom's always untidy.
Ma chambre est toujours en désordre.
My writing is untidy.
J'écris mal.

until prep
1 jusqu'à

He's here until tomorrow.
Il est là jusqu'à demain.

The supermarket is open until ten.
Le supermarché reste ouvert jusqu'à dix heures du soir.

2 (with "not")

avant

not until tomorrow
pas avant demain

When will it be ready? – Not until next week.
Quand est-ce que ça sera prêt? – Pas avant la semaine prochaine.

3 à

from nine until five
de neuf heures à cinq heures

---

from Monday until Friday
du lundi au vendredi

---

unusual adj
peu courant *m adj*
peu courante *f adj*

It's an unusual name.
C'est un nom peu courant.

---

up

up can be an adverb, an adjective or a preposition.

A adv
en haut

up on the hill
en haut de la colline

up to
jusqu'à

Let's count up to fifty.
Comptons jusqu'à cinquante.

up to now
jusqu'à présent

---

up here
ici
up there
là-haut
It's up to you.
C'est à vous de décider.

B adj (person)
levé *m adj*
levée *f adj*

I'm always up before eight.
Je suis toujours levé avant huit heures.

He's not up yet.
Il n'est pas encore levé.

C prep

The post office is up the road.
La poste est en haut de la rue.

The cat is up the tree.
Le chat est dans l'arbre.

upper adj
supérieur *m adj*
supérieure *f adj*

on the upper floor
à l'étage supérieur

---

upper sixth n

She's in the upper sixth.
Elle est en terminale.

In French secondary schools the years are counted from the **sixième** (youngest) to **première** and **terminale** (oldest).

Look at Language Plus on pages 283–308 for extra vocabulary.

A B C D E F G H I J K L M N O P Q R S T **U** V W X Y Z

a
b
c
d
e
f
g
h
i
j
k
l
m
n
o
p
q
r
s
t
u
v
w
x
y
z

upset

> **upset** can be an adjective or a verb.

Ⓐ adj
secoué *m adj*
secouée *f adj*

She's still a bit upset.
Elle est encore un peu secouée.

I had an upset stomach.
J'avais l'estomac dérangé.

Ⓑ vb
faire de la peine

I don't want to upset my granny.
Je ne veux pas faire de peine à ma grand-mère.

upside down adv
à l'envers

That painting is upside down.
Ce tableau est à l'envers.

upstairs adv
en haut

Where's your coat? – It's upstairs.
Où est ton manteau? – Il est en haut.

up-to-date adj
moderne

upwards adv
vers le haut

urgent adj
urgent *m adj*
urgente *f adj*

Is it urgent?
C'est urgent?

US n
les USA *mpl*

in the US
aux USA

to the US
aux USA

from the US
des USA

us pron
nous

Come with us.
Viens avec nous.

Tell us the story.
Raconte-nous l'histoire.

USA n
les USA *mpl*

in the USA
aux USA

to the USA
aux USA

from the USA
des USA

use

> **use** can be a verb or a noun.

Ⓐ vb
utiliser

You can use a spoon or a fork.
Tu peux utiliser une cuillère ou une fourchette.

Can we use a dictionary in the exam?
Est-ce qu'on peut utiliser un dictionnaire à l'examen?

Can I use your phone?
Je peux téléphoner?

Can I use the toilet?
Je peux aller aux toilettes?

Ⓑ n

It's no use.
Ça ne sert à rien.

use up vb
finir

We've used up all the paint.
Nous avons fini la peinture.

used adj
I'm used to getting up early.
J'ai l'habitude de me lever tôt.

🔑
I'm used to it.
J'ai l'habitude.
I'm not used to it.
Je n'ai pas l'habitude.

useful adj
utile

useless adj
nul *m adj*
nulle *f adj*

This map is useless.
Cette carte est nulle.

You're useless!
Tu es nul!

usual adj
habituel *m adj*
habituelle *f adj*

my usual seat
ma place habituelle

🔑
as usual
comme d'habitude

usually adv
en général

I usually wear trousers.
En général, je porte un pantalon.

utility room n
la buanderie *f*

A
B
C
D
E
F
G
H
I
J
K
L
M
N
O
P
Q
R
S
T
U
V
W
X
Y
Z

Look at Language Plus on pages 283–308 for extra vocabulary.

V

vacancy n
"no vacancies"
"complet"

vacuum cleaner n
l'aspirateur *m*

vague adj
vague

Valentine card n
la carte de la Saint-Valentin *f*

Valentine's Day n
la Saint-Valentin *f*

valley n
la vallée *f*

valuable adj
de valeur

a valuable picture
un tableau de valeur

van n
la camionnette *f*

*"Un camion" is a lorry. The ending
-ette shows that **une camionnette**
is smaller than a lorry.*

vandal n
le/la vandale *m/f*

vandalism n
le vandalisme *m*

vanilla n
la vanille *f*

vanilla ice cream
la glace à la vanille

varied adj
varié *m adj*
variée *f adj*

variety n
la variété *f*

There's lots of variety.
Il y a beaucoup de variété.

various adj
plusieurs

There are various possibilities.
Il y a plusieurs possibilités.

vase n
le vase *m*

VDU n
la console *f*

vegan n
le végétalien *m*
la végétalienne *f*
I'm a vegan.
Je suis végétalienne.

vegetable n
le légume *m*
vegetable soup
la soupe aux légumes

Would you like some vegetables?
Vous voulez des légumes?

vegetarian

vegetarian can be an adjective or a noun.

Ⓐ adj
végétarien *m adj*

végétarienne *f adj*

vegetarian lasagne
les lasagnes végétariennes

Ⓑ n
le végétarien *m*

la végétarienne *f*

I'm a vegetarian.
Je suis végétarien.

Susie's a vegetarian.
Susie est végétarienne.

verb n
le verbe *m*

very adv
très

very tall
très grand

not very interesting
pas très intéressant

🔑

very much
beaucoup
very soon
très bientôt
I'm very sorry.
Je suis vraiment désolé.

vest n
le maillot de corps *m*

vet n
le/la vétérinaire *m/f*

She's a vet.
Elle est vétérinaire.

You do not translate "a" when you say what someone's job is in French.

vicar n
le pasteur *m*

My uncle's a vicar.
Mon oncle est pasteur.

You do not translate "a" when you say what someone's job is in French.

video

video can be a noun or a verb.

Ⓐ n

1 (*film*)
la vidéo *f*

We're going to watch a video.
Nous allons regarder une vidéo.

2 (*cassette*)
la cassette vidéo *f*

I've got the video.
J'ai la cassette vidéo.

3 (*video recorder*)
le magnétoscope *m*

Can you switch on the video?
Tu peux allumer le magnétoscope?

Ⓑ vb
filmer

We're going to video the concert.
On va filmer le concert.

video game n
le jeu vidéo *m*

I like playing video games.
J'aime les jeux vidéo.

video recorder n
le magnétoscope *m*

A B C D E F G H I J K L M N O P Q R S T U V W X Y Z

Look at Language Plus on pages 283–308 for extra vocabulary.

video shop n
le vidéoclub m

view n
la vue f

There's an amazing view.
Il y a une vue extraordinaire.

villa n
la villa f

village n
le village m

in the village
dans le village

vinegar n
le vinaigre m

vineyard n
le vignoble m

violent adj
violent m adj
violente f adj

violin n
le violon m

I play the violin.
Je joue du violon.

virus n
le virus m

visit

visit can be a noun or a verb.

Ⓐ n
1 (to tourist attraction)
la visite f
a visit to Edinburgh Castle
une visite du château d'Édinbourg
2 (to country)
le séjour m

Did you enjoy your visit to France?
Ton séjour en France s'est bien passé?

Ⓑ vb
1 (person)
rendre visite à

I'm going to visit friends.
Je vais rendre visite à des amis.
2 (place)
visiter

We're going to visit the castle.
Nous allons visiter le château.

visitor n
l'invité m
l'invitée f

Today we've got a French visitor.
Aujourd'hui, nous avons un invité français.

vitamin n
la vitamine f

What extra vowel does the French word have?

vocabulary n
le vocabulaire m

voice n
la voix f
(pl les voix)

volleyball n
le volley-ball m

We sometimes play volleyball.
Quelquefois nous jouons au volley-ball.

volunteer n
le/la volontaire m/f

W

waist n
la <u>taille</u> f

wait vb
<u>attendre</u>

Wait Mathieu, it's not your turn.
Attends Mathieu, ce n'est pas ton tour.

Wait boys, I'm coming.
Attendez les garçons, j'arrive.

>
>
> **Wait for me!**
> Attends-moi!
> **Wait a minute!**
> Attends!
> **Wait a minute, children!**
> Attendez, les enfants!

waiter n
le <u>serveur</u> m

waiting room n
la <u>salle d'attente</u> f

waitress n
la <u>serveuse</u> f

wake up vb
se réveiller

Wake up, Marie!
Réveille-toi, Marie!

Wales n
le pays de Galles m

Swansea is in Wales.
Swansea est au pays de Galles.

When are you coming to Wales?
Quand est-ce que tu viens au pays de Galles?

Bronwen is from Wales.
Bronwen est galloise.

> *How can you tell that Bronwen is a girl's name?*

the Prince of Wales
le prince de Galles

walk

> **walk** can be a verb or a noun.

A vb
1 marcher

He walks fast.
Il marche vite.

Walk faster, Serge.
Marche plus vite, Serge.

Walk faster, children.
Marchez plus vite, les enfants.

2 *(go on foot)*
aller à pied

Are you walking or going by bus?
Tu y vas à pied ou en bus?

I walked 10 kilometres.
J'ai fait dix kilomètres à pied.

B n
la promenade f

Would you like to go for a walk?
Tu veux faire une promenade?

Look at Language Plus on pages 283–308 for extra vocabulary.

promenade is used in English to mean a road by the sea where you can go for a walk.

walking n
la <u>marche</u> f

My parents like walking.
Mes parents aiment la marche.

Walkman® n
le <u>walkman</u>® m

wall n
le <u>mur</u> m

There are posters on the wall.
Il y a des posters au mur.

wallet n
le <u>portefeuille</u> m

want vb
<u>vouloir</u>

Do you want some cake?
Tu veux du gâteau?

I don't want to play.
Je ne veux pas jouer.

What do you want to do tomorrow?
Qu'est-ce que tu veux faire demain?

What do you want, Marie?
Qu'est-ce que tu veux, Marie?
What do you want, boys?
Qu'est-ce que vous voulez, les garçons?

war n
la <u>guerre</u> f

wardrobe n
l'<u>armoire</u> f

warm adj
<u>chaud</u> m adj
<u>chaude</u> f adj

warm water
l'eau chaude

It's warm.
Il fait chaud.
I'm warm.
J'ai chaud.

was vb, *see* **be**

wash vb
1 (*thing*)
<u>laver</u>

I'll wash the grapes.
Je vais laver le raisin.
2 (*oneself*)
<u>se laver</u>

At seven I get up, wash and get dressed.
À sept heures je me lève, je me lave et je m'habille.

Notice how my is translated in the next two examples.

I'm going to wash my hands.
Je vais me laver les mains.

I want to wash my hair.
Je veux me laver les cheveux.

Wash your hands!
Lave-toi les mains!

washbasin n
le <u>lavabo</u> m

washing machine n
la <u>machine à laver</u> f

washing-up n
Who's going to do the washing-up?
Qui va faire la vaisselle?

I often do the washing-up.
Je fais souvent la vaisselle.

wasn't = was not see **be**

wasp n
la <u>guêpe</u> f

waste n
It's a waste of time.
C'est une perte de temps.

wastepaper basket n
la <u>corbeille à papier</u> f
Put your chewing gum in the wastepaper basket.
Mets ton chewing gum dans la corbeille à papier.

watch

> **watch** can be a noun or a verb.

Ⓐ n
la <u>montre</u> f
I haven't got a watch.
Je n'ai pas de montre.
Ⓑ vb
<u>regarder</u>
I watch television on Saturday mornings.
Je regarde la télévision le samedi matin.

> 🔑
> **Watch me, Mum!**
> Regarde-moi, maman!

watch out vb
<u>faire attention</u>
You need to watch out.
Il faut faire attention.

> 🔑
> **Watch out!**
> Attention!

water n
l'<u>eau</u> f
a glass of water
un verre d'eau

wave n
la <u>vague</u> f
There are sometimes big waves.
Il y a parfois des grosses vagues.

wavy adj
wavy hair
les cheveux ondulés

way n
❶ (to place)
le <u>chemin</u> m
I don't know the way.
Je ne connais pas le chemin.
Ask the way.
Demande le chemin.
Can you tell me the way to the station?
Vous pouvez me dire comment aller à la gare?

> 🔑
> **It's a long way.**
> C'est loin.
> **Which way is it?**
> C'est par où?
> **It's this way.**
> C'est par ici.

A B C D E F G H I J K L M N O P Q R S T U V W X Y Z

Look at Language Plus on pages 283–308 for extra vocabulary.

a
b
c
d
e
f
g
h
i
j
k
l
m
n
o
p
q
r
s
t
u
v
w
x
y
z

2 (manner)

la façon f

What's the best way to learn French?
Quelle est la meilleure façon d'apprendre le français?

Do it this way, Sophie.
Fais-le comme ça, Sophie.

way in n
l'entrée f

way out n
la sortie f

Where's the way out?
Où est la sortie?

we pron

> *There are two ways of saying "we". In spoken French on is used more often than nous.*

1 nous

We're staying here for a week.
Nous restons une semaine ici.

2 on

Shall we start?
On commence?

wear vb
porter

She's wearing a hat.
Elle porte un chapeau.

I wear glasses.
Je porte des lunettes.

weather n
le temps m

because of the weather
à cause du temps

What's the weather like today?
Quel temps fait-il aujourd'hui?

The weather's not very nice.
Il ne fait pas beau.

What's the weather like?
Quel temps fait-il?
The weather's nice.
Il fait beau.

weather forecast n
la météo f

website n
le site web m

wedding n
le mariage m

It's my cousin's wedding today.
Aujourd'hui, c'est le mariage de ma cousine.

wedding anniversary n
l'anniversaire de mariage m

Wednesday n
le mercredi m

It's Wednesday today.
Aujourd'hui, c'est mercredi.

on Wednesday
mercredi
on Wednesdays
le mercredi
every Wednesday
tous les mercredis
last Wednesday
mercredi dernier
next Wednesday
mercredi prochain

Days of the week are not written with a capital letter in French.

week n

la <u>semaine</u> f

two weeks
deux semaines

this week
cette semaine
last week
la semaine dernière
every week
toutes les semaines
next week
la semaine prochaine
in a week's time
dans une semaine

weekday n

on weekdays
en semaine

weekend n

le <u>week-end</u> m

What are you doing at the weekend?
Qu'est-ce que tu fais ce week-end?

at weekends
le week-end
last weekend
le week-end dernier
next weekend
le week-end prochain

welcome adj

Welcome!
Bienvenue!

Welcome to Scotland!
Bienvenue en Écosse!

Thank you! – You're welcome!
Merci! – De rien!

well

> **well** can be an adverb or an adjective.

A adv
<u>bien</u>

The team is playing well.
L'équipe joue bien.

as well
aussi

We're going to Chartres as well as Paris.
Nous allons à Paris et aussi à Chartres.
B adj (in good health)
He's not well.
Il ne va pas bien.

I'm not very well at the moment.
Je ne vais pas très bien en ce moment.

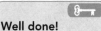

Well done!
Bravo!
Get well soon!
Remets-toi vite!

well-behaved adj
<u>sage</u>

wellies npl
les <u>bottes en caoutchouc</u> fpl

wellingtons npl
les <u>bottes en caoutchouc</u> fpl

A
B
C
D
E
F
G
H
I
J
K
L
M
N
O
P
Q
R
S
T
U
V
W
X
Y
Z

Look at Language Plus on pages 283–308 for extra vocabulary.

well-known adj
<u>célèbre</u>

a well-known film star
une vedette de cinéma célèbre

Welsh

> **Welsh** can be an adjective or a noun.

A adj
<u>gallois</u> m adj
<u>galloise</u> f adj

She's Welsh.
Elle est galloise.

Welsh people
les Gallois

> **gallois** is not spelled with a capital letter except when it means a Welsh person.

B n (language)
le <u>gallois</u> m

Welshman n
le <u>Gallois</u> m

Welshwoman n
la <u>Galloise</u> f

went vb, see **go**

were vb, see **be**

weren't = **were not**, see **be**

west

> **west** can be an adjective or a noun.

A adj
<u>ouest</u> m, f, pl adj

the west coast
la côte ouest

B n
l'<u>ouest</u> m

in the west
dans l'ouest

West Country n
le <u>sud-ouest</u> de l'Angleterre m

western n
le <u>western</u> m

I like Westerns.
J'aime les westerns.

West Indian adj
<u>antillais</u> m adj
<u>antillaise</u> f adj

She's West Indian.
Elle est antillaise.

> The adjective **West Indian** is spelled with a capital letter, but **antillais** is not.

West Indies npl
les <u>Antilles</u> fpl

wet adj
<u>mouillé</u> m adj
<u>mouillée</u> f adj

wet clothes
les vêtements mouillés

I'm wet.
Je suis mouillé.

It's wet today.
Il pleut aujourd'hui.

whale n
la <u>baleine</u> f

what

> **what** can be a pronoun or an adjective.

A pron

1 qu'est-ce que

What are you doing, children?
Qu'est-ce que vous faites, les enfants?

What's happening?
Qu'est-ce qu'il se passe?

What's the matter?
Qu'est-ce qu'il y a?

Take a card and tell your partner what it is.
Prends une carte, et dit à ton partenaire ce que c'est.

2 quel *m pron*

quelle *f pron*

What's your phone number?
Quel est ton numéro de téléphone?

What's the capital of Belgium?
Quelle est la capitale de la Belgique?

B adj *(which)*

quel *m adj*

quelle *f adj*

What letter does it start with?
Ça commence par quelle lettre?

What colour is it?
C'est de quelle couleur?

🔑

What?
Comment?
What is it?
Qu'est-ce que c'est?
What do you want?
Qu'est-ce que tu veux?
What's the weather like?
Quel temps fait-il?
What's your name?
Comment tu t'appelles?
What time is it?
Quelle heure est-il?
What day is it today?
Quel jour sommes-nous?

wheel n
la <u>roue</u> f

wheelchair n
le <u>fauteuil roulant</u> m

when adv
<u>quand</u>

When it rains we stay in the classroom.
Quand it pleut nous restons dans la classe.

When's your birthday?
C'est quand, ton anniversaire?

You can also say:
Ton anniversaire, c'est quand?

where adv, conj
<u>où</u>

où can come first or last.

Where's Emma today?
Où est Emma aujourd'hui?

Where are you going?
Tu vas où?

🔑

Where do you live?
Où habites-tu?

which

which can be an adjective or a pronoun.

A adj
quel *m adj*

quelle *f adj*

Which flavour do you want?
Quel parfum est-ce que tu veux?

Which number is it?
C'est quel numéro?

B pron
lequel *m pron*

laquelle *f pron*

Which would you like?
Vous voulez lequel?

A B C D E F G H I J K L M N O P Q R S T U V W X Y Z

Look at Language Plus on pages 283–308 for extra vocabulary.

Which is your car?
C'est laquelle, ta voiture?

Which do you prefer, cricket or football?
Qu'est-ce que tu préfères, le cricket ou le football?

while conj
pendant que

While you're here we can do some sightseeing.
On peut faire du tourisme pendant que tu es là.

whipped cream n
la crème fouettée f

whiskers npl
les moustaches fpl

white

white can be an adjective or a noun.

Ⓐ adj
blanc m adj
blanche f adj

He's wearing white trousers.
Il porte un pantalon blanc.

My shirt is white.
Ma chemise est blanche.

He's got white hair.
Il a les cheveux blancs.

Colour adjectives come after the noun in French.

Ⓑ n
le blanc m

The bride is wearing white.
La mariée est vêtue de blanc.

white coffee n
le café au lait m

Whitsun n
la Pentecôte f

who pron
qui

Who wants to start?
Qui veut commencer?

Who's that?
C'est qui?

You can also say: **Qui est-ce?**

whole adj
tout m adj
toute f adj

the whole class
toute la classe

the whole afternoon
tout l'après-midi

the whole world
le monde entier

whose pron, adj
à qui

Whose pencil case is this?
À qui est cette trousse?

Whose turn is it?
C'est à qui le tour?

Whose is this?
C'est à qui?

why adv
pourquoi

Why are you crying?
Pourquoi tu pleures?

That's why I can't come.
Voilà pourquoi je ne peux pas venir.

Why not?
Pourquoi pas?

wide adj
large

a wide road
une route large

widow n
la veuve f

widower n
le veuf m

wife n
la femme f

She's his wife.
C'est sa femme.

wild adj
sauvage

a wild animal
un animal sauvage

will vb

It will soon be my birthday.
C'est bientôt mon anniversaire.

It'll soon be the holidays.
C'est bientôt les vacances.

I'll come with you.
Je vais venir avec toi.

Do you think he will come?
Tu crois qu'il va venir?

Colette won't come.
Colette ne viendra pas.

Will you help me?
Est-ce que tu peux m'aider?

win vb
gagner

I've won!
J'ai gagné!

wind n
le vent m

There is a lot of wind.
Il y a beaucoup de vent.

window n
la fenêtre f

Look out of the window, boys.
Regardez par la fenêtre, les garçons.

a shop window
une vitrine

windy adj
a windy day
un jour de grand vent

It's windy.
Il y a du vent.

wine n
le vin m

a bottle of wine
une bouteille de vin

a glass of wine
un verre de vin

white wine
le vin blanc

red wine
le vin rouge

winner n
le gagnant m
la gagnante f

winning adj
the winning team
l'équipe gagnante

winter n
l'hiver m

last winter
l'hiver dernier

in winter
en hiver

A
B
C
D
E
F
G
H
I
J
K
L
M
N
O
P
Q
R
S
T
U
V
W
X
Y
Z

Look at Language Plus on pages 283–308 for extra vocabulary.

a
b
c
d
e
f
g
h
i
j
k
l
m
n
o
p
q
r
s
t
u
v
w
x
y
z

winter sports npl
les sports d'hiver mpl

wintertime n
l'hiver m

> 🔑
>
> **in wintertime**
> en hiver

wish

> **wish** can be a noun or a verb.

A n
le vœu m
(pl les vœux)

Make a wish!
Fais un vœu!

with best wishes, Kathy
bien amicalement, Kathy

> 🔑
>
> **"best wishes"**
> "meilleurs vœux"

B vb

I wish I could!
Si je pouvais!

witch n
la sorcière f

with prep
1 avec

Come with me.
Venez avec moi.

Tea with milk?
Du thé avec du lait?

It begins with "b".
Ça commence par un "b".
2 (at the home of)
chez

We're going to stay with friends.
Nous allons loger chez des amis.

I live with my dad.
J'habite chez mon père.

without prep
sans

I drink coffee without sugar.
Je bois mon café sans sucre.

without a coat
sans manteau

without speaking
sans parler

wives npl
les femmes fpl

wolf n
le loup m

woman n
la femme f

three women and two men
trois femmes et deux hommes

won vb, see **win**

wonder vb
se demander

I wonder where Caroline is.
Je me demande où est Caroline.

wonderful adj
formidable

won't vb = will not; see **will**

wood n
le bois m

wool n
la laine f

It's made of wool.
C'est en laine.

word n
le <u>mot</u> *m*

Repeat the words, everyone.
Répétez les mots, tout le monde.

I've forgotten the word.
J'ai oublié le mot.

What's the word for "shop" in French?
Comment dit-on "shop" en français?

I don't know the word.
Je ne connais pas le mot.

the words
(*lyrics*)
les paroles

We're going to learn the words of a song.
Nous allons apprendre les paroles d'une chanson.

work

work can be a verb or a noun.

Ⓐ vb
1 (*person*)
<u>travailler</u>

She works in a shop.
Elle travaille dans un magasin.

2 (*machine, plan*)
<u>marcher</u>

The heating isn't working.
Le chauffage ne marche pas.

Ⓑ n
le <u>travail</u> *m*

He's at work at the moment.
Il est au travail en ce moment.

I've got a lot of work to do.
J'ai beaucoup de travail à faire.

at work
au travail

worker n
She's a good worker.
Elle travaille bien.

worksheet n
la <u>feuille d'exercices</u> *f*

Max, have you got a worksheet?
Max, tu as une feuille d'exercices?

world n
le <u>monde</u> *m*

the whole world
le monde entier

He's the world champion.
Il est champion du monde.

worried adj
<u>inquiet</u> *m adj*
<u>inquiète</u> *f adj*

She's very worried.
Elle est très inquiète.

worry vb
<u>s'inquiéter</u>

Don't worry, Mum!
Ne t'inquiète pas, Maman!

worse

worse can be an adjective or an adverb.

Ⓐ adj
<u>pire</u>

The weather is worse in Scotland.
Le temps est pire en Écosse.

Look at Language Plus on pages 283–308 for extra vocabulary.

a
b
c
d
e
f
g
h
i
j
k
l
m
n
o
p
q
r
s
t
u
v
w
x
y
z

B adv
plus mal

I'm feeling worse.
Je me sens plus mal.

worst adj
the worst
le plus mauvais

> Use **la plus mauvaise** if the noun
> is feminine.

I always get the worst mark.
J'ai toujours la plus mauvaise
note.

Ten! My worst score.
Dix! Mon plus mauvais score.

Maths is my worst subject.
Je suis vraiment nul en maths.

would vb
1 (in offers)
Would you like to play with me?
Tu veux jouer avec moi?

Would you like coffee, sir?
Vous voulez du café, monsieur?

2 (in requests)
I'd like a hot chocolate, please.
Je voudrais un chocolat chaud, s'il
vous plaît.

My friend would like a coke.
Mon ami voudrait un coca.

What would you like, Sir?
Vous désirez, Monsieur?

What would you like, dear?
Qu'est-ce que tu veux, ma chérie?

> You can also say:
> **Que veux-tu, ma chérie?**

3 (in polite orders)
**Would you give out the books,
Hugues?**
Tu peux distribuer les cahiers,
Hugues?

Would you close the door please?
Vous pouvez fermer la porte, s'il
vous plaît?

wrapping paper n
le papier cadeau m

write vb
écrire

Write your names.
Écrivez vos noms.

Write to me soon, Roxanne.
Écris-moi vite, Roxanne.

I'm going to write to my penfriend.
Je vais écrire à ma correspondante.

> **Write soon!**
> Écris-moi vite!

write down
noter

I'll write down the address.
Je vais noter l'adresse.

**Can you write it down for me,
please?**
Vous pouvez me l'écrire, s'il vous
plaît?

writing n
l'écriture f

I can't read your writing.
Je n'arrive pas à lire ton écriture.

wrong

> **wrong** can be an adjective or an adverb.

Ⓐ adj
Number 2 is right, but number 3 is wrong.
Le numéro 2 est juste, mais le numéro 3 est faux.

I got three questions wrong.
J'ai eu trois questions fausses.

You're looking at the wrong page.
Tu n'es pas à la bonne page.

That's the wrong answer.
Ce n'est pas la bonne réponse.

Ⓑ adv
mal

You're saying it wrong.
Tu le dis mal.

Have I spelled it wrong?
Je l'ai mal écrit?

What's wrong?
Qu'est-ce qui ne va pas?
What's wrong with you?
Qu'est-ce que tu as?

Look at Language Plus on pages 283–308 for extra vocabulary.

X

Xmas n
Noël *m*

X-ray

X-ray can be a verb or a noun.

Ⓐ vb
faire une radio de

They're going to X-ray my leg.
Ils vont faire une radio de ma jambe.

They X-rayed my arm.
Ils ont fait une radio de mon bras.

Ⓑ n
la radio *f*

I'm going to have an X-ray.
Je vais passer une radio.

Y

yacht n

1 (*sailing boat*)
le voilier *m*

2 (*luxury motorboat*)
le yacht *m*

yard n
la cour *f*

in the yard
dans la cour

year n
l'année *f*

next year
l'année prochaine

*There are two words for year:
année and an. Use an with
numbers.*

a hundred years
cent ans

an eight-year-old child
un enfant de huit ans

this year
cette année
I'm ten years old.
J'ai dix ans.

I'm in Year 6.
Je suis au CM2.

She's in Year 5.
Elle est au CM1.

> In France children start
> primary school at the age of
> 6. The first year is **CP**,
> followed by **CE1** and **CE2**.
> The last two years are **CM1**
> and **CM2**.

yellow

*yellow can be an adjective or a
noun.*

A adj
jaune

I'm wearing yellow shorts.
Je porte un short jaune.

*Colour adjectives come after the
noun in French.*

B n
le jaune *m*

Yellow is my favourite colour.
Ma couleur préférée, c'est le jaune.

yes adv
oui

Do you like it? – Yes.
Tu aimes ça? – Oui.

Answer yes or no.
Réponds par oui ou par non.

yesterday adv
hier

When? – Yesterday.
Quand? – Hier.

A
B
C
D
E
F
G
H
I
J
K
L
M
N
O
P
Q
R
S
T
U
V
W
X
Y
Z

Look at Language Plus on pages 283–308 for extra vocabulary.

a
b
c
d
e
f
g
h
i
j
k
l
m
n
o
p
q
r
s
t
u
v
w
x
y
z

I was absent yesterday.
Hier, j'étais absente.

> 🔑
>
> **yesterday morning**
> hier matin
> **yesterday afternoon**
> hier après-midi
> **yesterday evening**
> hier soir

---

yet adv
encore

I haven't finished yet.
Je n'ai pas encore fini.

Have you finished yet, children?
Vous avez fini, les enfants?

> 🔑
>
> **Not yet.**
> Pas encore.

---

yoghurt n
le yaourt m

you pron

> *Only use **tu** when you're talking to your family or to someone of your own age, or younger. Use **vous** when you're talking to several people, or to an adult you don't know very well. The teacher calls you "**tu**", but you call the teacher "**vous**".*

1 (*singular and subject of verb*)
tu

Do you like football, Nina?
Tu aimes le football, Nina?

Do you understand, Michelle?
Tu comprends, Michelle?

2 (*singular and object of verb*)
te

I know you.
Je te connais.

> *te changes to **t'** before a vowel sound.*

I love you.
Je t'aime.

3 (*singular and after a preposition*)
toi

I'll come with you.
Je viens avec toi.

It's for you, Xavier.
C'est pour toi, Xavier.

She's younger than you.
Elle est plus jeune que toi.

4 vous

Do you understand, children?
Vous comprenez, les enfants?

Are you listening, Gaëlle and Richard?
Vous écoutez, Gaëlle et Richard?

Could you move out of the way please, miss?
Vous pouvez vous pousser s'il vous plaît, madame?

Can I help you?
Est-ce que je peux vous aider?

It's for you, children.
C'est pour vous, les enfants.

---

young adj
jeune

You're too young.
Tu es trop jeune.

---

younger adj
plus jeune

He's younger than me.
Il est plus jeune que moi.

youngest adj
plus jeune

my youngest brother
mon plus jeune frère

To say that someone is the youngest, use le plus jeune for a boy and la plus jeune for a girl.

Hugo's the youngest.
Hugo est le plus jeune.

She's the youngest in the class.
C'est la plus jeune de la classe.

your adj
1 *(to someone you call "tu")*

When you want to say something like "your name", "your house", or "your hair" in French, you need to know if "name", "house", "hair" are masculine, feminine or plural, because there are three possible words for your.

ton *m adj*

Is that your brother?
C'est ton frère?

ta *f adj*

Is that your sister?
C'est ta sœur?

tes *pl adj*

your parents
tes parents

ta becomes ton before a vowel sound.

your friend Éléonore
ton amie Éléonore

2 *(to people you call "vous")*
votre *sing adj*

your house
votre maison

When's your birthday, miss?
Quelle est la date de votre anniversaire, madame?

vos *pl adj*

Take your things out.
Sortez vos affaires.

Notice how your is translated in the next two examples.

Wash your hands, Laura.
Lave-toi les mains, Laura.

Wash your hands, children.
Lavez-vous les mains, les enfants.

yours pron
1 *(to someone you call "tu")*
à toi

Is this yours, Frank?
C'est à toi, Frank?

Whose is this? – It's yours, dear.
C'est à qui? – À toi, chéri.

2 *(to people you call "vous")*
à vous

Is this yours, sir?
C'est à vous, Monsieur?

These tickets are yours.
Ces billets sont à vous.

Whose is this? – It's yours.
C'est à qui? – À vous.

yourself pron
1 *(to someone you call "tu")*
te

You'll make yourself sick!
Tu vas te rendre malade!

te changes to t' before a vowel sound.

Are you enjoying yourself?
Tu t'amuses bien?

After a preposition, use toi instead of te.

toi

Tell me about yourself!
Parle-moi de toi!

Look at Language Plus on pages 283–308 for extra vocabulary.

A B C D E F G H I J K L M N O P Q R S T U V W X Y Z

2 (*to someone you call "vous"*)
vous

Help yourself, Mrs Day!
Servez-vous, Madame Day!

Tell me about yourself!
Parlez-moi de vous!

yourselves pron

1 vous

Did you enjoy yourselves?
Vous vous êtes bien amusés?

2 vous-mêmes

Do it yourselves!
Faites-le vous-mêmes!

youth club n
le centre de jeunes m

at the youth club
au centre de jeunes

youth hostel n
l'auberge de jeunesse f

We're going to stay at a youth hostel.
Nous allons loger dans une auberge de jeunesse.

Z

A
B
C
D
E
F
G
H
I
J
K
L
M
N
O
P
Q
R
S
T
U
V
W
X
Y
Z

zebra n

le <u>zè</u>bre *m*

zero n

le <u>zé</u>ro *m*

zoo n

le <u>zoo</u> *m*

We went to the zoo on Saturday.
Samedi, nous sommes allés au zoo.

Look at Language Plus on pages 283–308 for extra vocabulary.

MAP OF FRANCE

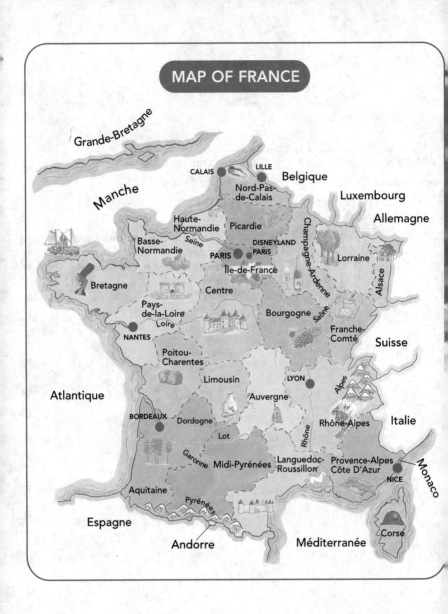

Grande-Bretagne

Manche

CALAIS   LILLE
Nord-Pas-
de-Calais   Belgique

Luxembourg

Allemagne

Haute-
Normandie   Picardie
Basse-
Normandie   Seine   DISNEYLAND
PARIS   PARIS   Lorraine

Bretagne   Île-de-France   Champagne-Ardenne   Alsace

Centre   Saône
Pays-
de-la-Loire   Bourgogne   Franche-
Comté   Suisse
Loire   NANTES

Poitou-
Charentes

Atlantique   Limousin   LYON   Alpes

Auvergne   Rhône-Alpes   Italie

BORDEAUX   Dordogne   Rhône

Lot

Garonne   Midi-Pyrénées   Languedoc-
Roussillon   Provence-Alpes
Côte D'Azur   Monaco
NICE

Aquitaine   Pyrénées

Espagne   Corse

Andorre   Méditerranée